RECOGNIZING REALITY

SUNY Series in Buddhist Studies
Matthew Kapstein, editor

RECOGNIZING REALITY

Dharmakīrti's Philosophy and Its Tibetan Interpretations

Georges B. J. Dreyfus

State University of New York Press

Published by
State University of New York Press, Albany

Printed in the United States of America

For information, address State University of New York Press
State University Plaza, Albany, NY 12246

Production by Dana Foote
Marketing by Dana E. Yanulavich

Library of Congress Cataloging-in-Publication Data

Dreyfus, Georges.
Recognizing reality : Dharmakīrti's philosophy and its Tibetan interpretations / Georges B. J. Dreyfus.
p. cm. — (SUNY series in Buddhist studies)
ISBN 0-7914-3097-9 (hc : alk. paper). — ISBN 0-7914-3098-7 (pb : alk. paper)
1. Dharmakīrti, 7th cent. 2. Buddhist logic. 3. Buddhism—China—Tibet—Doctrines. I. Title. II. Series.
B133.D484D74 1997
181′.043—dc20 96-14258
CIP

10 9 8 7 6 5 4 3 2 1

CONTENTS

PREFACE AND ACKNOWLEDGMENTS

This work began more than twenty-five years ago, in 1970, when I first studied Buddhist philosophy with Tibetan teachers in India. For the next fifteen years, I followed the traditional Tibetan curriculum for Buddhist monks, learning a great deal from many Tibetan teachers. I have thus been able to benefit from the unfortunate situation of this exiled community. I became interested in the study of philosophical topics pertaining to logic, epistemology, and philosophy of language. This interest developed over the years during which I had the privilege to study these topics with some of the most knowledgeable Tibetan scholars. Although I cannot mention them all by name, I am deeply grateful to each one. In particular I would like to mention Ge-shay Rabten, who set me on the path that includes this present work; Ge-shay Lati Rimbochay, who supported my efforts consistently; and Gen Lo-sang-gya-tso, Principal of the Tibetan Institute of Dialectics, where I spent many of my most formative years. I would also like to express my deep appreciation to his Holiness the Dalai Lama, who helped and guided me throughout my years spent in the Tibetan community. Finally, in Ge-shay Nyi-ma-gyel-tsen I encountered an incomparable mind. Through contact with him I learned a great deal, given my personal limitations.

This work does not, however, just report on the training I underwent during these very formative years. In the process of inquiring into the diversity of Buddhist logico-epistemological traditions, I gained some valuable insight into materials with which I have been familiar for quite some time, but that in some ways eluded me. This work is an attempt to bring together the varied aspects of my philosophical education. One of the questions central for the integrated understanding I seek is the problem of universals. This current work explores this topic in the context of Buddhist tradition. I can only hope that I have been able to communicate part of the enthusiasm this work has evinced in me.

By entering Western academia in 1985, after completing my Ge-shay degree, I have been able to learn about Western philosophy. This has allowed me to find the vocabulary with which to explicate Buddhist philosophical concepts that would otherwise have remained buried under the weight of exegetical details. Several people have contributed to my ongoing process of philosophical translation. I want to acknowledge Dr. Joshua Tonkel, who helped me to understand the aspects of Anglo-Saxon analytical philosophy especially relevant to this work. I also learned a great deal from Professors Cora Diamond, James Cargile, Robert Schlarleman, Jamie Ferreira, and other philosophical minds from the University of Virginia. I also want to thank Matthew Kapstein, professor at Columbia University, for his insightful philosophical remarks and helpful comments. Last, but not least, I would like to acknowledge Jay Garfield, professor at Hampshire College. A great deal of the clarity and philosophical accuracy of this book is due to his help.

My academic training has also familiarized me with modern philological and historical methods and exposed me to Sanskrit literature. These tools have been of great use to me in successfully completing my Ph.D. dissertation ("Ontology, Philosophy of Language and Epistemology in Buddhist Tradition," University of Virginia, 1991), on which this book is based. I would like to thank the people who have supported my inquiry into the Buddhist logico-epistemological tradition with their knowledge. In particular, I owe a great deal to Tom Tillemans, professor at the University of Lausanne. Our prolonged discussions over the course of several years have been a great source of insight for me, and his help with Sanskrit sources, invaluable. I would also like to mention Professor Jeffrey Hopkins, my advisor, who guided my work with great patience and competence, as well as Professors Karen Lang, Paul Groner, and so many others who helped me to deepen my grasp of the material. I thank Professors Ernst Steinkellner from the University of Vienna, Richard Hayes from McGill University, and Leonard Van der Kuijp from Harvard University for their help in my endeavor, as well as Helmut Krasser from the University of Vienna and John Dunne from Harvard University. I thank Professor Katsura from Hiroshima University for helping me with some particularly difficult passages as well as Professor Mikogami for sharing with me his views on some aspects of the later aspects of Indian tradition. Thanks also to the late Richard Martin, South Asia bibliographer at the University of Virginia, for his tremendous patience and helpfulness in providing support for this lengthy project. Finally, thanks to Dr. Gareth Sparham from the University of British Columbia for procurring for me a copy of a rare text and to the monastery of La-brang Dra-shi-kyil (*bla 'brang bkra shis 'khyil*) in the Amdo province of eastern Tibet for giving it.

I would like to acknowledge the support of a Fulbright-Hays Doctoral Dissertation Research Fellowship that enabled me to study more deeply Indian and Tibetan sources in India. My stay at the Sa skya College in Rajpur was decisive in broadening my understanding of the variety of Tibetan traditions. The kindness and competence of Gen Migmar Tsering, head of the Sa skya College, was crucial to the success of my project. I learned a great deal from him as well as other Sa-gya scholars such as Ken-po Abe and Ken-po Gya-tso, whose help was invaluable. I am also grateful to His Holiness Sakya Trizin, head of the Sa-gya order, for encouraging my research. I would like also to thank Dr. K. K. Mittal of Delhi University.

Finally, I would like to thank all those who at various stages of this project provided much needed help in many forms, such as editing, proofreading, and moral support: Katherine Rogers, Darcy Philips, Katherine Pfaff, Bill Magee, and John Powers. I also want to acknowledge Paul Hackett from the University of

Virginia, whose careful reading has greatly improved the quality of this work. Finally, I want to express my deep gratitude to *ma compagne* Natasha Judson, who has helped me enormously to make this work understandable to a broader audience. Her patience and support are largely responsible for successfully concluding this enterprise.

TECHNICAL NOTES

Throughout this text my practice is to transliterate Sanskrit names in a standard fashion, and phoneticize Tibetan names when they occur in the body of the text and cite them, within parentheses, in transliteration at their first occurrence. I follow the system of transliteration, with the minor modification in that no letters are capitalized, devised by Turrell Wylie (see "A Standard System of Tibetan Transcription," *Harvard Journal of Asiatic Studies* 22 [1959]: 261–67). The pronunciation system used is a modified version of the "essay phonetic" system developed by Jeffrey Hopkins in *Meditation on Emptiness* (London: Wisdom, 1983), pp. 19–21.

Technical expressions used by Indian and Tibetan thinkers are introduced in the text in their English translation. Their original expressions are italicized in parentheses using either Sanskrit or Tibetan depending on whether the author who uses these expressions is Indian or Tibetan. Their equivalents in the other source language (either Tibetan or Sanskrit) is given whenever available. Thus, I have avoided the use of Sanskrit reconstruction of original Tibetan concepts. I have also not provided Tibetan equivalents for Non-Buddhist concepts, except for those most current in the Tibetan literature.

This work is not a translation of original sources but an explanation of their content. However, I liberally quote from original sources and provide this material in notes so that my reader can check my conclusions. For the Sanskrit material, I have used critical editions as they were available to me. When quoting these editions, I also give the Tibetan version on which I often rely in my translations and arguments. Throughout this work I emphasize the Tibetan reception of Dharmakīrti's tradition, an orientation which limits my use of Sanskrit sources. I have tried, however, to use as often as I could both Sanskrit original and Tibetan translations while translating passages from Dharmakīrti's works. I have often used Tibetan commentaries to help the translation. In using critical editions, I adopt the following notation: Dharmakīrti, *Commentary*, III: 25–6 should be read as *Commentary*, chap. III, stanzas 25 to 26. In texts which are only partially edited, I use the edition as well as the Tibetan translation provided in the Derge or the Peking editions of the Den-gyur *(bstan 'gyur)*.

When translating a passage quoted from either Tibetan or Sanskrit in a note, I provide the passage from the source language in a non-italicized form from which I made the translation. I have tried to remain fairly literal in my translations, using the same terms to translate the same words as much as possible. I have not followed this policy in my explanations, in which I use more freely terms that reflect less literally the originals but provide insight into their meanings.

All titles of texts cited are translated into English; at the first occurrence the Tibetan and Sanskrit (if it was originally a Sanskrit work) title of the texts are provided, citing the Sanskrit first. Further citations only provide the English abbreviated title, which is also used in the translation of the quoted passages regardless of how it is cited in the original text. At the first occurrence, reference to the full long form of the title as well as transliteration of the author's name are provided. The notation I have chosen for some often mentioned works is the following: volume is indicated by a "." and chapter by a ":". Follows the page number, which is usually completed by the line number when relevant. For example, Gyel-tsap, *Revealing*, I.13–.14 should be read as *Revealing*, vol. 1, p 13 to 14. Similarly, Śākya Chok-den's *Defeater*, II.215.3–.4 should be read as *Defeater*, volume two (of this work, not of the Collected Works), page 215, lines 3 to 4. Texts in traditional folio format are quoted with the inclusion of the side number. For example, Gyel-tsap, *Essence*, 26.a.1 should be read as *Essence*, folio 26, side one, line 1. On the other hand, Kay-drup, *Ocean*, I:112.a.3–.4 should be read as *Ocean*, chapter I, folio 112, side one, lines 3 to 4. In referring to often quoted works such as Śākya Chok-den's *Defeater*, the volume number refers to work itself, not to the collected works, unless explicitly mentioned.

Indian Logico-Epistemological Tradition

The following is a list of the thinkers belonging to the Indian logico-epistemological lineages mentioned in this work. The Buddhists are listed on the left and a few of their orthodox Hindu interlocutors are mentioned on the right. As often in Indian history, these dates should be taken as approximate at best. Most dates are taken from K. Mimaki, *La Réfutation Bouddhique de la Permanence des Choses* (Paris: Institut de Civilisation Indienne, 1976).

	Śabara (fourth–fifth centuries C.E.)
	Vātsyāyana (fourth–fifth centuries)
	Bhartṛhari (fifth century)
Vasubandhu (400–480)	
Dignāga (480–540)	
	Kumārila (sixth–seventh centuries)
	Uddyotakara (550–610)
	Praśastapāda (560–610)
Dharmakīrti (600–660)	
Devendrabuddhi (?)	
Śākyabuddhi (?)	
Vinitadeva (630–700)	
Śubhagupta (720–780)	

Prajñākaragupta (740–800)
Śāntarakṣita (725–783)
Kamalaśīla (740–795)
Dharmottara (750–810)

Trilocana (tenth century)
Vācaspatimiśra (tenth century)
Śrīdhara (950–1000)

Jetāri (950–1000)
Jina (tenth century)
Śaṃkarānanda (eleventh century)
Mokṣākaragupta (eleventh–twelfth centuries)
Śākya Śrībhadra (1127–1225)

Sa-gya Lineages

The following is a list of the authors belonging to the Sa-gya logico-epistemological lineages mentioned in this work. The followers of Sa-paṇ are in the left column, and the Sa-gya thinkers who have followed the realist interpretation of Dharmakīrti are in the right column. Bo-dong's position on the extreme right is meant to signify his particular situation, outside the main lineage, despite being nominally a Sa-gya. Although most of the ideas of the Seventh Karmapa Chö-drak-gya-tso (1454–1506) are similar to those of Sa-paṇ, I do not include him in the Sa-gya lineage. Most of the dates are taken from L. van der Kuijp, *Contributions to the Development of Tibetan Buddhist Epistemology* (Wiesbaden: Steiner, 1983) and D. Jackson, *The Entrance Gate for the Wise* (Vienna: Arbeitkreis für Tibetische und Buddhistische Studien, 1987).

Śākya Śrībhadra (1127–1225)
Sa-gya Paṇḍita (1182–1251)

U-yuk-ba-rik-bay-seng-gay (?–1253)
Rik-bay-ray-dri (1250–1330)
Nya-wön-gun-ga-bel (1300–1380)

Yak-dön-sang-gyay-bel (1348–1414)

Ren-da-wa (1349–1412)

Rong-dön Śākya-gyel-tsen (1367–1449)

Bo-dong (1376–1451)

Dak-tsang Lo-dza-wa (1405–?)
Śākya Chok-den (1428–1507)

Go-ram-ba Sö-nam-seng-gay (1429–1489)
Tuk-je-bel-sang (?)
Lo Ken-chen Sö-nam-hlün-drup (1456–1532)
Ngak-wang-chö-drak (1572–1641)

Ga-dam-ba and Ge-luk Lineages

The following is a list of the authors belonging to the Ga-dam-ba and Ge-luk logico-epistemological lineages mentioned in this work. I have grouped these two traditions together to indicate the close connection between some of the main ideas of the early Tibetan epistemologists and Ge-luk thinkers. I have also added some of the Sa-gya thinkers (in the right column) who have been more particularly influential in the formation of the Ge-luk tradition.

Ngok Lek-bay-shay-rap (?)
Ngok Lo-dza-wa Lo-den-shay-rap (1059–1109)
Cha-ba Chö-gyi-seng-gay (1109–1169)
Kyung-rin-chen-drak (?)
Dzang-ngak-ba (?–1171)
Gang-ba-se-u (?)

U-yuk-ba-rik-bay-seng-gay (?–1253)
Nya-wön-gun-ga-bel (1300–1380)
Ren-da-wa (1349-1412)

Dzong-ka-ba (1357-1419)
Gyel-tsap-dar-ma-rin-chen (1364–1432)
Kay-drup-jay (1385–1438)
Ge-dün-drup (1391–1474)
Jam-yang-chok-hla-ö-ser (fifteenth century)
Se-ra Jay-dzün-ba (1469–1544)
Paṇ-chen Sö-nam-drak-ba (1478–1554)
Jam-yang-shay-ba (1648–1722)
Jang-gya-röl-bay-dor-jay (1717–1786)
Gön-chok-jik-may-wang-bo (1728–1791)
Tu-gen Lo-sang-chö-gyi-nyi-ma (1737–1802)

Den-dar-hla-ram-ba (1759–1840)
Gung-tang Jam-bel-yang (1762–1823)
Ngak-wang-bel-den (1797–?)
Pur-bu-jok (1825–1901)
Jam-bel-sam-pel (?–1975)

The following list contains all the Tibetan names appearing in the text in "essay phonetics" followed by a transliteration:

A-gu Shay-rap-gya-tso	a ku shes rab rgya mtsho
Bang-lo-drö-den-ba	dpang blo gros brtan pa
Ba-tsap Nyi-ma-drak	pa tshab nyi ma grags
Bel-den-drak-ba	dpal ldan grags pa
Bu-dön-rin-chen-drup	bu ston rin chen grub
Bo-dong Chok-lay-nam-gyel	bo dong phyogs las rnam rgyal
Cha-ba Chö-gyi-seng-gay	phya (phwya or cha) pa chos kyi seng ge
Chö-drak-gya-tso	chos grags rgya mtsho
Chim Jam-bel-yang	mchims 'jam dpal dbyangs
Dak-bo Ga-gyü	dwags po bka' brgyud
Dak-tsang Lo-dza-wa	stag tshang lo tsa ba
Den-dar-hla-ram-ba	bstan dar lha ram pa
Döl-bo-ba Shay-rap-gyel-tsen	dol po pa shes rab rgyal mtshan
Dor-jay Gyel-bo	rdo rje rgyal po
Dra-shi-hlün-bo	bkra shis lhun po
Drak-ba-chok-wang	grags pa mchog dbang
Dre-bung	'bras spungs
Dri-gung ba	'bri gung pa
Dri-gung Jik-den-gong-bo	'bri gung 'jig rten mgong po
Drom-dön Gyel-way-jung-nay	'brom ston rgyal ba'i 'byung gnas
Dzang-ngak-ba	gtsang ngag pa
Dzong-ka-ba	tsong kha pa
Ga-dam-ba	bka' gdams pa
Ga-gyü	bka' rgyud
Gang-ba-se-u	gangs pa se'u
Ga-den	dga' ldan
Ga-den-ba	dga' ldan pa
Ge-den-ba	dge ldan pa
Ge-dün-chö-bel	dge 'dun chos dpal
Ge-dün-drup	dge 'dun grub
Ge-luk	dge lugs
Ge-shay	dge bshes
Go-mang	sgo mang
Gön-chok-gyel-bo	dkon mchog rgyal po

Gön-chok-jik-may-wang-bo	dkon mchog 'jigs med dbang po
Gön-chok-dze-ring	dkon mchog tse ring
Go-ram-ba Sö-nam-seng-gay	go rams pa bsod nams seng ge
Gö Lo-dza-wa Shö-nu-bel	gos lo tsā ba gzhon nu dpal
Gung-tang Jam-bel-yang	gung thang 'jam dpal dbyangs
Gyel-tsap-dar-ma-rin-chen	rgyal tshab dar ma rin chen
Jam-bel-sam-pel	'jam dpal bsam 'phel
Jam-gön Kong-trul	'jam mgon kong sprul
Jam-yang Kyen-tse-wang-po	'jam dbyangs mkhyen tse'i dbang po
Jam-yang-chok-hla-ö-ser	'jam dbyangs phyogs lha 'od zer
Jam-yang-shay-ba	'jam dbyangs bzhad pa
Jang-gya-röl-bay-dor-jay	lcang skya rol ba'i rdo rje
Jay-dzün-chö-gi-gyel-tsen	rje btsun chos kyi rgyal mtshan
Jo-nang-ba	jo nang pa
Ka-tog Tse-wang-nor-bu	ka' thog tshe dbang nor bu
Kay-drup-jay	mkhas grub rje
Kyung-rin-chen-drak	khyung rin chen grags
Long-chen Rap-jam-ba	klong chen rab 'byams pa
Lo Ken-chen Sö-nam-hlün-drup	glo mkhan chen bsod nams lhun grub
Lo-sang-gya-tso	blo bzang rgya mtsho
Lo-se-ling	blo gsal gling
Ma Lo-dsa-wa Ge-way Lo-drö	rmā lo tsā ba dge ba'i blo gros
Mi-gyö-dor-jay	mi bskyod rdo rje
Mi-pam Gya-tso	mi pham rgya mtsho
Ngak-wang-bel-den	ngag dbang dpal ldan
Ngak-wang-chö-drak (Ngak-chö)	ngag dbang chos grags
Ngak-wang Lo-sang Gya-tso	ngag dbang blo bzang rgya mtsho
Ngok Lek-bay-shay-rap	rngog legs pa'i shes rab
Ngok Lo-dza-wa Lo-den-shay-rap	rngog lo tsā ba blo ldan shes rab
Ngor-chen Kun-ga-sang-bo	ngor chen kun dga' bzang po
Nya-wön-gun-ga-bel	nya dbon kun dga' dpal
Nyi-ma-gyel-tsen	nyi ma rgyal mtshan
Nying-ma	rnying ma
Pa-mo-dru-ba	phag mo gru pa
Paṇ-chen Sö-nam-drak-ba	paṇ chen bsod nams grags pa
Pur-bu-jok	phur bu mchog
Ra-dö	rwa stod
Rang-jung Dor-je	rang byung rdo rje
Ren-da-wa	red mda ba
Rik-bay-ray-dri	rig pa'i ral gri
Rong-dön Śākya-gyel-tsen	rong ston śākya rgyal mtshan
Śākya Chok-den	śākya mchog ldan
Sa-gya	sa skya
Sa-gya Paṇḍita	sa skya paṇḍita

Sang-pu-ne-u-tok	gsang phu sne'u thog
Se-ra Jay	se rwa byes
Se-ra Jay-dzün-ba	se rwa rje btsun pa
Shang Tsal-ba	zhang tshal pa
Sha-wa Lo-dza-ba Seng-ge-gyel-tsen	zhwa ba lo tsā ba seng ge rgyal mtshan
Si-tu Chö-gi-jung-ne	si tu chos kyi 'byung gnas
Sö-nam-dzay-mo	bsod nams rtse mo
Sum-ba Ken-po Ye-shay-bel-jor	sum pa mkhan po ye shes dpal 'byor
Tai Si-tu Jang-chup gyel-tsen	tai si tu byang chub rgyal mtshan
Tāranātha	Tāranātha
Tsul-trim-nying-bo	tshul khrims snying po
Tu-gen Lo-sang-chö-gyi-nyi-ma	thu'u bkwan blo bzang chos kyi nyi ma
Tuk-je-bel-sang	thugs rje dpal bzang
U-yuk-ba-rik-bay-seng-gay	'u yug pa rigs pa'i seng ge
Ü-ba Lo-sel	dbus pa blo gsal
Yak-dön-sang-gyay-bel	g.yag ston sangs rgyas dpal

Introduction I

A Few Methodological Considerations

Purpose and Content

During what could be considered the golden age of ancient Indian civilization, Dignāga and Dharmakīrti articulated and defended Buddhist philosophical principles. They did so probably more systematically than anyone before their time, the fifth to the seventh centuries C.E. In this work I analyze this Buddhist tradition and its relevance to a wider history of human ideas. My perspective is more philosophical than philologico-historical, though I do consider history as it relates to the evolution of ideas. My choice of a primarily philosophical mode of analysis reflects my own prejudices and preoccupations, but more significantly, it captures an important aspect of these philosophically inclined thinkers.

Previously scholars' efforts have tended to focus on basic Indian texts by Dignāga, Dharmakīrti, and their direct commentators. This work undertakes the quite different task of studying their ideas from the point of view of their later Tibetan reception. This work does not deal extensively with Dignāga, for the Tibetan thinkers important to my perspective have understood him mostly through the grid of Dharmakīrti's interpretations. Nevertheless, I do consider Dignāga's ideas on occasion to provide some background for Dharmakīrti's efforts and to indicate the relationship between the two authors. The main focus of this work, however, centers upon Tibetan articulations of Dharmakīrti's system as it pertains to epistemology, the domain of philosophy examining the nature of knowledge, in Indian terms the nature of *pramāṇa* (valid cognition or means of valid cognition). In addition to epistemology, Dharmakīrti's system addresses related fields such as ontology, philosophy of language, and logic (the aspect of Dharmakīrti's system that this work does not address).

My discussion attempts to capture the range and movement of Dharmakīrti's whole tradition. Even so I emphasize Tibetan thinkers working between the end of the fourteenth and the end of the fifteenth centuries. This is the heart of the period described by David Ruegg as the classical period of Tibetan Buddhism, representing "the high point of philosophical penetration, exegesis and systematic hermeneutics, accompanied by the final constitution of the Tibetan religious schools . . ."[1] At this time, Tibetan thinkers provided conflicting interpretations,[2] many of which prove advantageous to an understanding of Dharmakīrti's thought. I find this period particularly revealing of some of the most philosophically interesting questions raised by Dharmakīrti's system.

Among the wide array of Tibetan authors, I consider mostly thinkers belonging to the Ge-luk (*dge lugs*) and Sa-gya (*sa skya*) schools, opposing the realism of the former to the antirealism of the latter. This choice of schools is mandated by several considerations. Together, they largely encompass the range of ideas within which Tibetan epistemological thinking has evolved. Historically, these two schools do not subsume the whole of Tibetan epistemological thinking. Prior to and during the fifteenth century, there were several other epistemological traditions but they later disappeared. Of the four contemporary schools of Tibetan Buddhism, the remaining two, Ga-gyü (*bka' rgyud*) and Nying-ma (*rnying ma*), tend to follow the Sa-gya views with a few minor modifications. Moreover, through their lively and often vehement disagreements, the Ge-luk and Sa-gya schools effectively articulate diverging interpretations of Dharmakīrti. Thus, focussing on these two schools allows me to avoid unnecessary dispersion as well as to present Tibetan epistemology in its diversity.

In considering Tibetan contributions to the understanding of Buddhist epistemology, I do not mean to suggest that Indian and Tibetan traditions are identical. The great cultural and historical distance separating India and Tibet is undeniable, but this does not warrant a systematic assumption of incommensurability between the two traditions. Hence, it is meaningful to speak of Indian and Tibetan thinkers as belonging to a connected but not identical tradition of philosophical inquiry. Tibetan thinkers stand within an ongoing tradition of inquiry historically connected with the Indian original works. They belong to a milieu in which explanations, debates, doubts, and interpretations have been passed on through generations of highly qualified interpreters. This connection with the Indian tradition does not preclude Tibetan thinkers from developing their own original thought, but in doing so these thinkers proceed by commenting on Indian sources. Hence, it is not possible to study Tibetan logic and epistemology in isolation from the original Indian models. Tibetan thinkers do not write their philosophical works based only on their personal reflections. Rather, they develop their ideas by commenting directly or indirectly on basic Indian texts. These texts are approached through a commentarial tradition that consists of a first level of Indian commentaries and a second layer of Tibetan commentaries. This exegetical apparatus is completed by the use of textbooks (*yig cha*) that reflect the viewpoint of a scholar's school or even monastery. Therefore, Tibetan scholastic achievements must be appreciated in the light of the original Indian texts to which they relate.

Attending to interacting Tibetan interpretations assists my attempt to throw some light on Dharmakīrti's thought, as they describe some of the otherwise unacknowledged aspects of his philosophy. For example, I evince that his view of reality (the by now famous or infamous *svalakṣaṇa* or specifically characterized phenomenon) is complex. I also present an aspect of his theory of *apoha* (elimination) that has not been studied fully yet. In these ways, Tibetan commentary and scholarly tradition help identify Dharmakīrti's views and indicate their implications. Examining Tibetan ideas in light of the originals on which they comment is revealing not only of the achievements of the Tibetan tradition, but it also contributes to understanding the original model.

More important, Tibetan commentators bring out the philosophical content of and problems in Dharmakīrti's thought. They offer rich conceptual explorations of Buddhist epistemology on the basis of their ongoing participation in the Buddhist philosophical tradition. Although Tibetan thinkers are informed by historical considerations, their main strength is their ability to explore the philosophical content and implications of Dharmakīrti's works. In doing so, they help us appreciate some of the philosophical insights of the Buddhist epistemological tradition. For those patient enough to follow them, the intricate discussions of Tibetan thinkers provide a rich exercise in analytical and critical skills and serve as a guide to important philosophical questions. Hence, I hope that the audience of this book, which addresses the concerns of scholars and students interested in fields such as Tibetan civilization, Buddhism, and Indian philosophy, will not be limited to "Tibetologists" and other "Buddhologists." The use of a standard Western philosophical vocabulary is meant to allow nonprofessional readers to penetrate this often difficult but rewarding material.

The Commentarial Style of Indian and Tibetan Philosophical Traditions

While approaching this work, those philosophically inclined readers who are less familiar with Buddhist scholastic philosophy will have to keep in mind the commentarial nature of Indian and Tibetan philosophical style, one of the particularities of these traditions to which I have already alluded. An Indian or Tibetan philosophical system is usually close-knit and complicated, with boundaries and details that have been well elaborated over centuries. It is, however, hard to distinguish a clear philosophical method that characterizes Indian or Tibetan philosophical systems. Mohanty explains:

> In such a system, it is often a frustrating experience to look for an absolute beginning. Should the point be the scriptural texts which are then explicated and rationally justified? Should it be a primary cosmological and/or spiritual intuition which is then conceptually elaborated and defended against rival intuitions? Should the beginning be in the epistemological theory of *pramāṇas* or means of *knowledge* (with which the classical exposition began) from which the ontology, or theory of *prameya* (or objects of such knowledge) then follows? Or is the theory of *pramāṇas* itself a consequence of the implicitly presupposed metaphysics? Or, as may appear not unlikely to readers of Sanskrit philosophical texts, do the philosophers begin with ordinary experi-

ence and ordinary language, *lokānubhava* and *lokavyavahāra,* and then unravel their implications by a peculiar combination of description, analysis and transcendental argument?[3]

In the great diversity of methods, considerations and arguments used by Indian and Tibetan philosophers, only one fact clearly emerges: all philosophical activities rely on and are intended to validate the framework given by the tradition. Philosophical problems are not discussed only on the basis of their philosophical merits but in relation to and under the form of commentaries to some basic text formative of the tradition. This is also the case of the area of Indian and Tibetan philosophical traditions to be described here. On the Hindu side, epistemologists comment on the *Nyāya-sūtra* or other basic texts. On the Buddhist side, thinkers elaborate their system by commenting on Dignāga's or Dharmakīrti's texts.

This explicit and fairly narrow reliance on a pregiven system distinguishes Indian and Tibetan philosophical traditions from, for example, pre-Hellenistic Greek philosophy, where reliance on tradition is more diffuse.[4] Aristotle relies on Plato, but often in a negative way, and proposes his own independent system of thought. This is not the way in which Indian and Tibetan philosophers proceed. For them, to do philosophy is not to examine philosophical propositions independent of any traditional framework, but always to examine other systems from within one's own and to defend or develop one's own positions. This is, for this tradition, responsible philosophizing as distinguished from irresponsible sophistry.

The importance of commentary is a well-known feature of religious traditions that are shaped by the authority of certain scriptures. Michael Fishbane describes the religious imagination as "an imagination whose creativity is never entirely a new creation, but one founded upon older and authoritative words and images."[5] So-called Eastern and Western religions often are based on a corpus of normative teachings in which the historical experience of their founder(s) is recorded, transformed, and given atemporal dimensions. This is an ongoing creative process, which must have a fixed point, provided in most traditions by scriptural authority. The atemporal claim to authority of scripture is the basis for the constant reappropriation of the content of the tradition which is carried on through commentarial reinterpretation. The famous Jewish scholar Gershom Scholem summarizes this process when he says that "revelation needs commentary in order to be rightly understood and applied."[6] Commentary is seen by its authors as an act of retrieving a truth that has been given once and for all and needs to be reappropriated. It does not overtly innovate but rests its enterprise on a perennial truth grounding the whole tradition. This ongoing process of reinterpretation renews the life of a tradition and keeps scriptures relevant to changing circumstances, thus facilitating the continuation of that tradition.

The commentarial character of Indian philosophy is due not only to the religious character of its conflicting systems, for commentary in India applies to domains of thought that have little soteriological value. Even discussions of logic, grammar or medicine often take the form of commentaries on a basic text. The study of Indian and Tibetan epistemological traditions follows this model. An obvious assumption of this model is that the texts commented on are authoritative. These texts are worthy of being commented on because they present a true and complete picture of the field one wishes to study. In the Buddhist case, commentators take Dignāga and Dharmakīrti as authorities, assuming that they provide a true and complete picture of Buddhist epistemology. That is, to get them right is tantamount to being right. In this perspective, philosophical disagreements become arguments about the meaning of Dharmakīrti's pronouncements. But this assumption of authority presupposed by the commentarial method goes further. Not only does it hold that what Dharmakīrti says is right, it also assumes that what is right in logic and epistemology must be said by Dharmakīrti. Hence, we will see Ge-luk thinkers arguing for their own interpretations of Dharmakīrti on the basis of mostly logical considerations. These scholars will feel no compunction in interpreting the numerous passages disagreeing with their interpretations, for they assume that there is a necessary congruence between Dharmakīrti's texts and truth in the field of logic and epistemology.

The assumption of authority granted to the texts formative to the tradition has limitations, especially in the case of the Tibetan interpretations of Dharmakīrti. There, thinkers often are quite aware that their basic views of reality partly differ from Dharmakīrti's. This divergence is usually handled through a doxographical model which I will examine later. For instance, most Sa-gya and Ge-luk thinkers describe themselves as Mādhyamika. They also recognize that Dharmakīrti is a Yogācārin and hence does not share some of their views. Nevertheless, they use his thought in the domains of logic, epistemology, and philosophy of language. They do so because, in a tradition in which philosophy is commentarial, a philosophical point cannot be made without being properly grounded in a previous tradition. In the logico-epistemological domain, Dharmakīrti provides this authoritative grounding. Tibetan thinkers are quite aware of his limitations but realize that there is no epistemological tradition within Indian Buddhism rich enough to provide a viable alternative. Hence, when dealing with Dharmakīrti's thought, Tibetan thinkers will assume that Dharmakīrti is right, except for matters that reflect his doxographical limitations.

An implication of this situation is that the opinions defended by commentators represent their own views to a certain extent. On some topics, particularly those concerning ontology, Tibetan thinkers will argue about what is right and wrong more in relation to Dharmakīrti's texts than in relation to their own opinions. For example, Ge-luk and Sa-gya thinkers commenting on Dharmakīrti will agree that partless atoms are real and argue about whether objects of commonsense, such as a jar, are real or not. Such views should not be understood as reflecting their own personal views but, rather, as commentaries on Dharmakīrti's philosophy. As Mādhyamikas, these thinkers mostly reject Dharmakīrti's distinction between the real and the conceptual. Thus, according to their own system, neither atom nor jar has any reality over and above its conventional status. Nevertheless, while discussing Dharmakīrti's philosophy, these authors suspend their own ontologies and argue about this point in implicit reference to Dharmakīrti's system. This allows them to use Dharmakīrti to deal with more strictly logico-epistemological matters where he is assumed to be right, everything else being equal. Therefore, throughout this work the reader should understand that my descriptions of Tibetan thinkers' views do not refer always to their positions, but to their commentarial interpretations of Dharmakīrti.

This commentarial style also has definite implications for this work. Since the views I examine are genuinely philosophical as well as commentarial, I will assess them from both standpoints. I will compare these views to the original they comment on, mostly Dharmakīrti's thought, as well as evaluate them on their own merit. When discussing the problem of universals, for example, I will explain Ge-luk and Sa-gya interpretations. I will compare them to Dharmakīrti's thought, stating which one is closer to the original model than the other. I will also present a more strictly philosophical evaluation of these traditions, showing their conceptual strengths and weaknesses.

Another noticeable feature of the material we will examine here is its great complication. This is partly a function of the commentarial nature of the tradition. Every philosophical point must be made in reference to some text, which has to be discussed in order to make the argument understandable. But there is more. The commentarial style encourages a highly technical style of philosophy that is best described as scholastic. This word, which has been used derogatorily by the Western Enlightenment, should be understood here to refer colloquially to a style of philosophy in which discussions involve highly developed analytical skills. In such a tradition, a technical question such as the problem of universals can receive great attention. A similar type of philosophy is found in the writings of Aristotle and his school, Islamic, Christian, and Jewish Medieval scholastics, as well as modern analytical philosophers. Hence, it is among these thinkers, particularly the last group, that I have found revealing similarities.

A common but mistaken assumption is that a scholastic philosophy is necessarily sterile and fruitless. Although scholasticism leads to a proliferation of subtle distinctions and is in danger of losing sight of important questions,[7] such a reproach can be made of any philosophical tradition. We could even argue that such a danger reflects the nature of philosophical inquiry itself. Whatever is the truth of this overly general statement, it remains that despite its limited popularity in these days of "fast thinking," technical analytical philosophy as practiced by European scholastics, Indian paṇḍits, Tibetan lama-scholars, or modern logicians has manifested the vigor of philosophical thinking.

The problem with scholastic philosophy is that describing its arguments is difficult, for they involve distinctions that are hardly understandable to those not specially trained. Throughout this work, I have tried to reach a compromise between excessive simplification and utter scholasticism. The reader should be aware that often I have simplified the complicated positions, and the arguments supporting them, to make them fit into my narrative. I have tried, however, to preserve some of the flavor of the scholastic voices presented in this text.

Scholarly Context

In underlining the philosophical strength of the Tibetan tradition, I have relied greatly on both modern and traditional scholars. This work is not, however, a summary of their impressive accomplishments but, rather, presents a new picture of the Tibetan epistemological tradition. Of particular significance is the dialogue between the various Tibetan schools and the interactions between history and philosophy. In making these points, I see myself as continuing the dialogue between Tibetan scholarly tradition and modern academic scholarship started by David Ruegg, Katsumi Mimaki, and others.

The study of Tibetan Buddhism is a recent endeavor that has benefited greatly from the forced exile of learned Tibetan teachers. Their misfortunes have raised Tibetan studies to an unexpected level for such a young field, particularly in the domains of Buddhist philosophy, where the considerable knowledge of Tibetan scholars has allowed scholars such as Jeffrey Hopkins and Anne Klein to present significant explanations of the Tibetan epistemological tradition in a well-informed manner. Their studies, however, have focused mostly on the contributions of the the Ge-luk tradition, in isolation from other schools, and largely has left aside their historical context. Other scholars such as David Jackson and Leonard van der Kuijp have contributed invaluable historical studies of Tibetan epistemological traditions. They also have provided interesting glimpses into the rival Sa-gya tradition but have not explained its philosophy in great detail.

The excellent works of all these scholars have provided students of Buddhist thought with rich material, which was previously totally inaccessible. Nevertheless, there is ample room for further improvements. An example is the need to articulate in a clear philosophical language the views of Tibetan traditions, which Tom Tillemans, Paul Williams, Roger Jackson, and others have begun for the Ge-luk views, whereas the views of Sa-gya epistemology have remained mostly absent from the discussion.

More important, I believe that it is time to move toward a more encompassing approach to the study of the different Tibetan traditions. Instead of attending to the views of each school in isolation, we may now attend to the interactions between traditions. This approach to Tibetan Buddhism was not possible in the earlier stages, when correctly describing the views of the various traditions was most pressing. This task, although not complete, has been well carried on. We may now aim for a more contextualized view of the Tibetan tradition, so that its diversity is well accounted for and relations among its strands are not obscured. The Tibetan tradition is not a juxtaposition of self-enclosed schools but consists of a rich dialogue among competing traditions. It is also important at this point to relate historical and philosophical developments to each other, putting ideas in relation to their proper socio-political contexts and better understanding their evolution.

This work is indebted not only to Western scholarship. My study of Buddhist epistemology began during the 1970s when I became a full-time student in the

Ge-luk tradition. I am fortunate to have spent my most formative years as a student there, in a milieu that had inherited the study of Buddhist philosophy through generations of highly qualified scholars. For seven years, I spent several months each year studying Dharmakīrti's texts, together with the best of the Ge-luk commentaries, under the guidance of these scholars. I am particularly indebted to the many teachers who patiently helped me develop my philosophical abilities through these studies. Ge-shay Rabten, Lati Rimbochay, Ge-shay Lo-sang-gya-tso (*blo bzang rgya mtsho*) and Ge-shay Nyi-ma-gyel-tsen (*nyi ma rgyal mtshan*), among many others, were particularly helpful in this regard. This work attempts to acknowledge the immense value of the scholarly tradition they have represented so well.

This indebtedness creates its own set of problems. The close link that I and many other students of Tibetan Buddhism have forged with traditional scholars is one of the greatest attractions of studying Tibetan Buddhism. Instead of being limited to texts, we have been fortunate to have access to well-informed scholars. As my colleagues surely recognize, this has been, and still is, a source of enormous strength from which we all have benefited. This closeness, however, can be an obstacle to a more mature understanding of Tibetan tradition. There is a danger of becoming dazzled by the quality of the scholarly expression and the personalities we encounter, which may in fact obscure the limitations of the positions asserted.

Living Tibetan traditions are institutions that make their own claims to authority. I find it necessary to be critical of these claims. I have attempted to do this in several ways, two of which seem particularly relevant here: placing their interpretations within the development of the overall Tibetan tradition, and keeping sight of the historical and political character of Tibetan schools. Failure to attend to such concerns could lead to an absolutizing of the viewpoints of Tibetan scholars. In actuality, although their views are valuable, they share the limitations of any interpretation. Establishing a degree of critical distance has allowed me to attempt to contribute to this tradition by bringing it into dialogue with modern academic scholarship.

Therefore, it should be clear that my use of Tibetan sources in no way implies an acceptance of the authority of this tradition. Although I rely on the insights of Tibetan commentators to understand the material I study, Dharmakīrti's ideas included, I do not claim that the truth about Dharmakīrti and his tradition is their sole possession. Nor am I arguing for a wholesale adoption of their interpretations, however "enlightened." On the contrary, this work presents a critical picture of the strengths and limitations of their approaches, even as it draws on them in developing an analysis and critique of Dharmakīrti's philosophy.

In this way, I attempt to give Tibetan traditions serious consideration within a sustained dialogue across boundaries. In the process, I do not intend merely to repeat the conclusions of Tibetan commentators. Hans-Georg Gadamer makes an important point when he says, "It is enough to say that we understand in a different way, if we understand at all."[8] Hence, whatever is of value here must involve more than mere repetition: it must reflect some degree of insight into the material.

It is perhaps obvious that works of interpretation, this one included, reflect the limitations of the historical situations in which they have been written. It may be less apparent that our position as modern interpreters and that of traditional scholars are no different in this respect. Our understanding has historical limitations that are similar (but not identical) to those of ancient interpreters. However methodologically refined our works may be, they do not come into existence from a position of absolute neutrality but reflect our historical situation. As the ethicist Alasdair MacIntyre says, "[I]t is an illusion to suppose that there is some neutral standing ground, some locus for rationality as such, which can afford rational resources sufficient for enquiry independent of all traditions. Those who maintained otherwise either have covertly been adopting the standpoint of a tradition and deceiving themselves and others into supposing theirs was just such a neutral stand-ground or else have simply been in error."[9] Ethically and methodologically useful at times, the injunction to absolute neutrality usually given to modern scholars obscures the epistemological nature of the interpretative process. Understanding a text is not accomplished by eliminating all expectations and preformed ideas—that would be strictly impossible—but by unearthing them. As good interpreters we do not empty our minds to understand what an author means but check existing ideas and judgments against the evidence provided by the text and the context and confront our opinions against those of other informed interpreters. Therefore, the search for the meaning of a text or a system is not just an analytical process but involves a dialogical dimension as well.

This work considers Tibetan commentators to be partners in the kind of dialogue necessary for greater understanding. Because of their participation in an ongoing tradition of inquiry in the philosophy of Dharmakīrti's tradition, these highly educated interpreters are ideally suited to a dialogue with modern methodologically aware interpreters.

The dialogical dimension of scholarly work is particularly relevant to my own experience. After finishing my studies of the traditional curriculum offered by Ge-luk monastic universities, I continued my study of Buddhist epistemology while engaged in academic work in the United States. There my previous understanding of Dharmakīrti confronted that of modern scholars such as Bimal Matilal, Ernst Steinkellner, Masaaki Hattori, Masatoshi Nagatomi, Nandita Bandyopadhyay, Dharmendra Shastri, Richard Hayes, Ernst Vetter, Rita Gupta, and many others. In the process, I could not but notice the discrepancies between their views and the interpretations to which I had been exposed previously. I also noticed that these differences often corresponded to the points that I had felt had not been resolved adequately during my previous training. All this obliged me to go back to the study of Dharmakīrti's own texts. In the process I developed a diversified comprehension of Buddhist epistemology. I came to understand some of the sources and rationales for the discrepancies I had noticed earlier, realizing that they arose due to difficulties internal to Dharmakīrti's own system. This gave me a realization of the richness of Dharmakīrti's tradition that would have been difficult to develop solely through the study of his texts. I hope to share with my readers some of the enthusiasm that has taken me down this path.

The Hermeneutical Significance of Comparison

Another methodological concern I would like to address is the partially comparative nature of my work and the resulting difficulties. Despite the problematic nature of this methodology, it remains at the center of the humanities. Let me make a few general remarks, following the penetrating analysis of Jonathan Z. Smith, a contemporary historian of religions.

Smith starts his investigation of comparison by underlining its cognitive importance: "The process of comparison is a fundamental characteristic of human intelligence. Whether revealed in the logical grouping of classes, in poetic similes, in mimesis, or other like activities—comparison, the bringing together of two or more objects for the purpose of either similarity or dissimilarity, is the omnipresent substructure of human thought. Without it, we could not speak, perceive, learn, or reason."[10] Despite its primordial importance, the role of comparison in the humanities is problematic. Comparison has led us astray at times, as for example in the comparative study of mysticism in which similarities have tended to be overemphasized. Nevertheless, despite its problematic nature and the disrepute into which it has fallen,[11] comparison remains a privileged tool of the humanities.

The first point to make is that comparison involves not only similarities between two or more elements but also dissimilarities. Comparison does not consist of saying "this is like that." This simplistic approach inevitably invites the unfair but devastating question mentioned by Smith,[12] "and so what?" If we want to avoid being either trivial or groundless, we have to take into account differences as well as similarities. This seems to have been ignored by many comparative studies of mysticism, which have assimilated different forms of religious experiences while relegating their differences to linguistic and cultural superstructures.

Such an assimilative approach to comparison falls into the extreme of presuming an overwhelming degree of similarity between mystical phenomena. Despite their transcendent vocations, however, even these cannot escape the status of cultural object. To be more fruitful, comparison must walk the finer path described by Dilthey: "Interpretation would be impossible if [past] expressions of life were completely strange. It would be unnecessary if nothing strange were in them. It lies, therefore, between these two extremes."[13] Whereas something utterly alien could not be understood, something identical is self-evident and requires no interpretation. Comparison requires the presence of some differences, "a methodological manipulation of difference, a playing across the 'gap' in the service of some useful end."[14] This play of differences and similarities answers the "how" question, but leaves open the "why." Why do we compare? How can we avoid the "so what" response mentioned earlier?

Dilthey's passage suggests that the main purpose of comparison is hermeneutical. Comparison is required by the nature of cultural objects, which require interpretation. This is most obvious in the field of religion, where the student is faced with a bewildering diversity of myths, beliefs, and practices. This alienness of cultural objects is not, however, limited to the unfamiliar domains explored by history of religions or anthropology. It affects any cultural object whose significance goes beyond the most basic level of communication.

Confronted by an unfamiliar object, we use comparison: we notice similarities and, more significant, differences. We situate the object, understanding it as belonging to a certain type or genre. We also notice differences that set this object apart from others. We thereby start to form certain anticipatory prejudgments,[15] which lead and inform our enquiry.

This work uses such a comparative method. It is not intended, however, as a full-blown comparative enterprise. My concern here is not to attempt a symmetrical comparison across cultures, extensively comparing Indian, Tibetan, and Western philosophies. Rather, I focus on Indian and Tibetan thinkers, using comparisons to determine the vocabulary of the enquiry.[16] Indian and Tibetan concepts are discussed using a standard Western vocabulary, and comparisons are briefly suggested rather than thematically developed. For example, I make extensive use of the opposition between realism and conceptualism concerning the problem of universals to reveal the logic of ideas in a tradition in which interpretative issues sometimes hide the more purely philosophical questions. Although the use of such terminology is not explicitly comparative, it involves an implicit comparison made to frame the vocabulary of my inquiry.

I also use some more explicit comparisons. For instance, I compare Dharmakīrti's philosophy to modern empiricism not just as a rhetorical device to introduce Dharmakīrti's ideas nor to present the alien through what is already known (because of the specialized nature of this work, it is in no way certain that most of my readers will know Locke better than Uddyotakara or Dharmakīrti!). My intention is to suggest a view of Dharmakīrti's tradition that facilitates its integration into the history of human ideas. Too often discussions of Indian philosophies fail to retrieve the philosophical content of the thoughts they examine. This leads to the unfortunate situation in which Indian thought is ignored by the philosopher and historian of ideas as being irrational, illogical, and altogether nonsensical.

It seems to me that one of our tasks as students of Asian thought is to present the material we examine so that it gradually becomes integrated into the larger history of ideas. There is a need for presenting non-Western ideas in terms that can be related to the concepts of other cultures. This task is not, however, without problems, for the "larger" scheme through which "the history of humankind" is written is hardly neutral. The "history of philosophy" is written from a perspective formed in ancient Greece and developed in Europe and, therefore, is heavily connected with a cultural context from which Asia (not to mention other non-Western cultures) has been largely excluded.

Integrating Indian or other cultures to a history written from this perspective is not without danger. For in introducing etic concepts we incur the risk of damaging beyond repair the material we intend to retrieve. For example, in comparing Uddyotakara with Aristotle and choosing a standard Western vocabulary to present the two systems, I run the risk of obliterating the particularities of the Nyāya philosophy (such as its close association with Sanskrit linguistics).

Still, it seems to me that the risk has to be taken, for the alternative, irrelevance, is hardly desirable. As a Western scholarly community, we cannot avoid using etic concepts in examining the ideas of other cultures. We have to use our own words, with all their history and associations, and face the prospect of transforming the traditions we examine. This risk cannot be escaped and is implied by the increasing cross-cultural dialogue characteristic of the contemporary situation. What we can do is to be careful not to succumb to the temptation of believing that the description we obtain by using a standard Western vocabulary is normative, that it is the last word on the question, which allows us to pass a judgment on the traditions we study. Rather, it seems to me that this is the first step, after which a deeper exploration of the tradition can take place.

The Structure of the Work

For its central theme this work explores the problem of universals, including the consequences various interpretations of this notion hold for epistemology and semantics in the Buddhist logico-epistemological tradition. The procedure I follow is straightforward: for most of the topics I examine I open with an introductory chapter discussing my terminology as well as the Indian context of Dharmakīrti's ideas. The next chapter discusses Dharmakīrti's philosophy, and the following ones compare his views with those of Tibetan scholars. This order is largely expository, however. It does not reflect the reality of the interpretive process underlying my thinking in this work. My understanding of Dharmakīrti's ideas is not independent of that of traditional Tibetan scholars, as it is based mostly on a philosophical reading of the Tibetan versions of his texts and their Tibetan commentaries. Nevertheless, my view of Dharmakīrti is not reducible to the Tibetan interpretations either. Although this work focuses the Tibetan reception of Indian Buddhist epistemology, it also investigates the Indian side of the story. By consulting some of the Sanskrit texts and the views of modern scholars on the topic, I have tried to present a philosophically meaningful interpretation of Dharmakīrti that is more than the sum total of the scholarly contributions on which I have relied.

The work is divided into two books. Book I analyzes the problem of universals from an ontological perspective, and investigates the importance of this question for the philosophy of language in the Buddhist logico-epistemological tradition. Book I is divided into three parts. Part I deals with the ontology of Dharmakīrti's tradition. There, I analyze Dharmakīrti's antirealist philosophy and the sharp contrast it makes between the real and the conceptual. I also contrast Dharmakīrti's anti-realist view with the moderate realism of the Ge-luk tradition. Part II of Book I deals with the problem of universals per se. I contrast realism and antirealism, showing how many doctrinal conflicts in the Tibetan tradition relate to this opposition. Part III of Book I examines the semantic consequences of realism and conceptualism. In particular, I analyze the famous *apoha* theory, the hallmark of Buddhist philosophy of language.

Book II considers the epistemologies implied by conflicting views of universals. It is divided into two parts, organized around the concepts of valid cognition and perception. The first part examines valid cognition, which is central to Dharmakīrti and his tradition. I consider the conflicting interpretations of valid cognition, showing how Dharmakīrti's rejection of universals makes it difficult for him to provide a convincing account of knowledge. I also show how this difficulty provides the basis for further discussions among his later Indian and Tibetan followers. Finally, the second part of Book II completes this analysis by considering the theory of perception. I analyze the opposition between representationalism and direct realism, showing how this opposition informs debates among Tibetan philosophers. I also investigate the views of Dharmakīrti and his followers concerning reflexivity. This allows me to draw out some of the possible soteriological dimensions of his work.

At the completion of this long investigation, though we may not have resolved the problem of universals, we will have learned a great deal about Buddhist epistemology. Moreover, the impossibility of reaching any final conclusion in such a discussion is by itself a great philosophical lesson. This is not only my own conclusion but that of the Tibetan tradition. The historical background of this discussion is the task of the next introductory section, which discusses the place of Dharmakīrti and his followers in the Indian and Tibetan traditions.

Introduction II

Dharmakīrti's Tradition in India and Tibet

The Epistemological Turn in Indian Philosophy

Having sketched some of the methodological presuppositions of this work, let us start our study of the Buddhist tradition of logic and epistemology by locating the place of Dharmakīrti's tradition within Indian philosophy and Buddhism. This tradition was started by Dignāga around 500 C.E.[1] Although before him Buddhist thinkers such as Nāgārjuna and Vasubandhu dealt with these topics, Dignāga was the first to explicitly formulate a complete Buddhist logico-epistemological system. His tradition provided the standard formulation of Buddhist logic and epistemology in India and Tibet. The importance of this system in India is suggested by the continous references by later Buddhist thinkers and the numerous attacks it received from orthodox Hindu thinkers, such as the Mīmāṃsaka Kumārila Bhaṭṭa and the Naiyāyika Uddyotakara. Answering this criticism was left to Dharmakīrti, whose elaboration of Dignāga's system became the reference point for Buddhist epistemology, so that Dignāga's ideas have tended to be viewed through Dharmakīrti's eyes.[2]

Dignāga's and Dharmakīrti's contributions are significant within the overall evolution of Indian philosophy, not just for Buddhist thought. Both authors wrote at a time when Indian philosophy turned toward logic and epistemology as a way to defend existing doctrines. Starting from the discussions of the *Nyāya-sūtra* and Vātsyāyana's commentary, great attention was paid to argumentation and the theory of inference. This resulted in the establishment of a logic that gained wide acceptance, so much so that it provided intertraditional standards of validation. These developments created the relatively neutral framework within which competing claims of Indian philosophical schools, such as Nyāya, Mīmāṃsā, Jain, and Buddhism, could be assessed.

In some ways this is not unlike the situation of modern Western philosophy. From the beginning of the modern era, marked by Descartes's "epistemological turn," philosophers have turned away from metaphysics to study scientific knowledge. In this process, a common framework for discussing conflicting claims was developed. Philosophers turned away from the traditional religious and metaphysical questions and toward new areas of human knowledge. This allowed a discussion between empiricists and rationalists in almost purely logical and epistemological terms. Overtly religious or metaphysical topics, which had become undecidable, were avoided. These concerns did not, however, disappear but remained in the background, where they continued to inform the competing logico-epistemological systems.

In recent times, analytical philosophy has taken over the task of defining a tradition-neutral framework. This new way, created by Gottlob Frege (1848–1925), has been well described by Richard Rorty as a "linguistic turn."[3] In it, philosophers no longer deal with epistemological questions about the justification of knowledge claims. At this point, these had become overly psychologized. Instead modern analytical thinkers turn to the study of mathematical logic and formalized languages. The effect of this change has been twofold. First, new questions about the philosophy of language, mathematics, and formalized logic have come to the fore. Second, old problems, such as that of the essential-accidental distinction, also have come to be studied in the more aseptic environment of linguistic and logical analysis.

The appearance of Dignāga and Dharmakīrti represented a somewhat similar paradigm shift. Their works helped create an epistemological turn that was part of a broader movement affecting the whole of Indian philosophy. These two authors were part of a vast movement of thinkers, Hindu and Jain as well as Buddhist, who turned away from traditional metaphysical questions such as the nature of the self and the path to liberation. Instead they devoted themselves to the study of epistemology. After this turning point, the philosophical quest seemed to bear less on metaphysical truth claims than on the basis for making such claims. The new concern with validating philosophical and religious claims through argumentation motivated thinkers to elaborate theories about the sources and types of knowledge.

In other ways, however, the epistemological shift in India differed from that of the West. This epistemological turn was not based on the demotion of theology and the rise of scientific thinking, as in modern Western philosophy. Rather it was built on new developments in a long linguistic tradition. These provided the technical tools for discussion of new problems or new ways of discussing old doctrines. Such discussions have focused on the question of knowledge, phrased in terms of *pramāṇa* (means of valid cognition or valid cognition).

Dignāga and Dharmakīrti are often presented as Buddhist logicians. This is not false, but it is bound to be misleading without some explanation. It wrongly suggests that these authors were interested primarily in the formal properties of reasoning. There is no denying that there is an important logical side to their works, but it must be understood that this logical side is always subordinate to pragmatic concerns. The primacy of the practical in the classical Indian study of reasoning is apparent in the origins of logic in India. These had to do with the validation of sacred texts. This emphasis on the practical is visible in the Nyāya school as well, where correct arguments, in conformity with the norms, free the soul.

This is a different use of the word *logic* than is commonly assumed in contemporary analytical discussions. In these discussions, logic is a discipline whose central problem is the study of arguments according to their logical form. Lukasiewicz says: "Only syllogistic laws stated in variables belong to logic, and not their application to concrete terms. Logic is devoid of any *hule* (matter) and is concerned only with form."[4] In the modern analytical usage, logic is not preoccupied with the content of the propositions it posits but with their form. It is interested in the deductions that are drawn from propositions, not in the truth or falsity of the propositions. Its primordial object is not material truth but formal necessity.

This concern for formal validity over material truth does not concern just modern logic. Despite its differences with modern formalism, Aristotelian logic was already preoccupied with formal validity over soundness. Thus, Carnap is quite justified in saying, "All the efforts of the logicians since Aristotle have been directed to the formulation of rules of inference as formal rules, that is to say, as rules which refer only to the form of the sentences."[5] This is why the primordial concern of Western logic has always been mostly deductive. It is only in deduction that absolute (for Aristotle) or formal (for Carnap) necessity can be found. Such has indeed been the focal point of the Western logical tradition.

The concern of Indian "logicians" is quite different. They intend to provide a critical and systematic analysis of the diverse means of correct cognition that we use practically in our quest for knowledge. In this task, they discuss the nature and types of *pramāṇa*. Although Indian philosophers disagree on the types of cognition that can be considered valid, most recognize perception and inference as valid. Within this context, which is mostly epistemological and practically oriented, topics such as the nature and types of correct reasoning that pertain to logic in the large sense of the word are discussed.[6] In this work, I have chosen to leave aside this aspect of Dharmakīrti's thought to focus on the overall epistemological framework of his system.

The Place of Dharmakīrti in Indian Buddhism

The turn in Indian philosophy toward logic, epistemology, and the philosophical study of language coincided with a similar change within Buddhist tradition, which can be understood as developing over three stages.[7] In the first centuries of its existence, Buddhists focused on differentiating their view from competing traditions (Brahmanical or nonorthodox such as Jain and Ājīvika). Therefore, they attempted to prove the truth of the Buddhist tradition rather than assume it. The resulting intersectarian discussions tended to use a simple and direct language, with little of the technicality that would become the hallmark of classical Indian philosophy.

The second period focused more on intrasectarian developments. During this time the foundations of what later became known as the four schools of

Buddhist philosophy (Vaibhāṣika, Sautrāntika, Yogācāra, and Madhyamaka) were laid down. Toward Aśoka's time (third century B.C.E.), Buddhism gained the institutional recognition that guaranteed its place as a separate tradition. Its emergence as a major school of Indian thought created the context in which major Buddhist thinkers tended to assume the truth of their tradition and focus on intratraditional dispute. For sure, some attention was given to discussion of non-Buddhist views. The focus, however, departed from intertraditional discussion in which the tradition as a whole must be defended. It centered instead around discussions between competing Buddhist schools, largely around issues in the Abhidharma. In the earlier stages, most thinkers shared a similar view of reality. They insisted on the ideas basic to the Buddhist tradition (impermanence, selflessness, etc.) and held a view of reality as being reducible to building blocks (the *dharmas*), which the Abhidharma listed. All other phenomena were declared to be unreal projections. The debate centered around conflicting listings of the basic components of reality. Gradually, however, more radical views emerged that brought this view into question.

Nāgārjuna (second–third centuries C.E.), the founder of the Madhayamaka school, is typical of the later part of that second period of Indian Buddhism. He set forth a radical view that rejected any trace of substantialism. According to his view, all phenomena, including the building blocks of the Abhidharma, are essenceless. All phenomena lack intrinsic identity and exist only relationally. Although Nāgārjuna refuted some aspects of the Nyāya system,[8] he focused mostly on debating Abhidharmic schools. His view set the stage for new developments within Buddhist philosophy. Many were not quite ready, however, to go as far as he had, and yet they could not revert to the simpler views of the Abhidharma.

Asaṅga and Vasubandhu (400–480 C.E.) offered an important contribution to this current, the Yogācāra philosophy, which attempts to include a more radical element in the Abhidharmic tradition. According to this view, all phenomena are essenceless only inasmuch as they do not exist independent of consciousness.[9] Like the old Abhidharma views, the Yogācāra system distinguishes real entities (in this case consciousness), the equivalent of the old Abhidharmic building blocks, from less real mental projections. Only the latter are essenceless in the literal sense of the word. The former are real. In this way, the key Abhidharmic distinction between the real and the conceptual is maintained. We will see that such a distinction is central to Dignāga's and Dharmakīrti's system, where it serves as the basis of an epistemological foundationalism. Hence, I describe their view as Yogācāra, despite the problems involved in this description.[10]

The third period (around 500 C.E.) within Indian Buddhism was marked by a return to the pattern of intersectarian disputes. This development was probably prompted by the development of more sophisticated philosophical tools with which traditions could reopen old disputes. In this domain Dignāga, who was supposed to have been Vasubandhu's disciple, and Dharmakīrti excelled, providing a well-articulated defense of Buddhist philosophical principles against the rising tide of Hindu philosophy. In the process, their tradition became an important school of Indian Buddhism in its own right, producing several major thinkers including Śāntarakṣita, Dharmottara, and Prajñākaragupta (all around the eighth century C.E.). Its influence, however, was not limited to their followers. Other Buddhist schools adopted its vocabulary. Hence, it has central importance for understanding later developments in Buddhist philosophy.

The influence of the logico-epistemological tradition was already clearly noticeable in Bhavya (500–570). He reconsidered Madhyamaka doctrine in the light of Dignāga's logical system. Jñānagarbha (700–760) offers the example of a Mādhyamika who has adopted many of the key Dharmakīrtian epistemological concepts we examine here. His works mark a strong shift toward epistemology within the Madhyamaka tradition. His use of concepts such as the performance of a function (*arthakriyā, don byed pa*) to define correct relative truth and self-cognition (*svasaṃvedana, rang rig*) betrays the extent to which Dharmakīrti's vocabulary had penetrated other Buddhist traditions.[11] Not all Mādhyamikas, however, agreed on this use of Buddhist logic and epistemology. Candrakīrti (540–600) in particular saw this use of Dignāga's system, which is, as we will see, committed to an essentialist ontology and a foundationalist epistemology, as contradicting the Madhyamaka rejection of essentialism. For Candrakīrti, Mādhyamikas should undermine, or, to use a by now worn out word, deconstruct, concepts that presuppose an idea of essential identity. Consistent Mādhyamikas should not aim at providing a complete system, but rest happy with pragmatically endorsing the philosophical tools that can further their task of undermining essentialism.

This work will not analyze extensively Candrakīrti's philosophy but will focus on the very different philosophy of Dharmakīrti and his tradition. In this way, we may contribute to undermining the reified view of Buddhism as a tradition unified in its rejection of essentialism. Although such a view is found in Candrakīrti, it does not represent the view of the majority of Indian thinkers, who often adopted a systematic and constructive approach even while suscribing to Madhyamaka tenets. Consequently, Indian Buddhist thinkers had not been very impressed by Candrakīrti, at least up to around 1000 (when his works seem to have received greater attention), having favored Dharmakīrti's systematic and constructive approach instead.

The situation was quite different in Tibet, where many thinkers have considered Candrakīrti central to their understanding of Nāgārjuna's philosophy. This became the case especially after Ba-tsap's (*pa tshab nyi ma grags*, 1055–1145?) translation of Candrakīrti's works. Even then, however, Dharmakīrti's influence remained considerable. For, although many Tibetan thinkers have adopted Candrakīrti's Madhyamaka, they have been reluctant to follow him in his rejection of Dignāga's epistemology. This use of Dignāga's and Dharmakīrti's system within a philosophy whose overall orientation is opposed to the latter's philosophy is one of the paradoxes of Tibetan tradition that we will have to examine, particularly in our conclusion.

Most of the Tibetan philosophical discussions reflect Dharmakīrti's strong influence. They presuppose his vocabulary even when discussing Madhyamaka philosophy. Dharmakīrtian concepts such as valid cognition (*tshad ma, pramāṇa*) and elimination (*sel ba, apoha*) are used often in monastic debates on a variety of topics. The debate format, which is still very popular among Tibetans, also is based largely on Dharmakīrti's logic,[12] and so is most of the basic vocabulary used by Tibetan students in their education. This has provided Tibetan philosophers with a standard terminology that is used as a framework for inquiry into various areas of Buddhist philosophy. All this shows the considerable influence of Dharmakīrti on the later part of the Indian and Tibetan traditions.

The importance of Dignāga and Dharmakīrti within the evolution of Indian Buddhist thought lay in their ability to formulate a defense of basic Buddhist principles within the relatively tradition-neutral framework emerging around that time. Dharmakīrti's assertion that Buddhist doctrines can be justified was historically an important contribution. In his famous "Establishment [of Buddha] as Valid" (*pramāṇasiddhi, tshad mar grub pa*),[13] he argued that there are consistent reasons for holding that reality conforms to Buddhist teachings. This provided a reference point for other Buddhist thinkers asserting their viewpoints in the face of Hindu reaction.

This defense is carried within a philosophical vocabulary widely accepted in India. It uses relatively tradition-neutral terms (such as universals *versus* individuals and conceptions *versus* perceptions) that are understandable to non-Buddhist philosophers and applicable across much of Buddhist discussion as well. Participating in such wide discussions affects the relation of Dignāga and Dharmakīrti's tradition to the schools within Indian Buddhism. They often relied on what I would describe as a minimal interpretation of Buddhist philosophy. That is, an interpretation acceptable to most Buddhist schools. Rather than focus on their own view, a form of Yogācāra idealism, they most often, but not always, propounded a doctrine of the reality of external objects that does not necessarily correspond to their opinion. On a deeper level, however, they did not retain these objects. This results in a rather surprising articulation of two seemingly contradictory positions.

The first view, defended throughout Dignāga's and Dharmakīrti's texts (Yogācāra passages representing only a small fraction of the texts), is often described as Sautrāntika.[14] It seems to be so-named for the sake of integrating it within the usual doxographical scheme of four Indian Buddhist schools. In fact, it is different from the view usually ascribed to Sautrāntika. This discrepancy is well perceived by Tibetan scholars, who attempt to explain away this discrepancy by describing Dharmakīrti as a "Sautrāntika following reasoning" (*rigs pa'i rjes 'brang gi mdo sde pa*).[15] This oxymoronic term illustrates the difficulty in pinning down Dignāga's and Dharmakīrti's views in terms of tenet systems. It reflects the limitations of doxographical considerations, and also the difficulty of the project of these two thinkers; namely, the articulation and defense of a Buddhist epistemology in terms broadly acceptable both inside and outside Buddhist tradition. Dignāga and Dharmakīrti allowed themselves to use metaphysical standpoints that are contradictory from a doxographical point of view to further this project.

Since Stcherbatksy's famous *Buddhist Logic*, it has been customary to divide Dharmakīrti's Indian commentators into three traditions: the school of literal exegesis of Dharmakīrti's disciple, Devendrabuddhi (630–690 C.E.), and the latter's student Śākyabuddhi;[16] the religious school of Prajñākaragupta (740–800 C.E.); and last, the philosophical tradition of Dharmottara (750–810 C.E.) and Śaṃkarānanda.[17] Although the differentiation between the three latter authors is less clear, a clear difference lies between the first tradition and the later commentarial traditions. Whereas the former attempts a literal rendering of Dharmakīrti, the latter present a comparatively remote stage of interpretation. Here, the necessity to respond to repeated criticism from Hindu orthodoxy has taken precedence over literal gloss. This second group differentiates itself from Devendrabuddhi, whom they accuse of having misinterpreted Dharmakīrti's thought.[18] In this work, they will offer a transition between the early views of Dharmakīrti and his first commentators and elaborations by later Tibetan thinkers. To Stcherbatsky's grouping into three, a fourth group should be added, Śāntarakṣita (725–783) and his disciple Kamalaśīla, who contributed to a transformation of the *apoha* theory we will document in this work. They also strongly influenced a group of later Indian commentators who interpreted Dharmakīrti as a Mādhyamika.[19] Early Tibetan commentators adopted this idea and tended to interpret Dharmakīrti's text in the light of the Madhyamaka idea of essencelessness.

Dharmakīrti's Tradition in Tibet

In Tibet, Dharmakīrti and his school have occupied a different place in the Buddhist tradition than the one they had among Indian Buddhists. Whereas in India, Buddhist thinkers used Dharmakīrti's thought successfully as a way to defend their tradition against their adversaries, Tibetan Buddhists have not had to argue philosophically for Buddhism. From the eleventh century at the latest until recently, the supremacy of Buddhism in Tibet has been well established. No other tradition challenged this dominance. Therefore, one of the main reasons for justifying the study of Dharmakīrti's tradition, namely, the defense of Buddhist philosophy against its Hindu critics, is missing in Tibet.

Several Tibetan thinkers have felt that Dharmakīrti's thought was not relevant to their situation. Atīśa for one, whose influence on the formation of Tibetan Buddhism is difficult to overestimate, distrusted Dharmakīrti's tradition. He considered it a purely intellectual tradition without much relation to Buddhist practice. For him, Dharmakīrti's texts had been written for the sake of refuting Hindu opponents and had been successful. Since these adversaries did not exist in Tibet, however, there was no need to refute them. Hence, there was no need to study this tradition: "Such texts as the ones produced by Dharmakīrti and Dharmottara were made by learned men for the sake of refuting Non-Believers. Therefore, there is no need of [knowing] epistemology for meditating on the ultimate. I will not explain what has [already] been stated elsewhere."[20] Atīśa's view has had a large following in Tibet. There Dharmakīrti's tradition has often been perceived as a purely intellectual pursuit on a par with other worldly branches of learning, such as grammar and medicine. This suspicion has continued up to present times in certain Tibetan circles.[21]

This attitude, however, has been counterbalanced by another more sympathetic appraisal of Dharmakīrti with an equally large following in Tibet. This interest in philosophy in general and epistemology in particular originates with the famous Ngok Lo-dza-wa (*rngog lo tsā ba blo ldan shes rab*, 1059–1109). Despite belonging to the Ga-dam-ba (*bka' gdams pa*) tradition of Atiśa and Drom-dön-ba (*'brom ston rgyal ba'i 'byung gnas*, 1005–1064), Ngok was deeply interested in scholarly studies, which he promoted in Tibet.[22] Under his influence Tibetan Buddhism became more philosophically oriented. Ngok's tradition of philosophical studies centered around the monastery of Sang-pu (*gsang phu ne'u thog*), founded in 1073 by his uncle Ngok Lek-bay-shay-rab (*rngog legs pa'i shes rab*), one of Atīśa's direct disciples.[23] Ngok made extensive translations, but he also wrote several commentaries on Dharmakīrti's *Ascertainment*.[24] In this way he established a new tradition of logic and epistemology (*tshad ma gsar ma*) that supplanted its uninfluential predecessor.

Starting with Ngok, Dharmakīrti's thought greatly influenced philosophically inclined Tibetan thinkers. Dharmakīrti's importance was further strengthened by Cha-ba (*phya pa chos kyi seng ge*, 1182–1251), who brought about important developments due to his acute and original intellect.[25] Cha-ba is credited with writing the first Summary (*bsdus pa*) of Dharmakīrti's thought in Tibet, called *Clearing of Mental Obscuration with Respect to the Seven Treatises on Valid Cognition (tshad ma sde bdun yid gi mun sel)*.[26] With this work, Cha-ba initiated a literary genre of Summaries that has proven immensely successful. Sa-gya Paṇḍita (*sa skya paṇḍita*), Kay-drup (*mkhas grub*), and Ge-dün-drup (*dge 'dun grub*) all wrote important summaries. This genre of summaries can also be considered the ancestor of the Collected Topics (*bsdus grwa*)[27] type of literature. It in turn became very important in the curriculum of several traditions (including the tradition that later became known as Ge-luk). Cha-ba is also credited with settling the form of debate practiced by Tibetans. He is said to have been the first to propose debate through consequences (*thal 'gyur, prāsaṅga*), instead of using the formal arguments of Indian logicians.[28]

Neither Ngok's nor Cha-ba's works are available, making it difficult to determine their exact impact on Tibetan logico-epistemological studies. Still their influence can hardly be over-emphasized, as this work will demonstrate. Their epistemological contributions thrive to this day in the tradition nowadays known as Ge-luk (*dge lugs*), a school that currently has an extremely vital scholarship. Before introducing this tradition, however, I would like to describe the Sa-gya (*sa skya*) tradition, which had been the great rival of the Sang-pu tradition of Ngok and Cha-ba.

Foundation of the Sa-gya Scholastic Tradition

In the same year (1073) that Sang-pu was founded, its future rival, the monastery of Sa-gya was established by Gon-chok-gyel-bo (*dkon mchog rgyal po*). During the eleventh and twelfth centuries, however, the monastery of Sa-gya was not yet the important philosophical center that it later became. The Sa-gya tradition of this time essentially remained focused on tantric pratices, centered around the Path and Result (*lam 'bras*) tradition based on the Hevajratantra cycle. Sa-gya became a major scholarly tradition only during the thirteenth century under the influence of the fourth of five great Sa-gya masters (*sa skya gong ma lnga*),[29] Sa-gya Paṇḍita (1182–1251 C.E.). He stressed critical acumen (*shes rab, prajñā*) as central to the Buddhist path and the role of study in its development. In particular, he promoted the study of Dharmakīrti's thought as both a propaedeutic to the study of other systems of Buddhist philosophy as well as to a Buddhist account of knowledge.

Sa-gya Paṇḍita (henceforth abridged as Sa-paṇ) was a figure of considerable importance in several respects. Politically, Sa-paṇ was the first ruler of a unified Tibet since the collapse of the Tibetan empire in 842. He was chosen by the Mongolian prince Godan to govern Tibet under Mongolian domination and was summoned to the Mongolian court, where he spent his last years. Religiously, Sa-paṇ played an important role in bringing together the monastic and tantric aspects of Tibetan Buddhism. In his *Differentiation of the Three Vows,* he furthered Atīśa's attempt to harmonize these two traditions by describing the practice of tantra from a monastic perspective.[30] This work does not address these important accomplishments, however, but rather, looks at Sa-paṇ's promotion of the study of Dharmakīrti's tradition in Tibet.

Sa-paṇ is arguably the most important Tibetan thinker in the field of logic and epistemology. His main contribution in this context is the promotion of Dharmakīrti's *Commentary on Valid Cognition (pramāṇavārttika-kārikā, tshad ma rnam 'grel)* as the primary text of Tibetan logico-epistemological studies. Whereas previously the *Ascertainment of Valid Cognition (pramāṇa-viniścaya, tshad ma rnam par nges pa)* was predominant, Sa-paṇ's influence was decisive in the primacy assumed by the *Commentary* in Tibet. Throughout his life as a scholar Sa-paṇ remained devoted to this text, which he is said to have taught every day. He is the main source of all the lineages of Dharmakīrti's *Commentary* existing in Tibet.[31]

Sa-paṇ's contribution is not, however, limited to the diffusion of Dharmakīrti's *Commentary* in Tibet. He is also possibly one of the greatest commentators on the works of Dharmakīrti, as evinced by his masterpiece, the *Treasure on the Science of Valid Cognition (tshad ma rigs gter).*[32] In this text, Sa-paṇ reveals his mastery of Dharmakīrti's difficult works. Rather than rely on commentaries, Sa-paṇ directly quotes the master. The opinions of other commentators are summarized, but they are not usually taken as evidence for what Dharmakīrti meant. This apparently unique (in Tibet) feature of Sa-paṇ's work seems to arise out of his historical position. According to the official account, Sa-paṇ studied with the Indian paṇḍit Śākya Śrībhadra (1127–1225). The paṇḍit had come to Tibet fleeing the destruction of Nālandā Monastic University by Muslim invaders. Through his long study with the paṇḍit and his knowledge of Sanskrit, Sa-paṇ discovered that the Tibetan interpretations of Dharmakīrti (such as those of Ngok and Cha-ba) he had been taught corresponded only partially to Dharmakīrti's real thought. To correct these misinterpretations, Sa-paṇ wrote his famous *Treasure.* The prime target of this work was the Tibetan realist interpretation of Dharmakīrti and its attempt to reintroduce real universals into Buddhist epistemology.

Although Sa-paṇ was revered, his epistemology was not given the same consideration as some of his other contributions. His promotion and translation of Dharmakīrti's *Commentary* was well accepted, but his critique of Tibetan realism was by far not as well regarded.[33] Realism, which was propounded in Tibet by Cha-ba and his followers, remained the dominant view despite Sa-paṇ's opposition. Accordingly, Sa-paṇ's *Treasure,* which was a critique of realism, did not receive the attention it warranted for quite some time. Rather it was perceived by early Tibetan scholars as a problematic work.[34]

Around the turn of the fifteenth century, interest in the *Treasure* appears to have increased under the influence of Yak-dön (*g.yag ston sangs rgyas dpal,* 1348–1414).[35] In a commentary heavily criticizing Tibetan realism, he complained that misinterpretations of Dharmakīrti were so pervasive among Tibetans in his time that: "Those who know [should] speak having unerringly realized the meaning of those points [of Dharmakīrti's system]. Nowadays in this Land of Snow I am the only [such informed speaker]."[36] Throughout this work Yak-dön criticized those who, following Cha-ba's *Summaries,* supported a realism regarding universals and commonsense objects that corresponds neither to Dharmakīrti's ideas nor to Sa-paṇ's explanations. To expose the groundlessness of their interpretations, Yak-dön wrote a literal commentary on Sa-paṇ's *Treasure* and its *Auto-Commentary.*[37]

Yak-dön's critique of earlier Tibetan interpretations seems to have been partly responsible for increased interest in the *Treasure*. It opened the way for Sa-gya thinkers to take Sa-paṇ's critique of Tibetan realism seriously. These thinkers included Rong-dön (*rong ston śākya rgyal mtshan,* 1367–1449) and his disciples Go-ram-ba and Śākya Chok-den. They wrote a number of commentaries in that century, helping the *Treasure* gradually to become the basis for the study of logic and epistemology among the Sa-gya. Henceforth, it is included in the list of eighteen texts studied in the Sa-gya tradition known as the "Eighteen [Texts] of Great Renown" (*grags chen bco brgyad*).

A Conflict of Interpretations

The growing interest in Sa-paṇ's *Treasure* made it difficult to ignore. Some scholars chose to confront the difficulty head on and explicitly criticized Sa-paṇ.

Others tried to reinterpret certain passages of the *Treasure* that contradicted their own views. Śākya Chok-den mentioned that many centers maintained the study of the Summaries à la Cha-ba in combination with the *Treasure.*[38]

Among those who were explicitly critical of Sa-paṇ's views as undermining the validity of inferential knowledge and its ontological support, one of the most vocal was Bo-dong (*bo dong phyogs las rnam rgyal,* 1376–1451). Despite being a Sa-gya, this very prolific writer repeatedly criticized Sa-paṇ for being too nihilistic in his ontology and failing to adequately account for the validity of conceptual knowledge. Nevertheless, despite his criticisms, Bo-dong also followed the Zeitgeist in his attempt to establish a synthesis between Sa-paṇ and the realist interpretations dominatant in his time. He also seems quite often to have followed Rik-bay-ray-dri (*rig pa'i ral gri,* 1250–1330), particularly in his description of universals as being real negative properties.

Others felt that they could not criticize Sa-paṇ openly. Nonetheless his interpretations were not acceptable, for they contradicted the more realist interpretation of Dharmakīrti that they favored. Sa-paṇ's importance and the rising interest in his text made it imperative, however, for these thinkers to be able to explain his text without openly contradicting his views. Accordingly, many scholars interpreted them instead. In the attempt to make Sa-paṇ's views compatible with those of Cha-ba and his tradition, some extremely dubious glosses were put forward.[39] The main disciples of Dzong-ka-ba (*tsong kha pa,* 1357–1419, the founder of what later became known as the Ge-luk school), Gyel-tsap (*rgyal tshab dar ma rin chen,* 1364–1432), Kay-drup (1385–1438), and Ge-dün-drup (1391–1474) took this approach. They provided the major epistemological treatises of the tradition, each attempting to show that Sa-paṇ's text is compatible with a realist interpretation. Hence, they usually refrained from explicitly refuting Sa-paṇ. Rather he was made out to be a forerunner of Dzong-ka-ba, even though their views on epistemology were quite different. In his *Ornament,*[40] Kay-drup asserted that his presentation corresponds to Sa-paṇ's true intention; other interpretations distort the master's views as they are expressed in his difficult *Treasure.* To underline this assertion, Kay-drup modeled the outline of his systematic exposition in *Clearing* on Sa-paṇ's outline in *Treasure.*[41]

The reason Tibetan thinkers have had difficulty accepting Sa-paṇ's epistemological ideas is that these ideas suffer from the same problems as Dharmakīrti's system. They offer only restrictive ontological bases for logical reasoning. They also face epistemological difficulties in explaining the validity of conceptual knowledge. Such logico-epistemological difficulties, already sharply highlighted by orthodox Hindu critics, led later commentators to reinterpret Dharmakīrti's system in a way that would provide a stronger support in reality for logic and epistemology. A great deal of this work will be devoted to assessing this revision, begun in India and continued by Tibetan thinkers.

Another example of such revisionist attempts to appropriate Sa-paṇ while ignoring his critique of realism is Gyel-tsap's commentary on Sa-paṇ's *Treasure.*[42] This work, which has not been available for a long time, recently reappeared in

Tibet. The work appears to have been Gyel-tsap's attempt to reconcile Tibetan realism with Sa-paṇ's *Treasure.* Its polemical intent is clear. Gyel-tsap starts by saying that he intends this work for those of "feeble minds" (*blo dman pa*)[43] who cannot understand Sa-paṇ's *Treasure* despite its clarity! Although no names are mentioned, Gyel-tsap was probably referring to Yak-dön and his attempt to put Sa-paṇ's critique of realism in sharp relief.

Gyel-tsap was by far not the only one to interpret Sa-paṇ's work according to the tenets of the Summaries. Many important Sa-gya thinkers such as Nya-wön (*nya dbon kun dga' dpal,* 1300–1380) and Ren-da-wa (*red mda ba gzhon nu blo gros,* 1348/9–1412) are to be included on the list of thinkers attempting to reconcile the rising *Treasure* with the accepted views of Cha-ba's tradition.[44] Therefore, at the end of the fourteenth and the beginning of the fifteenth centuries, a conflict of interpretations opposed the partisans of Tibetan realism to those who followed Sa-paṇ's antirealism. Śākya Chok-den alluded to this situation when he complained about authors who, although claiming to uphold the tradition of the *Treasure,* nevertheless made it the target of their indirect criticism.[45] He further complained that by his time (end of the fifteenth century) the terminology of logico-epistemological studies had become hopelessly contaminated by the bizarre inventions of Cha-ba and his followers.[46] Although, as Jackson remarks, these comments must be read with care, it seems that Śākya Chok-den's complaints are well founded. In the later literature there are occasions when Sa-paṇ's words have been used with little regard for the intentions of their author.

The conflict of interpretations may have started with the criticism directed against Sa-paṇ by Bo-dong and others. This prompted Yak-dön and Rong-dön to propose a defense of Sa-paṇ's *Auto-Commentary.* This in turn prompted Gyel-tsap and Kay-drup to propose their own interpretations of the "true meaning of Sa-paṇ's thought." The most detailed Sa-gya answer to this challenge came at the end of the fifteenth century, when Go-ram-ba and Śākya Chok-den developed their critique of Gyel-tsap's and Kay-drup's interpretations.

This whole debate hinged on the interpretation of the *Auto-Commentary*, written by Sa-paṇ to complement his *Treasure.* Although the root text reflects Sa-paṇ's antirealism, its brevity makes it easier to interpret as supporting realism. The *Auto-Commentary,* however, is much more explicit in its rejection of realism. Moreover, there are a number of discrepancies between the root text of the *Treasure* and the version found in the *Auto-Commentary*, raising the question of which version is authoritative.[47] Given these uncertainties, some scholars cast doubt on the authenticity of the *Auto-Commentary*. Others held that the text had been corrupted by interpreters. For example, Gyel-tsap said: "With reference to this [*Auto-*] *Commentary,* some of my mighty and learned teachers stated that [this text] is difficult to posit [as Sa-paṇ's work, saying] 'this text is not [Sa-paṇ's] *Auto-Commentary.*' Nevertheless, I have [explained Sa-paṇ's text] in accordance with [his own] commentary. It is clear, however, that there are some passages conflicting with the root-text which have been introduced by some ignoramus. Accordingly, I have left out [these passages whose] mistakes cannot be but rejected."[48] In this way Gyel-tsap attempted to discredit the antirealist interpretation of Sa-paṇ indicated by the *Auto-Commentary*. Contrary to what this passage may suggest, however, Gyel-tsap's commentary does not consist of a sustained analysis of the offending passages in Sa-paṇ's *Auto-Commentary*. Rather, his work briefly mentions a few passages of the *Treasure* that seem to conflict with the antirealism presented in the *Auto-Commentary*.[49] Gyel-tsap's refutation of antirealist interpretations of Sa-paṇ's *Treasure* was done mostly on philosophical grounds. Therefore, his strong statement does not signal an attempt at close textual interpretation. Rather it is validating the free interpretation of Sa-paṇ's text necessary to the realist interpretation of Dharmakīrti dominant in Tibet at that time. As I will show in this work, such an interpretation rests mostly on commonsense arguments, though it is not completely devoid of support in Dharmakīrti's or Sa-paṇ's works.

Sa-gya Commentators

Among several prominent Sa-gya thinkers,[50] I focus mostly on Rong-dön's two rival disciples, Go-ram-ba (*go ram pa bsod nams seng ge,* 1429–1489 C.E.) and Śākya Chok-den (*gser mdog paṇ chen śākya mchog ldan,* 1428–1509 C.E.).[51] They have provided a well-argued defense of Sa-paṇ's system as well as a detailed examination of their opponents' systems. Their works played a decisive role in finally determining the meaning of Sa-paṇ's ideas. Due to their contribution, which is clearly recognized by the modern tradition, the Sa-gya tradition acquired the views that have remained largely unchanged to the present. Their works greatly highlighted the differences between the Sa-gya tradition and the Ga-den (*dga' ldan*) school, which was later to be called Ge-luk. By raising the significant questions concerning epistemology that we examine in this work such as the problem of universals, Go-ram-ba and Śākya Chok-den contributed doctrinally to the polarization between schools unfolding on the political level.

Go-ram-ba was one of the thinkers most influential in delineating what differentiates Sa-gya from Ge-luk tradition. Modern Sa-gya scholars recognize him as the main among Sa-paṇ's many commentators. Those with whom I spoke hold Go-ram-ba's words to reflect accurately and precisely Sa-paṇ's ideas. The reality is probably slightly different, although on many issues Go-ram-ba's claim to be Sa-paṇ's orthodox interpreter is not far from the truth, at least in the domain of logic and epistemology. Although his activities remained primarily religious and philosophical, Go-ram-ba was also involved in the politics of his time. He supported the Ring-pung family and his contemporaries attributed great political significance to his comings and goings between Tsang and central Tibet. His death before the age of sixty was a considerable shock for his tradition. Some must have considered it a result of his involvement in the escalating politico-religious warfare between the forces of Tsang and central Tibet.[52]

Śākya Chok-den, whose thought has had a considerable influence on this work, occupies quite a different position within the Sa-gya tradition. He is often perceived as a controversial figure by its members due to his unorthodox interpretations of Sa-paṇ. The main historical reason for Śākya Chok-den's status of enfant terrible of the Sa-gya tradition is his provocative writings on Sa-paṇ's *Differentiation of the Three [Types of] Vow.* Here Śākya Chok-den put forth a controversial list of questions on Sa-paṇ's work, effectively challenging the views of other scholars.[53] Because initially he did not give his own answers, many Sa-gya scholars resented this gesture as undermining the credibility of Sa-paṇ himself. Despite Śākya Chok-den's disclaimers that he did not intend for this list to refute Sa-paṇ but to challenge contemporary scholars (mostly his rival Go-ram-ba), his writings were seen as provocative and contentious. Since then the Sa-gya tradition has tended to give Go-ram-ba's works primacy over those of Śākya Chok-den. This lack of enthusiasm toward one of the best philosophical minds in the Tibetan tradition was deepened by Śākya Chok-den's alleged conversion to the emptiness-of-other view (*gzhan stong gi lta ba*) under the influence of the Seventh Kar-ma-ba Chö-drak-gya-tso (*chos grags rgya mtsho,* 1454–1506).

The unusual nature of Śākya Chok-den's philosophical project is illustrated by the difficulty that later Tibetan thinkers have had in pinning down his view. For example, the Ge-luk scholar Tu-gen Lo-sang-chö-gyi-nyi-ma (*thu'u bkwan blo bzang chos kyi nyi ma,* 1737–1802) divides Śākya Chok-den's career into three stages: Mādhyamika, Cittamātra, and Jo-nang-pa. The Sa-gya commentator Ngak-wang-chö-drak (*ngag dbang chos grags,* 1572–1641), however, refuses this description and claims that Śākya Chok-den was attracted by the emptiness-of-other view during his entire life. There is even some doubt as to the sincerity or at least the depth of his acceptance of the emptiness-of-other view. Some contemporary Sa-gya scholars speculate that Śākya Chok-den might have been pushed or even forced by the Seventh Kar-ma-ba to accept a view that did not correspond to his real opinion. Ngak-chö claims that Śākya Chok-den's allegiance to the teaching of emptiness-of-other was only provisional.[54]

In the face of such a divergence of opinions it is quite difficult to come to any definite conclusion. The examination of Śākya Chok-den's main works persuades me, however, that his thought did really evolve. Whereas his early works on epistemology and Madhyamaka do not mention the concept of emptiness-of-other, his middle ones show an interest for the topic and his later ones endorse it repeatedly and unequivocally. In the face of this partial evidence, which will have to be further examined, I believe tentatively that Tu-gen's three-stage evolution is not unreasonable, although I find his polemical description inadequate. In Śākya Chok-den's early works on epistemology and Madhyamaka, particularly in his masterful commentary on Sa-paṇ's system, the *Defeater*, a work composed when he was forty-six (1474) that will play an important role in this book, Śākya Chok-den does not mention the concept of emptiness-of-other.[55] Similarly, in works on Madhyamaka contemporary with this commentary, he presents the usual emptiness-of-self (*rang stong*) view of Madhyamaka found in other Sa-gya thinkers.[56]

A change appears in later works, which could be described as belonging to the middle period. For example, in his major Madhyamaka commentary, the *Dharma Treasury*,[57] Śākya Chok-den mentions without endorsing it the view of emptiness-of-other, which he describes as being a Yogācāra-Madhyamaka view. By this term he does not mean Śāntarakṣita's attempt to integrate Yogācāra and Dharmakīrti's philosophy in the Madhyamaka tradition but the view found in several of Maitreya's treatises. Śākya Chok-den describes this view as focusing on the experiential side of the nondual gnosis (*jñāna, ye shes*) and characterizes it as being Yogācāra False Aspectarian[58] (*rnam rdzun pa,* which he distinguishes from Cittamātra). He recognizes that this is not the final Madhyamaka view, which he claims is to be found rather in Nāgārjuna's five treatises.[59] A similar attitude is found in Śākya Chok-den's contemporaneous epistemological works, where he suggests the emptiness-of-other view without further comment.[60] At this point in his life, Śākya Chok-den seems to have begun exploring the emptiness-of-other view, which must have been perceived by Sa-gyas as radically opposed to Sa-paṇ's view and, hence, off limits. Śākya Chok-den is not yet ready, however, to commit himself to this extremely controversial view, merely suggesting that it is not as far away from Sa-paṇ's view as thought in the Sa-gya tradition.

This reserve later disappears in the works written after his first meeting (at the age of fifty-six) with the Seventh Kar-ma-ba in 1484. In these later works, such as the *History of the Madhyamaka* (between 1484 and 1490) and *The Distinction Between the Two Traditions* (1489),[61] Śākya Chok-den explicitly introduces and advocates the view of emptiness-of-other, claiming it is a more appropriate way to account for the experiential side of the realization of emptiness. This orientation is also noticeable in Śākya Chok-den's subsequent works on logic and epistemology (such as the *History of Valid Cognition* composed in 1502) where Dharmakīrti is presented as propounding an emptiness-of-other view.[62]

Even then, however, his view cannot be assimilated to the Jo-nang view associated with Dol-bo-ba (*dol po pa shes rab gyel tsan,* 1292–1361), contrary to what Tu-gen polemically asserts, for under the label of emptiness-of-other one can find a number of conflicting views. The Jo-nang-ba historian Tāranātha (1575–?) mentions twenty-one differences between Dol-bo-ba's and Śākya Chok-den's views. Although Tāranātha minimizes these distinctions, some of them are quite significant.[63] For example, whereas Dol-bo-ba holds that emptiness-of-self is merely a preliminary to understanding the profound view, which is exclusively emptiness-of-other, Śākya Chok-den holds that the two views are equally profound. That is, emptiness-of-self and emptiness-of-other basically come to the same point, the experience of the nondual gnosis. Similarly, whereas Dol-bo-ba holds that gnosis is eternal, permanent, and stable, Śākya Chok-den denies this, holding that as a cognition it must be momentary. Therefore, it is clear that Śākya Chok-den's emptiness-of-other should not be assimilated to the Jo-nang view. It is also clear that the emptiness-of-other is more than a provisional standpoint or passing interest for our author.

The Rise of the Ge-luk Tradition

On the Ge-luk side, I focus on the works of Dzong-ka-ba's direct disciples, Gyel-tsap, Kay-drup, and Ge-dün-drup. They were instrumental in setting forth what can be described as "Ge-luk" views on logic and epistemology. It is quite accurate to say that, after these three thinkers, the tradition has merely repeated and refined the views expressed by them regarding epistemology and philosophy of language. The contributions of major textbook (*yig cha*) authors of the main Ge-luk monasteries is limited to the restatement of positions taken by one of these three founding figures of the Ge-luk tradition of epistemological studies.[64]

Such textbooks assist in the study of difficult texts, but their significance should not be overemphasized. Some modern scholars have relied excessively on these simplified compilations, considering them representative of the Ge-luk tradition. This approach detracts from a complete understanding of it. Several modern scholars wrongly believe that most Ge-luk scholars limit themselves to textbooks to the exclusion of earlier, more significant texts. Although this misperception unfortunately is grounded partly in reality, it would be a gross distortion to believe that most well-trained Ge-luk scholars rely mainly on textbooks. Especially in the study of logic and epistemology, textbooks are not widely used even by average scholars.[65] Thus, the Ge-luk views on logic and epistemology are to be found in the texts of Gyel-tsap, Kay-drup, and Ge-dün-drup, which have formed the tradition, not in later compilations whose acceptance is partial at best.[66]

Among these three thinkers, the first is by far the most important and influential. His works are recognized by Ge-luk scholars as setting forth the orthodox view on most questions of logic and epistemology. Despite this prominence, I use Kay-drup's works more often because they set forth a clearer and more interesting view. This choice is due to several considerations to which I will have the occasion to return. One difference is the genre of literature in which the two authors work. Whereas Gyel-tsap writes commentarial guides to Dharmakīrti's and Sa-paṇ's works, Kay-drup also presents his own summary. This offers a better opportunity for the properly philosophical mode of explanation that I favor in this work.

The main difference between the two authors, however, lies in their style. Whereas Kay-drup presents his ideas clearly without shying away from the difficult points, Gyel-tsap tends to limit himself to strictly commentarial tasks. He explains basic texts and refutes conflicting opinions. He rarely, however, explores issues in a purely philosophical style but tends to explain his view exactly but tersely, contrary to Kay-drup who delights in confronting difficult issues head on. For instance, in his commentary on Sa-paṇ, for example, Gyel-tsap never seriously discusses the many passages in which Sa-paṇ criticizes realism. He just sets forth the correct explanation and glosses over the contentious passages.

My choice reflects my personal admiration for such an independent thinker as Kay-drup, who, like Śākya Chok-den, forcefully engages issues. Frequently, his explanations offer greater insights into the Ge-luk views than Gyel-tsap's tighter elaborations. An examination of Kay-drup's explanations often leads to a better understanding of the rationale behind Gyel-tsap's positions. In any case, it is clear that the difference between these two authors is less one of content than of style. As the analysis of Gyel-tsap's commentary on Sa-paṇ's *Treasure* reveals, Gyel-tsap often holds positions similar to the ones usually associated with Kay-drup.[67]

A striking element in Kay-drup's writing style is the biting tone of the polemical remarks he addresses to his adversaries. These comments are not expressions of contempt or dishonest attempts to disqualify the adversary. As I hope to show, Kay-drup is a forceful but honest thinker who is not afraid of depicting his position in the clearest possible terms and who is ready to face the difficult issues. I find a rather similar tone of voice and quality of thinking in Śākya Chok-den. Although this polemical element doubtlessly expresses a sectarian standpoint, it also corresponds to a typical attitude within the Tibetan dialectical tradition. It is often introduced to make a text or a debate more lively. Biting remarks may not be entirely innocent but they are less offensive for trained debaters, who understand them to be artifacts of the dramatization that is part of any good debate. Similar practices are found in monastic institutions to this day. In the three great seats of Ge-luk-ba learning (i.e., Dre-bung, Ga-den, and Se-ra), for example, debaters do not hesitate to hurl the worst insults at each other as a way to strengthen their dialectic. Ad hominem arguments are viewed as a way to bring some life to the debate and are rarely taken personally.

Another choice that may surprise my reader is how infrequently Dzong-ka-ba is mentioned in this work. This limited presence of the founder of the Ge-luk tradition is not due to some idiosyncratic choice but merely reflects that Dzong-ka-ba wrote very little concerning logic or epistemology. Because his few minor writings on this topic are not considered important by the tradition itself,[68] Dzong-ka-ba will not be a major figure of this narrative. For sure, there are oral reports that attempt to compensate for the limited contribution of the founding figure, according to which Gyel-tsap and Kay-drup wrote their works under the guidance of Dzong-ka-ba. Contradictions between these two authors are then attributed to Dzong-ka-ba's passing down to them two conflicting traditions of exegesis of Dharmakīrti, one to each.

As I will show in the part devoted to the study of perception, it is true that there are two currents of exegesis in the Ge-luk epistemological tradition. They are usually associated with Gyel-tsap and Kay-drup and are said to have been given by Dzong-ka-ba on the basis of Dharmottara's and Devendrabuddhi's commentaries respectively.[69] Although this description seems partly warranted, nothing other than oral reports directly connects these two interpretative systems to Dzong-ka-ba himself. This is insufficient grounds for accepting the historical character of this connection.

Moreover, the doubtful character of such oral reports is clearly shown by the mistaken attribution of these two subtraditions to Gyel-tsap and Kay-drup. This does not seem to be correct, for the same views usually attributed to Kay-drup are also found in Gyel-tsap's commentary on Sa-paṇ's *Treasure* (assuming that the attribution of authorship is genuine). Certainly, these views are not defended in Gyel-tsap's other works and are even sometimes explicitly criticized. Hence, there is some doubt about whether Gyel-tsap was completely committed to all the views found in his commentary on Sa-paṇ's *Treasure*. Nevertheless, it remains that Gyel-tsap was willing to defend these views in print at the end of his life.[70] Therefore, the attribution of the second current to Kay-drup alone is mistaken. It reflects a later situation, in which Gyel-tsap's commentary on Sa-paṇ's *Treasure* was no longer available. Thus, it seems more than probable that these oral reports are later attempts to compensate for Dzong-ka-ba's limited role in the elaboration of a Ge-luk logico-epistemological tradition.

Concerning the two currents in Ge-luk epistemology, we should not speak of two conflicting views associated with two authors but, rather, of two ways of interpreting Dharmakīrti's system. The first, usually attributed to Gyel-tsap and generally taken as the more orthodox, is closely connected to Cha-ba's tradition of Summaries and its offspring, the Collected Topics. The second, defended by Kay-drup (and also by Gyel-tsap in his commentary on Sa-paṇ's *Treasure*), is critical of this first current. It refutes several of the concepts introduced by Cha-ba in his discussion of epistemological typologies. This second system of interpretation represents a more explicit attempt to reconcile Sa-paṇ's ideas to the realism dominant in Tibet at the time. As we will see, however, the differences between these two currents are limited. They agree on the essential point of the Ge-luk view; namely, the importance of interpreting Dharmakīrti in a way compatible with realism.

Another reason it is unnecessary to attribute a special role to Dzong-ka-ba in this field is that the views defended by Dzong-ka-ba's disciples were unexceptional for their times. They advocated an already predominant realist view in Tibet and defended it against those who were attempting to emphasize Sa-paṇ's antirealism. Contrary to Madhyamaka, where Dzong-ka-ba's large and original impact is impossible to miss, there seems to be little that is original to the Ge-luk tradition in the domain of logic and epistemology. Gyel-tsap, Kay-drup, and their followers mostly repeated the views elaborated by earlier thinkers. Before ever meeting Dzong-ka-ba, Gyel-tsap was a well-trained scholar in the Sang-pu tradition of Summaries. Dzong-ka-ba himself was trained in the dominant tradition of logic and epistemology. He studied at the monastery of Tze-chen (*rtse chen*)[71] where his teacher Ren-da-wa[72] emphasized the study of Sa-paṇ's text in combination with U-yuk-ba's commentary, which reflects a realist approach.[73] Hence, there seems to be no need to posit any special role for Dzong-ka-ba. The Ge-luk tradition adopted its view on logic and epistemology less out of a deliberate philosophical choice than due to its historical position in a tradition where realism was the accepted view.

However, a few important differences exist between the earlier Tibetan and later Ge-luk thinkers that the readers may wish to keep in mind. One concerns the tenet system through which Dharmakīrti's works are interpreted. Whereas, for early Tibetan thinkers, Dharmakīrti is Mādhyamika, for later Ge-luk as well as later Sa-gya thinkers, he is a proponent of Yogācāra doctrine, with most passages in his work defending a Sautrāntika position. For example, Gyel-tsap describes

Dharmakīrti's *Commentary* as a text common to both Sautrāntika and Yogācāra *(mdo sems thun mong ba).*[74] Outside of a few minor points,[75] Ge-luk thinkers agree on this doxographical description. They also reject Cha-ba's theory of perception, which is similar to the Vaibhāṣika view in that it allows direct apprehension of external objects as well as the coexistence of subject and object.

This Ge-luk position is due, as we will see, to Sa-paṇ, who describes Dharmakīrti as advocating a system in which Sautrāntika and Yogācāra ideas are mixed. For Sa-paṇ, Dharmakīrti's comments on emptiness do not imply the non-substantiality of all phenomena but refer to the absence of duality between subject and object *(gnyis su med pa'i stong pa nyid, dvayaśūnyatā).*[76] I believe this doxographical description to be better suited to the foundational character of Dharmakīrti's epistemology than the earlier one. Although Dharmakīrti uses the idea of essencelessness, it is clear that he is not ready to give to this idea its maximum extension, as Nāgārjuna and Candrakīrti do.

Despite these important differences between Ge-luk thinkers and earlier Tibetan epistemologists, a number of similarities remain between them. In retaining several of the views that were part of an earlier Tibetan synthesis of Madhyamaka and the logico-epistemological tradition, Ge-luk authors have developed a view that is not purely a continuation of Cha-ba's tradition but, rather, a compromise between Sa-paṇ's more literal interpretation of Dharmakīrti and Cha-ba's more creative new epistemology. Among Ge-luk thinkers, the predominant current tends to more closely follow Cha-ba's views on perception, as described previously. The second current tends to diverge from Cha-ba's model. Both, however, adopt his epistemological vocabulary, his new conception of perception, and his description of thought as bearing on reality as a consequence of a realist interpretation of Dharmakīrti's system. Both also refuse to adopt Cha-ba's doxographical model for explaining Dharmakīrti's epistemology. In doing so, they have developed a distinctive view that is peculiar to their tradition but still retains the main elements of Cha-ba's tradition.

The Origin and Significance of Sectarian Divisions

Discussing the various approaches to interpreting Dharmakīrti's thought in Tibet involves differentiating the various schools of interpretation. This task is not, however, as straightforward as distinguishing individual interpretations, for it involves a level of philosophically convenient generalization that often conflicts with the actual historical "details." In this work, I will use quite liberally labels such as "Ge-luk" or "Sa-gya," despite my awareness of their problematic nature. For example, the group of thinkers to which I refer as "Ge-luk-ba" did not think of itself as such but, rather, as *Ga-den-ba* (*dga' ldan pa*); that is, "those from [the monastery of] Ga-den." Later on, this group became known as *Ge-den-ba* (*dge ldan pa*) and *Ge-luk-ba* (both mean "the Virtuous Ones"). This is clearly a loaded transformation of the original name. Thus, calling Dzong-ka-ba and his direct disciples "Ge-luk" is an obvious anachronism. I do it nonetheless to convey the essential philosophical continuity between the early group of the Ga-den-bas and their later Ge-luk interpreters (such as the authors of the different monastic textbooks).

Similarly, the use of the term "Sa-gya" is not without problems. Here, when dealing with logico-epistemological matters, I use the term to refer to the group of thinkers who follow literally the logico-epistemological system established by Sa-gya Paṇḍita (the *sa lugs*). Such usage is restrictive because it ignores the great diversity of opinions among Sa-paṇ's interpreters during the classical period, when scholars with widely conflicting interpretations all considered themselves Sa-gya. Many members of the Sa-gya tradition such as Bo-dong openly and stridently opposed Sa-paṇ's views. Even Sa-paṇ's direct disciple U-yuk-ba disagreed with Sa-paṇ's *Treasure*.[77] In this work, I have chosen to restrict the label *Sa-gya* to those thinkers who follow Sa-paṇ closely and literally (such as Yak-dön, Rong-dön, Go-ram-ba, Śākya Chok-den, and Lo Ken-chen), excluding those (such as Ren-da-wa, Nya-wön, and even Gyel-tsap or Kay-drup) who attempt a conciliation between their own views and those of Sa-paṇ. This simplistic but convenient usage of the label *Sa-gya* is meant to reflect as well the usage of the modern Sa-gya tradition.

The use of these labels creates problems of anachronism and overgeneralization. By now, furthermore, the labels have become reified. This makes using them to describe the evolution of the Tibetan logico-epistemological tradition during the fifteenth century particularly delicate. Such usage wrongly suggests that the schools of Tibetan Buddhism were already separated by the rather rigid boundaries that currently divide them. Yet, there is no easy solution to this problem, for by now sectarian distinctions have acquired a solidity and an immediacy that cannot be easily ignored. This puts us, scholars of Tibetan Buddhism, in a double bind. If we use these labels, we seem to reinforce the most dubious aspects of Tibetan sectarianism. If we do not use them, we fail to make our work relevant to the present situation of Tibetan Buddhism. With either approach, it is difficult to avoid distortion.

In this work, I have chosen to use the labels despite their obvious disadvantages. One reason for allowing an emphasis on sectarian differences in this case relates to the nature of my main topic, the problem of universals. Unlike some other topics, it brings forth differences among Tibetan thinkers that largely do follow sectarian lines. Book I of this work investigates mostly the conflict of interpretations about universals between Sa-gya and Ge-luk thinkers. This topic, which I examine for its philosophical interest, lends itself to an overemphasis of intersectarian differences at the expense of the differences that separate thinkers considered part of the same tradition. The analysis of the more specifically epistemological part of this work (Book II) provides an opportunity to partly correct the unfortunate impression created by the first part. It underlines the importance of intrasectarian differences, thus giving a more balanced view of both inter- and intrasectarian discussions in the Tibetan logico-epistemological tradition.

Problems in the use of sectarian labels and categories can be traced to the radical changes undergone by the Tibetan tradition between the fourteenth and the seventeenth centuries. During this time, the sectarian divisions that characterize contemporary Tibetan Buddhism crystallized. Let me explain this process to highlight the importance of political considerations in the overall transformation of Tibetan Buddhism and the emergence of strong sectarian divisions. I believe scholars and lay people interested in this tradition cannot afford to underestimate these considerations.

The classical period of Tibetan Buddhism was exceptionally productive in the areas of philosophy and doctrine. Buddhism was by then solidly established in most parts of Tibet. The enormous task of translating the canonical and commentarial literatures had been accomplished. The fourteenth century became a time during which the enormous mass of teachings transmitted from India was systematized. The canon (*bka' 'gyur*) was determined by Rik-bay-ray-dri, Bu-dön-rin-chen-drup (*bu ston rin chen grub,* 1290–1364), and others after several controversies over whether the Nying-ma tantras (*rnying ma'i rgyud 'bum*) should be included or not.[78]

Parallel to the process of canonical organization, a process of doctrinal systematization was started. The Third Kar-ma-ba Rang-jung Dor-je (*rang byung rdo rje,* 1284–1339), Long-chen Rab-jam-ba (*klong chen rab 'byams pa,* 1308–1363), and Dzong-ka-ba produced masterful and original treatises that organized the whole mass of teachings that had come from India. Descriptions and classifications of the elements of the tradition became available, thus making a systematic presentation of Buddhism possible in Tibet.

A common characteristic of the traditions of this period, one that is particularly in evidence in the biographies of Long-chen and Dzong-ka-ba, is the eclectic character of the times. Scholars traveled to monasteries belonging to other denominations and studied with teachers from different schools. Doctrinal differences were not yet understood to reflect deep sectarian divisions, but rather were taken as differences between teachers and lineages both inside and outside of a given school.

The political situation of the fourteenth century, however, was far less ecumenical. The power of the Sa-gya hierarchy, which had dominated Tibet since Sa-paṇ was chosen by the Mongolian Prince Godan as the regent of Tibet, declined throughout the first half of the fourteenth century. Then a powerful person, Tai Si-tu Jang-chup-gyel-tsen (*tai si tu byang chub rgyal mtshan,* 1302–1364) from the Pa-mo-dru-ba (*phag mo gru pa*) family established new dominance in Tibet (1358). This ascendency did not last long but it did create a new political climate. Tai Si-tu attempted to establish a strong rule that could unify Tibet in relative independence from the outside interventions that had been plaguing Tibet for a great part of its history. After his death in 1364, the hold of the Pa-mo-dru-ba family on the rest of the country diminished. Consequently the Ring-pung family established its rule, leaving only nominal power to the Pa-mo-dru-ba family. But the impulse to establish a strong rule in Tibet did not disappear. It remained to have a dramatic influence on the development of the Tibetan tradition.

The period that follows can be seen as a transition between the more open atmosphere of the fourteenth century and the confrontations of the later period. Around the turn of the fifteenth century, Dzong-ka-ba started to become a popular teacher, making an enormous impression on his contemporaries. He had a large following in central Tibet, including the Pha-mo-dru-ba family and allied groups. He also had a circle of devoted students such as Gyel-tsap and Kay-drup. In the first years of the fifteenth century, the group around Dzong-ka-ba started to become organized. In 1409, Dzong-ka-ba and his disciples instituted the Great Prayer festival (*smon lam chen mo*) and in 1410 founded the monastery of Ga-den to serve as a center for their group.[79] Shortly after, other disciples founded the monasteries of Dre-bung (*'bras pung*) and Se-ra (*se rwa*). Thus, by the end of Dzong-ka-ba's life (1419), the new Ga-den-ba school seems to have been organized as a partly separate group, although it is unclear how self-conscious this was.

Despite criticism by Rong-dön against Dzong-ka-ba's ideas, the relations with the other groups seem to have been friendly. The Ga-den-bas did not see themselves as completely separate from other schools. There was a particular lack of differentiation from the Sa-gya school, to which Dzong-ka-ba and most of his disciples belonged. In these institutions students seem to have examined Sa-paṇ's and Dzong-ka-ba's systems without clearly differentiating between the two.[80] It is hard to know the degree to which sectarian labels were even applicable to this time.

The situation seems to have started to change in the 1430s. In 1432, Kay-drup became the leader of the Ga-den community on which he started to put his stamp. After Dzong-ka-ba's passing away in 1419, Gyel-tsap had been chosen as the holder of the abbatial throne of Ga-den. As such, he was Dzong-ka-ba's successor and must have had a considerable influence on the nascent Ga-den community. Gyel-tsap seems to have been gentle and well disposed toward other schools. He was also quite open-minded, as evinced by his writing at the end of his life a commentary on Sa-paṇ's *Treasure*, a text unrelated to Dzong-ka-ba's tradition. This catholic atmosphere seems to have changed when Kay-drup became the holder of the throne of Ga-den after 1432. Kay-drup differed from Gyel-tsap. He is often depicted as having a fiery temper and was certainly quite outspoken. As a leader of the community of Dzong-ka-ba's followers, he started to become quite active in enforcing a stricter orthodoxy, chastising some disciples for not upholding Dzong-ka-ba's pure teachings. This insistence on a strict orthodoxy and a differentiation from other schools must have contributed to the change of atmosphere that seems to have taken place around that time. Moreover, in 1434, a dispute concerning the succession in the line of the Pa-mo-dru-ba was decided by the Ring-pung faction, creating a great deal of animosity among rival groups in Tsang and central Tibet. All these events were signs of the much more severe confrontations that were to follow in which the new school would be pitted against other religious groups competing for political influence and economical support.

During the rest of the fifteenth century, the Ring-pung, with the support of the Kar-ma-ba branch of the Ga-gyü and some Sa-gya groups, expanded its power over the province of Tsang and into central Tibet. Toward the end of the century, a bitter struggle ensued with the forces of central Tibet supported by the Ge-luk, which by then seem to have become a clearly separated school. During this period monasteries from the different schools were attacked and converted from one sect to the other following the flow of political events. For instance, the Seventh Kar-ma-ba Chö-drak-gya-tso narrowly escaped being killed when central Tibetan forces supporting the Ge-luk school destroyed a newly established Kar-ma-ba monastery near Lhasa.[81] The Ring-pung forces retaliated by occupying Lhasa between 1492 and 1517, forbidding Ge-luk monks to take part in the Great Prayer Festival.[82]

During the sixteenth century the regency of Tsang replaced the Ring-pung family as the most powerful group among the forces from Tsang, but this did not improve the situation. Intermittent war with central Tibetan forces supported by the rising power of the Ge-luk monastic establishment continued. The situation was complicated by the involvement of rival Mongol groups enlisted by the warring factions. The balance of power further deteriorated at the beginning of the seventeenth century, when Lhasa again was occupied several times. The protracted struggle became a veritable civil war. Several Ge-luk monasteries were forcefully converted into Kar-ma-ba establishments. The situation of the Ge-luk forces became so precarious that a delegation was sent to the Mongol tribes to request support. At this point, the support of Gushri Khan decisively changed the situation. His tribe, the Qoshot, wiped out the rival Chogtu tribe, which had supported the Regent of Tsang. The door was now open for Ge-luk victory. This occurred in 1642 when the Regent of Tsang was made prisoner by the alliance of central Tibetan and Mongol forces. The same year, the Fifth Dalai Lama Ngak-wang Lo-sang Gya-tso (*ngag dbang blo bzang rgya mtsho,* 1617-1682) received the supreme authority over Tibet from Gushri Khan.[83]

This victory for the forces from central Tibet prompted the staunchest among Ge-luk supporters to demand reparations from the groups that had supported the forces of Tsang. The Great Fifth seems to have been tolerant and hence unwilling to suppress other schools. He nevertheless agreed to a number of measures aimed at curbing the influence of the groups that had opposed the Ge-luk school most openly. The Jo-nang-ba were directly suppressed. This was probably due to the close association of its main figure, the polymath Tāranātha (1575–?), with the anti-Ge-luk party of the Regent of Tsang. The Kar-ma-ba school was more fortunate. It escaped complete proscription due to Drak-ba-chok-wang's (*grags pa mchog dbang,* 1618–1658) skillful diplomacy.[84] Nevertheless, its activities were curtailed, and the number of its monasteries, limited. The Kar-ma-ba hierarchs' freedom of movement was restricted by assigning them residency at Tshur-pu in central Tibet.

The Sa-gya tradition was also targeted, although probably less than the Ga-gyü. The monastery of Na-len-dra, for example, was put under the direct rule of the Dalai Lama's government.[85] It steadily declined under governmental rule, unable to compete with the great Ge-luk seats of learning, Dre-bung, Se-ra, and Ga-den.

Its fate illustrates the decline of the non-Ge-luk schools in the domain of philosophico-dialectical studies. This decline is due to political circumstances such as the loss of support and protection. Great learning centers require the active support and protection of powerful groups to thrive. By the end of the seventeenth century, the Sa-gya tradition had lost the level of support necessary for the vitality of its large learning centers.[86]

The "ideological" restrictions imposed at that time also contributed to a decline in scholarship. In particular, the writings of Dzong-ka-ba's critics such as Go-ram-ba, Śākya Chok-den, the Eighth Kar-ma-ba Mi-gyö-dor-jay (*mi bskyod rdo rje,* 1504–1557), and others were proscribed. Consequently they became unavailable for a long time in most parts of Tibet. The nineteenth century Ge-luk scholar A-gu Shay-rap-gya-tso mentions Go-ram-ba's and Śākya Chok-den's commentaries on Sa-paṇ's *Treasure* in his list of rare books.[87] This shows that by the mid-nineteenth century these texts were not commonly available, even to students in Sa-gya and Ga-gyü monasteries. Only toward the end of the nineteenth century were some of these works reprinted.[88] The ban on these important writings together with the other measures of proscription had obvious consequences for the non-Ge-luk traditions. Although not limited to them, this is especially the case for Sa-gya scholars. Deprived of material and scholarly resources, they could not sustain the high level of scholarship that had characterized their tradition.

The sectarian situation that characterizes the Tibetan tradition at present is largely a result of political struggles and intellectual proscriptions such as these. These events mark the beginning of an increasing sectarian polarization. Instead of being exposed to a variety of viewpoints, students began at this time to be limited to a single tradition. The atmosphere became such that even considering, not to speak of adopting, the views of other schools would amount to a political betrayal. Recently, the restrictive atmosphere has been exacerbated. Contemporary monks are often limited to the views of a single monastery within the same tradition. We are far from the open and ecumenical atmosphere of the fourteenth century!

Such narrow-mindedness is bound to have long-term consequences for the vitality of the tradition as a whole. Although Tibetan scholastic traditions still exhibit a remarkable vigor, signs of decay are unmistakable. Many Tibetan scholars avoid studying views that conflict with their system. And even if they pursue such studies, they are careful to keep quiet about it to avoid creating political waves. Only some of the most courageous monks such as Ge-dün-chö-bel (*dge 'dun chos dpal,* 1895–1951) have been able to withstand the pressure to conform to the "party" line. I believe the vested political interest that prompts Tibetan scholars to assume their particular tradition to be entirely right is partly responsible for the current intellectual stagnation of these traditions relative to their own past. The polymath Jang-gya Röl-bay-dor-jay (*lcang skya rol ba'i rdo rje,* 1717–1786) expressed such forbodings already in the eighteenth century: "Present-day logicians, not valuing the great texts highly, take refuge in mere deceptive entanglements. They take a garland of foam—dry consequences which do away with the essential meaning—as the best of essences. Such people see only a portion [of the meaning of the great texts by Dharmakīrti and so forth]; the actual thought is beyond their ken. Therefore, for them the scriptures have become like diamond words [impossible to penetrate]."[89] I believe that the lack of creativity that seems to threaten Tibetan Buddhist thinking is due mostly to the sectarianism that has plagued this great tradition.

This is not to deny that other more ecumenical tendencies are at work in the Tibetan tradition. Openness has continually manifested its influence in all schools. The spirit of openness has manifested most visibly in the Nonsectarian (*ris med*) movement, which took place during the nineteenth century around the person Jam-gön Kong-trul (*'jam mgon kong sprul,* 1813–1899) and Jam-yang Kyen-tse-wang-po (*'jam dbyangs mkhyen tse'i dbang po,* 1820–1892). Such a tolerant spirit can also be found among Ge-luk scholars such as Jang-gya and even Tu-gen Lo-sang-chö-gyi-nyi-ma (*thu'u bkwan blo bzang chos kyi nyi ma,* 1737–1802).[90] Despite its admirable qualities, however, this tradition of more tolerant Tibetan thinkers never succeeded in eliminating the heavily sectarian atmosphere created by the civil war between Tsang and central Tibet.

Although this work deals with ideas more than with historical or political facts, the reader should be aware that the ideas I am exploring often have political significance among Tibetans. For example, the differences between Sa-gya and Ge-luk thinkers concerning the problem of universals are philosophically interesting (whatever this might mean). They parallel similar preoccupations among Western thinkers and as such have cross-cultural significance. Philosophy is not, however, the only reason they became a hot topic of controversy among Tibetan thinkers. They were brought up by Go-ram-ba and Śākya Chok-den to emphasize the differences between Sa-gya and Ge-luk traditions. Thus, they became philosophical markers of largely political disputes. Later, they remained ideological markers of differences that were essentially political.

The history of Western philosophy offers similar cases of philosophical topics, of apparent interest only to specialists, acquiring enormous cultural and political significance. For example, the problem of universals was at the center of philosophical discussions during the second half of the Middle Ages. It had important theological implications. The type of realism defended by Aquinas became very popular in the church because it was understood to imply an affirmation of a strong connection between human beings, God, and the world through the Catholic Church. Ockham's nominalism, by contrast, was interpreted as a denial of the possibility of such a link. The political implications of these views are fairly obvious; it is no surprise that the Catholic Church embraced Aquinas and distanced itself from Ockham.[91]

In Tibet, the importance that the topic of universals acquired was due partly to its influence upon the status and prestige of the Tibetan scholastic traditions. Each tradition claimed to truly represent Indian Buddhism, which is venerated by Tibetans as the source of their traditions. Since the problem of universals is so central to Dharmakīrti's philosophy, its correct interpretation became a sign among Tibetan scholars of having inherited the enormous prestige of Indian Buddhist masters in general and Dharmakīrti in particular. This is all the more true in a commentarial tradition like the one existing in Tibet, where any philosophical elaboration must be presented as a commentary on an authoritative text. Therefore, Ge-luk views could never be presented on their own philosophical merits but only as authoritative commentaries. In this perspective, being right as an interpretation mattered a great deal. It was taken as a justification of the superiority of the claims to preeminence of this school over the claims of other schools. Refuting these interpretations became a way for the adversaries of this tradition to score political points and advance their own tradition. The political dimensions of the problem of universals were intensified by the practice of debate in Tibet. Debates were significant events in India, where kings attended encounters between important rival thinkers. Although this institution did not survive unchanged in Tibet,[92] dialectics retained some of its political importance. In particular, the Ge-luk school was able to derive considerable prestige from the dialectic abilities of its scholars.

Thus, although probably devoid of any intrinsic political meaning, the problem of universals came to have political significance. It became the focus of debates in which the competing status and prestige of the Tibetan scholastic traditions were at stake. In this way, this topic became a convenient way to question *via* philosophical debate the political supremacy achieved by the Ge-luk school after the seventeenth century. Since then, the question of universals has been continually raised for both its philosophical interest and its political impact. In this century, the "renegade" Ge-luk scholar Ge-dün-chö-bel, for example, repeated some of the objections formulated by Śākya Chok-den against the Ge-luk doctrine of universals. His critique has been perceived as an outrage by some Ge-luk scholars, who took it as a sign of betrayal.

I certainly would not make the reductionist claim that the meaning of debate practices or philosophical discussion derives solely from political dimensions. Nevertheless, political considerations are relevant to this work, forming part of the picture I am sketching. An awareness of the political aspects of intersectarian differences is important to students and scholars of Tibetan Buddhism alike. We must not fail to perceive the true nature of the differences between the schools of Tibetan Buddhism. The philosophical differences between schools are real but rather small when appraised against the important similarities. I am committed not to blow out of proportion philosophical differences or mislead readers by ignoring the political origins of sectarian differences.

One thing that my reader will have to keep in mind is that I take for granted that the similarities between them vastly outweigh the differences. My insistence on differences has to be appreciated against this background. Nothing is further from my intention than falling into sectarianism, which unfortunately plays an undue role among those interested by Tibetan Buddhism. I hope that these few explanations of the development of sectarianism in Tibet have helped the reader to realize that the distinctions between different schools are first and foremost political. This is not to deny that there are philosophical and religious differences, some of which are explored here. Nevertheless, these differences remain slight in comparison to the overwhelming similarities between Tibetan lineages.

My personal experience has been that studying different traditions has greatly enhanced my understanding of Tibetan Buddhism. In my studies of Dharmakīrti, I have found reading Sa-gya scholarship to be illuminating. It has greatly helped me in my reconsideration of Dharmakīrti's ideas. I was particularly enriched by reading Śākya Chok-den's enormously insightful work as well as by studying Sa-paṇ's *Treasure*. This in turn has allowed me to see the Ge-luk commentarial tradition in a new light, as revealing of the problematic areas in the thought of Dharmakīrti and his tradition. It is to such an exploration that I now invite my reader.

Book One

Ontology and Philosophy of Language

PART I

Ontology

1

Ontology and Categories

Indian Philosophy and the Pramāṇa Method

Dharmakīrti's major work, the *Commentary on Valid Cognition* (*pramāṇa-vārttika*), defends and explains Dignāga's *Compendium on Valid Cognition* (*pramāṇa-samuccaya*). Like his model Dignāga, Dharmakīrti questions the nature of knowledge. In the Indian context, this question is formulated as, What is the nature of *pramāṇa* and what are its types? Whereas his Hindu opponents tend to present a realist theory, which liberally allows for a diversity of *pramāṇa*, Dharmakīrti offers a more restrictive view in accordance with his antirealism. The interpretation of the word *pramāṇa* is itself a topic of debate among Buddhist and Hindu thinkers. For the former, *pramāṇa* means "valid cognition,"[1] whereas for the latter, this word refers to "means of valid cognition," in accordance with its grammatical form. Regardless of how the term *pramāṇa* is interpreted, a question considered later,[2] the essential preoccupation of the thinkers whose ideas we are examining is epistemological. They discussed the nature of *pramāṇa* and the types of knowledge allowable in philosophical inquiry.

The scope of the discussion of *pramāṇa*, however, is not limited to the analysis of knowledge, but constitutes a veritable philosophical method used in investigating other fields of inquiry such as ontology and philosophy of language. Matilal describes this *pramāṇa* method: "i) There are accredited means of knowledge (*pramāṇa*) such as perception and inference, on the basis of which we make assertions about what exists and what is true, and ii) there are knowables (*prameya*), i.e., cognizable entities, which constitute the world. Each knowable entity can be revealed or grasped by our knowledge-episodes."[3] The heart of the *pramāṇa* method is that all pronouncements about the world and our ways of knowing it must rest on some attested forms of knowledge, such as perception and inference. No one can just claim truth but must be able to establish statements by pinning down their epistemic supports. For example, when Buddhist epistemologists claim, along with other Buddhists, that all things are impermanent, they cannot just invoke the Buddha's religious authority or individual religious experience to support this claim. Rather, they must indicate the epistemic basis (in this example, inference) for their conclusion. The discussion can then proceed by assessing the epistemic basis of such a statement, rather than directly discussing the statement itself.

This *pramāṇa* method of evaluating statements is remarkable in more than one way. First, it provides intertraditional standards of validation. This explains what I have called the *Indian epistemological turn*; namely, the development of a relatively neutral framework within which philosophical and metaphysical claims can be assessed without regard to religious or ideological backgrounds. Second, the *pramāṇa* method puts a premium on analytical thinking. Statements are not evaluated as elements within a global theory in which criteria may include aesthetic considerations such as simplicity or elegance. Rather, statements are appraised on their own merits by taking apart their components. For instance, the Buddhist claim that all things are impermanent is discussed by investigating the inference that supports it. Such an investigation examines each element of the reasoning posited in supports of this claim, looking for possible formal or material flaws.[4]

Third, the *pramāṇa* method is remarkable in that it entails a foundational mode of thinking. We are to evaluate statements in terms of our ability to relate them to some well-established cognitive mode. Cognitive modes in turn are evaluated in terms of being grounded in reality. In ultimate analysis, all systematically elaborated statements are appraised according to their relation to reality, through the channel of some established cognitive form. Hence, our analysis will proceed in two steps. First (Book I), we will consider together the ontological foundation of Dharmakīrti's epistemological system and other related issues such as the philosophy of language that this ontology supports. Then (Book II), we will discuss the established cognitive modes through which knowledge can be reached.

Epistemology and Ontological Commitments

Although the term *ontology* was not invented until the seventeenth century, its topic, the philosophical study of "what is," has long been at the heart of philosophical inquiry both in Europe and India. Our ordinary attitude assumes that existence and reality are given to our intuition and refuses to differentiate between what is more and less real. Dignāga and Dharmakīrti are not satisfied with this attitude, for to give all phenomena equal ontological status leads to the undesirable multiplication and reification of entities. Accordingly, one of the important tasks of the philosopher is to distinguish what to accept as real, in the full sense of the word, and what to consider as conceptually constructed.

Dignāga, and after him Dharmakīrti, base their systems on the distinction between real individual objects, called *specifically characterized phenomena* (*svalakṣaṇa, rang mtshan*), and conceptual constructs that do not exist in a specific way, called *generally characterized phenomena* (*sāmānyalakṣaṇa, spyi mtshan*). Distinguishing the real from the conceptually constructed provides the ontological basis of the Buddhist logico-epistemological system. Its main function is to support an epistemology that distinguishes two types of knowledge, perception (*pratyakṣa, mngon sum*)[5] and inference (*anumāna, rjes dpag*). These two types of cognition are distinguished on the basis of their objects: whereas perception relates to real individuals such as shape, taste, and so forth, through experience, inference apprehends conceptual constructs that are general, but unreal, on the basis of reasoning. Hence, the ontological and epistemological levels of Dignāga's system are connected.

One of the most important ontological questions raised by this distinction between real individuals and unreal conceptual constructs is the status of these constructs, known as *universals*. The nature of universals, which has been an important question in both Western and Indian philosophies for a number of centuries, will be at the center of our preoccupations. Dharmakīrti and other Indian philosophers approach this problem from two distinct domains of philosophical inquiry, ontology and the philosophy of language, a distinction that we will follow in our discussion.[6]

Ontology is closely linked to the question of whether universals exist. Most people willingly grant the existence of particular objects such as jars, trees, and computers. They are more hesitant about species such as human being and horse, properties such as being a tree, and relations such as being wiser than somebody else. The latter entities (supposing they exist) are abstract and general in nature, that is, they are universals, and the person who accepts their real existence is a realist. Ontologically, such entities can be considered properties that individuals instantiate. Linguistically these entities can be thought of as designated by general terms. I first present universals through an analysis of the ontology of Dharmakīrti's tradition and then discuss them in reference to language.

We must first be clear that, for Dignāga and Dharmakīrti, the formulation of a Buddhist epistemology in a broadly accepted framework is the essential task. Determining the ontological basis of the system is not an end in itself. Although Dignāga and Dharmakīrti are Buddhist scholars, they do not see the development of a Buddhist metaphysics as their most important contribution. They are ontologists only inasmuch as their epistemology requires them to be. They even seem to feel free to alternate between several conflicting metaphysical standpoints. For example, in most parts of their works, Dignāga and Dharmakīrti adopt a so-called Sautrāntika standpoint, presupposing the existence of external objects. In other parts of their works, however, they shift their ontological framework and move to a Yogācāra rejection of external objects. Such an unusual attitude toward ontological commitments is not due to a confusion or lack of logical rigor but to the nature of their project. For them, ontology remains subordinated to epistemology. Hence, they feel free to shift their ontological framework following a strategy that I will describe as an ascending scale of analysis. Lower, more commonsensical levels are introduced for the sake of convenience and withdrawn to be replaced by higher but more counterintuitive schemes. Thus, there is a certain flexibility in Dignāga's and Dharmakīrti ontological commitments. Nevertheless, their epistemology does entail certain ontological commitments that require careful examination.

Among modern analytical philosophers, W. V. Quine (1908–) has a similar attitude toward ontological commitments. Like Dharmakīrti, Quine thinks that holding a certain view commits oneself to asserting the existence of certain types of entities. This does not mean that there is no flexibility in our choice of ontological frameworks. The use of certain names or expressions does not need to imply an ontological commitment. For example, the use of the name "Pegasus" does not commit us to accept an entity corresponding to this name. There are, however, limits to this flexibility. Abstract pseudo-entities such as universals is where Quine, like Dharmakīrti, draws the line. These pseudo-entities cannot be accepted, for they do not have any identity conditions. Hence, they lead to a hopeless multiplication of entities.

For Quine, asking, What kinds of entities are there? is an important question that can prevent philosophical confusion. This question is particularly relevant to logic and mathematics, which are based on decisions about the type of entities to allow into a formal system. Do we accept numbers, sets, classes, or only individuals and sum-totals of individuals? As Quine himself remarks, these questions are not unique to modern mathematics but address more fundamental philosophical problems such as the question of universals.[7] Not surprisingly, the answers of modern analytical philosophers often parallel the positions taken by medieval philosophers such as realism, nominalism, or conceptualism. This similarity allows us to compare the philosophies of these modern thinkers to Indian and Tibetan views.

This seriousness concerning ontological commitments is far from being universally accepted. Rudolph Carnap (1891–1970), for one, finds that Quine's mode of questioning confuses internal questions, which frame a problem in relation to a given theoretical system, and external questions, considered in abstraction of any given system.[8] The first type is legitimate and meaningful, for it admits a definite answer through a precise method. For example, the question Do numbers or classes exist? makes sense in relation to a mathematical theory, where a decision to accept abstract entities such as numbers is a practical matter. Within a mathematical theory we can interpret, Do numbers exist? to mean, Should we adopt a mathematical theory that presupposes numbers? When this question is asked in abstraction of any framework, there is no precise and recognized method for settling the question. Hence, it is actually meaningless.

Although a similarly pragmatic tendency is present in Quine's work, he takes ontology much more seriously than Carnap, for he holds that the acceptance of certain theories commits one to an ontology. Philosophical decisions about which entities to admit into a system is not a pragmatic matter. Rather, it is to be decided in the light of one's philosophical beliefs. Thus, whereas Carnap sees the question of ontological commitment as either pragmatic and trivial or metaphysical and necessarily confused, Quine thinks that ontological commitments are important. Quine says, "To be assumed as an entity is, purely and simply, to be reckoned as the value of a variable. In terms of the categories of traditional grammar, this amounts roughly to saying that to be is to be in the range of of references of a pronoun."[9] In our theoretical explanations, we admit the existence of certain entities without which we could not make sense of the world. We may use a number of expressions as convenient descriptions that can be paraphrased. This does not commit us to the entities literally described. Nevertheless, they do commit us to asserting the existence of some types of phenomena. We are bound to acknowledge that certain things exist. Those things, which we find indispensable for the expression of our beliefs, are the entities our beliefs commit us to.

Similar attitudes concerning ontological commitments are found within the Buddhist tradition. For example, Candrakīrti is willing to accept any entity as real provided it is implicated in certain linguistically embedded practices. This pragmatic readiness is not unlike Carnap's ontological *désinvolture*. For Candrakīrti, "to be real" can have two meanings: conventionally, it means to be assumed by practical conventions. This does not entail any privileged ontological status. Individuals such as cows and trees as well as universals such as being a cow or a tree qualify. Ultimately, the very assumption that certain things are real is problematic and no entity qualifies.

Dharmakīrti's view is quite different. Like Quine, Dharmakīrti is not unwilling to accept several possible ontological frameworks. Nevertheless, he is committed to draw a strict boundary between real individuals and unreal universals. Admitting the latter among real elements could only lead, for Dharmakīrti, to the reification and multiplication of entities feared by Quine. To understand Dharmakīrti's view, let us examine briefly the philosophical context his views address, with a particular focus on the Nyāya realism, which is one of Dharmakīrti's main targets.

Indian Schools of Philosophy

Dharmakīrti's work addresses a number of different views, not all of them Hindu. For example, he often criticizes the Materialists (*cārvāka, rgyang 'phen*), who reject any form of knowledge other than perception. Nevertheless, his major opponents are Hindus. Among the six schools of Hindu philosophy, not all schools will be equally relevant here.[10] For example, because Śankarācarya's Vedānta became important only after Dharmakīrti's main commentators had spelled out the intricacies of Buddhist epistemology, it is given little consideration in Tibetan scholarship.

The Sāṃkhya (*grangs can pa*), together with its sister school the Yoga, are more relevant to our discussion. Dharmakīrti often refers to this school, which may have been one of the earliest to develop a logico-epistemological system. Reconstructing early Saṃkhya thought on this topic from fragments found in Dignāga and Jinendrabuddhi's works, Frauwallner has given us a few glimpses of an early epistemological attempt by a Saṃkhya philosopher whom he identifies as Vṛṣagaṇa (also known as Vārṣagaṇa, probably at the beginning of fourth century C.E.).[11] Here, we find a genuine epistemological concern in the study of inference. Unlike most Indian philosophers (Buddhists included), Vṛṣagaṇa held inference (*anumāna, rjes dpag*) to be the first *pramāṇa*. This unusual move prepares the ground for the establishment of the major theses of the Sāṃkhya system. For this school, reality is composed by the duality of Nature (*prakṛti, rang bzhin*) and Self (*ātma, bdag*). Whereas the latter is multiple, permanent, and immaterial, the former is the one universal ground of all phenomenal manifestations. In its primordial state, this Nature is constituted by three balanced qualities (*guṇa*). The manifold phenomenal world comes out of the unbalance of these three components. Since these theses cannot be established by experience but only through inference, this school favors inference.

Despite its early contributions, this school has not been very important in the field of logic and epistemology. Perhaps it was larger prior to Dignāga's time. In any case, this school was neither influential in Dharmakīrti's time nor has been since. Curiously enough, Tibetan scholars often seem quite fond of the Sāṃkhya. Raised in an exclusively Buddhist culture, contemporary Tibetan thinkers do not "feel the bite" of the other Hindu schools, particularly the Nyāya system, which they often tend to dismiss. They are more sympathetic to the Sāṃkhya, which shares certain similarities with the Tantras, which are at the center of their religious life. A bias for Sāṃkhya is reflected in explanations given by some contemporary Tibetan teachers, which can be seen in Klein's excellent *Knowlege and Liberation.* This predilection for Sāṃkhya is not shared, however, by classical authors such as Sa-paṇ, Gyel-tsap and Śākya Chok-den and is lamented by the nineteenth century scholar Ngak-wang-bel-den when he says, "Although nowadays [scholars] are slightly familiar with the Sāṃkhya system, they are not [so familiar with] the Vaiśeṣika system which is not extensively explained in [Jam-yang-shay-ba's] *Great Exposition of Tenets. . . .*"[12]

The school of the Mīmāṃsā (*spyod pa ba*) is more relevant. This school proposes an elaborate system of Vedic interpretations. Its main point is that the Vedas are self-sufficient and eternal sources of truth. In support of this view, the Mīmāṃsā offers an elaborate analysis of language, which we examine in our analysis of the *apoha* theory. For the most part, however, the Mīmāṃsā views are fairly similar to those of the Nyāya and, hence, will not require special attention.

Nyāya Realism and the Importance of Categories

Among all the Hindu schools, the Nyāya (*rigs pa can pa*, the word means "reasoning") school, together with its sister school, the Vaiśeṣika (*bye brag pa*), is by far the most important in our inquiry. Although Dharmakīrti sometimes refutes the doctrines of other philosophers (Sāṃkhyas, Grammarians,[13] and so on), the bulk of his argument is directed against the Nyāya positions. Historically, this school had become important through the systematization of its basic text, the *Nyāya-sūtra,* and Vātsyāyana's authoritative commentary. It received a further boost from the partial support of the Mīmāṃsā's most important thinker, Kumārila, and from the Naiyāyika Uddyotakara, both probably living shortly before

Dharmakīrti. Barlingay describes the importance of the Nyāya school in the field of logic and epistemology: "Though they [philosophers of other Hindu orthodox systems] rejected the metaphysical tenets, they accepted the general methodology of Nyāya-Vaiśeṣika school and soon, thanks to their efforts, instead of remaining a mere school of philosophy, it attained a position of pre-eminence in the science of methodology. Thus in ancient India a pupil was first required to learn grammar and then Nyāya or logic. Unless a student took lessons in Nyāya he was not supposed to be competent to study Pūrva Mīmāṃsā or Vedānta."[14] The influence of the Nyāya is evident in the way other systems use its categories. Even Buddhist[15] philosophers frame their arguments using concepts, such as substance and universals, that come out of the Nyāya categorical system. As Aristotle's categories permeates the Western discourse, the Nyāya categories have permeated the philosophical discussions of ancient India.

We often take the vocabulary of an investigation for granted, and easily forget that philosophical concepts are rarely neutral, having acquired their significance as part of a tradition. Aristotle's categorical scheme is the clearest example of a vocabulary that has become so integrated within our worldview that we no longer see it as a system of reference but as the very structure of the world.[16] In India, the Nyāya school has provided the categorical framework referred to by most Indian philosophers. The Nyāya divides all phenomena among six categories (*padārtha, tshig don*): substance (*dravya, rdzas*), qualities (*guṇa, yon tan*), actions (*karma, las*), universals (*sāmānya, spyi*), individuations (*viśeṣa, bye brag*), and inherence (*samavāya, 'du ba*). To this list, absence is often added.[17]

This list is not a heuristic catalogue of a variety of entities. Rather, it is based on a genuinely categorical analysis of reality. In its own view, the Nyāya does not just delineate useful philosophical notions or principles, but puts forth notions that reflect the way in which reality is articulated. In general, the word *category* can be used in a trivial sense as meaning concept, notion, or cognitive class. The Nyāya notion of category is stronger, for its classification reflects the necessary divisions of our cognitive schemata that provide form but no content to our discourse. This is the way Nyāya typology sets limits to what can properly be said. Categories are *padārtha*, the object of possible types of expression that are classified by an analysis of language that reflects the way in which the elements of reality are put together. Hence, the Nyāya's list of categories is distinguished from the Sāṃkhya cosmogonical list of twenty-five elements, which offers a description of the evolution of the world based on a correspondence between the macrocosm and the microcosm. It also differs from the phenomenological[18] list of elements found in the Buddhist Abhidharma that aims to present a list of the building blocks of the universe.

The Nyāya categories presuppose a strong realistic approach to universals, for the articulations found in language are said to be more than a reflection of our conceptual framework. They are considered fully real and exist in the way in which we conceive them. For example, when we see a red object, we do not just encounter a particular but apprehend it through the universal of being red. Whereas

Dharmakīrti holds this articulation to be entirely due to our conceptual apparatus, the Nyāya insists that such a distinction is real. Its philosophy relies on a strongly realist principle: Whatever we experience must exist as we conceive it to be. Accordingly, the Nyāya emphasizes that whatever exists must be intelligible, as illustrated by the saying, "Whatever is, is knowable and nameable."[19] That is, a thing exists in accordance with the way it can be known and named. Accordingly, the task of the philosopher is to correctly describe the reality of such a thing in accordance with the way we conceive of it. The Nyāya gives all entities and distinctions full ontological status, systematizing these distinctions with a spirit that vindicates commonsense reality, regardless of the difficulties this objectification entails (as will be illustrated shortly by a brief discussion of the relation between whole and parts). But, what can *realism*, a word with a bewildering variety of usages, mean?

The Meanings of Realism

It is possible to distinguish at least[20] five possible meanings of the words *realism* and *realist*, some of which will apply to the Indian discussion more than others. (1) Ontologically, realism accepts the reality of external objects, in opposition to idealism, which maintains that they are mentally created. I sometimes call this view *metaphysical realism.* (2) In another sense of the word, *realism* advocates the reality of general and abstract entities or universals, such as being a cow or being impermanent, in opposition to nominalism and conceptualism, which assert that universals are linguistically or mentally created. (3) Epistemologically, direct realism asserts that perception is able to perceive its object without an intermediary, in opposition to representationalism and phenomenalism, which argue that perception has no direct access to the world and needs the mediation of representation. (4) In the domain of the philosophy of science, realism asserts the reality of the theoretical entities postulated by science, which are seen as more real than commonsense objects. This view is opposed by instrumentalism, which denies the reality of theoretical entities. (5) Finally, realism can be a privileging of the objects of commonsense over those of abstract thoughts. The Nyāya is realist in the three senses of 1, 2, and 5 since it holds that both universals and external commonsense objects are real.

In my explanation of Indian and Tibetan epistemologies, I refer primarily to realism as described in 2, and secondarily to realism as described in 5, for the two are connected in the Indian and Tibetan contexts. This choice is dictated by the nature of my work, which concerns Dharmakīrti's system and its traditional interpretations. I use the realism of 2 and 5 to differentiate Dharmakīrti's philosophy, which is antirealist, from some of its later interpretations. In particular, I describe the Ge-luk interpretation as realist as described in 2 and in 5. The Ge-luk tradition is also realist as described in 3, as we will see later. I refer less often to the realism of 1, despite the obvious connection between the realism of 1 and 5, for there is remarkable unity among traditional commentators about Dharmakīrti's view on this topic. All agree that Dharmakīrti advocates the reality of external objects on some level and denies it on some others. Hence, I will be less concerned with this form of realism in this work and will focus mostly on *realism* as described in 2 and 5.

Nyāya Realism and the Status of Wholes

To better understand the nature of the Nyāya realism and Dharmakīrti's rejection of this view, we must come back to the twin problems of ontology and ontological commitments. In our lives, we all encounter a variety of entities. The entities that seem to affect us most directly are described as middle-order entities. They are neither extremely small, like atomic components, nor extremely large, like galaxies. One of the problems of ontology is the status of these common-sense objects. Are items such as persons, chairs, trees and mountains real? Or are they constructed out of more real elements? If we were to take the pragmatic attitude, which we encountered in Carnap and which in this respect is not unlike Candrakīrti's, we could dismiss the problem as being either trivial or meaningless. Philosophical inquiries cannot analyze reality from an absolute standpoint, but must presuppose an accepted vocabulary, a language game, that uses certain concepts. To ask a question such as Do tables really exist? makes sense only within a particular language game and is then answered on empirical grounds. Any larger use of this question rests on a misuse of language and can lead to only the confusion typical of philosophy.

Dharmakīrti and his Nyāya adversaries have a very different attitude toward ontological commitments. Like Quine, they hold that our beliefs imply a commitment to certain entities, which are real in the strong sense of the term. That is, these entities exist not just within the framework of certain agreed-upon practices, but have an ontological status that goes beyond these practices and support them. For Dharmakīrti and his Nyāya adversaries, to limit the reality of entities to a conventional framework is to put the cart before the horse. It is to renounce one of the main roles of philosophy, which is to explain and justify the validity of human practices. Renouncing such a role also entails a limitation of philosophy to a piecemeal reflection on conventional practices and language games.

Dharmakīrti and his Nyāya adversaries agree on rejecting this casual attitude toward ontology. They disagree, however, on the entities to be admitted in their ontology. Their disagreement revolves around the identity of the entities that we encounter in our experience and the degree to which this identity should be reified. The question of identity becomes particularly crucial in the case of broadly spread objects. Let me explain this point. One day, we see an extended surface of water and identify it as a lake. Later on, we come to another lake and say "this is a lake, too." In referring to these objects, we attribute a unified identity to objects spread over space and time. The lake is made up of a vast number of smaller entities, water molecules, but we need to attribute such a common identity to these spread entities. Similarly, we need some ascription of unity to refer to the same lake the next day. Finally, we need some description to deal with a plurality of similar objects. Otherwise, we would be reduced to pointing to objects without any way to determine the spatio-temporal spread or the nature of the objects we encounter. This would deprive us of the ability to integrate the objects we relate to into meaningful patterns.

In accordance with their restrictive ontology, which we will examine in the next chapter, Dharmakīrti and his antirealist followers are reluctant to admit the existence of these commonalities. Like Quine, they reject the third type of commonality, the universal. Unlike Quine,[21] however, they are not ready even to admit cross-time identities. They hold that the time slices of the object we called *a lake* are temporally located objects that confuse us by their quick arising into positing some stable identity. They endorse Hume's words that "the objects, which are variable or interrupted, and yet are supposed to continue the same, are such only as consist of a succession of parts, connected together by resemblance, contiguity or causation. For as such succession answers evidently to our notion of diversity, it can only be by mistake that we ascribe to it an identity."[22] For Dharmakīrti and his antirealists followers, duration is a conceptual fiction due to the quick arising of discrete moments looking alike. We are deluded by the arising of different moments looking alike in believing that the object we perceive endures. Such a mistake has practical benefits, in that it allows us to attribute to the external world the stability that is necessary to human activity. This practical usefulness does not make it real, however, but exposes it as the product of our ways of conceptualizing a world made of momentary events.

Many, but not all, Buddhist antirealists go further and hold that the commonsense identity we attribute to the water molecules at any one time, the object we refer to by the word "lake," does not correspond to anything real. It is just a convenient label used to identify a spread of real elements. This view is quite counterintuitive. It also lends little support to the elaboration of a convincing epistemology, the main task of Dharmakīrti and his tradition. Hence, this restrictive ontology has been criticized both inside and outside of the Buddhist tradition.

The Nyāya view is quite different. In accordance with its strong realism and its appreciation for common sense, Nyāya holds that, in all three cases, the common identities that we impute to spatio-temporally spread objects are fully real. The first two cases are accounted for by the doctrine of substance (*dravya, rdzas*), and the third case by real universals. The lake is a real substance, a unified whole (*anavayin, yan lag can*), whose reality is not reducible to that of its parts. In the third case, the commonality is not concrete but abstract. It is accounted for by the presence of a real universal, a kind (*jāti, rigs*) whose nature we will investigate in our discussion of universals. The Nyāya goes further, however, and holds that these unitary identities exist separate from the elements they unify. Let me explain this position in relation to the notion of wholes, for this latter view illustrates the extreme realism of this tradition, as well as the concrete and empirical orientation that distinguishes this tradition's realism from other forms of realism.

The Nyāya recognizes the difference between the concrete spatio-temporal identity of substances, which are the basic elements of Nyāya ontology, and the abstract identity of universals, which we will analyze later. These substances are the concrete and unitary wholes that we observe empirically as being spread over space and time. For example, a jar is a substance characterized by particular qualities (color, shape, etc.), universal attributes (jarness), and so forth. The jar is a unitary whole made by the aggregated partless atoms that cohere to form a larger unit. The final stage of aggregation is reached when the two halves of the jar are put together. At this stage, the jar is a whole and constitutes an object that is not a mere collection of its parts, as Buddhists would have it, but that has a unitary identity of its own distinct and even separate from that of its parts.

The stress on the unity of objects is an important part of the Nyāya theory of substance. Following the realist principle that to any valid experience must correspond some real entities, the Nyāya wants to find in the external object a support of our intuition of unitary objects. This support is found in the reality of substances existing as wholes distinct from their parts. A cloth, for example, is the result of an aggregation of threads but is not reducible to them. It is a substance that exists as a synthetic whole over and above the collection of its parts. Moreover, argues the Nyāya, it is a new unity that does not pre-exist in its causes, the threads. Since the cloth is produced from the threads and since in this system causes and effects must be different, the unlikely conclusion that the cloth is entirely different from the threads is irresistible within the classical Nyāya framework. Thus, to vindicate realism, the Nyāya is ready to assert that cloth and threads coexist in the same space, despite being different.[23] The obvious objection that we do not perceive them to be different is met by asserting they are bound by the relation of inherence (*samavāya*). This rather ad hoc position reflects the reificatory character of this philosophy. As Shastri says, "it is realism with a vengeance."[24]

The doctrine of substance is the basis for a systematic distinction made by the Nyāya between substance and characteristics. This distinction is fully real, argues the Nyāya, independent of any conceptual system. Substances are the subjects;[25] that is, substrata (*dharmin, chos can*) of predicates (characteristics, *dharma, chos*)[26] that inhere in them. It is quite ordinary to differentiate objects from their qualities: We think of a chair as distinct from its color, shape, and so on. This difference is reflected in the Nyāya ontology: Substances are the prior bases of their characteristics, existing independent of them, at least for very short moments. Śrīdhara says: "apprehension of substanceness is just an apprehension of having independent existence."[27]

The Nyāya uses three different criteria of substance. Substances (1) have independent existence, (2) support qualities and actions, and (3) act as substrata of change. We perceive things changing and attribute change to the objects themselves. We say "this tree has changed so much in the last five years," indicating that we attribute the change to a support that does not undergo change, a substance. In all cases, the distinction between substance and characteristics is taken to be fully real, and provides the basis of the Nyāya categorical approach to reality. The distinction between individuals, that is, substances, and universals, which is central to our inquiry, depends on the differentiation between substances and characteristics. It is not, however, reducible to it, for the Nyāya holds that characteristics include more than universals.

Characteristics can be of five types: qualities, actions, universals, individuations or individuators, and inherence. Qualities are particular attributes (such as a particular object being white) that are not instantiable. For example, the white quality of a conch is particular to that conch and distinguished from its universal attribute, whiteness. Whiteness is not a quality in the Nyāya sense, but an instantiable property, a real kind (*jāti, rigs*), which the Nyāya holds to exist separately from its instances. Inherence is the relation that exists between elements that are never found apart, a kind of cosmic glue that can never be observed on its own. It binds together the different parts of a unitary object. It also relates substances to their properties and explains the relation between universals and individuals. Despite its invisibility, inherence is posited in the Nyāya system as a real and separate category. These five characteristics, plus substance, constitute the six categories of the old Vaiśeṣika ontology, which was adopted at an early stage by the Nyāya and other realist schools such as the Mīmāṃsā.[28]

Dharmakīrti's Critique of Substance

Dharmakīrti's philosophy is based on a refusal of the Nyāya ontology of substance. This refusal is deeply related to several of the central questions of our inquiry. In accordance with his rejection of the reality of universals, one of our central issues, Dharmakīrti refuses to accept categories as marking the true articulation of reality. Although recognizing that categories do seem to articulate the necessary elements in our way of experiencing the world, he denies that this articulation reflects anything more than our own predispositions. Hence, Dharmakīrti uses the notion of substance, but understands it in a different sense than the Nyāya.[29] A substance is not a substratum but an effective phenomenon, which must be understood less as a thing than as an event.

Dharmakīrti also rejects the Nyāya doctrine of whole, an overly reified concept that constitutes an easy target. Dharmakīrti delights in the opportunity to produce some memorable arguments. When you move a hand, do all the other members move? They should, according to the Nyāya view, which is that the body as a partless whole is entirely present in the moving hand. It must therefore move together with the hand. Otherwise, the body as a whole would not be partless anymore, since moving and unmoving parts could be differentiated. Since such a body, which is entirely moving (since it is moving and is partless), is also entirely present in other members, these must also be moving. Dharmakīrti cracks two other similar jokes at the expense of the Nyāya: Are all members covered when one part of the body is covered? Do all members change their colors when one is painted?[30]

Dharmakīrti's arguments are sharp. They expose a weakness in the Nyāya system, one corrected later by the Navya (New) Nyāya.[31] Even then, the problem of unitary objects, the question the doctrine of partless wholes was meant to solve, is not eliminated.[32] Dharmakīrti's philosophy is a response to this challenge. It is an attempt to build a logico-epistemological system without reifying entities. To succeed, Dharmakīrti has to provide a credible ontological foundation for his system. Let us examine his ontology and the explanations of his followers.

The next chapter focuses on Dharmakīrti's ontology, analyzing his understanding of reality to consist of causally connected individual thing-events. These individuals are further described by Dharmakīrti as specifically characterized phenomena and are sharply opposed to conceptual constructs, which are described as generally characterized phenomena. I also consider the criteria that Dharmakīrti proposes implicitly to distinguish the real from the conceptual. Chapters 3 and 4 both examine some of the areas left unclear by Dharmakīrti, using the resources provided by Tibetan commentators. Chapter 3 briefly discusses the concept of existence and its ambiguities. I contrast Tibetan interpretations, showing how their ontological commitments influence their interpretations of Dharmakīrti's works. Chapter 4 provides the reader with a more involved discussion of the nature and purview of the specifically characterized. I ask whether Dharmakīrti intends to reduce reality to a causal interplay of infinitesimally small moments of matter and consciousness or whether he intends to admit extended objects as well. This provides an opportunity to examine a remarkable feature of Dharmakīrti's philosophy, its readiness to use contradictory metaphysical frameworks concerning the reality or lack thereof of external objects. I show that this limited flexibility is due to Dharmakīrti's philosophical strategy, which I describe as following ascending scales of analysis. Chapter 5 concludes this part of Book I by discussing the ontology of the Ge-luk tradition. I emphasize the realism of this tradition, showing how its description of Dharmakīrti's ontology reflects this commitment. The realism of Ge-luk thinkers is also clear in their assertions that epistemology should be based on commonsense.

2

Dharmakīrti's Ontology

Momentariness and the Structure of Dharmakīrti's System

Despite much disagreement among Buddhist philosophers concerning questions of ontology, they all agree on their rejection of the Nyāya extreme realism we just examined. In particular, Buddhist thinkers disapprove of the Nyāya ideas of substance. Buddhist thinkers do not distinguish substances from characteristics, arguing that this distinction does not reflect a necessary articulation of reality but is relevant only to the ways in which we conceptualize the world. Hence, the distinction between substance and quality does not exist independent of our conceptual activities. Against the Nyāya ontology of substance, Buddhists adopt an ontology of evanescent phenomena-events in which material objects are made of infinitesimal temporal parts in constant transformation. A jar, for example, being an aggregate of evanescent atomic constituent-events is itself momentary (*kṣaṇika, skad cig ma*). Hence, it has no continuity as a real substratum. Similarly, consciousness is a succession of moments of awareness.

In asserting the primacy of change, Buddhism differs not only from the Nyāya but from most traditions, both in India and the West. Thinkers such as Plato, Aristotle, Uddyotakara, Kumārila, and Śaṅkarācarya all consider being as the central philosophical notion in relation to which fleeting elements must be explained. They also understand being to imply the existence of stable and unchanging entities such as substance, universal, form, essence, and substratum. Buddhism, by contrast, holds that change is more fundamental to reality than stability. Like Heraclitus,[1] Buddhists think that everything is in perpetual motion. For the Buddhists, this denial of stability is not necessarily a denial of being but an assertion that being must be understood first and foremost as change.

This denial of enduring stability is clear in the doctrine of selflessness, which is at the center of Buddhist soteriology.[2] The Buddhist denial of the existence of real substances is a direct consequence of this most basic tenet. The view that all phenomena are selfless (*anātma, bdag med*) does not just refuse the existence of a personal soul but also denies the existence of any unifying principle such as the substance or whole, as accepted by the Nyāya and the Mīmāṃsā, or universal substratum, as accepted by the Sāṃkhya. Thus, the Buddhist theory of selflessness is fundamentally a denial of Hindu orthodox philosophical theory. This has led to a protracted debate between the two sides that has greatly vitalized the Indian philosophical tradition. Whereas Buddhist thinkers consider the Hindu view as the expression of the reification that binds human mind, their Hindu opponents consider the denial of self to be tantamount to nihilism.

Selflessness also has implications for the status of universals, a topic that is central to this book. The denial of a reified self is based on an inquiry into the nature of the person that manifests a suspicion toward any synthesizing unity over and above causal regularity. When one looks for the person among his or her components, the aggregates (*skandha, phung po*), one fails to find any unifying element. Hume expresses very well this view when he says, "For my part, when I enter into *myself,* I always stumble on some particular perception or other, of heat cold, light or shade, love or hatred, pain or pleasure. I can never catch *myself* at any time without a perception, and never can observe any 'thing' but the perception . . . I may venture to affirm of the rest of mankind, that they are nothing but a bundle or collection of different perceptions, which succeed each other with an inconceivable rapidity, and are in perpetual flux and movement."[3] The presupposition of this inquiry is that, if the self exists, it must be findable among the components of the personality. Underlying this reasoning is the assumption that whatever is real must be an individual thing. If the self exists, it must be findable like the other components. In short, it must be a thing.

According to this view, the world is not made of enduring substances with changing qualities. Rather, change itself is the essence of reality. Things that appear to endure unchanged are, in fact, a succession of moments that arise and disappear in quick succession. Reality is made only of events that flash in and out of existence. Every real happening in the universe is due to the arising and disappearing of countless events that cause it. Even the continuity of things is due to successive phenomena-events that closely resemble each other. Each thing-event in passing away causes, in conjunction with other simultaneous moments, something that resembles it. Change is provided for in that the new thing comes into existence not only through the causal power of its chief cause but also through the influence of the entire causal complex. Nothing has causal power in isolation. This is the doctrine of dependent arising (*pratītyasamutpāda, rten 'byung*), a venerable doctrine in the history of Buddhist thought.

There are disagreements among Buddhist thinkers about the exact meaning of the doctrine of momentariness.[4] Some thinkers, often described as proponents of the Vaibhāṣika view, hold that momentariness is not incompatible with duration. Things are produced, endure and disappear. Vasubandhu (as well as other Buddhist thinkers often described as proponents of the Sautrāntika view), however, disagrees with this rather commonsensical view of change. He holds that no conditioned entity can endure more than a single moment, after which it stops existing. This is its disintegration (*vyaya*). Duration arises from the sequence of successive moments and has no other basis in reality. It is an illusion created by the succession of similar moments. For Vasubandhu, things are momentary by their very nature and hence require nothing other than their production to disintegrate: "Destruction of things is spontaneous. Things perish by themselves, because it is their nature to perish. Since they perish by themselves, they perish as they are produced. Since they perish by themselves, they are momentary."[5] This view of reality as being in flux is at the heart of Dharmakīrti's philosophy. His whole system is based on the idea of reality understood as implying change and causal relation. Real things are not stable entities like Nyāya substances but, rather, they are momentary material or mental events arising in dependence on a number of previous momentary factors.

Around this view of reality, which is widely accepted among Buddhist thinkers, Dharmakīrti organizes his ontology, which rests on a dichotomy between the real, understood as changing and causally efficient, and the constructed, understood as unchanging, causally ineffective, and hence less real. This dyadic structure, which runs throughout Dharmakīrti's whole system, can be expressed through a number of binary oppositions: impermanence (*anitya, mi rtag pa*)/permanence (*nitya, rtag pa*), thing (*bhāva* or *vastu, dngos po*)/nonthing (*abhāva, dngos med*), specifically characterized phenomena (*svalakṣaṇa, rang mtshan*)/generally characterized phenomena (*sāmānayalakṣaṇa, spyi mtshan*).[6] These oppositions yield several equivalencies, which are fundamental to Dharmakīrti's system: "thing," "impermanent," and "specifically characterized phenomenon" are equivalent terms. They designate real entities that are constantly changing, causally effective and individuated according to strict identity conditions. These entities are the ultimate elements of the universe. They are also, as we will see, the objects of perception. Similarly, "permanent," "nonthing," and "generally characterized phenomenon" are equivalent terms. They designate phenomena that are unchanging, ineffective, and lacking identity conditions. Since these phenomena lack the marks of reality, they are constructs, that is, pseudo-entities that have only conventional reality. They are the objects of inference. The reader will have to keep these equivalencies in mind, for they will be presupposed constantly in our analyses. For example, we will examine how Dharmakīrti argues that a phenomenon is a construct because it is a nonthing, or that a phenomenon is unreal because it is permanent (or vice versa). These conclusions, though far from being accepted by all philosophers, are basic to Dharmakīrti's system. They are true almost by definition.

In the next pages I examine the three equivalent dichotomies that constitute his system. I start with his notion of impermanence understood as momentariness and analyze Dharmakīrti's arguments for this view. I move then to his explanation of the concept of thing explained in terms of ability to fulfill a function (*arthakriyāsamartha, don byed nus pa*) and describe the ambiguity of this concept. Finally, I describe Dharmakīrti's notion of the specifically characterized and show that his system revolves around the problem of universals. It is based on the opposition between real, concrete, and individual things and unreal, abstract, and general constructs. Dharmakīrti's entire system rests on the opposition between these two chains of equivalents.

Dharmakīrti on Momentariness

Dharmakīrti's view of momentariness does not differ from the Sautrāntika view advocated by Vasubandhu. Dharmakīrti, together with Dignāga, is not original in his ontology but, rather, in the way in which he expresses it and articulates its epistemological consequences. Instead of using Buddhist terms such as "dependent arising" (*pratītyasamutpāda, rten 'byung*) and "compounded phenomenon" (*saṃskṛta, 'dus byas*), he prefers terms such as "substance" or "universal," which have wide acceptance among Indian thinkers. Dharmakīrti's philosophy is also interesting for the arguments he offers to support traditional Buddhist ideas. Following Tibetan commentators' explanations, let us examine his defense of the doctrine of momentariness. In the process, we will also notice the evolution of Dharmakīrti's arguments, which is less remarked on by Tibetan traditional scholarship.

In his early works, Dharmakīrti proposes the argument from disintegration as a refutation of a substantialist ontology à la Nyāya.[7] According to this substantialist view, substances come into existence in dependence on causes and conditions, endure, and only later disintegrate. Their disintegration depends on special causes of destruction (*vināśahetu, 'jig rgyu*). Until they meet these causes, substances abide without change. Only more fleeting qualities change. In this way, the continuity assumed by commonsense is explained. Against this substantialist view, Dharmakīrti proposes the following dilemma: Is the disintegration (*vināśa, 'jig pa*) of a substance related to the thing itself or is it merely a fortuitous occurrence, like the change of color that a cloth undergoes? If it is merely fortuitous, then why do all things meet their end in due time? If it is not fortuitous, then there must be a relation between a thing and its disintegration. What kind of relation is it? Is disintegration a cause of things or is it an effect? It cannot be a cause since it comes after these things. The commonsense view of things would tell us that the disintegration of things is a result of things.

Then, asks Dharmakīrti, how can we infer the future disintegration from the thing, which is the cause of the disintegration? This inference is, however, illicit for Dharmakīrti because it is an inference from cause to effect. Since one can never exclude the possibility of an unforeseen obstacle, one can never be sure that the result will follow from the causes. Dharmakīrti says, "Since it arises after [the fact, impermanence] cannot be the cause of a thing. Even if it is the effect, how can it be conclusive?"[8] That we are invariably able to predict the disintegration of things indicates that disintegration is constitutive of the things themselves. A jar's disintegration does not arise after the jar has been produced but is inherent to the jar itself. The disintegration of the jar requires no other causes than those necessary to its production.[9] Dharmakīrti expresses this by saying that disintegration is uncaused: "Since it does not [require any] cause, disintegration is concomittant with the nature [of things]."[10] This formulation has given rise to some misunderstanding. Some scholars seem to think that Dharmakīrti's view is that disintegration is completely uncaused. This is not Dharmakīrti's idea, for in this case disintegration would be permanent! Dharmakīrti's view is quite different; it is similar to Vasubandhu's idea that the disintegration of a thing requires no supplementary causes other than those required for its production. The misunderstanding comes from the intentional ambiguity of his formulation. His argument plays on the two possible meanings of the word "disintegration," as will be explained shortly.

In accordance with his process view of reality, Dharmakīrti holds that disintegration is the fact that the thing is produced in one instant and will not abide in the next moment. Understood in this way, disintegration is an aspect of the thing itself. Sa-paṇ explains Dharmakīrti's idea:

> *Question*: What is disintegration?
> *Answer*: [Disintegration] is not to be thought of as the state of disintegratedness [of something already] disintegrated, [for] this is a nonthing. Rather, the mere [fact] that [something] does not remain from the second moment onward after having been produced for a single moment from its causes is called disintegration. There is no separate phenomenon called *disintegration*. Accordingly, [Dharmakīrti] says in his *Commentary*: "In order to know that the disintegration of things does not rely on anything else, it is said that it [the disintegration] has no cause on the basis of mind superimposing a distinction [between the thing and its disintegration]."[11]

Since disintegration (understood in this unusual way) is not a separate entity but the nature of the thing itself, which exists only for a single instant, it does not have causes other than those of its production. To underline this, Dharmakīrti said that disintegration has no cause. One may wonder why he uses such a misleading description?

The answer is that Dharmakīrti attempts to present his concept of disintegration in ambiguous terms. In addition to his own understanding of disintegration as something being in the process of disappearing, Dharmakīrti wants to include in the word the more usual connotation of the concept, that is, that a thing has already ceased to be. This second and more usual understanding of the concept of disintegration is included to present the argument in the terms of his orthodox Hindu adversaries. They understand *disintegration* as describing the state of an already disintegrated thing. Sa-paṇ explains, "The word *disintegration* [can] also refer to that which is to disintegrate, a thing such as a jar or a tree. It [can] also refer to what does not exist [any more] after disintegration, which is a nonthing. Dharmakīrti spoke [of] the absence of cause in reference to the thing which is to disintegrate. Since this very disintegration is a thing, [Dharmakīrti speaks thus] having in mind that no other cause is required for the production of such a thing. When disintegration names the nonexistence [of something] on [its] disintegration, the absence of cause [is spoken by Dharmakīrti], keeping in mind the complete absence of cause [of such a nonthing. This is so] because such a disintegration is a nonthing."[12] Thus, Dharmakīrti's formulation is intentionally ambiguous. It is meant to accommodate two contradictory meanings of *disintegration* to "trick" his orthodox adversaries into assenting to his argument. The adversary will assent to the reason that the disintegration of things is uncaused believing Dharmakīrti to be talking about the state of something already disintegrated. In actuality, Dharmakīrti is referring to the process of disintegration. Despite the dubious nature of this dialectical trick, Dharmakīrti's position is clear and consistent: Disintegration is the process of disappearance of a thing. Hence, it is an expression of the processed nature of that thing and as such does not require any special cause to be produced. It is inherent to the thing it characterizes from the very incipience of that thing.

This understanding of impermanence is found in several works of Dharmakīrti, particularly his *Commentary.* In later works, Dharmakīrti adopts another presentation of momentariness, that of the inference from existence (*sattvānumāna*). Here, impermanence is argued not from the fact that disintegration does not require causes but from the fact that things exist.[13] For Dharmakīrti, things truly exist insofar as they are able to perform a function. To function is to be capable of producing an effect, a faculty possible only if the object is constantly changing. A static object is not acting on anything else nor is it being acted upon. Therefore, that something exists shows that it is momentary. In the *Science of Debate*, Dharmakīrti states this reasoning from existence: "Accordingly, all things that exist or are produced are impermanent, as for example jar, etc. Sound is also existing or produced."[14] This statement formulates two reasons for the impermanence of things: things are impermanent because (1) they are produced and (2) they exist. Sa-paṇ explains that these two reasons are equivalent. He states the reason for this: "Whatever exists disintegrates as [for example] a jar. Sound now exists. Thus [is] a reason of [identical] essence [stated]."[15] This reason is a reason of identical essence.[16] It is stated in regard to Hindu opponents, who do not accept that the words of the Vedas or that atoms are produced but who agree that they really exist.[17]

Steinkellner has argued that Dharmakīrti evolves from the early *Commentary,* which emphasizes the inference from disintegration (*vināśitvānumāna*), to later texts, which focus on the inference from existence.[18] In *Ascertainment*[19] and in *Drop of Logical Reason,* Dharmakīrti presents both reasonings, but in the later *Science of Debate,*[20] he uses only the inference from existence. Although Mimaki has demonstrated that this last reasoning becomes more influential in later authors such as Jñānaśrimitra and Ratnakīrti,[21] this evolution does not affect the concept of impermanence. Rather, the change occurs in the presentation of this concept and relates to a long-term dispute with the Nyāya school. Only the emphasis changes, since, as Mimaki remarks,[22] even in later texts the reasoning from disintegration remains present.[23]

The Causal Nature of Reality

The doctrine of momentariness is crucial in Dharmakīrti's system, permitting him to determine his basic ontology in accordance with classical Abhidharmic views. As explained earlier, Dharmakīrti equates reality with momentariness, for only momentary phenomena act as causes of other phenomena and thus make an observable difference. If permanent phenomena were to produce an effect, its production would have to be permanent also. As the effect would be changeless, it would either never be produced or endlessly repeat its production. The conclusion is that permanent phenomena cannot have any effect. Hence, they make no difference and are fictional, despite our notion that they exist.

In consequence, phenomena are real only inasmuch as they produce effects. A real thing is produced in dependence on a complicated network of causes and conditions. Once a thing is produced, it cannot stand outside this network. It in turn contributes to the production of further effects. This capacity to produce determines what is real according to classical Buddhist philosophy. Dharmakīrti adopts and systematizes this view to defend and explicate Dignāga's system, which lacked explicit criteria of reality.[24] Following traditional Buddhist ontology, Dharmakīrti defines thing (*vastu, dngos po*) as that which is able to perform a function (*arthakriyāsamartha, don byed nus pa*; literally, "readiness to do something"). Masashi Nagatomi has explained the double meaning of *arthakriyā* in Dharmakīrti's thought:[25]

> 1. In its ontological sense, it means causal efficacy. In this sense, *arthakriyā* is a criterion of reality. Dharmakīrti says: "That which is able to perform a function exists ultimately."[26] Only objects able to participate causally in the production of other phenomena are real.
>
> 2. In its epistemological sense, *arthakriyā* means to fulfill a practical purpose. As Dharmakīrti says in *Drop of Reasoning*: "Since correct [that is, valid] cognition is a prerequisite for achieving all human purposes (*artha, don*), I shall explain it."[27] Valid cognitions correctly identify objects and provide a cognitive basis for our successful activities. Real objects are called *artha* because they are the aim of practical activities such as cooking and burning.[28] *Artha* are not objects of theoretical knowledge, but practical objects. They are to be known in terms of whether they affect us positively or negatively.

These two meanings of *arthakriyā* do not conflict but refer to the functionality of real objects in two ways: Ontologically, real objects are distinguished from nominal ones on the basis of their having *arthakriyā*; that is, a causal capacity that exists in the objects themselves. Quasi-phenomena make no real difference and, hence, have only conceptually constructed "existence."[29] This causal capacity is also understood as it affects sentient beings. Hence, epistemologically, valid cognitions are differentiated from nonvalid ones on the basis of their objects having *arthakriyā*; that is, the ability to perform a function that can serve some practical purpose for somebody. This second sense is derived from the first, for only on the basis of their causal capacity can objects fulfill such a function. It underlines the importance of practical concerns in Buddhist philosophy. Reality is not an abstract domain of possibilities but one of practical importance to sentient beings. Things are real inasmuch as they potentially affect beings.

Nevertheless, an ambiguity and a tension remain in the term *arthakriyā* to be explored while investigating Dharmakīrti's epistemology. We will see how Dharmakīrti attempts to use this ambiguity to establish an epistemology that brings together the two halves of his system, the real-perceptual and the conceptual. This is one of the fundamental difficulties of Dharmakīrti's system. The ambiguity in *arthakriyā* is more than an accidental slip, it is a necessary consequence of Dharmakīrti's dualistic system.

Dharmakīrti's Ontology and Its Relation to the Problem of Universals

Dharmakīrti describes the fundamental opposition between the real and the constructed by using two terms that clearly indicate the connection between his ontology and the problem of universals. He names real things *specifically characterized phenomena* (*svalakṣaṇa, rang mtshan*) and constructs *generally characterized phenomena* (*sāmānayalakṣaṇa, spyi mtshan*) to indicate that the latter are universals (*sāmānaya, spyi*) and the former individuals.

These two concepts are known to classical Buddhist thought, for they are found in texts of the Abhidharma corpus,[30] practically applied to the identification of objects in meditation. In the Dignāga-Dharmakīrti school, these older ideas are transformed into new technical notions reflecting the ontology of this school. Accordingly, the two concepts no longer refer to properties[31] but mark the two basic types of "phenomenon":[32] The first category is equated with real effective phenomena (*arthakriyāsamartham, don byed nus pa*) and the second with fictional noneffective phenomena. Dharmakīrti says: "Those [phenomena] which are able to perform a function[33] are here [said to be] ultimately existent. Others are said to be conventionally existent. Those two [types of phenomena are] specifically and generally characterized."[34] The lines of Dharmakīrti's ontology are thus clearly drawn. Any phenomenon that is causally efficient is real and included among specifically characterized phenomena. Such a phenomenon is also called, somewhat misleadingly, a substance (*dravya, rdzas*). In the Buddhist context, the word "substance" does not have its usual meaning of something that exists independently and provides support for more fleeting qualities. Rather, the term "substance" refers to a momentary thing-event that is causally effective. Any phenomenon that is not causally active is conceptually constructed and included among generally characterized phenomena. Dharmakīrti says: "These [real things] are differentiated from other [things]. They are described as causes and effects. They are accepted as specifically characterized and generally characterized phenomena. Since these have as their fruits the adoption [of desirable objects] and the rejection [of undesirable ones], they are [the objects] to which all persons apply [themselves practically]."[35] The structure of Dharmakīrti's ontological system rests on the opposition between these two sets of categories, which constitutes a radical dichotomy (nothing can be both specifically characterized and generally characterized and everything is included in either).

Dharmakīrti, however, also states that these two types of phenomenon can be thought as two aspects of reality. They do not exist separately, like cats and dogs, but are two sides of the same coin. The simile, however, should not be pushed too far, for the two sides are not equally real. Specifically characterized phenomena exist and are apprehended through their own entity (*svarūpa, rang gi ngo bo*). That is, they have real, individual essences. Generally characterized phenomena exist and are apprehended only as being something else (*para-rūpa, gzhan gyi ngo bo*); that is, as having conceptual identities.[36] For example, a particular stone is perceived as an individual object. It can also be conceptualized as being an instance of a larger category such as stoneness, as in a case of predication. Conceptually, these two ways of understanding relate to two sides of the same stone. In reality, however, stoneness is merely a construct and only the individual stone exists.

As we will see, this ontological dyadic structure is complemented by the epistemological dyad of two types of valid cognition; that is, perception and inference. The former apprehends specifically characterized phenomena and thus offers an undistorted but limited access to reality. The latter apprehends generally characterized phenomena and provides a richer but distorted cognitive content. Dharmakīrti's entire system rests on the relation between ontological and epistemological binary oppositions.

Expanding on Dignāga's ideas, Dharmakīrti presents his ontology in the form of a critique of the Nyāya reification of identity. He confronts their realism by sharply distinguishing individual objects from synthetic principles, the universals or generally characterized phenomena. These he holds to be mental creations. Following up on his idea that the definition of reality is the capacity to perform a function, Dharmakīrti asserts that only individual objects are real. They alone can perform functions. Since these objects possess their own individual essences, they are called *specifically characterized objects*. Phenomena that do not possess their own characteristics cannot perform any function. Hence, they do not appear to perception, which is an accurate reflection of reality. They depend for their existence on the conceptual synthesis of individuals. These constructed entities, generally characterized phenomena, are not part of the fabric of reality but superimposed by our conceptual schema.

For Dharmakīrti, only individuals are objects of perception. Speaking of perception, Dharmakīrti says: "Its object is only the specifically characterized. The specifically characterized is the [kind of object] whose nearness or remoteness [creates] a difference in the appearance to the cognition. That alone ultimately exists because it performs a function, the defining property of things."[37] Dharmottara comments on this passage:

> *Question*: Why is the individuation the exclusive object of perception? Do we not know that we can see a fire that is the object of a conceptual thought? *Answer*: [Dharmakīrti] says: "That alone exists ultimately." [This means that

> it alone is] ultimate and unconstructed, that is to say, that it has a non-imputed (lit. not-superimposed) essence. Since it exists so, it exists ultimately. That object alone which produces the impression of vividness according to its remoteness or proximity, exists ultimately. Since it is also the object of perception, it is just this [thing which] is the specifically characterized.[38]

Perception experiences reality as it is. This experience is not the product of fabricated entities, such as wholes, substances, or universals. It is the result of encountering real individuals which make real differences in experience.

Dharmakīrti distinguishes the specifically characterized object through four criteria: (1) having the power to produce effects (*artha-kriyā-śakti, don byed nus pa*); (2) being specific, that is, individual (*asadṛśa, mi 'dra ba*); (3) not (directly) denotable by language (*śabdasyāviśaya, sgra'i yul ma yin*); and (4) apprehensible without reliance on other factors (*nimitta, rgyu mtshan*) such as language and conceptuality. Here, I will explain the first two of the four criteria stated by Dharmakīrti. I reserve the last two for my examination of the *apoha* theory.

Uncommoness and Identity Conditions

Since things have their own specific essence, they are said to be dissimilar (i.e., specific) from other real and unreal phenomena. By contrast, constructs have no definite criteria of identity. They are said to be "similar" to, that is, common and concomitant with, other phenomena. This characterization of specifically characterized phenomena as being uncommon and dissimilar has given rise to several misinterpretations. We will not dwell upon these for the moment. Let us briefly note, however, that contrary to what the great Russian scholar Stcherbatsky and others have asserted, uncommonness and specificity do not mean transcendental uniqueness. Specifically characterized phenomena are not unique in the absolute sense of the word. They are not completely beyond the reach of empirical determination.[39] Rather, each real thing is uncommon inasmuch as it is an individual with a determinate position in space and time, as well as a determinate essence. This it does not share with any other phenomena. Dharmakīrti explains: "Because all things essentially abide in their own essence, they partake in the differentiation between [themselves and the other] similar and dissimilar things."[40] This passage is said by the commentarial tradition to explain the nature of things (*dngos po'i gnas lugs*). Hence, it must be considered a particularly meaningful statement. An entity can be considered real if, and only if, it has its own distinctive essence. Moreover, such an essence must correspond to clear identity conditions. Tested in this way, individuals pass, but universals and abstract entities do not.

Dharmakīrti does not explicitly state what these identity conditions are. Passages in his work, however, point to such an explanation. Dharmakīrti implies three sets of identity conditions that directly answer the three ways in which the Nyāya reifies entities, as follows.[41]

1. Real things are spatially determinate (*deśaniyata, yul nges pa*);[42] that is, they occupy a definite spatial location (if they occupy any location at all).[43] The real fire I am seeing is either near or far, at my left or at my right. By contrast, the universal fireness, that is, the property of being a fire taken to be real by the Nyāya school, does not occupy a determinate position in space. The Nyāya view is that such a property is ubiquitous and can inhere in any particular that instantiates it. Dharmakīrti makes this ironical comment about the Nyāya position: "It is completely logical to say that [the universal], which was present elsewhere and did not move from its own place, exists in what has its origin in a place other than it!"[44] For Dharmakīrti, the impossibility of attributing a definite spatial location to fireness shows that it is not something that makes a real difference. Therefore, in accordance with the criterion of reality that something is real if, and only if, it can perform some function, such a universal is unreal from a spatial point of view. It is only a conceptual construct that we add onto experience for the sake of convenience.

2. Similarly, real objects are temporally determinate (*kālaniyata, dus nges pa* or *dus ma 'dres pa).* They come into and go out of existence at definite moments. This is not the case for universals, which are held by Naiyāyikas to exist regardless of whether particulars exist or not. This again shows for Dharmakīrti that such an abstract entity is unreal from a temporal point of view.[45]

3. Real things are determinate with respect to their entity (*ākāraniyata, ngo bo nges pa* or *ngo bo ma 'dres pa*), which is determined in causal terms. The entity of a thing is the result of a unique aggregation of causes (*hetusāmagrī, rgyu tshogs pa*) that have the ability to produce their own effects.[46] The entity is proper to the thing itself, it is not due to any property existing over and above the individual thing. For example, a white cow is a cow due to being produced by particular causes and having particular causal capacities.[47] It is not due to a "cowness" that it shares with black and brown cows, contrary to the Nyāya assertion. There is no real cowness over and above black, white, and brown cows. Dharmakīrti says: "[Words] do not refer to real things because all things abide in their own entities. The form of the multicolored [cow] does not exist in a brown [cow]. What is common to the two is the exclusion from [nonproduction of] an effect."[48] Dharmakīrti distinguishes between things that can be differentiated from the point of view of their spatio-temporal location and their entity and conceptual constructs that fail these identity conditions. Things have real identity because they can be clearly individuated from other things. Since conceptual pseudo-entities cannot be clearly distinguished, they cannot be real, as we will see when we analyze Dharmakīrti's arguments against the reality of universals.[49] This is as close as Dharmakīrti ever comes to providing a definition of the specifically characterized. If we put together the bits and pieces that Dharmakīrti and his commentators provide, however, we can define specifically characterized as that which "essentially abides in its own essence."[50]

Here again, there is here a striking parallel with Quine, for whom things can be said to exist only if they satisfy identity conditions. Entities are judged by clear criteria to assess their presence or absence in terms of spatio-temporal location. Only once these conditions are taken into account, we can understand the identity of things. Descriptions that seem to refer to abstract entities are in fact convenient shorthand for more complicated but ontologically more transparent descriptions, in what Quine describes as the identification of indiscernibles. Quine explains, "Objects indistinguishable from one another within the terms of a given discourse should be construed as identical for that discourse. More accurately: the references to the original objects should be reconstrued for purposes of the discourse as referring to other and fewer objects, in such a way that indistinguishable originals give way to the same new object."[51] Like Dharmakīrti, Quine proposes a sparse ontology to avoid the multiplication of entities entailed by accepting abstract entities such as universals. These pseudo-entities are individuals grouped together for the sake of convenience.

Before concluding, let us visit some of the implications of these criteria of reality. For Dharmakīrti, reality is made up of individual objects that are produced by causes and conditions, that undergo constant transformation, and that are devoid of any selfhood. Generally characterized phenomena, by contrast, have no definite identity. They are abstract constructs that are intelligible only in reference to a conceptual framework. As such, these universals are not real in the full sense of the word.

Accepting these criteria of reality commits Dharmakīrti to a radical rejection of realism regarding universals, for these criteria imply that real entities must be spatially and temporally localized and, therefore, constantly changing. Static entities, including universals, exist in the same state in different places and times. Thus, Dharmakīrti's criteria clearly imply the philosophical position of antirealism and the commitment to an event ontology. In a later chapter[52] we will analyze further the nature of Dharmakīrti's antirealism, and we will interpret it as a form of conceptualism.

The criteria, however, leave important questions unresolved. For example, Dharmakīrti distinguishes between real things and conceptual constructs. The latter are less real without being completely nonexistent. This raises the obvious but difficult question of the status of such quasi-entities. Do they exist? If they do not, how can they be part of Dharmakīrti's system, which is built on the correspondence of ontological and epistemological binary oppositions. Generally characterized phenomena are needed as the objects of inference. Without these conceptual entities his system would collapse. If, on the other hand, these conceptual entities, are said to exist, what kind of existence are we talking about? What does it mean for unreal entities to exist? The next chapter considers this question and analyzes the conflicting answers of Tibetan thinkers.

A second related problem is that Dharmakīrti's system does not make clear what kind of entity can count as having a definite spatial location. Does an entity that satisfies the criterion of spatial location need to be partless or does it need to have just a definite position in space and time? In the first case, only particles or moments of consciousness will be real. In the second case, larger objects such as colors and shapes will be real as well. We will see that both traditional and modern scholars have taken conflicting positions on this question, I believe in response to Dharmakīrti's own ambiguity.

Finally, a third problem left unresolved by Dharmakīrti is the metaphysical reality of the external world. Do Dharmakīrti's real things exist in the external world or are they moments of consciousness to which no external reality corresponds? Dharmakīrti's discussion of spatial position suggests that real things can be made of spatial parts. Nevertheless this requirement is not without ambiguity, as Dharmakīrti rarely commits himself to the existence of atoms, the building blocks of external objects. Chapters 4 and 5 investigate both problems in the light of the conflicting solutions provided by Tibetan epistemologists.

These problems are difficult points in Dharmakīrti's philosophy, and they have no easy solutions. It is, however, possible to clarify the issues by exploring the alternatives open to thinkers of his tradition. This is where the contributions of later Indian and Tibetan epistemologists become relevant. Here, as in other parts of my discussion, I will draw mostly upon Tibetan contributions. I will focus particularly on the debate between Sa-gya and Ge-luk thinkers during the fifteenth century, a time of great philosophical activity when the views of the Tibetan traditions crystallized.

3

The Ambiguities of the Concept of Existence

The Problems of Dharmakīrti's Concepts of Existence

Let us start our exploration of the difficulties in Dharmakīrti's ontological system by asking ourselves the question, What does it mean for an object to exist? An easy answer within the framework of Dharmakīrti's philosophy equates existence with reality, saying that to be means to be real and, therefore, effective. The existence of a thing lies in its having its own essence (*svabhāva, rang bzhin*), which is determined in terms of causal capacities.[1] For example, a fire exists because its essence is to be an object able to perform the function (*arthakriyā, don byed pa*) of burning. In Dharmakīrti's system, "existence" is used mostly in this sense, that is, as implying reality. This is illustrated by Dharmakīrti's discussion of the inference from existence (*sattvānumāna*) we have examined already. There, Dharmakīrti gives existence as a reason from which to infer the impermanence of sound. Therefore, in this sense of the word, to exist means to satisfy the three criteria of real identity.

This view of existence, however, is not sufficient to account for the complexities of Dharmakīrti's system. For his approach to work, it seems to require the view that among existents are included the conceptual constructs whose status we have begun to explore. His system requires that these constructed entities, that is, the universals that are the objects or contents of concepts, be given some status differentiating them from complete nonexistents (such as the famous horns of a rabbit). Accordingly, the concept of existence is ambiguous in Dharmakīrti's system. Most scholars have not been sufficiently attentive to this ambiguity in Dharmakīrti's thought and as a result have assumed that reality and existence are identical. We will see how to correct this oversight.

Although Dharmakīrti usually reserves the term "existence" (*sat, yod pa*) for designating real existence, he also accepts phenomena that are not real in the full sense of the term, yet not completely nonexistent. They can be said to exist in the secondary sense of the term, according to which existing is equivalent to being an object of comprehension *(prameya, gzhal bya)*. For example, when discussing the nature of universals (*sāmānya, spyi*), Dharmakīrti says: "[Contrary to] effective things which disappear, universals do not cease and do not perform any function. Therefore, they are not [real] objects despite [the fact that] they exist."[2] Since universals do not disintegrate, they cannot produce any effect and cannot perform any function. Therefore, they are not real. Nevertheless, they can be apprehended by inference. Since those are valid, their objects (*yul, viṣaya*) must be more than figments of the imagination, otherwise they would have the same epistemological status as delusive states of mind. Therefore, universals must somehow exist, inasmuch as they are objects of epistemologically valid activities.

Dharmakīrti refers to this notion of existence in a refutation of some Materialists. According to them, there cannot be two types of valid cognition since only specifically characterized phenomena exist. To this objection, Dharmakīrti answers: "[If you say that] since a nonexistent [thing] is not an object of comprehension there is only one [namely, the specifically characterized, we Buddhists] also accept this.[3] Since [for you] nonexistence[4] is ascertained [as a reason establishing that universals are not objects of comprehension, then your reason 'nonexistent'] is indeed inconclusive with respect to 'not being an object of comprehension'."[5] Dharmakīrti agrees with his materialist adversaries that ultimately there is only one type of object of comprehension. Only effective phenomena are really objects of valid cognitions. Nevertheless, universals must also be admitted as objects of comprehension despite being only conceptual constructs. Dharmakīrti makes this point by drawing his adversaries into contradicting themselves. He asks on what grounds they exclude universals as objects of valid cognition. The answer is, "universals are not objects of comprehension because they do not really exist." If this argument is correct, the predicate (not being an object of comprehension) must be entailed by the reason (nonexistence). Or, to use the more technical language of Indian argumentation, there must be pervasion (*vyāpti, khyab pa*) of the reason by the predicate. Moreover, this relation must be understood by a valid cognition. But, then, the terms of the entailment, nonexistence and not being an object of comprehension, would have to be identified by a valid cognition and would then be an object of comprehension. Therefore, the adversaries are forced to acknowledge that there are nonexistents, namely, universals such as not being a real existent, which require a special type of valid cognition.

When applied to his own system, this argument forces Dharmakīrti to concede that the conceptually constructed entities necessitated by linguistic and conceptual activities exist in some sense. Their denial would involve Dharmakīrti in the same self-defeating paradox as the Materialists. To explain how nonthings are excluded from reality, a realm of conceptually constructed entities has to be accepted on some level. These entities are not real in the sense that they cannot perform any function. They exist, however, inasmuch as they are objects of epistemologically valid cognitive acts.

Thus, it is clear that there are two possible understandings of existence in Dharmakīrti's works.[6] In its primary sense, "existence" refers to the causal effectiveness of real things. In its secondary sense, it refers to the epistemic validity of all phenomena (permanent as well as impermanent). In this second sense, existence includes mere nominal existence and is a nominally existent property. In both cases, existence is not an autonomous property characterizing entities. It either stands for the real causal nature of things or for their conceptually constructed nature of being an object of knowledge.

The presence of such an ambiguity is revealing of the difficulty, which we will encounter throughout this work, that Dharmakīrti's consistent antirealism has in explaining the nature of knowledge in a world without universals. As with other antirealists, Dharmakīrti finds it difficult to explain the role of thought in the cognitive process on the basis of his sparse ontology. From an antirealist standpoint, thought does not bear directly on a reality that consists of individual things. Thinking relates to abstract conceptual constructs without which a convincing epistemology cannot be delineated. The status of such constructs is, however, highly problematic in a system that holds that only things are real. Since constructs are not things, they are not real. Yet, they are required and thus must exist in a certain sense which we could call nominal.

This nominal existence is not unlike Meinong's concept of subsistence.[7] For Meinong, ideal objects such as propositions and numbers are objectives that do not exist like individual things but subsist (*bestehen*). For example, we see a cat on the mat and judge that "the cat is on the mat." The concrete object is the perceived cat, which is an individual existing in space and time. The object of my judgment is not, however, this individual but the proposition "the cat exists." Such an object is not real as an individual but exists as an object of true cognitive acts.[8]

Similarly in Dharmakīrti's epistemology, constructs are sometimes described as existents in the sense that they are objects of valid cognitions. The ontological status of these constructs is, however, problematic. Since they are not things, they are only quasi- or pseudo-entities. But what does this mean? To answer, Dharmakīrti, like Dignāga before him, uses the notion of *vikalpa* (or *kalpanā, rtog pa*),[9] our ability to think in dependence on language and thereby construct convenient fictions. Such constructs, whose nature we will have to investigate in the next two parts of this work, do not exist really, and yet, they have a kind of intersubjective validity that sets them apart from private fictions. Can we then say that they exist?

In Tibet, the tradition of antirealist thinkers who attempt to explain Dharmakīrti's system in a more literal fashion has wrestled with these issues in particular depth. This tradition must be differentiated from the more revisionist current that includes important Indian (Dharmottara) and Tibetan thinkers (Cha-ba and his followers including the whole Ge-luk tradition). In opposition to this latter, more interpretive trend, the former tradition attempts to solve the difficulties in Dharmakīrti's system while keeping to his overall antirealist commitment. One of the major challenges in this attempt is the notion of existence. Let us examine how this concept is articulated by Sa-paṇ, the leading proponent of the antirealist trend among Tibetan commentators.

Sa-paṇ's Controversial Views on Existence

In the epistemological traditions of India and Tibet, the concept of existence is usually explained in relation to that of being an object of valid cognition (*prameya, gzhal bya*). All epistemological schools focus on the concept of valid cognition (or means of valid cognition, *pramāṇa, tshad ma*) as the main concern of their philosophy and define existence in relation to valid cognition. Things exist if, and only if, they are apprehended by valid cognition. One might think that according to this definition of *existence*, objects come to be through being perceived by the mind. This would be idealism.

This is not, however, the meaning of this definition, for otherwise that would make it incompatible with the Sautrāntika (i.e., nonidealist) aspects of Dharmakīrti's system. In this view, the perception of an object does not materially constitute that object. Rather, it is only the necessary and sufficient condition for our being able to determine that the object exists. When we say a jar is in the room, we are implying that this is so because we correctly perceive such a jar, regardless of whether our perception has created the object or not. Thus, the definition of *existence* in terms of being an object of valid cognition is not an idealist statement about how the world is constituted. Rather, it reflects an analysis of our ordinary usage of words such as "is" and "exists." Such a definition is accepted by Buddhist epistemologists as a way to relate ontological and epistemological inquiries, regardless of whether they are idealists.

However, as Shah remarks,[10] this definition is quite formal. It must be fleshed out by an explanation of what is allowable as an object of valid cognition. Can constructs be objects of valid cognitions, or is this the exclusive privilege of real things? This question has been the focus of an intense conflict of interpretation among Tibetan scholars. This discussion is partly exegetical, attempting to find "what Dharmakīrti really meant." It also has, however, philosophical significance. It reveals the ambiguity of the concept of existence in Dharmakīrti's system. As an antirealist, Dharmakīrti is committed to denying that universals really exist. As a conceptualist, however, he still wants to find a place for them in his system. This tension explains why he uses the concept of existence in two contradictory ways.

Tibetan commentators have noticed these difficulties and tried to sort them out. Their discussion has been dominated by Sa-paṇ's controversial comments to the effect that to "exist," that is, to "be an object of valid cognition" (*tshad ma'i gzhal bya, prameya*) means to be real. This controversial position has been the target of sustained criticism within the Tibetan tradition. Such criticism has prompted some commentators sympathetic to Sa-paṇ to find a more moderate interpretation that allows for the existence of conceptually fabricated entities. Not all Sa-gya commentators have accepted this "moderate" interpretation and its seemingly neat conciliation of these two understandings of existence. I will examine Lo Ken-chen's[11] analysis of existence in terms of reality, which radically separates the two possible understandings of existence.

Let us first briefly summarize the general lines of Sa-paṇ's ontology. Sa-paṇ starts his ontological investigation by relating ontology to epistemology: "[Whereas] nonconceptual [cognitions] apprehend specifically characterized phenomena, universals are apprehended by conceptual [cognition]. With respect to this, specifically characterized phenomena are things [and] universals are not established as things."[12] Whereas conception apprehends only general entities, which have an imputed essence, perception, which is for the Buddhists nonconceptual, apprehends real phenomena. Those can be characterized in several ways. Sa-paṇ says, "Since [those things that are called] 'specifically characterized phenomena (*rang gi mtshan*), individuals (*gsal ba*), things (*dngos po, vastu*), substances (*rdzas, dravya*), distinguished [phenomena] (*log pa*),[13] ultimates (*paramārtha*), etc.' are the effective [phenomena] which are mutually unmixed substances, established as causes and effects, [and] the objects of engagement of the [actions] of developing and rejecting [what is desirable and undesirable], they are equivalent[14] to the meaning of thing."[15] Despite their difference in emphasis, these terms all refer to what Buddhists hold to be real. Some of the terms are part of the common Indian philosophical vocabulary. For example, *substance* and *individual* are favored by Naiyāyikas, who assert the reality of the difference between substrata and their properties. Other terms such as *differentiated, specifically characterized phenomena*, and the like are more specifically Buddhist, for they imply the unreality of the distinction of substrata or properties. However, most of these terms are used freely, irrespective of their original connotation. For example, Buddhists use the term *substance*, which they redefine in terms of causal efficiency.

Sa-paṇ provides a parallel list for the conceptual domain of generally characterized phenomena: universal (*spyi, sāmānya*), elimination of others (*gzhan sel, anyāpoha*), distinguisher (*ldog pa, vyāvṛtti*), preclusion (*rnam gcod, vyavaccheda*), indeterminate (literally "mixed," *'dres pa*), relation (*'brel ba, sambandha*), relative (*kun rdzob, saṃvṛti*). These phenomena do not exist in reality (*don la mi gnas pa*) for they are superimposed (*sgro btags pa*) by thought. Most of these terms will be clarified in the following chapters, when studying the problem of universals and the *apoha* theory. Suffice to say that according to Sa-paṇ, all these terms refer to the imputed entities which are objects of thought. They are spatially and temporally indeterminate and are constructed as unreal general entities.

Sa-paṇ's view on existence has to be understood within this classically Dharmakīrtian framework, which emphasizes the opposition between real things and conceptual constructions. For Sa-paṇ as for other epistemologists, to exist means to be comprehended by a valid cognition. For Sa-paṇ, however, conceptual contents are only quasi-entities, which are not really comprehended. Whereas individual things can be really known, contents are only conceived to be so. Sa-paṇ says, "Only specifically characterized phenomena are objects of comprehension."[16] In another passage, he is even clearer: "Since nonthings do not have any entity they do not exist [and] since they are entityless, they are not knowable. Accordingly, they are merely imputed on the absence of things."[17] Since permanent phenomena such as universals, which in Dharmakīrti's system are described as generally characterized phenomena, are without essence (*svabhāva, rang bzhin*), they are not knowable. They are conceptual contents we merely imagine to know. For example, I see a table and think "there is no elephant on this table." What is really known in this example is the real object, the table.[18] The absence of elephant is a conceptual overlay that I conceptually add on reality. Sa-paṇ summarizes his position: "That which is accepted as universal cannot be comprehended by valid cognition."[19] The conclusion to be drawn is that the objects of concepts do not exist at all. As one can imagine, such a view has fueled a great deal of controversy among Tibetan scholars, since it seems to involve Sa-paṇ in the self-defeating paradox explained previously. It is, however, not without support in Dharmakīrti's writings. In discussing valid cognition, Dharmakīrti asserts that nondeceptiveness (*avisamvādanam, mi slu ba*), the defining characteristic of valid cognition, consists of the capacity to perform a function in accordance with the way it is cognized by that cognition. Only causally effective phenomena (*vastu, dngos po*) have such a capacity. So, valid cognitions are nondeceptive inasmuch as they relate appropriately to real things (*svalakṣaṇa, rang mtshan.*) Therefore, the conclusion that only real, that is, specifically characterized phenomena are objects of valid cognitions is hard to resist. Dharmakīrti says, "Only specifically characterized phenomena are objects of comprehension."[20] The conclusion that only real phenomena are objects of valid cognition, which seems a straightforward interpretation of this passage, is not without problem, for Dharmakīrti also asserts that there are two types of valid cognition, perception and inference. He further states that perceptions relate to real phenomena and inferences to constructs as their primary object. Therefore, the conclusion that constructs are objects of valid cognitions is hard to escape.

Accordingly Sa-paṇ's remarks, which strongly suggest that constructs (universals) are not objects of knowledge and that only real things can be counted among phenomena, have drawn criticism from many Tibetan thinkers. Bo-dong, for example, strongly criticizes Sa-paṇ's view[21] for denying that generally characterized phenomena exist. He shows that Sa-paṇ's view (as he understands it) leads to contradictions with well-established points of Dharmakīrti's system. Such a view is not able to escape the self-defeating paradox afflicting the Materialist view.[22]

Moreover, Bo-dong clearly points out that generally characterized phenomena, constructs, must exist because they are objects. They are objects since they are cognized by a mental episode.[23] Bo-dong dramatically concludes: "Therefore, the acceptance of specifically characterized phenomena as the only objects leads to the [acceptance of absurdities such as] permanence being impermanent. Since correct contradictions become possible, [one is even led] to reject the reality of things, [as] I will extensively explain."[24] This indictment is an illustration of the strong rhetorical element that is an important ingredient in a lively debate. Exaggeration of this type is rather typical of polemics among Tibetans, who often tend to dramatically overstate their cases. An author who makes a slightly controversial move will be immediately accused of destroying Buddha's teaching, shaming his tradition, and other niceties. Such a move does not attempt to present a fair description of Sa-paṇ's view, but to impute to it as many faults as possible by drawing unwanted consequences from his positions. Some of these logically derive from his view. Others are forced on him on the basis of Bo-dong's own premises.

Dzong-ka-ba's main disciple in the field of logic and epistemology, Gyel-tsap, is less outspoken in his criticism, but he also implicitly criticizes Sa-paṇ's view. He points out that those who hold that generally characterized phenomena cannot be objects of comprehension are no better than Materialists, who reduce knowledge to perception. He further demonstrates the self-defeating nature of such a view by asking, Is the thesis that generally characterized phenomena are not objects of comprehension validated by a valid cognition? If this thesis is not so validated, it is false and its contradictory is true; hence, constructs are objects of valid cognition. If this thesis is validated by a valid cognition, it has to be a real thing! Gyel-tsap concludes: "Whatever reason is given to establish that generally characterized phenomena are not objects of comprehension does not overcome this [self-defeating] fault. This is similar to Bodhisattva Kamalaśīla's saying that 'The assertion that a nonthing cannot be either a proof or a thesis is like the mistake of training oneself in the practice of a self-destructive weapon'."[25] Gyel-tsap's conclusion is hard to resist. Those who accept the framework of Buddhist logic, in which inference and reasoning are based on constructed entities, but refuse to grant existence to these entities, face this contradiction. Since they accept logical reasoning, they must provide some proof supporting their rejection of the existence of constructs. But in doing so, they must use the very entities they deny. Therefore, as long as they operate within the framework of Buddhist logic, their position is involved in a pragmatic paradox and is self-defeating.

Defenses and Interpretations of Sa-paṇ

The presence of such obvious difficulties in a thinker of Sa-paṇ's quality makes us wonder whether these criticisms are true to Sa-paṇ's intentions or whether they focus on misleading comments. Sa-gya commentators have tried to explain Sa-paṇ's comments so as to avoid these difficulties but remain true to his thought. For example, the seventeenth century Sa-gya scholar Ngak-chö criticizes those[26] who take literally Sa-paṇ's comment that only specifically characterized phenomena are objects of comprehension. This, according to him, undermines Dharmakīrti's system correlating the two objects of comprehension, real and conceptual, with the two types of valid cognition, perception and inference.[27] How then should we understand Sa-paṇ's denial that conceptual constructs exist?

For Ngak-chö, Sa-paṇ's comments should be interpreted in this way: Only specifically characterized phenomena are *real* objects of comprehension (*don la gzhal bya yin*), since only they make a real causal difference in our lives. Conceptual constructs are not objects of comprehension *in their own right* but only in dependence on conceptual activities. They only exist nominally. Ngak-chö bases his interpretation on passages from Sa-paṇ such as this: "[Dharmakīrti] did not speak [of valid cognition] as being of two [types] due to the fact that there are [in reality] two [types of] object of comprehension. He declared that there are two [types of] valid cognition in consideration of the [two] modes [in which cognitions] realize [their objects]; namely, that evident specifically characterized phenomena are realized through their own [essence] and that hidden specifically characterized phenomena are realized through a different [conceptually imputed] essence."[28] Here, Sa-paṇ seems to adopt the more moderate position that generally characterized phenomena are indeed objects of comprehension, albeit only in dependence on conceptual activities. Understood in this way, Sa-paṇ's comments, which might have seemed at first so different from Gyel-tsap's insistence that both things and nonthings be included in the category of existing phenomena, do not actually conflict with the this view. This shared view, then, presents a more radical expression of Dharmakīrti's assertion of the ontological primacy of specifically characterized phenomena but does not deny the conventional existence of conceptual entities.

This interpretation appears quite "neat" and does take care of some of the evidence. It seems to be accepted by several contemporary Sa-gya scholars. Nevertheless, there is cause to wonder if it is compatible with all the evidence available from Sa-paṇ's texts. Lo Ken-chen, for one, does not accept this interpretation. He rather asserts that constructs do not exist at all. They are merely added to reality through a negative conceptual process, which we will describe later.[29] This explains why we conceive them to be but that does not entail that they somehow exist.

This interpretation finds support in another passage of Sa-paṇ's text. Discussing the inference from existence, Sa-paṇ criticizes the view of most Tibetan scholars asserting that nonthings exist. According to them, existence is an indeterminate reason (*ma nges pa'i gtan tshigs*) with respect to impermanence, since it is present in both permanent and impermanent phenomena.[30] Sa-paṇ objects to this: "What is this existence of non-things? If [non-things have] the ability to perform a function, they are things! If they do not have [this] ability, they do not exist. Therefore, they are indeed non-existent, although they are called existent."[31] Lo Ken-chen explains this passage by distinguishing two ways in which the word *exist* is used: (1) The real usage of the word is reserved for real things; (2) the figurative usage applies to nonthings as well, but since nonthings have no causal capacity, "they are not established [according to the true] meaning [of existence and are], therefore, figuratively existent."[32] Lo Ken-chen supports his interpretation by showing that many classical texts use the word "existence" only in the sense of thing. For example, Lo Ken-chen quotes the *Science of Debate* as saying "The defining property of existence is the capacity to perform a function."[33]

Lo Ken-chen's assertions that existence refers only to real existence turn us back to Bo-dong's criticisms of Sa-paṇ. Can we reconcile Lo Ken-chen's interpretation with the view that nonthings exist in a certain sense of the word? Commenting on Sa-paṇ's words, Śākya Chok-den answers this question:

> *Question*: Are we not to accept that the defining property of existence is that which is observed by valid cognition? If we do, it would absurdly follow that all knowables would be impermanent.
> *Answer*: We do accept this as the defining property [of existence]. The explanation of distinguisher phenomena (*ldog chos*, that is, the phenomena that exist as distinguishers, i.e., as conceptually constructed universals) as observed by valid cognition is made in consideration of their being observed from the viewpoint of elimination. However, in general [this is] not sufficient to establish [something] as observed by valid cognition since [such phenomena] are not apprehended by an omniscient wisdom.
> *Objection*: Does not Dharmakīrti explain that "Words do not refer to nonexistents"?[34]
> *Answer*: This statement is made in consideration of the fact that words relate to [phenomena] which are not nonexistent from the point of view of elimination.[35]

Śākya Chok-den's answer again takes up the idea that nonthings do not exist in reality. He introduces a further element by relating this to Buddha's vision. A Buddha would not see nonthings such as universals, space, and the like, since they do not exist in reality. Nevertheless, these phenomena exist from the viewpoint of elimination (*sel ngor*) which is the modus operandi of ordinary beings. Thus, nonthings do exist only from our ordinary viewpoint.[36]

For Śākya Chok-den, the use of the word "existence" in reference to nonthings is more than a metaphorical usage but, nevertheless, does not capture its essential meaning. Why then do Śākya Chok-den and other Sa-gya commentators (except Lo Ken-chen) insist on using the word "exist" in reference to nonthings? A remark quoted by Go-ram-ba might suggest a reason: "In this respect, the literal acceptance [by some scholars] of the pervasion of existence by impermanence is slightly uncomfortable given the [linguistic] conventions [currently used] in Tibet. [This is so for the following reason:] Existence and thing, which are stated as reasons establishing sound being impermanent, have the same Sanskrit equivalent, *bhāva*. Accordingly, this [term] is translated at times by 'existence' and at times by 'thing.' Nevertheless, the historical translators also have often used the convention of existence in reference to existence from the viewpoint of elimination. [For example, they have translated]: 'Universals have been declared to be existent . . .'"[37] For Go-ram-ba, the issue of whether constructs exist or not is merely semantic and does not involve substantive questions (as it does for other thinkers in the Sa-gya and Ge-luk traditions). The whole dispute can be solved by noticing the ambiguity in the Sanskrit original (*bhāva*). Historically, Tibetan translators have failed to distinguish between these two senses of the word. They have not reserved either *yod pa* (existent) or *dngos po* (thing) for either *sat* or *bhāva*.[38] And this is why Tibetan thinkers face this difficulty. All that one needs to do is decide on the appropriate vocabulary. Constructs do not exist really but as fictional objects of valid conceptual activities. If one wants to decide that this is what the word "exist" means, this is fine as long as one does not take such existence to have any real status.[39]

Let us notice, however, that the ambiguity is not only among Tibetan translators but in Dharmakīrti himself. He unsystematically uses both *bhāva* and *sat* to designate thing or existence (as applying to constructs).[40] The reason for this is that Dharmakīrti's concept of existence is ambiguous. Any attempt to make it more systematic remains artificial because of its ambiguity. This is not an accidental feature of Dharmakīrti's system but reflects a problem inherent to any antirealism, which must use the very pseudo-entities (the constructs) that it excludes. In privileging concrete things over abstract entities, antirealism makes it difficult to explain the ontological status of conceptual constructs that are necessary but without justification. What does it mean to say that constructs exist if they are not real? The answer that they exist because they are objects of valid cognitions will not do, for the question remains: Are the cognitions that validate concepts valid or not? If they are valid, then they must apprehend something that exists. If they are mistaken, how can they validate anything? It is the persistence of this kind of dilemma that explains the rise of revisionist interpretations of Dharmakīrti that attempt to get out of this quandary by reading his works in a more realistic way.

Before examining these attempts and the reactions that they provoked in Tibet, let us examine another problematic area of Dharmakīrti's system. A much disputed question considers the purview of "specifically characterized phenomenon" (the famous *svalakṣaṇa, rang mtshan*), to which I now turn.

4

The Purview of the "Real"

Atomic Theory

Earlier,[1] we delineated the criteria that separate the real from the conceptual. We noticed, however, that such criteria were far from unambiguous concerning the status of macroscopic objects. Let us now further inquire into Dharmakīrti's ontology by asking questions such as, What is to be considered part of the fabric of reality and what is to be excluded from this category? Are commonsense objects such as jars real? Or are they conceptual constructions? Rather than proposing a unified system, Dharmakīrti offers a variety of conflicting views which he sees as pragmatically compatible. These different strands have not been always recognized by both modern and traditional scholars, with the consequence that Dharmakīrti's system has been oversimplified. Following Śākya Chok-den's insight, I distinguish four strands in Dharmakīrti's ontology: Three assume the existence of external objects while the fourth one rejects this presupposition. I show how these four standpoints are articulated within his overall system according to a scheme of ascending scales of analysis. This allows me to throw some light on the role of the fourth level in Dharmakīrti's thought, his Yogācāra view. I ask the readers to bear with this rather involved discussion, for it often plays on subtle differences that are nevertheless important, for they will lead us to a better understanding of Dharmakīrti's overall philosophical strategy. The less specialized reader may chose to skip the more technical discussions, focusing on the first and last two sections of this chapter.

The ontological status of commonsense objects is a key topic of the debates that oppose Dharmakīrti's tradition to its Hindu opponents. There the Nyāya assert the notion of whole (*anavayin, yan lag can*), a notion the Buddhists reject. The Nyāya rejoin that Buddhist philosophers cannot account for the differences that we perceive between our experiences of aggregates (a bundle of threads) and those of unitary objects (a cloth). How can Buddhist thinkers account for such differences without accepting the reification of entities involved in the Nyāya view? To explain a possible Buddhist answer to this qualm, we have to explore how the tradition views the macroscopic objects that we experience as unities. How are they made from atoms (*paramāṇu, rdul phran*)?

In some respects, Dharmakīrti does not seem to have very original views on questions such as these. He accepts most of the standard Buddhist doctrines found in the Abhidharma texts and reinterpreted according to the Sautrāntika viewpoint. These include impermanence and dependent arising. He uses these as the basis of his logico-epistemological system. It seems quite likely that concerning the reality of atoms, Dharmakīrti would again follow the Sautrāntika reinterpretation of the Abhidharma view as explained by Vasubandhu in his commentary on his own *Abhidharma-kośa.*

The Abhidharma views material reality in two different ways: Ontologically, material reality is made of the atoms of the four elements (*bhūta, 'byung ba*) of earth, water, fire, and wind.[2] This schema does not, however, specify the status of material phenomena other than the elements. These macroscopic phenomena are just described as arising from elements (*bhautika, 'byung 'gyur*). They are included in another classification which describes these phenomena from a phenomenological point view according to how they are perceived through the senses. These objects are the five types of sensible phenomena apprehended by the five sense organs: form, sound, odor, taste, and touch. Among these five, sound is considered apart; it is not required for a material object to exist. The other four are necessarily present in any material object including sound. Thus, in our ordinary world of desire,[3] all material objects other than sound have eight components (four elements and four types of sensible phenomena). Sound has nine (the former eight plus sound).[4]

The Vaibhāṣika[5] system combines these two Abhidharmic typologies to create a list of building blocks for material reality, the dharmas. Consequently, this school holds that the five types of sensibilia are substances as real as the four elements. This grouping of two distinct typologies is a consequence of the Vaibhāṣika view of reality. The Vaibhāṣika school asserts that only phenomena that resist material destruction or analysis are ultimate (*paramartha-satya, don dam bden pa*).[6] The Vaibhāṣika school lists seventy-five phenomena that resist physical destruction or reduction to other elements. These are considered real. Included in this list are the four elements and five types of sensibilia apprehended by the five senses. Other phenomena are only conventionally or relatively real (*saṃvṛti-sat, kun rdzob bden pa*). A jar, for example, ceases to exist when broken. Other sorts of objects such as water cease to exist when analyzed into their atomic components. Such cessations signify that these synthetic things are not fully real. On the contrary, taste and smell retain their identity when reduced to their components. Hence, they are real.

Accepting objects such as color, smell and taste as building blocks of reality creates a tension in the Vaibhāṣika system.[7] These objects are not just atomic components but empirically observable entities; that is, sensibilia. They are sense-objects and they are called *spheres* (*āyatana, skye mched*) in that they are elements of a given sense sphere. For the Vaibhāṣika, they are real, despite being composed of atomic elements. This is problematic, however, for if colors, shapes, and tastes are collections of atoms, how can they be said to be real? Can they not be reduced to their atomic components? It would appear, then, that the Vaibhāṣika system is not coherent. It delineates reality according to contradictory criteria.

The Sautrāntika interpretation of Abhidharma presented by Vasubandhu seems to deal with this problem by reducing reality to simple elements. Vasubandhu refutes the Vaibhāṣika interpretation that large material objects are made up of eight substances. For him, this view is incorrect because it conflates two different senses of substance, ontological and phenomenological. Ontologically speaking, only the four elements are substances. From a phenomenological standpoint, by contrast, the four sense spheres can be called *substances*. This latter typology cannot, however, be assimilated to the former. Since we are here attempting to distinguish what really exists from what is merely conceptually added to reality, only the ontological meaning of substance must be taken into account. Vasubandhu thus eliminates the sensibilia (the spheres such as form) from the list of real phenomena. Among material objects, only the four elements are real. They are the building blocks out of which all macroscopic material objects are made. Consequently, they constitute these objects, which are not real in the full sense of the term. Our perceiving those objects is not due to their reality, but is the result of the causal efficiency of their constituent atoms. Hattori explains: "[Sautrāntikas] did not, like the Sarvāstivādins, consider as real what is seen by the organ of vision such as the blue color or the round shape; instead, by understanding as real that which has the efficacy to produce visual cognitions, they sought to resolve the difficulty inherent in the Sarvāstivādin atom theory."[8] According to this Sautrāntika explanation, only infinitesimal atoms and moments of consciousness are real. Everything else, such as a shape or a color, is real only inasmuch as it is taken as an object of conventional practice. This view is not unlike Wilfrid Sellars's claim that objects such as table, ice cubes, and colors do not really exist.[9] Our commonsense notions of such objects are false but cognitively useful. We will see that the parallel between Sellars and Dharmakīrti can be further extended to their theories of universals and perception.

This theory seems clear and unproblematic. And although Dharmakīrti never provides a detailed statement of his ontology, we could expect him to follow this Sautrāntika view. Several traditional and modern scholars have explained Dharmakīrti in this way, emphasizing that in his system reality is reducible to partless atoms interacting with moments of consciousness.[10] This causal relation explains our perceptions of extended objects. In reality, there is no extension but just the causal interaction of infinitesimal atoms with partless moments of consciousness. I call this interpretation of Dharmakīrti's ontology *the standard interpretation*.

Despite its strength, I believe that the standard interpretation does not account for some of Dharmakīrti's ideas concerning ontology. I am suggesting that Dharmakīrti's account is not unified. Conflicting elements in his view contradict the Sautrāntika account that he adopts in some parts of his work. These elements suggest an alternative view according to which spatially extended objects are to be included within the purview of the real. According to this view, material reality is not reducible to its atomic components but also includes extended objects such as shapes and tangible objects. I am not arguing that this is Dharmakīrti's view, but, rather, that this view is present in his work. It represents a level of his analysis which is often not recognized by scholars who tend to present his view as being more unified than it is.

I believe that there is a tension within Dharmakīrti's ontology between an atomistic reductionism, which is in accordance with his overall ontological parsimony, and a less reductionistic delineation of reality, which allows for the reality of extended objects. This tension is due to the very close connection between ontology and epistemology in Dharmakīrti's system. On the one hand, Dharmakīrti's ontology emphasizes the particular over the general. Accordingly, spatial extension, which materially subsumes real individual elements, cannot but be seen as ontologically secondary, an artificial construct. Therefore, on purely ontological grounds, it seems quite reasonable to deny the reality of any kind of extension. On the other hand, however, Dharmakīrti also holds that perception offers an undistorted reflection of reality. Accordingly, what is perceived by perception must exist in reality. This creates a problem for Dharmakīrti's ontology, for we do seem to perceive extended objects. Since this perception is an undistorted reflection of reality, the extended object we perceive ought to exist.

Dharmakīrti seems to recognize this tension and handles the problem through what I described as a strategy of ascending scales of analysis. This explains one of the most puzzling elements in Dharmakīrti's system, the adoption of several contradictory ontologies. Through most of his works Dharmakīrti presents himself as a realist concerning the existence of the external world. He defends a so-called Sautrāntika position. Within this view, he also seems free to move between conflicting accounts. Sometimes he follows the view described previously, reducing reality to the interaction of partless particles and moments of awareness. At other times, however, he includes extended objects such as colors or taste or even commonsense objects. Finally, at other times he seems to leave behind this form of realism concerning the external world to move toward a more radical antirealism, a Yogācāra idealism. I believe that these moves are made by Dharmakīrti to solve the difficult problems raised by the ontological consequences of his epistemology.

The existence of such a diversity within Dharmakīrti's ontology explains the diversity of views on this subject entertained by his commentators, traditional and modern. Here I will examine some of the Tibetan contributions to this question, delineating the conflicting opinions existing in the Sa-gya tradition concerning the reality of extended objects before explaining Śākya Chok-den's way of reconciling them. These conflicting interpretations are not idiosyncratic accounts given by commentators but reflect conflicting ideas that are clearly present in Dharmakīrti. I first examine briefly two passages that suggest that extended phenomena such as sensibilia are to be included among real things.

To discuss the ontological status of extended objects, I would like to distinguish four sizes of material objects. First, there are substantial atoms (*dravya-*

paramāṇu, rdzas kyi rdul phran). These are partless particles out of which all material phenomena are made. These atoms aggregate to form the second size, larger molecules (*saṃghātaparamāṇu, 'dus pa'i rdul phran*), which in turn form larger objects. When a sufficient number of molecules aggregate, they form the third type of material object, a collection (*samudāya, tshogs pa*). This collection is observable by perception. It is given to sense consciousness as sensibilia such as a patch of color, a shape, a taste, and the like. Such an object is markedly different from the fourth type of object, commonsense objects such as a jar. These objects, which are often described as coarse (*sthūla, rags pa*)[11] are synthetic objects constructed through the aggregation of the different sensibilia (colors, shapes, tastes, etc.). Although both collections and coarse objects are extended, they differ. Whereas the former is a mere aggregation of atoms of a similar kind, the latter is a synthesis of different kinds of sensibilia.[12]

An Alternative Interpretation

According to the standard interpretation of Dharmakīrti's ontology, both collections and coarse objects are unreal. Some passages in Dharmakīrti, however, do not fit this interpretation. The first passage I examine is found in Dharmakīrti's explanation of sense perception (*indriya-pratyakṣa, dbang po'i mngon sum*).[13] Here he examines the status of objects of sense perception in the context of refuting a Nyāya objection. The Nyāya adversary claims to have found a contradiction between the Buddhist textual tradition and its rejection of universals. This adversary argues that, according to the Abhidharma texts,[14] what a sense consciousness takes as its object is an aggregate (*saṃcita, bsags pa* or *saṃghāta, 'dus pa*). Such a collection (*samudāya, tshogs pa*), he argues, is nothing but a whole. It is determined as such by differentiating it from its parts. Such differentiation necessarily involves some conceptual determination based on universals. Dharmakīrti states the objection: "[*Objection*:] An aggregate (*saṃcita, bsags pa*) is an assemblage (*samudāya, tshogs pa*), [and] this is a universal. And there is a sense cognition of this [universal]. Now cognition of a universal must doubtlessly involve conceptualization."[15] For this Naiyāyika, Buddhists cannot maintain their assertion that perception is nonconceptual and ought to accept the existence of a determinate perception (*vikalpakapratyakṣa, mngon sum rtog pa can*) and its support in reality, real universals.[16]

Dharmakīrti answers that sense perception does not take as its object a genuine synthetic entity but only an aggregate of atoms. Atoms in isolation are not noticeable, for they do not have the capacity to generate a perception in ordinary beings. To do so they must act in a group. The Abhidharma refers to just such a group when it describes the object of sense consciousness as a collection. Not being the product of a conceptual synthesis, a collection is not a bona fide universal. Nevertheless, it can be called such since it subsumes a multiplicity of elements. Dharmakīrti says: "When different atoms are produced in combination with other elements, they are said to be aggregates. [And] indeed those [aggregates] are the causes for the arrival of [sense] cognitions. In the absence of other atoms, atoms have no special [noticeable] characteristics. Since cognition is not restricted to a single [atom], it is said to have a universal as its sphere of operation."[17] Since cognition cannot apprehend a single atom, it always perceives assembled atoms. This is why the Abhidharma describes cognition as having a universal as its object, although this object is not a real universal. For the Buddhist, as described by Dharmakīrti, sense perception depends for its object upon an assemblage of parts that collectively generate the awareness of an external object. These passages seem to suggest that the collection of parts must be included among the objects of perception. Hence, material reality is not reducible to atomic components.

A second passage suggests a similar conclusion. This passage answers a Nyāya objector, who argues that without unitary wholes we cannot account for the sense of unitary objects that we derive from experience. Dharmakīrti responds that large objects do not have to be wholes to be perceived: "If several [elements] are not apprehended simultaneously despite their [belonging] to a single sphere [of activity of a sense], how is it that many sesame seeds can appear to be apprehended simultaneously?"[18]

Dharmakīrti argues that a collection of atoms is the objective *relata* (the object condition, *ālambana-pratyaya, dmigs rkyen*) of sense perception. A heap of sesame seeds, for instance, can be apprehended by perception even though no synthetic entity pulls together the separate elements.[19] Furthermore, since these elements are apprehended together, they must be real not just on an individual basis but also as a collection. So, Dharmakīrti accepts that extended objects such as a heap of sesame seeds are perceived.[20] He also accepts that this perception corresponds to some element in reality. It is the cluster of atoms that corresponds to the extended objects we perceive. Commenting on a passage of Duveka Miśra's commentary on Dharmottara's *Commentary,* C. M. Keyt explains, "In conclusion, these last comments of Duveka Miśra leave no doubt that the sensory object is an aggregate of atoms *(paramāṇu)*. The cognition of an aggregate is free from both error and *kalpanā* or the mental operation in perception and is hence a sensory cognition. The atoms remain many and do not, simply because they are immediately juxtaposed, converge into some single, solidly extended thing. The singular solidarity of the sensum recording them is not a misrepresentation of them because this is the correct way for atoms immediately juxtaposed to be represented."[21] According to Keyt's interpretation, Dharmakīrti considers clusters of atoms to be effective and, therefore, specifically characterized phenomena. This is so because perception of extended objects is an undistorted reflection of reality. Certain macroscopic objects are effective inasmuch as they produce the perceptions that apprehend and validate them.

This conclusion is further supported by Dharmottara's comments on Dharmakīrti's *Drop.* Dharmottara differentiates, as we have seen, between individual real fires and the concept of fire.[22] His remarks indicate that the real fires to which he refers are not just atoms but extended objects that can be observed empirically. Thus Dharmottara appears to imply that reality is not limited to infinitesimal objects, but includes spatially extended objects as well. Reality consists of empirically available objects and, hence, is not reducible to atomic reality.

This conclusion is certainly surprising, for it goes against Dharmakīrti's tendency toward a maximal ontological sparsity. It also contradicts other passages, where Dharmakīrti seems to imply that material reality is reducible to atomic components. This latter view is Vasubandhu's account and seems more consistent. And yet, it is hard to ignore the existence of passages that clearly suggest a different account within Dharmakīrti's works. This apparent inconsistency is due, as I argued earlier, to a tension within Dharmakīrti's thought arising out of the double perspective that orients his thought: the ontological and the epistemological. Ontologically, Dharmakīrti tends toward an antirealist reduction of reality to simple elements. From this perspective, extension is reduced to infinitesimal particles. Epistemologically, however, such a reduction is harder to sustain. According to his fundamental thesis that perception accurately reflects reality, extension would seem to exist. Extension appears, after all, to perception. This seems to lead Dharmakīrti to accept at some level a minimal notion of extension.

This does not imply, however, that at this level of analysis commonsense objects such as a jar are real. These coarse, that is, commonsense, objects, which we usually take as being real individuals, are synthetic and thus unreal, since they are made by the aggregation of atoms that do not belong to the same sense sphere (*āyatana, skye mched*)[23] such as color, taste, and so forth. Hence, the reasoning that demonstrates the reality of collections (through the capacity of the atoms to collectively produce a perception) does not apply to these coarse objects. At this level, Dharmakīrti's acceptance of the reality of extended objects applies exclusively to objects such as color patches, which are made of similar elements. It does not include commonsense objects.

These commonsense objects are presupposed, however, to be real at other times. For example, while discussing the way in which causal relations are understood, Dharmakīrti shows how we understand the relation between fire and smoke by observing how smoke follows the presence of fire.[24] In this discussion, causal relations are described as involving commonsense objects such as smoke that are thus assumed at this level of analysis to be real. Hence, there seems to be a confusing diversity in Dharmakīrti's ontology. To gain some perspective, it will be useful to examine the opinions of Tibetan scholars. Our discussion focuses on the Sa-gya tradition, where revealing debates have taken place about whether extended objects are real in Dharmakīrti's system.

In the debates concerning the status of extended objects, all participants hold that partless particles and moments of consciousness are real. The disagreement concerns the reality, or lack thereof, of extended objects. The discussion has often been complex and arcane. For the sake of simplicity I will distinguish three positions: (1) Some Sa-gya scholars, such as Dak-tsang and in part Śākya Chok-den, hold the view that I have described as the standard interpretation. In it, only infinitesimal atoms or moments of consciousness are real. No extended object can ever be a specifically characterized phenomenon. (2) Other Sa-gya scholars such as Lo Ken-chen hold the view that I call the *collection view*. For them reality includes some extended objects (the sensibilia given to perception, such as, the collections of particles belonging to the same kind of physical object). They exclude from the purview of reality, however, commonsense objects such as houses and trees. These they describe as coarse.[25] (3) Finally, others such as Ngak-chö assert that reality includes even these commonsense objects. This view is defended by the Ge-luk traditions as well. In this chapter, I analyze these three views as they appear in the Sa-gya tradition as well as the way in which Śākya Chok-den reconciles them. I examine the Ge-luk argument in the next chapter. I conclude that all the three views are present within Dharmakīrti, but they do not function at the same level. They can be ordered according to an ascending scale of analysis.

No Extended Object Can Be Real

Śākya Chok-den defines the specifically characterized as that phenomenon which is ultimately able to perform a function. He defines generally characterized phenomenon as that which cannot do so.[26] Śākya Chok-den gives partless atoms and moments of consciousness as illustrations (*mtshan gzhi*) of the specifically characterized. Such specific existence also implies substantial existence (literally, substantial establishment, *rdzas grub*), and true existence (literally, true establishment, *bden par grub pa*).

In some parts of his works, Śākya Chok-den argues that no extended object can ever be real. Such an object always involves a synthesis of discrete elements. Dharmakīrti's arguments against the Nyāya wholes, which have been briefly examined earlier,[27] accordingly apply to any kind of extended object, even the mere collection of atoms. For if such a putative extended object existed, it would have spatial parts. It would have to be either substantially identical (*rdzas gcig*) with those parts or different. It cannot be either, however. If an extended object were substantially identical with its parts, in reality (*don la gcig*) it would be one with those parts. In that case, either it would become manifold or its parts would become one.[28] Since neither is possible, for such an extended object to really exist it would have to be substantially different from its parts. It would then exist apart from its parts like the Nyāya wholes. Therefore, Śākya Chok-den concludes:

> It is certainly not [possible] to accept that the special collection of the many substances that are its components and the continuum of moments grouped [together] are one substance [with their parts]. A description of them as existing substantially does not even exist in the texts of the author of the Seven Treatises [i.e., Dharmakīrti].
>
> *Question*: Can we accept in our system that everything that has parts must not be one substance?
> *Answer*: We should differentiate. We can accept that an object with substantial parts (*rdzas kyi cha*) must be so [not one substance], but we cannot accept this for objects with many distinguishers.[29]

All objects extended in space and time, even special collections of atoms and continua, are not real. They are made of different substances put together and are, therefore, reducible to such. Real objects are not associated with more than one point in space and time. Hence, they do not have real parts. Still, we may apply conceptual distinctions to them, such as being impermanent and being produced.

For Śākya Chok-den, all material objects exist only atomically (*rdul phran du gnas*) although we conceive (*rlom pa*) them as extended in time and space. Material reality is made of the atoms of the four elements (earth, water, fire, and wind). All material phenomena other than these elements are constructed from these basic building blocks and, therefore, are not fully real. In particular, the phenomena arising from elements (*bhautika, 'byung 'gyur*) are not real. They are extended, so they are reducible to their ultimate components, the four kinds of atoms. They are not real substances but exist nominally (*btags yod*).[30]

Up to this point Śākya Chok-den's position is similar to the standard interpretation of Dharmakīrti's ontology among modern Western scholars. The problem with this interpretation is that it makes it difficult to account for the status of extended objects. Once we grant that they are unreal, we have to admit that they are permanent and ineffective (since being a nonthing, permanent, a construct, and ineffective are equivalent almost by definition). While it is relatively easy to imagine a universal such as existence as permanent, it is more difficult to grant that colors and shapes are permanent as well! Most modern interpreters seem to have been unperturbed by this prospect, even though it seems to completely contradict our practical experience. They are ready to assert that for Dharmakīrti colors, tastes, and smells are not causally produced and perform no function. Rather they are conceptual overlays and as such they are changeless! Few Tibetan scholars find this prospect appealing. Strongly influenced by commonsense realism, they resist supporting a view that so directly contradicts our experiences of physical objects.

To solve this problem, Śākya Chok-den offers the following solution in some parts of his works, where he adopts Dak-tsang's view,[31] breaking down the dyadic structure of Dharmakīrti's system through the creation of an intermediary category. In addition to real things (specifically characterized phenomena) and ineffective conceptual constructions, is a third category, conventional things (*kun rdzob pa'i dngos po*). This category includes sensibilia such as color, taste, and tangible objects as well as commonsense objects such as jars and trees. These objects are generally characterized phenomena but are impermanent. They perform a function but only conventionally. All phenomena that have extension in space and time belong to this intermediary category. They are not really effective, for the performance of their function boils down to the functions performed by their constituent atoms.[32] Therefore, they are things but not specifically characterized phenomena. They are classified as nonassociated compositional factors.[33]

Śākya Chok-den's view has drawn criticism from other Sa-gya commentators. They have not failed to use this opportunity to distance themselves from such a controversial figure. Go-ram-ba, for example, argues against his rival that the binary distinction between the real and the conceptual at both the ontological and epistemological levels constitutes the basic structure of Dharmakīrti's system. Introducing a triadic structure changes this system. To put it in modern terms, Go-ram-ba argues that Śākya Chok-den's interpretation contradicts the hermeneutical maxim that a genuine interpretation must attempt to retain the basic structure of the system while confronting any tension therein. The dichotomous nature of Dharmakīrti's system creates several problems (such as the status of macroscopic objects or the existence of nonassociated compositional factors),[34] so the temptation is strong to establish an intermediary category. Nevertheless, a good interpreter, Go-ram-ba asserts, must resist the temptation to change the system even to solve its conceptual difficulties. Moreover, as Go-ram-ba gleefully observes, Śākya Chok-den's views conflict with Sa-paṇ's views, the highest authority in the Sa-gya tradition. The idea of conventionally effective things contradicts Sa-paṇ's emphasis on Dharmakīrti's dyadic system.[35]

I think that Go-ram-ba is quite right in his criticism. I find it even puzzling that Śākya Chok-den would advance this view, which contradicts his global view of Dharmakīrti's system as consisting of a variety of views arranged according to an ascending scale. For, if the acceptance of commonsense objects as real is a lower standpoint, as we will see shortly, what is the need of introducing this triadic structure? It is as if Śākya Chok-den sometimes is carried away by his investigation of a topic and loses sight of his own overall system. Although this fearless spirit of investigation makes his works particularly attractive, it sometimes makes a rendering of his views difficult. In this case, it is hard to know what to do with his triadic analysis. Although it is introduced at this point, it does not reappear later. This view also seems to be quite different from Sa-paṇ's ideas, which express the middle position that only some extended objects are real. Let us examine this position.

Some Extended Objects Are Real

Sa-paṇ seems to support what I have called the *alternative interpretation* or *collection* view. While refuting the Nyāya presentation of six types of relation, Sa-paṇ depicts a collection as the result of a gathering of elements:

> from the gathering of the separate components of a collection, a lump which is a collection is produced. [This is a case of] causes affecting an effect, as, for example, a mountain [is produced] from the gathering of atoms and a heap from the gathering of seeds . . . [Dharmakīrti says] in [his] *Ascertainment*:
>
> > Since the cause that establishes the collection
> > Is a component of the collection . . .[36]

Thus, Sa-paṇ seems to consider collections of atoms of the same kind (also referred to as *special collections*, *tshogs pa khyad par can*), as parts of causal reality. They are lumpy objects produced by the accumulation of parts. The parts act as the causes bringing objects into existence. Thus, for Sa-paṇ reality is not only made of partless entities. The reality of extended objects made by the aggregation of atoms is undeniable: "Atoms of objects and sense powers [form] collections whose every moment produces a consciousness which experiences [an object]. [Such] are the perceptions of ordinary beings."[37] Extended objects are performing the function of producing consciousness. As such they meet the criteria for reality.

Sa-paṇ's teacher Śākya Śrībhadra had already stated a similar position on his first meeting with Sa-paṇ. When asked what he thought about the idea that there is such a thing as mere blue (*sngo tsam*), Śākya Śrībhadra said: "Sometimes I do not know very much, but blue exists in reality."[38] He further adds that these comments contain the essence of the *apoha* theory.[39] The meaning and implications of these cryptic comments will have to be explained gradually. For now, suffice it to say that Śākya Śrībhadra seems to be committed to the idea that colors are real. This seems to imply that reality must include some extended entities.

If this is so, the next question is this: Are then commonsense objects (such as a jar) also included among the real? That is to say, is Dharmakīrti (according to this interpretation) a realist concerning commonsense objects? Lo Ken-chen gives an extremely lucid discussion of this question. Having criticized Śākya Chok-den's concept of conventional things, Lo Ken-chen discusses whether or not extended objects exist in reality. He distinguishes two types of extended objects:[40] those renowned to the world (*'jig rten la grags pa*) and those renowned to [philosophical] treatises (*bstan bcos la grags pa*).[41]

From the point of view of the world, substantial identity (*rdzas gcig*) concerns everyday objects such as jars and trees. They are substances. But when substances are analyzed from the point of view of their mode of apprehension, they are understood in terms of the spheres (*rdzas kyi skye mched*) apprehended by the senses as delineated by the Abhidharma texts.[42] Then the sense spheres are referred to as "substance," not the commonsense objects reducible to those spheres. Thus extended objects such as patches of color or tangible objects belonging to sense spheres are real but commonsense objects are not. Lo Ken-chen said:

> When engaged [in practical activities], one applies terms such as substance, thing, etc., [to objects such as pot]. Nevertheless, when they are explained in the treatises by differentiating specific [and] general [characteristics], they are not established as things for the following reason: since the eight sense spheres belonging to a jar, etc., exist independently, nonconceptual perceptions are produced individually. Accordingly, there is no single perception corresponding to the term "jar." [Moreover] while explaining Dignāga and others' thesis in [his] *Commentary on the Four Hundred*, [Candrakīrti] says: "Here, the logicians state: [an object such as] jar definitively does not exist [as an object of] perception. The specific characteristic of [its] form and so forth is not showable. It is called [object of] perception because it is the object of a visual consciousness, etc. Since a jar is merely named by the mind, it does not exist as a specifically characterized phenomenon. With respect to something which does not exist as a specifically characterized object, not only is there no real perception possible but even metaphorically perception is not feasible in such a case."[43]

We use convenient terms to designate objects we deal with in our daily life as if those objects were real and perceived as they are. These names are not given arbitrarily, but neither do they directly correspond to what exists. When we use the term *jar*, for example, we in fact refer to a component of the jar such as its shape or tangible aspect. We perceive such components, but not the jar itself which is a synthetic object constructed from eight components (four elements [wind, fire, water, and air] and four spheres of sensory objects [form, taste, smell, and tangible aspect]). Each of these exists on its own. Together they form what we commonly call *material objects*. These components are apprehended by different types of perception. For example, form (i.e., color and shape) is apprehended by visual consciousness, tangible objects by body consciousness, and so forth.

When we perceive the shape of a jar, we do not fully perceive that jar, which is constructed out of eight components. We perceive only some of these components, such as its form. This is because there is no overlap among the senses. The special capacities of the organs on which the senses rely are mutually distinct. Therefore, our vision of a jar is only the experience of color and shape and not that of the jar itself, conceptually constructed from the eight components. Similarly, when we touch the same jar, we experience only one aspect of that object, its tangible aspect. The label *jar* that we give to that object does not correspond to what we actually perceive. We refer to the jar as the sum total of its parts, but this totality is an abstraction unavailable to empirical experience. It is a label that we give for the sake of convenience.

Lo Ken-chen's exegesis explains how a jar as the sum total of its parts does not exist in reality, since it is not available in its entirety to any perception. Objects such as jars are conventional descriptions that we give to components such as color, taste, and the like, for the sake of coordinating our perceptions. This is a convincing account of what Vasubandhu means when he says: "In common usage, what is called 'earth' is the color and the shape."[44] The word *earth* is given commonly on the basis of what is in reality earth's color. Similarly, what we call *jar* is in reality a shape. These are convenient ways of speaking but do not reflect reality.

Extension in Space and Time

We are moving toward the examination of the third group of commentators. They hold a more realist position than Lo Ken-chen concerning commonsense objects. Let us pause to examine a question raised by Lo Ken-chen's claim that the collection of atomic elements is real. Does this real status apply to objects extended in time; that is, to continua (*rgyun, santāna*), which are collections of temporal parts, as argued by Gyel-tsap and Kay-drup? Among all groups of Sa-gya scholars the answer is unambiguously negative. Go-ram-ba explains: "Continua are also not [real] for the following reason: each part among the many parts [of the object] produces a single individual cognition as its effect. It is impossible that all the parts put together produce a single cognition as their effect."[45] According to Sa-gya thinkers, the temporal parts of an object cannot be treated in the same way as its spatial parts. Each type of part produces its effects in a different way. Spatial parts coexist and, therefore, are able to contribute to the production of a common effect. Since their effectivity is not reducible to that of their components, they have a reality as a collection. This is not the case with temporal parts. They do not exist at the same time and, therefore, cannot produce a common effect. The different moments that we string together to make a continuum have no effectivity as a collective body. Therefore, continua as such are necessarily unreal.

Moreover, as both Go-ram-ba and Śākya Chok-den remark, the arguments directed by Dharmakīrti against the Sāṃkhya and used by Sa-paṇ against Tibetan realists also refute the reality of continua.[46] If continua were real, they would have to be either one with their parts or different. In the first case, when the first moment disintegrates the continuum would disintegrate and hence would not be a continuum. Or it would remain for a second moment and, therefore, be permanent. Since neither is feasible and a continuum cannot be substantially different from its parts (for that would be a Nyāya whole), it must be unreal.

This argument is based on Dharmakīrti's refutation of a Sāṃkhya view. That view holds individuals to be one with their universal, Nature *(prakṛti, spyi gtso bo,* or *rang bzhin*), the all-inclusive substratum.[47] Dharmakīrti argues that individuals and Nature cannot be one entity since individuals keep coming into and going out of existence but Nature does not: "If they are not distinct, they would be produced and disintegrate together."[48] If Nature and individuals were one, that Nature would disappear when individuals do. However, this is not possible, for then it would not be the all-inclusive substratum imagined by the Sāṃkhya. If Nature remains when individuals disappear, it is of a different essence from those.

This argument, as well as Sa-paṇ's, relies on the explicitly stated premise that two phenomena cannot be substantially identical if they have different causes:

> It is contradictory for [two phenomena being] one substance to have different production and disintegration or different aspects. [Dharmakīrti says] in his *Ascertainment*: "It is not proper, when something is established, [for another thing which] is not established or [has] distinct causes to be [its] essence. The reality of things is to be distinct or [to have] different causes, [for] phenomena exclude [each other] or [have] distinct causes. If even that did not establish them as distinct, nothing would be distinct and everything would be one single block substance."[49]

Two phenomena are one substance if they are produced by the same aggregate of causes. This is so because the substance, that is, the essence (*rang bzhin, svabhāva*), of things is determined by the causal aggregate that produces them (*rgyu tshogs pa, hetusāmagrī*). Therefore, their essential identity or difference is also determined by their causes. Since two phenomena that are substantially identical must be produced by the same direct causes (*dngos rgyu tshogs pa gcig*), they must abide and disappear at the same time. Therefore, a continuum cannot be one substance with its parts. Since it cannot be different either, it cannot be real.[50]

Sa-paṇ reaches a similar conclusion by considering the temporal nature of continua, which are created by putting together past, present, and future moments. Only the present moment, however, is real. A continuum depending for its existence on unreal moments can be only unreal. It is like putting a jar between the two horns of a rabbit.[51] Such a synthesis cannot produce anything real!

Sa-paṇ does not indicate a source for his analysis of how continua lack reality. A text of Dignāga extant only in Chinese, however, has a similar view: "If a continuant were identical with [each of its successive members], a person—who is an example of a continuant—would have lost his whole being and existence when he left his babyhood behind and, after gradual growth, achieved boyhood; [therefore], a continuant cannot be identical with [its successive members]."[52] Dignāga expresses the same type of argument as Sa-paṇ against the view that continua are one substance with their parts. He also compares continua to wholes: Both are equally unreal since both are the products of synthesis.

Sa-paṇ's arguments rest on his refusal to accept a distinction made by Tibetan realists between oneness and substantial oneness. Sa-paṇ holds, for instance, that impermanence and thing are one in reality because they are substantially identical. Sa-paṇ does acknowledge four types of difference, but the realist distinction is not among them. They are (1) real things such as shapes and tangible objects are distinct (*tha dad*); (2) unreal phenomena such as nonthing and thing are merely not one (*gcig pa bkag pa*);[53] (3) impermanence and thing are distinct distinguishers within the same entity (*ngo bo gcig la ldog pa tha dad*), that is, they are conceptually distinct but in reality one; (4) moon and the Cooling Light[54] are equivalents whose names are synonymous (*don gcig la ming gi rnam grangs*).

Among these four, only the first distinction amounts to a real difference. Since the second distinction concerns quasi-entities, it is a quasi-distinction.[55] Nonthing is no different from thing, it is just not one with it. Sa-paṇ furthermore rejects the idea of Tibetan realists that these two phenomena are distinct within the same entity (*ngo bo gcig la ldog pa tha dad*), because they are not entities at all. Consequently, Sa-paṇ also refuses the idea that the moments of a continuum are one entity with the continuum. If they were, these moments would all become one thing.

All Extended Objects Are Real

Finally, the third group of Sa-paṇ's followers holds that all spatially extended objects (i.e., both the special collections of atoms of similar kind and the commonsense objects, but not continua) are real. This view is not, as we noticed earlier, without support in Dharmakīrti's works. There, he often uses commonsense objects such as jars, fire and smoke as examples of real things. Moreover, this is supported by commonsense as well, for after all, we believe that we see objects such as jars, tables, and trees. Tibetan thinkers find it more difficult to resist this appeal to commonsense than their Indian predecessors. As we will see, this realism concerning commonsense objects is precisely the position of Ge-luk thinkers.

Within the Sa-gya tradition, Ngak-chö, for example, expresses a view of this sort: "Obviously, jar and so forth exist substantially since they are specifically characterized phenomena."[56] For Ngak-chö, there seems to be little doubt that commonsense objects are real. Commenting on Go-ram-ba's passage, Ngak-chö states that a jar must exist substantially since it is a specifically characterized phenomenon. His position seems to be accepted by many contemporary scholars. They, like many other Tibetan thinkers, seem to feel the strong pull of commonsense. Even Go-ram-ba seems to feel this pull, although his position does not seem to be consistent. While commenting on Dharmakīrti's explanation on the identity conditions of real things, he takes jar as his illustration, thereby implying its reality.[57] In other passages, however, Go-ram-ba seems to express a contradictory view. While refuting the reality of universals, he lists a number of unreal phenomena. He includes in this list commonsense objects such as jar, which we just saw him include among the real![58] I believe that this last view is closer to what Go-ram-ba has in mind. This would make his position an instance of the middle view, holding only some extended objects to be real. His reference to an object such as jar is probably a convenient description of the different sensibilia made from components of a similar kind (*rigs mthun, sajātīya*).

Whatever the interpretation of his position, its internal contradictions are significant. They point to a general tendency among Tibetan thinkers toward a realism concerning commonsense objects. This insistence on commonsense objects as real does not correspond to what is found in most Indian texts. Śākya Chok-den, who does not accept this dominant tendency in Tibetan epistemological thinking, remarks that no Indian proponent of either the Sautrāntika or Vaibhāṣika view has accepted the reality of such objects on the ontological level. Only at the most common level of analysis can such objects be accepted, as when examples are given or the objects of cognitions are described. These objects cannot be accepted, however, within any slightly systematic ontological analysis.[59]

From an Indian point of view, the exclusion of commonsense objects from the domain of the real is not surprising. It is not unique to Dharmakīrti's school, but is a premise accepted by most Indian Buddhist philosophers, who hold onto the reality of external objects. This premise derives from the epistemological atomism of the Abhidharmic tradition, where material objects are described as formed by the aggregation of sensibilia. In this view, reality consists of partless components but is not reducible entirely to them. Extended objects such as shape and tangible objects (sensibilia) exist. They are apprehended by perceptions which offer a true picture of reality. We usually fail to pay attention to these experiences, instead remaining prisoners of conceptuality.

Stcherbatsky interprets this exclusion of commonsense objects from reality as indicating that Dharmakīrti views specifically characterized phenomena (*svalakṣaṇa, rang mtshan*) as some kind of transcendental a priori or unique instants. This is not the case. Rather, excluding commonsense objects from reality is the consequence of the epistemological atomism that runs through the Abhidharmic tradition. Lo Ken-chen quotes the Abhidharmic commentator Sthiramati as saying: "[Expressions] such as 'exist substantially, exists as [having its] own essence, exists ultimately' are equivalent. 'Persons' are [just] imputed, [they are] mere names [and] only exist conventionally. They do not exist substantially or as [having their] own essence."[60] This epistemological atomism is basic to Buddhist liberative strategy. Buddhism teaches that human beings can liberate themselves from suffering through a correct understanding of reality. We usually understand reality through perception and form wrong views, such as the substantial existence of persons, on the basis of these experiences. So the first step in a Buddhist liberative strategy is to gain a clear understanding of experience. This is achieved by developing mindfulness toward the four kinds of objects: body, feeling, consciousness, and mental factors.

Analyzing experience into different elements is essential to developing this practice. It permits us to disengage from our tendency to reify diverse elements into unities. To cure us of our constant reification the Abhidharma differentiates objects into spheres (*āyatana, skye mched*) and elements (*dhātu, khams*). In applying this teaching to experience, commonsense objects are found to consist of an aggregation of elements. These elements come apart through the power of mindfulness. The objects in which we have such strong confidence are found under analysis to be reducible to their components. Being real only to the commonsense world, they exist only at a superficial level. They are to be displaced by the practice of the path.

Who Is Right?

Our analysis reveals a surprising diversity among Dharmakīrti's Sa-gya commentators. Some, such as Dak-tsang, hold that only infinitesimal parts exist. Others, such as Sa-paṇ, seem to argue that sensibilia are also real, although not commonsense objects. Finally, a third group argues that even these objects are real. Who is right?

This diversity, I would argue, is less due to mistaken interpretations than to a multiplicity of views within Dharmakīrti's own work. Hence, in a certain way all three interpretations are partly right, although they are wrong to claim to represent Dharmakīrti's exclusive view. This seems to be Śākya Chok-den's approach in some parts of his work.[61] Such a view is quite helpful here. Contrary to other Sa-gya scholars and most modern commentators, he refuses to describe Dharmakīrti as opting exclusively for one or the other of the views we described here. Instead, he shows that Dharmakīrti's analysis of external objects is articulated around three levels of analysis: (1) At a commonsense level, objects such as jars and so on are said to exist. (2) At a deeper level, however, these preanalytical ideas cannot stand. When examined in relation to sense spheres (*āyatana, skye mched*), objects of commonsense disappear and the color of the fire is distinguished from the fire. This is the level of analysis corresponding to what I describe as the *alternate interpretation*. In the Buddhist tradition, this level is reflected in the Abhidharma, where commonsense objects are reduced to phenomenologically available entities. The ontological analysis, however, cannot stop there, for even entities such as color are not real. Therefore (3) at the deepest level, only their infinitesimal components are real. This third level corresponds to what I have described as the *standard interpretation*.

The important contribution to our inquiry is Śākya Chok-den's insight that Dharmakīrti does not chose between these different levels but uses them in dependence on the context of his inquiry. Thus, rather than following a logic of either/or concerning these views, Dharmakīrti pragmatically uses them according to his needs. This may sound at first surprising, to say the least, for these views contradict each other and Dharmakīrti knows it. How can a systematic thinker use views that undermine each other? Nevertheless, this is precisely what Dharmakīrti does. Throughout this work, we will encounter a similar strategy, which is basic to Dharmakīrti's way of doing philosophy. For example, Dharmakīrti discusses epistemological questions mostly on the ontological basis we are sketching here. This is the level described by Tibetan doxographers as the Sautrāntika view, which asserts that external objects exist. As we will see shortly, Dharmakīrti does not feel bound to always follow this view and sometimes introduces a conflicting Yogācāra view, which denies that external objects exist.

This mode of inquiry is not, as one may be tempted to think, an example of confusion or a deviant logic, for Dharmakīrti sees these positions as logically contradictory, but he also sees them as complementary or at least pragmatically compatible. The different levels (1), (2), and (3) function at different levels of analysis. When discussing epistemology, the first level is usually preferred for it is the closest to the way we conceive of things. At this level, we conceive of ourselves as perceiving objects such as jars. Such a description is not sustainable, however, for commonsense objects are not findable under analysis. Hence, we need to move to a higher level, at which our epistemic practices are redescribed as involving only phenomenologically available entities such as colors. But further analysis reveals that even these entities, which we usually think we perceive, are fictional. Hence, we need to move to a yet higher view, according to which only momentary particles are real (the standard interpretation) following a strategy of ascending scales. It is important to realize that Dharmakīrti does not believe that these levels are equally valid. Rather, for him, each level has its own limited validity within its own proper context of use. Ultimately, none of these three levels is valid, for they all assume the existence of external objects, a presupposition that Dharmakīrti ultimately rejects, as we will see shortly. However, Dharmakīrti does not refer to this ultimate but counterintuitive level very often. He prefers to move at a level more attuned to ordinary epistemic practices in accordance with his goal, the defense of the Buddhist logico-epistemological system first propounded by Dignāga.

Yogācāra in Dharmakīrti's System

So far this chapter has explored possible interpretations of Dharmakīrti's ontology. It has noticed a bewildering variety of views, suggesting that, on a certain level, Dharmakīrti's system might accommodate real extended objects. Accepting such objects would partly account for our spontaneous intuitions of perceiving unitary extended objects by showing that our notion of extension rests on some objective basis (the sensibilia). Nevertheless, this would only partly respond to the Nyāya objection that we cannot account for such intuitions without positing substantial wholes, since the collections we perceive (the sensibilia) are not unitary objects but mere clusters. Where does our sense of unity comes from?

For Dharmakīrti, ultimately, the answer to this question concerns reality itself less than our perception of it. Therefore, his answer moves toward an epistemological analysis of our subjective impressions of unitary objects. From this perspective, the relevant question is not about the objective support for our experiences of unitary objects. It is about the way in which these experiences arise. As we will see in our investigation of Dharmakīrti's theory of perception, we do not perceive objects directly but only through the intermediary of aspects (*ākāra, rnam pa*) that represent them. External objects provide the cause for such representations to arise in our minds. Thus, perception is really to be explained in causal terms.

Still, the question remains: What is the relation between our perception of objects as extended solid blocks of matter and their reality as aggregations of separate particles? How is the perception of extension generated? Does each atom contribute separately to the generation of such a perception or do they contribute collectively? Opinions among Indian Buddhist thinkers fall into two general categories. Some hold that atoms are merely parts of a collection (*saṃghāta, 'dus pa*) and that each atom contributes to a perception of unity without sharing in it. The other view holds that atoms form an aggregate (*saṃcita, bsags pa*) in which they acquire a dual aspect: On the one hand they keep their subtle aspect, while on the other hand, they collectively acquire a coarse aspect.

These two views are described respectively as the collection view and the aggregate view (or coalescence view). There is some confusion as to which schools entertain which view. Kalupahana seems to think that the Vaibhāṣikas accept the second while the Sautrāntikas hold the first.[62] However, Hattori and Keyt hold a contrary view.[63] Relying on the presentation of K'uei Chi, a disciple of the famous Chinese translator and pilgrim Hsüan Tsang, they assert that the Vaibhāṣikas hold the aggregate view and the Sautrāntikas the collection view. In any case, a presentation of these views in purely doxographic terms is probably too simplistic. It is likely to mask the complexity of the opinions held by individual thinkers.

Although both views differ in their explanations of extension, they rest on a similar metaphysical realism: Objects exist according to the way we perceive them. We have the gut feeling that we perceive objects that exist outside of our awareness, as if they were facing us. Metaphysical realism attempts to systematize this intuition by providing an account of external objects and their perception. This account is problematic, however, for our intuition concerning the perception of external objects conflict with other intuitions. We assume that our perception provides a true reflection of how external objects exist. We also assume, however, that external objects are made by aggregation. These two intuitions pull apart and lead to contradictions when systematized within a philosophical system. For if perceptions are unmistaken (*abhrānta, ma 'khrul ba*) reflections of reality, then the objects that they perceive should exist as they are perceived; that is, as unitary wholes. This unity is not confirmed, however, by an analysis of the way in which objects exist. When we analyze them, we discover that objects are not unitary but made of smaller particles. The collection view explains the nature of objects as being a mere collection of particles, whereas the aggregate view explains them as having a slightly greater degree of unity. Objects are aggregates of particles, which contribute together to the production of our impression of extension in a way that cannot be reduced to the contribution of individual particles. Both views attempt to explain how nonunitary objects made by collection or aggregation can give rise to perception of extension and unity. Both views face the same problem: If our perceptions are accurate reflections of the reality of external objects, how can these objects be made of atoms, which we do not perceive?

This tension is highlighted by Dignāga in his *Investigation of the Object.*[64] There, he proposes the following argument against realism concerning external objects, both in its collection and aggregate versions: Metaphysical realism is based on the intuition that our perception of external objects is accurate. External objects would exist then according to the way we perceive them; that is, as having extension and unity. This is not possible, however, since the individual particles, which compose the objects, cannot create individually the impression of extension. Since no individual atom has such an aspect, there is nothing in reality that corresponds to our impression of extension.

One might object that, although particles cannot produce individually perceptions of extended objects, they can collectively create the impression of extension. Against this, Dignāga proposes two possibilities: Either atoms form a mere collection (*saṃghāta, 'dus pa*), like a forest or an army, or they are aggregates (*saṃcita, bsags pa*), possessing their own collective structure. The collection cannot be, however, the external support of perception since it is not real. Like a forest, which is a mere name given to a bunch of trees without overall unity, it is a mere conceptual overlay on the individual atoms and, as such, does not exist substantially (*dravya-sat, rdzas yod*).[65] Since it is unreal, it cannot cause a consciousness to perceive extension. Similarly, the aggregate, the second alternative, cannot be the external support, for it is attributable to the cognition, not to the object. No collective structure in the object itself exists over and above its individual parts. Otherwise, we would have Nyāya wholes existing over and above their parts. Therefore, concludes Dignāga, both collection and aggregate accounts fail to vindicate the intuition that we have concerning external objects. Such intuition does not hold to analysis, despite its attraction. It is inconsistent to assume that external objects exist and that we perceive them correctly.

Dharmakīrti's thinking concerning external objects follows the same line as Dignāga's. He does not seem to distinguish an aggregate from a collection. For him, atoms remain what they are whether they are aggregated or not. How then does Dharmakīrti account for our impression of extension in external objects? Like Dignāga, he does so by maintaining that this impression does not reflect the way things exist but the way we perceive them. A material object is perceived through the intermediary of its representation or aspect (*ākāra, rnam pa*). Each of its atoms causes a perception that has such representation to arise so that we see such an extended object. Thus, the impression of extension is a result of the aspected perception, not a reflection of the way atoms exist.

This answer does not close the debate. If extension does not exist in the object, how can the perception to which the object appears as extended be unmistaken and completely objective? To solve this problem, Dharmakīrti makes a radically new move, introducing a Yogācāra view that constitutes a fourth level in his ontology.[66] Like Dignāga, he questions the assumption that external objects exist just the way we perceive them by denying the reality of the external world. In this way, he eliminates the source of the difficulty of knowing whether extended objects are real or not: "Therefore, the impression of coarseness (*sthūlabhāsa, rags snang*) does not exist in the cognition or in the object [because this coarse] essence is repudiated as existing in one [atom] and it does not exist either in many [atoms]."[67] The reasoning proposed by Dharmakīrti hinges on a simple assumption: If extended objects exist externally, they must be either identical with each of their parts or different from them. Extended objects cannot be identical with their atomic parts, since they are extended (assuming they exist) and atoms are infinitesimally small. They cannot be different either, for in this case they would exist apart from these atoms. Since no such object has ever been observed, we have to accept that extended objects are not different from their atomic parts. Since they are not one either, we have to conclude that extended objects do not exist externally. Why, then, are we perceiving extended objects if they do not exist? Dharmakīrti answers: "The appearance of a cognition, which is not distinct [from its object], as being so is indeed a distortion."[68] Our perception of extended objects is without support in the external world and therefore mistaken. Extended objects appear to exist separate from our consciousness, but in reality they do not exist externally. We perceive them as such, however, because our perceptions are distorted. This distortion does not concern just that we see extended objects but goes deeper to the root of the problem of distortion, the duality between subject and object. Dharmakīrti explains: "This [duality of objects existing independently of consciousness] is distorted [because] the dual [appearance] is also distorted. [The reason is conclusive because] the existence of objects different [from consciousness] depends on their appearance as distinct."[69]

Here Dharmakīrti confronts the objection that the reasoning he stated earlier (*Commentary*, III:211) shows that external objects do not exist the way we perceive them but does not establish that they do not exist. His answer is that the view that external objects exist depends on the realist assumption that they exist as they appear to our mind. On this basis of objects appearing to our mind as existing independent from consciousness, we decide that there are objects external to consciousness. Once this basis is questioned, the view that there are external objects is deprived of main support. We then understand the plausibility of the Yogācāra view that consciousness does not need any external support to perceive objects, not even that of infinitesimal atoms. The impression of extended external objects is not produced from external conditions but arises from innate propensities (*vāsanā, bag chags*) we have had since beginningless time. Under the power of these internal conditions, we constantly but mistakenly project the false impression that there are external objects existing independent of consciousness.

This denial of the reality of external objects is where Dharmakīrti finds a solution to the dilemma created by an impression of a solid extended object produced by atoms, which do not have any extension by themselves. The problem is solved by rooting out its source, the assumption that objects exist external to consciousness as a result of atomic aggregation. The Yogācāra view that objects exist only as reflections of consciousness is Dharmakīrti's answer to the problem created by extended objects.

Is Dharmakīrti Contradicting Himself?

This idealist solution differs from the so-called Sautrāntika view found throughout most of Dharmakīrti's works. There, Dharmakīrti assumes that external objects are real. He repeatedly articulates this position. All of our discussion has assumed this view. Nevertheless, at the crucial juncture of explaining the ontological status of spatial extension, Dharmakīrti appeals to a radically different view. Extension does not exist because there is no external world in which such phenomena could take place. Thus, it appears that Dharmakīrti holds two contradictory metaphysical views. Are they really contradictory or is it just we who see them as such? And if they are, how can Dharmakīrti maintain them in the same work?

It is tempting to believe these two views are not contradictory, for it is difficult to accept that an author takes two contradictory stances within a single work! This is precisely, however, what Dharmakīrti does repeatedly; for example, in *Commentary*, III:209–22, he states in short succession several conflicting views regarding the nature of aspects. Responding to the Nyāya charge that, in the absence of substantial wholes, experiences of unitary objects cannot be accounted for, Dharmakīrti answers that such experiences are due to the presence of aspects. The question of the status of these aspects is then raised: Are they real or not? That is, does this experience of extension have at least subjective validity or not? Dharmakīrti offers both answers without indicating a clear preference for either. Therefore, we have to accept that Dharmakīrti does introduce conflicting views within a single work.[70]

This is supported by several Tibetan sources, which understand Dharmakīrti's texts to articulate two points of view: External objects are accepted provisionally (the so-called Sautrāntika view) and refuted at a deeper level (the Yogācāra stance). This interpretation corresponds to what I have described as a strategy of ascending scales. Lower positions are introduced according to needs, with the understanding that they will yield to higher standpoints when the analysis is pushed further. This is confirmed by Dharmakīrti when he says: "[Buddha's] enacting the shutting of the eyes of elephants [leave] aside the meaning of the [ultimate] reality. [Acting] in a spirit of strict [agreement with] the world they display external activities."[71] This stanza comes at the end of one of the few passages reflecting a Yogācāra view.[72] It is important in that it indicates that Dharmakīrti does not take this Yogācāra philosophy as just a convenient element but holds it to be a deeper view of reality. Hence, the different standpoints in Dharmakīrti's philosophy reflect a definite hierarchy. More commonsensical views are subsumed by more critical but more counterintuitive views.

Still, a question remains: Why does Dharmakīrti rarely mention this deeper Yogācāra view, which he favors, preferring more commonsensical approaches? I believe that the scarcity of passages reflecting this view is not due to Dharmakīrti's belief in external objects but to a conscious strategic choice. For Dharmakīrti, this choice parallels Buddha's decision not to reveal the deeper meaning of reality in most of his teachings, instead focusing on simpler and pragmatically more appropriate teachings that do not provide an accurate vision of reality.[73] Dharmakīrti's choice is dictated by the nature of his audience. Like Dignāga before him, Dharmakīrti is engaged in elaborating an epistemology based on Buddhist principles but addressed to the larger Indian philosophical community of his time. He is also responding to non-Buddhist thinkers who had severely criticized Dignāga's thought. Since he is engaged in a debate with a wide variety of philosophers, mostly non-Buddhists, he cannot refer to his typically Buddhist Yogācāra idealism, for such a view would be completely unacceptable to most of his audience.

As Dignāga did before him, Dharmakīrti provisionally adopts a view, which later doxographers will describe as Sautrāntika, according to which external objects exist, while maintaining the Yogācāra denial of external reality in final analysis. Although these two views contradict each other, they are pragmatically compatible. They contribute to Dharmakīrti's task, the articulation and defense of a systematic epistemology embodying Buddhist principles within a generally accepted philosophical vocabulary. For this, he relies on the lowest common denominator between competing Buddhist views and uses as much as possible terms that have broad acceptance outside of Buddhist circles. This presentation of a common system is accomplished on the basis of a provisional acceptance of external objects. This less radical and more realistic view is introduced to create a basis of discussion acceptable to both sides. The discussion, however, will not stop at this level and the audience will be led gradually to realize that a sound theory of perception is incompatible with a realist acceptance of external objects.

Thus, the contradiction between this view and the Yogācāra view does not invalidate Dharmakīrti's system because they operate at different levels. Whereas the former Sautrāntika view offers a provisional basis for discussion, the latter Yogācāra view describes reality.

This seems to me the best explanation for Dharmakīrti's presentation of one view accepting the existence of external objects in most of his works and another view that clearly indicates the suspicion he ultimately bears toward such objects. This interpretation raises, however, another question: Given that Dharmakīrti is a Yogācārin, how important is this philosophy for him? Does Dharmakīrti develop a system that primarily aims at leading its auditors to realize the ultimate, the absence of duality between subject and object? Or does he offer a Yogācāra answer as a way to resolve certain epistemological problems? I will leave these questions aside for the time being, for they raise difficult problems such as the importance of Dharmakīrti's soteriological intentions. I will examine these in later chapters.

Suffice to say that I take Dharmakīrti's essential preoccupation to be epistemology not metaphysics. His interest in defining the nature of reality is to ontologically ground his epistemology. Essential to this purpose is the distinction between real individuals and unreal universals, a distinction that parallels and supports the one between the two types of knowledge, perception and inference. The exact nature of real entities (whether, for example, they are ultimately mind dependent or not) is a lesser concern. Although Dharmakīrti has a definite view on this topic, the epistemological nature of his project confines the articulation of this view to a system in which ontological commitments are kept to a minimum.

The nature of Dharmakīrti's enterprise explains why he left so many questions unanswered. It also accounts for the fact that his commentators came up with widely diverging interpretations. This last point will become clearer in the next chapter, where I examine the revisionist explanations provided by Dzong-ka-ba and his disciples.

5

Ge-luk Thinkers on Specific Ontology

Commonsense Objects and Universals

To conclude my investigation of the ontology of Dharmakīrti and his tradition, let me examine the Ge-luk presentation of this same topic. Ge-luk scholars' explanations are interpretations of Dharmakīrti's works. There are, however, certain differences between their interpretations and Dharmakīrti's views, which I begin to explore in this chapter and will revisit in my discussion of the nature of universals. The most significant of those differences is the realism of the Ge-luk tradition, which contrasts with the conceptualism of Dharmakīrti and Sa-paṇ. The first part of this chapter examines the status of extended and commonsense objects in the Ge-luk tradition. The second considers the Ge-luk interpretation of Dharmakīrti's notion of specifically characterized phenomenon.

The preceding chapter noted a realist tendency among Tibetan thinkers. For those of Sa-paṇ's followers who are influenced by this view, their realism concerns only commonsense objects. Realism has, however, a stronger hold on the overall philosophy of the Ge-luk tradition. Ge-luk thinkers are realists not only on the question of commonsense objects and continua, they are also realist on the question of universals. Their realism must be distinguished, however, from the Nyāya extreme positions. It is a more moderate form of realism.

The connection between these two related forms of realism, one regarding universals and the other concerning objects of commonsense, is less logical than conceptual. In the Indian and Tibetan contexts, coarse objects and continua are traditionally assimilated with universals. Realism about universals often entails a realism about commonsense objects. Such an assimilation is not necessary, however. Indeed, individual thinkers have adopted conflicting positions on this question, regardless of the traditions they belong to.

The assimilation between commonsense objects, continua and universals can be strict. It is found, for example, in Mokṣākaragupta's assertion that horizontal and vertical universals exist. For Mokṣākaragupta, the former (*tiryaglakṣaṇa*) is an unreal property such as being a cow, a conceptual construct we take to subsume a variety of individuals (hence, its name, "horizontal universal"). The latter (*ūrdh-*

vatālakṣaṇa) is a different type of universal. It is not a property subsuming separate individuals, but the synthesis of the different moments belonging to a single continuum.[1] For example, a cow seems to be an enduring object. As such, it is an unreal conceptual overlay, a vertical universal. Sa-paṇ seems to accept this typology and its implication that the concept of universal extends to commonsense objects and continua. He also differentiates between these two types of universals (*thad ka'i spyi* and *gong ma'i spyi*). According to this view, wholes and continua are vertical universals, whereas properties are horizontal universals. Both are bona fide unreal universals because of being conceptually constructed entities.[2]

Most Tibetan scholars have accepted Sa-paṇ's explicit connection between commonsense objects and universals. Sa-paṇ's acceptance of this typology is slightly surprising, however. Usually he bases his interpretations on elements explicitly found in Dharmakīrti's texts, but there is no explicit mention there of the concept of universal with regard to commonsense objects. Accordingly, some Sa-gya scholars have refused to assimilate the problem of commonsense objects to that of universals.

Śākya Chok-den is one such scholar. He remarks that commonsense objects and universals are often treated together because they concern "mere general entities that cover diverse elements."[3] Nevertheless, he claims, these are different questions. Commonsense objects are concrete identities that we impute to spatio-temporally spread concrete objects. Universals are abstract identities. Hence, asserting the reality of one type of generality does not commit one to accepting the other. Śākya Chok-den seems to doubt that Sa-paṇ's comments on the two types of universals reflect his (i.e., Sa-paṇ's) actual view, because such a division of universals is not found in Dharmakīrti.[4]

In the Ge-luk tradition, commonsense objects usually are not considered to be true universals. Nevertheless, they partake of the problematic regarding general entities that subsume (either logically or materially) other entities. Universals subsume logically their particulars because the particulars instantiate them. Coarse objects and continua materially subsume their parts because they are composed of those parts. Therefore, realism about objects of commonsense does not entail but parallels the assertion that universals are real. Dzong-ka-ba and Kay-drup, for example, argue at length for the similarity of these questions. They conclude that coarse objects, continua, and universals have some reality.

To mark the connection between these types of general entity, Tibetan epistemologists have elaborated a typology of universals that underlines the connection between commonsense objects and universals. Tibetan thinkers distinguish collection-universal (*tshogs spyi*), kind-universal (*rigs spyi*), and object-universal (*don spyi*). The last two are mostly genuine universals and will be considered in future chapters.[5] The first one is not considered to be a genuine universal by many epistemologists. Ge-luk thinkers consider this typology of universals to be metaphorical or terminological (*sgras brjod rigs kyi sgo nas dbye ba*) because collection-universals are not real universals. They are material objects such as jars and trees made of a collection of material parts. According to Ge-luk thinkers, these collections of material elements are coarse objects, and since they are for the most part individuals,[6] they do not need to be bona fide universals. Ge-dün-drup defines collection-universal as "the aggregate of several singles."[7] Pur-bu-jok gives a similar definition: "that coarse matter which is composed by several parts."[8] Objects of commonsense such as jars and mountains, which are made through an aggregation of atoms, are illustrations of such a "universal."

Not all Tibetan thinkers agree. Go-ram-ba, for example, holds that collection-universals are genuine universals, for they are formed by synthesis. He defines such an entity as "a superimposition that appears [to conception] as a coarse object on the aggregate of atomic substances."[9] Therefore, for him, collection-universals are not the individual objects we perceive but the conceptual entities that appear to the conceptual mind following perceptual experience. We use these concepts to organize the multiple sensibilia given to our senses. For example, we see a lump that has a certain shape, smell, feel, and so forth. These different sensibilia do not appear together, for they appear to different sense consciousnesses. We use the concept of jar to bring some regularity to the realm of chaotic experiences. Epistemologists call such a unifying principle a *collection-universal* (as well as an object-universal), according to Go-ram-ba. He identifies such a universal with Sa-paṇ's vertical universals (*gong ma'i spyi*).[10]

Śākya Chok-den does not accept this identification. He holds that collection-universals are not genuine universals, for that would relegate them to the realm of completely ineffective pseudo-phenomena.[11] Rather, they are the coarse objects that appear to our perception. These coarse "objects" are not real, for only infinitesimal particles are. Neither are they, however, completely unreal. They belong to this intermediary category posited by Dak-tsang and at times accepted by Śākya Chok-den of phenomena that are generally characterized phenomena despite being things. They do not ultimately perform a function but neither are they completely ineffective.[12]

Finally, Lo Ken-chen presents an intermediary position. Describing the threefold typology of universals, which is accepted by most Tibetan epistemologists (the difference being whether such a typology is metaphorical or not), he remarks that the term *collection-universal* (*tshogs spyi*) can be used in different ways: It can refer to real collections of atoms of the same kind or to the synthetic principle used to bring order to the diversity of perceptual experiences. In the second case (as argued by Go-ram-ba), the collection held as a single entity by conceptual thought is a universal; it is nothing other than the direct object (*dngos yul*) of a mistaken mind; that is, the object-universal. In the first case, the collection-universal is an individual object and cannot be a genuine universal.[13] In accordance with his ontology, Lo Ken-chen does not include commonsense objects in this category, contrary to Ge-dün-drup and other Ge-luk thinkers, who hold that such objects are collection-universals (but not universals).

The concept of collection-universal seems to be a Tibetan creation. Hence, the question of direct Indian sources does not arise. It is possible, however, to find indirect support for such a concept in Dignāga's and Dharmakīrti's texts. In particular, the passages we have examined, which suggest that collections of atoms of a similar kind are real, can be taken as sources for the concept of collection-universal. This passage, for example, seems to implicitly suggest a collection-universal: "Since cognition is [never] tied to a single [atom], it is said to have a universal as its sphere of operation."[14] Dharmakīrti is referring here to the plurality of atomic substances as a universal, although he does not seem to think that this plurality is a genuine universal. This is what he seems to imply when he says that such a collection "is said" to be a universal. This seems to be the usual connotation of the Tibetan concept of collection-universal.

Ge-luk Realism and Commonsense Objects

Having clarified the complex relation between commonsense objects and universals, let us start our investigation of the Ge-luk interpretations of Dharmakīrti's ontology by examining the views of the tradition on the status of commonsense objects. Our investigation of Dharmakīrti's ontology has revealed the existence of three views concerning the reality of material objects. Some thinkers deny that there are any real objects possessing spatial extension. For them, only infinitesimal atoms are real, all other objects are constructed. A second group of thinkers holds that spatial extension is not necessarily unreal. For them, the objects given to perception such as colors, shapes, and tastes are real, but commonsense objects are not real. Finally, a third group holds that reality must extend to commonsense objects as well.

As thinkers belonging to the third group, Ge-luk scholars assert the reality of commonsense objects such as tables, trees, and mountains. This tradition goes even further in its realism, for it asserts that objects have not only real spatial extension, but also duration. That is, the reality granted commonsense objects is extended to continua (*rgyun, prabandha*) as well, in opposition to the Sa-gya tradition. This realism always remains, however, moderate, in opposition to the more extreme Nyāya views. Let us start with Kay-drup's discussion of the reality of commonsense objects, keeping in mind these different forms of realism.

Kay-drup describes common sense objects as coarse (*rags pa, sthūla*). He explains coarse objects as being lumps that have several substances as their parts.[15] He is careful to distinguish these objects from the Nyāya wholes, which are partless entities totally distinct from the parts in which they nevertheless completely inhere. For Kay-drup, commonsense objects are not wholes in the Nyāya sense of the word but collections of different substances. Similarly, continua are occasions (literally, time, *dus*) that are constituted by the collection of several moments.[16] Kay-drup draws an explicit parallel between these two types of entity. He asserts that one is as real (i.e., effective) as the other. Coarse objects are collections of atomic particles, and continua are aggregates of moments. They are both real, just as common sense reckons.

A complication is introduced here because Kay-drup does not use the word *collection* in the same way as we have used it up to now. That is, his view is different from the view of the second group that the collection is real (the collection view). According to this alternative view, only collections of sensibilia of a similar kind, that is, belonging to the same sense sphere, are real. Thus, a color patch or a taste is real, for apprehending it involves no operation of synthesis, but the combination of these different sensibilia (the commonsense object) is not. Kay-drup, by contrast, uses the word *collection* to refer not just to the sensibilia belonging to the same sense sphere but also to the commonsense objects composed by the four sensible objects (sound is usually excluded) and the four elements. Collection in this wider sense is what Kay-drup considers to be real.

This description of commonsense objects as collections marks off the Ge-luk moderate realism from the Nyāya more extreme position. Kay-drup's collections, which are merely aggregates of atoms and sensible qualities, differ from Nyāya wholes, which completely inhere in parts. They are intermediary between the Nyāya whole and the mere collection of sensibilia of similar kind. They are less reified than the former but more than the latter.

Kay-drup is quite aware that many Indian sources characterize coarse entities as unreal and, hence, seem to contradict his point. He quotes, for example, Haribhadra's *Clear Explanation of the Meaning,*[17] where the author describes the position of the Mādhyamika's adversaries, the Proponents of Real External Objects (a group to which Dharmakīrti belongs when he elaborates the ontological status of external objects). Haribhadra describes how these adversaries deny the reality of notions such as killer and killed while maintaining the reality of karma and its effect. Their reason is that the identity of a person as a killer is not intrinsic to the person but determined in relation to other things (such as the killed person). Since such identity is relational, it is unreal.[18] If we apply this principle to the reality of material objects, we can see that the reality of coarse objects is difficult to maintain, for such objects depend on their parts and thus have only relational identity. Similarly, a continuum's identity is not intrinsic but determined in relation to the moments that constitute continua. Therefore, it would seem that neither coarse objects nor continua can be real.

Kay-drup answers this objection by making a subtle distinction (typical of Ge-luk scholasticism) between the intrinsic identity of a thing *as* a thing and its relational identity. In Haribhadra's example, a person's identity as a person is intrinsic but his or her identity as a killer or a killed is relational and, therefore, unreal. Similarly, an object that is coarse or a continuum can have a real identity even though its identity as a coarse object or as a continuum is not intrinsic. This distinction is based on the ways in which coarse objects are identified. A jar, for example, is identified by a visual perception, which apprehends a bulky object having a certain extension. Such a perception identifies this object, which is a whole (not in the overreified Nyāya sense of the word), as a jar, but it does not identify this object *as* a whole. This is so, Kay-drup argues, because to identify an object as a whole one must apprehend it as having parts. This requires that the object appear distinct from its parts. Such an appearance is impossible in the case of perception, which accurately reflects reality, for the object would then be in reality totally distinct from its parts. Since this is not the case, we must conclude that a whole *qua* whole cannot be perceived by a perception and, therefore, cannot be real.[19] However, the object, which is a whole, can still be real because it has a non-relational true identity apprehended by perception. Kay-drup concludes: "What are called universals, coarse objects, and continua are superimposed, generally characterized phenomena that do not exist substantially. Nevertheless, it is not contradictory [for something] that is a universal, a coarse object, or a continuum to be a specifically characterized phenomenon that exists substantially. Also, whatever is a universal, etc. does not have to be a generally characterized phenomenon. Therefore, one must know that phenomena such as jars are universals, coarse objects, and continua as well as specifically characterized phenomena but are not generally characterized phenomena."[20] Kay-drup's response underlines the realism of the Ge-luk tradition by drawing an explicit parallel between spatially and temporally extended objects (commonsense objects) and universals. Based on a subtle analysis of the different identities assumed by an object, Kay-drup offers a view typical of his tradition; that is, a realist interpretation of the antirealist doctrines defended by Dharmakīrti and most of his Indian followers. Since his views are commentaries on Dharmakīrti, Kay-drup offers textual arguments and defenses of his interpretations.

An obvious objection against this realist interpretation is that its acceptance of real coarse objects contradicts Dharmakīrti's arguments against the Nyāya wholes. Kay-drup answers that those arguments are directed against overreified entities that are partless and inhere in the totality of each part. Such wholes would be vulnerable to Dharmakīrti's argument that the movement of one part would entail the movement of the whole, since they are partless and wholly inhere in the moving part. Such is not the case with the Buddhist realist's assertion that coarse objects are real, because Buddhist realists (like Navya Naiyāyikas) do not hold that wholes are wholly present in their parts. Therefore, a movement affecting a part does not need to affect the whole, and Dharmakīrti's arguments do not conflict with the reality of coarse objects.

Realism and Momentariness

As suggested by Kay-drup, Ge-luk moderate realism is not limited to the acceptance of coarse objects as real. Their defense of commonsense extends to continua (*rgyun, prabandha*) as well. Things have duration in the same way that they have spatial extension. Contrary to most Buddhist epistemologists, who hold that duration is a conceptual construction, Ge-luk thinkers are willing to assert that momentariness is not incompatible with duration. Objects change from moment to moment without necessarily ceasing to exist. For example, consider a jar described by commonsense to have lasted for seven years. In opposition to Sa-gya thinkers, who hold that such a description is merely a convenient but wholly mistaken way to speak about the reality of infinitesimal moments that quickly succeed each other, Ge-luk realism holds that this jar has existed for seven years. It does not deny that this jar is made of a succession of infinitesimal moments that disintegrate as soon as they are produced but holds that the reality of such a jar cannot be reduced to its constitutive elements. The jar lasting for seven years is real as well. It exists as a continuum, that is, the collection of temporal parts. Thus, contrary to those who hold that only infinitesimally momentary objects are real, Ge-luk thinkers argue that commonsense objects are real and endure as continua constituted by a succession of moments. Let us examine Kay-drup's philosophical defense of this doctrine against challenges from Sa-paṇ's tradition.

Sa-paṇ's followers have argued, cogently in my mind, that this realism contradicts Dharmakīrti's conceptualism. They have argued further, but probably less cogently, that this discrepancy is revealed by Dharmakīrti's own reasoning, in particular that directed against the Sāṃkhya view. The target of Sa-paṇ's commentators has been the Ge-luk assertion that continua are one entity with their parts and yet distinct from them (*ngo bo gcig la ldog pa tha dad*).[21] Sa-gya thinkers have insisted that this view is similar to the Sāṃkhya view that individual objects partake in a universal Nature. Against this view, Dharmakīrti argues that individuals and universals cannot be the same entity, because the production and disintegration of individuals does not correspond to those of universals. Sa-paṇ's commentators have argued that this reasoning applies to the Ge-luk view as well.

Kay-drup responds to these critiques by showing that this argument does not apply to the entities defended by moderate realism. It applies, rather, to the more extreme Sāṃkhya idea that universal Nature (*prakṛti, rang bzhin*) is a permanent partless substratum. Since it is partless according to the Sāṃkhya, Nature completely abides in each individual. Hence, it must be indistinguishable from those individuals and, therefore, have the same production and disintegration. According to Kay-drup, this reasoning does not apply to coarse objects or continua, for those are not partless. Hence coarse objects do not completely abide in the individual parts or moments.[22]

Kay-drup also rejects a favorite argument of those who oppose the reality of continua. They argue that if an object exists at the first moment, it cannot still exist at the second moment without being permanent. Sa-paṇ, for example, takes a literal reading of Dharmakīrti's arguments establishing momentariness and holds that any real entity must cease to exist as soon as it comes into existence. Duration is a conceptual fiction due to the quick arising of discrete moments looking alike. Sa-paṇ recognizes that this idea is contradicted by our commonsense intuition, which holds, for example, that a jar lasting for seven years endures throughout this time, but argues that contradicting such an intuition is not decisive. Our intuition of duration is nothing but the product of our attachment to permanence. Hence, it can be discounted and should be eliminated. This is the very goal of the Buddhist tradition.

Kay-drup argues for a less counterintuitive understanding of momentariness. For him, objects change from moment to moment but the continua of these moments have a certain reality. Accordingly, the object constantly changes (and, therefore, is not permanent) but nevertheless endures. Take the example of a day. Does it not last for twenty-four hours? Ge-luk thinkers accept the validity of our common intuition about duration and explain it by positing the reality of continua. For them, denying the reality of collection or continua is one of the quintessential mistakes that a Buddhist philosopher can commit.

This view seems to contradict the well-known Buddhist doctrine of momentariness, at least as Vasubandhu and Dharmakīrti understood it. Are things not, after all, momentary? This objection, argues Kay-drup, is based on a misunderstanding of this doctrine. The meaning of momentariness is not that a thing must cease to exist right after it has begun to exist, for this contradicts our experience. Rather, a thing will not remain for a second moment after its time of establishment.[23] This time of establishment (*grub dus*) is not a short moment but the period required for an object to complete its function.[24] Gyel-tsap explains that the time of establishment of an object varies according to the object in question: "[Things] do not remain for a second moment after the time of establishment. This time of establishment when put together with a day has the duration of thirty *yud tsam* (40 min.). When put together with the smallest moment of time, it becomes an instant."[25] Time of establishment depends on the object. It might be as short as a single partless moment or as long as an eon. The meaning of momentariness is not in the short duration of the moment but in the reality of constant change. For things to be momentary means that their existence in time constitutes them, instead of being something merely external to them. For example, the jar is in existence for some time. Every moment of its existence brings it closer to its demise, which in itself implies that the jar is constantly changing.

In contrast, permanent phenomena are not constituted by temporality and hence are unchanging. This does not mean that they are eternal. Permanent phenomena do come into and go out of existence, but they do so without undergoing any change in their own essence. They are permanent because they are not causally produced and, therefore, are not completely real. They exist as mere imputation *(btags yod, vijñāptisat)* on the basis of really existing things. Thus, the coming into and going out of existence of permanent phenomena is not due to their own essence but to the changes occurring in the impermanent things on the basis of which they are labeled. The difference between permanent and impermanent phenomena consists in permanent phenomena being uncaused and existing merely by being superimposed on causal reality.[26]

A *permanent phenomenon* is defined by Ge-luk scholars as "that which is a common locus of phenomenon and nonmomentariness."[27] That is to say, a permanent phenomenon is an existent that is both a phenomenon and nonmomentary. Examples of permanent things include the classical illustrations given by the Abhidharma such as space and cessation. In Dharmakīrti's tradition, however, a number of phenomena not discussed by the Abhidharma literature are also considered permanent. All conceptual constructs are permanent since they are not real.[28] They are generally characterized phenomena and, therefore, not functional but exist merely due to being superimposed.

This understanding of impermanence and momentariness is accepted throughout the Ge-luk tradition. Dzong-ka-ba clearly articulates an interpretation of the doctrine of momentariness that reflects the overall moderate realism of his tradition. He defines impermanent things as "the things that will not endure for a second moment after their time of existence."[29] This formulation of the doctrine of momentariness does not mean that things can only exist for a short moment. Dzong-ka-ba is quite clear on this: "The momentariness which is spoken of as the defining property of impermanence is [the fact that something] will not remain for a second moment after its time of establishment. Momentariness does not mean [that something] will remain only for a short moment. Therefore, since a year needs twelve months to be completed and does not remain after that, the momentariness of all continua [consists of their] not remaining for a second moment after their time of establishment."[30] Dzong-ka-ba explicitly rejects the idea that the moments according to which things are said to be momentary can be only very brief instants. The briefness of the existence of things is not what makes them impermanent. The doctrine of momentariness does not mean that a mountain, for example, cannot exist for thousands of years. According to Dzong-ka-ba, momentariness means that things exist for the span of time during which they are established (*rang grub dus*). The momentariness of things consists of their constantly changing and yet remaining in existence during their time of establishment.

An important point to make is that the duration that Dzong-ka-ba posits is not identical to the one assumed by commonsense, although it is meant to be compatible with this latter understanding. Commonsense holds that things endure and then change. This view, argues Dzong-ka-ba, is correct in its assumption of duration but is mistaken in its holding that change occurs suddenly and adventitiously. For Dzong-ka-ba, objects do not endure unchanged. Rather, they endure as continua through a succession of changes.

Dzong-ka-ba presents this view by drawing a parallel between the status of commonsense objects and that of universals. In the same way that a universal subsumes its individual instances, so does a continuum subsume the moments that compose it. This parallel is highly significant for our study, for it reveals the sustained realism of the Ge-luk tradition. Its founder says: "For example, although the impermanence that is characterized by sound is not concomitant with a jar, impermanence is concomitant with both sound and jar. Similarly, although the jar existing in the preceding moment does not exist at a later time, it is not contradictory [for] the jar to remain at both times."[31] Dzong-ka-ba is making a point basic to the moderate realism of his tradition. A particular jar existing at time t does not necessarily exist at time $t + 1$. This does not imply that it is impossible for any jar to exist at both t and $t + 1$. There is a jar that exists as the continuum of t and $t + 1$ (assuming that they belong to the same continuum). In the same way, a particular jar has several properties such as being white, material, impermanent, and so on. Its particular properties (its particular whiteness, for example) are not concomitant with another jar, but general properties such as being white are. The reality of continua and collection mirrors that of universals.

Philosophy and the Validity of Conventions

This realist view of momentariness may seem surprising. It is different, I would argue, from Dharmakīrti's view. It is important, however, not to overstate the difference, for it does not concern the basic Buddhist insight that reality is ever changing. Contrary to what one might think, the basic Buddhist insight that things are in constant flux is retained here, for although objects remain in existence for extended periods of times, they do so only at the "price" of constantly changing. Accordingly, from a momentary perspective, things are being renewed constantly. When considered from the perspective of their continua (which is what we do in daily life) objects remain in existence.[32] The difference between this realist view and the more classical Sa-gya interpretation is that the latter considers the objects of daily activities, enduring commonsense objects, as constructs, whereas Ge-luk thinkers view them as real. What is at stake here concerns less the reification of entities than validity of commonsense intuition. Sa-gya and Ge-luk thinkers do not argue whether things change from moment but whether Buddhist philosophy should or should not accommodate commonsense intuitions and, if so, to what degree.

The more radical and classical understanding of momentariness, which accepts as real only strictly momentary phenomenon, contradicts common experience. We all seem to experience things as enduring. Sa-paṇ and his followers do not deny this, but hold that such intuitions do not constitute criteria for philosophical validity. For them, common sense is nothing but the product of attachment to permanence and self-grasping. Hence it is not normative, but, on the contrary, the source of our problems. To hold the doctrine of momentariness prisoner to our preanalytical intuitions destroys its very purpose, the overcoming of our limitations.

Sa-paṇ criticizes Cha-ba for holding that Dharmakīrti's epistemology should agree with conventions. Cha-ba proposes a system in which epistemology is established according to the Vaibhāṣika school, which often restates and systematizes common preanalytical intuitions. According to Cha-ba, ultimately Dharmakīrti is a Mādhyamika whose system must be established in relation to conventional valid cognitions[33] and, therefore, should be settled on the basis of what is renowned to the world.[34] Sa-paṇ answers: "If one relies on what is renowned as worldly convention, one contradicts the presentation of valid cognition."[35] Sa-paṇ's main point is that to interpret Dharmakīrti's epistemology to accord with our pre-analytical intuitions would destroy that epistemology, which is systematic and critical. Such a philosophy intends to overcome the limitations of commonsense. Hence it is absurd to hold it to the standard that it not only rejects but intends to overcome.

The Ge-luk understanding of the question is different. This tradition does not follow Cha-ba in explaining Dharmakīrti according to the Vaibhāṣika view. Neither does it hold that Dharmakīrti's system is Madhyamaka. Like Sa-paṇ's school, the Ge-luk tradition holds that Dharmakīrti's Seven Works reflect a partly Sautrāntika and a partly Yogācāra view. Still it has inherited from Cha-ba's tradition the idea that epistemology should respect, as much as possible, our precritical intuitions. For Ge-luk thinkers, Buddhist philosophy must rely on commonly accepted notions because of its commitment to philosophize on the basis of daily experience. The Ge-luk presentation of momentariness is an excellent example of this attempt to convey Dharmakīrti's insights without contradicting practical conventions. The doctrine of momentariness should not conflict entirely with common convention but only with the part of this convention corrupted by our attachment to permanence. Common conventions have a validity that is not the mere product of ignorance and cannot be contradicted by any philosophically informed interpretation of Dharmakīrti. This is the hallmark of a Ge-luk approach to Buddhist philosophy.

Realist Explanations of the Nature of the Specifically Characterized

The opposition between Ge-luk realism and Sa-gya antirealism, which has surfaced in the discussion of the status of commonsense objects, is clearly reflected in the explanations each tradition gives of Dharmakīrti's ontology. As examined in the preceding chapters, Sa-gya antirealism denies the reality of abstract entities and holds that only individuals are real. Accordingly, the Sa-gya tradition describes specifically characterized phenomena (*rang mtshan, svalakṣaṇa*) as real individuals and generally characterized phenomena (*spyi mtshan, sāmānyalakṣaṇa*) as conceptually constructed, unreal universals. These explanations, I would argue, correspond quite closely to Dharmakīrti's thought.

Ge-luk thinkers follow a realist interpretation of Dharmakīrti, which appears in their explanations of the nature of the specifically characterized. They refuse to identify the real with the individual, claiming that this identification does not correspond to Dharmakīrti's thought. Their characterization of the nature of the specifically characterized reflects this substantial but unacknowledged reinterpretation of the original system. It obliges them to fudge certain issues to support their interpretations.

Let us examine the problems surrounding the definition of the specifically characterized. Contrary to Dharmakīrti, Ge-luk thinkers do not define the specifically characterized in relation to the three sets of identity conditions, definite spatio-temporal location, and individual essence. Rather they give their own definition. For example, Ge-dün-drup says: "Therefore, the defining property of the specifically characterized is that which is ultimately able to perform a function."[36] Ge-dün-drup refuses to define the specifically characterized in terms of definite spatio-temporal location because having a determinate existence in space and time is not an exclusive property of specifically characterized phenomena. It is shared by all phenomena. Similarly, being common (*thun mong ba*), that is, being concomitant with other phenomena, cannot define the generally characterized, for some real phenomena, such as a jar, are concomitant with their particulars.

Similarly, Kay-drup refuses to identify reality and individuality. He asserts that having determinate existence does not establish something as being real. Kay-drup gives the following definition of the specifically characterized: "That thing which exists from its own side according to its own uncommon essence without being imputed by a conceptual cognition."[37]

Gyel-tsap is sometimes mistakenly thought to define specifically characterized phenomena in terms of determinate existence. This opinion, which is based on textual issues and does not reflect any significant philosophical difference, is defended by some modern Ge-luk scholars. It is mistaken, however, for it rests on a misinterpretation of Gyel-tsap.[38] Like other Ge-luk figures, Gyel-tsap does not identify real and individual things. While commenting on Dharmakīrti's *Commentary*, III:3, he gives this definition of the *specifically characterized*: "The subject, everything that is ultimately existing, ultimately exists within the context of this treatise because it is established from the side of the own mode of being of the object without being merely nominally [existent]. The subject, other [phenomena] that are empty of being effective, are called *conventionally existing* because they are established through mere imputation. There is a reason for these two aforementioned meaning-distinguishers (*don ldog*)[39] to be the defining properties of specifically characterized [phenomena] and generally defined [phenomena]; they are set forth that way by reason of the fact that the two defined objects are uncommonly and individually posited by these two meaning-distinguishers."[40] This mouthful of scholastic jargon indicates that, for Gyel-tsap, the specifically characterized is that which is established through its own essence. This may sound like Dharmakīrti, but Gyel-tsap's view is quite different. For Dharmakīrti specifically characterized phenomena are real inasmuch as they are individuals; that is, objects that exist without any construction. Anything that requires a synthesis, such as a commonsense object or a property, is unreal. Gyel-tsap understands construction differently. For him, we can be said to construct an object only when we artificially add something to the object. In the case of a commonsense object or a universal, we add nothing but simply capture the nature of the object. For example, we add nothing to a jar when we perceive it as such. Construction intervenes only when we hold a commonsense object or a universal to exist over and above its parts. Hence, both commonsense objects and universals can be real.

This reinterpretation of Dharmakīrti's view is related to the moderate realism of the Ge-luk tradition. Ge-luk thinkers interpret Dharmakīrti so as not to exclude the possibility that real properties exist in dependence on their instances. Strict determination in space, time, and entity entails that only individuals are real. Accepting these identity conditions would exclude the real and recurrent properties required for a moderate solution to the problem of universals. So, for the Ge-luk tradition, real things are not strictly determinate in space, time, and entity. They are determinate only inasmuch as they can be distinguished, conceptually or perceptually, from other phenomena. Taken in this way, determinate existence does not constitute being specifically characterized since it also applies to permanent, generally characterized phenomena.[41] Since any phenomenon (*chos, dharma*) is said to bear its own entity (*rang gi ngo bo 'dzin pa*),[42] it must be distinguishable from other entities. A permanent phenomenon exists in a determinate way since it is able, by definition, to bear its own entity. Hence, determinate existence cannot provide by itself a definition of reality. Taken strictly, it excludes too much. In the looser conception, it includes too much!

This does not mean that it is impossible to use the concept of determinate existence to define reality. Taken in the looser sense and with the suitable qualification, determinate existence can be used as an element in a definition of reality. For example, Dzong-ka-ba gives two definitions of the specifically characterized in his short introduction to the logico-epistemological studies: "The defining property of the specifically characterized is that which is ultimately able to perform a function, as, for example, [the color] blue. Or, it is that thing which exists unmixed in space and time."[43] Here, Dzong-ka-ba seems to accept a definition of specifically characterized phenomena based on the use of the three sets of identity conditions. This is not, however, the expression of an antirealist philosophy of universals, as it is for Sa-paṇ, for we have seen clear evidence of Dzong-ka-ba's realism.[44] Realism does not actually preclude a definition of reality based on the three criteria of definite existence but it does make it pointless. A realist perspective forces one to adopt a weak version of the criteria, thereby depriving them of their relevance. It still remains possible to elaborate a definition of the real on the basis of these three criteria, and Dzong-ka-ba's second definition is an example of such an attempt. With the addition of the suitable correctives (such as the addition of the word "thing" at the end of the definition) such a definition can be made extensionally correct. However, such an artificial attempt cannot restore the strength and significance held by the three sets of criteria in Dharmakīrti's system.

For Dharmakīrti, the real is that which is determinate in space, time, and entity. There is no need to add any qualification to that statement. Dharmakīrti does not give any other characterization of specifically characterized phenomena.[45] This is to say that these three sets of identity conditions play an extremely important role in Dharmakīrti's thought. This importance is partly recognized by Ge-luk scholars, who characterize *Commentary*, I:40 (the passage that characterizes real things as having a determinate existence) as a description of the nature of things (*dngos po'i gnas lugs*).[46] The tradition, however, finds it very difficult to substantiate this description. When asked what this means, most scholars respond that the nature of things is that they are distinguishable from other objects belonging to similar and dissimilar kinds. For example, a white cow is different from brown cows and horses. Still, it is not obvious how such distinctions, which according to this view apply equally to real things and constructs, constitute the nature of real things. For Dharmakīrti, the three sets of identity conditions define the real because real things and constructs are distinguished from each other on the basis of being or not being individuals. Accordingly, being determinate, that is, individual, is highly significant and deserves the characterization "nature of a thing." Since the identification between real and individual does not hold in Ge-luk philosophy, the description of the determinate as the nature of things loses its significance.[47]

According to Gyel-tsap, the correct interpretation of Dharmakīrti's statement that a thing is spatially determinate is the following: The western portion of a thing does not exist in the east and vice versa. Similarly, a thing is temporally determinate inasmuch as a thing that exists in the morning has ceased to exist in the evening. This does not mean that anything and everything existing in the morning must have ceased to exist in the evening. Finally, a thing has a determinate entity inasmuch as the entity of a particular object is not that of another object. For example, the entity of a black cow is not that of a multicolored cow. Although this characterization is certainly true, its significance is far from obvious. How can this distinction, which applies equally well to permanent phenomena regardless of their lesser ontological status, be a description of the nature of things?

According to Gyel-tsap, Dharmakīrti's characterization of things as determinate is not really meant as a definition of the nature of things but only as a refutation of the Nyāya view of universals. According to the Nyāya, universals are indivisible and omnipresent entities that inhere equally in all their instances. Since universals are partless, the Nyāya is committed, according to the Buddhist, to the idea that the entity of the white cow is identical to that of the black cow. This is, according to Gyel-tsap, all that Dharmakīrti has in mind when he proposes his three criteria!

Nominal Existence and Existence

In standard Ge-luk exegesis, the generally characterized (*spyi mtshan, sāmānya-lakṣaṇa*) is defined in opposition to the specifically characterized as "that which is not established as specifically characterized but is merely imputed by thought and language."[48] In the same way that the impermanent and the specifically characterized are said to be equivalent, the permanent and the generally characterized are also equivalent. Permanent phenomena include the items found in the Abhidharma (space and cessation) and also phenomena such as existence, common locus, or reasons, for all these phenomena lack causal reality and have, therefore, no mode of existence other than that constructed by conceptual and linguistic activities. Kay-drup defines the *generally characterized* as "That phenomenon which is a mere imputation by a conceptual consciousness and which does not exist as an entity from its own side."[49] Generally characterized phenomena do not truly exist, for they are not produced by causes and conditions. They can exist only in dependence on some conceptual activity. They are called *generally characterized phenomena* because they do not exist through their own characteristics but merely as general entities attributed to really existing things.[50]

In a certain way, this description of the nature of generally characterized phenomena captures Dharmakīrti's intentions. One crucial difference, however, concerns the status of universals. Dharmakīrti equates generally characterized phenomena and universals. Ge-luk thinkers differ, holding that real things like jar (or being a jar),[51] matter (or being matter), and the like can be universals. They can be instantiated by particulars and, therefore, are universals, despite being real. This view, which has given rise to intense controversies in Tibet, is characteristic of the Ge-luk approach. We will revisit it in the next chapters where we examine the problem of universals.

A last important point to be made of the subject of existence remains. In an earlier chapter, we discussed the ambiguities of the concept of existence in Dharmakīrti. We distinguished two understandings of this concept: existence as reality and existence as object of a valid cognition. In accordance with their realism, Ge-luk thinkers tend to emphasize the latter, broader understanding of existence. This view stresses that generally characterized phenomena, which have only nominal (or conceptual) existence, do exist since they are objects of knowledge. Whereas for most of their opponents this type of existence does not fulfill the requirements for existence, Ge-luk scholars hold that it is sufficient that an entity be nominally existent to exist.

Ge-luk thinkers define existence in relation to phenomena being objects of valid cognitions. They hold that both real and conceptually constructed entities are objects of valid cognitions and, therefore, exist. This description of existence as including both things and concepts represents a move away from Dharmakīrti's antirealist emphasis on the existence of individual things. Such a shift corresponds to the realism of the Ge-luk tradition: Existence is not restricted to concrete things but includes conceptual entities as well. Therefore, being intelligible rather than being a thing is emphasized as the criterion of existence.

This emphasis on intelligibility found in the discussions of the concept of existence among Ge-luk thinkers also reflects their more realist appreciation for the validity of conceptualization. Ge-dün-drup, for instance, gives a number of equivalents to existence: "Object, knowable, object of comprehension, definite existence, and established basis are equivalents."[52] He proceeds to define each of these equivalent *(don gcig)*[53] phenomena: *Object* is defined as that which is cognized by a mind. *Knowable* is defined as that which is fit to be the object of the mind; and *object of comprehension* is defined as that which is realized by valid cognition. Finally, *definite existence* is defined as that which is observed by valid cognition; and *established basis* as that which is established by valid cognition.[54] The meaning of these definitions can be summarized as follows: Phenomena are objects, knowables, existents, and the like, inasmuch as they are correctly cognized by consciousness.

Such descriptions of existence based on intelligibility can be found in Dharmakīrti and his followers. Most often, though, these authors equate existence with a reality understood as consisting of things. By contrast, Ge-luk thinkers tend to think of existence in a way that applies to both real and constructed entities. As heirs to Cha-ba's realist tradition, they have a marked preference for thinking of existence extensionally, without giving primacy to differentiating the sorts of entities that exist. Accordingly, both real and conceptual phenomena exist.

This does not mean that they exist on the same ontological level. Whereas the former really exist, the latter exist only in dependence on conceptual activities.

This difference in ontological status reflects the moderation of Ge-luk realism. More extreme forms of realism do not differentiate reality from existence, treating intelligibility as the criterion of both reality and existence. Ge-luk thinkers, by contrast, distinguish reality with its full ontological status from existence, which includes real as well as imputed entities. Existence is understood in terms of intelligibility, but intelligibility does not mean real. Imputed existence is enough, however, to qualify imputed entities as existents.

A Partial Reconciliation

This departure from Dharmakīrti has led some scholars to consider the Ge-luk view of existence as radically opposed to the original model. This assertion is not unsupportable. It is possible, however, to overemphasize a so-called Ge-luk conception of existence so that permanent and impermanent phenomena serve as mere subcategories of existence, now the all-encompassing category. Klein even goes so far as to assert that "However, the use of the word existent *(sattva)* as applying only to momentary or impermanent phenomena is foreign to them (Ge-luk-bas). In the Ge-luk enumeration of phenomena impermanent things are just one category among existents since this word (in Tibetan *yod pa*) includes permanent phenomena such as nonobstructive space or emptiness."[55] Klein's description does capture the thinking of a great part of the tradition, which places a strong emphasis on the existence of constructs. Moreover, her comments also reflect the opinion of what seems to be the enormous majority of contemporary scholars, who appear amazed when confronted with Dharmakīrti's inference from existence.[56]

However, she seems to imply that Ge-luk philosophy reifies existence to the extent that permanent and impermanent things become equally existent. This is not the case, because, even in the Ge-luk system, phenomena do not come to possess existence autonomously. Rather, existence is an imputed property created by linguistic and conceptual activities superimposed on the real (causal) characteristics of objects. Moreover, Klein's statement seems to suggest that Ge-luk thinkers have no concept of existence explained in terms of reality, whereas they do. Not having it would be problematic indeed for a Buddhist school, given the numerous Indian Buddhist references to existence as the equivalent of reality. Klein's comment does not accurately represent the Ge-luk point of view in its most lucid moments. Kay-drup, for example, considers two meanings of "existence," real existence and mere existence, and recognizes the first as primary. He says:

> *Question*: [Dharmakīrti says]: "Existence and effect are similar with respect to [the establishment of] perishability."[57] How is it that existence [in this passage] is said to be valid evidence establishing that sound is impermanent?
> *Answer*: [This passage] does not refer to the existence that is equivalent to being observed by a valid cognition as in [the passage] "existence is no different from observation."[58] [When used as an evidence for imperma-

> nence], the word "existence" [refers] to the autonomous existence of an entity and is [a case of] applying a general word to a [more] particular [situation]. Such an existence is said to be a valid evidence establishing that sound is impermanent.
>
> Therefore, there are two types of existence: (1) existence as being established as [having] an independent aspect, that is as establishing its own entity and (2) existence as the mere elimination of an object of negation. Since both are observed by valid cognitions, they are true [understandings of] *existence*. Nevertheless, when used strictly *(sgra dog 'jug),* the word "existence" applies to existence in an independent way, [that is,] by establishing its own entity, [a case of] a general word applying to a particular [case]. Accordingly, existence is explained as valid evidence establishing sound as [being] impermanent.[59]

Kay-drup distinguishes two uses of the word "existence."[60] Strictly speaking, existence should be reserved to designate real existence. In this sense, existence entails impermanence! However, this same word is also used by Dharmakīrti to designate mere existence, which is equivalent to being an object of comprehension *(gzhal bya, prameya).* These may be either permanent or impermanent. This second use has been adopted most of the time by Ge-luk scholars, particularly in the Collected Topics. In his later *Ocean of Reasoning*, in which he sometimes expresses a more typically "Ge-luk" standpoint than in his earlier *Clearing,* Kay-drup again defends a similar view. He compares the two uses of "existence" to that of "dependent arising." Used "loosely" it refers to all phenomena, but in its strict sense it refers only to real things.[61]

Thus, both these views of existence (as real and as object of cognitive activity) can be found among realists as well as antirealists. Realist views of existence are perhaps, after all, not so different from anti-realist ones. There is, however, a difference in emphasis that is not accidental. Whereas Dharmakīrti and the antirealists tend to equate reality and existence, Ge-luk thinkers tend to prefer a less ontological and more extensional view of existence as including both real and quasi-entities. This approach reflects not so much a reification of existence as an increased appreciation for conceptuality. For the antirealists, by contrast, conceptual constructs exist only from the point of view of a conceptual consciousness, which is inherently distorted. Since constructs rely on conceptual thought for their existence, they are not observed by enlightened beings. These beings have gone beyond conceptual thought. For them (but not for ordinary beings), constructs are no more existent than the horns of a rabbit. They are fictions imagined by ordinary beings that have little cognitive relation to reality.[62] From the Ge-luk point of view, the existence of constructs is not a concession to ignorance. A fully enlightened being still observes constructs, for these phenomena have an actual, albeit limited, validity. Although such nominal existents do not have full ontological status, they are not mere illusions. They exist in dependence on conceptual activities that partly relate to reality.

Conclusion

This investigation into the ontology of Dharmakīrti and his commentators has brought forth the diversity of views found within the Indian and Tibetan ontological traditions. In these chapters, I have attempted to sketch the ontological basis of Dharmakīrti's system as an introduction to my main subject, the problem of universals and its semantic and epistemological consequences. Before proceeding to this analysis, let me summarize some of the different views that have emerged so far.

The underlying structure of Dharmakīrti's system is based on the opposition between real, effective individual things and conceptual constructs, which are general and unreal in nature. This antirealism is not limited to the question of universals but extends to commonsense objects as well. Most Sa-gya commentators have followed this antirealist philosophy, attempting to solve the conceptual difficulties in Dharmakīrti's system without tampering with the refusal to accept abstract entities in the fabric of reality.

The Ge-luk tradition has taken a different approach. Its thinkers advocate a more revisionist line of interpretation, arguing not only for the reality of commonsense objects but even for that of universals. As will become increasingly clear in the following chapters, there seems to have been a long stream of commentators defending a realist interpretation of Dharmakīrti's system. Their commitment to a more commonsensical philosophy arises mostly from the difficulties that a consistent antirealist position entails for an explanation of the reasoning process. For if only individuals exist, how is it possible to justify the generalizations that are an inherent part of any sound reasoning? Some thinkers have attempted to solve this difficulty by weakening the antirealist commitment of Dharmakīrti's philosophy. Begun in India, this current has been particularly influential in Tibet. Therefore the Ge-luk school in its expression of this persistent current can perhaps best be understood as the heir of a Buddhist realist tradition. The strength of this tradition will become increasingly clear in the next chapters.

As our analysis has shown, Ge-luk thinkers do not proceed with a straightforward philosophical re-evaluation of Dharmakīrti's positions. Rather, through reinterpreting him, they attempt to solve the conceptual difficulties of the system by subtly changing the meaning of certain terms, such as the *specifically characterized*. The outcome of this complicated hermeneutical game is quite clear. The difference between real and conceptual phenomena no longer corresponds to that between individuals and universals; some universal properties are included among real elements. This realism is further confirmed by the status of commonsense objects. Accepting the reality of commonsense objects such as jars reinforces the view that reality does not consist only of individuals.

This realist move is different from the Nyāya view in that it maneuvers to avoid the excessive reification of general entities entailed by extreme realism. It is a moderate realism. As such its main goal is to accommodate the antirealist critique of reification while respecting commonly accepted notions. The question that we turn to next concerns whether such an approach is coherent. Is it possible both to avoid reification and follow commonsense intuition? Perhaps a response can be found in an examination of the nature of universals from realist and antirealist points of view. The next part takes on this task, providing a detailed analysis of the problem of universals in the Indian and Tibetan traditions. Chapter 6 defines the terms of the inquiry, examining the opposition between realism and conceptualism. It also provides the background for the discussion by considering some of the most significant views concerning universals in India.

Part II

The Problem of Universals

6

Introducing Universals

Three Dimensions in the Problem of Universals

This chapter discusses distinctions between realism and antirealism. It introduces the Nyāya realist view about universals, of particular significance for being the main target of Dharmakīrti's critique. This extreme realism is differentiated from moderate realism. Moreover, two forms of antirealism, nominalism and conceptualism, are compared and related to Dharmakīrti's tradition. Although epistemology, ontology, and semantics all provide bases for comparing these philosophical traditions, this chapter focuses on semantic concerns.

The variety of philosophical positions discussed here could be obscured by the use of terms such as *realism* and *nominalism.* Using them may even suggest a transhistorical and transcultural identity between vastly different positions and thinkers such Plato, Uddyotakara, Aristotle, Scotus, Kumārila, Samantabhadra, and Kay-drup. Not to use such terms in this book, however, would be even more misleading, for it would leave the significant philosophical differences between Tibetan schools buried among interpretive details. By showing that the Ge-luk interpretations of Dharmakīrti's ontology are realist and thus connecting them but not identifying them with their realistic cousins, I expose some significant characteristics of the Ge-luk tradition that might go unnoticed using a purely exegetical method. Similarly, delineating differences between moderate realism, extreme realism, and nominalism helps reveal the differences internal to Buddhist tradition.

Therefore, the use of an etic vocabulary probably is justified in this case, for it highlights some of the differences separating Tibetan epistemological schools without imposing too many distortions. It allows me to show how many seemingly obscure exegetical disputes between Tibetan epistemological traditions revolve around a problem that has been at the center of philosophical discussions in the West as well: the problem of universals.

But what is meant by the problem of universals? Let me first provide a simple and even somewhat misleading explanation. Our experience seems to indicate that we and the world we inhabit are not made up of disjointed individuals but of objects sharing common features. For example, we see a tomato and notice that it has a color similar to that of a red flag nearby. Are these two colors the same? Do these two objects share something in common? At first, the answer seems obviously positive, for they are both red. But what is this common element? Is it the property being red? This is where realism and antirealism part company.[1] Realism holds that the tomato and the flag share at least a common feature. Moreover, they argue, this property or universal is real. It is part of the "furniture" of the world and exists independent of any human mind. Nominalism and conceptualism deny this, holding common properties to be products of interaction between reality and human minds. Among Tibetan epistemological traditions, the lines of opposition between Ge-luk and Sa-gya traditions center on this problem of universals and its epistemological consequences. Whereas Ge-luk thinkers consistently propose a realist reading of Dharmakīrti, Sa-gya thinkers oppose this interpretation. Thus the problem of universals is essential to an investigation of the Tibetan interpretations of Dharmakīrti.

The preceding explanation is somewhat misleading in that it wrongly suggests that the only issue at stake here is whether things share common elements. This is, in one way, quite trivial. What does it matter whether the redness of the tomato is the same as that of the flag? The problem can be made more relevant. Consider two human beings. Do they share a common humanity? This question is less trivial. Even so, it does not yet explain why the status of universals has occupied the best minds of several sophisticated traditions. To understand this, we have to consider how such commonalities as we just discussed also contribute to our ways of experiencing the world. In our example, how do we come to know that the tomato and the flag are red? Initially this question may appear irrelevant, for it seems like we just come across these entities. We observe them as they are or, to put it in Russell's terms, we know them by acquaintance.

This attractive and simple picture exercises a strong fascination on our minds. I would call it a popular version of what Wilfrid Sellars calls the *Myth of the Given*, the idea that some elements of reality are given to us in their immediacy with absolute authority. This picture has been made more complicated by philosophers, in particular by empiricists who have tried to save this idea of the given through philosophical elaborations. Realizing that the claim to know commonsense objects by acquaintance is problematic, they have attempted to refine the myth by variously describing what is known directly as sense data, appearances, impressions, and so forth. We will examine these descriptions, some of which are also found in the Buddhist epistemological tradition, later while explaining the theory of perception. Suffice it to say here that all these different and complicated versions of the myth come down to the same view that certain knowledge events possess an authority of their own by virtue of the sheer giveness of what they apprehend. Sellars puts it in this way: "The idea that observation 'strictly and properly so-called' is constituted by certain self-authenticating episodes, the authority of which is transmitted to verbal and quasi-verbal performances when these performances are made 'in conformity with the semantic rules of the language' is, of course, the heart of the Myth of the Given. For the *given,* in epistemological tradition is what is *taken* by these self-authenticating episodes."[2] We know certain things directly, with absolute authority, and verbal statements are just ways to communicate what we know in isolation from conceptual schema, or to speak like some contemporary thinkers, in the privacy of our minds.

This picture is profoundly misleading. Let us consider for now its simple popular version. We come across the red flag and know it as such. This knowing cannot be in virtue of the object itself, for we do not know just an object but we know it *as* something. We know the flag as having a certain shape and color, as performing certain functions, and so forth. This is possible only if we already know the concept of flag with a certain degree of complexity. We must know how flags are used, for instance. To say that we perceive a piece of cloth which we call a flag would not change the issue. Even if we were to talk in terms of color patches, we would still need a concept to recognize them. Thus, we do not have a concept of something because we have become directly acquainted with that sort of thing. Rather, we have the ability to notice a sort of thing because we already have the concept of that some thing.

This is where the problem of universals becomes relevant to understanding our experience. For, if concepts or categories are involved in our very experiences of the world, the question of their status becomes important. Are categories such as "human" or "redness" the products of our human minds or do they exist independent of ourselves? This is what the problem of universals is really about. To discuss whether flags and tomatoes have the same redness or not is probably a philosophical indulgence. To discuss how it is that we know them as red is considerably more relevant. For, if our experience of the world depends on more than an acquaintance with some simple entities, then it becomes important to understand the nature of the entities upon which it does depend. These provide not just the categories of our experience but its norms as well. Thus, far from being irrelevant, the problem of universals is one of the central avenues of philosophical inquiry about the world, the way we know it, the norms to which we should conform, and more.

In this study, the problem of the status of universals will be examined through a triple approach: ontology, philosophy of language, and epistemology, distinctions which are purely heuristic since all three are intimately connected. Still, they help to bring some order to our discussion. They also coincide with the different areas of Western philosophical inquiry from which I draw my vocabulary. Let me provide a brief overview of these three approaches.

First, ontologically, the problem of universals can be stated in this way: What is the reality status of general entities? In our example, do the patches share a common property of being red? And if so, what is the ontological status of this property? Thinkers who are realists about universals assert the reality of general entities such as properties and classes, although they may disagree on how to explain this reality. Consequently, these thinkers hold that the world is not reducible to individuals but contains properties as well. Thinkers who are antirealist about universals reject this reification of commonality. They hold that the world is made of individuals. For example, the modern nominalist philosopher Nelson Goodman states: "For me, as a nominalist, the world is a world of individuals."[3]

This statement may appear at first clear and obvious. As Goodman himself recognizes, this is far from being the case. For what does it mean to be an individual? According to Dharmakīrti, being an individual means having clear identity conditions specifiable in terms of determinate spatio-temporal location and distinction in entity. That is, to occupy a definite portion of space, to exist at a specifiable time, and to have its own unique set of characteristics such as color, shape, and taste. In short, to be an individual is to be a specifically characterized phenomenon. General entities fail to satisfy these identity conditions and hence are rejected from the sphere of mind-independent reality. They are conceptual elaborations, indeterminate according to these criteria. To use Dharmakīrti's term, they are generally characterized phenomena.

The first part of this work has shown, however, that even such specificity does not yield always unambiguous determinations of what counts as an individual. Commonsense objects are excluded from reality by Dharmakīrti, except in certain circumstances, when they are introduced with the understanding that they can be reduced to their components. Similarly, the status of extended objects such as patches of colors, tastes, and smells is not without ambiguity. Are they individuals or not? Our investigation shows the difficulty of clearly separating individuals from other sorts of entities and the necessity of introducing several frameworks to account for the different ontological levels. Entities such as colors are accepted as individuals at a certain level of ontological analysis but ultimately reduced to their atomic components according to the scheme of ascending scales of analysis described earlier.

Second, ontology is not the only way to consider universals. Indian philosophers insist on understanding universals in relation to their semantic role as well. An important feature of language, made possible only if words are connected with universals, is its general applicability. If words acquired their meaning only in relation to individual things, language would be just a nomenclature of sound events pointing to directly present objects. There would be no way to say the same thing at different times or to refer to an object in its absence. It also would be impossible for different people to say the same thing. So it is necessary to posit a time-neutral element that allows people to understand utterances as something more than referential noise.

Western philosophers often call such a timeless element a *proposition*. Attitudes associated with these entities, such as thinking and believing, are propositional attitudes. Typically, propositions are composed of a subject on which a general property is predicated. For example, when we say "Bossie is a great Swiss cow," we refer to a particular object, Bossie, and predicate on it the general term "cow." This general term has a function, which is inexplicable except through the intervention of universals. Unlike the term "Bossie," which for the sake of simplicity can be thought of as referential,[4] the term "cow" does not operate by singling out an element. Rather, it functions by qualifying an element already singled out. This raises the following question: What is the meaning of general terms? The Nyāya answer is that general terms are meaningful because they signify real general properties. Antirealists reject this solution but are left with the difficulty of accounting for general terms in a world of individuals.

Third, Indian philosophers understand universals to play an epistemological role as well. Universals derive importance from their connection with knowledge, a connection understood differently by competing schools. For Naiyāyikas, the role of universals extends to all forms of knowledge. Even perception, they argue, requires the presence of universals. Without them, perception would boil down to a meaningless encounter with bare reality. It would be unable to bring about the categorization that practical activities require. Dharmakīrti disagrees with this point, which we will explore at length in our analysis of perception. He agrees, however, with his adversary on the role of universals in inference, the other form of knowledge he admits. Without real universals, though, how can he explain the success of inference?

But here I am running ahead of myself. Before examining the epistemological implications of the problem of universals, we must examine its semantic dimension.

Antirealism and Its Varieties: Conceptualism and Nominalism

Until now we have discussed antirealism as a single coherent position. This is actually a simplification, since antirealism covers a wide variety of positions. Two forms of antirealism, namely, conceptualism and nominalism, are particularly relevant to this work. Both hold that universals do not exist in reality, but they disagree on how to explain the commonality we seem to encounter. Nominalism holds that generalities can be adequately explained in terms of language. Commonality does not exist in reality but is created by the use of general terms. In our example the common redness does not exist in the tomato or the red flag but comes to be in the application of the general term "red." For sure colors do exist, but there is no overarching commonality, just similarity. Conceptualism agrees with most of this account but insists that the application of common terms requires conceptual intermediaries.

This distinction between nominalism and conceptualism should not be pushed too far. The opposition between these two forms of antirealism does not parallel the difference between the two forms of realism relevant to our discussion. Moderate and extreme realism clearly part company on a well-defined question: Are universals dependent on their instances or not? Conceptualism and nominalism are not so clearly separated. As Mackie observes, the line separating them is in fact rather thin.[5] What difference there is lies mostly in the degree of emphasis not in substantial differences. This difference in degree is not insignificant, however.

Let us explore the differences between nominalism and conceptualism a bit further.

Historically, the most famous nominalist is probably Ockham (1285–1349). For him, universals are to be understood in relation to the terms that signify individual things and stand for them in propositions. Only individuals exist; universals have no independent existence. They are just convenient ways of describing and categorizing the objects we encounter. This is also the view of modern nominalists such as Sellars, Goodman, and Quine.[6] All these authors share a similar distrust of abstract entities. For example, Sellars explains the world as consisting of the interaction of two types of entity: material and mental. As we saw earlier, Sellars's idea of knowledge is far from being a naive empiricism. He understands that we do not know individuals just by bumping into them, for the knowledge of objects involves concepts. To know a red color implies that we know the concept of red and use it to identify the object. The application of this concept identifies what is red and what is not, and provides a norm without which there is no knowledge. Sellars and the realist agree on this point, but they disagree on the way to explain the nature of this normative element. For the realist, the distinction between truth and falsity cannot be made without presupposing the existence of real norms existing independent of our human conceptions, inclinations, and the like. For example, the concept of being red is true when applied to certain red objects because such concept captures a real property, a universal, that is instantiated by red objects. This is what Sellars denies. For him, concepts do not refer to universals. The concept of red does not refer to the property of being red, except in the loose sense of the word. We do say that objects are red because they are red. We should not be misled, however, by these words into believing that there is some essential redness they all share. There is no such universal, except as a *flatus voci,* a convenient description.

What about concepts then? How does Sellars explain the normative element involved in knowledge? Sellars's response seems to be an explanation of the nature of concepts inspired by the later Wittgenstein.[7] Concepts are mental entities that do provide norms, but not by virtue of referring to some universals. Rather, they should be thought of in dispositional terms. A concept is a disposition or ability that we acquire to follow a rule or a procedure. For example, we acquire the concept of red when we come to know how to use the term "red" to describe certain patches of color. This acquisition is not simply the ability to point to some object and utter the noise "red." Rather, it involves the ability to place the object within a complicated conceptual network in which the recognition of perception conditions and social usage are involved. For example, to know that an object is red we must know that the light is right, our vision is unimpeded, and so on. We must also know how red is contrasted with other colors, such as brown and yellow. In short, we must be able to place the object "in the logical space of reasons, of justifying and being able to justify what one says."[8] Thus, the business of acquiring even a relatively simple concept is quite complicated. What it does not involve is a reference to some third world (that is, neither mental nor physical) entity such as a universal.[9]

As we will see, Dharmakīrti's view is not unlike Sellars's, Quine's, and Goodman's. Like them, Dharmakīrti understands that the crucial issue is the problem of concepts. He realizes that knowledge is not the result of an acquaintance with empirical entities and involves a normative element. Like Sellars, Dharmakīrti refuses to hypostatize concepts by relating them to some properties existing in the real world independent from human cognitive interests. Like Sellars, Dharmakīrti holds that terms such as "redness" are convenient descriptions of individuals. Dharmakīrti differs from Sellars and other nominalists, however, in his way of explaining the nature of concepts. And this is indeed the crucial issue, which we will examine in the following chapters. Whereas Sellars explains concepts without any reference to abstract entities, Dharmakīrti introduces universals in his explanation. These are the generally characterized phenomena, which are not fully real, but nevertheless exist in some weak sense of the word. They are less than fully real, but more than completely nonexistent. For the time being, we could call them *useful fictions.*

Dharmakīrti is often described nowadays as a nominalist. I do not object to such a description, provided the term is well understood. At the very least, a strong distinction must be maintained between moderate nominalism and extreme nominalism. Scholars who think of Dharmakīrti as a nominalist often understand his view to be extreme. They think that Dharmakīrti rejects not only the reality of the referents of general terms, which is true, but even their objective basis, which is wrong. That is, they hold Dharmakīrti to be saying that universals are not only fictitious but purely subjective a priori constructs applied to reality without any objective justification. I will show in the next chapter that this interpretation is mistaken, for it is contradicted by considerable textual evidence, as well as being philosophically untenable.

In this work I depict Dharmakīrti's antirealism as a form of conceptualism, for he emphasizes the mind-dependent nature of universals. Although they are not parts of the fabric of reality, they exist in some weak sense of the word. They are the objects or contents of concepts.[10] Therefore, Dharmakīrti's view is adequately described as form of conceptualism, a position Quine opposes to the more radical nominalistic objection to "admitting abstract entities at all, even in the restrained sense of mind-made entities."[11] I believe that his view can be compared quite fruitfully to that of Western conceptualists such as Locke, Berkeley, and Hume. Like them Dharmakīrti emphasizes the mind-dependence of concepts and the existence of resemblances as the basis for elaborating concepts, although he also differs from them in his recognition of the linguistic nature of conceptual construction.

Another feature of Dharmakīrti that I will stress is his constructivism. Whereas Western philosophers often describe the process of formation of universals as an abstraction, Dharmakīrti characterizes it as a process of construction. Universals are not part of the fabric of reality but are constructed by the mind on the basis of experiencing resemblances and in relation to linguistic usages, as will be shown in the next chapter. Universals are elaborated by thought, which is described as *vikalpa* or *kalpanā* (*rtog pa,* conceptuality), a word formed from the root *kḷp,* to prepare, arrange, construct, create.[12] Hence, throughout this work I will describe universals as being conceptual constructs elaborated in relation to linguistically embedded social practices but based on the experience of similarities.

Extreme and Moderate Realisms and Their Predicaments

Realists agree that universals exist independent of any conceptual scheme. Like antirealism, though, realism is not monolithic. Realists disagree primarily on how to describe the reality of universals. For extreme realists, universals exist independent, not only of human categories but even of their instances. In other words, universals exist over, above, and prior to things (*universale ante rem*). Extreme realists hold that in the case of red things, there is a property such as redness that exists independent of its instances.[13] Regardless of whether things are red or not, redness exists as an ideal property. Its being instantiated or not cannot affect it, argue these realists, for redness is an abstract property and hence cannot be changed by concrete transformations.

Historically, extreme realism seems to have been the earliest form of realism both in the West and in India. In Greece, Plato first defended an extreme realist position. For him, phenomena can be appraised in relation to ideal forms that provide eternal standards of judgment. Although rejected by Aristotle, this extreme realism dominated the early Middle Ages discussions (up to the end of the eleventh century). In India, too, the Nyāya and Sāṃkhya extreme realisms were first to arise, before being rejected by Buddhists or modified by Jains.

Moderate realists consider this account of universals too extreme. How can properties exist without any support in empirical reality, they ask? Consequently, they hold that universals exist in things (*universale in re*). Properties do not exist independent of their instances but come to be along with them. For example, the redness of the tomato and the flag do not exist independent of these objects, and neither are they just the products of conceptualization. This corresponds to our experience, argue these realists. For, we see a red tomato or a red flag but not redness itself. Only in thought does redness exists as a separate entity. In reality, things and properties do exist but not apart.

Historically, this more moderate position has arisen as a reaction to the perceived problems of extreme realism or antirealism. In Greece, Aristotle proposed such a view as an attempt to solve the difficulties in Plato's extreme realism. In Medieval discussions, thinkers such as Aquinas and Dun Scotus offered what they considered a more moderate form of realism as an attempt to find a middle ground between extreme realism and antirealism.[14] Similarly in India and Tibet, moderate realism arose in several traditions in response to the perceived excesses of Nyāya realism or Dharmakīrti's antirealism. Moderate realism, then, is a position of compromise looking for middle ground between realists and antirealists.

Let me say a few words about the nature of this moderate realist position and what I perceive to be its intrinsic difficulty.

Moderate realists are sympathetic to the antirealist's rejection of the extreme realist assertion that properties exist independent of the particulars that instantiate them. They are unwilling, however, to take the next antirealist step; namely, the rejection of abstract entities. Antirealists argue that properties are not only dependent on their instances, but they are also mere reflections of our conceptual schemes. Moderate realists, by contrast, hold that properties exist in their instances independent of whether we conceive of them. If properties did not have this sort of independence from conception, argue the moderate realists, our concepts would be arbitrary. To avoid this unwanted consequence, moderate realists hold that we must admit that properties exist independent of the mind.

Moderate realists are particularly uncomfortable with the nominalist assertion that universals do not exist independent of human linguistic practices but are merely abstractions derived from our use of general terms. For example, some nominalists go as far as saying that there is no universal redness, only a general term "red." But this is confusing or even incoherent. Consider this question: Are two words "red" spoken by different people instances of the same general term or not? To answer positively is not possible for the nominalist, for that would be tantamount to accepting that there are at least linguistic universals. And if there are words that are universals, why not accept external things as well? So, the nominalist answer to this question is bound to be negative. But then the question is this: In what way are these two terms general? Moreover, what is the nature of general terms? This account is problematic. It does not represent the nominalist's best account, but it offers the view that moderate realists feel they would be committed to if they adopted nominalism. Many nominalists would offer more credible responses to the realist's qualm. We already saw Sellars's explanation of concepts as being mental dispositions to follow rules and procedures. In later chapters, we will see Buddhist attempts to answer such questions, for they are crucial for the antirealists.

Moderate realists feel that, to avoid this problem, they must accept the reality of properties. Consequently, they refuse to reduce reality to individual material and mental entities or events and assert that properties, that is, universals, exist in things. Concepts are then explained as mental events that refer to some real universals. Unlike extreme realists, however, they refuse to dissociate properties from their instances, for we never apprehend such properties apart from their instances. This last point seems obvious but it raises a problem. That is, if universals and particulars are not separate, are they then identical? The answer, for moderate realists cannot be positive, for that would commit them to reducing properties to individuals. But then, what is the relation between individuals and universals?

This question represents the central difficulty facing moderate realism, what I call *the moderate realist's predicament*. To solve the problem, moderate realists have proposed a variety of solutions, which boil down to the creation of a new type of relation. This relation allows them to say that universals and individuals are neither completely identical nor do they exist apart. To do this, moderate realists must be able to find a type of relation that straddles the fence between the domain of individuals and the order of universals. This attempt is bound to be delicate, perhaps even artificial. Extreme realists hold a much simpler view that particulars and universals are completely different. Antirealists hold another comparatively simple view that universals are pseudo-entities, merely added to a reality of individuals.

Moderate realism is in a particularly difficult position arising from its attempt to conciliate these two extremes. It needs to find a way of bypassing the delineation between unity and distinction assumed by both extreme realists and nominalists. A great deal of the efforts of moderate realists such as Kumārila and Samantabhadra[15] in India; Cha-ba, Gyel-tsap, and Kay-drup in Tibet; and Aristotle, Aquinas, and Dun Scotus in the West is spent trying to elaborate such an intermediary relation. Scotus, for example, asserts that the distinction between particulars and universals is less than a real distinction but more than a mere mental differentiation. He describes the distinction as formal.[16] For Scotus, a real distinction can be found between things that are physically separable, as for example, two heads. A mental distinction may arise without any objective distinction, as when we distinguish the head as seat of thinking from the head as superior extremity of the body. Here there is no real distinction, just two expressions that describe the same thing. Dun Scotus's formal distinction attempts to create a space for a type of distinction that would lie in between these two clearly recognizable kinds of relation.

He takes for one example the distinction that obtains between different aspects of the soul that cannot exist separately, its sensitive and intellectual aspects. There is no intellect apart from feelings, and yet few would argue that the difference is merely nominal. For Scotus this distinction is less than real, since the two cannot exist apart, but more than conceptual, since the distinction is objectively true. It is formal. He holds that the type of distinction between universals and particulars is similar. Since no universals exist apart from their particulars, the difference between them is less than real. It is, however, more than purely subjective.

While interesting, this argument is less than fully convincing. Intellect and feelings are not the same, but one could argue that their distinction arises from a real difference which has yet to be understood. Even if one grants Scotus's point, his formal relation remains difficult to comprehend. What does it mean for a distinction to be less than real but more than conceptual? I hold this difficulty to be typical of the predicament of moderate realism, whether it is found in Europe, India, or Tibet.[17]

Realism in India

In India, the problem of universals has inhabited the center of philosophical discussions for a long time. Characteristically, these discussions have considered this problem from a semantic point of view. For example, pointing to a cow we say "this is a cow." The demonstrative "this" refers to the particular object in front of us, but what does the general term "cow" mean in this sentence? It does not seem to refer at all or at least not ostensibly. According to some Indian philosophers such as Kumārila and Bhartṛhari, universal cowness (*gattva, ba nyid*) is the meaning of this general word "cow." Others deny this, holding that universals are constructs. Both sides agree, however, on considering universals primarily as the objects of general terms.

Discussions about universals in India have opposed a wide variety of views, displaying the richness of Indian philosophical inquiry into language. Our purpose here, however, is not to fully describe this discussion but to contextualize Dharmakīrti's views. Hence, rather than attend to the full extent of this Indian philosophical and linguistic discussion, I will present the views that Dharmakīrti targets, just mentioning other views. Here, as in other parts of this work, Nyāya extreme realism is Dharmakīrti's main target. This view is taken by a number of other schools as a reference point as well. For example, Kumārila's Mīmāṃsā school of Vedic exegesis offers a less extreme realism than the Nyāya, but its view is, in fact, a modification of the Nyāya original position. So a discussion of the Nyāya offers a good vantage point from which to understand what has been for many centuries the dominant philosophical position in the Hindu tradition.

In general, the Hindu philosophical position concerning universals has been realist. This is not surprising, for realism corresponds philosophically to the Hindu religious idea of *dharma,* the general order of the universe. In the same way that *dharma* provides a general framework that yields context-sensitive guidance for particular situations, universals provide the general framework that guides linguistic and epistemic practices. Even the partly monist[18] view of the Sāṃkhya, which differs from the Nyāya, is a form of realism. Contrary to the Nyāya, which asserts a diversity of universals, the Sāṃkhya view holds that there is only one unique real universal. All other properties are constructed in reference to this ground. The Sāṃkhya view individuals as manifestations (*parināma, rnam 'gyur*) of an underlying reality, Nature (*prakṛti, rang bzhin*). Accordingly, things are said to be of the same essence as their universal, which is the ground for their existence.

The Sāṃkhya does not provide, however, as strong a philosophical support for the Hindu tradition as the Nyāya school. Hence, the Nyāya is especially important in the logico-epistemological domain. The Sāṃkhya view is epistemologically weak. In particular, it is helpless to explain predication, the basis of any contentful knowledge. Since there is only a single real universal, the diversity of predicates involved in predication is left with no objective basis. In that case, why not get rid of them entirely, as Dharmakīrti argues?

The Nyāya system attempts to remedy this situation by positing a multiplicity of universals. In doing so, the Nyāya has tended toward the opposite excess, the multiplication of unnecessary entities. This tendency has been singled out with great gusto by the Buddhists, as we saw in Dharmakīrti's polemic against the Nyāya idea of whole. In its debate with the Buddhists, the Nyāya school has had to curb its impulse towards multiplication. Still, it has retained its basic principle: No predication is possible without direct or indirect reference to a real universal. Let us examine this view more closely.

In the Nyāya school, universals[19] are called *kinds* (*jāti, rigs*),[20] and they play an essential role as objects of thought and language.[21] A kind is a real entity,[22] without parts (*niravayava*) and hence indivisible (*abhinna*),[23] without material form (*amūrta*), and unproduced (*anutpatti*). The most basic and contentious point is that a kind is absolutely different from its instances. A kind does not depend on its instances, for otherwise it could have no general application. Whether there are cows or not, the kind cowness exists. This point reflects well the Nyāya commitment to the realist principle that everything we correctly experience must exist in reality as we conceive it. Since we conceive of individuals and universals as different, they must be different in reality. The Nyāya point, however, goes deeper. It points to the fundamental difference between individuals and universals. The latter are not things but abstract entities that provide norms in reference to which statements can be assessed. Hence, from the Nyāya viewpoint, Dharmakīrti is profoundly mistaken in denying the reality of universals because they fail to satisfy identity conditions, for this presupposes that a real element must be a thing. For the Nyāya, this assertion is tantamount to a complete rejection of any normative dimension.

This important point raises an immediate objection: If kinds do not depend on their instances, they must exist even when they are not instantiated. Are they then ubiquitous? The Nyāya answers that kinds are indeed timeless and ubiquitous entities but they manifest only in their instances. Another way to say the same thing is to limit the relevance of spatio-temporal location to individuals. Only concrete things can described meaningfully as having a spatio-temporal location. This consideration is irrelevant to universals.

This, however, raises the following objection: If individuals and kinds are different, why are they never perceived apart? The Nyāya responds that, although universals and particulars are different, they are related by inherence (*samavāya*). This is the kind of relation uniting elements that are never found apart.[24] In this way, the Nyāya attempts to solve one of the most difficult problems confronting extreme realism: how to bridge the gap between individuals and universals. Although a form of extreme realism, in this regard the Nyāya view does not share the extreme position of ancient Western thinkers. In particular, the Nyāya does not share Plato's apparent dismissal of concrete reality. Individuals are no lesser objects of knowledge than universals. Rather, knowledge implies the participation of two equally important elements: individual substances and their kinds. The former are never found apart from the latter, but they are not identical. For instance, a cow is never seen apart from its cowness. The two are inseparable, despite being entirely different (since one is a changing substance and the other is a permanent norm). Therefore, contrary to Plato, the Nyāya assert that universals are not transcendent forms. Norms are part of this empirical world despite being entirely different from individuals.

According to the Nyāya view, permanent universals fulfill several roles. Semantically, they are required to account for predication. Universals form the support in reality for the use of common terms. Naiyāyikas think that common nouns have objective *relata*, universals, that are the causal underpinnings of our notions. Any particular substance becomes inherently associated with its coexistent universals. Through these relations a substance acquires its identity, allowing the predication of general terms. For example, the cow Bossie is a cow because cowness inheres in it. Accordingly it is called *a cow*.

The role of universals in support of predication requires that universals lack differentiable parts. If they were constituted by parts, they would constantly rearrange, leading to their continuous disappearance and re-emergence.[25] Moreover if universals had parts, the part predicated of one individual would be different from that predicated of another. In that case, predicating a single general term (such as "cow") of different individuals would be impossible. Accordingly, a true kind has to be an undefinable element that cannot be analyzed.

Universals play an epistemological role for Indian philosophers. For example, we see a cow and take note of it. The characterization of this object as a cow is conceptual and hence involves a universal. There is not much debate among Indian epistemologists on the role of universals in conceptual knowledge, even though they disagree on their ontological status. Unlike moderate realists or nominalists, the Nyāya assert that conceptualization truly reflects reality. Cowness is not just conceptualized, it is a given at the level of the perception of individual cows, although not necessarily in a clearly articulated form. Thus, the universal is a principle of intelligibility present even at the level of perception, for it is an intrinsic part of reality without which knowledge would be impossible.

Moderate Realism in Indian Traditions

The most vocal opponent of this view has been the Buddhists. Although antirealism has been the dominant position within this tradition, we will see attempts among Indian and Tibetan followers to transform Dharmakīrti's rejection of the reality of universals into a moderate realist view that accepts universals but refuses their reification. Other Indian schools have also developed modified views on the topic.

Kumārila offers a moderate interpretation of Nyāya extreme realism. Like moderate realists, Kumārila attempts to find a middle ground between extreme realism and its rejection. The problem with the Nyāya view is that it fails to convincingly explain the relation between kinds and individuals. Once universals and individuals are taken apart, the problem is how to reconnect them. Since we do not perceive them apart (nobody has seen cowness apart from a cow), they must be connected in some way. The Nyāya solution, the relation of inherence, is obviously ad hoc. Kumārila's view is an attempt to retain a realist view of universals without going to the extreme of radical separation between individuals and their universals.

He achieves this by creating a new type of relation that combines the two modes of relation, real and conceptual. His view is that universals and individuals are mutually dependent. One cannot be without the other. Therefore, individuals and universals are not externally related (as the Nyāya assert) but internally through a relation of identity in difference (*bedhābedha*).[26] Although a universal is objectively different from its individuals (being permanent and partless), it is also conceptually identical with them. It is said to have a relation of identical nature (*tādātmya*) with those (the individuals).

Nevertheless, Kumārila's Mīmāṃsā realism is strong enough to disqualify it as genuine moderate realism. The Mīmāṃsā view considers universals to be permanent, partless, and omnipresent. Hence, its conception is quite similar to that of the Nyāya. It is, in fact, an attempt to rid the Nyāya view of its most extreme positions. It is more an attempt to avoid the main difficulty in the Nyāya system (i.e., relating universals to particulars) than a real alternative to the extreme realism of the Nyāya.

A more genuine form of moderate realism is held by some Jain philosophers such as Samantabhadra. He describes generality and particularity as relative notions.[27] That is, nothing is absolutely a universal. Only aspects or modalities of substances can be either universals or individuations, according to the context. Thus, the difference between universals and individuations is neither absolute nor purely conceptual. Universals and individuations exist, but not independent from each other. Universals cannot exist independent from the substances they characterize. By themselves they are pure abstractions, separable only in thought.

Why Bother with Universals?

Two of the most striking points about the various theories of universals are the abstruse character of the discussion and the persistence of the problem. Despite centuries of sustained philosophical effort and numerous claims to final solutions, the question of universals has remained "unsolved." Under these circumstances it is a great temptation to ignore the problem, as did thinkers during the Enlightenment.

During the sixteenth and seventeenth centuries the shift away from metaphysics to a greater emphasis on empirical enquiry became distinct. This shift meant that scholasticism and the problems of universals were increasingly left aside. Concordantly, the prominent role of philosophy, previously the primary source of knowledge other than Christian revelation, changed. Once science displaced religion as the leading worldview, the task of the philosopher was no longer to capture the essence of things in a *logos* but to define a clear and precise language as a tool for scientific inquiry. Under the influence of the new scientific spirit, philosophers became increasingly skeptical about the possibility of finding the real essence of things. They considered it completely arbitrary to choose certain properties among the many properties of a horse and declare them to constitute the essence of horse.

This skepticism, however, does not successfully avoid the problem of universals. Rather it follows the antirealist rejection of universals. In accordance with the new scientific spirit, the British empiricists hold as almost self-evident that real universals do not exist. Their arguments do not attempt to demonstrate this point. Rather taking it for granted, they attempt to demonstrate compatibility between the nonexistence of universals and the objectivity of scientific activity. Locke, for example, says, "Since all things that exist are merely particulars, how come we by general terms?"[28] If the philosopher is able to provide an account of general terms without using universals, the case against real universals may be taken as established.

Modern thinking is characterized by such a move away from ontology toward a more epistemologically or linguistically oriented approach. In contemporary discussions, universals are understood less as elements of reality and more as concepts through which we deal with reality. Like Indian philosophers, contemporary analytical thinkers often focus on this linguistic approach in their discussion of universals. For them, universals are discussed in relation to general terms. The question is no longer "does redness exist?" but "what does 'redness' mean?"[29] In making this move, however, the problem of universals is neither solved nor bypassed but relocated to a new context. Therefore, the problem of universals keeps recurring, prompting thinkers to constantly reopen the question. Let us do just this in relation to Indian and Tibetan Buddhist traditions.

Our discussion of universals continues in Chapter 7 with an analysis of Dharmakīrti's antirealism. There, I describe it as a conceptualism based on a resemblance theory of universals. This is followed in Chapter 8 with the Sa-gya interpretation of Dharmakīrti's conceptualism, since this tradition follows Dharmakīrti's antirealism quite closely. Chapter 9 discusses Ge-luk moderate realism, an attempt to solve the difficulties inherent in Dharmakīrti's position. Moderate realism has its own predicament as well, however, as we will see. The analysis of universals concludes in Chapter 10 with a closer historical look at the causes and reasons for the proliferation of realist interpretations of Dharmakīrti in Tibet. There, I show that, though these interpretations differ from Dharmakīrti's original system, they should be understood less as corruptions of Dharmakīrti's ideas than as attempts to correct their deficiencies.

7

Dharmakīrti on Universals

Logic and Ontology

Dharmakīrti's fame is mostly due to his contributions to Indian logic, the part of Indian philosophy that focuses on the distinction between correct and incorrect types of reasoning. So, a complete study of Dharmakīrti's thought ought to examine fully his doctrines of logic and relate them to his ontology, epistemology, and philosophy of language. Such a task exceeds the purview of this work, which more narrowly addresses the interface between Indian and Tibetan traditions concerning more strictly epistemological matters. For this reason, I do not consider the relation between Dharmakīrti's ontology and his theory of logical reasoning. Still, to contextualize the views of Tibetan interpreters on universals I examine some passages on logic that directly relate to universals. Consideration of the most delicate points of Dharmakīrti's logic, such as his presentation of the reasoning of (identical) essence (*svabhāvahetu, rang bzhin gyi rtags*),[1] I have had to leave aside.

This choice is based essentially on practical considerations, but it rests on methodological and interpretative reasons as well. While Dharmakīrti is a logician, he is a conceptualist philosopher as well. His ontology should not be subordinated to considerations of logic or dialectics, since for Dharmakīrti dialectics is concerned with the conceptual, which is unreal. In other words, logic does not bear directly on reality but concerns only conceptuality. Logic applies only to conceptually constructed pseudo-entities that are superimposed on reality, not to reality itself. Indeed, the ontological implications of Dharmakīrti's logical doctrines may be in tension with his ontological doctrines. Hence, in a discussion of ontology, such logical doctrines should not be given as much weight as the passages directly relevant to ontology.

This interpretative strategy, which is primarily heuristic and so must await further confirmation, has philosophical implications. Although a focus on logic does not necessarily lead to a different view of ontology, it certainly favors the development of a realist interpretation. As we will see,[2] some elements in Dharmakīrti's logic do tend toward a more realistic ontology. Nevertheless, following Śākya Chok-den's distinction between theoretical and practical considerations and its implications for the inferential process,[3] it is possible to explain these more realistic elements in a way compatible with the antirealism depicted here as Dharmakīrti's view.

Dharmakīrti's Arguments Against Realism

Against Nyāya realism, Dharmakīrti develops a conceptualist theory of universals. The essential difference between the two lies in that, whereas for the Nyāya universals are real, for Dharmakīrti they are not. Dharmakīrti holds that universals have only nominal existence. They are constructed by conceptuality on the basis of our experiences of resemblances. In short, they are generally characterized phenomena.

Dharmakīrti offers several arguments against the Nyāya philosophy of universals in the third chapter of his *Commentary.* There he argues that the universals posited by the Nyāya are unreal for the following reason: Since universals are taken by Nyāya to exist separately from their particulars, universals cannot be related to their particulars. This is so because, for Dharmakīrti, two phenomena can be related in only two ways: Either they have an identical nature such as being impermanent and being a thing, or they are distinct but related through a causal connection. For the Nyāya, universals exist separately from their instances. Hence, a universal cannot have a relation of identical essence with its instances. Neither can it have a causal connection with them, since universals and particulars coexist (cause and effect are always sequential for Dharmakīrti). Hence, they must be unrelated.[4] But, by definition, a universal is related to individuals because individuals instantiate it.

Thus, universals as posited by realists have contradictory attributes, a clear sign that they fail to satisfy the identity conditions of real phenomena.[5] Therefore, they are not real. Dharmakīrti explains: "If [this universal] is distinct from [its particulars], then it is unrelated to them. Therefore, it is established as being essenceless. It does not follow [from that] that nonexistents are kinds because they do not depend on their [particulars]. Therefore, this kind which is unreal and constructed on the basis of [real] entities is revealed by words for the sake of relating to particulars."[6] Universals are not real because they are not part of the causal network that is reality. If we were to inventory the elements composing reality we would find no universals. Only when a thinking mind intervenes do universals come to be. Then categorical notions such as being a color and being impermanent become relevant. Before this we just have individual things causally connected. Therefore, universals cannot possibly have the same reality as the objects that are part of this causal network.

This rejection of real universals is seized upon by the Nyāya opponents as a complete denial of general concepts. If universals are unreal, they do not exist at all. In that case nonexistents such as the horns of a rabbit could be universals. What then would be the difference between saying "Bossie is a cow" and "Bossie is the horn of a rabbit"? Moreover, where would the normativity necessary for knowledge come from if reality is reducible to a collection of individuals?

Dharmakīrti does not deny that knowledge involves norms, but he holds that, in a world of individuals, norms do not derive from real universals. Like Sellars, he holds that norms derive from our use of concepts. Unlike Sellars, however, he is not ready to completely eliminate any reference to abstract entities. Universals are not totally nonexistent, but they are fictional conceptual constructs. They do not have full ontological status but they still exist in some weak sense of the word. We may wonder why Dharmakīrti, in opposition to nominalists such as Ockham, Goodman, Sellars, and Quine still want to retain abstract entities? Why reintroduce universals in a world of individuals?

The answer, I believe, is to be found in the epistemological nature of Dharmakīrti's enterprise. As we will see later, epistemology is the study of knowledge in relation to its object. Dharmakīrti wants to account for two forms of knowledge: perception and conception. The former can be accounted for in terms of real individuals. The object of the latter, however, is more problematic. To account for the object of conceptual knowledge, Dharmakīrti must introduce some abstract entities. Since they are the objects of conceptual knowledge, universals must be accepted to exist at least in the sense of being the object of a valid cognitive activity. This validity does not entail, however, that universals are parts of the fabric of the world. For example, the thought that Bossie is a cow is mistaken in imputing a universal on a particular, but this distortion has some validity. Hence, contrary to a nonexistent, its *relata,* the universal cowness exists, not as a real thing, but as a fictional object of a valid cognitive activity. To use Dharmakīrti's language, universals are generally characterized phenomena superimposed onto causal reality. Dharmakīrti explains: "The distinction 'this is a universal, this is a particular,' is the object of the imagination. Even the distinction among characteristics is conceived with regard to just that on the basis of an exclusion of other [phenomena]."[7] Universals do not exist as objects awaiting human discovery but are mind dependent. They are the objects posited by the conceptual distinctions formed through encounters with individuals, which in and of themselves do not share anything in common. Thus, for Dharmakīrti and his antirealist followers, universals do not have any extramental reality, they are not completely nonexistent either. They are constructs, the fictional and convenient objects of valid conceptual activities, and as such they have the same semantic role as the Nyāya real kinds.

The Roles of Universals

As we recall, the role of universals is double: semantic and epistemological. First, universals are the *relata* of general terms. They qualify an element already introduced into the realm of discourse; for example, when we say "this is a cow." This semantic role raises the following question: What is the meaning of general terms? The Nyāya answer is that general terms are meaningful because they signify general properties. This answer is unproblematic for the Nyāya school, since it holds that general properties are real. Dharmakīrti refuses this reification but the epistemological nature of his project obliges him to keep universals in some attenuated form. His solution allows universals to be the unreal but necessary semantic respondents of general terms. Since universals are fictional constructs, there is no danger of a multiplication of entities. The existence of unreal constructed universals does not compromise the Buddhist ontology of causally connected individuals. Universals are not real, but they do exist enough to give meaning to general terms and allow for predication.

Second, universals are understood by most Indian epistemologists to play an important epistemological role. Dharmakīrti refuses to follow the Nyāya account of knowledge, arguing that perception relates only to individuals. He agrees, however, that conceptual knowledge, that is, inference, bears on universals. How can he then explain the success of inference if he denies the reality of universals? To examine his answer, let us examine a typical example of inference: We see smoke coming from a hill and infer that there is fire. The argument can be formally stated in this way: On the smoky hill there is a fire because there is smoke, just as in the case of putting pine needles in a camp fire. In this reasoning, a property (fireness) is inferred on a given locus (hill) on the basis of its relation with another property (smokeness) understood in an example.

Indian logicians understand this inferential process to involve the pervasion (*vyāpti, khyab pa*) of one universal by another one. We do not infer a particular fire from a particular smoke. We do see a particular smoke on the hill but the inference does not proceed from this particular smoke to a particular fire. Otherwise, we would have to know already that particular fire and there would be nothing left to infer. Rather, on the basis of the perception of a particular smoke, we infer the presence of a general property, smokeness, and from it the presence of another, fireness. That is, when we see a particular smoke on the hill we realize that smokeness is instantiated on this hill and deduce that fireness must be as well. Therefore, the inferential process starts from the particular and moves to the universal before going back to the particular. It is based on the apprehension of universals that are connected and applied to a particular situation.

Since Buddhists deny the reality of universal properties, how can they explain our successful inference of general properties? The Buddhist answer, first proposed by Dignāga and later expanded by Dharmakīrti, is the famous *apoha* (exclusion) theory about which we will have much more to say. Suffice it for now to indicate the essential point of this theory, which is that concepts do not exist naturally but are constructed negatively (hence, the name of the theory) and linguistically. Thought relates to its objects, general properties or universals, which are not real. Nevertheless, such a construct is not completely nonexistent either. It differs from the object of a dream or a fantasy in that it is intersubjectively valid. It is a convenient fiction, a shared myth that allows us to function in the world. Such a construct is constructed by thought (*kalpanā, rtog pa,* from the Sanskrit root *kḷp,* to prepare, arrange, construct, etc.) on the basis of language.[8] This imaginative construction amounts to less than an apprehension of the objectively given, and yet, it is more than a purely private subjective imposition. It is a kind of public creation, a second-order reality, different from both the given of unmistaken perceptual experience and the purely imaginary realm of errors, dreams, and illusions. This intermediary realm of conceptuality is social; it is made of agreed on fictions, myths, and convenient labels, all of which are created in relation to language. Such constructs do not exist really, and yet, they are "not shattered when reality is properly understood."[9]

Moreover, according to Dignāga's *apoha* theory, such a construction is negative in nature. When we think of a particular fire, for example, we are not thinking about a real individual object. All that we are considering is a general property, fireness, which we know to be instantiated in a particular situation. This general property is not given, but constructed in a negative way by excluding the individual from the class (nonfire) to which it does not belong. Hence, in the inferential process we do not come to know of any real entity, but we conclude to the presence of, say, a fire by eliminating the deniability that fire is absent. Hayes articulates this very well: "We are not to conclude that x (standing for the locus on which fire is inferred) is qualified by the fire universal, but rather we are to conclude that x is qualified by the presence of at least one particular fire, which can also be expressed as the deniability of the absence of every particular fire."[10] Inference, the only conceptual form of knowledge in Buddhist epistemology, does not concern real entities but constructs, which are linguistically constructed on the basis of a process of elimination. These pseudo-entities are similar to the universal asserted by the Nyāya realist with two important differences: (1) they are not real, for nothing real exists over and above individuals, and (2) they are not positive entities. This last feature is the central point of the *apoha* theory. A universal is not a positive entity but is constructed by eliminating all the features whose presence can be denied in every particular that instantiates it. Before going into the details of this ingenious theory, let us further explore Dharmakīrti's position on the problem of universals and further characterize the specific contribution of our author to Buddhist epistemology.

Universals and Similarities

It is often said that Dharmakīrti is a nominalist. Dravid, for example, says about him: "However, it must be granted that the Buddhist is the most thoroughgoing nominalist in the history of thought."[11] As we have seen, it is difficult to give a strict definition of nominalism and distinguish it from conceptualism. My point here is not to quibble over whether Dharmakīrti is actually a nominalist or a conceptualist. Rather, we need to understand the type of antirealism that Dharmakīrti holds regarding universals. In doing so, we will see that Dravid's representation of Dharmakīrti is misguided, for it overlooks several of Dharmakīrti's contributions to Dignāga's system, such as his development of a resemblance theory and his emphasis on the role of mental events. On the basis of these elements I describe Dharmakīrti as a conceptualist.

According to Dravid's interpretation, Dignāga and Dharmakīrti hold that the real is completely unknowable and that, therefore, the only kind of knowledge we can have is the kind we construct. Concepts are the life of knowledge but have no objective counterparts. They are, according to Dravid, the products of creative thought without any objective support in the real world onto which they are arbitrarily projected.[12] Real things, Dravid *dixit*, offer no support whatsoever for our a priori projections since "identity and diversity, similarity and dissimilarity are attributed to them by our thought. Thus, the identity of cows, for example, as also their differences from horses, etc., are merely conceptual."[13]

Dravid's presentation of the Buddhist view of universals, according to which language and conceptuality are arbitrary and a priori projections, is not without some basis. Dignāga presents a system based on the distinction between individual real things and conceptual constructs. As the initiator of this system, Dignāga sharply emphasizes the gap between the two domains. He also stresses the constructed and linguistic nature of universals, without providing much discussion of their objective basis. For example, while discussing inference,[14] Dignāga describes the process as proceeding almost entirely in the conceptual space of reasons and justifications. Inference here involves the deduction of concepts from other concepts on the basis of a conceptual hierarchy resting on linguistic conventions. Any word divides the world of concepts into two: those that are excluded and those that are not. The excluded group is an open-ended set of contrary possibilities that cannot be inferred from the nodal point defined by a particular word. The nonexcluded group, is further divided into the concepts that are implied by a particular expression, the higher or coextensive concepts in the conceptual hierarchy, and those that imply it, the lower concepts. Thus, using a word allows us to exclude certain expressions and imply others. For example, using the word "tree" allows us to exclude an object from the classes formed by expression such as "human" or "animal." It also allows us to infer from its use that further expressions higher in the conceptual hierarchy such as "material" or "impermanent" can be used to characterize the object. In using concepts, however, we do not characterize things positively but only locate them negatively in a linguistically constructed conceptual space.

This explanation of the inferential process is nominalist in its emphasis on the linguistic nature of concepts. People use concepts on the basis of socially transmitted linguistic usages accepted in a given community. The logical links between concepts are not based on a connection between real properties but are mostly a matter of linguistically embedded social practices.[15] Hence, to a certain extent Dravid's description is not without some basis, despite its lack of emphasis on the social nature of conceptuality. It does capture Dignāga's insistence that universals, the objects of conceptual constructions, are not given but linguistically constructed.

Dravid's interpretation, however, completely fails to appraise the particularity of Dharmakīrti's project; namely, the defense of Dignāga's *apoha* theory against intense Hindu criticism. Dharmakīrti's project is not just to restate Dignāga's view but to show that the rejection of real universals does not exclude the possibility of grounding knowledge in reality. Although concepts relate only to fictional properties, they are causally related to our experiences of reality. Hence, Dravid's description is particularly inappropriate to Dharmakīrti, who is no extreme nominalist, at least in Dravid's sense of the term. Dharmakīrti agrees with Dignāga that concepts are linguistically constructed but holds that this construction has an objective basis, the experiences of resemblance that causally effective things present us with. One of Dharmakīrti's main contributions to Buddhist epistemology is establishing this basis as a way to defend Dignāga, who had not given a clear answer to the charge that in a world of particulars conceptuality can be only arbitrary.

The unreality of universal properties, which is a clear implication of the *apoha* philosophy, does not imply that these mentally created distinctions are totally arbitrary, contrary to what Dravid thinks. In this respect, Dharmakīrti and his Nyāya adversaries agree: Conceptuality and language are not arbitrary. Once conventions have been established, we apply general terms, such as "flower" or "cow," on the basis of some criterion or justification. The two sides disagree on how to explain the perceived regularities of concepts and words. The Nyāya view is realist in that it holds that this nonarbitrary application of general terms to individual things can be explained only if these things share a common property. This is a recurrence theory of universals since it asserts that the application of general concepts and terms can be explained only in reference to the recurrence of general properties in individual objects. In this theory, properties are primary. Resemblances between individual things, based on their shared universal attributes, are secondary.

Dharmakīrti, by contrast, defends a resemblance theory of universals that holds that concepts are based on similarities from which properties are construed. Dharmakīrti describes these similarities (*sādṛśya, 'dra ba*)[16] among things in terms of their having "a [common] effect."[17] Similarity between cows, for example, comes from their capacity to perform similar functions, not from the inherence of a universal cowness.[18] For example, we see large beings that provide milk, carry loads, produce a manure usable as fuel, and so forth. We are struck by the similarities, and we construct the unitary concept of cowness to account for these similarities. These similarities in experience are primary and provide the basis for the construction of properties. Thus, contrary to what an extreme nominalist thinks and contrary to what Dravid holds Dharmakīrti to be saying, concepts do have a basis in reality, the similarities in our experience of reality. These resemblances exist not because we think they do but due to the nature of our experiences. Dharmakīrti says: "Certain [things] are essentially (*svabhāvena, rang bzhin gyis*) determined as producing common results such as being contemplated as the same [object], being understood as having the [same] function, etc., even though they are distinct, just as sense bases, etc. For example, certain medicines, taken separately or together, despite being distinct, are seen to cure fever, etc.—[whereas] other things do not."[19] Dharmakīrti argues that, despite being distinct, things can produce similar results on the basis of which abstract properties are constructed. These similarities are not our own projection but exist essentially or naturally, as is made clear by Dharmakīrti's use of the term *svabhāvena* (*rang bzhin gyis*). To illustrate his point, Dharmakīrti examines two cases, namely, the production of the vision of a flash of lightning and the efficacy of medicinal herbs, in which a seeming commonality can be explained without any recourse to real universals. Since the second example is clearer, let me examine it first. Various medicinal plants such as the *harīkata* and the *abhaya* can cure fever through their natural therapeutic powers. The common element in these plants is their remedial effect. Nothing over and above such resemblances regarding their medicinal effects is required to explain how these plants are all remedies.[20]

The first example is more surprising: Dharmakīrti compares seeing things as instantiating a similar property to the production of a visual experience of lightning through the cooperation of many causal factors such as sense basis, object, and attentiveness.[21] At first this does not seem to be a very good example, for sense, object, and the like do not resemble each other. However, the example becomes clearer when we understand that Dharmakīrti is not using it to illustrate similarities but another important point of his doctrine, one that a recurrence theory of universals tends to hide: Things that are similar remain different. This is so because similarities are a matter of degree. We perceive things, which are different, to be more or less similar. Therefore, resemblances cannot depend on identities, for these do not allow degrees. The essential likeness that things share is a comparative likeness, not an identity. The pine and the maple perform similar functions in that they are more similar to each other than they are to nontrees. On the basis of real things that resemble each other and yet are different, we create concepts such as "being a tree," "being a medicinal plant," and so forth.

Dharmakīrti's position in its general outline is not unusual. Many philosophers have asserted a resemblance view of universals. The most famous of these in the West are Hobbes, Berkeley, and Hume. Although their views are not identical, these three share the idea that only particulars are real and that general terms are to be explained in relation to concepts derived from similar uses of real particulars resembling each other. Hume says: "When we have found a resemblance among several objects, that often occur to us, we apply the same name to all of them, whatever differences we may observe in the degrees of their quantity and quality, and whatever differences may appear among them."[22] Hume primarily considers similarities among objects. Dharmakīrti holds a similar view, with one important difference.

Dharmakīrti does not spell out similarities in relation to the characteristics of the object, but in relation to our experiences of them. We might expect him to explain functional similarities in terms of observable effects, like producing milk and being able to carry a load. Instead, he refers to certain things as naturally producing cognitive results such as being understood as one kind and being known to have the same function. Dharmakīrti is positing resemblances among objects in terms of the perceptions they generate. This is surprising, for it appears to make Dharmakīrti's account of resemblances circular. Moreover, two levels of discussion seem to be collapsing into one: the level at which objects have functional similarities, and the level at which perceptions apprehend them as having these similarities.

Dharmakīrti spells out similarities in terms of our perceptions to clarify that similarities are not things existing "out there" but products of our interactions with the world. Strictly speaking, there is no such thing as a similarity,[23] no special entity that supports our judgment of similarity. Otherwise, similarities would be real properties. There are only similar perceptual experiences. Still, these perceptions are not arbitrary but are the direct results of the causal capacities of objects. Moreover, these perceptions are accurate reflections of reality. Hence, they testify to the objective basis for perceiving similarities; namely, individual objects with similar causal capacities.[24] This explanation points to the fact that the similarity Dharmakīrti has in mind cannot be understood in terms of things. It is not a similarity in color or shape but rather a similarity in our experience of them. We are struck directly by similarities and differences and our concepts are artificial ways to deal with this preconceptual experience. Thus, even our concepts of similarity and difference are constructs, but they are the closest to our actual experiences.

To further understand this twist in Dharmakīrti's discussion of similarity we have to replace it in its original context: a discussion with the Nyāya. The realism of this school is extreme. Not only do its proponents hold that the existence of real universals is required to explain knowledge, they also insist that even the causal process leading to knowledge cannot be accounted for in the absence of universals. Compelled by their extreme realist view, they tend to collapse the cognitive and ontological aspects of resemblances. They want to explain cognition with a single factor, a universal, as both object and cause of cognition. For example, when we think of several animals as being cows, there must be a single factor, the universal cowness, that is both the object and the cause of this cognition.[25] To Dharmakīrti's assertion that thinking is produced in the absence of universals, Naiyāyikas object that thinking about the unity of distinct individuals would be causeless.

Dharmakīrti disagrees, for conceptions of things as sharing a common property are produced in dependence on individual objects.[26] In our example, we see individual animals and develop an idea of cowness. This conception is caused indirectly by the individual animals we have encountered. The Nyāya, however, is not satisfied with this answer. It argues that since a conception of cowness conceives a single object, its cause must also be a single object.[27]

Dharmakīrti's response follows the Naiyāyikas' in collapsing the two levels of similarities, physical and epistemic. Responding to the Nyāya argument, Dharmakīrti describes the relevant similarities that account for the construction of a common property as the apprehension of things as similar. His answer explains simultaneously how causes without any common element can produce something and how the apprehension of different things as being the same can arise without any real common element. Both are possible since things have similarities in their causal capacities and thereby induce in us the experience of their similarities and dissimilarities. According to Dharmakīrti, this is our basic experience, and it is the basis for the conceptual activities through which we construct properties.

The recurrence theorist has a classical objection to make against such a resemblance theory: Without a property with respect to which it is possible to evaluate similarities and dissimilarities, it makes no sense to speak of similarities. Bossie is similar to other cows in being a cow, but dissimilar in other regards such as, for instance, having more spots. This objection is true but not decisive. It is true that we cannot evaluate similarities without a conceptual scheme, but we may still be struck at a preconceptual level by resemblances. In the final analysis, Dharmakīrti points to the sheer giveness of this type of experience as providing the basis in reality for the construction of our conceptual frameworks.

An Assessment of Resemblance Theory

Before moving on to the Tibetan analyses of this theory, allow me to briefly pursue my philosophical investigation into Dharmakīrti's resemblance theory, highlighting its merits as well as some of its problems. One advantage we have seen already. A resemblance theory can explain that the likeness we perceive among objects is a similarity, not an identity. Another strong point of resemblance theories is they allow for the possibility of overlapping typologies. Realist accounts, by contrast, presuppose a fixed order of things that may be either understood or ignored.

A resemblance theory allows for the possibility that different classifications can be right in their own ways. Things have a plurality of functions and so can be perceived as similar in various ways, according to the kinds of effects considered. For instance, the similarity of different types of wood can be appraised from different standpoints: the sample's constitution, its ability to perform certain function, its beauty, and so forth. Therefore, in a resemblance theory things can be categorized differently according to our aims and expectations. These diverging typologies are not arbitrary but limited by the essential qualities of things. The functionality of things imposes constraints on our experience of similarities and hence on our classificatory schemes.

A resemblance theory has another advantage. Its explanation of common concepts as based on similarities parallels the way we learn concepts. A cognitive psychologist describes the way in which we actually learn through exemplars: "Many experiments have shown that categories appear to be encoded in the mind neither by means of lists of each individual member of the category, nor by means of a list of formal criteria necessary and sufficient for category membership, but, rather, in terms of a prototype of a typical category member. The most cognitively economical code for a category is, in fact, a concrete image of an average category member."[28] We do not learn by rules or criteria but by exemplars which we connect with each other through similarities and dissimilarities. When we encounter a new phenomenon, we are struck first by its similarities and dissimilarities with other things we know already. Thus, our categorical scheme emerges out of a fuzzy network of resemblances that we pin down by constructing properties. Such a network of similarities sufficiently accounts for our success in identifying corresponding objects or activities. Real universals are of no use in explaining this process. This argument refutes recurrence theories like the Nyāya that hold universals to participate in the learning process by causing our conceptions of commonality.

This argument does not refute all recurrence theories, however, for not all realists need be committed to such a view. A modern Platonist could argue that the inability of universals to participate in the learning process is irrelevant. Universals are meant to provide objective norms and criteria irrespective of the way in which humans come to know them. Humans may learn by resemblances more than by rules. This hardly proves that such criteria do not exist. Thus, the argument from learning does not solve the problem of universals. It strikes at the heart of only a certain type of realism, the one Dharmakīrti is directly addressing.

Resemblance theories have major drawbacks as well as advantages. For instance, such a theory does not present a very convincing account of natural kinds. We feel that certain things are similar to others in a more substantial way than merely sharing similarities. For example, we think of individual cows as intrinsically similar simply due to their biological constitution. Sharing a natural kind, such individuals possess a similarity that is difficult to explain in terms of functional similarities. The similarity of cows is more than the mere fact that they produce milk. Dharmakīrti's resemblance theory finds it extremely cumbersome to account for this. Suppose someone produces a machine able to perform all the functions of cows. Would anyone consider this machine actually to be a cow? This is not likely.

This argument is not decisive either, for the resemblance theorist can answer in the following way. First, perhaps we would be ready to call such a machine a cow. Second, even if we were not ready to call it a cow, this would not prove that natural kinds are the basis of our categorical schemes. It would demonstrate just our unwillingness to change some of the notions that are more central to our ways of dealing with the world. Hence, here again, the discussion does not end. Both sides keep elaborating more sophisticated theories and arguments. Like many other philosophical questions, the problem of universals is no closer to resolution than it was in Plato's or in Dharmakīrti's times. Some find this lack of resolution frustrating. Others, such as myself, find such ongoing discussion an enriching way to keep the mind open and flexible. In any case, I hope the reader is convinced by now of at least one point; namely, that Dharmakīrti's philosophy is not a form of extreme nominalism. Contrary to what Dravid, Stcherbastky, and others have asserted, Dharmakīrti acknowledges that our concepts have a basis in reality. That basis is the complicated network of resemblances between individuals. Whether such a view is correct or not is open to debate. Before doing this, however, we should attempt to get Dharmakīrti right and avoid reading him through the eyes of his Nyāya opponents.

Here we have reached an important point in our investigation. Dharmakīrti's view of universals is central to the later Buddhist philosophical tradition. This theory of universals delineates the later Buddhist philosophy of language and underlines its ontology. The theory also has important epistemological repercussions. The remaining chapters analyze the implications of Dharmakīrti's philosophy and the conflicting interpretations to which it has given rise. First, the debate between Ge-luk realists and their Sa-gya opponents that dominates the reception of Dharmakīrti's philosophy in Tibet reveals some of the difficulties and contradictions in his system. The interpretations offered by remarkable thinkers such as Kay-drup and Śākya Chok-den reflect more than just episodes in the intellectual history of Tibet. They reveal aspects of Dharmakīrti's system that may not be obvious to modern interpreters. Let us start with an analysis of Sa-gya antirealism, focusing on Sa-paṇ's arguments and Śākya Chok-den's analysis of predication.

8

Sa-gya Antirealism and the Problems of Predication

Sa-paṇ's Refutation of Realism

This chapter investigates the tradition of Tibetan commentators who, following Sa-paṇ, have adopted a strictly antirealist interpretation of Dharmakīrti's philosophy.[1] This tradition has been confronted by the problem of how thought and reality can be related in the absence of real universals. If reality is limited to individuals, how can thoughts such as inference, which rely on general entities, successfully operate?

Dharmakīrti answers by attempting to link conceptuality to reality through experience. As we will see, this explanation is problematic. Hence, much of the later history of Dharmakīrti's tradition is an attempt by his followers to provide more satisfactory answers. Starting in India and continuing in Tibet with much greater vigor, a tradition of realist thinkers (such as Cha-ba, Gyel-tsap, and Kay-drup) has offered a realist reinterpretation of Dharmakīrti's thought. This tradition attempts to solve the problem of the validity of thought by attenuating the strength of Dharmakīrti's antirealist stance. Sa-paṇ and his followers also attempt to account for the validity of thought, but without sacrificing the rejection of real universals, which they consider the cornerstone of his thought. This chapter investigates the ways in which Sa-gya thinkers have dealt with the difficulties raised by their rigorous view.

The antirealist stance of the Sa-gya tradition is a natural consequence of its ontology.[2] Only individuals (*gsal ba, vyakti*) are real. Thus universals, being generally characterized phenomena and not specific individuals, can be only unreal. They are conceptual characteristics (known as *distinguishers, ldog pa, vyāvṛtti*) through which we categorize things. The reason generally characterized phenomena are unreal is they do not meet the three sets of identity conditions delineated by Dharmakīrti.[3] Śākya Chok-den, for example, defines a universal as "that unique distinguisher which is the mere preclusion of [things of] discordant kinds."[4] A universal is a distinguisher;[5] that is, it is not a real property but a negatively constructed one. For example, the universal cowness is not some essential property that all cows would share but merely the exclusion of all cows from a class (noncow) to which they do not belong.

These antirealist thinkers target the moderate realist views of their contemporaries. Sa-paṇ in particular attacks a disguised form of moderate realism according to which individual blue objects are the individuations of "mere blue" (*sngo tsam*). This "mere blue" is posited by some Tibetan realists as a real but negative property that subsumes all particular instances of blue.[6] This form of moderate realism, which we will examine in Bo-dong, distinguishes between real negative properties, which are allowable, and positive properties. Those are the kind of overreified universals that are not allowed in Buddhist epistemology. They are posited by Hindu realists and are the targets of Dharmakīrti's arguments.

For Sa-paṇ, such a distinction cannot be maintained. Any assertion that universals exist is bound to face the same problems incurred by Hindu realists. Let us examine briefly some of his rather abstruse arguments, which relate to Dharmakīrti's refutation of the Sāṃkhya. As we recall, the Sāṃkhya differs from the Nyāya in being partially monist. Whereas the Nyāya holds that individuals and universals are different, the Sāṃkhya holds them to be identical in their essence. Individuals are manifestations of the underlying Nature (*prakṛti, rang bzhin*). Hence, they are of the same essence as their unique universal, which is the ground for their being.

Against this position, Dharmakīrti argues that a real entity cannot be fully present in different instances.[7] If Nature were fully present in its instances, either they would become one or Nature would be manifold. The first possibility is excluded because things having distinct spatio-temporal identities are not identical. The second possibility is similarly excluded because Nature, being the universal ground of all phenomena, cannot be multiple. Therefore, individuals and their universal cannot be identical. Moreover, argues Dharmakīrti, if individuals were identical with their universal (Nature), they would lose their distinct identities. A rose and a tulip would have the same essence of flower and thus be identical. This is so because, their Nature being one and indivisible, there can be no distinction between the essence of the two flowers. Since they have the same essence, they must be the same thing (i.e., the same substance).

Buddhist moderate realists hold a different but related view. Their view, which will be explored in the next chapter, is that individuals and universals are the "same entity" (*ngo bo gcig*). By this they do not mean that universals and individuals that instantiate them are identical, as one would expect it. Nor do they mean, like the Sāṃkhya, that the universal is totally present in its instances. Rather, they use this term technically to designate the type of relation between individuals and universals implied by their moderate realism. Individuals and universals have the same entity because the latter are instantiated by and cannot exist apart from the former. Although this sounds similar to the Sāṃkhya view, there is an important difference in that Buddhist moderate realism is not monist. Accordingly, there is a plurality of universals. Moreover, these universals are not partless, permanent, and ubiquitous, contrary to the Nature posited by the Sāṃkhya. For Buddhist realists, universals do not abide entirely in their instances. At some level, universals and their instances are distinguishable, despite their substantial identity. This differentiates this view from Sāṃkhya monism.[8]

Sa-paṇ, however, refuses to make these distinctions. For him, this form of realism is a disguised acceptance of the Sāṃkhya view according to which individual things are the manifestations of the universal they instantiate. Therefore, Sa-paṇ argues, Dharmakīrti's reasonings against the Sāṃkhya apply equally to this supposedly more moderate form, as follows. If individuations are substantially identical with their universals, they must appear and disappear together. For example, if all blue objects are substantially identical with the mere blue they instantiate, they all must be produced and disappear at the same time, for this is what Buddhists mean by substantial identity; that is, being the same thing.[9] The absurdity of this position shows that individuals cannot be substantially identical with their universals. Since they cannot be different either it follows that universals are not real.

Śākya Chok-den takes Sa-paṇ's refutation of Buddhist realism to apply to his Ge-luk adversaries. He adds some further arguments of his own: If yellow and the real universal color are substantially identical, then either other colors are substantially identical with yellow (and are yellow) or they are substantially different from yellow and therefore, from color itself. This latter view is not acceptable, for it would follow that the others would not be part of the category color. Śākya Chok-den's conclusion is that the universal color is not to be understood in terms of substance but as a purely conceptual distinction.

Śākya Chok-den develops a similar argument concerning time. Imagine a jar existing at moment *t*. If this jar were substantially identical with jar in general then other jars existing at $t + 1$ would be either substantially identical with jar existing at *t* (which would then be permanent because of existing for more than a single moment), or substantially different and, therefore, substantially different from jar itself. For Ge-luk thinkers, the latter alternative is as unacceptable as the former. As moderate realists, they hold that individual jars are the real individuations of jar, which exists as a universal only in dependence on its instantiations.

All these arguments, which are typical of the highly technical, not to say arcane, style of philosophy that Tibetans have developed, hinge on the assimilation of the Buddhist moderate realist position to the Sāṃkhya view. This assimilation has considerable rhetorical power, for it amounts to accusing Buddhist realists to be philosophical heretics. Logically, however, it seems much less cogent and proceeds from a style of argumentation in which a debater forces conclusions on his adversary not in virtue of the latter's own position, but in relation to his own view. Sa-paṇ's or Śākya Chok-den's arguments are not drawn from the premises of their adversaries but from their own. For example, take the argument that if yellow and the real universal color are substantially identical, then either other colors are substantially identical with yellow (and are yellow) or they are substantially different from yellow and, therefore, from color itself. This argument works on the assumption that if *x* and *y* are substantially identical then *x* and *y* must be identical in all respects. This assumption certainly makes sense within an antirealist system. This is not, however, the view of the realists Śākya Chok-den is arguing against. It is his own assumption that he thrust on his adversaries on the ground that it corresponds to the way things are.

From the Buddhist realist's perspective, these arguments miss the crucial distinction between substantial identity and identity (more on this in the next chapter). Antirealists refuse to see that Dharmakīrti's arguments would apply to the Buddhist realists' view only if these thinkers held universals and individuations to be identical. For these thinkers, however, universals and their instances are substantially identical but they are not identical. Hence, Dharmakīrti's arguments do not apply directly to their view. Moreover, Dharmakīrti's arguments also presuppose that universals are partless entities that entirely abide in each of their instantiations, as the Sāṃkhya holds. This is not the Buddhist realists' view. Hence, they can claim in good faith that the reasonings directed at the Sāṃkhya do not apply to their own positions. This answer is obviously not final, for as we will see in the next chapter, the coherence of the distinction between identity and substantial identity is questionable. Nevertheless, the arguments developed by Sa-gya thinkers against Buddhist realism appear to be far from unproblematic.

Sa-gya thinkers seem to be on stronger grounds when they argue that realism is unsound as an interpretation of Dharmakīrti's ideas. Go-ram-ba denounces one of the main Ge-luk interpretive moves: that which differentiates universal (*spyi, sāmānya*) and generally characterized phenomena (*spyi mtshan, sāmānyalakṣaṇa*). No such distinction is ever made by Dharmakīrti, argues Go-ram-ba. On the contrary, Dharmakīrti repeatedly identifies these two. For example, Dharmakīrti specifies three types of generally characterized phenomena: "Since they rely on either thing, nonthing, [or] both, these universals are also threefold."[10] This division serves as a typology of both universals and generally characterized phenomena. It suggests no difference between the two. Therefore, their separation is without solid basis in Dharmakīrti's system. Universals can be no more real than generally characterized phenomena.

Go-ram-ba's controversy against his Ge-luk opponents sometimes takes a more sarcastic overtone, as when he bitingly remarks that several Ge-luk thinkers are too sheepish to even acknowledge their realism. They shy away from the term *real universals* (*spyi dngos po ba*), claiming that their view is that there are no real universals but that some universals are real.[11] Go-ram-ba says: "Some Tibetan [scholars say], 'No real universal of tree exists but we do accept that there is a common locus between the universal of tree and real things.' We shall refute [this position] by taking the tree that is the universal of individual trees as the subject [of refutation], in accordance with the screen of such words."[12] For Go-ram-ba, no amount of interpretive gimmicks can ever change the basic issue, which is that Dharmakīrti's system is incompatible with any realism whatsoever.[13] Go-ram-ba concludes his indictment of Buddhist realism by quoting from Śākyabuddhi's *Explanation*: "In [his] explanation of [Dharmakīrti's verse] 'this is distinguished from the others,'[14] Śākyabuddhi says: 'There is nothing whatsoever that is real and [can be called] a "universal."' Think whether this contradicts [your position] or not!"[15] Here Go-ram-ba reaffirms the antirealist commitment of Sa-paṇ and his disciples. Universals are not part of reality but are superimposed on it by thought and language. In the next pages, I examine the significance of this view in relation to the important question of predication.

Śākya Chok-den on Predication

Predication (*khyad gzhi khyad chos sbyar ba*) is often, and rightly so, thought to be an essential support of most forms of thinking. As we saw in the preceding chapters, most forms of thought relate to timeless entities (or pseudo-entities), called by Western philosophers *propositions*. For example, when several people (referring to the same object) say "this is a cow," they put forth statements that signify a single proposition: that this is a cow. Typically,[16] such a proposition is made of a subject (*chos can, dharmin*) of which a property or universal is predicated. This is the predicate (*chos, dharma*).[17]

In our example, the word "this" designates the basis or subject of which being a cow is predicated. This basis is called *substance* (*rdzas, dravya*) by Vaiśeṣikas and *distinguished* (*ldog pa, vyāvṛtti*) by Buddhists. The term *subject* is accepted by both Buddhist and non-Buddhist thinkers as ontologically neutral.[18] Matilal describes how this concept gradually evolved in India: "Nyāya and Buddhist logicians (notably Dignāga) developed the concept of *dharmin* 'property-possessor,' which was the nearest Indian analogue for a 'logical-subject'. This concept was regarded as neutral to ontological beliefs of the logicians."[19] Substance, as opposed to subject, is specific to particular systems. Since every Indian school has its own definition of *substance*, it is easier to refer to subject for the sake of discussion.

Realists feel that the structure of predication strongly supports their view that universals are real. They see thought as proceeding by subsuming particulars in more inclusive real properties. Antirealists have greater difficulty explaining this fundamental structure of thinking, since they deny the reality of properties. How can Buddhist antirealists explain predication?[20] Let us consider Śākya Chok-den's technical but piercing analysis.

Śākya Chok-den responds by making a fundamental difference between subject and predicate.[21] For him, predication does not relate two entities of the same ontological level, but conceptually differentiates a single subject. This entity is differentiated by negating the contradictory of what is being asserted in the predication. This is to say, predication does not relate two entities but excludes an individual object from being what it is not. When I say "this is a cow," I am only seemingly relating an individual to a property instantiated by this individual. More accurately, I am excluding an individual cow from being a noncow. Śākya Chok-den says: "When [something] is posited as being a universal and a distinguisher in relation to a subject, it is only a mental property *(blo chos)* in relation to that subject and cannot be a real property (*don chos*)."[22] In this explanation, predication does not entail two real entities. Only the individual is real. The universal is only a conceptual construct.

Similarly, when we predicate impermanence of several individual entities, we are not relating these entities to any shared real property. Rather, we consider them to share the common conceptual characterization of being impermanent. Or, to use a more Buddhist terminology, we say that they share a common exclusion from being permanent. Again the predicate is not a real thing but a conceptual construct. Therefore, Śākya Chok-den says: "When we say 'sound is impermanent' or 'sound is produced,' being produced and impermanent are taken from only a strictly eliminative point of view (*sel ngo*). They are universals (*spyi, sāmānya*), distinguishers (*ldog pa, vyāvṛtti*), eliminations of other (*gzhan sel, anyāpoha*) in relation to the subject sound taken from both elimination (*sel ngo*) and real (*snang ngo*)[23] points of view. Moreover, [both] expressions are definitively predicate expressions (*chos brjod kyi sgra*) and kind expressions (*rigs brjod kyi sgra*) in relation to this [subject]."[24] In the act of predication, individuals are subsumed under universals. But, for the Buddhist epistemologist, this does not concern the real world, only the conceptual domain in which individuals are conceptually subsumed by properties that are predicated of these individuals. These properties are not real entities but conceptual distinctions imposed on individual objects. For example, when we consider a yellow patch we see something that it is a color and say "this is yellow." The realist mistakenly assumes that there must be something corresponding to being a color we predicate of a particular color. Mesmerized by the linguistic structure, the realist wants to find something real that corresponds to color when we say of a yellow color that it is a color.

For Śākya Chok-den, this is the wrong way to look at things, for, when we see this color as a color, there is nothing that corresponds to the general color except the yellow color itself. We should not be misled by the predication to assume that the description of an individual as a color necessitates more than a single real entity. In our example, the individual patch of yellow is the only real color relevant to our situation. There is no existing color aside from the yellow. Śākya Chok-den says: "If there is a color that is substantially identical with yellow, this cannot be anything else except yellow [itself]."[25]

Accordingly, universals, which are the properties predicated of individual things, are simply the conceptual characterizations of these things. A real universal is a contradiction in terms, for if something is real it must have a definite essence. As we saw earlier, universals have no clear identity conditions (explained in terms of definite spatio-temporal location and definite entity) and hence are unreal. They can be explained only in terms of conceptual differentiations or, to speak technically, in terms of distinguishers (*ldog pa, vyāvṛtti*). Dharmakīrti says: "According [to our view] too, words as well as cognitions conform to conventions whether [they refer to] distinguishers or to distinguished [things]."[26] Dharmakīrti's remark addresses the Nyāya contention that, although Buddhists first deny the reality of universals, they reintroduce them when they talk about distinguishers (*vyāvṛtti, ldog pa*) and the things thereby distinguished (*vyāvṛtta, log pa*). From the Nyāya point of view, the Buddhist negative way of describing predication is an attempt to disguise the reintroduction of a distinction between universals (distinguishers) and individuals (distinguished).

Dharmakīrti answers that predication does not relate real entities but conceptually differentiates individual things according to linguistic conventions and the intentions of the speaker. In accordance with the principle of ontological parsimony (Ockham's razor), there is no reason to allow any entity than it is not strictly necessary. Since predication can be accounted for without introducing spurious entities such as (real) properties, there is no need of real universals. Take our example, "this is a cow." This predication does not require a real cowness. It is a negative operation in which we exclude a real individual from being something it is not (noncow). What the Nyāya misrepresent as a real universal is, in fact, a conceptual distinguisher through which an individual cow is excluded from the class of nonanimal. The negative description does not reintroduce real universals in disguise but avoids being trapped by language.

At this point we can imagine a Nyāya objection. The Buddhist use of the language of exclusion cannot mask that the exclusion of an individual from what it is not seems to be in virtue of having a property. For example, we exclude an individual from not being a cow. This presupposes the property of being a cow in relation to which the concept of noncow is elaborated. Hence, the Buddhist explanation does not solve anything but just attempts to disguise the problem by adopting a negative language.

This objection is, however, not as decisive as one may think. We will have the occasion of exploring a more developed Buddhist answer when we deal with the *apoha* theory. Suffice it to say that the Buddhist point is not that negative properties somehow manage to escape the problems of positive properties. Rather, what the Buddhists are indicating is that the negative formulation is epistemologically more transparent than the positive one. Instead of misleading one to believe that there is a real property over and above individuals, it draws the attention to the constructed nature of the predicated properties. This process of construction starts from our experiences of similarities and dissimilarities. We are struck by the fact that certain individuals (cows) seem to be more similar to each other than to others. At this preconceptual level the predicative process has not started yet, all we have is an experience of similarities and dissimilarities. Predication starts when we construct (either newly or by learning) a concept (cowness) that accounts for this perceived gap. At this level, we start organizing our perceptive experiences through categories. These are not real entities that we discover in the real world but are constructed as a result of our experiences of similarities and dissimilarities. Thus, the question "in virtue of what is the exclusion done?" misses the point of the *apoha* theory, which is not to posit some new entities but to draw our attention to this process of construction. The exclusion is done in virtue of a property constructed on the basis of perceived similarities and dissimilarities.

Predication and the Validity of Thought

These explanations seem to give a convincing antirealist account of predication. There is, however, a deeper problem with this account: the assumption that the real individual is the subject of predication. This is highly problematic in

Dharmakīrti's antirealist system, where thinking or language can never relate directly to reality, in opposition to perception. How can then predication be described as the exclusion of an individual from being what it is not if such an individual is not available to the conceptual process of exclusion?

An easy solution would be to ground the process of predication on a form of direct reference. In our example, we could imagine that the word "this" directly refers. This solution is not, however, available to Buddhist antirealists who draw a radical distinction between the real and the conceptual domains. Śākya Chok-den amplifies this point by drawing a distinction between real substances, as they exist independent of our conceptual frameworks, and the concept of these substances which we take as subjects of predication.[27] Only those can be subjects of predication. Since thought cannot relate directly to real individual substances, it conceptualizes them through an intermediary.

We may find this surprising, for in our example, "this is a cow," it seems that conceptual mediation intervenes only at the level of the predicate. The use of the indexical ("this") seems to ensure that our words and thoughts are put in direct relation with the real world. A moment of reflection, however, undermines this confidence. Even the use of an indexical presupposes some conceptual description in the background. Otherwise, how would we know that we are pointing to an animal rather than its color, particular shape, or the like? Therefore, even in this simple case, reference presupposes the ability to locate an object within a conceptual space and, hence, mediation. Śākya Chok-den describes this conceptual intermediary as a conceptually understood substance (literally, "the substance considered from the point of view of exclusion," *sel ngo'i rdzas*). This pseudo-substance is an elimination (*sel ba, apoha*); that is, it is an unreal universal. It is an individuation (*bye brag, viśeṣa,* more on this shortly) whose conceptual nature provides the actual basis of predication and, hence, is called the *actual subject* (*song tshod kyi chos can*), but it is nothing but a conceptual construct. This concept is mistaken as the real substance, even though it is not. When this subject is mistaken as real, it is designated as the *assumed subject* (*rlom tshod kyi chos can*); that is, the subject (falsely) assumed to be real.

For Śākya Chok-den and other consistent Dharmakīrtian antirealists, this mistake of taking the actual subject to be the real substance is at the heart of the conceptual process. Thinking is always and necessarily mistaken because it involves a confusion between two radically incommensurable domains, the real and the conceptual. We believe that we are able to refer directly to reality, but this is an illusion. In referring to an entity, we use (implicitly or explicitly) a concept, which bears on an artificial construct. For example, when we say "this cow," we feel that we are in direct touch with reality. The truth of the matter, however, is that we are not. The content of the concept we use to identify the object does not exist in reality. Nothing in real cows corresponds to our concept. Thus, our identification is always mistaken.

And so is the whole process of predication. First, it rests on mistaken identification. We believe that we directly refer to a real object, whereas we merely locate the (conceptual) individuation of that object within the logical space of reasons. Second, we predicate a property to this subject, believing that such a subject instantiates this property. This is also a mistake since the real object, which we conceive to be the subject, and the constructed property have nothing to do with each other. For example, when we say "this table is impermanent," we believe that we have (1) singled out a real object in the world and (2) predicated a property instantiated by such an object. Both beliefs are, however, mistaken. This is so for two reasons: (1) We cannot identify things as they are but only project our concepts onto a reality beyond our conceptualization, and (2) the properties we predicate are not instantiated by real objects. The real table does not instantiate impermanence. It is impermanent in that it changes constantly, but this does not mean that there is a property, impermanence, that this object shares with other things.

The two mistakes are not, however, exactly on the same level. Whereas the subject expression is necessarily taken to refer to a real object, the predicate term need not be taken in this way, for its sole function is to characterize an entity already introduced into the realm of discourse. To put it in a slightly different way, whereas the subject expression is the name of an object, the predicate expression is not. Although naming is conceptually mediated and, hence, mistaken, it remains true that the subject expression has to be conceived to name something. For example, when I say "this is a cow," I cannot but conceive of "this" as singling out a real object. Without such a mistake, thinking cannot proceed. The situation is different for the predicate expression, which does not name anything. In our example, "cow" does not name anything, not even a property such as cowness, but characterizes an entity already introduced within the realm of discourse. Hence, the object of this expression, the predicate, cannot be said to be real even from a conceptual point of view. This is different from the subject, which can be said to be real from a conceptual viewpoint.

These explanations raise an immediate and obvious objection: How can thinking, which is inherently distorted, be considered valid? If predication involves no more than the subsuming of an object under an artificial concept on the basis of a mistaken identification and if conceptual knowledge rests on predication, how is conceptual knowledge possible? If, when I think that this is a cow, I merely subsume an unreal concept under another unreal concept, how can I be said to learn anything through this operation about reality?

The antirealist answer is mostly pragmatic. Thinking is valid inasmuch as its mistakes do not preclude its having a pragmatic value. Thinking directly relates only to constructs that are mistaken as substances. Still these constructs help us to think about real substances, or to use Śākya Chok-den's technical language, they are nondeceptive with respect to specifically characterized phenomena (*don rang mtshan la mi slu ba*) because they causally relate to reality.[28] This is why they are called *substance*. Moreover, the distortions entailed by the conceptual process belong to the innate (*lhan skyes*) level of our thinking.[29] They are inherent (*ngo bo nyid kyis 'khrul pa*) to thinking and are shared by all of us as thinking beings. We cannot but proceed through mistaken concepts and hence those are valid from our limited point of view. To put it briefly, we agree to do the same mistakes.

These innate distortions are the condition of the possibility of thinking. We cannot start thinking without presupposing that our concepts identify real things. The very act of asking a question about the validity of language presupposes that we have accepted to proceed in the domain created by such mistakes. Hence, the ultimately mistaken nature of thinking does not preclude its conventional validity. To put it in an often misused Kantian language, thinking is transcendentally mistaken but empirically valid.

Śākya Chok-den develops this answer by fleshing out Sa-paṇ's distinction between [practical] application (*'jug pa*) to the object and [critical] explanation (*'chad pa*) of such application.[30] To clarify this technical distinction, which is important to explain the status of reasoning in this antirealist interpretation, let us take a more complex example, the case of the following inference: The language of the Vedas is impermanent because it is produced, just like a jar.[31] When we say this, we speak from a conceptual and hence mistaken point of view. The mistake is that we take the subject of the argument, the language of the Vedas, as being the actual object and proceed on this basis. This mistake, however, is unavoidable and, moreover, it is pragmatically adequate since it is shared by our audience. It can be exposed only by critical examination, differentiating real entities from constructs. When this distinction is made, the mistaken nature of thinking is exposed, and thinking comes to a halt.

This distinction between precritical application and critical examination provides a basis for an antirealist explanation of inference. For Buddhist logicians, inference does not deal directly with reality. To put it in their terms, inference does not establish or refute anything in direct reference to a real substance (*rdzas la dgag sgrub mi byed*).[32] Accordingly, reasoning involves conceptual creations, which are the direct *relata* of our thoughts, and reasoning works on the basis of our mistaking them for real entities.

In examining the ontology and epistemology implied by our use of arguments, we must be careful to distinguish between the actual (*song tshod*) and assumed (*rlom tshod*) terms of the reasoning. These are the subject (*chos can, dharmin*), the predicate of the probandum (*sgrub bya'i chos, sādhyadharma*), and the reason (*rtags, liṅga*). The actual subject, predicate, and evidence are constructs, but reasoning can proceed only when these concepts are applied to reality. We do not abstractly deduce constructs from constructs, but rather, we do so by applying them to reality. For instance, in our example, we infer impermanence from the property of being produced. The actual reason (*song tshod kyi rtags*) is the property of being produced. Since it is conceptual, it is permanent and we may wonder how we can deduce impermanence from it. We come to such a conclusion by mistakenly applying this construct. That is, we think that Vedic language is impermanent because it is produced, ignoring that we are really dealing with universals, not real things. In the process, we conceive the actual reason, the construct, as being real and proceed on this basis. This assumed reason (*rlom tshod kyi rtags*; that is, the actual reason mistakenly assumed to be real) is not real, however. It is nothing but a useful fiction.

This distinction between practical application of concepts and their theoretical understanding is crucial to Śākya Chok-den's interpretative strategy. It allows him to brush aside suggestions that real properties exist in Buddhist logic. We will see that there is some evidence in Dharmakīrti's logic to suggest that reasoning presupposes the establishment of real properties. Śākya Chok-den takes these suggestions about the existence of real properties to refer to the context of practical application. At the level of practical application of reasonings properties are assumed to be real. Recognizing the mistaken identification of conceptual and real entities involved in predication comes later, at the analytical level. In this way Śākya Chok-den preserves the coherence of his antirealist interpretation of Dharmakīrti. The ontological basis of Dharmakīrti's system is not established at the practical level at which we reason, but at the theoretical level where real and conceptual entities are strictly distinguished. The mistake made by realist interpreters of Dharmakīrti is to run together the preanalytical and the critical standpoints.

As we can see, Śākya Chok-den offers a radical antirealism, which is in the mainstream of Buddhist epistemology. It is quite remarkable, however, that, in his emphasis on a thorough rejection of universals, Śākya Chok-den goes back to a formulation of Buddhist epistemology, which in certain respects is closer to Dignāga's than to Dharmakīrti's. Although Śākya Chok-den does not reject Dharmakīrti's resemblance theory and the causal link between reality, experience and conceptuality, he does not stress these points, like Dharmakīrti does. Like Sa-paṇ and his contemporary Go-ram-ba, Śākya Chok-den's essential preoccupation is to emphasize the gap between conceptuality and reality. Locked in an interpretive struggle about the meaning of Dharmakīrti's thought with realist commentators, Śākya Chok-den rejects the realist claim that thought can capture reality. Hence, he has little interest in stressing the elements that relate thought and reality. Although he does not deny these elements, which are essential for Dharmakīrti, his focus is different; namely, to emphasize the gap between the two domains that realism tends to conflate.

This is not to say that Śākya Chok-den holds the extreme nominalism described by Dravid. It is doubtful that any important thinkers hold such a view. Śākya Chok-den does not deny that thought has a causal support in reality,[33] but he emphasize the idea that thought or language do not mirror reality. Thought proceeds by synthesizing separate elements. This operation creates quasi-entities that are abstractions with no correspondence to anything real. Similarly, the logical operations, which we hold to be basic to our way of seeing the world, are nothing but useful fictions. For example, we hold that x and non-x are contradictory.[34] We also hold that they follow the principle of the excluded middle. Neither is there something that is both or neither. Moreover, we think that this law of the excluded middle reflects a deep structure of reality rather than the organization of our conceptual apparatus. This is an illusion, argues Śākya Chok-den on the basis of the following argument. Imagine that x is real. Then non-x is unreal. How can their opposition exist in reality? Opposition is not a reflection of how things are but is solely a product of our logical imagination. Like any other category, the so-called laws of logic are just convenient ways we have to order reality.[35]

The radical nature of Śākya Chok-den's account is immediately apparent. His view contradicts some of the assumptions we strongly hold to concerning the ways in which language and logic apply to reality. As indicated previously, being counterintuitive does not bother Buddhist antirealists, who understand their work to be to undermine the reifications that form the basis of the commonsense view of language. Contrary to realists, Śākya Chok-den holds that thought and language do not mirror reality. Hence, it is a delusion to hold theory prisoner of commonsense. Rather, we should recognize the gap between language and reality and move toward a view of concepts that recognize their inherent limitations.

We may wonder, however, whether Śākya Chok-den's account is satisfactory. Does he really provide an account of the validity of concepts or is he just positing such a validity? Is not his pragmatic justification just a way to bypass philosophical investigation by pointing to what we do as the last answer? Dharmakīrti's realist interpreters would not hesitate to answer positively to this last question. They think that such an explanation just begs the question and betrays Dharmakīrti's foundational project, for to say that thought is just pragmatically valid is to refuse to answer the question, Why are we successful in our use of thinking? Before examining the views of these interpreters, let us complete our discussion of universals in the Sa-gya tradition.

Are Distinguishers Parts of Reality?

The outline of the ontology of this tradition should be quite clear by now. Universals are explained as conceptual distinctions superimposed on things, in opposition to the realist view that they are predicated on them. Let us begin to contrast the views of this tradition with those of its adversaries. Two rather technical topics provide the context for our examination: the concept of distinguisher (*ldog pa, vyāvṛtti*) and the nature of individuations. The importance of these topics (particularly the former) in the Tibetan tradition warrants the effort of confronting these rather abstruse discussions. The reader less interested in the overly technical details of these two sections may want to proceed directly to the next chapter, where Ge-luk realism is examined.

For Sa-paṇ and his tradition, a distinguisher is a conceptual distinction, which can be predicated on a subject. This predication is not, however, an instantiation but a mistaken identification. For example, when we think that the Vedic language is impermanent, we apply the distinguisher, that is, the concept of impermanence, to the Vedic language. This application is not an actual instantiation, for no real thing can ever instantiate conceptual constructs. Those can be applied only through mistaken identification, as described earlier.

The tradition of the Collected Topics, started by Cha-ba and continued by the Ge-luk school, developed a rather different understanding of this concept. As with many of its topics, the Collected Topics presentation of distinguishers (*ldog pa ngos 'dzin gyi rnam bzhag*) did not originate in the Ge-luk tradition. It is a legacy from the earlier tradition of Cha-ba. This topic is found in all Ge-luk textbooks and occupies an important role in the dialectical training of beginners, who take great joy in unraveling its apparent paradoxes. It seems to be a Tibetan indigenous creation, born out of the practice of debate.[36]

According to the Collected Topics,[37] a distinguisher of a phenomenon is its conceptual identity. It is the property of a phenomenon being not what it is not. For example, a jar is distinct from everything else. This is explained by the Collected Topics to be its distinguisher. Since such a distinguisher is a distinction made by thought, it is conceptual. Its being unreal does not prevent it, however, from being instantiated by a real thing, the object that it distinguishes. Take the example of a jar. That jar is said to instantiate its own distinguisher because that jar is that which distinguishes that jar from everything else. Similarly, every existent is posited as the instance of its own distinguisher.

The point behind this conception of distinguisher seems to be the following. Take the terms "being impermanent" and "being a thing." They designate the same real things, but nevertheless they differ. According to a Ge-luk analysis, this difference necessitates an analysis of the terms in extensional and intensional terms.[38] Although "being impermanent" and "being a thing" have the same extension, that is, they pick out the same objects, their intensions or connotations differ. Whereas "being a thing" connotes the property of being a causally effective thing, "being impermanent" connotes change. For Buddhist realists, this intensional distinction is conceptual but indirectly reflects the structure of reality. The difference between these two terms is not just conceptual, for they identify two properties, being impermanent and being a thing. These entities are real and different from each other, even though they do not exist apart. To use terms that we will investigate in the next chapter, these two properties are substantially identical but they are not identical. Their difference is described as a difference in distinguisher, which is distinguished from a difference in real entity.

This distinction plays an important role in Ge-luk thinking. It is in agreement with the moderate realism of this tradition concerning the nature of predication. Contrary to Sa-paṇ and his followers, Ge-luk thinkers hold that predication is not a case of mistaken identification but instantiation. That is, when we predicate existence of a sound, we are not just superimposing a construct on an incommensurable reality. Rather, we are instantiating the concept of existence on one of its instances. Similarly, distinguishers are understood not just as a superimposed property but as being instantiated by real things despite being conceptual.

One of the surprising consequences of this idea is that the distinguisher of, for example, a jar is necessarily permanent even though its unique instance (the jar) is impermanent. That is, we cannot infer that a distinguisher is impermanent from the fact that its only instance is impermanent. This move (distinguishing between the phenomenon itself, which may be permanent, and its instance, which may be impermanent) is used repeatedly throughout Ge-luk scholasticism. For example, a commonly accepted truth of Dharmakīrti's system is that the terms of a reasoning (the subject, predicate, and evidence) are all unreal. In this case, how can we apply an argument and expect thereby to understand reality? Sa-paṇ explains this by pointing to our mistaken identification of real objects with concepts. Ge-luk thinkers are not satisfied with this explanation, which deprives thinking of any direct ontological support. They use the preceding distinction to explain Dharmakīrti's view in a way compatible with moderate realism: Although the entities involved in a reasoning are unreal, their instances are real.[39]

This distinction parallels the Sa-gya differentiation between assumed (*rlom tshod*) and real (*song tshod*) entities. The subject is unreal in reality but real from the point of view of our conceptions. The difference is that, for Sa-paṇ's tradition, this distinction does not reflect the way things exist but only the mistaken way we conceive them to be. Sa-paṇ criticizes the assertion that distinguishers exist in real things. Since they are conceptual, distinguishers are not characteristics of things but are superimposed by us on them: "Distinct distinguishers such as 'sound, being impermanent, being produced' are differentiated by mind and do not exist in reality."[40] Sa-paṇ criticizes the idea that distinguishers exist in real things despite being conceptual.[41] If distinguishers such as being impermanent and being produced existed objectively (*don chos*), they would be one entity in reality. They would then be substantially identical[42] and indistinguishable. Thus, the assertion that distinguishers characterize real things leads to the cancellation of the distinctiveness of these distinguishers.[43]

For Sa-paṇ, the only coherent way to maintain a conceptual distinction between impermanence and thing is to separate the conceptual from the real. Sa-paṇ agrees with his adversaries that impermanence and thing have distinct distinguishers but denies that this has any direct bearing on reality. The distinction is purely conceptual. This is what Sa-paṇ means when he says that thing and impermanence are substantially identical. This is not unlike Quine's idea that entities which are indiscernible are identical.[44] For Quine and for Sa-paṇ, terms such as "being impermanent" and "being produced" do not refer to different properties but identify the same real objects. They are informative descriptions of the same things. Since these two terms are extensionally equivalent, that is, since they apply to the same real things, their objects are indiscernible and, hence, identical.

Śākya Chok-den repeatedly criticizes the Ge-luk presentation of distinguisher. He rightly points out how different it is from Dharmakīrti's concept of distinguisher.[45] In particular, he criticizes the Ge-luk assertion that a thing instantiates its own distinguisher (*rang rang gi ldog pa yin pa*).[46] This is not possible, he says, because if it were, we would have something that is both a thing and a universal. For Śākya Chok-den, a real jar cannot be a distinguisher because it is an individual. The construct jarness is a distinguisher but not its own distinguisher. Śākya Chok-den says: "When one says that a golden jar is a jar, we accept that jar is a distinguisher. However, it cannot be its own distinguisher, for we accept it as the distinguisher of that golden jar, etc."[47] When we say that "a golden jar is a jar," we are referring, mistakenly as we saw earlier, to a real object and predicating a property (being a jar). This property conceptually distinguishes the golden jar from everything else and hence is its distinguisher. It is not, however, its own distinguisher in the same way that the concept of a golden jar is not the concept of that concept. The idea that things instantiate their own distinguishers is confused. It corresponds to neither real nor conceptual order.

This mistake, Śākya Chok-den adds, results from a failure to differentiate the practical understanding of things from critical examination. Practically, jar is not distinguished from its distinguisher. Critically, thought is found to be dealing with unreal universals. When we say "a jar is a thing," the assumed subject is the real jar and the actual subject is the distinguisher or universal of jar. In the context of practical application, these two subjects are assumed to be identical. But in reality they are not. Without this fundamental distinction, thought cannot be granted any validity. According to Śākya Chok-den, ignorance of it has led Ge-luk thinkers to create artificial concepts that have little support in Dharmakīrti's thought.

This artificial creation is all the more surprising in light of the Ge-luk recognition of Dharmakīrti's own usage of the concept of distinguisher. Gyel-tsap, for example, puts the passage in Dharmakīrti's *Commentary*, I:40 under the heading "Responding to the debate [that argues that] distinguisher and distinguished are identical to individuations and universals."[48] Gyel-tsap's reference to this Nyāya objection, which argues that Buddhists are just hiding their acceptance of real universals by calling them *distinguishers* makes it clear that he is not unaware that Dharmakīrti equates universals with distinguishers. Similarly, Kay-drup describes a distinguisher phenomenon (*ldog pa'i chos*) as "a phenomenon that is merely imputed."[49] And yet, they do not hesitate to replace this well-established understanding of distinguisher as a conceptual distinction by the more idyosyncratic view described earlier.

The Conceptual Nature of Individuations

The antirealism of Sa-paṇ and his followers applies not only to universals but to individuations (*bye brag, viśeṣa*) as well. They argue that the distinction between universals and individuations must remain confined entirely to the conceptual realm. Since universals are unreal conceptual distinctions, individuations cannot be real things that instantiate universal properties (as they are for Ge-luk thinkers). Rather, they are restricted distinctions made in relation to broader differentiations. Since such a distinction exists only in dependence on the other phenomena in relation to which it is made, it is relational and hence cannot be real but is superimposed on real individuals. To put it in Medieval scholastic terms, an individuation is not an individual substance but is its conceptually determined specificity (*haecceitas*).

Śākya Chok-den defines *individuation* as "that assemblage of [at least] two distinguishers that are different not only from their discordant kinds but also [from things] among concordant kinds."[50] Let us again take an example: "this cow is an animal." Here, the concept of being an animal is the universal of the cow and the concept of being a cow is the individuation of that universal. Let us notice that in accordance with his theory of predication, Śākya Chok-den rejects the idea that the real cow is an individuation. Only realists hold to such a crude idea, ironizes Śākya Chok-den. An individuation is the basis on which a universal is predicated. Hence, it can never be real. It is just a narrower conceptual differentiation (being a cow) posited in relation to a more general distinction (being an animal). Accordingly, an individuation is described as a "common locus (*gzhi mthun*) between two distinguishers," not to be confused with the individuals that are differentiated, for both individuations and universals are conceptual entities.[51] It is also referred to as a *collection of two distinguishers* (*ldog pa gnyis tshogs kyi bye brag*).[52] This contrasts with a universal, which is a single distinguisher. As such, an universal eliminates less than an individuation and, hence, is more inclusive. Hence, the word *unique* in Śākya Chok-den's previously stated definition of universals where he describes them as "unique distinguisher" (*ldog pa cig kyang*).[53]

The translation of *bye brag (viśeṣa)* is particularly difficult, for the word has different meanings according to different schools and contexts. Sa-gya antirealists hold that *bye brag* does not refer for the most part to individuals but to the conceptual differences. Hence, for them, *bye brag* should be translated as "individuation." Bo-dong and Ge-luk-bas hold, however, that the word refers to individuals and is equivalent to *gsal ba (vyakti)*. Accordingly, the translation should be "particular." Both uses are present in Dharmakīrti's work.[54] Nevertheless, I use "individuation" as a translation of *bye brag,* hoping that this word will help the reader to remember the two possible meanings of *bye brag.* The problem in translation, however, is not so easily resolved, for Śākya Chok-den does not deny that this word is often applied to individuals and, hence, means "particular" in that context.[55] He maintains, however, that this use is only a loose way of talking (as when we say "a particular cow"). It reflects the practical point of view (*'jug pa'i tshe*) in which real and conceptual entities are confused. This common usage differs from the philosophical concept of individuation, which is made from the point of view of critical examination (*'chad tshe*). The philosophical use of *individuation* should differentiate real from conceptual entities rather than conflate them.

For Śākya Chok-den, philosophical understanding cannot rest satisfied with the common practical understanding of individuation but must seek a critical standpoint, for, when pointing at a jar saying "this golden jar is a jar," the actual subject of predication is not the real jar but the conceptual distinction of such a jar as opposed to other jars. Thus, according to Śākya Chok-den, an individuation is not the instance of a general property, as common folk and realists assume it to be. Rather, it is the conceptual distinction made inside a class already determined by a universal. Śākya Chok-den says: "To summarize, what is called 'an individuation' is not the individual substance. Rather, the diverse distinguishers [that are assumed] when language and factual thought distinguish several distinguishers on the [basis of] a single substance are what are called 'individuations.' The unique distinguisher that is the mere elimination of what is not [this substance] on [the basis of] that substance is called a 'universal.' Otherwise, the assertion that 'the different substances are the individuations' is [an example of] the exalted [position of] non-Buddhists [such as] Vaiśeṣikas."[56] For Śākya Chok-den, it is a mistake to identify individuations and individuals. Rather, one should keep in mind that individuations exist only in relation to universals. Hence, they must be conceptual like universals. This strong antirealist philosophy of universals is consistent with Śākya Chok-den's overall approach. It is quite different from the more realist approach of the Ge-luk tradition to which I now turn.

9

Ge-luk Realism

Universals in the Collected Topics

The preceding chapters gave us ample evidence of the realism of the Ge-luk tradition. We noticed that its moderate realism is markedly different from Dharmakīrti's antirealism, despite its claim to interpret the latter in the most orthodox way. We also examined the refutations of Ge-luk views proposed by their adversaries. We have yet to examine their defense. This chapter analyzes the Ge-luk arguments. This provides the occasion for a philosophical exploration of what I have called the *moderate realist's predicament.*[1] Let us start our investigation of Ge-luk moderate realism by exploring the way in which this tradition defines and discusses the concept of universals.

In his Ge-luk Collected Topics Pur-bu-jok defines a *universal* as "that phenomenon which is concomitant with its manifold individuals" (*gsal ba, vyakti*).[2] Such an entity may also be called a kind-universal (*rigs spyi*), which is defined as "that phenomenon which is concomitant with its manifold instances" (*rigs can*; literally typified).[3] This rather formal way of putting things is not especially informative philosophically. It refers to the simple fact that a universal is something instantiated by its individuations (*bye brag, viśeṣa*).[4] For example, jar is instantiated by individual jars. These are its *gsal ba*; that is, specific appearances that reveal the essence of jar.[5] As universals are here defined in relation to their individuations, we must next examine the nature of individuations.

An *individuation* (*bye brag, viśeṣa*) is defined as "that phenomenon which has a kind by which it is subsumed" (literally pervaded, *khyab pa*).[6] A jar, for example, is the individuation of impermanence since it is subsumed by impermanence, its kind (*rigs, jāti*) or universal (*spyi, sāmānya*, the two terms being synonymous). This formal way of defining universals in relation to individuations and vice versa is circular and uninformative unless we can identify individuations without reference to universals. Such a noncircular account is found in the literature in the form of criteria for individuation (*bye brag yin pa'i 'gro tshul*). These are standards that phenomena must satisfy to be individuations. A phenomenon x is an individuation of y if, and only if, it satisfies the following three criteria: (1) x must be y, (2) x must have a relation of essential identity (*bdag gcig 'brel, tādātmya*)[7] with *y*, and (3) there must exist several other instances of *y* that are not *x*.[8] For instance, a jar is an individuation of thing (*dngos po, vastu*) because (1) it is a thing, (2) it has a relation of essential identity with thing, and (3) there are many things that are not jar.

The first and third requirements are quite easy to understand. The first necessitates that a given individuation be an instance of the phenomenon it instantiates. The third requirement necessitates that an individuation be of smaller extension than its universal. The second requirement, that of having a relation of essential identity, is more obscure. It rests on a delicate distinction between individuations and universals. This is the Ge-luk way of solving the moderate realist predicament, the equivalent of Kumārila's identity in difference and Scotus's formal distinction. It is technically described as a relation between two entities that are distinct distinguishers within the same entity (*ngo bo gcig la ldog pa tha dad*). This way of spelling out the difference between individuals and universals is the Ge-luk attempt to articulate a type of relation that distinguishes universals and particulars without separating them. It will require a detailed investigation of the several possible ways the distinction between identity and difference can be drawn. This investigation will be undertaken in the next section.

Before going into this, let us make sure that we have understood the importance of these criteria of individuation for the Ge-luk tradition. They offer what the definition could not provide, a noncircular way to understand universals: Phenomenon *x* is the individuation of another phenomenon *y* if, and only if, it satisfies the three criteria of individuation in relation to *y*. Jar is an individuation of thing because jar is a thing, jar has a relation of essential identity with thing, and there are things that are not jars. Therefore, it is possible to know that jar is the individuation of thing before knowing that thing is a universal. Once we know that jar is the individuation of thing, then we understand that thing is a universal.

This noncircular way of positing universals from individuations seems in itself unexceptional. It leads, however, to a view that is unusual within the Buddhist logico-epistemological tradition. Since individual colors satisfy the three criteria of individuation in relation to impermanence *(mi rtag pa)*,[9] they are individuations of impermanence; impermanence is their universal. We may assume that as individuals, colors are unproblematically real. But what about impermanence? What is the nature of that entity, which is shared by individual colors? Is it real or not?

Dharmakīrti's likely answer would be that impermanence is unreal inasmuch as it is predicated of particulars. Predication is a conceptual relation that has little bearing on reality. It is a useful depiction of the similarities between individuals (colors) that is important in practical contexts where reasonings are used. There, we can identify general properties as being predicated on individuals. We can even talk about properties being instantiated by particulars but we have to recognize, however, that this is no more than a practical use of concepts that does not reflect their true nature. In actuality, properties are not instantiated by real things but superimposed on them. Hence, predication does not warrant the ontological assertion that impermanence as a real entity is the universal of individual colors. Dharmakīrti apparently does not consider the possibility that some universals are real. Locked in a contest with Naiyāyikas, who assert that universals are real and independent from their particulars, Dharmakīrti's strategy is to grant that universals are different from their particulars but to deny them any reality. It is extremely important to Dharmakīrti not to admit that any universals are real, for that would support the Nyāya contention that at least some general properties must be accepted as real![10]

Ge-luk thinkers view this topic in a different light. They take predication much more seriously, understanding it as an actual instantiation of properties by particulars. For them, the assertion that colors instantiate impermanence is not a shorthand for depicting the similarities between individuals. It is a description of the relation that obtains in reality between impermanence and its particulars. Therefore, they assert that some entities such as impermanence are universals predicated of particulars, despite being themselves real.

A general agreement on this point seems to be basic to the Ge-luk interpretation of Dharmakīrti. All the major thinkers share this realism.[11] Dzong-ka-ba is quite explicit: "there are two [types of] universal: that which is a nonthing and that which is a universal [and] a thing that is concomitant with specifically characterized particulars."[12] Kay-drup offers an extensive defense of this view on the basis of both textual and logical arguments. Although less expansive, Gyel-tsap argues that this is the correct interpretation of Dharmakīrti's works as well as that of Sapaṇ's *Treasure.*[13] Ge-dün-drup states a similar view when he says: "Although universal is [itself] not a thing, every universal does not need to be a nonthing *(dngos med).*"[14] Jay-dzün-ba says that "it is taught that universal and thing have a common locus."[15]

These Ge-luk thinkers' realism, however, is moderate, for they do not go to the extent of asserting that real properties exist separate from their instances. Moreover, they deny any intrinsic difference between universals and particulars. When we consider that jar is impermanent, jar is the particular of a real property (impermanence), but when we consider a yellow jar as being a jar, jar is then a universal. Particulars and universals are relative notions that derive from conceptual distinctions. Hence, even though these notions are grounded in reality, they do not directly reflect its structure. This raises a question, which is central to moderate realism: What is the relation between particulars and universals?

One and Many

This is a delicate question for any form of moderate realism, and the Ge-luk view is no exception. When we say of yellow that it is a color, we are predicating a universal (color) of an individual thing. According to the Ge-luk view, both universal and individual colors really exist. This immediately raises the question of the relation between the individual color and color in general, for color in general does not exist apart from the individual colors. Is it then identical?

The response to this question about the relation between universals and their instances is expressed by the second of the three criteria of individuation. It is a relation of essential identity. This is type of identity must, however, be differentiated from identity simpliciter; hence, the necessity to discuss the different types of relation accepted in Buddhist philosophy and the problem of identity and difference in general.

According to Dharmakīrti's tradition, a phenomenon *x* is related to another phenomenon *y* if, and only if, *x* cannot exist without *y* (*med na mi 'byung ba, avinābhāva*). Such a relation can occur in two possible ways: *x* can have a relation of origination (*de byung 'brel, tadutpatti*) with *y* or a relation of essential identity.[16] We can leave aside the former, which is a relation in which *y* causes *x*. A relation of essential identity between *x* and *y* is explicated as (1) *x* must be distinct (*tha dad, bhinna*) from *y* but the same entity (*ngo bo, rūpa*) as *y*. (2) Moreover, it must be impossible for *x* to exist if *y* does not exist.[17] Leaving aside the second requirement, which simply indicates that *x* is related to *y*, we must inquire into the meaning of the first criterion. What does it mean for two things *x* and *y* to be distinct and yet the same entity (*ngo bo gcig la ldog pa tha dad*)?

Antirealist interpreters of Dharmakīrti understand this relation of identity as being strictly about conceptual differentiation. For example, impermanence and being produced have a relation of essential identity because they are conceptually distinct but in reality are the same thing. To put it in Quine's terms, they are identical because they are indiscernible.[18] Hence, for these interpreters, a relation of essential identity concerns less real entities than conceptual distinctions. In fact, relation itself does not concern reality but only the conceptual domain. This is so because reality is made of things individuated through their intrinsic, that is, nonrelational, identities. Since relation can be established only in relation to other phenomena, it is necessarily conceptual and hence unreal.

Ge-luk thinkers reject this consistent antirealist understanding of relation. They point out that this view is counterintuitive and threatens to undermine the basis of Buddhist philosophy. If relation concerned solely the conceptual domain, causal relations would be unreal as well. How could then reality be defined by causality? In accordance with their realism, Ge-luk thinkers hold that relations concern reality, although relation in itself may be conceptual.[19] This is also the case of the second type of relation between two essentially identical phenomena. This relation concerns two phenomena that are distinct and yet the same entity. How is this possible? How can two phenomena be distinct and yet the same thing?

This question raises larger problem of identity and difference. This is one of the most persistent problems in the history philosophy in the "East" as well as in the "West." This problem arises from the philosophical attempt to make sense of the unity and multiplicity that exist in our experiences. It is particularly acute for moderate realists, for it goes to the heart of their enterprise. Moderate realism holds that universals are real but do not exist apart from their instances. But, since the terms designating universals and their instances do not have the same extension, they must be distinct. And yet, they are not found apart. What kind of distinction is this? Answering this question is what I called the *moderate realist predicament*. Scotus's answer is that this distinction is formal; that is, less than real but more than conceptual.[20] Kumārila's answer is that universals and particulars have a relation of identity in difference. The Ge-luk answer is the notion of phenomena being distinct and yet the same entity. Let us further investigate this notion to raise the fundamental question: Is this notion coherent? Or is it simply an untenable compromise?

The Ge-luk tradition has developed a sophisticated conceptual apparatus inherited from Cha-ba for drawing the distinction between one (*gcig, eka*) and many (*du ma, aneka*) or, rather, identical (*gcig, abhinna*) and distinct (*tha dad, bhinna*).[21] Here, I simplify this discussion by considering only real entities and contrasting two types of identity and difference: substantial and conceptual. These two types correspond to the two epistemic ways of making valid distinctions among things.[22] Substantial identity and difference are involved in the distinctions made by perception; for example, a cow and a horse are substantially different since they can be differentiated by perception. Conceptual identity (or, to speak more technically, identity of distinguisher, *ldog pa gcig*) and difference are involved in the distinctions made by conceptions; for example, being a cow and being a thing and being impermanent are conceptually distinct albeit substantially identical.

Realists and antirealists agree on this last point. They disagree, however, on its implications. Antirealists hold that conceptual difference does not amount to actual difference. For them, two phenomena can be said to be different only if they are substantially different; that is, if they can be observed apart in reality as cow and horse. Thing and impermanence do not qualify as different since they are never observed apart. Difference and identity is ontological and must be decided on the basis of an observation of the real. Nominal differences are irrelevant to the way in which things exist and hence have no bearing on whether two phenomena are identical or not.

In conformity with their realist outlook, according to which conceptuality is an at least partly accurate guide to reality, Ge-luk thinkers hold that identity and difference are conceptual. In opposition to Sa-paṇ and his followers, Ge-luk thinkers hold that two phenomena are identical if, and only if, they cannot be distinguished conceptually.[23] Thus, that two things are not observed apart is not sufficient to establish them as identical.[24] They have to be identical conceptually to qualify as identical. For example, thing and impermanence are never observed apart, but, nevertheless, they are not identical.

Perception is understood to have undistorted epistemic access to reality. Nevertheless, it does not establish identity but only substantial identity. Two things are substantially identical if, and only if, they cannot be taken apart from the point of view of perception. Refuting an adversary, Gyel-tsap indirectly suggests this meaning of substantial identity: "It [absurdly] follows that [according to you] the subject, parts and wholes, are substantially different because they appear differently from the point of view of what a nonmistaken cognition (i.e., a perception) holds."[25] Implicit in Gyel-tsap's argument is that two things are substantially different if, and only if, they appear (or, better, can appear) different to a perception. Entities that cannot come apart in a perceptive experience are substantially identical. For example, a yellow color cannot be distinguished from its impermanence from the point of view of perception, and therefore, both are substantially identical. However, they are not identical, for we can make a conceptual distinction, and this has some relevance to reality.

This idea of substantial identity has some basis in Dharmakīrti's thought and yet it differs from his view. For him, identity and difference concerns reality and, hence, is not conceptual but perceptual. Two entities are identical when they cannot be observed apart. For Dharmakīrti, this means that they are the same individual. Whenever we see or touch one, we, eo ipso, see or touch the other. Dharmakīrti says: "In all cases, there is only a [verbal or conceptual] difference [between] what describes substances (subjects) and entities (properties). Thus, in all cases there is no [real] distinction whatsoever in the denotation of these two [types of] word."[26] A single object can be described in different ways. For example, we can describe a yellow patch as a color, a form, an impermanent thing, and so forth. All these characteristics apply to the same particular yellow patch. They are distinct ways of speaking about the same thing. This patch is said to be substantially identical with its form, its being impermanent, and the like because they are all different ways of describing the same individual.

This notion of substantial identity, which for Dharmakīrti means identity simpliciter, is reinterpreted by Ge-luk thinkers to support their realism. They consider the distinction between yellow and impermanence to be more than merely different ways to conceptualize the same thing. These are two distinct phenomena. The distinction made by thought between them is not merely conceptual but has a validity that extends past the conceptual domain to the real. This is entirely in accordance with the realism of this school. As realist thinkers, Ge-luk philosophers tend to stress the importance of intelligibility as a criterion of existence. Due to the moderation of their realism and their historical situation as commentators of a conceptualist system, they do not go, however, as far as equating intelligibility and reality, as extreme realists do.

Accordingly, particulars and universals are described as being distinct. Nevertheless, they cannot exist apart. Hence, they are said to be substantially identical. For example, an individual color is substantially identical (*rdzas gcig*) with the more general color (its universal) because the two are indistinguishable by perception. Still, they are conceptually distinct. Combined, these two types of distinctions, conceptual and perceptual, explain the relation between individuals and their properties. Since conceptual distinctiveness is the sufficient and necessary condition for actual distinctiveness, it takes precedence. Hence, an individual and a general color can be said to be distinct within being substantially identical (*rdzas gcig la ldog pa tha dad*).

Perception is the unmistaken reflection of reality and it does not distinguish individuals from their properties. So, properties and individuals must exist inseparably. This does not mean, as the antirealist has too quickly concluded, that they are exactly the same. It means that they are substantially identical.[27] And yet, they are also different. In this way, the objectivity of the distinction between universals and particulars is maintained without having to accept the multiplication of entities entailed by the extreme realist view that properties exist independent of their instances.

This argument for moderate realism rests on the characterization of identity in conceptual terms. The distinction between individuals and their properties collapses if being conceptually distinct is not a sufficient condition for being distinct (as asserted by Sa-gya antirealists). The distinction between individuals and their properties would then be strictly limited to the conceptual domain. It would have no bearing on reality. By asserting that things are actually distinct because they have distinct distinguishers, the Ge-luk tradition is attempting to use the concept of distinguisher, which originally reflected an antirealist view, to get out of the predicament of moderate realism.

We are now in a position to realize the significance of the view found in the Collected Topics, that distinguishers can be instantiated by real things despite being themselves unreal. Individuals and properties are distinct because they have distinct distinguishers. Since those are not just projected by thought but actually exist in the individuals, the distinctions that relate to them can be taken as actual distinctions. Accordingly, for Ge-luk thinkers a conceptual distinction is an actual distinction.

The Ge-luk case is well defended by Kay-drup in a long polemic against a position quite similar to that put forth by Śākya Chok-den and Go-ram-ba.[28] Kay-drup's main point is that his opponents, the antirealists, fail to differentiate substantial from conceptual identities. They ignore the difference between these two types of identity, and this leads them to confuse substantial identity (*rdzas gcig*) with identity in general (i.e., oneness, *gcig*). Kay-drup attributes this confusion to his adversary's oversight. He says: "Moreover, the thesis that anything being substantially identical must be one rests in the final [analysis] for its evidence on the following [assumptions: (a) Things that are] substantially identical such as sound and its impermanence, etc., are observed as [being one] by the perception that apprehends them. (b) If something is observed as one by an unmistaken cognition it must be one [in reality]. This simply misses the distinction between (i) being observed as being one by an unmistaken cognition and (ii) not being observed as being distinct [by such a cognition]."[29] Kay-drup identifies the unwarranted assumption on which his adversaries' argument rests. They assume that things that are substantially identical are observed as such by perception. In assuming this, they fail to differentiate (a) not being observed as distinct and (b) being observed as one. They also assume that if two things really exist, they must be seen as one if they are not seen as distinct. This assumption is unwarranted, argues Kay-drup, for the perception of sound does not hear sound and impermanence as one but is just unable to distinguish them. To fail to make a distinction is not the same as actively noticing an identity. If they were the same, argues Kay-drup, the perception of sound would perceive sound as having a self (*bdag yod*) since it does not perceive it as selfless.[30]

Kay-drup's ingenious diagnosis stops short of completely identifying the assumptions separating him from his antirealist adversaries. The antirealists do not just commit a dialectical blunder. Rather, they have a different idea of what is real. For them, something is real if, and only if, it is an individual thing. Thus, when we say that jar and impermanence are substantially identical, that means they are the same real thing; that is, the same individual. Within an antirealist framework, therefore, substantial identity necessarily implies identity.

The moderate realist view Kay-drup defends is an attempt to find a middle ground between extreme realism and conceptualism. It depends on finding a differentiation of universals and particulars that straddles the fence between the usual ways in which we distinguish things. This is Scotus's formal distinction and Kumārila's identity in difference. The Ge-luk answer is closer to the latter than to the former. For, it does not offer a completely new way of drawing distinctions but, rather, combines the two usual ways of distinguishing things.

The accusation of artificiality often raised against Scotus's formal distinction also applies to the Ge-luk presentation. However, inconsistency (the problem faced by Kumārila) is of greater concern. In authors such as Śākya Chok-den and Go-ram-ba, the distinction between same and different entities is easy to make since it corresponds to what Aristotle calls *identity* or *difference in number* (and to our common notion of identity).[31] The Ge-luk distinction between substantial identity and difference does not correspond to our commonsense differentiation; it is a technical distinction whose boundaries are hard to determine. We could even wonder if this distinction is coherent.

Ge-luk students are familiar with the many debates on this topic. For example, a jar and impermanence are substantially identical. What about the jar and its smell?[32] Jar is usually considered by Ge-luk scholars to be an example of a form sphere (*gzugs kyi skye mched, rūpāyatana*).[33] Form and smell are distinct spheres,[34] and as such they are considered substantially distinct. Since jar and its smell are instances from distinct spheres, should they not also be substantially different? Whereas scholars from Sera Jay College usually answer positively, those from Dre-bung Lo-se-ling respond negatively.

The view that a jar and its smell are substantially different is consistent with the assertion that different spheres are distinct entities. But it goes against the Buddhist assertion that parts and wholes can never be substantially different. It even gets uncomfortably close to the Nyāya philosophy of separate wholes. The view that a jar and its smell are substantially identical is consistent with the requirement for parts and wholes. It has difficulty, however, in explaining how a jar, which is a form, and its smell can be inseparable from the point of view of perception!

These difficulties illustrate the problems that the distinctions created by moderate realists face. They show the tension in a type of relation created by the combination of two conflicting ways of making distinctions. These tensions illustrate the predicament of the moderate realist view in its attempt to retain real properties without paying the price of ontological reification. Moreover, these tensions reveal a problem more particular to Ge-luk philosophy, which arises from its historical situation in a commentarial tradition. This problem is how to defend a moderate realist reading of a conceptualist author (Dharmakīrti). This predicament becomes clearly visible in the complicated topic of predication, which I address later in this chapter. Before going into this, however, let us examine the arguments given by Ge-luk thinkers to support their view.

Arguments for Moderate Realism

The arguments used by Ge-luk thinkers to defend their moderate realism reflect the nature of their enterprise. This enterprise is philosophical but it is also commentarial. In Tibetan traditions, these two aspects go together. Therefore, the Ge-luk tradition must support its interpretations textually, showing that its views correspond to what Dharmakīrti really intended. In addition to these textual arguments are more purely philosophical arguments presented independent of any textual references.

One of the main Ge-luk textual arguments rests on the interpretation of a passage where Dharmakīrti argues that individual cows do not have a common essence. Nevertheless, they share something in common: "The form of the multicolored [cow] does not exist in the brown [cow]. What is common to the two is the exclusion from non[performance of] a function."[35] This passage is puzzling for its last two verses seem to contradict its first two. If there is no form (*rūpa* means both shape and entity) shared by the individual cows, how can Dharmakīrti assert that they have something in common? This passage has given rise to a number of interpretations: Go-ram-ba and other antirealists interpret it as denying that anything real is common to individuals. The common element is purely conceptual, as indicated by the negative language used by Dharmakīrti.[36]

Tibetan realists take this passage to express the opposite view, that there is something common to discrete individuals. Bo-dong, for one, takes this passage to indicate that the common entity is a negative but real property. Brown and white cows have in common that they are not noncows. This non-noncowness, which is referred to as mere *cowness* (*ba tsam*), is a real entity. It is instantiated by all individual cows but is not a cow. It is also different from cowness, which is the concept of cow reified by Indian extreme realists.[37]

Gyel-tsap points to this passage as proving that Dharmakīrti cannot be an antirealist. Otherwise, the last two verses of the passage would contradict the thesis expressed in the first two verses. Accordingly, the first two verses are understood not as denying any commonality between individuals, as the antirealists assert. Rather they deny the reified commonality imagined by Hindu realists. There is no separate cowness common to all cows, for each has its own specific spatio-temporal existence. Nevertheless, they have something in common: that they are all cows. This is not something we superimpose but something intrinsic to the individual cows' identities. Hence, cow is real despite being a universal.[38]

Although Ge-luk realism is introduced as an interpretation of Dharmakīrti, its main and most cogent support is not textual but philosophical.[39] As I will show in the next chapter, the realism of the Ge-luk school is due mostly to the historical situation and background of its founders. Dzong-ka-ba, Gyel-tsap, and Kay-drup were realists because they were members of traditions in which a realist interpretation of Dharmakīrti had dominated for long time. They kept to this tradition, based on such an unlikely interpretation less as the result of a close reading of Dharmakīrti than of a philosophical reflection about the problems in Dharmakīrti's system. In a tradition in which philosophy is mostly a commentary on some preexisting tradition, such reflection takes the form of an interpretation. In our case, realism is offered as the authoritative interpretation of Dharmakīrti's works. Nevertheless, the arguments for adopting this interpretation are more philosophical than textual. Let us consider these arguments.

Gyel-tsap argues that, if universals were not real, reasoning that rests on them would not apply to reality. If this is so, hidden phenomena such as infinitesimal atoms and the subtle aspect of impermanence could not be established since they are neither perceivable nor inferable. Reality then would become limited to what can be perceived, an unacceptable position for a Buddhist. Gyel-tsap further criticizes the answer that reasoning operates by holding to unreal entities but, nevertheless, leads to practical success. How can one get to the real by merely holding to some fiction? The understanding produced by correct evidence must connect with reality; otherwise, it would be similar to contradictory evidence (*'gal rtags*).[40]

Similarly, Dzong-ka-ba argues for a realist interpretation of Dharmakīrti on the grounds that antirealism makes it impossible to understand reality in a way that is conducive to the practice of Buddhism. Antirealism makes it difficult to identify reality, for it excludes commonsense objects as well as universals from the purview of the real. Identification of reality, like any identification, presupposes a categorization that allows us to classify the individual objects we encounter. Without such classification, knowledge becomes impossible. Since, for the antirealist, categories are superimposed by our conceptual schema, such classification becomes groundless. Moreover, denying the reality of spatio-temporal extended objects makes it impossible to explain the causal connections that we observe in daily life. How can we explain the causal relations that we observe if we exclude duration from the real?

Moreover, argues Dzong-ka-ba, antirealism makes it difficult to elaborate an account of our cognitive practices. In particular, it makes it difficult to explain how conceptions seem to bring us knowledge.[41] How can thought that is limited to constructs ever be correct? How do we explain that we do seem to acquire knowledge by reasoning?[42] How do we explain that reasoning seems to lead us toward greater understanding of the impermanent or selfless nature of reality? To say that we just conceive of things in certain ways that work for us is no explanation but the recognition of one's incapacity to provide a convincing answer!

Kay-drup argues at length for the existence of real universals (*spyi dngos po ba*). His arguments are mostly appeals to commonsense. Things (*dngos po, vastu*) exist with their own unique essence (literally, unmixed with other things, *dngos po gzhan dang ma 'dres pa*). This, argues Kay-drup, does not exclude the possibility that some things may be concomitant with individual instances. Kay-drup says: "There is no contradiction for jar, thing, etc., to be concomitant with their individuals and exist itself unmixed in location, time, [and] entity. Therefore, anything that is a thing must be a specifically characterized phenomenon. Moreover, there is no contradiction between being a specifically characterized phenomenon and being a universal that is concomitant with its individuals."[43] If real things cannot be concomitant with several instances, it would be impossible for several things of the same kind to exist simultaneously, which would be absurd. Moreover, anything real would have to be absolutely numerically unique.

Kay-drup argues that nothing in the meaning of *universal* prevents universals from being real. To be a universal is to exist as something that at least two phenomena share in common. Therefore, just being concomitant with two other phenomena is enough to establish a thing as a universal. Being concomitant with at least two things does not conflict with being real. For example, thing itself is concomitant with jars, trees, and the like and, therefore, is a universal.

How may a universal be real? As we already noticed,[44] one of the key moves in the realist interpretation of Dharmakīrti is to separate the meanings of universal (*spyi, sāmānya*) and generally characterized phenomenon (*spyi mtshan, sāmānya-lakṣaṇa*). A generally characterized phenomenon is an essenceless construct. To be a universal means to exist in common, not to be an essenceless construct. Therefore, some real phenomena may be universals.

For Kay-drup and other Ge-luk thinkers, a universal is not necessarily a superimposed factor, although universals qua universals are unreal. Red color is real since its identity as a color (*kha dog gi cha*) derives from the causes that produce it. As a universal, however, red color is unreal since its identity as a universal (*spyi'i cha*) depends on a conceptual framework. Dignāga's and Dharmakīrti's critiques of universals does not refer to the universals qua things but to the universals qua universals. Hence, being a universal is not incompatible with being real.[45]

This distinction between the identity of a thing as a thing and its identity as a universal is quite different from Dharmakīrti's view, for he leaves these two identities undifferentiated and globally denies any reality to universals. The subtle distinction drawn by Kay-drup between the real identity of a thing as a thing and its relational identity as a universal reflects the moderate realism of the tradition, which posits that universals and particulars are relative.[46] It is a somewhat artificial attempt to give a realist reading of an antirealist tradition.

Such a reading is not, however, without explanatory power. An important argument for a realist interpretation of Dharmakīrti is that it is able to provide an adequate ontological basis to reasoning, a task beyond the power of antirealism. One of the key points of Dharmakīrti's logic is that the terms of a reasoning, the subject, property, and evidence, are unreal. The obvious question is this: How can the use of unreal terms yield any knowledge about the real world? Śākya Chok-den answers that the use of concepts is mistaken but pragmatically useful. Ge-luk thinkers finds such an answer wholly lacking, for it is tantamount to an admission that Dharmakīrti's theory is unable to justify the validity of reasoning.

Ge-luk realism offers a viable alternative by distinguishing between the unreal identity of the term qua term of reasoning and its real identity. For example, the subject of our reasoning (the Vedic language is impermanent because it is produced just like a jar), the Vedic language, is unreal as subject but real as a thing. This distinction is captured in an elegant if somewhat abstruse way by the the notion of distinguisher understood à la realist. The subject of the reasoning is then said to be unreal as far as its own distinguisher (*rang ldog,* that is, *ldog pa*) is concerned but real as far as its basis distinguisher (*gzhi ldog*; that is, its instance) is concerned. In this way, Dharmakīrti's logic is set on a firm footing. A reasoning can be valid because it captures real properties instanciated by real entities. Its terms are unreal only as far as they are taken as terms, but they are part of the fabric of reality as far as their real essence is concerned. In our example, the Vedic language is unreal inasmuch as it is taken as a term of reasoning. This does not prevent it from being real. Reasoning can take as its terms real properties instantiated by real entities. In the process, these properties and entities acquire superimposed conceptual identities. This entails that reasoning contains a certain amount of distortion. Thought cannot understand reality exactly as it is. It does, however, get in touch with reality, not with some separate conceptual domain, as antirealists would have it. Hence, the distortions of thought do not prevent its validity.

Another interpretive strategy used by the Ge-luk tradition is to hold that the numerous denials of real universals by Dignāga and Dharmakīrti are directed against the overreification of universals by Hindu thinkers. According to their extreme realism, universals are real and independent of their instances. Such putative entities do not exist at all. They are negated from both ultimate and conventional points of view. Kay-drup says: "The refutation of the reality (*bden grub*) of universals is twofold: [universals such as] the [Sāṃkhya] Nature, etc. imputed by non-Buddhists are negated both conventionally and in reality. Universals in our own system are [only] refuted in reality, not conventionally . . ."[47] Since Dignāga's and Dharmakīrti's numerous statements denying the reality of universals can be interpreted in these two ways, these passages do not conclusively support the view that universals must be unreal. If there are two plausible interpretations of a statement, the sounder one is to be chosen. The interpretation that no universal can be real is philosophically less plausible than the interpretation accepting the reality of some universals; hence, we must follow the second interpretation.

Subject and Predicate

We have examined the nature of Ge-luk moderate realism and the arguments that support it. A final topic to consider in this tradition is its analysis of predication. Looking at this topic will give us the opportunity to understand the particularity of the Ge-luk view as a moderate realist interpretation of a conceptualist system. Let us start by examining Dharmakīrti's view of predication together with its Nyāya background.

It is a realist principle that every element we experience has a correspondent in reality. In accordance with this principle, the Nyāya school holds that the distinction between subject and predicate is not just a reflection of linguistic structures. We speak of "a cow being impermanent" and "the cow's impermanence."[48] Both imply that a subject (a substance such as a cow) possesses another object (being impermanent). The Naiyāyikas argue that such expressions involve two real and separate entities: an individual (cow) as subject and a property (impermanence) as predicate. The information provided by predication cannot be accounted for if we do not accept a real difference between subject (substance) and predicate (property).

Buddhist epistemologists think that predication involves no more than a peculiar way of differentiating an individual. Dharmakīrti articulates this view in *Commentary*, I:60: "Although both [subject and predicate expressions can] describe the same real entity, under the influence of a [grammatical] case [such as the genitive] the impression that there are distinct objects is created."[49] There is no need for two elements to account for expressions such as "a cow being impermanent." When somebody asks whether this cow is permanent, we answer that the cow is impermanent. The difference between the predicate expression (*chos brjod kyi sgra*) "being impermanent" and the subject expression (*chos can brjod pa'i sgra*) "a cow" is merely grammatical and reflects no real distinction. There is only one object to which we are referring, a cow, and it can be described in several ways.

We might then wonder the following: If the difference between the predicate and the subject does not reflect any real distinction, why are we so strongly tempted to assume that there are different objects corresponding to the different expressions? Kay-drup answers: "It is due to the strength of the influence of habituation to seeing the many times we use the genitive in [expressions] such as 'Ḍittha's jar' in [cases with] subjects and predicates that are substantially different."[50] Kay-drup attributes our desire to find real correspondents for linguistic expressions to the distortion of conceptuality. Our compulsion to assume a correspondence between what we say and what there is comes from a long habituation to naming different things by different names.

In the expression "the cow's impermanence" there are no separate objects corresponding to both parts of the expression, cow and impermanence. Yet we vainly try to find such objects to make this expression fit the "standard" situation in which we do use different terms to name separate objects. Cases such as "cow's impermanence" expose the ways in which we have become trapped by language. This entrapment is due to a fascination with a particular view of language, a model that depicts linguistic activity as a succession of ostensively defined names of objects. Moreover, it presumes that we know these objects by direct acquaintance. This compulsion to make reality fit language reflects the inherent distortion that characterizes conceptuality. It is what distinguishes conceptuality from direct experience, which is the only cognitive mode that fully reflects reality.[51]

This explanation of predication is certainly not going to convince the Nyāya realists, whose aim is to find a direct correspondence between real and linguistic orders. The Nyāya retorts that, if the different parts of our expression do not describe different objects, then why bother with these different descriptions? Against this objection, Dharmakīrti states the Buddhist point of view in *Commentary*, I:61: "Exclusion and non-exclusion of other characteristics are the basis of these two [types of] different conventions which are subordinated to the intentions of the [person who] understands [them]."[52] Different ways of describing the same thing are expressions of the hearer's interests and the speaker's intentions. We could just consider a cow as a cow. We might also wonder aloud whether a cow is impermanent or not. We would then be told about "a cow being impermanent." This way of presenting things just answers our qualm. It also excludes other characteristics from the field of inquiry. Or, we may inquire about the cow in relation to its other characteristics. We then talk about "the cow's impermanence." In any case, there is only a cow and it characteristics. There is no separate "impermanence," for the only entity observed is a cow.[53]

Kay-drup's explanation of these passages restates the central point of Dharmakīrti's philosophy: the dissociation between the linguistic and real orders of things. But, as a moderate realist, his view differs from Dharmakīrti's analysis. For Dharmakīrti there is only a single entity in predication, the subject. The predicate expression does not introduce another element but merely characterizes an already introduced entity. Kay-drup's point seems to be slightly different. As a moderate realist, Kay-drup remains committed to the existence of a certain distinction between subject and predicate. The predicate expression is more than a useful characterization of the subject. And yet, it does not introduce a separate element. Hence, Kay-drup interprets Dharmakīrti as arguing that the predicate expression does not introduce a categorically separate property (although it does introduce an element that cannot be reduced to the subject). Let us examine his analysis of predication to understand the peculiarities of Ge-luk moderate realism.

Kay-drup explains Dharmakīrti's stanzas as playing on the permutation of the two expressions "a cow being impermanent" and "the cow's impermanence." Dharmakīrti is responding to an adversary who argues that there is an intrinsic difference between subject and predicate. According to Kay-drup's interpretation, Dharmakīrti takes the first of the two phrases and argues that, if there is an intrinsic difference between subject and predicate, then cow (which is, for Kay-drup, the subject in the first phrase) and impermanence (which is the predicate in the first phrase) would always have to be subject and predicate in all synonymous phrases. This is not the case because cow is the predicate and impermanence is the subject in the second sentence ("the cow's impermanence"). This sentence is stated to a person who, for example, on hearing *impermanence*, asks whether it is the impermanence of a cow or a buffalo. We answer that we are talking about the impermanence of a cow. Here, according to Kay-drup, impermanence is the subject and cow the predicate.

Accordingly, it is not possible to explain the expression *the cow's impermanence* as the conjunction of a separate property (impermanence) with a particular cow. If it were, there would be no explanation for how "a cow being impermanent" and "the cow's impermanence" are synonymous, even though the subjects and predicates are different.

How does Kay-drup's explanation compare with that of dedicated antirealists such as Śākya Chok-den? Two things need to be stressed. First, Kay-drup's explanations are true to Dharmakīrti's most essential point; that is, that predication does not mirror the structure of reality. Whereas the grammatical structure of predication suggests that we are dealing with two separate entities, the Buddhist view is that there is no intrinsic difference between subjects and predicates.[54] Rather, a phenomenon is either a subject or a predicate depending on whether it can be described by a predicate expression or a subject expression. Predication pertains to the conceptual domain and has no immediate correspondence with reality.

In accordance with this view, Kay-drup defines *predicate expression* as "that word which indicates the very object singled out by the speaker and the hearer's intentions as a predicate."[55] An example is the word *cow* in *the cow's impermanence*. Similarly, a subject expression is a word that indicates an object as a subject, for example, the word *cow* in *a cow being impermanent.*

This rather formal way of putting things can be clarified by examining the ways these two types of expression introduce their object. Dharmakīrti explains a predicate expression as "eliminating other characteristics" (*khyad par gzhan spongs*). As Kay-drup says: "Words do not make their speakers [express themselves] unwillingly, but indicate things in accordance with the intentions of the speaker and [the interests of] the hearer. In reference to this, [the expression] 'eliminating other characteristics' means that when we introduce this object as a characteristic we eliminate [the possibility for this object to] appear as the subject acting as a support for other characteristics."[56] Subject expressions are said "not to eliminate other characteristics" because they introduce their objects as possible bases for positing other properties. Predicate expressions are said to "eliminate other characteristics" inasmuch as they eliminate the (subjective) possibility for this object to appear as a support of other characteristics. For Dharmakīrti, the difference between the two types of expression is that a subject expression introduces an object in the universe of discourse whereas a predicate expression qualifies the object already introduced.

This view is accepted equally by Sa-gya and Ge-luk thinkers, despite their differences. The Ge-luk view is realist only inasmuch as it posits that the truth of predication necessitates the existence of some real properties. It does not agree with the extreme realist view that subject and predicate are intrinsically separate. In our example, cow and impermanence do not exist apart from each other. Hence, the articulations of our ideas does not mirror the structure of reality.

And yet, this is the second point to be made here, Kay-drup's view is not identical to Śākya Chok-den's and other antirealists. In accordance with his moderate realism, Kay-drup introduces a realist twist to his otherwise orthodox explanations. This is noticeable in his explanation of subject and predicate in the aforementioned two sentences given as examples of stanza I:61: "a cow being impermanent" and "a cow's impermanence." Whereas in the former cow is the subject, it is the predicate in the latter.

Śākya Chok-den vehemently disagrees with Kay-drup's interpretation of this stanza. Śākya Chok-den argues that, even if a person inquires whether we are talking about the impermanence of a cow or a buffalo, the subject cannot be impermanence. The distinction between subject and predicate is not only grammatical or pragmatic but also semantic. There is no denying that predication is complex and involves a grammatical distinction that follows linguistic conventions and a pragmatic dimension based on the context of the inquiry.[57] These distinctions should not obscure the semantic of predication, however. In a lengthy refutation of this particular point in the Ge-luk presentation,[58] Śākya Chok-den argues that cow is the subject and impermanence is the predicate independent of how the phrase and the inquiry are formulated. Otherwise, it would absurdly follow that when one understands the second sentence, one would take impermanence as a subject and predicate cow of it. This is not a correct predication since that would be tantamount to negating noncow on the subject, impermanence. Noncow cannot, however, be correctly negated of impermanence since impermanence is a noncow. Hence, cow cannot be correctly predicated of impermanence.[59]

This argument is by far not as decisive as Śākya Chok-den wants us to believe. For Kay-drup could answer that, in the second sentence, we are not asserting that impermanence is cow, but merely that impermanence belongs to the cow. Nevertheless, Śākya Chok-den's larger point stands. For Kay-drup's analysis seems to overlook the semantic difference between subject and predicate expressions. Whereas Śākya Chok-den holds that the former is a name and the second is not, Kay-drup assimilates the functions of the predicate expression to that of the subject expression. For him, the function of a subject expression is to designate the subject and that of a predicate expression is to designate a predicate. Both name their objects. Thus, when I say "a cow is impermanent," I may be not introducing a separate real element (as the Nyāya view would want) but I am introducing a real entity that cannot be reduced to the subject. When I predicate impermanence of a cow, a full account requires two elements: an individual and a property, which does not exist apart from the former but is not reducible to it either. Otherwise, predication would be a tautological assertion of identity. To say "a cow is impermanent" would be the same as saying "a cow is a cow."

Śākya Chok-den argues that this move, which is customary to most forms of realism, is problematic, for it fails to realize that the two expressions are semantically different.[60] Whereas the subject expression introduces an object in the realm of discourse, the predicate expression does not introduce anything. Its sole function is to further characterize an already introduced object. The mistake, argues Śākya

Chok-den, is not to understand the fundamental difference between individuals and properties. Whereas the former are concrete objects that have identity conditions, the latter are not things. They are abstract and cannot be individuated. Hence, they are not real. This is not to deny that they are relevant to our conceptual activities, but that this relevance does not entail any ontological commitment.

This analysis of predication shows the peculiarity of Ge-luk moderate realism. The idea that a predicate expression designates a property distinct from the subject is usually held by extreme realists such as the Naiyāyikas, who assert a radical difference between individuals and properties. It is also asserted by moderate realists such as Aristotle or Samantabhadra, who accept that there is a categorical difference between subject and predicate. It is more unusual to find the view that the predicate expressions designate real properties combined with a denial of an intrinsic difference between subject and predicate.[61]

This reflects the peculiar historical and philosophical situation of the tradition. Because Ge-luk thinkers are heirs to Dharmakīrti's conceptualist system, they do not accept a categorical framework. On the basis of Dharmakīrti's *apoha* theory, they refuse to accept the Nyāya distinction between substance and properties. Accordingly, they understand the difference between subject and predicate to be nominal. Nevertheless, because predicate expressions designate real entities, both subject and predicate must be real. Since predicates are real, real universals serving as the referents of predicate expressions must also be accepted.

Philosophy and Linguistic Ambiguities

In concluding this chapter, I would like to wonder about the reasons for the Ge-luk adoption of a realist interpretation of Dharmakīrti. Why did Dzong-ka-ba and his disciples adopt such an unusual position?

A first hypothesis is that the Ge-luk view is due to an influence of the linguistic medium in which it is expressed. The reader has probably noticed that I have used some rather unfelicitous "English" expressions to describe what Ge-luk thinkers were saying in Tibetan. For example, I have said "jar is impermanent" to translate the Tibetan *bum pa mi rtag pa yin*. To what does this "jar" (*bum pa*) refer? Does it mean *a* jar, *the* jar, or *jars*? Moreover, I have also encountered difficulties in the translation of words such as *mi rtag pa* (impermanence, but also that which is impermanent). These phrases show some of the natural ambiguities of the Tibetan language.

We often perceive Tibetan language as ambiguous due to the absence of two grammatical distinctions found in the English language. English distinguishes "a jar" from "the jar."[62] We also like to differentiate abstractions such as impermanence from concrete things. For example, we distinguish impermanence from the things that are impermanent. Tibetan does not systematically mark either of these distinctions.

Interestingly enough, Sanskrit marks the second of the two distinctions, differentiating *anitya* (impermanent) from *anityatā* (impermanence). The Tibetan language has a technical way of translating this by differentiating *mi rtag pa* (*anitya*) from *mi rtag pa nyid* (*anityatā*), and the tradition can give a philosophical exposition of this difference. These two expressions, however, are not communicative of any difference in meaning in Tibetan. They mark a technical difference that plays no part in Tibetan discussion or debate.

Hence, we might wonder about the influence of this ambiguous formulation in the production of a view of universals. For Indian thinkers, the difference between a concrete entity (an impermanent phenomenon) and an abstract entity (impermanence) was naturally marked by the language in which they were thinking. That difference has not been there for Tibetans. They artificially created the distinction but it did not take hold in the language as it was used. Have not Tibetan thinkers then tended to ignore this distinction in their thinking? Has this situation lead to a position, moderate realism, whose philosophical problems partially derive from linguistic ambiguities?

The response must be nuanced, though essentially negative. It would be quite wrongheaded to suggest that this ambiguity is the only, or even the main, factor that led to the acceptance of a realist position in a large segment of the Tibetan tradition. It is likely that the ambiguity of the Tibetan language has been a contributing factor, encouraging thinkers to accept the moderate realism we have been discussing here. It is clear, however, that the main reasons for the development of moderate realism in Tibet have to be sought elsewhere. The next chapter undertakes this search, showing that this unlikely interpretation of Dharmakīrti is not a Tibetan fabrication but the continuation of an interpretive strand already existing in India.

10

Realism in Buddhist Tradition

Two Early Tibetan Realists

The preceding investigation has shown the nature of and some of the rationale behind Ge-luk moderate realism. It would be wrong, however, to think that Gyel-tsap's and Kay-drup's realist interpretations of Dharmakīrti were unusual in Tibet. Realism did not originate with Ge-luk thinkers but was part of a well-established intellectual tradition that predated them. This is confirmed by the location of the Ge-luk view of universals mostly in the Collected Topics, texts that have a propaedeutic character. These texts have their origins in the tradition started by Cha-ba and his disciples. Often these texts do not express the full-blown Ge-luk position on a given topic. It would be tempting to declare that this view does not represent the more mature point of view of the tradition. Nevertheless, no other theory of universals appears to exist in the tradition. This suggests that the view of universals found in the Collected Topics (and defended by Kay-drup) represents the tradition's authoritative view.

This conclusion is reinforced by the fact that a similar view is found throughout the Tibetan logico-epistemological tradition. It was by no means limited to those outside the Sa-gya tradition, such as Cha-ba's followers or the Ge-luk-bas.[1] Rather, it was widespread even among thinkers inside the Sa-gya tradition prior to the fifteenth century, despite Sa-paṇ's vigorous antirealism. Although most post-fifteenth century Sa-gyas took Sa-paṇ's antirealism for granted, not all thinkers within the tradition have shared this view.

This chapter analyzes this phenomenon historically and philosophically, showing its reasons and significance. I ask questions such as these: Where, why, and how did this interpretation of Dharmakīrti's system emerge? Only a detailed study of the logico-epistemological texts of early periods (before Sa-paṇ) could give a complete answer. This, however, falls outside the scope of my work. Hence, I will make just a few scattered remarks that suggest some of the characteristics of Tibetan realism prior to the rise of the Ge-luk tradition. To illustrate the situation of the Tibetan tradition prior to this time, I examine two early realist commentators, Sa-paṇ's direct disciple U-yuk-ba and the polymath Bo-dong. Both were members of the Sa-gya fold, even Bo-dong, who was Sa-paṇ's most vocal critic. In these pages, I do not present a detailed analysis of their positions but just a few impressionistic glimpses of their views, which are typical of this period. I also review some of the key interpretive moves made by Tibetan realist interpreters of Dharmakīrti.

One of these moves is to distinguish extreme from moderate realism. This move is essential because it deflects Dharmakīrti's critique of universals toward the reified properties posited by Hindu extreme realists. U-yuk-ba makes such a move in the process of explaining Dharmakīrti's refutation of real universals. He distinguishes between real universals (*don la yod pa'i spyi*) and mental universals (*blo la yod pa'i spyi*). An instance of a real universal is the similarity shared by all individual pots. U-yuk-ba says: "'Universal' is mentioned [in reference to] the similarity that all pots share with non-nonpot. [Such a universal] pervades all [instances of being a] pot."[2] Something is common to all pots that does not exist in anything not a pot. This property of being a pot, or to speak in more Buddhist terms, the fact of not being a nonpot, is the universal of individual pots. According to U-yuk-ba, Dharmakīrti refers to such a universal in stanza I:68. There he states that a mind that apprehends several individuals as being of one kind depends on the individuals that appear identical. U-yuk-ba reads Dharmakīrti to say that the real things on which this mind depends have something in common that it apprehends. Accordingly, Dharmakīrti's denial of real universals refers to mental universals. U-yuk-ba says: "The second [mental universal] is the unitary appearance held [by] thought in reference to the appearance of pots [which appear under] different aspects. This is certainly an [example of a mental universal] because it [consists of] the fusion as one [entity] of [the different things that are of] similar kind. That this very [mental universal] is indicated here [by Dharmakīrti is shown by] the quote 'it appears as if it were not distinct'."[3] U-yuk-ba attempts to reconcile his realist stand with Dharmakīrti's antirealism. He does so by narrowing Dharmakīrti's view to a denial solely of the reality of mental universals. Those are the concepts we impose on things to unify their diversity and they are reified by Hindu realists. However, says U-yuk-ba, another kind of universal exists in the objects themselves. They share something in common beyond simply being conceived to be of the same type by human beings. All pots share in common that they are not nonpots. Without the existence of such real properties our thinking would be arbitrary, for it would have no objective basis.

This attempt to develop a moderate realism within the Sa-gya tradition is criticized by Go-ram-ba. In his comments on the same passage (*Commentary*, I:68–70), Go-ram-ba quotes U-yuk-ba's explanations without naming him and briefly explains that U-yuk-ba is wrong to believe that Dharmakīrti refers to objective universals in this passage. Dharmakīrti merely identifies universals as distinguishers. Moreover, adds Go-ram-ba, Dharmakīrti's refutation of real universals would apply to both kinds of universals that were artificially distinguished by U-yuk-ba.[4] Interestingly, Go-ram-ba does not refute U-yuk-ba at length. A probable explanation for this moderation is that he is not willing to emphasize differences within his own tradition, even though he refutes the similarly realist position of another school. Go-ram-ba's main target is the Ge-luk view of universals we have already examined.

Another variant of early realism can be found in the works of Bo-dong, whose realism is quite similar to the position examined previously. It also presents the supplementary interest of being closer to the realism of early Tibetan thinkers than that of U-yuk-ba. Hence, it is quite close to the position often criticized by Sa-paṇ. This explains the vivacity of Bo-dong's reactions. I will not enter into the details of Bo-dong's complex presentation but just sketch some of his main points.

Although I have introduced Bo-dong as a realist, he himself would refuse the label. I call him a realist because, as we may remember, Bo-dong distinguishes between generally characterized phenomena and universals. Although most universals are generally characterized, not all are so, for some are real. Moreover, some generally characterized phenomena, such as the distinguisher of the pot in front of me, do not have a plurality (at least two) of instances. Hence, they are not universals.[5] For Bo-dong, this suggests that universal and generally characterized phenomenon are not equivalent. That is, some generally characterized phenomena are not universals and vice versa. This dissociation between universal and generally characterized phenomena is one of the main interpretive moves made by realist commentators.[6]

Nevertheless, and here is where Bo-dong would deny being a realist, he criticizes other Tibetan thinkers for introducing a realism that is in fact a disguised Sāṃkhya view.[7] He argues that this view is not feasible because it necessitates the existence of a partless universal. Such a universal cannot be part of reality, since being effective requires the presence of parts. Moreover, Bo-dong argues, the classical Buddhist critique of real universals applies to the type of positive realism found in the Ge-luk tradition.[8] If, for example, jar and thing really were substantially identical, as claimed by Ge-luk thinkers, they would have to be so in final analysis. But this is not compatible with their having a relation of particular and universal. For, universals and particulars are necessarily distinct. Hence, we are faced with this choice: Either jar and impermanence are real and they cannot be particular and universal, or they are fictional.[9] In either case, realism fails!

These comments could lead us to think that Bo-dong shares Sa-paṇ's antirealism. Bo-dong makes clear, however, that he is not in agreement with Sa-paṇ, whom he characteristically accuses of nihilism (literally, denial, *skur 'debs*).[10] Bo-dong's criticism mostly repeats his previous attacks on Sa-paṇ's ontology; namely, that without any real universals, reasoning becomes completely unsupported by reality. Against the answer that reasoning does not rest on evidence that exists in reality but on reasons that exist in the conceptual sphere (literally, from an eliminative point of view, *sel ngor*), Bo-dong points out that this entails a denial of the validity of reason and inference. Moreover, if the same analysis were followed to its logical consequences, the reality of causes and effects would be threatened. Bo-dong rejects both Sa-paṇ's antirealism and the type of moderate realism we have seen in the Ge-luk tradition. What is his position? How can one entertain a position that would avoid the faults of both extremes?

Bo-dong's "miraculous" solution is to formulate the relation between particulars and universals in negative terms. Thing is not the universal of pot but mere thing (*dngos po tsam*), which is the negation of nonthingness, is the universal of pot.[11] For Bo-dong, mere thing is not a conceptual entity. It is an objective elimination (*don rang mtshan gyi gzhan sel*), which is, as we will see later, something both real and an elimination.[12] Such a thing participates in the fabric of reality since it is produced from causes and is causally effective. It is also and more surprisingly a distinguisher. This is so because it is "the factor of opposition to [phenomena belonging to] a discordant kind" (*rigs mi mthun las bzlog pa'i cha*).[13] That is, "mere thing" is the real property that negates nonthing. Bo-dong's negative solution to the problem of universals avoids, he claims, the mistakes of the positions he criticizes. Since these negative universals are real, Sa-paṇ's nihilism is avoided. Since they are conceptually differentiated from other real entities such as pot or thing, the extreme of positive realism is avoided.

It seems to me, however, that Bo-dong's claims cannot resist a searching investigation. First, it does not seem possible to accept his claim to present an original position. When examined, his view is seen to be quite similar to that criticized by Śākya Śrībhadra during his first meeting with Sa-paṇ. Asked if mere blue (*sngo tsam*) exists, the Indian master was puzzled by this expression. He sarcastically answered that sometimes he does not know very much, but he knows one thing: Blue exists in reality.[14] That is, the fabric of reality contains individual objects such as a patch of blue. Inasmuch as an entity such as mere blue is instantiated by these real individuals, it can be only conceptual. Thus, it seems clear from Śākya Śrībhadra's response that Bo-dong's claim to originality is unfounded. Moreover, his position is quite similar to that articulated by Rik-bay-ral-dri.[15]

Second, and more important, Bo-dong's position is unable to escape self-contradiction. For, if a negative universal is real, then it must be a either substantially identical with or different from its particulars. The faults adduced by Bo-dong himself against positive universals would then apply equally to these negative entities. It seems that in this case the recourse to negative language cannot prevent the difficulties that confront realism.[16] Once one has granted that the criterion for being a universal is "to be instantiated by individuals" (and not to be constructed as such by thought without any direct objective support), the use of "negativeese" cannot prevent this criterion from applying equally to thing and mere thing.

Perhaps Bo-dong's negative realism is best explained as an attempt to distinguish properties from individual things, thus resolving the ambiguity that seems to exist in Tibetan where abstract and concrete entities are not marked separately. Whereas *thing* refers to individuals, *mere thing* describes the property of being a thing. As the negation of nonthing, mere thing is the property instantiated by all the particular things. Hence, whereas mere thing is a real universal, thing can be only a particular. However, this attempt to use the *apoha* theory, which is based on a refusal of any real categorical difference, to make a categorical distinction between individual and property is difficult in Dharmakīrti's tradition, despite its philosophical justification.

Moderate Realism in Tibet and Madhyamaka

Whatever the truth of the matter is, the main point of these few scattered remarks is not to provide a precise description of Bo-dong's realism. Rather, it is to illustrate the extent to which realism has been, prior to the fifteenth century, the dominant interpretation of Dharmakīrti's philosophy. Tibetan thinkers have adopted this view despite their different backgrounds and sectarian affiliations. Realism is not the privilege of any tradition, but has been widely accepted among Tibetan thinkers. Hence, the realism of the Ge-luk tradition is not as extraordinary as it might at first seem. It is less the result of a deliberate philosophical choice made by Dzong-ka-ba, Kay-drup, or Gyel-tsap than the product of these authors' association with a certain intellectual milieu in which realism was the accepted view. This point requires emphasis. Ge-luk realism was unexceptional in its time. The period during which this tradition was being formed is marked by the pervasive acceptance of realism in Tibet. The dominance of this view relates to the fact that the antirealist character of Sa-paṇ's contribution had not yet been established. Rather it remained the topic of sustained inter- and intrasectarian debates. Only after the fifteenth century did Sa-paṇ's antirealism become well accepted within his tradition and sharply opposed to Ge-luk realism.

We now understand the place of Ge-luk realism within the Tibetan tradition. However, other questions remain: Why and how did realism become dominant in Tibet? One may be tempted to respond by postulating socio-political reasons. We could wonder, for example, about the relation between Ge-luk realism and the political ambitions of this school. Mark Hobbart has speculated on such a connection between philosophy and politics in general. An essentialist view of things would favor rulers and a nominalist view would be more useful to those in revolt.[17] At the time, however, when the Ge-luk views were being formulated its political authority had not yet been established. And although political motivations might play a role in the formation of this tradition, they do not seem directly pertinent to the question of realism.[18] Thus, political concerns are much less relevant to the acceptance of realism than is the philosophical situation at large.

At the end of the fifteenth century,[19] I would suggest, politics did become intertwined with the realist versus antirealist debate. Through the works of Go-ram-ba and Śākya Chok-den, antirealism became the accepted interpretation of Sa-paṇ's thought. This created a polarized situation in which realism became a political issue, a sign of sectarian appurtenance. Henceforth, realism characterized the Ge-luk tradition. Other traditions tended to emphasize their opposition to this school by adopting Go-ram-ba's and Śākya Chok-den's antirealist interpretations of Sa-paṇ. It remains the case, however, that prior to this more polarized situation (which continues to the present) many thinkers who saw themselves as Sa-paṇ's followers did not accept his rigorous interpretation of Dharmakīrti. At the time of its incipience, Ge-luk realism did not differ substantially from its contemporaries.

These considerations suggest that the Ge-luk school adopted a realist interpretation of Dharmakīrti from their intellectual heritage. Still we are left to wonder about the origins of this realist heritage and the way in which it became so pervasive in Tibet. Is realism a Tibetan peculiarity within the Buddhist logico-epistemological tradition? Or does realism as a countercurrent within the tradition reach back to India? Although the former view merits some attention, I find the latter finally much more convincing.

It is possible but mistaken to attribute realist interpretations of Dharmakīrti's logico-epistemological tradition to a Madhyamaka influence. In particular one might speculate that the so-called Prāsaṅgika interpretation of Madhyamaka might have been influential in this regard, especially since it seems to have been so important in Tibet after the twelfth century. Furthermore, this explanation might seem plausible in view of the distinctive role played by Madhyamaka in Tibet. Contrary to India, where this philosophy never received universal acceptance, Madhyamaka has been accepted by almost all schools of Tibetan Buddhism. Can the realism in Tibetan interpretations of Dharmakīrti, who is not a Mādhyamika, be due to the influence of this philosophy? Let us examine this question historically.

If we want to demonstrate a connection between Madhyamaka and realism in Tibet we need to establish that realist interpretations came to be formed under the influence of Madhyamaka ideas. As we have seen, realism seems to have been pervasive in Tibet since the early times. This means as early as Cha-ba, as Śākya Chok-den suggests. He describes realism as pervasive in Tibet right from the time of Cha-ba: "All thinkers from Cha-ba and Dzang-ngak-ba[20] up to modern [times] agree that individuations and universals are substantially identical on the basis of [their] being one thing."[21] Since the works of most early Tibetan logicians and epistemologists are not presently available and since Śākya Chok-den is hardly a disinterested observer, it is hard to draw definitive conclusions. Nevertheless, circumstantial evidence supports Śākya Chok-den's claim that realism was prevalent prior to the appearance of Sa-paṇ's *Treasure,* and originated in Tibet with the school of Cha-ba and his followers. They mark the beginning of a sustained realist tradition of logic and epistemology in Tibet. Was this beginning, which was strongly realist, influenced by Madhyamaka ideas?

A discussion of Cha-ba's Madhyamaka philosophy is not easy.[22] Since his works are not extant, we have to rely on secondary sources such as the works of Śākya Chok-den. These are not always clear or consistent in their description of the positions of this thinker. Cha-ba seems to have been influenced by Madhyamaka thought in his interpretations of Dharmakīrti. For example, on the conventional level he criticizes the representational view of perception. Specifically, he criticizes the Sautrāntika and Yogācāra view that perception's access to the world is mediated by the aspect (*rnam pa, ākāra*) of an object. Instead he proposes a direct realism similar to the Vaibhāṣika view. On the ultimate level, Cha-ba understands the entitylessness asserted by Dharmakīrti as a nonimplicative negation (*med dgag, prasajyapratiṣedha*).[23] Hence, some of the seminal thinkers of the Tibetan logico-epistemological tradition were favorably disposed toward Madhyamaka interpretations of Dharmakīrti's system. One may wonder then whether the enthusiasm for realism was not due to a Madhyamaka influence?

The influence of Madhyamaka does not, however, seem to be the main reason for the predominance of realism in Tibet. Mādhyamika thinkers such as Śāntarakṣita, Prajñākaragupta and Mokṣākaragupta, who inflected early Tibetan interpretations of Dharmakīrti toward Madhyamaka views, do not accept the realist interpretation of Dharmakīrti propounded by Cha-ba. It is true that Candrakīrti supports a realist view and that realism quite accords with a Prāsaṅgika view of universals as it appears in Candrakīrti. The realist's assertion of an ontological equality between universals and particulars moves in a way toward the Prāsaṅgika view of the mutual dependence of universals and particulars. By accepting real phenomena such as pot and impermanence as universals realism refuses to privilege particulars. Particulars and universals are given the same ontological status.[24] This contrasts with the ontological privilege Dharmakīrti accords particulars.

These philosophical considerations, however, do not demonstrate a significant connection between realism and Prāsaṅgika thought in the Tibetan logico-epistemological tradition. This would require Candrakīrti's ideas to have influenced the formation of that tradition's ideas. Although Candrakīrti's influence is considerable among later thinkers (and particularly among Ge-luk-bas), early Tibetan epistemologists do not seem to have been influenced by his Prāsaṅgika philosophy.[25] Cha-ba is quite critical of Candrakīrti, tending more toward Svātantrika than Prāsaṅgika.

The turn toward Prāsaṅgika that we normally associate with Tibetan Madhyamaka seems to have occurred right after Cha-ba. It is noticeable among Cha-ba's disciples such as Dzang-ngak-ba but does not seem to have been influential previously.[26] The Madhyamaka influence on the early Tibetan epistemologists responsible for the formation of the logico-epistemological tradition comes not from Candrakīrti but from thinkers such as Śāntarakṣita and Prajñākaragupta. These thinkers do not support realism. Hence, the realism evident in Tibet at this time does not seem strongly tied to a Madhyamaka influence. Historical considerations do not show a significant link between Prāsaṅgika and the origins of realism in Tibet.

An examination of the sources adduced by realist thinkers confirms the lack of connection. The presentation of universals by realists does not purport to present the Prāsaṅgika view on the topic as one would expect if realism and Prāsaṅgika were intertwined from the start. Rather it sets out to capture the view of universals as it is found in the tradition of Dignāga and Dharmakīrti. For example, Jam-yang-chok-hla-ö-ser (*'jam yang phyogs lha 'od zer*), the author of one of the earliest and most authoritative Ge-luk Collected Topics, quotes the passage we have examined earlier in Dharmakīrti's *Commentary* (I:88) as a source for his discussion of universals and particulars.[27] Thus, a careful examination of the accounts given by Tibetan thinkers also shows no reason to link the realism characteristic of early Tibetan epistemologists with a Prāsaṅgika (or Madhyamaka) influence.[28]

This conclusion is certainly clear; it does not, however, explain the existence of a strong realist trend in Tibet. Until now we have assumed that Buddhist realism, which is quite unorthodox in the logico-epistemological tradition, is a typically Tibetan phenomenon. Under this assumption, we have been looking for some explanation relating realism with peculiarities on the Tibetan tradition, attributing the difference between Tibetan and Indian interpretations to the cultural distance separating India and Tibet. This assumption is, however, unjustified. Other elements suggest a rather different answer.

Go-ram-ba[29] and Śākya Chok-den offer another explanation. They find traces of the realism they criticize in their Tibetan contemporaries in Bhavyarāja,[30] a Kashmiri scholar with whom the translator Ngok studied. Both Go-ram-ba and Śākya Chok-den[31] characterize the views of Bhavyarāja as contaminated by non-Buddhist elements. They thereby discredit this realist view as unorthodox in the Buddhist tradition. According to Go-ram-ba and Śākya Chok-den, realism in Tibet is due not to Tibetan peculiarities but to a Hindu influence on late Indian Buddhist thinkers, thinkers who were instrumental in transmitting Buddhism to Tibet. These comments, however, have to be taken with a grain of salt due to their polemical intent against Ge-luk and other thinkers who follow Cha-ba's ideas.

I would like to suggest that the view influential in early Tibetan epistemology, found in the Ge-luk tradition as well as in Bhavyarāja, is not as exceptional as Go-ram-ba and Śākya Chok-den suggest. That even Sa-paṇ's direct disciple U-yuk-ba shares this view is an indication that realism is not just a local corruption of Buddhist tradition. Rather it corresponds to an older and more "legitimate" trend. Let us trace some of the sources of this persistent realist trend within the Buddhist tradition.

Moderate Realism in India

Our examination should start with Dharmakīrti himself, for although he was certainly not a realist, his works are not without support for realism. The ambiguity of his concept of existence, which we examined earlier,[32] illustrates the actuality of the realist temptation in Dharmakīrti's works. Although Dharmakīrti explains existence mostly as equivalent to reality, at times he shifts to a different meaning of existence, now understood as equivalent to intelligibility. This slip shows the difficulty that such an antirealist thinker as Dharmakīrti has to avoid realism while involved in the study of logic and epistemology. To discuss inference and its support, reasoning, Dharmakīrti cannot but assume the existence of properties. Although this does not necessarily entail realism, it does raise the question of the status of these entities. Many passages illustrate this difficulty.

For example, in a discussion of a sophistic reasoning proposed by the Materialist,[33] Dharmakīrti refers to the presence of the property of the probandum *(sādhyadharma, sgrub bya'i chos)* in the subject. The Materialist, whose real agenda is to demonstrate the unreliability of inference, invokes several pseudo-parallels with Buddhist logic. One element in Buddhist logic he invokes is a well-known point we have encountered already. The property to be inferred in relation to the subject is to be taken generally, without qualification. For example, when a sound is inferred to be perishable (*vināśa, 'jig pa*) on the basis of being produced, the property of the probandum is perishability simpliciter. It is not the perishability of the sound (the subject) or that of the pot (the example). Dharmakīrti states the Materialist's objection and responds: "[Objection:] But it is analogous for the [*sādhya*] 'perishability' too if one conceives it in terms of the particular cases, sound and vase. [Reply:] No, it is not [analogous], for through an established perishability there is a proof that sound has this [property, perishability]."[34] In this passage, Dharmakīrti speaks of the establishment of a property (perishability) in the subject (sound). Taken at its face value, this and other passages[35] suggest that there is an element (perishability) that is common to both sound and pot. Ge-luk thinkers take such assertions literally, arguing that dialectic would be impossible without the existence of some common properties.

Śākya Chok-den contends that this is a convenient means to refer to the conceptual process in which real and conceptual entities are mistakenly conflated. Although his explanation seems to accord with the overall character of Dharmakīrti's philosophy, it remains true that elements in Dharmakīrti's texts point to an acceptance of real properties as a way to support the inferential process. A realist interpretation has advantages over the antirealist alternative. Accepting real properties allows us to ground logic more strongly in reality. It thus answers the criticism that conceptual knowledge is groundless in Dharmakīrti's system without having to accept more extreme forms of realism.

In another passage, Dharmakīrti makes a related move when he asserts that universals can be indirectly cognized by perception.[36] Since the impermanence of things does not exist apart from them, it is indirectly understood when these things are established by experience. This does not mean that impermanence is directly cognized by experience, for it is only a conceptual construct. Nevertheless, because a property such as impermanence depends on the concrete things it characterizes (conceptually?), it is established when these things are established. A similar move is found in Mokṣākaragupta, who asserts that universals can be indirectly realized by perception.[37] Although Dharmakīrti and Mokṣākaragupta do not actually assert the reality of universals, they move in that direction. If perception apprehends things as they are and if universals are indirectly cognized by perception, then the conclusion that universals must have some reality is hard to resist.

Indications of a persistent realism in Buddhist thought are found in other authors as well. Realism seems to be present, for example, in Śaṃkarānanda. He is quoted by Jay-dzün-ba in support of the Ge-luk view of universals. In his *Explanation of Dharmakīrti's Commentary,* Śaṃkarānanda comments upon Dharmakīrti's declaration that "since all things abide in their own entity . . ."[38] He explains that "[Dharmakīrti's words] 'all things' refers not only to individuals but also to universals."[39] Such a passage shows that the Ge-luk view of universals is not a Tibetan deformation of an original Indian model, but continues a conceptual evolution started in India.

Furthermore, there is also evidence that the presence of this realism in Buddhist epistemology cannot be attributed exclusively to the influence of non-

Buddhists, despite its unorthodoxy. To begin with, the realist view of universals found in Śaṃkarānanda is present in several other Indian Buddhist authors as well. In an excellent article,[40] Franco presents a fascinating picture of a group of Buddhist logicians who propounded the existence of real universals. Franco finds mention of their surprising view in a non-Buddhist work (Jayarāśi's *Tattvopaplavasiṃha*), as well as in refutations of their views by Śāntarakṣita and Kamalaśīla. This little known group of Buddhist thinkers lived, according to Franco, after Dharmakīrti and before Śāntarakṣita.

Participants in this group seem to have been led to an assertion that real universals exist by their understanding of Dignāga's view of conceptual cognition *(kalpanā, rtog pa)*. Let us take a brief look at the discussion in the Buddhist tradition that ensues. In his *Auto-Commentary,* Dignāga elaborates his well-known definition of perception (*pratyakṣa, mngon sum*) as being free from conceptual construction (*kalpanāpoḍha, rtog pa dang bral ba*).[41] Explaining what absence of conceptual construction means, Dignāga says: "What then is this 'conceptual construction'? The association of name *(nāma, ming)* and kind *(jāti)* etc.[42] In the case of arbitrary names *(yadṛcchāsabda, 'dod rgyal ba'i sgra)* a thing is singled out by [its] name such as in 'Ḍittha.' In the case of kind words, [a thing is singled out] by its kind such as [in] 'cow' . . ."[43] Dignāga does not define conceptual thought but gives five examples. Among these, the second, just quoted, is a conceptual cognition that identifies its object through a kind; that is, through a universal. Śāntarakṣita[44] and Kamalaśīla mention some philosophers[45] who, drawing on Dignāga, hold that universals are real because they can be instrumental in identifying objects. These philosophers reject Dharmakīrti's characterization of conceptual thought in his *Ascertainment* as "that cognition which is [characterized by] words" (*rtog pa mgnon par brjod can gyi shes pa; abhilāpinī pratītiḥ kalpanā*).[46] They consider this an incomplete description of conceptual thought, holding that there must be a second type of thought that connects a thing to its universal.[47] This universal would be real since it would be instrumental in identifying the object.

Since these proponents of real universals rely for their description of conceptual thought on Dignāga's discussion and since they are refuted by Kamalaśīla on the basis of scriptural authority, they must have been Buddhist and even followers of Dignāga. Franco concludes that "certain Buddhists did allow universals as real entities, and on top of that, justified their position by appealing to the authority of Dignāga himself."[48] Thus, Śāntarakṣita's and Kamalaśīla's discussion reveals another side of the Buddhist logico-epistemological tradition. Although the dominant view propounded by Dignāga and Dharmakīrti has always rejected the existence of universals, there has been a current attempting to find a place for real universals within the framework of Buddhist epistemology.

Thus, throughout the history of Dignāga's and Dharmakīrti's tradition, a current of epistemologists have accepted the existence of real universals. Although the group of logicians referred to by Śāntarakṣita and Kamalaśīla were specifically concerned with the interpretation of Dignāga, their views have applications well beyond the question of textual interpretation, finding echoes in many important commentators as well as in several passages in the works of Dignāga and Dharmakīrti themselves. The presence of this unorthodox view in the Buddhist tradition may even have been continuous. It is not a unique and anomalous phenomenon but rather reflects some of the deepest problems that beset Buddhist epistemology.

The Role of Universals in Inference

To understand the sustained support within Buddhist tradition for real universals let us briefly examine the philosophical problems and discussions that led to this position. These are rooted in Dharmakīrti's ontology and epistemology.

Dharmakīrti has the view that universals are mere conceptual constructions. They do not exist really as specifically characterized phenomena (*svalakṣaṇa, rang mtshan*) but have a mere nominal existence as generally characterized phenomena (*sāmānyalakṣaṇa, spyi mtshan*). This ontological dichotomy between real individuals and unreal universals is paralleled on the epistemological level by a dichotomy between perception and inference. It is a basic tenet of Dharmakīrti's epistemology that specifically characterized phenomena are objects of perception (*pratyakṣa, mngon sum*), whereas generally characterized phenomena are objects of inference (*anumāna, rjes dpag*). An inference is a consciousness that apprehends something hidden *(parokṣa, lkog gyur)* from us, on the basis of some evidence (*liṅga, rtags*). An inference is correct only if it rests on correct evidence; that is, evidence that satisfies the threefold criteria (*trairūpya, tshul gsum*).[49]

Among the three criteria, the last two, the two pervasions, are the most difficult for Dharmakīrti's conceptualist system to handle. To illustrate the difficulty, consider the example of the inference of impermanence from its being produced. In this case, the evidence satisfies the second criterion of forward pervasion (*anvaya, rjes gro*) on the basis of a concrete example: Whatever is produced must be impermanent, as, for example, a pot. Understanding this pervasion involves much more than realizing a link between particulars. It requires an understanding of a general relation, in which universals are implicated. But since universals are not real, what is the basis on which reasoning rests?

This fundamental objection to Dharmakīrti's logico-epistemological system challenged Dharmakīrti's followers to find ways to answer it, generating an expansion of the conceptual resources handed down by Dignāga and Dharmakīrti. This expansion has taken the form of an elaboration of new distinctions. To solve the problem, Dharmakīrti's epistemology has been modified to allow an indirect grasp of universals by perception. Mokṣākaragupta makes this move when he asserts that universals can be indirectly determined (*adhyavaseya*) by perception. He posits two types of object of perception: the held object (*grāhya*) and the indirectly determined object (*adhyavaseya*). Individual objects are the held objects, whereas the universal pervasion is indirectly determined by perception and manifestly known when conceptual thought (*vikalpa*) intervenes in the cognitive process.[50]

A similar epistemological move is made by Dharmottara, one of Dharmakīrti's most important commentators. Dharmottara is often taken by the Ge-luk tradition (Gyel-tsap in particular) as the main commentarial authority on logic and epistemology. He attempts to give a more ontologically grounded answer, transforming the theory of universals to give more ontological support to the logical system. In his *Examination of Valid Cognition,* Dharmottara struggles with the forward pervasion. Dharmottara describes the problem: "*Question*: If there is no [real] momentariness or anything else, how is anything to be established by a reason of nature (*svabhāvahetu, rang bzhin gyi gtan tshigs*)?"[51] That is, if universals such as momentariness and impermanence are unreal, how can a reasoning such as "sound is impermanent because it is produced" work? Since impermanence and production are unreal universals, it is impossible to perceive the relation between them. To this Dharmottara answers: "*Answer*: The momentariness of sound is not completely nonexistent. What does not exist is the kind [of universal] that is constructed as a unity of several individual moments and which is excluded from what is not momentary. As for the individual characteristics of blue, etc., they are definitely existing. Nevertheless, whatsoever is a universal can only have the nature of an individual. Insofar as it exists, a universal is to be apprehended only on the basis of some particulars. If there are no particulars or if they are not apprehended, there [can] not be any universal nor [can] it be apprehended. Therefore, if there are particulars, universals [can] exist, and if there are no particulars, no universal [can] be."[52]

Dharmottara's solution is to distinguish two kinds of universals. The universals posited by the Nyāya view as real entities, separate from their instances and partless,[53] are fictional. These universals lack any real essence, existing only as the fictional supports of our conceptual activities. This is not, however, the only kind of universal. Real elements such as the properties of colors including impermanence characterize real things. These properties must really exist, despite being universals. They do not constitute real universals in the Nyāya sense of the word despite being real, for they do not exist apart from their instances. Rather, they completely depend on them. Dharmottara acknowledges that, since they cannot exist without their particulars, universals that are real have a lesser ontological status than their particulars. Nevertheless, they are real and as such can be apprehended by perception. By modifying the theory of universals in this way, Dharmottara attempts to strengthen the ontological basis of Dharmakīrti's logical system without conceding the Nyāya point that separate universals are real.

This position taken by Dharmottara in order to account for knowledge of a pervasion seems quite similar to the Ge-luk view of universals. Since it is hard to know how much weight to give to Dharmottara's passage, we should refrain from completely identifying the two views. Nevertheless, the similarity is quite striking.

Conclusion

It would then appear that the idea of real universals is not a Tibetan creation. Rather it was taken by Tibetans from Indian responses to criticism provoked in orthodox Hindu circles by the works of Dignāga and Dharmakīrti. In the process of defending Dharmakīrti's original model, commentators such as Dharmottara and Śaṃkarānanda were obliged to expand the conceptual resources bequeathed to them by Dharmakīrti, sometimes transforming the original concepts.[54]

This realist current was transmitted to Tibet by later Indian scholars such as Bhavyarāja. Their views represented less a Hindu influence on Buddhist tradition than an internal evolution of the Buddhist tradition due to the necessity for Indian Buddhists to respond to their orthodox opponents' criticisms. Once transmitted to Tibet, this realist view took on a life of its own there. In the absence of a well-articulated alternative, this interpretation became the accepted view. When Sapaṇ wrote his *Treasure* to refute realism and vindicate Dharmakīrti's antirealism, realism was already the standard interpretation of Dharmakīrti, which Tibetan scholars found difficult to discard.

The reason Tibetans found the realist interpretation so compelling, despite its problems as a bona fide interpretation of Dharmakīrti's thought, relates to the inherent difficulty antirealism faces in accounting for human reasoning. When we infer, for instance, the presence of fire from that of smoke, we seem to rely on something more than individual objects or fictional concepts. Such a reasoning involves considerations that pertain to universal as well as particular aspects of reality. An epistemological account of the success we have in epistemic practices has to explain the relation between these practices and reality.

Realism does not find it difficult to account for inferential knowledge. This knowledge relates to the particular as well as the universal aspects of reality. Since both are considered part of reality, the success of reasoning can be explained by its ability to grasp both aspects of reality. The relation of our epistemic practices with the general aspects of reality is much more difficult for antirealism to explain, since it reduces reality to individuals. Its economical ontology provides no basis for the universal statements involved in inferential reasoning. For example, when we infer fire from smoke, we rely at least implicitly on a universal statement of this type: Wherever there is smoke, there is fire. Such a statement is not about particular fires but about a general connection between fireness and smokeness. Antirealism finds it difficult to account for how this relation between general entities or properties can obtain in a world where no such entities really exist.

This has been a preliminary investigation of some of the elements relevant to the dispute over universals in the Tibetan Buddhist tradition. It suggests some of the philosophical reasons for the development of a moderate realism in a strongly conceptualist tradition. The Indian and Tibetan examples demonstrate the difficulties of a rigorously conceptualist position. Such a position may be ontologically elegant, inasmuch as it does not lead to an unnecessary multiplication of entities. It is difficult to sustain, however, when one deals with logical and epistemological issues. The temptation then becomes strong to reintroduce some of the entities considered ontologically undesirable. The repeated appearance of realist interpretations of Dignāga and Dharmakīrti's conceptualist system testifies to the strength of this temptation.

This concludes the part of this work in which the problem of universals occupies a central place. In the remaining chapters I investigate the semantic and epistemological consequences of conflicting views regarding universals. I discuss the ways in which realism and antirealism yield conflicting epistemologies and philosophies of language. The next and final part of Book I is devoted to the latter question, the philosophical analysis of language, which I examine in relation to the *apoha* theory. I start by laying out the background of the discussion, briefly touching on the importance of linguistics and grammar in Indian philosophy. I present the main elements of the *apoha* theory as they appear in Dignāga. I show that his theory contains two elements, a negative and an intuitional, that are in tension. The later chapters of Part III will examine how later developments of this theory are attempts to solve this basic tension.

Part III

Philosophy of Language

11

Introduction to *Apoha*

The History of Apoha *and Its Reception*

The central problem of the debate between Dignāga and Dharmakīrti, and their Hindu adversaries focuses on the status of universals, which play a central semantic role. The Nyāya and the Mīmāṃsā schools assert the necessity of real universals to explain the semantics of general terms. Dignāga's and Dharmakīrti's rejection of real universals necessitates on the part of these authors an account of how general terms can be meaningful in a world of individuals. Such is the purpose of the *apoha (sel ba)* theory created by Dignāga and developed by Dharmakīrti and his followers. In the next few chapters, I sketch out the evolution of this theory, presenting some of its more complex and difficult aspects and the discussion they have provoked among both traditional and modern scholars. I make no pretense of covering the topic in detail; rather, my aim is to present a few among the many revealing points of the theory.

Recently, Dignāga's *apoha* theory has received a great deal of attention from modern scholars. Hattori,[1] Hayes,[2] and Katsura[3] have significantly advanced our understanding of Dignāga's view. Since there is no point in duplicating their excellent work and since this book is devoted to the presentation of Dharmakīrti's philosophy in relation to later Tibetan sources, I will not focus on Dignāga's view. In the study of the *apoha* theory, however, it is not possible to completely ignore this author's seminal contribution, which determined the evolution of the later tradition. Hence, in this chapter I start with a brief introduction to his *apoha* theory, showing that his view combines two elements, a negative and an intuitional, whose relation is far from obvious. This tension sets the stage for the efforts of Dharmakīrti and his later followers to clarify and defend the *apoha* theory, a topic I take up in the following chapters. While explaining Dignāga's view, I also lay out the linguistic background for this discussion, showing the importance of the grammatical contribution to the *apoha* theory.

Since the publication in 1935 of Mookerjee's *Buddhist Philosophy of Universal Flux,* the history of *apoha* theory has often been understood to contain three stages, each dominated by one of three views: (1) negativism, which Mookerjee attributes to Dignāga and Dharmakīrti; (2) the positivism of Śāntarakṣita and Kamalaśīla; and (3) the dialecticism of Jñānaśrīmitra and his disciple Ratnakīrti. Mookerjee's schema is based on Jñānaśrīmitra's and Ratnakīrti's descriptions of two extreme views. The negativist view is that negation is primary.[4] Elimination is essentially negative and does not rest on any positive identification or mental image. The positivist view asserts that elimination is not only negative but has positive elements as well. According to this view, the essential element of the *apoha* theory is not the pure negation but the mental image through which this negation is made. According to this view, affirmation followed by negation is primary. Whereas there is some reason to believe that the latter view can be attributed to Śāntarakṣita and Kamalaśīla, the identities of the negativists seem much more problematic.

Until now, this threefold schema has been the accepted account of the *apoha* theory's historical development. Recently, however, Katsura has expressed some reservations about this theory which seem to me quite convincing. He says: "After reading through Jñānaśrīmitra's *Apohaprakarana*,[5] I had an impression that there was really nothing new about his theory of *apoha* in comparison with Dharmakīrti's. As a matter of fact, Jñānaśrīmitra quotes extensively from the works of Dharmakīrti in order to justify his understanding of the *apoha* theory. When examined more closely, most of his arguments stem from Dharmakīrti at least in germs."[6] Following Katsura's suggestion, I will assume here the following picture of the development of the *apoha* theory, which differs from Mookerjee's three stages. Dignāga initiated the *apoha* theory, which was met with a barrage of criticism from his Hindu opponents, who used some of the ambiguities of his view such as the presence of two elements (a negative one and an intuitional one) to refute it. As opponents also repeatedly emphasized, the *apoha* theory threatened to isolate thought and language from reality in a purely conceptual realm. Dharmakīrti and his followers were left with the task of solving these ambiguities and responding to such attacks from the orthodox Hindu camp. As they did so, these thinkers came upon new formulations of the *apoha* theory, although the basic insights derived from Dignāga.[7]

Another reason for not using Mookerjee's theory is that this work is devoted to the reception of Dharmakīrti's ideas in Tibet. Authors such as Jñānaśrīmitra and Ratnakīrti represent a relatively late stage of the theory, which does not seem to have been very influential in Tibet. Tibetan scholars seek their sources in earlier commentators, such as Devendrabuddhi or Śāntarakṣita. Accordingly, I will not use the contributions of later Indian thinkers here but will consider instead the developments of the *apoha* theory by Dharmakīrti, Śāntarakṣita, Kamalaśīla, and later Tibetan thinkers. But what is the *apoha* theory about?

Grammar and Philosophy of Language in India

To put it succinctly, the aim of the *apoha* theory is to explain how conceptuality, which relates to universals, can provide knowledge in a world of individuals. Hence, it is vital to Buddhist epistemologists since it allows them to explain thought and language in the absence of real universals. The role played by the *apoha* theory in explaining thought is addressed in the following chapters. In this chapter I consider the role of *apoha* mostly in explaining language, thus underlining the importance of the grammatical speculations that form the background out of which it arose.

The importance of grammatical and linguistic studies for the understanding of Indian philosophy does not need to be emphasized here. Biardeau, Matilal, and others have described how philosophical questions arose out of a highly abstract linguistic thought. A transition from Pāṇini's (between sixth and third centuries B.C.E.) more grammatical concerns to the philosophically oriented works of Śabara, Vātsyāyana (fourth century C.E.), and Bhartṛhari (fifth century C.E.) took place with Kātyāyana's *Vārttika* and Patañjali's *Mahābhāṣya* (first century B.C.E. or C.E.). A question raised by the philosophical transformation of grammar and of great relevance to the *apoha* theory is posed by Patañjali: "What is the object of the word (*padārtha*)?"[8]

To greatly simplify,[9] we could say that traditionally there have been two types of answer in India to this question. These two views have come to be associated with Vyādi and Vājapyāyana,[10] respectively. They are denotationism, which asserts that individual substances are the objects of terms, and connotationism, which holds that language first and foremost signifies through universal attributes. According to the denotationism first defended by Vyādi the word cow is meaningful due to its ability to refer to an individual cow. It does this not directly or through the intermediary of a universal but by eliminating the contradictory of cow; that is, noncow. Kumārila describes Vyādi's theory as asserting that "the import of words is *bheda* or the mutual exclusion of the word-meanings."[11] The word *white* in *white cow*, by this view, does not indicate a connection with whiteness but denies all other colors to the cow.

The important point to keep in mind is that Vyādi's theory is not philosophical. Vyādi's object is not the status of universals. He is a linguist, not a philosopher. He is concerned with explaining the way language functions, not with the ontological consequences of his linguistic views. Hence, his disagreement with Vājapyāyana does not concern the ontological status of universals, but the primary function of language. Is language primarily about reference or about sense? Vyādi's view embodies one of the intuitions that we have about language, that we can use it to single out individual objects. Focusing on practical uses of language, Vyādi holds a denotationist view. For example, when we say "bring me the cow," we seem to use language to single out a particular object. Vyādi held such examples to be paradigmatic of the way in which language functions.[12]

His opponent Vājapyāyana asserts that reference is not the primary function of language, but only one of its many possible uses. His view embodies another intuition that we commonly have about language, that it is first and foremost meaningful. This latter intuition, which emphasizes connotation over denotation, partly conflicts with the former. Whereas a denotationist such as Vyādi following the first intuition holds that sense is a consequence of denotation, a connotationist such as Vājapyāyana holds that the latter has primacy over the former. As Kumārila asserts, words primarily signify universal attributes. Application to particular things is a secondary function of language, which rests on sense. For example, the word *cow* primarily signifies the universal cowness, giving rise to a single conception subsuming particular cows irrespective of their particularities. Particular cows are understood through their instantiating a universal property (cowness) and in function of their being contextually implied (*ākṣepa*). Therefore, sense is primary in language and reference is only secondary.

A similar view is found in Bhartṛhari, who asserts that the primary locus of linguistic meaning is the sentence, not the word. Isolated words have meaning only through abstraction out of a sentential context. The basic semantic unit is the sentence meaning, which is a unitary whole that Bhartṛhari calls *pratibhā* (*snang ba*). On hearing a sentence, we perceive the meaning of that sentence in a flash, without having to construct its meaning by relating the individual words composing it. The content of this immediate intuition is, according to Bhartṛhari, the real meaning of the sentence and is called *ideational meaning* (*pratibhā*). For Bhartṛhari, the object of a word can be only a universal, for that is the object we have in mind when we speak. Since universals, however, are associated with individual things, those wrongly appear to be the object of language.[13]

These opposed views gradually became the focus of more strictly philosophical discussions. They were adopted by competing schools and discussed in relation to their ontological consequences. The Nyāya view, for example, is complex, not to say confusing. It mostly but not exclusively adopts the denotationist view that reference is primary. For the Nyāya, terms can signify both individuals and universals.[14] When a term signifies the multiplicity, it primarily refers to individuals and secondarily to their kinds. For example, when we say "a group of cows standing in the meadow," the referent of the word "cows" is essentially the individual cows, and the kind informs our speech only in a secondary fashion. Similarly, when we say "bring this cow," the referent is an individual cow qualified by the universal property of being a cow. But when I say "cow is an animal," "cow" then primarily, but not solely, refers to the kind. Since no kind can be perceived in isolation from its instances, some individuals are necessarily implied by it. By and large, however, the Nyāya understanding tends toward a denotationist view, which was criticized by Dignāga and Dharmakīrti.

Dignāga on Apoha

For Dignāga[15] and Dharmakīrti,[16] meaningful linguistic entities[17] do not refer directly to individuals without the mediation of concepts. Otherwise, words would be tied down to the particulars they express, and we would have to identify each particular object anew. For example, if the word "cow" were to directly signify an individual cow, it would be impossible to use the same word to denote another one.

Since the word I learned directly referred to the particular I first saw, I would not be able to apply it to any other cow. And since the particular cow I first identified is long gone, it would be difficult for me to use the word "cow" again. Language is used so that we can identify things as what they are. For example, we learn how to identify a cow. Once we have mastered this concept, we are able to apply it to other individuals. Thus, language must have general application.[18]

The opponent may answer that denotation is not constituted by a single individual but by the collection of all the objects to which the word applies. If that were the case, we would have to identify all the individuals that a word denotes to know what the word means. Since we have not the capacity to identify all particulars, we would never be able to learn general words. Thus, for the Buddhist philosophers of language, things are not directly signified by terms, either individually or collectively.

For language to function, it must be generally and consistently applicable. This suggests that language is primarily about sense. This is difficult from Dignāga's and Dharmakīrti's viewpoint, however, for only individuals are real. Their ontology provides no place for the existence of senses or other intensional[19] entities that could support the use of meaningful linguistic units. Such ontological support was not essential for a linguist such as Vājapyāyana. It is, however, much more important for Dignāga and Dharmakīrti, who intend to offer a complete Buddhist account. A philosophical description of language focusing on sense is essential to their project.

This puts them, however, in a paradoxical situation in which they must argue for a connotationist view within an ontology that tends to favor a denotationist view.[20] Dignāga's and Dharmakīrti's connotationist view of language is problematic because they cannot find in their system any entity (such as a universal) that can support the meaningfulness of language. Since universals are unreal and since denotation is not primary, the question remains: On which basis does language rest?

A possible solution would be to deny that language rests on anything at all. That is, to hold that the only basis for the meaningfulness of language is the practices in which humans engage. For example, a phrase such as "bring the cow" does not function on the basis of an entity such as "sense" or "meaning" but just on the basis of the uses we make of it. There is no such thing as meaning, there are just meaningful sentences. This "solution," which roughly resembles the views expressed by Wittgenstein in his *Investigations,* is not unknown in Indian philosophy. Candrakīrti and probably Nāgārjuna held a view according to which language is entirely conventional.

Dignāga and Dharmakīrti, however, do not share this view. They do accept that language is conventional inasmuch as its meaningfulness is not natural. The link between language and the world is conventional. But to say that language is based just on human practice will not do, for it does not explain anything at all. It merely describes what people do. To say that a sentence is meaningful because it is used in this way by people does not account for its meaningfulness. It merely states the case without providing a philosophical explanation of that practice. Merely stating the case is precisely what Candrakīrti intends to do, for he does not think it is possible to do anything more than describe conventional practices. Any attempt to go further ends up destroying the conventional practices we are trying to explain. For Candrakīrti, all we can do is provide a thick description (to use a Geertzian anachronism)[21] of how people use language. Anything else involves us in a hopeless metaphysical quagmire (to use another anachronism).

Dignāga and Dharmakīrti believe that philosophy should go beyond mere description and provide a complete account of epistemic practices by grounding them in reality. Epistemology should not just describe our successful uses of language but explain how and why we are successful in speaking. Dignāga and Dharmakīrti believe that epistemology must provide a deeper justification of human epistemic practices, pointing out their ontological bases and specifying the ways in which we connect with such bases. In short, Dignāga and Dharmakīrti believe that epistemology must be foundationalist to be philosophically meaningful. A similar approach is evinced by their philosophy of language. Since it is based on the primacy of sense, it must provide an account of the nature of sense and explain how it is grounded in reality.

True to their rejection of Nyāya realism, they hold that real and separate universals cannot be the direct object of language since they do not exist. Even if they were to exist, they would bear no relation to the things referred to by language. Since unchanging and separate universals have no effect on empirical reality and since language must be explainable in function of this reality, abstract universals cannot account for language being meaningful. How can Buddhists, who deny that language directly refers to individuals, explain how we use language to describe things without reference to real universals? In other words, how can Buddhists avoid the epistemological price of their ontological parsimony?

A decisive Buddhist answer was given for the first time by Dignāga through his *apoha* theory. The gist of his solution is that language does not describe reality positively through universals but negatively by exclusion. Language is primarily meaningful and this suggests that we should be able to provide some support for intensional entities such as senses. This does not mean that there are real senses but, rather, that we can posit agreed-upon fictions that we construct to categorize the world according to our purposes. "Cow" does not describe Bossie through the mediation of a real universal (cowness) but by excluding a particular (Bossie) from the class of noncow. Matilal describes Dignāga's view: "Each name, as Dignāga understands, dichotomizes the universe into two: those to which the name can be applied and those to which it cannot be applied. The function of a name is to exclude the object from the class of those objects to which it cannot be applied. One might say that the function of a name is to locate the object outside of the class of those to which it cannot be applied."[22] Although linguistic form suggests that we subsume an individual under a property, analysis reveals that words merely exclude objects from being included in a class to which they do not belong. The function of a name is to locate negatively an object within a conceptual sphere. The impression that words positively capture the nature of objects is misleading.

Dignāga forms his *apoha* theory based on a reflection on the grammatical discussions about the object of words that are part of the general cultural background of classical India (in a similar way as geometry was a standard branch of learning in classical Greece). There, Dignāga finds the conceptual resources needed to formulate a philosophy of language consistent with his rejection of realism. Two views seem to have had a particular influence on Dignāga.

In Vyādi's view, Dignāga finds a theory in which a word signifies an individual without the intervention of a universal. A word refers to an object by eliminating the contradictory of the object referred. Dignāga develops his own version of a negative theory of language by assimilating communicative knowledge to inference. For Dignāga, the function of words is similar to that of an inferential evidence (*liṅga, rtags*): "[Knowledge] based on verbal communication is not [a type of] valid cognition different from inference. Accordingly, [a word] signifies its object through the elimination of other [things], just as [the fact of] being produced [signifies impermanence]."[23] Take for example the case of a classic formal argument: The subject, a sound, is impermanent because it is produced. Here the reason (*hetu, rgyu mtshan*) or evidence (being produced) proves a thesis (*pakṣa, phyogs*) or a probandum (*sādhya, bsgrub bya*), that sound is impermanent. Being produced establishes the fact of being impermanent for sound by eliminating what is incompatible with the indicated property.[24] Likewise, language reveals its object through a similar process of elimination.

Although this theory provides an important insight into the eliminative process through which language is formed, it cannot provide the complete account sought by Dignāga, for it does not explain sense. As we saw, Dignāga rejects denotationism as being unable to account for the iterability of language. He holds a connotationist view, which he finds in Bhartṛhari's idea that the sense of a sentence is the intuitional idea associated with it. This second major influence on Dignāga's philosophy is clearly revealed in this passage: "The meaning of the word is constructed from the sentence through [analysis]. [For] the sentence meaning which is called idea (*pratibhā*) first arises by dint of that [meaning of the word]."[25] For Dignāga, *pratibhā* is the sense of a sentence in that *pratibhā* is what the sentence signifies (*vāk, brjod*). Words or, rather, sentences, signify sentence meanings, not individual things. Individuals cannot be the object signified by words, for even without external objects various sentences can be formed. Hence, denotation is not the primary function of language but just one of the main ways in which it can be used. The denotationist is deluded into believing that language is primarily referential because of assimilating language to a process of naming individual objects. Language is not, however, a nomenclature of names put together, but rests on the meanings that we form through signs.

This is the *sphoṭa* theory of language, which plays a central role in Bhartṛhari's holistic philosophy. This theory further argues that language (*śabda, sgra*) is mostly an internal articulation of meaning; it is not just external sounds expressing speaker's intentions. Language is first an internally delineated sphere of intelligibility, the *sphoṭa,* which is understood all at once. Such internal conceptual space forms a whole out of which individual sentences can be carved out. Those in turn can be further analyzed into words. Hence, for Dignāga, as for Bhartṛhari, the meaningful semantic unit is not the word but the sentence. The meaning of a sentence is apprehended holistically, in a flash (*sphoṭaḥ*). The meaning of individual words is then artificially constructed from that sentence. When a sentence is formed, it serves as the basis for the use of audible noises, which in turn reveal the internally formed meaning of the utterance. Thus, this internal entity, which is more a conceptual ground or sphere than a thing, is comparable to a light which both reveals the meaning of the external sounds and is revealed by them.

This internal nature of language does not entail its subjectivity, however, for the *sphoṭa* is not the speaker's private property, completely shut off from everybody else. Rather, it is an intersubjectively available sphere of meaning that is present in all those who participate in a linguistic community. Thus, for Bhartṛhari, language is a domain of internal intelligibility that is communicated, but not formed, by external sounds. Real language is internal and pre-exists its external vocalization. Only in a secondary sense is language a set of communicative sounds. But what is the role of this internal element in Dignāga's system?

His theory seems to combine two heteroclite and contradictory elements that have no apparent intrinsic relation to each other. The negative aspect of Dignāga's theory is taken out of Vyādi's denotationist theory of language. Dignāga does not, however, believe in denotationism. On the contrary, he holds the opposite connotationist view, according to which language is based on the idea of an intuitive understanding of the sentence as a unit. The relation between these two heteroclite elements—*apoha* and *pratibhā*—is an obvious difficulty in Dignāga's system inherited by Dharmakīrti and other commentators.

An obvious but I believe mistaken explanation of how these two elements are combined would hold that the *apoha* theory concerns primarily the meaning of individual words, whereas ideational meaning (*pratibhā*) concerns all sentences. This view is not correct, however, for it contradicts Dignāga's fundamental intuitions concerning language: that it is first and foremost meaningful and that sentences, not words, are the basic meaningful units. Dignāga must apply the *apoha* theory, which he sees as central to his system, to the actual meaningful units, the sentences. He cannot reserve the *apoha* theory to words, since those are only abstractions. Not only does Dignāga apply the *apoha* theory to sentences as well as the meaning of individual words, he also applies Bhartṛhari's idea of ideational meaning (*pratibhā*) to words, inasmuch as they can be abstracted from their sentential contexts. At the close of his discussion on ideational meaning, Dignāga says: "Ideational meaning (*pratibhā*) is accepted as the meaning differentiated from the meaning of other sentences."[26] Hence, the problem of explaining how these two composite elements—*apoha* and *pratibhā*—are articulated cannot be solved by relating *apoha* to word meaning and *pratibhā* to sentence meaning. The problem remains, and this difficulty did not go unnoticed among Dignāga's opponents.

Hindu Reactions: The Mīmāṃsā View

Dignāga's *apoha* theory was submitted to a barrage of criticism from orthodox thinkers. They attacked it for undermining the validity of language and thereby the Vedic revelation itself. In addition to these religious concerns social issues were also at stake, further explaining the vehemence with which orthodox opponents reacted to Dignāga's theory. To fully understand this controversy, a bit more must be said of Dignāga's main critic. Unlike the discussion of ontology and the problem of universals, Dignāga's main opponent here was not the Nyāya but the more orthodox Mīmāṃsā. Its leading proponent, Kumārila, formulated the most incisive critique of the *apoha* theory. This critique is important to the discussion, as it subsequently became the target of Dharmakīrti's response. The vehement tone of Kumārila's reaction was largely due to the doctrine addressed by the *apoha* theory; namely, the authoritative status of the Vedas, an idea particularly important for orthodox Hinduism. The Mīmāṃsā opposition to *apoha* theory was primarily a philosophical defense of Vedic authority.

Like the Nyāya, Mīmāṃsā ontology is realist and pluralist. It is based on the distinction between substance and properties. Of the six or seven categories formulated by the Nyāya, the Mīmāṃsā school adopts five (substance, quality, motion, universal, and nonexistence), leaving out two (individuations, because they are either substances or limited universals, and inherence, which is too obviously ad hoc). We already have noticed its position on universals, which is less extreme than the Nyāya. For the most part, however, the views of the two schools are rather similar.

Their views are not similar, however, as far as philosophy of language is concerned. There, the Mīmāṃsā view has a more extreme but also a more consistent position than the Nyāya. Contrary to the Nyāya school, which asserts a complex view combining denotation and connotation, the Mīmāṃsā asserts a well-articulated, though at times surprising, connotationist philosophy of language. This philosophy played an important role for the tradition because it allowed a defense of one of the most cherished religious views of orthodox Hinduism, the self-sufficient status of the Vedas.

The main point of dissension between the Mīmāṃsā and other schools is a well-known philosophical topic already debated by Plato in *Cratylus*; namely, whether language is conventional. The Mīmāṃsā, whose point of view is the most orthodox, strongly rejects the view defended by Buddhists and Naiyāyikas that language is conventional. For the Mīmāṃsā, language is naturally meaningful. In other words, it has an inherent capacity to signify its meaning. This view may surprise a modern reader not accustomed to Indian philosophy, for this issue has been decided long ago in the West in favor of language as conventional; nobody has resuscitated the dead issue. This is not the case in India, where the question has remained open to debate for a long time. To comprehend this, the reader should keep in mind the socio-religious underpinnings of the issue. At stake is not only the nature of language, but the status of the Vedic revelation and the validity of the social order based on this revelation. As we can see, the stakes are quite high. Let me explain.

The (Bhaṭṭa) Mīmāṃsā view subscribes to a view contrary to the holistic view of meaning supported by Dignāga and Bhartṛhari. For the (Bhaṭṭa) Mīmāṃsā, language is composed primarily of words that combine to form sentences in accordance with rules of syntactical relations. This is the word plus syntax theory.[27] (It is also accepted by the Naiyāyikas and probably by Dharmakīrti as well.) According to this view, to understand a sentence is to grasp the objects indicated by individual words and to grasp the relations among these objects indicated by the syntax. For the Mīmāṃsā, the primary objects of words are not individuals, for individuals change constantly and hence cannot be the proper objects of language. Language requires the ideal constancy provided by timeless elements, such as universals.

This is nothing unusual, but what follows is peculiar. For, the Mīmāṃsā view holds that not only universals but words themselves are permanent. They are ideal articulations of meaning that do not change, though their phonic expressions (*dhvani*) may vary. For example, the word *cow* is a constant articulation of the universal cowness. Its phonic or graphic realization may change. We could even imagine a language that does not have such a word. But the word itself does not change, only its material realization. Consequently, the link between words and universals is essential (*svabhāvika*).[28] Words have an inherent capacity (*śakti*) to signify the universals to which they are internally related. Hence, language is not conventional. It is not an instrument created by humans, but is naturally meaningful. Moreover, it is fully transparent, at least when presented in a well-formed idiom, Sanskrit, the well-formed language (*saṃskṛta*) par excellence.

The religious implications of this view are obvious. For Hindus, language is grounded in the Vedas, the source of their culture. The intense preoccupation of Indian culture with grammar and linguistics derives largely from this Vedic connection.[29] By asserting that language is naturally meaningful, the Mīmāṃsā vindicates the orthodox view that the Vedas are *śruti* (revelation).[30] Contrary to other important texts such as the *Bhagavadgītā,* the Vedas are not composed. For the Mīmāṃsā, this is indispensable to their perfection, for human-made things are usually flawed. At least, they must be tested independently. This is the case of a *smṛti* (tradition) text such as the *Gītā,* which can be tested against the Vedic corpus.

No such recourse exists in the case of the Vedas, for they are the ultimate source of spiritual knowledge concerning *dharma.* There is no means to test or verify them. Their topics are beyond human faculties of reasoning, and recourse to other texts would open an obvious regression ad infinitum. We are then faced with this choice: Either we declare that humans cannot know *dharma* (the modern secular view), or we must accept that they can know spiritual matters through revelation. In that case, we must accept the intrinsic validity of the Vedas.[31] These texts are the conditions of a meaningful spiritual and moral existence. Therefore, the Vedas are not only eternal (language itself is eternal) but also self-sufficient. This means that contrary to other texts, which are composed by combining permanent words, the Vedas have no authorship. Hence, their source is flawless and they are necessarily true.[32] And so is the social order that the Vedas command.

The Buddhist *apoha* theory is a direct attack against this essential point. In denying that language is naturally meaningful, the Buddhists refuse to grant the Vedas any privileged epistemological status. The Nyāya view avoids going as far by holding that the perfection of the Vedas comes from its author, God.[33] The Buddhists reject this Nyāya move, too, and deny the validity of the Vedas all together. They even take great pleasure in pointing out the apparent contradictions and non-senses in the text, engaging in provocative anti-Vedic polemics.

Against the threat represented by *apoha,* Hindu thinkers develop vehement and incisive critiques. Kumārila, for example, devotes a whole chapter to the refutation of the *apoha* theory in his main philosophical work, the *Śloka-vārṭtika.*[34] His (and Uddyotakara's) attacks provoke Dharmakīrti's response, which in turn is submitted to virulent counterarguments by Jayanta, Vācaspati, and others. Much of the philosophical conversation over the next five centuries (fifth–tenth) centers on this question.

Kumārila proposes three powerful counterarguments to the the *apoha* theory. He argues that it is (1) counterintuitive, (2) circular, and (3) useless. That is, *apoha* contradicts our intuition that the meaning of a positive word is positive. For, what is negative about the phrase *this is a cow*? Only where something is negated can a negative entity be taken as the meaning of the words.[35] Moreover, argues Kumārila, if the understanding of *x* necessitates the elimination of non-*x*, then this presupposes in turn the knowledge of non-*x*. But since one can understand only via elimination, the understanding of non-*x* will entail the knowledge of non-non-*x*. This in turn is nothing else than the knowledge of *x*.[36] Finally, and for our purposes most important, the *apoha* theory is useless. Since, according to Dignāga's own theory, the meaning of a sentence is the intuitional idea (*pratibhā*), why bother with *apoha* at all. Kumārila says: "Even in the absence of the corresponding external object there is *intuition* signified by the sentence; similar may be the case with what is expressed by the word also; why should the *apoha* be postulated at all?"[37] As accurately indicated by Kumārila, the *apoha* theory has been marked by an ambiguity from its incipience. If the significance of words is to be explained negatively, what is the role of the intuitional element in the theory? If, on the other hand, the theory is understood mainly on the basis of its intuitional aspect, why bother with the negative element?

Similarly, the Naiyāyika Uddyotakara raises a number of extremely technical objections against the *apoha* theory that are important for understanding later developments. Most significant, Uddyotakara questions the ability of the *apoha* theory to account for reference and to explain the relation between conceptuality and reality. In accordance with the denotationist orientation of his school, the Nyāya philosopher argues that if the word *cow* primarily bears on a negative entity, either this entity is a cow in disguise or it is different from a cow. In the first case, the *apoha* theory would just be a negative way to express what the Nyāya and common sense hold; that is, that language is used to single out phenomena from the universe of discourse. In the latter case, the word cannot refer to a real cow, making it difficult to see how any linguistic item can refer to reality. Conceptuality is then isolated in its own self-created fictional sphere unable to bring about knowledge of the real world.[38]

Dignāga's followers attempt to respond to these challenging criticisms by making more subtle distinctions among the elements of Dignāga's theory. The next four chapters examine their efforts. Chapter 12 focuses on Dharmakīrti's response. The *apoha* theory of this author, though, has already received considerable attention from the scholarly community.[39] So rather than reduplicate these efforts, I attempt to present his views on *apoha* in relation to the aforementioned critiques of the theory and its later developments. Chapter 13 continues to consider the defense of *apoha*, in relation to Śāntarakṣita's analysis of the concept of negation and his distinction between three types of elimination. Since Śāntarakṣita's presentation has been extremely influential in Tibet, I describe his views together with the diverging interpretations of Tibetan scholars. Chapter 14 pursues this investigation by further examining Tibetan views on the concept of negation. It focuses on the concept of object universal (*don spyi*), which lies at the center of a controversy opposing Ge-luk realists and Sa-gya conceptualists. Finally, Chapter 15 delves into the philosophy of language proper. My main topic, the distinction between sense and reference, gives me the opportunity to revisit the evolution of the *apoha* theory. I examine Dharmakīrti's ideas about reference and show how his concerns differ from Dignāga's. I also show how later Sa-gya interpretations represent an unsuspected return to Dignāga's early views, although they rely mostly on Dharmakīrti. Finally, I contrast the Ge-luk interpretations with the preceding views, once more revealing the realism of this tradition.

12

Dharmakīrti on Concept Formation

Thought and Language

My examination of Dharmakīrti's *apoha* theory focuses on a single question, that of concept formation. I make here no pretense of giving a complete account of Dharmakīrti's *apoha* theory. Rather I present his views on the relation between thought and language as a response to Uddyotakara's and Kumārila's critiques of the *apoha* theory and in the light of later Tibetan views. In this regard, Dharmakīrti's suggestions concerning the articulation between *apoha* and ideational meaning (*pratibhā*) are of particular concern. My discussion of this articulation draws from Dharmakīrti's treatment of *apoha* theory in *Commentary* III, a text that has not received as much attention from the scholarly community as has his discussion in *Commentary* I.[1] As a result of this neglect, excessive emphasis has been placed on the negative aspect of the *apoha* theory at the expense of the more positive elements, which have been largely ignored.

The challenge for Dharmakīrti's philosophical program is to show that the absence of real universals is compatible with a valid epistemological theory. The *apoha* theory is one of the main elements of this program, for it explains how conceptual knowledge is possible in the absence of universals. To understand his view we have to keep in mind the basic structure of Dharmakīrti's epistemology, which sets in sharp contrast conception and perception, a fundamental point we will have to examine later.[2] Suffice it to say here that, for Dharmakīrti, there are two radically different ways in which mental episodes apprehend their objects: (1) A mental event can apprehend its object positively, engaging in the object as it is. This is the way perception applies to its object. Or, (2) a mental episode can operate by elimination, engaging the object through the intermediary of a conceptual construct. This is the way thought considers things. This description of these two elements, however, is slightly misleading in that it wrongly suggests that thought and perception have an equal though different access to the same reality. This is not the case. The difference between thought and perception is not restricted to the mind's mode of operation, positive or negative, but also concerns its object. Whereas perception apprehends real entities, universals are the objects apprehended by thought.

This two-tier system makes it impossible to talk about the single way that mind understands things. We must distinguish between the essentially accurate but passive realization of real things by perception and the active but mistaken formation of concepts by thought. As we will see later,[3] Dharmakīrti understands perception to merely reflect things as they are, without interpreting them. Conception, on the other hand, categorizes the objects perceived and synthesizes them. In this way it brings signification to the bare data apprehended by perception. Unlike perception conceptual activity does not mirror reality but relates to universals, which it mistakenly projects onto reality. In this way, conceptuality constructs the universe of meaning in which humans live. The problem with this account is that it isolates conceptuality in its own sphere, making very hard to understand how thought can apply to reality. Overcoming the gap between the real and the conceptual is one of Dharmakīrti's central concerns. His theory attempts to establish a bridge between the two realms by establishing an indirect causal link between reality and the domain of negative conceptual construction, responding in this way to Hindu critiques of the *apoha* theory.

Dharmakīrti's conceptualist and constructivist bent also concerns language, which like thought is based on conceptual activity. For Buddhist epistemologists, language and thought (*kalpanā, rtog pa*) are intimately related to the extent that they are often equated from an epistemological point of view. Dharmakīrti says: "The way in which words signify universals is the same as [the way] thought [apprehends its object]."[4] Language signifies through conceptual mediation in the same way thought conceives of things. We speak with the intention of saying something; we say it through the concepts we have in mind. The hearer listens to the speaker's utterance and gets the ideas that the speaker intends to communicate. The hearer's mind forms a concept similar to the one the speaker has in mind. Effective communication is accomplished by the matching of concepts in speaker and hearer. A contemporary hermeneutician, E. Betti, expresses a similar view when he says: "In fact, human beings get to the point of understanding one another . . . by reciprocally putting into motion, each one of them, the same link from the chain of his own representations or conceptions, and—to adopt a figurative image—by touching in each other the same string of each individual mental instrument, as if to sound a chord, so that ideas corresponding to those of the one who speaks or writes will be stimulated in the one who listens or reads."[5] In this way the speaker's intentions of saying something are realized. According to Dharmakīrti, that language is spoken by individuals using it to signify their intentions is highly significant. For him, this shows the conventional nature of language, a view opposed by Kumārila and Bhartṛhari. The meaning of what we say is determined by our intentions, which we express in accordance with the linguistic conventions of the linguistic community to which we belong. The meaning of words is not essential but derives from pragmatic considerations in which speaker's intentions figure prominently.[6]

Language, however, serves more than a communicative purpose. We do not first understand things independent of linguistic signs and then communicate this understanding to others. Dharmakīrti's philosophy recognizes a cognitive import to language; through language we identify the particular things we encounter and in this way we integrate the object into the meaningful world we have constructed. When we become part of a linguistic community, we acquire the capacity to mark certain experiences with certain words. This gives us the ability to categorize objects and to understand, for example, a certain particular object that has branches and a trunk as a tree.[7] The cognitive import of language is particularly obvious in the acquisition of more complex concepts, such as that of universal or new concepts such as virtual reality. In these cases, clearly nothing in experience could possibly give rise to these concepts without language. Without linguistic signs thought cannot keep track of things to any degree of complexity. Dharmakīrti also notes that we usually remember things by recollecting the words associated with those things.[8] In fact, concepts and words mutually depend on each other. The concept of virtual reality is dependent on a word, while, at the same time, the word depends on the concept to acquire its meaning.[9]

This close connection between thought and language inherited from Dignāga differentiates Dharmakīrti from empiricists such as Locke and others, who believe in what we described, following Sellars, as the Myth of the Given.[10] Locke, for example, holds that concepts and words are linked through association. The word *tree* gets connected with the idea tree, which is nothing but the mental image of a tree, by the association established by repeated use. For Locke, the representation of the tree is not formed through language but is given to sensation (Dharmakīrti's perception). We understand a tree as a tree through mere acquaintance with its representation without recourse to concepts. The representation of the tree is given as already meaningful with absolute authority.

Dharmakīrti's philosophy is quite different, for it emphasizes the constitutive and constructive nature of language. This distinction must be stressed, for there are similarities between Dharmakīrti and the British empiricists at the level of ontology and the understanding of perception. Like the British empiricists, Dharmakīrti emphasizes that universals are not real and products of the mind. They are elaborated on the basis of the resemblances we perceive. He also holds a view of perception, that is, sensation, not unlike that of the empiricists. For Dharmakīrti, perception holds its object and hence provides an undistorted view of reality. There is, however, a crucial difference, which is that for Dharmakīrti perception does not identify its object but merely holds the object in its perceptual ken. Hence, perception does not provide any cognitive content by itself but merely induces conceptual activities through which content is constructed. This is quite different from empiricism in the strict sense of the term, which is based on the premise that knowledge is the internalization of experience. We encounter the world that impresses on us its content. This is not Dharmakīrti's view, for such a view forgets that the meaningful world in which we live is constructed. This construction, Dharmakīrti insists, is largely linguistic. To understand this last point, let us examine Dharmakīrti's definition of thought.

Two Definitions of Thought

The close connection between thought and language appears clearly in the definitions of thought proposed by Dharmakīrti. His works reflect two different though related definitions of thought (i.e., conceptual cognition, *kalpanā, rtog pa*). These two definitions are not conflicting but do introduce different emphases, which illustrate Dharmakīrti's anti-Mīmāṃsā polemic. Let me explain these two definitions in the light of later Tibetan commentarial contributions.

The first definition is found in *Commentary* III, where Dharmakīrti emphasizes the close connection between thought and universals, the objects of concepts. He gives the following account: "Conceptual cognition is that consciousness which apprehends the object [indicated by] words in relation to the [actual thing]."[11] Here a thought is an awareness that conceives an actual thing indirectly by applying a concept. For example, we think about a particular tree by evoking the concept of this tree. Thought cannot conceive the tree as it is but only via this conceptual intermediary. In addition to being an intermediary, the concept provides the meaning of what we say on describing a tree. Accordingly the object of the concept, the exact nature of which we will examine later, is called the *object* (indicated) by words (*śabdārtha, sgra don*). A consciousness that apprehends such an "object" is a conceptual cognition.

In his later *Ascertainment,* Dharmakīrti gives a different account. Here he emphasizes the relation between thought and language rather than thought and concept. He defines *thought* as the apprehension of the combination of a representation and a word: "Conceptual cognition is that consciousness in which representation (literally, appearance) is fit to be associated which words."[12] Thought identifies its object by associating the representation of the assumed object with a word. That is, when we conceive of an object, for instance, a jar, we do not apprehend the jar directly. Rather, we apprehend it through the mediation of its appearance to our mind. The appearance of the jar, however, is not the jar itself but its representation, also often and somewhat misleadingly called its *image*, which we identify by associating it with a linguistic sign.

To better understand how thought operates in dependence on representations, we have to realize that in Dharmakīrti's philosophy objects do not appear directly to consciousness. Rather, they appear to consciousness via a representation, variously described by Dharmakīrti as the reflection or the aspect (*ākāra, rnam pa*) of the object. This aspect is the imprint left on consciousness by the object. It is also described as the objective aspect (literally, the held aspect, *grāhyākāra, gzung rnam*) in distinction to the subjective aspect (literally, the holding aspect, *grāhakākāra, 'dzin rnam*), which we will leave out for the time being. In both perceptual and conceptual cases, we apprehend things through an aspect. This process of representation, however, proceeds quite differently for the two types of cognition, conceptual and nonconceptual. For nonconceptual cognition, as we will discover later,[13] representation relies on a direct causal link with reality. External objects are perceived by directly producing their representations. Here, though, we are not discussing perceptual representations but conceptual ones; that is, the representations that arise in conceptual mental states.

Like perception, conception proceeds through representations, but the process of mediation is different. Contrary to perception, there is no direct correspondence between external objects and their representations in conceptual consciousness. That is, the representation does not arise through the direct causal power of the object, as in the case of perception, but by close association with a linguistic marker. Moreover, as we will see shortly, the way in which a representation stands for its object is different in the case of conception than in the case of perception.

To summarize these two approaches to defining thought: In his *Commentary*, Dharmakīrti features the conceptual side of thought, depicted as dealing with fictional entities. This preeminence of the conceptual is well in keeping with his conceptualist theory of universals. In the later *Ascertainment,* Dharmakīrti elucidates thought in relation to language. Although this later definition places a greater emphasis on the linguistic than the conceptual, there is no contradiction between the two points of view. But why did Dharmakīrti give two definitions? Let us examine the conflicting opinions of later commentators.

Tibetan interpreters agree to define conception according to Dharmakīrti's second definition of universals in relation to *sgra don (śabdārtha)*. They disagree, however, on the meaning of *sgra don*. Ge-dün-drup, for example, understands it to mean "terms(*sgra*) and objects(*don*)"; that is, as a conjunctive compound (*dvanda*).[14] For him, *object* refers to object universal (*don spyi*), which he understands as the appearance of an object to a conceptual cognition. *Term* refers to term universal (*sgra spyi*), the conceptual appearance of a term to a conceptual cognition. According to this interpretation, the definition of conceptual cognition is "that cognition which apprehends a term-[universal] and an object-[universal] as fit to be associated."[15]

In this view, most conceptual cognitions apprehend their objects through a combination of both term and object universals. Some such cognitions hold their objects only through the intermediary of an object universal, as in the case of a child with no linguistic training. Mokṣākaragupta, for example, argues that babies have simple concepts that allow them to perform certain basic functions.[16] Similarly Śāntarakṣita holds that the word *fit* was added by Dharmakīrti to include the conceptions of babies, who have concepts but no linguistic training. Their concepts are fit to be verbalized, but are not actually associated with words.[17] To use Tibetan terms, a conceptual cognition apprehends "term and object universals as suitable to be associated" although it does not necessarily associate them. According to these commentators, the word *fit* must be added to the definition to include all these cases.

Kay-drup disagrees forcefully with this interpretation: "It is not correct to hold that the words 'term' and 'object' refer to term- and object-universal."[18] Kay-drup understands *sgra don* in the definition of conceptual cognition to mean "object of a word," making it a genitive compound (*tatpuruṣa*), not a conjuctive one. Such an object designated by words is considered an object universal.[19] Thought, then, conceives its object through an object designated by words. Hence, it is to be defined as "that cognition which apprehends the object [designated by] words."[20]

Kay-drup does not object to the general distinction between term and object universals. He agrees with the standard Ge-luk view of term universal: When a person who has not yet learned what the word *jar* means hears this word, the conceptual reverberation of it in that person's mind is a term universal.[21] Since that person understands the word as a communicative form rather than as a mere noise, the term universal is present. Since that person does not understand the meaning of the word, the meaning universal is absent. Thus, Kay-drup does not refuse to distinguish term and object universals, but he does not consider this distinction relevant to the definition of conceptual cognition given by Dharmakīrti in his *Commentary.*[22] In that case, however, how is it possible to explain Dharmakīrti's use of *fit* (*yogya, rung ba*) in the *Ascertainment* definition?

Go-ram-ba's remarks may provide an answer. He objects to Ge-dün-drup's interpretation of *fit* as intended to account for the conceptions of linguistically untrained people. For Go-ram-ba, the word *fit* is not necessary to make the definition correct in all cases. Rather, the use of *fit* is meant to emphasize the following point: The association of a representation with its object does not take place in reality but only in the conceptual realm. Representations are considered fit to be associated with words because links between the two are entirely conventional. Indeed, no essential or natural limitation is placed on the capacity of representations to become associated with terms. Accordingly, the definition of conceptual cognition can be stated with or without the word *fit* without any effect on the extension of the definition.[23]

This explanation helps us to realize the issue behind Dharmakīrti's use of the word *fit*. Go-ram-ba and Kay-drup are probably quite right to argue that Dharmakīrti does not intend to address the case of linguistically untrained people, despite the arguments made by Śāntarakṣita and many Tibetan commentators. Rather, refuting the Mīmāṃsā seems to be his foremost concern. According to the Mīmāṃsā view, as we may recall, a permanent and essential relation exists between words and their meanings. Moreover, the inherent fitness (*yogyatā, rung ba nyid*) that abides between words and meaning is not due to any human or divine agency.[24] Against this realism, Dharmakīrti argues that the fitness between words and meaning is not inherent but conventional. Nothing inherent in the Vedic words "One who desires heaven should offer the fire sacrifice (*agnihotra*)" compels us to understand these words as a command to perform a certain ritual. For, these words are equally fit to make the provocative statement "one should eat dog meat."[25] Nothing in the words themselves mandate the first meaning and forbid the second. This is a purely conventional matter in which the speaker's intention is primary. We begin to realize that the use of the word *fit* in the definition of thought plays an important role inasmuch as it supports Dharmakīrti's anti-Mīmāṃsā polemic, which is at the center of his *apoha* theory. We also understand that the issues raised by this debate are by no means insignificant. Nothing less than the authority of the Vedas is at stake!

For Dharmakīrti, the capacity of a word to express any meaning seems unlimited. Since signification is purely conceptual, it relies strictly on convention and not in any way on the word itself. Furthermore, Dharmakīrti seems to hold a view of unlimited fitness. Words can mean whatever the speaker intends them to mean. We may wonder how widely Dharmakīrti intends to apply the speaker's intention. What role is played by the hearer's ability to understand or social conventions, for instance? Does Dharmakīrti include them in the conventional framework? Factors other than the speaker's intention are obviously relevant, but their role within Dharmakīrti's account of the relation between words and meaning seems less than clear.

The important point, however, is that Dharmakīrti's assertion of the primacy of the speaker's intention aims primarily at refuting the Mīmāṃsā view and asserting the conventional nature of language. The way in which other factors relate to a speaker's intentions is a secondary detail that can be factored in once the conventional nature of language has been established. It remains true, however, that a speaker's intention figures prominently in Dharmakīrti's understanding of language. Language is not natural but concerns human constructs. Thought conceptualizes its objects with these linguistically constructed concepts acting as intermediaries.

This constructed and linguistic nature of thought concerns only conception and not perception, which is entirely free from conceptuality. This latter form of cognition provides a bare contact with reality without any articulation. Contrary to the Nyāya realist theory, Dharmakīrti does not accept that perception categorizes the objects it perceives. For example, we do not see that this table is made of wood. Rather, we sense a bulky object that we categorize conceptually as being made of wood. This process of categorization is conceptual; it is entirely different from the perceptual process that involves a bare contact with real individual objects. Then how is it, asks the Naiyāyika, that discrete individuals can produce in the mind a single category?

The Negative Nature of Conceptuality

Here, Dharmakīrti applies the *apoha* theory first propounded by Dignāga. This theory explains how the emergence of propositional knowledge takes place without the presence of real properties shared among objects. As we shall repeatedly emphasize, propositional knowledge is not given at the perceptual level but is due to the conceptual categorization of experiences, which are in themselves free from conceptuality, on the basis of an association with language.

One of the particularities of Buddhist epistemology is that, contrary to the other Indian systems, it holds that conceptual thinking is essentially negative.[26] The process of constructing concepts, which characterizes thinking, is negative in nature: conceptual constructs are formed by eliminating their contradictory. For example, the concept tree is constructed by eliminating nontree. This process requires thought to create a dichotomy between a conceptually constructed property (being a tree) and its contradictory (not being a tree). By eliminating this contradictory, a constructed property is determined in association with a linguistic sign. Dharmakīrti says: "[This universal] appears as being these [real things] or is held to as the real object. This distorted [concept] is projected through beginningless habituation to seeing [real things in this way]. That which is a universal of [real] things has the characteristic of being excluded from others. It is what is signified by these words [and] it is without any reality (*rūpa, ngo bo*; literally without any form)."[27] The concept that has been formed in an essentially negative way is projected onto real things. In the process of making judgments such as "this is a tree," the real differences that exist among the different trees come to be ignored and the similarities are reified into a common universal property, which is nothing but a socially agreed-on fiction.

One of the important consequences of this explanation is that any form of thinking is dichotomous, since it apprehends a construct formed on the basis of a dichotomy. For Dharmakīrti, as long as one remains within the conceptual realm, there is no possibility of overcoming dichotomies. Only perception is not dichotomous, but as we will see, it provides no cognitive content. Thus, knowledge in ordinary beings is always dichotomous and can never pretend to accurately reflect reality. Dharmakīrti's own system is no different and hence should not claim any privileged status, although it does. Moreover, as we will see in the second part of this work, this is not the only problem created by the dichotomies. Dharmakīrti's whole system is based on a strict differentiation between real and conceptual realms. We will find this radical separation particularly troubling while explaining Dharmakīrti's epistemology. There, we will see how dichotomies tend to proliferate in his system, thereby threatening to jeopardize his epistemological enterprise.

A frequent source of confusion for both traditional and modern critics of the *apoha* theory lies in misunderstanding the negative character of thought to be psychological. For example, Kumārila accuses the *apoha* theory of being counterintuitive because introspection does not reveal the thinking process as negative. Kumārila and many others hold that this objection decisively refutes the *apoha* theory. This is a mistake, for the negative nature of thought described by the *apoha* theory is epistemological rather than psychological. Go-ram-ba draws our attention to this confusion. He explains that thought is eliminative in its nature not because it directly excludes the contradictory (non-*x*) of its object (*x*). Rather, thought is negative because it depends on this elimination.[28] Go-ram-ba does not explicate, however, the nature of this dependence.

In my opinion, it is not inappropriate to explain the dependence of thought on elimination in terms of validation. Let us consider our example, "this is a cow." In this expression we have two elements, the subject and the predicate expressions. The predicate expression, here the word "cow," does not signify a particular cow but cowness in general. This property (cowness) is not some positive entity that can be found in the world but only a difference that conceptually obtains between certain individuals. What about the subject expression? The validation of the subject expression is a bit more immediate since it refers to a real individual. This reference, however, is not direct. The subject expression does not refer directly to a real individual, but only locates the conceptual individuation of this individual within the conceptual space by eliminating the other possible subjects of predication. Hence, for both expressions, the validation is negative, although in different ways.

Allow me to illustrate this through the following pedagogically useful explanation. Let us assume that the process of validation is like the exchange of titles at a bank. When we come to the epistemological bank, we cash in our expressions for entities. We give the teller the subject expression "this" and we are told to exchange our title for something equivalent to a cow at another counter. We then give the teller the predicate expression "is a cow," but the teller tells us that he or she has nothing more to give us. We insist that there must be something since there is an expression, but the teller does not demur. There is nothing real to exchange for the predicate expression. All we have is a way of differentiating the same entity from other phenomena. Hence, the pseudo-entity designated by the expression "being a cow" is only fictional and can be reduced to a negative construct.

The eliminative nature of thought and language is psychologically revealed when we examine the learning process. The word "cow," for instance, is not learned only through a definition but by a process of elimination. We can give a definition of cow, but the definition works only if its elements are known already. For example, we can define cows as animals having dewlaps, horns, and the like. But how do we know what counts as a dewlap? Not just by pointing to the neck of a cow, but by eliminating the cases that do not fit. In this way, we establish a dichotomy between those animals that fit and other animals or things that do not. On the basis of this negative dichotomy we construct a fictive property, cowness. The *apoha* theory does not hold that this negative learning process remains psychologically evident. Hence, the argument that the *apoha* theory is counterintuitive misses the mark. Nevertheless, Dharmakīrti still has a lot of explaining to do before he can claim that his theory is vindicated. One of the main questions he must face is: If conceptuality is mistaken and proceeds by self-constructed fictional conventions, how can it ever apply to reality?

Formation of Concept

The clearest discussion of concept formation, which seems to be one of Dharmakīrti's dominant preoccupations, in opposition to Dignāga who does not seem to deal extensively with this question, occurs in an extremely important passage in *Commentary* III that has often been overlooked by modern scholarship.

This oversight seems to have had two related effects. First, the evolution of the *apoha* theory has not been adequately appreciated by modern scholars, who have either assumed a complete identity between Dignāga and Dharmakīrti or, on the contrary, have tended to exaggerate the gap between these two authors. This in turn has obscured the place of thinkers such as Śāntarakṣita, whose ideas are often mistakenly presented as standing far apart from Dharmakīrti's. As I will argue here, Śāntarakṣita's *apoha* theory represents a new development of elements already found in Dharmakīrti. Second and more important, the ignorance of the view implied by this key passage has allowed a whole stream of influential scholarship to present concept formation in Dharmakīrti as a priori and arbitrary. In this way, Dharmakīrti's specific project, the grounding of concepts in reality through a causal relation with experience, has been left out.

For Dharmakīrti, the conceptual process is neither arbitrary nor groundless, even though it does not reflect reality. Conceptuality does not arise out of nothing but results from experience. As we may recall, things such as trees, for instance, have functional similarities. Categorizing an object as a tree is brought about from these similarities. In dependence on our experiences in which the functional resemblances of things are registered, we construct concepts. Thus, conceptuality arises as a result of our experiences. In this way, conceptual thoughts are connected indirectly to reality.

This answer raises an objection from an adversary. This adversary argues that the existence of a causal link between things and our concepts of them contradicts the basic Buddhist epistemological tenet that words do not relate to real things but to fictional entities. Indirectly, the adversary is also questioning how the Buddhist epistemologist can explain the referential function of language. How can language apply (*pravṛtti, 'jug pa*) to the real world if all language has access to are agreed-on fictions? In response to this objection, Dharmakīrti says: "Although a word does not rest on an elimination [found in] external [things] that has the capacity [to perform a function], it is related to the [object's] reflection [provoked] in conceptual thought [by words], which rests on this [elimination existing in external objects].[29] Therefore, since it rests on an elimination of others, a word signifies an elimination of others. That which pertains to the reflection[30] of the object appears to the cognition [arising] from words similar to the elimination [of others], but it is not the real object, [for] it arises from mistaken latencies."[31] This passage raises a number of important issues. It also has provided the basis for later developments of the *apoha* theory such as Śāntarakṣita's distinction between three types of negation. Before examining these issues in greater detail, let me briefly gloss the passage itself.

In his response Dharmakīrti grants that language and conceptuality do not bear directly on reality. Yet he insists on the mediating function of the representation, the concept as a mental event, here described as reflection (*pratibimba, gzugs brnyan*), which is central to linking conceptuality to reality. Thought cannot directly conceive reality, but proceeds by constructing and superimposing agreed-on fictional commonalities onto discrete individuals. Such constructions, however, are not groundless, for they arise as results of the indirect causal connection between real things, our perceptions of them, and our thoughts. There is no connection between perceptions and universals, the objects of concepts, for those are of two different orders, but experiences and concepts are connected and thus provide a bridge between the two realms (the conceptual and the real). Let me explain this important point by examining a simplified version of the acquisition of a concept.

As stated earlier, our starting point is our experience of things and their mutual resemblances. These experiences give rise to a diffuse concept of similarity. To account for this sense of similarity, we construct a more precise concept by correlating conceptual representations with a single term or sign previously encountered. This creates a more precise concept in which the representations are made to stand for a commonality that the objects are assumed to possess. Let me illustrate this key move in Dharmakīrti's account of concept formation, emphasizing that this example does not intend to illustrate how we acquire language in general but how we learn a particular concept.[32] We see a variety of trees and apprehend a similarity between these objects. At this level, our mental representations have yet to yield a concept of tree. The concept of tree is formed when we connect our representations with a socially formed and communicated sign and assume them to stand for a treeness, which we take individual trees to share. In this way experiences give rise to mental representations, which are transformed into concepts by association with a linguistic sign. The formation of a concept consists of the assumption that mental representations stand for an agreed-on imagined commonality.

Two points must be emphasized here regarding concept formation. First a concept, which is nothing but an assumption of the existence of a fictional commonality projected onto things, comes to be through the conjunction of two factors: the experience of real objects and the social process of language acquisition. Hence, the process of concept formation is connected to reality, albeit in a mediated way. Second, a concept is mistaken. It is based on the association of a mental representation with a term that enables the representation to stand for a property assumed to be shared by various individuals. The individuals, however, do not share the common property which is just projected onto them. The property is manufactured when a representation is made to stand for an assumed commonality, which a variety of individuals are mistaken to instantiate. This property is not, however, real. Nor is it reducible to a general term. That is, the commonality we project onto things does not reside in using the same term to designate discrete individuals. For, on analyzing the notion sameness of terms, we realize that identifying individual terms as being the same presupposes the concept of sameness of meaning, in relation to which the individual terms can be identified. For example, we identify different tokens of the word *cow* as being the same because they identically signify cowness. Thus, commonality is not due simply to a term but requires the formation of concepts on the basis of the mistaken imputation of commonality onto discrete individuals.[33]

This account raises several questions: The first, which I will address extensively in the next chapter, concerns the textual interpretation of Dharmakīrti's reference in the preceding passage to "an elimination [found in] external [things] that has the capacity [to perform a function]." Does Dharmakīrti hold that eliminations can be real? Some later commentators such as Śāntarakṣita think so and propose the concept of objective elimination (*arthātmaka-svalakṣaṇānyāpoha, don rang mtshan gyi gzhan sel*) to capture what they perceive to be an essential element of the *apoha* theory.

Another, and at this point more directly relevant, question is this: What is the nature of concepts? Are they mental entities; that is, Dharmakīrti's reflections? Are they eliminations? Here Dharmakīrti is not explicit, and as a result his commentators differ on the relation between reflections, concepts, and elimination. Using Go-ram-ba's ideas, which I explicate fully later,[34] I can offer this clarification: Concepts are mental events that take universals as their objects. Hence, concepts are neither universals nor eliminations, for eliminations are unreal in Dharmakīrti's system. This reply helps clarify the ways in which the term *concept* can be used in relation to Dharmakīrti's thought. Yet, my reader should remain aware that, in proceeding to clarify Dharmakīrti's ideas, I am making them clearer than they are.

Thus, conceptual representations are mental events. Dharmakīrti technically describes them as aspects (*ākāra, rnam pa*) as well as reflections. They are also sometimes described by modern interpreters, somewhat misleadingly, as mental images. Being mental events, concepts are real and individual in nature. Hence, they are different from their objects, the universals, which are general in nature. Such concepts are based on a "standing for" relation in which mental representations are made to stand for the agreed-on commonality that individuals supposedly share. This "standing for" also exists in the case of perception but in a different way, for a perceptual representation stands for its object through a direct causal connection. In the conceptual case, the "standing for" is not a direct connection between a thing and its representation. Rather, it is an indirect relation between a representation and a fictive property assumed to be instantiated by individuals. This relation comes about in a roundabout way through a process of mediation well described by Pierce as semiosis; that is, a process involving a sign.[35]

The Mistaken Nature of Concepts

This explanation that a concept is formed on the basis of a mistaken "standing for" relation provokes an objection from an opponent (identified by Go-ram-ba as Buddhist),[36] who opposes Dharmakīrti's explanation of thought as inherently distorted. This opponent argues that the role of representation in the conceptual and perceptual processes is identical. Mediation between external reality and mental states requires nothing but the production of representations or aspects, which stand for individuals. Dharmakīrti responds by emphasizing the mistaken nature of conceptuality: "When this [reflection] is signified by a word, an objective factor is understood. If it is not understood, there is no point in naming [anything]. [If one objects]: 'How [can] a statement signify an objective factor?' We answer [through] the elimination of others. Since the aspect does not exist in the object, how could it have any role in signifying an object? A statement has [as its] effect [the obtainment of] connected [things] through [a relation to] those connected things. This [aspect], however, has no such connection, for it is not distinct from the mental episode being the manifestation of the habituation to seeing [objects]."[37] The purpose of language is not only communicative but also cognitive and constructive. That is, we use words not only to communicate to others what we have understood already, but also to identify the objects we encounter in the world through the construction of concepts.[38] Concepts, however, are different from perceptual representations. In perception a representation, that is, a reflection or an aspect, stands for a real individual object in a one-to-one, direct causal correspondence. No such relation exists in the conceptual case, for conception is essentially imaginative and constructive. It does not require the existence of a real something to be derived. Hence, the representation existing in a conceptual cognition does not stand for an individual. What does it stand for?

Conceptual representation stands for the commonality, which is merely assumed to be instantiated by individual objects. In a world of individuals, commonality among different objects does not exist actually but is superimposed on the reality of individuals. It is constructed when a representation is (mis)taken for a property and that property is assumed to be instantiated by individual objects.[39] In this way a pseudo-entity is fabricated and superimposed (*adhyāropa, sgro 'dogs*) on the representation. The property is taken to exist in reality, but this is a mistake. There is no commonality outside of our imagination. Nevertheless, subjectively assuming commonality between objects is a necessary condition for thought and language to relate successfully to the objects.[40] We cannot conceive of things directly but only by subsuming them under fictional commonalities. Even if we were to point at something saying "this," the object is identified by falling under a tacitly implied minimal description. The description always contains a general term that designates a property, which is assumed to be shared by several individuals. Only on the basis of this confusion is thought able to relate to real objects through concepts.[41] This is the best epistemology Buddhists can hope for in the absence of real universals.

Notice that Dharmakīrti is not arguing that subjective concomitance is a sufficient condition for appropriate conceptualization. To ensure that a thought relates adequately to a real object, at least two conditions must be fulfilled: The thought must be indirectly related to the object via factual experience, and there must be a subjective concomitance between appearance and object. The representation fulfills the first condition but not the second. Incorrect, or inadequate, thoughts or words fulfill the second but not the first. Thus, legitimate thought is not arbitrary, despite the necessary mistake that it involves.

In another, well-known part of his work Dharmakīrti describes the mistake that lies at the basis of conceptuality. Thought proceeds by unifying discrete objects into a single kind, thereby covering up real differences. Having imposed its own form on the individuals, thought creates the impression that these things are really the same, whereas they are not. Thus, conceptual consciousness distorts reality by making it fit into artificially created categories. It thereby obscures the fundamental differences between the objects that we judge to be similar.[42]

Dharmakīrti does not go any further than that. In particular, he does not give any indication as to whether all concepts are acquired or whether certain concepts are innate.[43] He just describes the tendency to project these concepts onto reality as innate. This disposition is inborn in each of us and forms an integral part of our way of coping with the world. That does not mean that the concepts themselves must be inborn. It is possible instead that concepts arise out of innate tendencies (such as desire or aversion) and are shaped by the particular circumstances we encounter in life. This is not to say that this is Dharmakīrti's position, but that this view is compatible with Dharmakīrti. Dharmakīrti himself is mute on the topic.

Conclusion: Dharmakīrti's Response to the Hindu Critique

I have attempted to explain Dharmakīrti's response to the Hindu critique of Dignāga's *apoha* theory. How does Dharmakīrti's explanation, which emphasizes the role of concepts, fit within the *apoha* theory? That is to say, what is the relation between a concept, which stands for an object indicated by words (*śabdārtha, sgra don*) and the elimination of others (*apoha, sel ba*)?

As we have seen, Dignāga's original *apoha* theory seems to be an unstable combination of two elements without apparent connection: elimination (*apoha, sel ba*) and intuitional ideation (*pratibhā, snang ba*). Kumārila uses this unstable combination to argue against Dignāga: If intuitional ideation were the meaning of terms there would be no need for the *apoha* theory.[44] I believe that Dharmakīrti hints at the resolution of these two elements when he says: "Since the elimination of the other is realized through understanding what is superimposed [as a real] thing, once again, there is no contradiction in saying that 'this [appearance] is indeed the object of words.' The false appearance to the mind caused by the influence of words is connected with the factual object. Therefore, a word eliminates [something] else."[45] Our knowledge of the world does not boil down to a bare encounter with reality but requires concepts. We identify something as being a tree, for instance, by using the concept of tree. This mental entity allows us to identify objects by creating a property, treeness. This property is not, however, a positive entity but a fiction we tend to conceive positively. When we do so, we are misled into believing there is some real positive treeness. This is a mistake, for there are only individuals excluded from being what they are not. This is shown by the way in which the expression *being a tree* can be validated. When we examine how this expression is validated, we discover that the only way to validate it is through the negative process of understanding that real trees are not nontrees.

A concept is elaborated negatively through misidentifying representations as standing for an agreed-on property that real individuals are assumed to instantiate. Such a concept, which is a real mental event, has a content, which is nothing but the fictional universal assumed to be instantiated by real individual objects. Such a constructed universal can be considered in two ways. First, it can be taken as the content of the concept. This is the universal qua conceptual content, which is also called *object* (indicated) *by words* (*śabdārtha, sgra don*), since it is constructed through language. Such a conceptual content is taken by Dharmakīrti to be Dignāga's intuitional ideation. Second, such a universal can also be taken as a property. Such a property appears as a real phenomenon in its own right but is nothing but an agreed-on fiction, which can be validated only in a negative way. There is no other way to validate the notion of, for example, cowness outside of saying that it is an abstraction derived from the fact that any real cow is not a non-cow. Since it rests on a negative process of validation, such an abstract pseudo-entity is called an *elimination*. This is the universal qua pure elimination. Thus, the two concepts of elimination and ideation do not stand apart, as Kumārila had mistakenly assumed. Rather, they are two distinct but equivalent ways to describe the same abstract pseudo-entity.

In this way Dharmakīrti stresses the link between reality and conceptuality, thus answering some of Uddyotakara's criticisms. Thought and language proceed by constructing fictional commonalities that are mistakenly projected onto real objects. This construction is not groundless, however, but proceeds in close causal connection with reality. Here, concepts are elaborated as a result of experiences. Thus, Dharmakīrti's solution to the problem of thought and meaning is conceptualist. It argues that, in a world of individuals, there are only constructed intensional entities but conceptual construction is also a product of experience. Hence, far from advancing an a priori view of conceptualization, Dharmakīrti's theory gives the mediating role between language and reality to concepts qua real mental events arising from our encounters with reality.

Such a conceptualism is similar to a Lockean conceptualism in that it holds that the link between concepts and experiences is causal. It is different in that it emphasizes the constructive but mistaken nature of conceptuality. This emphasis on the distortion involved in concept formation shows the problematic position of conceptuality in Dharmakīrti's system. Although thought helps us achieve our practical aims, conceptuality as a whole is viewed with suspicion. Although Dharmakīrti recognizes its practical value, his overall attitude toward thinking remains fundamentally distrustful. K. Jarter quite rightly says: "A . . . difficulty we noticed in *apohavāda* was its tendency to reduce to anti-conceptualization; insight seemed to require giving up conceptual thinking altogether. But the Buddhist was forced to this because he refused to admit universals, and absences, into the external world. This conclusion is only necessary for someone like the Buddhist who believes in the momentariness of everything that exists."[46] Although Jarter's statement needs to be nuanced, it reflects an important and even predominant tendency in Indian Buddhism. Contrary to both Aristotle and Bhartṛhari (as well as many other thinkers), who assert the primacy of conceptual thinking in the cognitive process, traditional[47] Buddhist epistemology allows only a limited validity to conceptual thinking. Since it relates to unreal entities and since it involves concepts that are without objective correspondents in reality, conceptual thinking cannot but involve distortion despite its practical value.

This concludes our investigation of Dharmakīrti's *apoha* theory. In the next chapters, I move to the later developments of this theory. Chapter 13 further examines Śāntarakṣita's distinction among three types of elimination. Chapter 14 considers Tibetan interpretations of some aspects of the *apoha* theory, and Chapter 15 concludes by using these ideas to explain language and making a few comparisons with standard Western theories.

13

The Concept of Negation and the Evolution of the *Apoha* Theory

Are Negation and Elimination Equivalent?

In the preceding chapter, we examined Dharmakīrti's conceptualist explanation of how representations mediate between the real and the conceptual realms. We noticed the lack of clarity in Dharmakīrti's formulations, which explains the development of conflicting theories among his later followers. In this chapter, I delve into the important contributions of Śāntarakṣita and his direct disciple Kamalaśīla, whose new developments of the *apoha* theory are of great theoretical interest[1] and provide an important link to the Tibetan views on the subject.

In further developing the *apoha* theory, Śāntarakṣita seems to have been motivated by a desire to provide a decisive response to Kumārila and Uddyotakara's objections. He introduces his discussion by clearly stating their objections, quoting their works at length. He then proceeds to answer systematically their criticisms against the *apoha* theory. Here, I examine just Śāntarakṣita's response to Kumārila's three criticisms; namely, that *apoha* is counterintuitive, circular, and useless. I also compare Śāntarakṣita's views to those of later Tibetan thinkers whom he greatly influenced. I attempt to explain the discussion as simply as possible. Nevertheless, I must confess that, despite my best efforts, this chapter remains quite technical. The reader less interested in the evolution of the *apoha* theory than in the philosophical insights of this tradition may chose to move directly to the next chapter.

On the question of negation, Indian philosophy is divided into two main groups: the realist and the antirealist. In spite of certain differences, the Nyāya-Vaiśeṣika and the Bhaṭṭa-Mīmāṃsā systems belong to the former group (realist). They conceive of absence (*abhāva, dngos med*)[2] as a real and separate category. As such it is the corresponding object of negative cognition (*abhāvadhi*). The second group is constituted of the later logicians led by Dharmakīrti and the Prabhākara-Mīmāṃsā.[3] They hold that negation is not a separate reality but arises as a consequence of a negative conceptual characterization of reality.

Dharmakīrti's tradition as a whole belongs to the second group, for which negation is more epistemic than ontological. Even for the Ge-luk tradition, negation comes to be as a result of the negative characterization of an object (the basis of negation). A negative characterization is added onto such an object of negation on the basis of nonobservation (*anupalabdhi, ma dmigs pa*) of the putative object to be negated. For example, I see a mountain on which no restaurant can be found and sadly think "there is no restaurant on this mountain." Thus, the negation is epistemic, reflecting how we know rather than what we know.

Śāntarakṣita's *apoha* theory follows this general Buddhist view. However, it also represents a new development in the history of the *apoha* theory, which takes further elements introduced by Dharmakīrti. As we saw already, one of Dharmakīrti's major preoccupations is the necessity to establish a link between the real and the conceptual realms. Dharmakīrti does this by stressing the mediating role of conceptual representations (concepts qua mental events). For Dharmakīrti, the mental representation does not seem, however, to be an actual elimination but just provides the causal link that supports the purely conceptual realm. Hence, the meaning of elimination (*apoha*, understood as being equivalent to conceptual construct) does not seem to be changed.

To respond more fully to the Hindu critique, Śāntarakṣita takes Dharmakīrti's ideas further but, in the process, transforms the very notion of elimination. For Śāntarakṣita, something is an elimination not because it is a conceptual construct which can be validated only in a negative way (as it is with Dignāga and Dharmakīrti), but because it is understood through a psychologically observable process in which a putative object of negation is eliminated. Hence, Śāntarakṣita's use of the concept of negation (*pratiṣedha, dgag pa*) explains less how concepts are validated than the psychological nature of elimination. Hence, Śāntarakṣita also extends elimination to include real phenomena. I document this evolution from Dignāga to Śāntarakṣita through Dharmakīrti in this chapter.

Śāntarakṣita explicates the notion of negation by differentiating two types of elimination: *paryudāsa* (*ma yin dgag*) and *prasajya-pratiṣedha* (or *niṣedha, med dgag*). As he informs us,[4] these two eliminations are two types of negations (*pratiṣedha, dgag pa*). Therefore, for him elimination and negation are equivalent and even synonymous. He takes these terms from discussions relating to the analysis of ritual injunctions in the Mīmāṃsā school. Some injunctions are essentially negative in import and called *prasajya.* These statements are pure prohibitions in which the negation is bound to the verb (*prasajya*). *Do not look* is an example of such verbally bound negation.[5] *He shall not say "hello" at dawn* is an example of nominally bound negation (*paryudāsa*), in which affirmation is primary (he shall say "hello" but not in the morning).[6]

The distinction between two types of negation was introduced within the framework of Buddhist philosophy for the first time by Bhavya.[7] In Buddhist philosophy, these terms are taken quite differently from their original exegetic context. The Buddhist theory of negation does not concern moral command or ritual injunction but the epistemology of negation, with no judgment of value.

This distinction between two types of negation is used by Śāntarakṣita in the context of the *apoha* theory to respond to the indictment of the *apoha* theory by Kumārila and Uddyotakara.[8] Śāntarakṣita starts by differentiating the two types of eliminations: "Accordingly, elimination is of two types: implicative and nonimplicative negations. Implicative negation is of two types due to a difference in the mind and in the object."[9] The gist of this answer is that eliminations are not solely negative in import. In his indictment of Dignāga, Kumārila has forgotten, argues Śāntarakṣita, that negation is not just an elimination but can also have positive implications. To support his point, Śāntarakṣita distinguishes those negations that are exclusively negative in import, which he calls *prasajya (med dgag,* here translated as "nonimplicative negation") from those that have a positive import (*paryudhāsa, ma yin dgag,* here translated as "implicative negation"). In this case, negations do not concern words exclusively but are applied to universals and perhaps even to actual entities in the world. Nonimplicative negations do not imply a commitment to the existence of any positive entity, merely negating the assertion to be negated.[10] For example, the negation of the existence of the horn of a rabbit does not imply the existence of any positive entity whatsoever. Implicative negations have a positive import in that they imply a commitment to the existence of some positive entity. An example of this type of negation is a mountain without a restaurant. Such a negation negates the presence of an entity (the restaurant) and also implies the existence of another, positive entity, the mountain. The ignorance of this type of negation lies behind Kumārila's critique. Once the different types of negation are differentiated, the *apoha* theory can be shown to be neither counterintuitive nor circular nor redundant.

Objective Elimination

To make his point, Śāntarakṣita further develops the concept of negation by differentiating two types of implicative negation: The first, mental implicative negation, relates to the ideational meaning (*pratibhā, snang ba*) proposed by Dignāga. Here, mental elimination (*buddhyātmakānyāpoha, blo'i gzhan sel*) is, in the context of the *apoha* theory, nothing other than a conceptual representation; that is, a reflection (*pratibimba, gzugs brnyan*). The second, objective negation, has to do with the thing itself. The objective elimination (*arthātmaka-svalakṣaṇānyāpoha, don rang mtshan gyi gzhan sel*) of a thing is the thing itself, when it is negatively characterized. Hence, now we have three types of negation: nonimplicative negation (what is usually meant by negation) and two (objective and mental) implicative negations. Let us first consider Śāntarakṣita's concept of objective elimination.

Through a conceptual reflection of an object, a person indirectly apprehends a real object. For Śāntarakṣita, this real object is a negation inasmuch as it is distinguished from its contradictory. When we conceive a real object x we do not conceive the object as it is but merely get at x by negating its contradictory, non-x. Accordingly, an object x is x because it is not non-x. From this conceptual point of view, x can be considered an elimination.[11] This type of negation is called an *objective elimination* (*arthātmaka-svalakṣaṇānyāpoha, don rang mtshan gyi gzhan sel*).

What are the ramifications of the view that negations can be real entities? The exact nature of Śāntarakṣita's ideas is a topic of debate among later Tibetan commentators, and their opinions will help formulate and evaluate the different possible interpretations. Here I briefly spell out two alternative interpretations and explain my preference between them.

First, *objective eliminations are real.* Śāntarakṣita could be saying that a real object *x*, such as a jar, is not itself a negation; still, such real things can be negations (or even negatives) when considered from an eliminative standpoint. This opinion is accepted by most Ge-luk scholars. They assert that real things can be objective eliminations. Furthermore, Gyel-tsap,[12] Kay-drup in his later phase, Ge-dün-drup,[13] and all the authors of the monastic textbooks agree that, despite being real, objective eliminations are actual negations. The existence of objective eliminations has thereby become a self-evident truth for the members of the present-day Ge-luk tradition.[14] Ge-dün-drup, for example, expresses this view when he defines *objective negation* as "A thing that is an elimination is an implicative negation established from its own side without being a mere [mental] imputation."[15] An objective negation is a real object conceived negatively. This negative object truly exists, for it is not a mere conceptual creation, even though it is conceived negatively. This view brings about a modification of the sense of negation *(dgag pa, pratiṣedha).*[16] Negation is not merely conceptual but capable also of concerning the real world. Although negations relate primarily to our propositional attitudes, they are not strictly limited to these attitudes, having objective counterparts as well.

This transformation, however, is only partial, for even while Ge-luk thinkers assert the reality of negations, they maintain the essential point of the Buddhist presentation of negation, which is that negation is not a real, separate category. Negation remains primarily epistemic. Although negations can be real things, the difference between negation and affirmation is conceptual. A jar and a 'distinguished from nonjar' are not two things but substantially identical.[17]

Second, *objective eliminations are not real.* Go-ram-ba has quite a different view. He takes Śāntarakṣita to be saying that a real object can be called an *elimination* when understood conceptually, though it is not. Being part of the actual fabric of the world, a real thing is not an actual elimination. Its mode of existence does not depend on the way in which conception applies to it. Hence, a real object exists independent of any elimination of a contradictory.

An elimination is always an essenceless conceptual entity. A real thing can be called an elimination although it is not.[18] Mokṣākaragupta seems to hold a similar point of view. He says: "An external object such as a jar as conceptually determined (*yathādhyavasāyam*) is called *apoha,* the term being understood as in 'the other or dissimilar is discriminated from this'."[19] Mokṣākaragupta suggests that an external object is not really an elimination but is called so to indicate the basis for making a differentiation. According to this interpretation, the presentation of elimination applies to an external object inasmuch as the object is appropriated through a conceptual elimination. This is the only actual elimination. Similarly, mental eliminations are not real eliminations, since they are mental events, but are so called inasmuch as they are the mental elements that exclude things from their dissimilar instances. Accordingly, a mental representation is called *elimination* because it is the aspect of a mental state that appropriates an object by excluding one thing from being something else.

By taking Śāntarakṣita's presentation to be metaphorical, these authors considerably downplay the importance of his contribution. His division of elimination is reduced to a terminological typology whose philosophical significance is dubious. The reasons for presenting three types of elimination from a terminological point of view are, according to Go-ram-ba, to present a formal framework within the *apoha* theory according to which a conception can be determined as factual or not. This interpretation, however, does not do full justice to Śāntarakṣita, who sees himself as proposing not a mere terminological typology but the correct interpretation of Dignāga's *apoha* theory. Let us try to determine the import of Śāntarakṣita's opinion.

Here I will proceed simply and merely state what Śāntarakṣita's *Compendium* says. It is always difficult to know how much weight to attribute to the statement of an author without an in-depth study of his thought. Since such a study is beyond the scope of the present work, my conclusions are only provisional. There seem to be indications, however, that Śāntarakṣita takes his presentation of the three eliminations more seriously than some of his interpreters.

For Śāntarakṣita, an objective elimination is an elimination even though it is a real thing. Two facts support this reading. First, Śāntarakṣita does not hold that elimination must be conceptual in all instances. For him (as we will see in the next section), a representation or aspect of an object in a conceptual mental state is clearly an elimination. It is even the main element in the *apoha* theory, despite being a mental event and, therefore, a real thing.[20] Therefore, that something is real is no reason in itself for excluding it from the purview of Śāntarakṣita's *apoha* theory.

Second, while explaining objective elimination, Śāntarakṣita asserts that a specifically characterized phenomenon "is called an *elimination*."[21] Although this statement might suggest that a thing is, in fact, not an elimination but just called so, Śāntarakṣita's disciple Kamalaśīla interprets it otherwise: "This [passage] (stanza 1009) indicates that the reference to specifically characterized phenomena as elimination [is to be understood] in its primary sense."[22] Kamalaśīla takes Śāntarakṣita to be saying that a real thing is called an elimination in the primary sense (*mukhyat, dngos*) of the term and that, therefore, a real thing is an elimination. Although there is no guarantee that Kamalaśīla always remained truthful to the intentions of his teacher, the close link between the two thinkers gives Kamalaśīla's explanations considerable weight. In the absence of any decisive counterevidence, the conclusion that Śāntarakṣita holds objective eliminations to be actual eliminations is difficult to resist.[23]

This description of Śāntarakṣita's position on the question of elimination confirms our previous characterization of Śāntarakṣita's position as one that emphasizes the psychological nature of *apoha*. It also supports Mookerjee's opinion that what Jñānaśrimītra describes as the positivistic view of elimination is to be ascribed to Śāntarakṣita.

Śāntarakṣita holds that negation is not restricted to the conceptual realm but concerns real things as well. Real objects can be considered negations (here they are negatives as well) inasmuch as they can be negatively conceptualized. On this issue, Śāntarakṣita is in agreement with most Ge-luk thinkers that negations can be real. By contrast Go-ram-ba's idea that this threefold typology of elimination is not to be taken literally fails to capture Śāntarakṣita's intent. The presentation of the three eliminations is not just a terminological way to present a difficult topic. It is an original framework meant to provide a clear, exhaustive Buddhist answer to Hindu criticism of the *apoha* theory. Go-ram-ba's interpretation suffers from the assumption that Dharmakīrti and Śāntarakṣita have an identical view, when actually there are substantial differences between the two.

Dharmakīrti does not deal explicitly with the concept of an objective elimination. Nevertheless, his texts do mention an elimination existing in external objects. For example, Dharmakīrti refers to "an elimination [found in external things] that has the capacity [to produce an effect]."[24] We should not jump to the conclusion, however, that Dharmakīrti accepts the idea that real objects can be eliminations. It is quite difficult to determine what Dharmakīrti means by his few references to this topic. Does he really think that external objects can be eliminations or does he introduce the idea of an elimination existing in things merely as a way to introduce real objects into the *apoha* theory?

I prefer the second alternative, for it quite adequately explains Dharmakīrti's comments. The Ge-luk interpretation of the question, although it has become standard for this school, does not seem relevant to authors writing prior to Śāntarakṣita. I find support for this preference in Ge-dün-drup's own explanation:

> *Question*: With respect to this [objective elimination], why is [such an elimination] called "elimination"?
> *Answer*: In this [matter], [such an elimination] is called "elimination" because it is the basis [on which] other [entities] are eliminated. Śākyabuddhi [says]: "In this [matter], specifically characterized phenomena are indeed distinguishers because they eliminate other [entities." Such an explanation] is made from the point of view of etymology, [for] something that is the basis of an elimination does not need to be an elimination.[25]

Ge-dün-drup is explaining how real things can be called *eliminations*. In the process he quotes Śākyabuddhi, who writes prior to Śāntarakṣita, saying that real things are referred to in this way because they are the basis in reality on which universals are differentiated. From this perspective, all things can be called *elimination*. This explanation does not fit Ge-dün-drup's purpose, however, for it offers no means to distinguish objective eliminations from positive phenomena, which he requires. Ge-dün-drup compensates by saying that Śākyabuddhi's comments are made in relation to an explanation of the etymology (*sgra bshad*) of *elimination*, not from the point of view of the extension (*sgra 'jug*) of the word.

This slightly embarrassed and inelegant explanation by Ge-dün-drup suggests that Śākyabuddhi's opinion is in fact different from his own. The former probably understands discussions about eliminations in real things as just a way to introduce real things into the framework of *apoha* theory. Unlike Śāntarakṣita, he does not understand eliminations in real things to refer to a special class of elimination. If this is indeed his understanding of the matter, it may well have been Dharmakīrti's opinion as well. This would confirm the difference between Dharmakīrti and Śāntarakṣita regarding the status of negation.[26]

Śāntarakṣita on Representations

In addition to his description of negations as real entities, another element of Śāntarakṣita's *apoha* theory justifies our characterization of his view of elimination as more positive and psychologically oriented than Dharmakīrti's. This second element is his insistence on the role of representations (or reflections, *pratibimba, gzugs brnyan*) in the conceptual process.[27] Although Dharmakīrti introduces this concept, he does not make it the main element of his *apoha* theory. For Śāntarakṣita, the concept of representation becomes the central element. Let us examine his viewpoint on the question.

Following Dharmakīrti, Śāntarakṣita explains that things, despite their differences, can give rise to a unitary conception through their resemblances. Relating this idea to the cognitive role of conceptual reflection, he writes: "On this basis, a cognition [arises] to which appears a conceptual reflection of the object. [This reflection] is conceived as 'the object' even though the objective nature is absent in it."[28] Kamalaśīla comments on this stanza: "*On this basis*: on the basis of similar things such as [medicinal plants like] *Harītakī,* etc., that is to say through the power of the experience [of these things], which acts as causes [of the experience], arises a conceptual cognition. To this [cognition] a reflection of the object appears as being in reality the object. And it is this [conceptual reflection] which is called elimination (*apoha, sel ba*)."[29] For Śāntarakṣita, the word *elimination* does not refer to just the elimination of the contradictory of a thing (non-*x*) but also to the representation that acts as a support of the conceptual process. In fact, Śāntarakṣita understands the word *apoha* to denote primarily the representations that arise in our minds. Now, how are these representations, which are real, eliminations? Śāntarakṣita gives two reasons: "Because it is distinct from the other appearances [and] it is the cause of obtaining things that are excluded from others . . ."[30] The first reason Śāntarakṣita gives for calling a conceptual representation an elimination is that it is psychologically distinct from other conceptual appearances, excluding them from the field of attention. Kamalaśīla comments on this passage: "[This point] is explained through four reasons: (1) directly, because it itself appears as distinct from the other appearances superimposed by other conceptual thoughts, it is an elimination . . ."[31] When someone thinks about something, the representation that arises in that person's mind completely occupies the field of attention, precluding other images from appearing to the mind. Such a conceptual reflection is an elimination because it excludes other representations from appearing to the mind.

The essence of *apoha* doctrine in general is that thought does not relate to its object directly, as does perception. Thought apprehends its object by creating a double dichotomy. Logically, thought apprehends *x* through differentiating between *x* and non-*x*. Psychologically, the reflection of *x* is distinguished from other reflections. Between these two dimensions of the theory, Śāntarakṣita puts greater emphasis on the latter. Hattori aptly explains: "It is not that Śāntarakṣita disregarded the process through which the concept is formed. . . . However, he is chiefly concerned with the psychological fact that the image of an object appears immediately in the mind of the man who hears a word."[32] Śāntarakṣita presents elimination primarily from a psychological point of view. For him, the main element is the (conceptual) representation, or reflection, which he understands as an actual negation.

This explanation seems different from Dharmakīrti's explanation of the nature of concepts. For him, unreal universals are the contents of concepts. Hence, for Dharmakīrti concepts are seen mostly as supports in the construction of universals. Śāntarakṣita does not disagree but tends to emphasize the psychological nature of concepts. Whereas Dharmakīrti stresses that concepts take universals as their objects, Śāntarakṣita emphasizes concepts as mental events. This is at least how we interpret Dharmakīrti, but in fact his words are less than clear. He says: "That which pertains to the reflection of the object appears to the cognition [arising] from words similar to the elimination [of others], but it is not the real object, [for] it arises from mistaken latencies."[33] This passage seems to be open to two possible interpretations: the one we gave following Go-ram-ba and some other Tibetan commentators in arguing for a differentiation between reflection and elimination and the one given by Śāntarakṣita. According to the latter's view, the representation, that is, the concept, is the actual elimination. This does not mean, however, that it is a universal, for it is a real mental episode. Thus, the meaning of elimination has shifted from an epistemological description of concepts to a psychological explanation of the real entities involved in the thinking process and their relations to the external world.[34]

Referring back to the passage from Śāntarakṣita, we find there a second reason for calling a representation an *elimination*. A representation is an elimination because it leads to obtaining something that is being excluded from others. For example, when we hear "this maple is a tree," these words create a representation in our consciousness. It is an elimination because it leads to our seeing, using, and so forth an actual maple tree, which is excluded from nontree. Kamalaśīla says that our calling the representation an *elimination* is a case of giving the name of the effect (the obtainment of a real thing that is excluded from its contradictory) to its cause (the representation that we form in our mind to help us to deal practically with real things).[35] By this view, the representation is the actual elimination that enables one to obtain a real thing.

Its existence allows Śāntarakṣita to give a quasi-mentalist explanation of the relation most basic to language, that of signifier-signified (*vācaka-vācya, brjod byed brjod bya*). For Śāntarakṣita, the signifier is the meaningful linguistic unit and the signified is the object of the words; that is, the representation. The relation between these two entities is causal. The signifier produces a representation that stands for the actual thing. This view is different from a Lockean mentalism (hence, the qualification *quasi*) in that Śāntarakṣita does not hold that universals are representations, for, otherwise, they would be real.

Yet, Śāntarakṣita's description of reflections (representations) as being actual eliminations differs from Dharmakīrti's insistence on the constructed nature of eliminations. Śāntarakṣita explains: "The cognition of the reflection of the object in that form is produced from the word. This thing, [the relation of] signifier-signified is established as having a causal nature."[36] Kamalaśīla comments, expanding on the relation of signifier and signified: "The reflection, which is of the nature of the mind and which is in relation [to the word], is produced from the word. That is to say, when [this reflection] arises, that is, when a signified arises due to a signifier, [their] relation is established as being [one of] effect to cause. Accordingly, since the word produces the reflection, it is said to be the signifier [of this reflection] and since this reflection is produced by the word it is said to be the signified."[37] Śāntarakṣita and Kamalaśīla explain the process of conceptual mediation without relying on metaphysical entities such as universals, purely on the basis of the causal relation between individuals. Thus, contrary to the Ge-luk tradition, where the assertion of the existence of real negations tends to reflect a realist agenda, Śāntarakṣita's interpretation of elimination as negation reflects no similar tendency to accept real properties. Rather, the meaning of elimination has shifted from an epistemological to a psychological perspective.

The Evolution of the Apoha *Theory*

Through his presentation of the three types of elimination, Śāntarakṣita can claim that he simultaneously answers all of Kumārila's three charges. He accomplishes this by demonstrating that Kumārila's criticisms are based on a misunderstanding of the notion of elimination. Kumārila does not realize that there are several types of elimination and assumes that elimination is necessarily a mere elimination, what Śāntarakṣita calls *nonimplicative negation*. But implicative negations, such as ideational meaning (*pratibhā, snang ba*), and objective negations are also eliminations. Thus, when Kumārila asks "Why do you talk about elimination of others (distinguished from non-*x*) when you can talk about ideational meaning?" Śāntarakṣita can answer, "Because thought involves all three types of elimination!" Since neither the purely negative element nor ideational meaning by itself can provide a complete explanation of conceptuality, all three types of eliminations must be considered.

Śāntarakṣita's theory also responds to Kumārila's charge that the *apoha* theory contradicts our common intuition. His revised *apoha* theory does not contradict our precritical intuitions. Our intuition tells us that, in an expression like *this is a tree*, the import of the words is positive, whereas in an expression like *don't do this!* negation is primary. Against Kumārila's recourse to precritical intuition, Śāntarakṣita argues that the revised theory accommodates this intuition because external positive objects are also the objects (albeit indirectly) of conceptual thought. Therefore, in the case of positive utterances, the import of words is positive, and the negative elements come only by implication. The element felt to be positive is the appearance, which in turn leads us to understand by implication the negative content of the cognitive process.[38] Thus, Kumārila's appeal to common intuitions is shown to be inconclusive, since the *apoha* theory is able to account for them.

Last, the *apoha* theory is also free of the fault of circularity, one of the main charges: If conceptual understanding involves negation of *x*, then understanding *x* will presuppose that of non-*x*, which in turn presupposes that of non-non-*x*. And this is nothing but understanding *x*. Against this objection, Śāntarakṣita applies the distinction between two kinds of eliminations. When the words *this maple is a tree* are spoken, a conceptual representation arises in the mind of the hearer. This idea is the primary object of the words. As such, this idea is able to make us understand by implication that this maple is not a nontree. Therefore, since the understanding of tree does not necessitate that of nontree but just that of the ideational meaning of tree, there are no grounds for adducing a vicious circularity against the *apoha* theory.[39] The whole controversy can be shown, according to Śāntarakṣita, to be a result of the misunderstanding by Kumārila and Uddyotakara of Dignāga's true intentions.

Śāntarakṣita's theory marks an important stage in the evolution of *apoha* theory. Dignāga produced an unstable synthesis of two apparently heterogeneous elements, *apoha* and *pratibhā*. The instability of the combination accounts for how different thinkers could use the *apoha* theory according to their needs and inclinations and could come up with conflicting formulations. Dignāga himself places the emphasis mostly on the logical aspect of *apoha*.[40] This is reflected in his insistence to connect his *apoha* theory to the analysis of inference. Elimination is a way to explain how inference is possible despite the absence of real universals. It is also a way to explain how language can be meaningful in a world without real intensional entities. In using the notion of elimination, Dignāga always insists on the inferential model. Thus, the logical component of the theory (elimination as elimination of non-*x*) receives greater emphasis as the basis for inference.

Next, Dharmakīrti emphasizes a different aspect of *apoha* theory; namely, its epistemological dimension. His whole philosophy relies on the explanation of concepts as providing a support for thought and language. One of his dominant preoccupations is to respond to criticisms of Dignāga's *apoha* theory as isolating the conceptual domain from reality; hence, Dharmakīrti insists on the importance of concepts as mental phenomena whose objects are the fictional universals to which thought and language relate. Through their causal connections with real things, these mental entities link conceptuality to reality. And yet, Dharmakīrti's mentalism is different from Śāntarakṣita's psychologization of the concept of elimination. For, Dharmakīrti does not think, like Śāntarakṣita does, that elimination is to be understood in terms of negating a putative object of negation. Rather, a construct is an elimination not because it negates some putative object but because it is conceptual and, hence, unreal. For example, the notion of knowable is an elimination, not because it negates any assertion, but because it is a conceptual content whose mode of existence depends entirely on a conceptual dichotomy. Hence, the eliminative character of universals is not psychological, but is a consequence of their being the exclusive objects of thought. Nevertheless, by insisting on the role of the mental representation as the objective basis of conceptual construction, Dharmakīrti opens the door to Śāntarakṣita's later psychologization of the *apoha* theory. By insisting on the idea that concepts qua mental events are real phenomena causally connected to experience, Dharmakīrti emphasizes the role of mental representations in the *apoha* theory. Although for him, such representations do not seem to be actual eliminations (since they are real), these elements play a central role as the support of fictional entities, thus establishing a bridge between the conceptual and the real domains.

Śāntarakṣita continues the same mentalist line of thought but, in the process, comes to modify the theory quite considerably. Śāntarakṣita's attempt is also a response to Kumārila's criticisms, an attempt to vindicate Dignāga's theory. But, in the process, Śāntarakṣita further transforms the concept of elimination by including the concept qua mental event in it. The conceptual representation is not just the objective support of necessarily conceptual eliminations, as it is for Dharmakīrti, but becomes an actual elimination. In his hands, the theory is less a way to explain how Buddhists can have a valid epistemology in a world of individuals than a psychologically oriented explanation, focusing on the nature of actual entities involved in the conceptual process. Hence, Śāntarakṣita uses extensively the concept of negation to explain *apoha*.

This view, which was severely criticized by later Indian thinkers such as Jñānaśrīmitra, has had an enormous influence in Tibet. Let us examine how later Tibetan thinkers have dealt with the questions raised by Śāntarakṣita's ideas. In this chapter I will deal only with their views about negation in general and the notion of an objective elimination, reserving the examination of the concept of mental elimination, which plays an extremely important role in the Tibetan tradition, for the next chapter.

Ge-luk Views of Negations

In the Tibetan epistemological tradition, the role of Śāntarakṣita is quite important since several Tibetan thinkers take his ideas as the basis for their understanding of the *apoha* theory.[41] This is particularly the case in the Ge-luk tradition, which finds in this author a presentation of the *apoha* theory more favorable to its realism, even though Śāntarakṣita himself is no realist. Śāntarakṣita offers a support for a realist interpretation of the *apoha* theory because he moves away from the equation between elimination and conceptual fiction and introduces the idea that some real phenomena may be eliminations. I have argued that this is a move away from Dharmakīrti's more strictly epistemological ideas, in which elimination is understood as a way to explain the conceptual and fictional nature of universals. By psychologizing the concept of elimination, Śāntarakṣita breaks this equation and thus opens the door to a further revision of the *apoha* theory, in which the status of actual elimination can be extended not only to real individual phenomena (as for Śāntarakṣita) but also to real universals. Thus, the Ge-luk tradition's reliance on Śāntarakṣita comes as no surprise.

For instance, Ge-dün-drup, for his entire presentation of elimination and negation, relies on the premise that these two are equivalent. Referring to Kamalaśīla's comments on Śāntarakṣita's stanza 1004, Ge-dün-drup states that elimination is equivalent to negation.[42] Ge-dün-drup then defines negation as "that which is realized by explicitly eliminating an object of negation."[43] Following Śāntarakṣita, he further divides negation into implicative and nonimplicative negations. He defines the latter as "That which is realized through an explicit elimination of an object of negation and does not suggest some other positive phenomenon in place of its object of negation."[44] A nonimplicative negation negates its object but does not imply the existence of any positive entity. For example, I say, "there is no restaurant." This negates an assertion without implying any commitment to the existence of any positive entity. Such nonimplicative negation is not limited to trivial uses: In the Madhyamaka system, emptiness is a nonimplicative negation. The Ge-luk school places particular emphasis on this last point, for it insists that without understanding emptiness as a nonimplicative negation, the process of investigating ultimate reality can never reach its final point.[45]

Following Śāntarakṣita, Ge-luk thinkers hold that the concept of nonimplicative negation also has significance in epistemology, since conceptual cognition is related to both implicative and nonimplicative negations. To every phenomenon *x* corresponds a nonimplicative negation that can be formulated as the absence of a common locus between *x* and non-*x*. Gyel-tsap gives as an example of such an elimination "the absence of nonjar on the basis of jar."[46]

Implicative negation is differentiated from nonimplicative negation by its implication of the existence of a positive phenomenon in place of its object of negation.[47] The exact determination of what constitutes a positive implication is a topic of highly technical debate among Ge-luk scholars. According to Ge-dün-drup, for example, a negation such as 'a mountain which is without a restaurant' is not an implicative negation because the positive entity mountain is not suggested in place of the restaurant. Rather, it is the basis on which one appreciates whether another phenomenon is or is not implied (*chos gzhan 'phen mi 'phen brtsi ba'i gzhi).* On the other hand, 'a mountain without a restaurant' is an implicative negation because the entity mountain is implied by the negation of the object of negation (restaurant).[48] Whatever the exact details of this presentation, the Ge-luk view is quite simple: Phenomena are to be divided into positive and negative entities according to the way in which they are conceptualized. Elimination and negation are equivalent and divided into two categories, implicative and nonimplicative negation.

Following Śāntarakṣita, the Ge-luk tradition distinguishes two types of implicative negations: objective and mental eliminations. Among these two concepts, the latter plays an extremely important role within the Tibetan tradition and, hence, will be treated separately. Let me say a few words on the Ge-luk view of objective elimination, however, before examining the Sa-gya view of negation.

Almost all the thinkers belonging to the Ge-luk tradition use this distinction, which as we will see in a following chapter, plays an important role in the philosophy of language of the tradition and supports the realism of the tradition. Let us nevertheless notice that, although the two positions on universals and on negations have affinities, the former does not entail the latter.[49] Kay-drup, who is so candid in his realism, denies in his *Ornament* that real things can ever be negations.[50] There, Kay-drup refutes a proposed definition of elimination: preclusion of one's contradictory (*dngos 'gal gcod pa*). This cannot be the definition of negation because then all phenomena would be eliminations. He then continues: "This refutes the opinion that a specifically characterized phenomenon [can be] an elimination, for such an opinion completely disregards the texts of the master [Dharmakīrti], who on many occasions explains that all eliminations are [mental] imputations."[51] Whereas according to the interpretation of most Ge-luk thinkers an objective elimination is a negation, according to Kay-drup in *Ornament,* an objective elimination is little more than a negative way to talk about something that positively exists.

In his later *Ocean of Reasoning,* however, Kay-drup changes his mind and accepts the existence of objective elimination: "Those who assert that anything that is an objective elimination is a metaphorical elimination show that they have not seen the masters' texts, despite [their] stating [this idea] as the masters' thought."[52] Quoting Kamalaśīla's explanations, which we examined previously, Kay-drup argues against those who, like himself earlier, assert that an elimination is necessarily conceptual. Kay-drup sets forth this argument: Let us posit an entity, 'assemblage of jar and the elimination of nonjar'. If this entity is not an elimination, it is not a negation. This is not possible, however, for such an entity is identified as eliminating an object of negation, which by definition entails its being a negation. If this entity negates something, then it also eliminates something. Hence, it is an actual elimination.

Outside of Kay-drup's early work, all the Ge-luk texts that I have seen rely on the concept of an objective elimination. The disagreement between them concerns the precise way of positing an objective negation. Ge-dün-drup gives 'that which is distinguished from nonjar' (*bum pa ma yin pa las log pa*) as an example of an objective negation.[53] Such an entity is a phenomenon that is both coextensive with jar and a negation. This entity is a real jar negatively characterized. It is different from the 'distinguisher of a jar' (*bum pa ma yin pa las ldog pa*), which is not a jar but its conceptual characteristic. Most Ge-luk epistemologists accept this interpretation in asserting that the distinguished object of the first example is both real and an object of perception. The textbooks from the Go-mang College disagree, for they hold that such a distinguished jar is neither a real thing nor an object of perception. Accordingly, their example of an objective elimination is a jar that is not permanent.[54] Aside from this slight difference, the main Ge-luk textbooks all accept the existence of negations that are real.

Other Tibetan realists similarly support the idea of objective elimination. For Bo-dong, for instance, an objective elimination is nothing other than a negative universal. Like most Ge-luk thinkers, he also considers it the most important element in the *apoha* theory.[55] Objective elimination is essential because it allows mental eliminations, that is to say, ideas, to be included in the *apoha* theory. Such a mental picture is not negative by itself. It is negative because it relies on a negative element, the real thing qua elimination. Bo-dong finds support for this view in several passages of Dharmakīrti's *Commentary*. The most revealing is probably *Commentary*, III:163.bc–173.[56] In this passage, Dharmakīrti speaks of "an elimination [found in] external objects that has the capacity [to perform a function]."[57] This seems to refer to an elimination that is real, since it is functional. Dharmakīrti also describes a mental reflection (*pratibimba, gzugs brnyan*) as relying on this elimination, furthermore receiving its identity as an elimination through this reliance.[58] Bo-dong takes this passage as well as several others to indicate that Dharmakīrti accepts objective elimination.

Thus, we can see a large agreement between Śāntarakṣita and later Tibetan realists on the existence of objective elimination and on the understanding of the *apoha* theory through the psychological concept of negation. Their agreement is not complete for, whereas Śāntarakṣita refuses the possibility of real universals, Tibetan realists are ready to entertain this idea. Moreoever, on the subject of mental elimination, as we will see, Śāntarakṣita does not have the same idea about mental elimination. Finally, he does not share in differentiating the implicit and explicit levels of understanding as developed by Cha-ba and accepted by the Geluk tradition.[59]

Several later Ge-luk thinkers hold that three eliminations are simultaneously present in a single conception. For example, when I think about a jar, the mental elimination of that jar is the direct or appearing object (*snang yul*) of the conceptual cognition apprehending that jar. The second and third eliminations are the objective elimination, that which is distinguished from nonjar, and the nonimplicative elimination, the mere absence of any common locus between jar and nonjar. Both are implicit objects (*shugs yul*) of the conception.[60] As we will see, Go-ram-ba and other Sa-gya thinkers hold that the epistemology of explicit-implicit realization (*dngos shugs la rtogs pa*) is a creation of the early Tibetan thinker Cha-ba and is without foundation in classical Indian texts.[61]

Śāntarakṣita does not distinguish the content of a mental state at a given time into implicit and explicit aspects. He holds, rather, that the direct object of such state is positive and the cognition of the mere negation comes after by implication, as follows: Conceptual consciousness, operating through the intermediary of a conceptual reflection, creates a logical dichotomy between *x* and non-*x* and apprehends the object as not being non-*x*. In the process it apprehends the purely negative concept that there is nothing in common between *x* and non-*x*.[62] This is a nonimplicative negation (*prasajya, med dgag*), the third type of elimination. This negation is exclusively negative in import and is not understood directly by the mind. For example, when I point to a jar and say "this is a jar," a mental state is presented directly (*sākśāt, dngos su*) with a positive image through which it understands the negative implication of what has been said. The understanding of the positive element is primary and prior; the negative import is understood later, by implication (*sāmarthyatas, shugs kyis*).[63]

Sa-gya Views on Negations

As in other matters, Sa-paṇ and his followers have tried to remain close to what they perceive to be Dharmakīrti's view. Due to their historical position, however, they are confronted with the interpretations elaborated by authoritative Indian commentators. Because they belong to a tradition in which philosophy is understood mostly as commentary on the tradition, they find it difficult to reject the authority of prestigious Indian commentators. Accordingly, instead of bluntly stating the differences between these commentators and Dharmakīrti, they try to conciliate conflicting views by subtle but often artificial exegeses.

In the case of the *apoha* theory, the difficulty comes from the difference between Dharmakīrti's epistemological theory, which Sa-gya thinkers are trying to follow, and Śāntarakṣita's more psychological orientation. Whereas Ge-luk scholars are at ease with this latter perspective, which they have adopted as an interpretation of Dharmakīrti's theory, Sa-gya thinkers find it difficult to explain the concept of elimination in light of negation without jeopardizing their system. This explains the artificial nature of some of their interpretations. The introduction of the concept of negation greatly complicates their explanatory task.

Both Śākya Chok-den and Go-ram-ba give complicated explanations attempting to distinguish negation (*dgag pa, pratiśedha*) from affirmation (*sgrub pa, vidhi*). They are attempting to relate Dharmakīrti's theory, in which elimination is the object of conceptuality, to the new theory, in which elimination is explained by the notion of negation. Affirmation, the opposite of negation, must then be the object of perception. Accordingly, affirmation is equivalent to the real thing and negation to the unreal construct. When the distinction between affirmation and negation is understood in this way, negation and affirmation are radically different: Whereas affirmation is real, negation is merely conceptual. Within this framework, it is possible to assert negation and elimination to be equivalent.

This is not, however, the way in which negation is usually understood. For example, we speak of affirming or negating an assertion, thereby implying that both affirmation and negation are conceptual. To speak technically, the equation of affirmation and reality, and negation and unreal construct does not concern the way in which both affirmation and negation are taken as direct objects (*dngos yul*) of conceptual activities. When we speak of affirmation and negation in this way, we are merely referring to unreal quasi-entities, for real things are beyond either affirmation or negation (*dgag sgrub kyi dngos rten mi byed*).[64] According to this way of understanding affirmation and negation, both are said to be eliminations and therefore fictional quasi-entities. Go-ram-ba says: "When affirmation and negation are established as direct objects of affirmations and negations by valid cognitions, both cannot but be eliminations. [This is so] because, since specifically characterized phenomena are mere appearances, perceptions cannot engage in affirmation and negation. Ascertaining consciousnesses induced by this [perception] and inference affirm and negate."[65] Here, the Sa-gya idea is that affirmation and negation are best understood as conceptual contents, not as real. Whereas affirmation is positively inferred, negation is inferred from the nonobservation of the object of negation.

This view of affirmation and negation as conceptual distinctions, and therefore as eliminations, makes sense within Dharmakīrti's *apoha* theory. It leads, however, to some difficulties when integrated within the theory of the two types of negation. Since an affirmation qua conceptual content is an elimination, it must be a negation.[66] It is not a negation in the usual sense of the term, however, since it does not seem to negate anything. Thus, this approach to negation and affirmation seems to contradict the ordinary usage of these terms.

To explain this discrepancy, Śākya Chok-den rather artificially proposes to integrate this unusual type of negation into Śāntarakṣita's theory of the two types of negation, implicative and nonimplicative. His attempt posits two types of implicative negation: First, when implicative negations are opposed to nonimplicative negations within the division of conceptual negation, implicative negations are understood as negations (in the usual sense of the word) that imply the existence of some positive entity. Such implicative negations are called *mere negation* (*dgag pa rkyang pa*) and are then defined as "that which is to be realized by elimination only and which implies a positive phenomenon in place of its object of negation."[67]

The second type of implicative negation is called a *combination of both affirmation and negation* (*dgag sgrub gnyis tshogs*).[68] It consists of conceptual contents that are usually thought of as affirmations.[69] An example of such a negation that is both an affirmation and a negation is the knowable (*shes bya*). Since to assert that something is knowable is to assert that something can be known, knowable should be considered an affirmation. However, since knowable does not exist independent of thought, which is epistemologically negative, it is an elimination. And since elimination and negation are equivalent, it is also a negation. The curious consequence of this interpretation is that negations and affirmations are not exclusive of each other. For, although affirmation and nonimplicative negation[70] are without common locus, a single universal can be both an affirmation and a implicative negation.

The artificiality of this attempt to integrate Śāntarakṣita's new view into Dharmakīrti's is reflected in Śākya Chok-den's definition of implicative negation as "that negation or elimination which does not exclude an affirmation or does not reject an implicative phenomenon."[71] This definition does not explain very much, which is hardly surprising for it is meant to hide more than to explain. It is stated to reconcile two conflicting theories: Śāntarakṣita's psychological understanding of eliminations as negations and Dharmakīrti's epistemological view of eliminations as conceptual entities, validated through a negative process. Whereas for Śāntarakṣita negation is something we intuitively understand as eliminating something, for Dharmakīrti elimination is an epistemological concept that is not necessarily understood through a psychologically negative process. An elimination is a quasi-entity that comes into "existence" through a conceptual discrimination, regardless of whether or not we have the intuition that such a discrimination has taken place. This difference between a psychological and an epistemological understanding of the *apoha* theory is also present in the Tibetan treatment of the concept of mental elimination, to which I now turn.

14

Object Universal and Concept Formation

Importance of the Notion of Object Universal in the Tibetan Tradition

The psychological transformation of the concept of elimination described in the previous chapter influenced both Indian and Tibetan traditions. Nevertheless, most thinkers did not completely accept Śāntarakṣita's ideas. In India, his views were severely criticized by later thinkers such as Jñānaśrīmitra and Ratnakīrti. Tibetan thinkers have been less directly critical of Śāntarakṣita. They have used several of his concepts, such as the two types of negation and the three types of elimination, but they have not always followed his conclusions.

In the preceding chapter we compared Śāntarakṣita's views with those of later Tibetan authors. In this way, we were able to better identify the particularities of his interpretations. Our investigation suggested a similarity of views between him and most Ge-luk authors on the meaning of elimination, especially regarding the notion of objective elimination. It also revealed important differences between the mentalist conceptualism of Śāntarakṣita and the realism of the Ge-luk approach. Let us again consider the nature of mental elimination, this time in relation to object universals.

The concept of object universal plays a determining role in Tibetan explanations of thought and language. The term object universal (*don spyi, arthasāmānya*) is not a Tibetan invention. It is found in Dignāga's writings, where it plays an important semantic role.[1] Dignāga analyzes a linguistic entity as being composed of two abstract elements: the term universal (*śabdasāmānya, sgra spyi*) and the object universal. Whereas the former is the word or sentence as the abstract communicative form imparting meaning, the latter is the abstract content imparted by the abstract form (more on this later). What is most surprising is that this semantic analysis of language, which seems quite logical given the rejection of real universals, does not seem to have been adopted by most later Indian authors, Dharmakīrti included. The notions of term and object universals appear in a few definitions of thought in Vinītadeva, Śāntarakṣita, and a few other Indian thinkers,[2] but seems to play no significant in post-Dharmakīrtian semantics.

Thus, it comes as a surprise to see this term being revived by Tibetans, possibly under the influence of Cha-ba and his followers, as a way to support their interpretation of Dharmakīrti's *apoha* theory. Cha-ba and his followers used this term, which does not seem to be found in Dharmakīrti's writings, to explain the latter's thought. In the process, these early Tibetan thinkers extended its purview considerably. More important, they understood it in a way that contradicts Dharmakīrti's antirealism and representationalism. As with universals, Sa-paṇ noted this discrepancy and objected to what he perceived to be a Tibetan innovation. Still he did not reject the term altogether but rather proposed his own understanding of it, maintaining that Cha-ba's realist interpretation betrayed Dharmakīrti's antirealism. In doing so, Sa-paṇ offered an understanding of object universal which in certain respects goes back to Dignāga but uses the term as a general explanation of conceptuality in Dharmakīrti's system. In this way, the notion of object universal became a significant topic of controversy between Sa-paṇ's antirealist followers and Cha-ba's heirs, among them Kay-drup, Gyel-tsap, and their Ge-luk followers.

This chapter analyzes this debate over the meaning of *object universal*, which is a crucial part of the Tibetan analysis of thought and language. Exploring it allows us to further delineate the Ge-luk realist interpretation of the *apoha* theory and Sa-gya objections. It further clarifies the nature of concepts, a crucial element in Dharmakīrti's understanding of the nature of thought. It also introduces the topic of the next chapter, which explores the philosophies of language of the respective traditions around the notion of object universal.

The issue in this debate is the following: The Ge-luk view asserts that the appearance of an object to a conceptual consciousness is an object universal. Sa-paṇ's followers disagree, holding that the appearance is not an object universal but the representation of an object in consciousness, also called a *reflection* or *aspect*. For them, the object universal is the mistaken identity attributed to a representation by thought.[3] Let us begin to explore this issue by examining the Ge-luk view.

Object Universal in the Ge-luk Tradition

According to the Ge-luk tradition, an object universal is the conceptual appearance of a thing. It is called an *object universal* because it is an object [indicated by] words (*sgra'i don, śabdārtha*) and has the nature of a generally characterized phenomenon (*spyi mtshan, sāmānya-lakṣaṇa*). As such it is permanent and not real.[4] Pur-bu-jok defines the object universal of a jar as "that factor of superimposition that is the appearance to the conceptual cognition [of something] as a jar despite its not being a jar."[5] This mouthful of a definition simply means that, when a conceptual thought considers a jar, its primary object is not the real jar but the conceptual appearance of that jar. This appearance of a jar cannot function as a jar despite appearing to be a real jar. It is mistaken and hence unreal. This has the rather counterintuitive consequence that it is unchanging, since by definition in

Dharmakīrti's system only real things change. Kay-drup therefore describes the object universal of jar: "The appearance of a golden jar as a jar to the conceptual cognition apprehending a jar is also the object [indicated by] words. [Moreover], the appearance of that appearance to that [conceptual cognition] as not being a nonjar is also the object [indicated by] words."[6] According to Kay-drup, thought takes a conceptual appearance as its direct object. This appearance mediates between reality and thought by appearing as the real object. For example, when we think about a jar we do not see the jar directly. Rather, we have in our mind an appearance of the jar that appears as jar. Confusing the appearance of the conceptual object for the real object is what enables us to conceive of things. This appearance is both the object indicated by words and the object universal.

This explanation of the distorted nature of thought partially corresponds to Dharmakīrti's idea, but not completely. For Dharmakīrti and his antirealist interpreters, the mistake of conceptuality does not lie just in the fact that the appearance of a jar appears as a real jar, for instance, but, rather, because the appearance is construed as a real property by individuals. From Kay-drup's realist standpoint, this is not a mistake, since such real properties exist. Therefore for Kay-drup the distortion imposed by conceptuality concerns not what thought apprehends but the way the object appears to thought.

The issue is further complicated because realists and anti-realists understand differently the notion of appearance. Dharmakīrti and his Sa-gya interpreters hold a position we will describe later as representationalism, which postulates that awareness is directly in contact with only representations, what Dharmakīrti calls *reflections* or *aspects*. By contrast Kay-drup holds a direct realist view, according to which mental episodes are in direct contact with objects. Hence, the reflection of a thing in consciousness is not a representation but the revelation of that thing itself.

This distinction is relevant mostly to perception, as we will see in the last part of this work. It also concerns conception, however. Whereas for Dharmakīrti and Sa-gya thinkers the conceptual reflection of an object is a representation mistaken for a property, Ge-luk thinkers hold that real objects appear to conceptual cognitions, albeit in an indirect fashion. For example, when I think about my favorite rocking chair, a chair seems to appear to my mind. At least two analyses of this can be postulated. Dharmakīrtian representationalists argue that this description is misleading, for what appears to my mind is not the chair itself but its representation. In the case of a conception, the chair does not appear but only a representation on the basis of which the idea of chairness is mistakenly constructed, as explained earlier. This construct is then applied to identify the real object. Ge-luk direct realists reject this analysis, which they argue entails a curtain between us and the world. They hold that the chair in our example does appear to the mind, although only indirectly via a partly deceptive conceptual appearance. Hence, for the Ge-luk tradition, an object universal is a partly transparent appearance, not an image, as unfortunately suggested by some Western interpreters of Ge-luk tradition who translate *object universal* (*don spyi*) as "generic image."[7] By this term, they understand a sort of internal image or picture that we form when we think about things. This description is, however, misleading for it suggests that the conception does not really conceive of the external object but just apprehends an image representing the external object. This is not Kay-drup's or Gyel-tsap's view, for they insist that real objects appear to conceptual mental states.

This analysis of thought as conceiving of real objects corresponds quite well to some of our common sense assumptions. It becomes more problematic when used as an interpretation of Dharmakīrti's *apoha* theory. Interpreting the *apoha* theory, however, is just what Kay-drup and before him Cha-ba are aiming for when they interpret the object universal as the unreal conceptual appearance of its object. Kay-drup takes the appearance of an object to be an unreal conceptual quasi-entity, and he explicitly identifies this construct with what Dharmakīrti describes as a reflection (*gzugs brnyan, pratibimba*) and an eliminative universal (*gzhan sel ba'i spyi*).[8]

In making this identification Kay-drup seems to be using Śāntarakṣita's idea of mental elimination to interpret Dharmakīrti. There are, however, important differences between these three authors. For Dharmakīrti, a reflection is a real individual mental event, not a universal. It also does not seem to be an elimination, although this point seems to me less certain than the previous one. For Śāntarakṣita, a reflection is a mental elimination but it is not a universal since it is real. Kay-drup takes Śāntarakṣita's mental elimination to be what Dharmakīrti describes as a reflection, which is correct. Moreover, he takes the reflection, which he describes as the appearance of an object to conception, to be an unreal construct. He further identifies this appearance as the object indicated by words (*sgra don, śabdārtha*), thereby providing the support for the notion of object universal. These last two moves are much more questionable, for Śāntarakṣita holds that a mental elimination is a real thing, despite being an elimination. Hence, for him, a reflection cannot be a universal.

In his explanations, Kay-drup assumes that Śāntarakṣita's mental elimination is an unreal construct, the object indicated by words and, hence, the object universal. He identifies this notion of object universal with Dharmakīrti's idea of reflection and assumes this is what Dharmakīrti refers to as unreal universals. In this way he and the Ge-luk tradition can claim that their realism about universals is compatible with Dharmakīrti's assertion of the conceptual nature of universals. To support this claim, the Ge-luk tradition sets forth a threefold typology of universals: collection universal, kind universal, and object universal. Among these three, the latter two relate directly to our topic. Kind universals are what we have called *universals* until now; that is, the properties that Ge-luk thinkers take to be real in the case of things and their impermanent properties.[9]

Such realism is bound, however, to face this question: If universals are real, how should we understand Dharmakīrti's claim that universals are unreal? As we have seen already, the Ge-luk tradition proposes several strategies for responding, such as the distinction between extreme and moderate realisms and the difference between a thing's identity as a thing and that thing's identity as a universal.

Object universals provide another answer. For example, when I think about my favorite rocking chair I do not see it directly, but it appears to my mind. Ge-luk thinkers analyze this by saying that the object universal, that is, the appearance of the chair, appears as the real chair even though it is not. Hence, this appearance is unreal. It has no essence of its own, but is simply a mistaken identity that arises as the result of conceptual activity. The unreal status of conceptual appearances makes them fit Dharmakīrti's description of universals as unreal eliminations. Thus, as Kay-drup explains, there are two types of universals: "Therefore, [for each individual jar], there are two [types of] universals concomitant with the individual jars, a real one and an unreal one. Whereas jar is the real universal (*spyi dngos po ba*) concomitant with individual jars, this very appearance [of something] as a jar is the unreal universal concomitant with the individual jars."[10] Each thing has two universals: a real kind universal that it instantiates and an unreal object universal to which Dharmakīrti refers while discussing universals as unreal constructs. In this way, Dharmakīrti's critique can be deflected from the real properties and redirected toward object universals.

An examination of the concepts of kind universal and object universal reveals, however, the difference between Dharmakīrti's antirealism and Ge-luk realism. Dharmakīrti's universal is an unreal conceptual construct, akin to the description of object universal given by Sa-gya scholars (see later). In the Ge-luk tradition, a universal is a kind universal that can be real and is instantiated by its particulars. Thus, the very concept of universal has undergone a transformation only partially masked by Kay-drup's interpretive attempts.

The Ge-luk explanation of object universal raises an obvious objection: How can an appearance be unreal? We all understand that an appearance can be delusive but does this make it unreal? Consider, for instance, the apprehension of a mirage. The mirage appears as water. Now, it is true that the mirage is not real water, but it would be difficult to maintain that the mirage as a delusive appearance is unreal (i.e., ineffective). Similarly in the case of a conception, an object appears to our mind. This appearance is what Dharmakīrti calls *a reflection* and what we have described as a concept. This concept is taken to stand for the property that defines the object (answering to questions such as "Is it a table, a cow, or a pig?"). It is quite feasible to say that the appearance qua object is unreal, for the representation is mistakenly assumed to stand for a commonality that does not exist in real objects. This is, in fact, how Sa-gya thinkers understand an object universal. They argue that the appearance of the object to a conceptual consciousness is not the unreal object universal, but the real aspect or representation of the object in consciousness. To argue that the appearance qua appearance is unreal seems much more unlikely.

Nevertheless this is what Ge-luk thinkers seem to attempt. They disagree with the Sa-gya analysis of appearance, for they hold that it is based on at least three fallacious assumptions. First, the Sa-gya view is flawed since it holds that mental states cannot apprehend reality directly and thereby are isolated into a separate domain of representations. For Gyel-tsap and Kay-drup this is a mistake, because mental states do not take representations as its objects but real things. Otherwise, mental episodes would be able to perceive nothing but themselves and thus they would be cut off from the external world.

Second, the Sa-gya analysis mistakenly identifies the appearance of an object with its aspect. Gyel-tsap and Kay-drup, by contrast, hold that the appearance of an object is not the aspect of a cognition, for the aspect is nothing but the form of a cognition. If the appearance were the aspect, it would be the same entity as the consciousness itself. This is not possible, for it would entail a confusion between agent and object since the appearance is something that appears to a consciousness. Hence, for example, the reflection of a jar appearing to a conception cannot be that conception or that conception's aspect but must be its object.[11] Since the reflection is not the real individual jar or the property jarness, it must be the conceptual universal to which Dharmakīrti refers when he explains that conception takes a universal as its object.[12]

Third, the Sa-gya view assumes that the notion of appearance is similar in both its conceptual and nonconceptual cases. To return to the example of a mirage, the appearance of the mirage to a nonconceptual cognition is real. It is the mirage itself. Ge-luk thinkers hold, however, that this analysis of nonconceptual appearance cannot be applied to conceptions. There, the appearance qua appearance is unreal. The reason for this difference in the ontological status of distorted appearances is to be found in the causes of the mistakes. Although both conceptual and nonconceptual appearances are distorted, their mistakes are different, for the causes of the mistakes are different. In the case of the mirage, the cause of distortion is superficial, having to do with external conditions such as heat and light. In the case of conception, the mistake is internal to the cognition itself. It is the very nature of conceptions to have mistaken appearances. The mistaken in conceptual appearance is not fleeting and external but intrinsic and internal. Hence mistaken conceptual appearances are not real; they do not exist in virtue of their own independent essence but depend wholly on conceptual activities.

And yet, despite these arguments, the Ge-luk description of object universal seems to remain problematic. Its difficulties have not gone unnoticed in the Ge-luk tradition, where they are often taken as the subjects of debate. Several members of the tradition I am acquainted with find it difficult to make sense of this point and have attempted to phrase alternative interpretations. Some have suggested that it is not the appearance itself that is the object universal but the delusive part of that appearance (much like what the Sa-gyas argue). They are not willing, however, to put forth their views officially, which may be perceived as undermining the official Ge-luk view. This would in turn be taken as a betrayal of the orthodoxy, an essentially political act.

Object Universal in the Sa-gya Tradition

This explanation of object universal, which is well accepted by Ge-luk thinkers, has received considerable critical attention from Sa-gya thinkers. Let us examine their view, which provides a more viable explanation of object universal than the one we have just explored. As with the topic of universals, the Sa-gya view of object universals differs from Ge-luk realism. Śākya Chok-den and Go-ram-ba do not accept the Ge-luk presentation of an object universal as the conceptual appearance of an object. They suggest, rather bitingly, that this view is yet another inaccuracy of Cha-ba's legacy enshrined in the Ge-luk tradition.[13] Go-ram-ba is particularly critical of the distinction between kind universal and object universal. He says:

> *Qualm*: Although [it is true that] any cognition taking an object universal as its appearing object is a conceptual cognition, it is not the case that any cognition taking a kind universal as its object must be conceptual.
> *Answer*: The idea of a kind universal not included in an object universal is like the idea of an ocean not included in water. It is like the confusion created by the intoxication of a bad teacher, for a kind universal cannot exist outside of the imputation that confuses the appearance and the denomination.[14]

For Go-ram-ba, it is not possible to distinguish kind universal from object universal. The world is made of individuals and there are no real properties. All we have are conceptual representations that are taken to stand for commonalities that we assume real objects possess. This mistaken assumption is based on confusing appearance (representation) with denomination (the mistaken identity imputed on the appearance mostly on the basis of its association with a term). Śākya Chok-den agrees with this view. He argues that the Ge-luk presentation rests on a confusion between concept and its object. He says: "It follows that the subject, the appearance to a conceptual consciousness [of something] as not being a nonjar, is not the elimination [belonging to] a jar because it is the mental aspect of a conception apprehending a jar."[15] For Śākya Chok-den, an appearance is a conceptual reflection. It is a real mental event, produced by causes and conditions. Moreover, such an appearance changes over time. For example, the appearance of a jar to my mind can become clearer or murkier. Thus it is impermanent and hence, by definition, real. In fact, the appearance is the aspect or form that the conceptual consciousness takes in apprehending its object. Therefore, this conceptual appearance cannot be an actual elimination, nor a universal, nor an object universal.

Śākya Chok-den further argues against the Ge-luk analysis of object universals as conceptual appearances appearing, claiming that it leads to an infinite regress. If the conceptual appearance of a pot appears as a pot, we then have the appearance of the appearance of a pot, which in turn appears, and so on. This leads to an infinite regress. For Śākya Chok-den appearances do not appear, they are just representations. They do not appear to mental states but are the forms that those take.[16] This is what Dharmakīrti describes as aspect or reflection.

These representations are understood by Śāntarakṣita to be eliminations even though they are real. Like Go-ram-ba, Śākya Chok-den does not accept this description as literal. According to Sa-gya thinkers, neither mental (*blo'i gzhan sel*) nor objective eliminations (*don gyi gzhan sel*) can be actual eliminations, for to be an elimination presupposes that one cannot be validated by experience but only by thought. Hence, to be an elimination excludes being real and vice versa. Nevertheless, Sa-gya commentators recognize that conceptual representations are involved in the process of constructing universals.

The role of conceptual representations, that is, concepts, is explained by Go-ram-ba when he distinguishes two aspects of conceptual representations: the representation, that is, the appearance as an appearance of an object (i.e., as a real mental event), and the content of that appearance. He says: "Now, is the objective aspect of the conceptual cognition a [real] appearance[17] or is it an [unreal] elimination? Here, [I would like to distinguish] two factors: a cognitive factor and a factor superimposed onto the external jar. Among those two, the former is a [real] appearance because it is the object that is taken as an object of self-cognition (*rang rig, svasaṃvitti*) of a conceptual thought. The latter is an elimination because it is an imputation."[18] The conceptual representation of the object is the objective aspect, a real mental event. It is Dharmakīrti's reflection and, hence, not an actual elimination. Thus, the mental elimination presented by Śāntarakṣita is not an actual elimination because it is a real mental event, a causally effective thing. For Go-ram-ba, we can identify concepts with representations and aspects (in the case of conceptions). We can also understand these entities to be real mental events and, as such, positive. These real entities have to be contrasted with their unreal content. This content can be variously characterized as eliminations, universals, or properties. All these descriptions are equivalent: Concepts relate to constructs, the universals or unreal properties assumed to be instantiated by individuals.

These universals can be understood in two ways: as the content of concepts or as properties instantiated by things. These two descriptions do not entail any significant difference, they are just distinct but equivalent ways of understanding universals. For example, cowness can be taken as the content of the concept of cow or it can be described as the property shared by cows. In the first case, universals are taken as the mistaken identifications of the representation and the property that the representation is assumed to stand for. This is the object universal of cow. In the second case, the universal is understood as a property assumed to be instantiated by things. Since this property can be validated only in a purely negative way, it can be reduced to the mere elimination of the contradictory of the object considered (non-non-*x*). This is the universal as pure elimination.[19]

Comparative Conclusion

This investigation of concept formation in Buddhist epistemology has given us the opportunity to confront alternatives available to the epistemologist to account for general notions in a universe of individuals. As a conclusion, I would like to summarize the main points of the explanations given by Sa-paṇ and his followers concerning this problem and relate them to some Western views. I believe that the Sa-gya view, which is based on the concept of object universal, represents an interesting

Buddhist contribution to the problem of abstract entities in a world of individuals.

To summarize, we can say that, according to this view, universals are not real but false constructs formed through language. When we experience things, we mark the objects of our experiences through linguistic signs. These signs allow us to categorize on a practical level the diversity of individual objects we encounter. When we do this, we think that we apprehend common properties (kind universals). This apprehension of commonality is not a direct reflection of the way things exist. It is only a convenient way to account for our experiences of similarities. Through it, we are able to categorize individual things in accordance with our inclinations and interests.

This conceptualization proceeds through representations. Since representations are mental events, they are not universals. As Go-ram-ba rightly points out, moreover, the creation of concepts occurs not just by the mere presence of representations resembling represented objects. It requires as well the imputation of a false identity onto those representations. The object universal is the content of the concept that arises out of this misidentification. Thus, conceptualization does not consist merely in the association of representations with external objects. Representations are concepts only inasmuch they are taken to stand for a commonality mistakenly assumed to be instantiated by individuals. Hence, in the case of conception, the relevant point is not whether the representation looks like the object it represents. That is, a concept does not function in virtue of its similarities with the objects it is assumed to represent but in virtue of standing for a commonality that individual objects are assumed to instantiate. For example, the concept of a rocking chair does not need to be constructed on the basis of a resemblance between it and its representation (although it may), but it is constructed on the basis of the representation being taken as chairness.

It may be helpful to compare this Buddhist view with the philosophies of the British empiricists. As a reaction against medieval metaphysics, Locke proposes that universals can be explained as mental ideas. The referents of general terms are not to be found in external reality but in our own general ideas. According to critics such as Berkeley, Locke never succeeds, however, in explaining the nature of general ideas. His trouble lay in his understanding of ideas as mental "things" (events) associated with external things. Accordingly, general ideas would be mental events of a certain type. The question is then: What do such general ideas look like? Locke's answer is that we reach a general idea by abstracting particular features so that at the end of the process we are left with only general features. Because such a general idea is a particular mental idea, it seems difficult to understand how it could ever become abstract. Locke never solves this conflict, or so claims Berkeley and other critics.

Berkeley's solution is to do away with general ideas. How then can one account for the difference between particular and general terms? Berkeley's answer is that general and particular terms are distinguished on the basis of their use. Terms are general not because they refer to some universal but because they are used to refer to several individuals. For example, the concept of a triangle is created by the particular use that we make of a particular mental image. Commenting on Berkeley's philosophy, Stanton explains: "If we refrain from taking into account in our reasoning any of the properties of the triangle we imagine other than its being triangular, then our reasoning will apply to all triangles, irrespective of whether they share the peculiarities of the particular triangle we imagine."[20] If I understand Berkeley's point correctly, his view presents interesting similarities and differences with the view of Sa-gya thinkers. For both sides, a representation is not a universal, since it is a real individual. For Berkeley, a universal is the content of a concept. Such an entity comes to be when an idea is used to stand for several particulars. Similarly, for Go-ram-ba or Śākya Chok-den, a concept is a particular representation taken to stand for the property assumed to be instantiated by individuals.

This latter solution to the problem of general terms, however, has a specifically Buddhist (i.e., Dignāgian or Dharmakīrtian) twist. It is based on the distinction between passive but accurate perception and active but mistaken conception. Contrary to empiricists such as Locke, Buddhist epistemologists hold that conceptual activity is not an internalization of external reality but proceeds from its own inherent mistaken tendency to confuse conceptual representations for real things. Like Kant, they hold that perception does not deliver any meaningful content in isolation from concepts. The meaning of experiences is not given but constructed by thought, which proceeds by synthesizing discrete elements. Hence, the general use of a particular representation is based less on an idea of similarity, as asserted by British empiricists, than on the constructive activity of thought, which is largely linguistic. Unlike Kant, however, Buddhist thinkers do not hold the synthesis produced by thought to be legitimate but view it with skepticism. It obscures reality, since it is inherently distorted. This mistake "explains" how certain images can be made to stand for certain general properties, even though these images have no special characteristics that would differentiate them from other images. In the ultimate analysis, however, it is an obstacle to the realization of the nature of reality.

Sa-paṇ captures this insistence on the distorted nature of thought when he says: "Any conception inherently mistakes its object without a basis, like a falling hair or [an object] of dream."[21] In the same way that we see a falling hair under the influence of ophthalmia or in the same way that objects appear during the dream state, we conceive of similarities and differences that do not exist in reality. Our conceptual activities do not mirror reality and are largely (though not solely) products of our inner mistaken tendencies (though they may have an objective causal basis). Moreover, and this is where such a view, which is not unlike Humean skepticism, becomes specifically Buddhist, such mistakes can be removed by the practice of the Buddhist path. Through meditation, we can come to a true insight into the nature of things. We are then able to act in the world not on the basis of our distorted conceptual constructs but on the basis of a spontaneous attunment of the mind to reality. Such attunment is complete only in a Buddha. Other less advanced practitioners can partake only partially of this spontaneity.

This Buddhist "solution" to the question of general terms and conceptuality creates its own set of problems and difficulties. If thought is distorted by an inherent mistake, how are we to justify the reliance that we place in thinking? Is such reliance an illusion, or does thinking have some value despite the distortion that inherently besets it? A similar question concerns language, which is epistemologically equivalent to thinking. Does language, which is central in the construction of concepts, have value despite the distortions imposed by the concepts that support it? To explore possible responses to these questions brought up by the *apoha* theory, let us examine Dharmakīrti's philosophy of language as well as that of his Tibetan commentators.

15

Philosophy of Language

The Terminology of the Inquiry

Questions relating to language hold an important place in Indian philosophy. We have seen the impact of grammatical and linguistic discussions on the development of a philosophical inquiry concerning universals. We have seen how Indian Grammarians and philosophers have struggled with the relation of language to reality. We have yet to examine, however, the implications of the *apoha* theory for the philosophical understanding of language. Let us clarify some of the terms used to study language in the Indian and Tibetan traditions, and then further examine the philosophy of language of Dharmakīrti and his followers. In this way we summarize the whole development of the *apoha* theory, from Dignāga to later Tibetan thinkers.

For Indian grammarians, language has two functions, the *vācaka* (*rjod pa*) function of signification and the *vṛtti* (or *pravṛtti, 'jug pa*) function of application. A word or sentence is said to *vāc* (signify or express) an object if the listener becomes aware of that object on listening to the speaker. On the other hand, a word or sentence is not limited to the conceptual domain but also applies to the real world. This is its *vṛtti* (application) relation, in which it applies to an object.[1]

This difference between signification and application partially corresponds to the distinction between sense and reference introduced by Frege in 1892.[2] Like application, the reference of an expression is the object named or denoted by it. This object is to be distinguished from the sense of the expression, which Frege explains as the mode of presentation of the object. For example, the planet Venus is the reference of expressions such as *the morning star* and *the evening star*. Each of these expressions, however, has a specific mode of presentation, its sense, which distinguishes it from the other expressions, even though their reference is identical. This distinction was elaborated by Frege as a way to resolve puzzles relating to the problem of identity raised by the designation of a single entity by synonymous expressions.[3] It was also, and more important, drawn to explicate the nature of propositional attitudes. It has become an accepted part of Western philosophical vocabulary, where a discussion of the philosophy of language is bound to make some reference to this distinction.

The Indian distinction between signification and application, however, does not always correspond to the one between sense and reference. In Kumārila's Bhaṭṭa system (and in the Grammarian school), where a word or a sentence signifies a universal and is applicable to particulars, the signification and application distinction parallels the sense and reference distinction. The parallel is less clear in the Nyāya system, where a word signifies a particular qualified by a universal. It is not always clear in Buddhist philosophy, where the term *signification* is sometimes used loosely to mean application. This confusion between signification and application is due sometimes to a lack of systematicity in the use of words. Sometimes, however, it reflects a realist commitment, as in the case of some Geluk thinkers such as Ge-dün-drup and Jang-gya.[4] Thus, the distinction *vṛtti-vācaka* does not always recover our sense-reference distinction. Still it is sufficiently close to facilitate our use of the sense-reference distinction in the Indian context.

Like other comparisons, the similarity with Frege's sense and reference distinction should not be pushed too far, for there are many differences between Frege, who is in certain respects a realist, and Dharmakīrti or Sa-paṇ. The value of such a comparison does not lie in the establishment of a strict correspondence between two sides, which proceed from very different contexts but in drawing attention to some features of Buddhist accounts that have not been given sufficient attention. In using this distinction, I argue that Buddhist epistemology provides an insightful view of sense. Buddhist explanations of reference are not as strong, although neither are they nonexistent, contrary to the opinions of some modern scholars. In fact, one of the noteworthy features of Dharmakīrti's contribution to Buddhist epistemology is his attempt to establish a theory of reference.

Another related distinction, which is missed even by some Tibetan scholars, should be made here. That is, signification (*brjod pa, vācaka*) differs from indication (*bstan pa, nirdeśa*). Words explicitly indicate (*dngos su bstan pa*) things but do not directly signify (*dngos su ma brjod*) them, for that would make real things into direct objects of signification by language. Go-ram-ba sarcastically criticizes those Tibetans who, "wanting to refute Dharmakīrti's position," assert that specifically characterized phenomena are directly signified by language because they are explicitly indicated. Go-ram-ba continues: "This [position] is not correct, for [something] explicitly indicated does not need to be directly signified. [This is so] because the meaning of being explicitly indicated is to be directly understood on the basis of an expression, and the meaning of being directly signified is to directly appear to the conceptual cognition that arises after the perception that hears the expression. Therefore, one should know without confusion that there are two ways of indicating [something, namely,] explicit (*dngos bstan*) and implicit indicated [objects] (*shugs bstan*) as well as two [objects] of signification, namely direct signified (*dngos kyi brjod bya*) and conceived signified (*zhen pa'i brjod bya*)."[5] *Signification* is an epistemological term that describes the relation of a term with its object. Something is directly signified if, and only if, it appears directly to the speaker's and the hearer's minds. To use Fregean terms, the signification of a term is a function of its sense. Tibetan Buddhist epistemology explains this sense as the object universal held by the speaker and the hearer.

By contrast, *indication* is an exegetical term that describes the way in which a text is to be understood by its interpreter. A text explicitly indicates something if, and only if, that something can be immediately understood from the text itself. That which is understood indirectly by implication is not explicitly indicated. For example, when I say "this is a cow," my words indicate that this animal is a cow. This fact is explicitly understood by the listener, but it is not directly signified. Only the conceptual construct, the Tibetan object universal or Frege's sense, is directly signified. Thus, indication does not concern the distinction between sense (unreal constructs) and reference (real individuals). Rather, indication is a notion of a different order that encompasses both sense and reference, much like our colloquial *meaning*. I have tried to make this difference between signification and indication clear by using different English words to translate the same Tibetan word (*dngos*). I say that something is "explicitly indicated" (*dngos su bstan*) rather than "directly indicated," but I say that something is "directly signified" (*dgnos su brjod*) rather than "explicitly signified."

Having clarified some of the basic terms, let us begin our analysis of Dharmakīrti's philosophy of language. As we already have noticed, Dharmakīrti is ambivalent toward thought and language: On one hand, he views them suspiciously as products of distortions; but on the other hand, he realizes that they are indispensable to the fulfillment of practical (both mundane and religious) aims. One possible way to resolve this tension is to provide an account of the referential function of language, explaining how language (and thought) can apply to reality despite its inherent distortions. This is, however, a highly problematic endeavor in a philosophy that assumes a radical gap between things and concepts. But how radical is this gap? Let us examine this question, which relates to one of the most famous tenets of the Mahāyāna tradition,[6] the claim that reality is ineffable.

Ineffability

A basic tenet of the *apoha* theory is that language does not relate directly to reality. Language always requires conceptual mediation and, hence, can never be free from distortion. Dharmakīrti says: "Words do not relate (*pravṛtti, 'jug pa*) [directly] to individuals for [these individuals] are discrete [entities]. Therefore, the object of words relates solely to conventions."[7] We cannot directly refer to real individual things, but only through the intermediary of conceptual mediation. For example, we point to a cow saying, "this is a cow." Even in this case, the indexical *this* refers successfully only in dependence on some tacitly accepted description, which allows the speaker and the hearer to single out the features relevant to the situation. Since such a description involves an unreal universal, it has no direct application to reality. Hence, reference is always mediated and distorted. This entails that, for the Buddhist epistemologist, reality is beyond the direct scope of thought and language. Accordingly, reality is said to be unutterable, ineffable, transcending description, and so forth. The Buddhist epistemologists express this point by saying that the specifically characterized (*svalakṣaṇa, rang mtshan*) is not the direct object of language.[8]

Faced with these claims of ineffability two attitudes are possible. These claims can be taken at face value or they can be seen as incomprehensible in isolation and necessitating interpretation as parts of the system in which they acquire their meaning. The first attitude takes the claims of ineffability literally. It constitutes what I will call a *strong* version of the ineffability claim. The second attitude does not accept the ineffability claim as literally true, seeking instead a way to understand it as a function of the system of which it is an integral part. This second hermeneutical strategy takes ineffability claims to be *weak* claims.

A similar distinction can be made in the context of interpreting Dignāga and Dharmakīrti's philosophy. A strong version of ineffability claims that language and judgment do not reach anything real at all and that "the unique particular cannot be signified by any word."[9] Gupta defends this point of view when she says: "Words do not have any function of denoting external things' svalakṣaṇas. The meaning of a word consists only in its producing a concept that tends to be applied to external things."[10] According to this interpretation, the gap between the conceptual order and reality is radical and unbridgeable. Reality utterly transcends thought. Gupta continues: "As far as I understand, however, the svalakṣaṇas are not nameable at all, either from the ultimate or the conventional point of view. Words do not, according to the Buddhists, name anything. To say that a word is meaningful is not to say that it names anything, either externally or internally. To say that it is significant is just to say that it evokes a certain idea in our mind . . ."[11] According to this interpretation, this is what Dharmakīrti means when he says that words do not relate to real objects. They relate only to conventions and have no bearing on reality. The most famous example of such an interpretation is Stcherbatsky's comparison of the specifically characterized to Kant's transcendent noumenon. The specifically characterized is described as qualityless, without extension, a thing-in-itself. Stcherbatsky says: "A deeper insight into what happens in our everyday cognition has led the Buddhists to establish behind the veil of empirical reality the existence of its transcendental source, the world of things as they are by themselves."[12] Like Kant's noumenon, the specifically characterized is an absolutely transcendent entity, propertyless, whose real modalities are unknowable. For example, the reality behind a fire is something akin to a moment of pure energy, which we imagine to have a certain shape, and so on.

An alternative interpretation does not take ineffability claims at face value, instead considering them weak. According to this interpretation, language is able to refer to the real world but indirectly. Ineffability claims are taken not literally but as expressions of the Buddhist attempt to ward off any danger of reifying entities. As we will see, both Sa-gya and Ge-luk traditions present consistent attempts, each in its own very different way, to interpret ineffability claims in a way that preserves some validity to language. I take this to be Dharmakīrti's opinion as well.

According to a weak ineffability claim, language and thought do relate to things but only indirectly and with distortion. As we saw earlier, Dharmakīrti draws a strong distinction between two types of knowledge, perception and conception. Whereas the former has direct access to reality, the latter bears on reality only through the mediation of fictional constructs. Similarly, language signifies reality only indirectly. Dharmakīrti argues that, if, for instance, a conceptual consciousness conceptualizing a jar had direct access to the real jar, it would ascertain that jar as it is, including all its qualities (shape, color, and the like). That would include even the impermanence of the thing, which is, after all, nothing more than the constant transformation undergone by the object. If thought were to size up an object as it is, there would then be no need for further investigation of its different characteristics.

An obvious objection to this argument is that, despite perception's unmediated apprehension of reality, there is still the need for further investigation. Dharmakīrti answers by insisting on the difference between perception and thought. Whereas the former does not identify its object but merely holds it in the perceptual ken without ascertaining it, the latter actively conceptualizes its object without having any direct access to such an object. Perception operates positively, holding the object as it is. It is not able to ascertain things as they are, however, because perception does not determine anything. It just holds things for conception to ascertain step by step. In contrast, conception operates by elimination. It constructs categories on the basis of dichotomies. Objects are characterized by eliminating their contradictories. For example, thought conceives of a jar as blue by eliminating nonblue. That particular thought, however, does not conceive of anything other than nonblue, since it is not able to hold the object as it is, in its totality. An additional conceptual cognition is required to conceive of that jar as round and so forth. Hence, if a single conception had unmediated access to a thing as it is, it would have to be able to ascertain all the aspects of the thing.[13]

Tibetan scholars have expanded Dharmakīrti's distinction between perception and conception into a more formal framework. Here nonconceptual cognitions are understood as subjects of full engagement (*sgrub 'jug, vidhipravṛtti*) and conceptual cognitions as subjects of eliminative engagement (*sel 'jug*).[14] This presentation of full and eliminative engagement applies in different ways to mind, language, and for some thinkers even persons,[15] but let us briefly examine these concepts with reference to mind.

Minds of full engagement relate to things in their totality. Such a mind is defined by Go-ram-ba as "that subject that engages in its object through a mere appearance without depending on the preclusion of a different type."[16] Nonconceptual cognitions (perceptions as well as false nonconceptual cognitions) are minds of full engagement. A mind of eliminative engagement relates to its object by eliminating an object of negation. Conceptual cognitions qualify as such because they relate to objects only by eliminating the contradictory of the object they apprehend. Ge-dün-drup characterizes such a mind as "that which engages in its object by differentiating its parts."[17] A conceptual thought is eliminative because it does not apprehend its object as it is with all its characteristics. Rather, it conceives of its object by selecting a particular feature. It focuses on this feature by eliminating the contradictory of the feature.[18]

Both Sa-gya and Ge-luk thinkers agree on this distinction. They also agree that a similar distinction applies to language. They disagree, however, on the way to understand this distinction. In accordance with their realism, Ge-luk thinkers hold that thought and language capture real features of the world, albeit in a distorted fashion. Thinking proceeds by differentiating properties that exist in the real world. By contrast, Sa-gya thinkers deny the reality of these properties, and hence hold that thought merely apprehends conceptual fictions. This seems, however, to entail that thought, together with language, is entirely cut off from a reality that is utterly beyond the reach of conceptuality. As argued earlier, one of Dharmakīrti's main preoccupations is to overcome this gap between the two realms and account for the objective basis by which concepts are applied to reality. Let us examine his account of the naming process and the implicit theory of reference it contains, before examining Tibetan views on language.

Dharmakīrti on Name and Reference

An account of naming seems to play an important role in Dharmakīrti's work but has not yet received adequate scholarly attention. Whereas in several domains Dharmakīrti's views are partly similar to Dignāga's (or, at least, to what he understands Dignāga to be saying), in the domain of the philosophy of language, Dharmakīrti seems to adopt views that differ from and even contradict Dignāga's. Whereas the latter often tends to follow Bhartṛhari and the Grammarians in their analysis of language, Dharmakīrti does not and disagrees on a number of issues with this group. For example, contrary to Dignāga's view, Dharmakīrti seems to hold the view that words, not sentences, are the primary meaningful units. Similarly, Dharmakīrti seems to hold that language is composed of words made by sequences of sounds that convey meaning rather than an internal articulation, as argued by the proponents of Bhartṛhari's *sphoṭa* theory and Dignāga.

Although a full analysis of these important differences is beyond the scope of this work, let me nevertheless put down a few words on Dharmakīrti's views of naming and the primacy of words over sentences. In general among Indian philosophers, three views concerning the primary linguistic unit have been defended:[19]

> 1. Dignāga and the Grammarians hold a holistic view of meaning, according to which the sentence is the primary linguistic entity. Words have meaning only in the context of sentences. Hence, sentence meaning is primary and word meaning is an abstraction resulting from semantic analysis.[20] This is the consequence of the *sphoṭa* view that language is primarily a conceptual sphere of intelligibility in relation to which material sounds are meaningful.

2. Kumārila and the Naiyāyikas hold the opposite, atomistic view. This is the word plus syntax view (*abhihitānvayavāda*), according to which the word is primary. A sentence is a complex of words arranged in accordance with the semantic and syntax that obtain among words. They argue that, since one cannot understand a sentence without grasping the meaning of the individual words that compose the sentence, individual words must be the fundamental building blocks making up the sentence. This capacity to understand the sentence meaning from the meaning of individual words, which are finite in number, explains how we can understand an infinite number of sentences.

3. The Prabhākara school holds an intermediary position, the related designation theory (*anvitābhidhānavāda*), which attempts to recognize the intuitions contained in both views. Hence, sentence meaning is not an impartite whole but is constituted by the individual contributions of words. Those words, however, have no meaning in isolation. For when we learn to speak we do not learn the meaning of individual words but how to use complete sentences. Hence, the meaning of a sentence is not a function of isolated words. Rather, sentence meaning is a function of the related meanings of the words that compose it.

There is some uncertainty as to which of these three views Dharmakīrti and his followers adopt. Whereas Hattori has argued that Śāntarakṣita adopts the word plus syntax theory, Siderits has made a cogent argument that Śāntarakṣita opts for the related designation theory.[21] Whatever the truth is on this point, an important point has often been overlooked: The rejection of Dignāga's holistic account of meaning does not begin with Śāntarakṣita. Dharmakīrti already moves away from Dignāga's view to hold that individual words have meaning (either in isolation or in the context of a sentence). He also adopts a different view, in which language is not an internal articulation but a series of voice sounds (*ghoṣa, dbyangs*) that express meaning, in dependence on the conventions within a linguistic community. Following Vasubandhu's so-called Sautrāntika view, Dharmakīrti refuses to differentiate an internal meaningful communicative form from its externalization. The phonemes indicate the meaning of an utterance, not some putative conceptual communicative form such as Bhatṛahari's *sphoṭa* or the Vaibhāṣika name (*nāman, ming*, which is the internal illumination of a meaning in turn manifested by the voice). For Dharmakīrti, the formulation and communication of meaning relies on the abilities of speakers to express their intentions through phonemes and those of the listeners to understand these intentions.

The shift away from Dignāga's holistic philosophy of language, as primarily an internal conceptual formulation, toward a more atomistic view of language creates difficulties in a philosophy that limits the real to momentary individuals. How can the difference between short and long phonemes be explained? Even individual phonemes are not just single moments but composed of several moments and, hence, unreal. Furthermore, how can Dharmakīrti explain how phonemic unities emerge out of the aggregation of moments of sounds? We do not just hear a succession of sounds, but elements that seem to have a communicative unity regardless of their semantic content. Where does such unity come from? To answer these questions Dharmakīrti appeals to the idea, which we will explore later, of self-cognition (*svasaṃvitti, rang rig*).[22] He argues that we hear the moments composing long phonemes individually but the impression of length arises from the ability of self-cognition to experience the individual moments of hearing and keep track of them. Therefore, the perception of phonemic units arises, which leads to phonemes being conceptualized as expressing the speaker's intention and, hence, as having meaning.

This view of language as being composed of empirically observable phonemic entities also obliges Dharmakīrti to pay closer attention to the naming process than has Dignāga.[23] Since language is made up of individual phonemes and words are the primary meaningful units, the temptation to fall prey to the fallacy of conceiving of language as a nomenclature of noises pointing to present objects becomes stronger. Hence, Dharmakīrti insists that naming is not primarily a process of denotation.

Concerning the meaning of names, a distinction between proper names and general names is customarily made by modern Western philosophers. John Stuart Mill (1806–1873), for example, argues that proper names have no connotation but just denote. This view is rejected by Frege, who holds that any meaningful linguistic entity has a sense. The view of Buddhist epistemologists is similar to Frege's. They do not differentiate between proper names and general names, for they hold that any name has a sense. Conceptualists such as Ockham and Hobbes also develop their theories on a similar neglect for the difference between proper and general names. But whereas they assimilate general names to proper names, Buddhists assimilate proper names to general names. In both cases, a name excludes individuals from certain classes to which they do not belong.

If for a Buddhist philosopher there is nothing particular to names, why does Dharmakīrti focus on them? The answer has to do with his Naiyāyika adversary's position, which most directly threatens his own. As a denotationist, the Naiyāyika holds that language is primarily a process of naming. Language first and foremost denotes real substances. This view represents a threat for Dharmakīrti, for like the Naiyāyika, he holds that individual words are primary. He further believes that words are first and foremost sequences of sounds that communicate meaning insofar as there is agreement among speakers. Hence, his position is closer in certain respects to the Nyāya denotationist view than to Dignāga's. To establish his account, Dharmakīrti must differentiate his view from Nyāya denotationism. Dharmakīrti does this by showing that names do not just denote individual objects. The naming process requires the construction of meanings, without which the iterability of names would be inexplicable. Once the denotationist view is refuted with regard to names, Dharmakīrti can easily show that the Nyāya view is unable to account for more complex linguistic entities such as sentences. He is then in a position to offer his own account of naming. This provides the central element of a more general account of language, in which language is made of words combined according to syntactic rules.

Dharmakīrti's account of naming centers around the recognition that names must refer to some time-neutral element to be used in different circumstances (or by different people). When a term is introduced, it is given to an object, arbitrarily or not, by a person or a group of persons. The connection between the term and its object is then made for the first time in a purely conventional manner on the basis of the speaker's intention. A name thus introduced in the linguistic community is called an *agreed-on convention* (*saṃketa, brda*). When the word is used after having been introduced in the linguistic community, it is known as an *established convention* (*vyavahāra, tha snyad*). Naming can function only on the basis of some commonality between the introduction of a convention and its use.[24]

One may wonder why we need to assume that a name used at different times is the same name? The answer is that the aim of introducing a name is not just communicative. Communication of our intentions is an important function of language but not the only one. Language is not the externalization of what is conceived independent of it but plays cognitive and constructive roles.[25] Language does not just verbalize ideas but constitutes them. Without language, we could not form complex concepts and would be reduced to facing the chaos of contentless experiences. Thus, language in general and names in particular are used to provide stability and content to our experiences. This function involves a time-neutral element. Dharmakīrti explains: "Words communicate [their objects] as agreed upon convention for the sake of recognizing [them at the time of using] the established convention. At that time the individual object [in reference to which the convention was made] does not exist [any more]. Therefore, the convention does not take this [thing] as its [object]."[26] A cognitive purpose for language presupposes that language is not reducible to noises pointing to objects directly present. Words can help us to organize our perceptions only if they capture a time-neutral element common to the different contexts in which the name is used. The real individual object in reference to which the convention was introduced cannot provide this commonality for it does not remain; it will have disappeared when the convention is used. Within the context of the doctrine of momentariness, a time lag between the establishment of a convention and its use is necessary. Since the real object remains for no more than a moment, it is never present when the convention is used. The real objects in relation to which a name is introduced cannot be assumed to remain until the name is used. Hence, the commonality required by naming cannot be provided by real individuals. For a realist such as Kumārila this is not problematic, for real universals provide commonality. These general entities are the primary objects of language. Reference achieved by a name is a function of the sense of the word; that is, of the universal signified by the name.

In an antirealist framework, such a commonality is harder to account for, since universals are not real. They are posited, however, as the fictional objects of valid conceptual activities, as the ideational meaning of words. As such, universals provide the commonality required by the naming process. Thus, the object to which an agreed-on convention primarily relates is not a real individual but a fictional construct, which is superimposed onto reality. Since such a construct is permanent, it can exist when the agreement is created as well as when the convention is used. This fictional entity provides the commonality necessary to the naming process, the sense necessary for successful reference.

This answer, however, gives rise to a more difficult question: If such an entity is fictional, on what basis can language be applied to reality? Dharmakīrti answers this question by appealing to the causal relation between our experiences and the conceptions they give rise to. Dharmakīrti describes the process in this way: "The [individual] things are the main causes of such [unitary] consciousness due to their essence. Although [individual things] are distinct, [their commonality] is considered by consciousness. Similarly, cognitions are conceived as one though they are distinct. Therefore, [the commonality of individuals consists of their] being concomitant with the exclusion of the absence of effect, not of one single real entity."[27] For Dharmakīrti, the notions of commonality that we form on experiencing things does not reflect reality. No real universal supports or warrants our conceptions, which assume commonalities. This does not mean, however, that our concepts are arbitrary or a priori projections. On the contrary, thoughts are causally connected to the different individual objects that they synthesize.[28] They are based on the presence of certain recognizable effects of these individual objects. Or, as Dharmakīrti puts it, thoughts are concomitant with the exclusion of the absence of effects. For example, our conception of tree is connected to the different trees we have come across while forming this concept. When we see different individual things that produce similar effects, we coalesce the representations of these different objects with some word, thereby creating a fictional commonality that we impute on the real things themselves on the basis of a causal link with perception. Dharmakīrti says: "[A term] gives rises to a mental episode, which has the appearance of [having] functional things as its objects despite their not being so. [Such a mental episode] is grounded in the mere individuality of things. Though it is produced [by language], it is taken to be nondeceptive with respect to things because it relies on the things [that exist] individually [and] because it is a means of eliminating that which does not perform the function of these [individual objects]. Therefore, [a term] has an elimination as its object since it is based on that which performs the [function of individual objects]."[29] For Dharmakīrti, terms apply to things through the intermediary of directly signified constructs. The commonality thus assumed is not real. Nothing is actually in common between things not even their being similar. Nevertheless, we are struck by how certain things resemble each other. The elaboration of common properties is our way to conceptualize these experiences, which are preconceptual. The process of categorization proceeds on the basis of these experiences of reality. Thus, our conceptions of commonality are products of the objects we experience in their individuality. They have a limited but real validity based on their indirect causal connection with individual things, which allow practical activities to be successful.

Although these experiences of similarity are not rigidly fixed, they are determined within a certain range. Conceptual activity takes place in an already partially predetermined situation. The objective similarities (i.e., the real objects experienced as similar) that exist in the world constrain the range of conceptual classification we can elaborate. Our inner dispositions also partially determine our situation. The objectivity of human conceptuality in Dharmakīrti's system has to be understood against this double background.

We can find here an implicit Dharmakīrtian theory of reference. Words, which are the primary linguistic units, have first and foremost meaning, or to use Frege's terminology, *sense*, which is for Dharmakīrti the unreal conceptual content. Words also have reference, however, for they can be applied to real objects on the basis of their causal relation with these objects. For example, I see an object, say, a tree, and use the concept of tree to identify it. In this case, the description I use applies to a real individual through the intermediary of a fictional property ("treeness"). Nevertheless, indirectly my words manage to single out a real object on the basis of the experiences of similarity that lead to the construction and acquisition of the concept of tree. The causal links between the real tree, my perceptual experience, and its conceptual elaboration ensures that my words succeed in picking out a real object, despite the fictional nature of the construct I use to describe the situation.[30]

We are now in a better position to realize how mistaken is the view that Dharmakīrti is an extreme nominalist who refuses any objective foundation to conceptuality and holds to a strong view of ineffability. This interpretation systematically underestimates the objective basis of the creation and application of concepts. In doing so, it follows the Hindu description of Buddhist views.[31] It is not difficult to see why Hindu thinkers have described Buddhists as supporting the view that conceptual thought is arbitrary and without relation to reality. In doing so, however, these thinkers do not describe the Buddhist understanding but force their own conclusion on the Buddhists. Although this conclusion may be justified, it is not Dharmakīrti's view but its unwanted consequence. The description *extreme nominalism* is particularly inadequate in relation to Dharmakīrti, whose very project is to ground conceptuality in reality as a way to defend Dignāga.

My point here is not to defend Dharmakīrti's views and offer them as unassailable truths. On the contrary, I intend to show their limitations. Although Dharmakīrti is less extreme in his views than some scholars have made him out to be, his antirealism is quite radical. This leads to great difficulties, which we have started to explore through our investigation of Śākya Chok-den's views. But before exposing Dharmakīrti's weaknesses, we must at least understand his view. In consistently misrepresenting Dharmakīrti's view, scholars such as Dravid and Gupta have systematically left out the causal link present in his account. In doing so, they have not only misrepresented his philosophy and ignored its specificity in relation to Dignāga's, but they have missed its real problem. The difficulty of Dharmakīrti's philosophy is not that conceptions are without foundation in reality. It is that such foundation requires something that is in principle impossible for Dharmakīrti; namely, the coordination of the two halves of his system, the domain of reality-perception and conceptuality.

Let me give an example to illustrate this crucial point, to which we will have the occasion to return. I see a snowy mountain and think, "this is a snowy mountain." How is this useful idea different from the much less relevant thought, "this is a mountain of sugar"? The commonsense answer is that, whereas the former captures an actual feature of the real world, the latter fails to do so. But this explanation is not possible in Dharmakīrti's system, for it presupposes real properties such as being a snowy mountain that can be captured by thought. Dravid and Gupta are right to interpret Dharmakīrti as rejecting this realist assumption, but they are wrong in holding that this entails that thought is utterly foundationless.

Dharmakīrti holds that conceptions are not randomly produced but are the natural results of individual things. We see a real individual thing (e.g., a snowy mountain),[32] and this perceptual experience induces in our mind a conceptual judgment whose validity is ensured by its being the result of our experience. This answer will not do, however; for the postulation of causal links between thought-language, perception, and the world cannot ensure the validity of conceptuality. For, my two conceptions of the mountain (as snowy and as sugary) are both produced by similar perceptions. Thus the mere fact that an idea comes to my mind after seeing an object in no way guarantees that I have used the right concept.

We require something stronger than mere causal link; namely, that conceptions apprehend the same object (the snowy mountain) as perceptions. Such a cognitive cooperation between perception and conception, however, is impossible in Dharmakīrti's system, based as it is on a radical dichotomy between conception and perception:[33] Whereas perception apprehends real individual things, thought and language relate only to conceptual quasi-entities. Thus, there seems no way for Dharmakīrti to account for the cooperation between conception and perception that his system requires.

Signifier and Signified: A Sa-gya View

This is the problem Dharmakīrti's system faces, not the imputation of arbitrariness. Also the persistence of such problems explains the continuous existence of a realist commentarial tradition. But, before examining this revisionist trend in Buddhist philosophy of language, let us examine the more classical antirealist view of the Sa-gya tradition. In defending a rigorous antirealism, Sa-gya thinkers attempt to capture Dharmakīrti's thought. In doing so, however, they use concepts such as term universal and object universal that often bring their views closer to Dignāga than to Dharmakīrti.

One of the basic tenets of the *apoha* philosophy of language is that sense is primary and reference secondary. Dignāga and Dharmakīrti, like Bhartṛhari, hold a connotationist view, which asserts that reference depends on the language's ability to make sense. This ability is internal to language and does not involve direct reference to external objects but only signification of conceptually constructed entities. This means that language is not a nomenclature of names referring to objects. Rather, it is a system of conventional signs whose meaning is conceptually constructed in dependence on the meaning of other terms.

To clarify this view, it may be useful to introduce Saussure's account of language. Like Dignāga, Saussure holds that language consists of a system of linguistic signs. A sign is a combination of signifier and signified. A signifier is less a sound than a sound image associated with the physical sound that makes an impression on our senses. Saussure explains: "The linguistic sign unites, not a thing and a name, but a concept and a sound-image. The latter is not the material sound, a purely physical thing, but the psychological imprint of the sound, the impression that it makes in our senses."[34] A noise is meaningful only when it is combined with a communicative form that expresses its content. To communicate an idea, a meaningful noise must be part of a system of conventions, part of a system of signs. The sign is the union of a signifying form, which Saussure calls *signifiant* or signifier, and a signified idea, the *signifié* or signified.

A similar description of the nature of sign is found among Buddhist epistemologists, who distinguish signifier (*vācaka, rjod byed*) from signified (*vācya, brjod bya*). This distinction is strongly emphasized by Sa-gya thinkers, who describe the communicative form (Saussure's *signifiant*) as the direct signifier (*dngos kyi brjod byed*). This is also known as the *term universal* (*sgra spyi*), which we have already encountered in our description of thought. Its direct object of signification is not an object in the real world but the mental content that we successfully convey through the words (Saussure's *signifié*). This is the object universal (*don spyi*), also called the *directly signified* (*dngos kyi brjod bya*) or the *object* [indicated] *by words* (*sgra don, śabdārtha*). Go-ram-ba explains: "The appearance of a word as expressing the idea 'this word signifies this object' to the conceptual consciousness arising after the perception that hears the word is the direct signifier. [Similarly] the appearance as the signified object is the direct object of signification."[35] This distinction between signifier and signified is important, for it reveals that signification does not relate directly to the real world but is internal to the conceptual domain and applied to reality only on the basis of a mistaken superimposition.

A difficulty with this view is that it seems to enclose language entirely within a conceptual realm. When we use language, however, we do not conceive of our words as relating to purely conceptual entities, assuming rather that they relate to real individual things. Saussure's followers have struggled with how language relates to reality and so have Dharmakīrti's disciples.

The responses given by Tibetan thinkers vary. In accordance with their antirealism, Sa-gya thinkers hold that language does not capture reality but applies to reality on the basis of the distortion inherent in conceptuality. This does not mean, they argue, that language does not refer. They explain the referential function of language pragmatically by differentiating two levels in the concepts of signifier and signified. This distinction parallels that already introduced with reference to the subject of an inference, where conceived and actual subjects are differentiated. Go-ram-ba distinguishes the conceived signified (*zhen pa'i brjod bya*), which is the real external object, from the direct signified (*dngos kyi brjod bya*), which is the concept or object universal.[36] In a parallel way, he distinguishes the conceived signifier (*zhen pa'i brjod byed*), which is the actual physical sound, from the actual signifier (*dngos kyi brjod byed*), which is the sound image or term universal. Similarly, Śākya Chok-den distinguishes the actual (*song tshod kyi*) signified (the concept) and the conceived or assumed (*rlom tshod kyi*) signified (the real thing).[37]

These two levels of the concepts of signifier and signified are actually different. From the point of view of what actually takes place in the mind (*song tshod*), words signify only conceptual universals and do not bear on reality. Hence, from an ultimate standpoint, reality is completely ineffable. And yet, we fail to make this distinction when we use concepts, and in fact, this is what allows us to think. From the mistaken point of view that we assume (*rlom tshod*), words refer to real things. Thus, language is not limited to signified concepts (described as the objects [indicated] by words, *sgra don, śabdārtha*) but refers to reality on the basis of a confusion between concepts and real things. From this conceptual point of view, names do name things and reality is not utterly ineffable.

Sa-gya thinkers hold that making such a distinction is important for preserving the integrity of Buddhist epistemology. For them, reducing language to only one dimension would misrepresent Buddhist philosophy as either realism or extreme nominalism. By asserting that things are conceived signified, that is, are signified from the conventional point of view of conception, Buddhist epistemology can pretend to do justice to our precritical intuitions, which we use language to refer to reality. By asserting that ultimately the direct object of signification is the unreal object universal, Buddhist epistemology can prevent us from falling into the realist temptation of holding that reality can be captured by language.[38]

This Sa-gya view, which is an interpretation of Dharmakīrti, seems to be here, probably unbeknownst to them, closer to Dignāga's view than to Dharmakīrti's. Like the former, Sa-gya thinkers see language as being primarily a matter internal to the conceptual realm. They explain the nature of language as being an internal articulation involving a communicative form and a signified concept. This seems to be close to Dignāga's view, which is similar to the *sphoṭa* view of the Grammarians, that language is an internal abstract articulation (the term universal), with sounds being reduced to the externalization of what is conceived internally. In this view, understanding language is based on the hearer's conceptual ability to partake in the sphere of intelligibility internally articulated and communicated through external sounds. This differs from Dharmakīrti's view of language as being made of vocal indications of what is in the mind of the speaker.

Sa-gya thinkers also tend to pay less attention to Dharmakīrti's insistence on the objective basis of concepts and to minimize Dharmakīrti's insistence on the importance of intention and mental comprehension. By appealing to the distinction between practical and theoretical standpoints, Sa-gya thinkers seem to leave out Dharmakīrti's contribution to the *apoha* theory, his insistence on the causal connection between concepts and our experiences of reality. As we saw earlier, Dharmakīrti insists on the centrality of a speaker's intention in determining the meaning of an utterance. He also stresses that the understanding of a sentence is due to the hearer's abilities, past habituation, memories, and predispositions.[39] In both speaker and hearer, Dharmakīrti stresses the importance of real mental events as supports of the process of understanding. This is not to say that Dharmakīrti ignores the conceptual side, but that he wants to relate the conceptual to the real as a response to Hindu criticisms. Hence, he emphasizes concepts (Dharmakīrti's reflections or representations) as being real mental events supporting the process of conceptual construction.

The Sa-gya explanations do not seem to rely very much on this aspect of Dharmakīrti's thought. Locked in a contest with their realist adversaries, Sa-paṇ and his followers seem preoccupied mostly with rejecting any suggestion of real universals. So, they pay less attention to Dharmakīrti's insistence on connecting the conceptual realm with experience. Although they recognize such a connection,[40] this element seems to play a more restricted role in their explanations, which are aimed at refuting realist adversaries. Hence, when explaining language Sa-gya thinkers seem quite happy to rely on the schema signifier-signified thereby minimizing Dharmakīrti's causal elements.

The reason for this difference of emphasis and orientation in both authors is to be sought in the nature of Dharmakīrti's and Sa-paṇ's projects. Sa-paṇ focuses on rejecting the sort of realism common among Tibetan thinkers. In doing so, he comes back to some of Dignāga's formulations. This is no surprise, since Dignāga's and Sa-paṇ's preoccupations are similar; namely, the rejection of realism (Hindu for the former and Tibetan for the latter). Hence, they tend to emphasize the distance between conceptuality and reality. Dharmakīrti's project is quite different. He intends to respond to the Hindu accusations of arbitrary conceptuality leveled against Dignāga. Hence, he emphasizes the connection of conceptuality with experience, seeking to bridge the gap without minimizing it. But even that bridging is, as we will see, quite problematic. For, if the application of concepts to reality is explained on the basis of mistaken identifications, it is difficult to account for some identifications working while others do not.

Moderate Realism and Language

A realist commentarial tradition comes into being to solve such difficulties. Taking Dharmakīrti's critique of the reification of universals to refer to universals as posited by Hindu extreme realists, Buddhist realist commentators open the possibility for an epistemology based on real properties intelligible to thought. According to this reinterpretation, which began in India and has come to play an important role in Tibet, conceptions are valid not just because they stand in the appropriate causal relation with reality but because they capture properties that are part of the fabric of reality. Thought and language do not, however, capture reality as it is but only in a mediated and distorted way. For example, when I say, "this is a cow," my words suggest the existence of two separate entities: a subject and a predicate. As we have seen, however, this is not accurate. Although there are two entities, they are not separate. Thus, thought and language distort reality but do not prevent it from being intelligible. In this view, reality is only very weakly ineffable.

This explanation, which makes a great deal of sense philosophically, is more problematic as an interpretation of Dharmakīrti's view. Hence, the Indian and Tibetan revisionist tradition that offered such a view has drawn complicated distinctions so that their reinterpretation would be both philosophically and textually correct. Ge-luk thinkers share in this revisionist tradition, developed in Tibet by Cha-ba and his disciples. They understand Dharmakīrti, rather idiosyncratically, to provide a realist explanation of how language applies to reality. Let me examine briefly some of the salient points of their analysis of naming.

The realism of Ge-luk thinkers plays an important though often unacknowledged role in their interpretations of Dharmakīrti's explanation of naming. As we have seen, names are conventional. They are not applied to individuals by virtue of some inherent link between reality and language but on the basis of a conceptual construction superimposed on a reality of discrete individuals. Moreover, names are applied on the basis of a causal connection with experience. Ge-luk thinkers agree that language is conventional and connected to experience. They also agree with Dharmakīrti's view of language as being composed of strings of sounds expressing the speaker's intention and understood in function of the hearer's own dispositions. Hence, in certain respects Ge-luk thinkers can quite legitimately claim to follow Dharmakīrti. Where they differ from the latter is in rejecting the antirealist rejection of the reality of properties, which they take to be a misinterpretation of Dharmakīrti.

Ge-luk thinkers argue, not without some reason, that antirealism makes it difficult to account for the distinction between true and false designations. How do we differentiate calling cows *cows* from calling them *horses*? Ge-luk scholars hold that this distinction can be preserved only if language is understood to capture real features of the world. True to their commentarial style of philosophy, they proceed to interpret Dharmakīrti's *apoha* theory in this realist way. To explain his theory in such a manner, they have to find a way to couch the notion of property in the negative language characteristic of the *apoha* theory. As we will see, however, the connection they draw is artificial, for their view does not require such a negative characterization. Nevertheless, most Ge-luk thinkers insist on using negative language, which seems to be necessary only from an exegetical perspective. They find the ideal tool in Śāntarakṣita's concept of objective exclusion (*don rang mtshan gyi gzhan sel, arthātmaka-svalakṣaṇānyāpoha*).[41] According to Ge-luk interpretations, the naming process succeeds inasmuch as it captures objective exclusions, understood as real negative properties. For example, individual cows are called such on the basis of their being not noncows (literally, differentiated from noncows, *ba ma yin pa las log pa*). This negative depiction is not meant, as one might suspect, to mask the presence of a realist element in the theory. Rather it is a way to integrate such a realist element into Dharmakīrti's *apoha* theory. It also has the virtue of marking the negative character of the conceptual process involved in naming. As we have seen, Ge-luk thinkers accept that language is eliminative but limit the importance of this point.

Ge-dün-drup explains how the objective exclusion is the basis of the naming process: "There is disagreement [between Buddhists and non-Buddhists] on the reason [for which] we are [later] able to understand [an exemplar]. For the Buddhists, the objective elimination, [for example] the [fact that a cow is] not a noncow, is the object of the agreed upon convention. Since this [objective exclusion] is present in all cows, [we are later able to] understand something as a cow."[42] According to Ge-dün-drup, the object of both the agreed-on convention (*brda, saṃketa*) and the established convention (*tha snyad, vyavahāra*) is the objective negation. By *object*, he means the feature that the name singles out and that allows its iterability. Like Dharmakīrti, Ge-luk thinkers are connotationist and thus hold that reference is secondary to sense. Reference to individual objects does not explain naming, for those objects are fleeting. Language requires a more stable element, which Dharmakīrti finds in unreal constructs.

Ge-luk philosophers do not deny the role of such constructs, the object universals, which they accept as being part of linguistic meaning. They argue, however, that the meaning of language is not exclusively conceptual but includes real elements as well. They find a real component to linguistic meaning in the notion of objective exclusion. For example, a young child learns that both gray and black cows are to be called *cow*. The individual cows are the basis (*gzhi*) on which the name is given. They are not the feature in virtue of which these individuals are called *cows*. This feature, which Ge-luk thinkers describe as the object of convention (*brda'i yul*), must be a common element shared between these individuals. This common element is the objective negation, that is, that they are not non-cows. On the basis of this shared element, the name *cow* can be given successfully. The process of learning a name rests on such a common property, which is the main (*gtso bo*) object of convention, whereas the object universal is the secondary (*phal pa*) object.

Ge-dün-drup further explicates the naming process by contrasting Dharmakīrti and his Hindu adversaries on the question of naming. By his account, both sides agree on the purpose of naming and consider a naming successful if it allows the person for whose benefit the naming is done to identify a similar object later. They disagree on the reason why naming is successful. To explain the successful use of language, we must be able to account for the general applicability of names to different objects.[43] Such an account requires that we be able to find an element common to all the situations in which the name is or will be used. Whereas Hindu thinkers find this common element in real universals existing independent from their particulars, Dharmakīrti finds it, according to Ge-luk thinkers, in objective eliminations, which are negative common properties existing in dependence on their instances.

The difference between this view and Dharmakīrti's antirealism appears clearly when we compare their explanations of the naming process. For Dharmakīrti, the only common element that can serve as the direct object of a convention is the unreal conceptual content, for there are no real common properties.

By contrast, for Ge-luk thinkers, a common element is to be found within the things themselves. To be sure, the fictional concept still plays a role. It is the mediating element that makes it possible to conceptualize and categorize things and indirectly connects thought with reality. When we name something, we have in mind an object universal representing the relevant feature of the object. Through this construct, we apply the name to different individuals. According to Ge-luk thinkers, the main object of convention (*brda'i yul*), that is the relevant feature in virtue of which the name applied to individuals, is not the object universal itself but a real property. Otherwise, our naming would be delusive, since we would give, for instance, the name *cow* to a conceptual entity that cannot function as a real cow. Correct naming requires that names capture some feature of the real world.

As we can see, the Ge-luk explanation of naming does not require negative properties. The object of convention can be described positively (as being a jar) or negatively (as not being a nonjar). The issue remains the same: The name *jar* names a real element common to all instances of jar. Gyel-tsap and Ge-dün-drup adopt a negative way to describe this common element to mark that the process of naming is negative: Thought identifies something by eliminating what it is not. Ge-dün-drup describes the common element as an objective elimination, such as a non-noncow. Accounting for how we identify a black cow even though the convention "cow" was not applied to it at the time of our learning the word *cow*, Ge-dün-drup says: "There is no fault in not understanding it [i.e., the black cow] as a cow despite the fact that the convention 'cow' was not applied directly to it at the time when the convention [was introduced]. The convention was directly applied to the non-noncow at the time of [using] the convention and a black cow is also not a noncow."[44] The gray cow on which the convention was first introduced was not the direct object of naming but only the basis on which the name was introduced (*brda sbyar ba'i gzhi*). The direct object of naming is the objective exclusion that is the thing itself.

The use of a negative characterization does not, however, change the basic issue; the necessity of positing real properties. Kay-drup puts forth a similar position without the negative description used by Gyel-tsap and Ge-dün-drup: "The object to which the name is applied [is to be understood in this way]: When we introduce the convention 'cow' we take a white cow as a basis to which we apply [the name] cow."[45] For Kay-drup, the object of the name is cow itself (not a cow or the concept of cow).[46] Or to put it in a clearer way, it is the property of being a cow. The white cow is just the concrete exemplar to which the name applies. Since this individual is not concomitant with all instances to which the name can be applied, it is not the object of the convention.

Although the object universal of cow is concomitant with all cows, it is only conceptually so. Hence, it is not the object (or at least not the main object) to which the name is applied, for it is unable to fulfill the function that the name is meant to capture. Hence, it does not allow a distinction between true and false descriptions. If names applied only in virtue of unreal concepts, there would be no way to distinguish true from false naming. Kay-drup says: "Therefore, when [a name] is applied on the basis of a white cow, the main object of the convention is cow plus the [objective] elimination non-noncow.[47] The object [indicated by] words, the appearance of [something] as not being a noncow, is only just the object of convention (*brda'i yul tsam*)."[48] For Kay-drup, names apply in virtue of real properties. The unreal conceptual construct (the object universal) is only an element of mediation. Kay-drup extends this realist view to explain the relation between signifier and signified. All phenomena are signified by words, which acquire their meaning through an original name giving that establishes a convention.[49] Each successive correct name giving is such in function of its ability to designate the common feature in virtue of which the name is given to a variety of individuals.

Thus, the Ge-luk point is not that language naturally signifies reality, as argued by the Mīmāṃsā, but that conventional signification requires an ability to capture features of reality. Naming cannot just signify fictional concepts but requires the justification derived from capturing real properties. Against the opinion that only conceptual contents are signified, Kay-drup argues: "With respect to the opinion that words cannot signify specifically characterized phenomena there is indeed much counterevidence. Nevertheless, I have already said a lot in preceding [passages]. How could I [go on] infinitely? However, [I will grant that] specifically characterized phenomena are not the direct object of signification (*dngos kyi brjod bya*) of words, for then they would [absurdly] be appearing objects of conceptions (*rtog pa'i snang yul*)."[50] Real things are neither the objects directly signified by language nor are they the objects that we directly conceive. Nevertheless, they are the conceived signified (*zhen pa'i brjod bya*) of words; that is, they are the objects we conceive through language.[51] Here Kay-drup seems to be close to Go-ram-ba's view, but the similarity is partial. Whereas Go-ram-ba holds that language applies to reality only in virtue of the mistaken reification of concepts, Kay-drup holds that language applies in virtue of the world's real features. Hence, his realist understanding of the notion of conceived-signified markedly differs from Go-ram-ba's conceptualism. It is also different from the Mīmāṃsā extreme realism, for in Kay-drup's view, signification is conventional. As with the question of universals, his view on naming, which is also the view of the whole Ge-luk tradition, is an attempt to find a middle ground between antirealist and extreme realist positions.

Although these interpretative attempts to solve crucial conceptual difficulties within Dharmakīrti's system have some support within his work,[52] they transform his system. They are parts of a realist revisionist current that seeks to weaken Dharmakīrti's commitment to the reality of individuals by reinterpreting the meaning of the specifically characterized (*svalakṣaṇa, rang mtshan*) so that it can include universals. This current also transforms Dharmakīrti's explanation of language, which attempts to explain the iterability of names in a world of individuals.

In Tibet, the Ge-luk tradition has continued the revisionist trend started in India by arguing that it is the only way to make sense of Dharmakīrti. Its Sa-gya opponents, refusing this interpretative strategy, have argued for a more literal reading of Dharmakīrti, which preserves his critique of reification. This tradition is faced, however, with the same problems that besieged Dharmakīrti's original system; namely, the necessity of giving a credible account of the validity of knowledge. Can an antirealist philosophy give a convincing explanation of epistemic practices, which for the most part involve concepts?

To examine possible answers to this question, let us now turn to Dharmakīrti's epistemology. My discussion is divided into two parts. Part I focuses on the notion of valid cognition, which is central to Dharmakīrti's work. I analyze the ways in which epistemology is understood in India; that is, understood as the investigation into the nature, scope, and types of *pramāṇa.* I also analyze the different interpretations of the concept of *pramāṇa* and the issues that they raise. In Part II, I examine Dharmakīrti's theory of perception and the conflicting interpretations of it given by his Indian and Tibetan followers.

BOOK TWO

Epistemology

Part I

Valid Cognition

16

Dharmakīrti's Epistemology of Valid Cognition

Mental Terminology and the Mind-Body Problem

This discussion of *pramāṇa* (*tshad ma*), the central notion in Dharmakīrti's system and in the larger Indian logico-epistemological tradition, consists of three parts. The first examines relevant Indian terms in comparison with similar English words. The next part examines the problems raised by Dharmakīrti's multiple accounts of *pramāṇa*, where I distinguish a pragmatic understanding and an intentional understanding of this term. Finally, I examine the typology of *pramāṇa*, which is central to Dharmakīrti's epistemology.

But first we should ask, What is meant by *epistemology* in the Indian context? Epistemology is a branch of philosophy that systematically investigates the nature, scope, presuppositions, basis, and reliability of knowledge. In ancient Greece, some sophists claimed that no fixed standards exist to evaluate knowledge. Protagoras, one of their leaders, held that appearances are the only reality, as expressed in his saying "man is the measure of all things." Plato answered this challenge by positing standards of evaluation, the ideal forms. In the *Meno* and the *Theatetus*, Plato asserted that a knower must be able to give the *logos*, or an account of the essence of the known object. Knowledge is more than factual opinion; true belief needs to be grounded in reality to be knowledge. However, Plato never succeeded in giving a clear explanation of what a proper *logos* should be. In the seventeenth century, Descartes and other epistemologists identified knowledge with justified true belief, a definition that has become standard in the Western tradition. In recent years, Edmund Gettier has raised significant questions concerning this definition, which still provides the framework of many discussions.[1]

Similarly, classical Indian philosophers have been concerned with defining knowledge, or the Indian equivalent, *pramā*, right cognition, and *pramāṇa*, its means. There are differences, however, between concepts of knowledge and *pramāṇa*. A common Sanskrit word that is often translated into English as "knowledge" is *jñā* (in Tibetan, *shes*), which means to be aware or to cognize. I think the preceding translation is misleading since this word does not imply the truth entailed by "knowledge." Instead I translate *jñā*, and its equivalents such as *bud-*

dhi (blo) and *saṃvitti (rig pa)*,[2] by a variety of words such as "mental states," "mental episodes," "cognition," "consciousness," or "awareness." I even use the word "mind." Rather than being a general reservoir of information or just mechanisms of the brain that produce thought and ideas, here a mind consists of individual moments of knowing or the continuum of moments of awareness bearing upon their objects. Each mental episode gives rise to a following one, constituting a mental continuum or stream of awareness (*saṃtāna, rgyud*).

Similarly, I use *consciousness* in a particular way. Instead of meaning a mental state involving self-awareness, the word *consciousness* here refers to mental states understood as phenomenologically[3] observable entities or, better, processes apprehending objects that thereby are revealed to them. Hence, my readers should be aware that these words are used here to designate states of awareness that apprehend objects. In general, the translation of mental terminology is problematic, for mental terms are highly culturally specific. Rather than refer to a more precise but artificial vocabulary, I have chosen to use current English words to translate Indian and Tibetan terms, even though the connotation of these terms is often different in English.

The mental episodes that compose a stream of awareness take as their objects either real or fictional entities. This object-directedness character of mind has been called *intentionality* by some Western philosophers and has been proposed as a criterion for the mental. Brentano says: "Every mental phenomenon is characterized by what the scholastics of the Middle Ages called the intentional (and also mental) in-existence (*Inexistenz*) of an object (*Gegenstand*), and what we would call, although not entirely in unambiguous terms, the reference to a content, a direction upon an object (by which we are not to understand a reality in this case), or an immanent objectivity."[4] According to Brentano, only mental phenomena are intentional; no physical phenomena manifest anything similar, and hence they are not conscious. All acts of awareness bear on an object, regardless of whether this object exists or not. We cannot think, wish, or dread unless our mind is directed toward something that appears to it.

A similar view of consciousness (*jñāna, shes pa*) as intentional is brought out by most Indian epistemologists. For example, Dharmakīrti says: "Apprehension of an object is the [defining] characteristic of consciousness."[5] Tibetan epistemologists have elaborated this definition of consciousness as "that which is clear and cognizes."[6] *Clear* (*gsal*) refers to the ability that mental states have of revealing things.[7] As we will see, this clarity can be understood in several ways. Dharmakīrti understands the clarity of mental states as their ability to represent external objects. He also understands clarity as being the ability of cognition to free itself from distortion in its apprehension of its object. For Dharmakīrti, there is a kind of natural fit between awareness and reality. This fit is less actual than potential. To actualize it we need to free ourselves from obstructions. The minds of all beings have the potential for reaching an unimpeded attunement to reality. Hence, they have clarity. His realist interpreters understand clarity as the ability of mental states to see their objects directly.

Cognize (*rig*) describes the faculty of mental episodes to apprehend things that appear to them. For Dharmakīrti, objects that are directly apprehended by mental states are not external objects, but their representations. Some interpreters give a realist account according to which mental states apprehend external objects that appear to them. All agree, however, in describing mental states as having the ability to reveal objects that appear (*snang*) and that they apprehend (*'dzin*).[8] In this way, mental states cognize objects; hence they are intentional. They are also momentary, disappearing the next moment, making a place for other moments of awareness.

Contrary to the modern Western tradition of acute mind-body dualism, the Indian tradition is less concerned with this problem, although it is not unknown. The Materialists, for instance, reduce the mental to physical events. Most thinkers, however, refuse to accept this reduction, arguing that the mental can neither be eliminated nor reduced. These views do not, however, necessarily amount to a classical mind-body dualism, for Indian philosophers often hold that the mental is partly material. For example, the Sāṃkhya metaphysics is based on the duality between material Nature and conscious Self.[9] The dichotomy is radical but does not coincide exactly with the modern Western mind-body division.[10]

Buddhist thinkers do not explain our changing mental life in terms of a changeless self. Since they reject such a self, they see mental life as consisting of a succession of related intentional states of awareness, constituting a stream or continuum of consciousness (*saṃtāna, rgyud*). Such a stream is not material. Hence, Buddhists seem to come the closest among Indian philosophers to a mind-body dualism. Nevertheless, Buddhist philosophers partake of the general Indian reluctance to separate the material and the mental. Hence, they do not hold that the divide between the material and mental spheres is absolute. Moreover, they do not believe in an ontology of substances, but argue that reality is made of things consisting of a succession of evanescent moments. Thus, mental and material events interact in a constantly on-going and fluctuating process.

Knowledge and Pramāṇa

In Indian philosophy a more central question than the mind-body problem is the nature of knowledge or, rather, its Indian analogues, *pramā* or *pramāṇa.* These technical words are derived from the root *mā,* to measure or cognize,[11] and the prefix *pra* indicating excellence or perfection.[12] The word *pramā* designates a state of being factually aware of something, and should be literally translated as "knowledge event." The adjunction of the suffix *ana*[13] makes the word *pramāṇa,* which literally signifies the means or instrument of bringing about the knowledge event (*pramā*).

Here again, these words differ from the English *knowledge.* Neither *pramā* nor *pramāṇa* is understood as referring to an endurable quality possessed by the knowing person, as *knowledge* does, but to a mental event that cognizes the object as a momentary knowledge event. Bilimoria explains: "Knowing *qua* cognizing here is understood as a phenomenologically continuous process, which is . . . transitory, remaining and disappearing in the duration of the particular mental mode, much as an experience or a mood of the person come and go, so to say."[14] Indian and Tibetan thinkers understand knowledge as a succession of moments of passing knowledge-events. Once a knowing state has passed, the person is left with only the traces of the knowledge event, which in turn can produce recollection (*smṛti, dran pa*).[15]

Another significant difference between the Western concept of knowledge and the Indian *pramā* or *pramāṇa* is that, whereas the former is analyzed in terms of belief (knowledge is justified true belief), the latter is analyzed in terms of certainty. *Pramā* or *pramāṇa* is cognition described as realizing or understanding (*adhigam, rtogs pa)* its object.[16] That is, it is able to lead to the correct identification of its object and bring about certainty (*niścita, nges pa*, or *adhyavasaya, nge shes*) with respect to it. For example, I see a jar in front of me. My visual perception enables me to correctly identify the seen object as what it is (a jar). I know that this object is a jar, and I do not have any doubt with respect to this fact.

Most modern Western accounts of knowledge do not hold certainty to be a necessary condition of knowledge.[17] Therefore, the Buddhist definition of the equivalent of our term *knowledge, pramāṇa,* does not correspond to the standard tripartite characterization of knowledge as justified true belief. Similarly, the standard tripartite definition of *knowledge* as justified true belief does not apply to the Indian idea of *pramā*. Consequently, the domain covered by Indian epistemology does not completely overlap with what Western epistemologists have studied, the theory of knowledge and of justification.[18]

Nevertheless, the Indian concept of *pramāṇa* corresponds for the most part to our concept of knowledge. Both concepts are based on a similar understanding of truth and on the intuition that some of our beliefs or experiences are true in a way that is not fortuitous. Moreover, as we will see, similar problems are raised by Western and Indian philosophers concerning the definition of *knowledge* and its Indian analogue, *pramāṇa*. Finally, the discussions concerning the types of knowledge admitted in both traditions are comparable, although not identical. For example, the Buddhist thesis that there are only two forms of knowledge, perception and inference, is similar to what most Western epistemologists assume. All this shows that the name *Indian epistemology* given to the study of the Indian equivalent of knowledge, *pramāṇa,* is more than a convenient label.

Indian epistemology examines the nature of *pramāṇa,* its scope, basis, reliability, and the like. This is the central concern of Dharmakīrti and his followers. In his *Drop of Reasoning*, the master starts his inquiry by saying: "Since right cognition is the prerequisite to the fulfillment of all human purposes, I shall explain it."[19] Dharmakīrti's inquiry focuses on knowledge understood as valid cognition. His questions are clearly epistemological: What is *pramāṇa* and what are its different types? Which type of valid cognition is most fundamental? Does each type bear similarly on the empirical world? Let us examine these questions in order, starting with the first, What is *pramāṇa*?

Defining Pramāṇa

To greatly simplify, we could say that *pramāṇa* is understood by the diverse Indian schools of epistemology in two ways. Jhā explains: "In philosophical literature, this term 'Pramāṇa' has been used somewhat promiscuously: sometimes in the sense of the *Means* of Cognition, the etymology of the word being given as '*pramīyate jñānate anena*'[20]–while sometimes it is used in the sense of Valid Cognition itself–with the etymology '*pramīyate yatt*'."[21] The Bhaṭṭa Mīmāṃsā, and most Hindu schools, hold *pramāṇa* to be an instrument or means of knowledge. *Pramāṇa* means both the factor most relevant to knowledge or the dominant cause of knowledge and the criterion (the right measure) that allows us to assert that we have knowledge.[22] For instance, in our example of seeing a jar, the visual perception is the *pramāṇa,* that is, the means that allows the knower (*pramtṛ*), the self, to rightly evaluate the jar as a jar. This instrument brings about the certainty that this object is a jar. This is the result (*phala*) of the *pramāṇa,* the knowledge event (*pramiti*) of the jar as a jar.

Pramāṇa can also mean valid cognition[23] itself, in which case it is the equivalent of correct cognition (which the Nyāya would describe as the *pramiti*) rather than a means to it. Both the Buddhist and the Prabhākara Mīmāṃsaka epistemologists have chosen this second understanding as demonstrated by their explanation of *pramāṇa* as either nondeceptive cognition (*avisaṃvādi-jñāna, mi slu ba'i shes pa*) or right cognition (*samyagjñāna, yang dag pa'i shes pa*). This understanding of *pramāṇa* as an item of knowledge event (*pramiti*) is reflected in Dharmakīrti's explanations. He characterizes *pramāṇa* as a cognition that is nondeceptive (*avisaṃvādi-jñāna*): "Valid cognition is that cognition [which is] nondeceptive (*avisaṃvādi, mi bslu ba*). [Nondeceptiveness consists] in the readiness [for the object] to perform a function."[24] This statement emphasizes that *pramāṇa* is not the instrument that a knowing self[25] uses to know things. There is no separate knowing subject but just knowledge, which is *pramāṇa.* According to this account a cognition is valid if, and only if, it is nondeceptive. But, what does *nondeceptive* mean?

Dharmakīrti responds that nondeceptiveness (*avisaṃvādanam, mi slu ba*) consists of an object's readiness to perform a function that relates to the way it is cognized. One may wonder why Dharmakīrti speaks of the nondeceptiveness of the object when he should be describing that of the consciousness. Śākya Chokden gives this technical but useful explanation: nondeceptiveness is of the object but can be extended to the consciousness. The subject's nondeceptiveness consists of its apprehension of the object in accordance with the latter's causal dispositions.[26] For example, the nondeceptiveness of a fire is its disposition to burn, and so forth. The nondeceptiveness of the perception of the fire is its apprehension of the latter as burning, which is nondeceptive since it practically corresponds to the object's own dispositions. By contrast, the apprehension of the fire as cold is deceptive because it grasps the object in an inadequate way. Notice the practical and even behavioral emphasis in Dharmakīrti's account. Appropriateness and adequacy or lack thereof are functions of the cognition's success or failure in appropriating the object in ways that correspond to the objects' own disposition to behave in certain ways.

One implication of Dharmakīrti's account is that the objects with respect to which cognitions are deceptive or nondeceptive must be real, because only real things, that is, causally effective phenomena, have the capacity to perform functions. The relation between an object and its cognition can be either conceptually unmediated, as when we observe real objects, or mediated, as when we infer something through reasoning. In either case, the relation between valid cognition and real things is to be understood in practical terms.

This understanding of *pramāṇa* seems to be different from the intentional description of mental events we examined earlier. By saying that validity in cognitions is a practical matter, Dharmakīrti views mental life as being composed of representations standing in the appropriate causal relation with their objects. In this account, to know an object is less an intentional or normative relation than a pragmatic one in which successful or unsuccessful outcomes decide the epistemological status of cognitions. The contradiction, however, is only apparent, for in another passage, Dharmakīrti characterizes valid cognition quite differently: "Or, [i.e., another explanation is that *pramāṇa*] is the revealing of a [yet] unknown thing."[27] Here a cognition is valid if, and only if, it reveals some hitherto unknown aspect of reality and makes us understand something that is first true and second new. According to this account, these two aspects, truth and novelty, are necessary and sufficient conditions for a cognition to be valid.

In this second account, Dharmakīrti appeals to a normative notion of truth that is not reducible to a pragmatic dimension. He depicts valid cognition not as bringing about the right result in dependence on an appropriate causal relation with its object, but as intentional; that is, as being directed toward an object. To be valid, a cognition must reveal an object (*artha, don*) that really exists. That is, a valid cognition must be directed toward its object in accordance with the nature of the object. It is the agreement between the cognition's intentionality and the nature of the object that constitutes the truth necessary to the validity of the cognition. This does not necessarily mean, as we will see later, that this second account is committed to a so-called correspondence theory of truth. It does entail, however, a commitment to a normative dimension.

Though necessary, truth is not sufficient for *pramāṇa.* The content revealed by a cognition must be new. A mental episode that just repeats previously known information can be useful. It also can be true, but it is not valid in the technical sense of the word, for it does not bring anything new to the cognitive process. Hence, it is cognitively irrelevant. For example, memory (*smṛti, dran pa*) is not valid for Dharmakīrti and for most schools of Indian philosophy.[28] It is excluded from being valid on the ground that it is a mere conceptual repetition of previous knowledge without any demonstrable link to reality to ensure its validity.[29] Hence, it is notoriously deceptive and unfit to be valid. Memory may be relevant to the production of further knowledge. For example, memory is involved in inferences, but the knowledge that results from the inferential process is a new conclusion.

Dharmakīrti's second account is well known in Indian philosophy. For example, the Nyāya school defines cognition (*jñāna, shes pa*) as the revealing of an object.[30] Nevertheless, these two accounts seem to be in tension. This difficulty is not just the result of Dharmakīrti's having two accounts but reflects the tension that exists between several of our intuitions. On the one hand, we hold the commonsense view of cognition, particularly in its perceptual form, as an awareness directed to an immediately present object. On the other hand, we also assume that such a cognition is the result of a contact with external reality. In this case, however, cognition could not be in contact with the object it apprehends since this object would cease to exist when the cognitive act occurs, since it is its cause. Systematic epistemology is an attempt to sort out these intuitions, which pull apart, and come up with a coherent and complete account of epistemic practices.

Indian and Tibetan commentators have struggled at great length with these two apparently conflicting accounts, arguing how to reconcile them. Devendrabuddhi, for example, argues that Dharmakīrti offers a choice. Either definition will do. By contrast, the later commentator Prajñākaragupta (740–800 C.E.) seems to argue that Dharmakīrti's *Commentary* defines valid cognition by combining the two statements.[31] Modern scholars have entered the discussion as well. Katsura, for example, argues that Dharmakīrti's two accounts provide two definitions: a pragmatic view that includes both perception and inference as performing pragmatic functions and an epistemological account that includes only perception. Whereas the former viewpoint reflects the commonsense view, according to which we come to know things either perceptually or conceptually, the second reflects the reality of causal interactions between mental states and infinitesimal point instants. Hence, it does not concern inference, which can be valid only from a commonsensical perspective.[32]

My explanation will differ from the latter view. Following Śākya Chokden, I would like to explain Dharmakīrti's view by combining his different accounts. According to this unified account, a cognition must meet the following three criteria to be valid: (a) nondeceptiveness understood in a practical way, (b) a normative idea of truth relying on the idea of intentionality, and (c) novelty, which we can leave aside for the time being.[33] This is the account that Dharmakīrti provides in his later *Ascertainment.* There, he combines his two previous statements, characterizing valid cognition in both practical and intentional terms. Speaking of the two types of valid cognition, he says: "[Perception and inference are valid cognitions] because they are nondeceptive with respect to the purpose [of the action] in the application [toward an object] after having determined it."[34] This account gives a double characterization of valid cognition. The first is practical: a cognition is valid inasmuch as it helps us to fulfill a purpose. Here a cognition is correct because we can rely on it to accomplish a practical goal. The second introduces a more explicitly intentional or normative element: a cognition is valid if, and only if, the object we are seeking is determined (*bcad pa*) correctly. According to the *Ascertainment,* a valid cognition combines these two independent elements (practical value and cognitive capacity to reveal an object) to characterize all valid cognitions. Each one taken in isolation is a necessary but not a sufficient condition for knowledge.

We may wonder, Why does Dharmakīrti think that both practical and intentional elements are required? To understand this, let us examine Dharmottara's commentary on this passage. Dharmottara starts by explaining the nondeceptiveness of valid cognition: "We should understand that just as in the world where nondeceptiveness consists of putting [us] in touch with the promised object, nondeceptiveness for a cognition consists of [its] putting [us] in touch with the indicated object."[35] In this passage, Dharmottara interprets Dharmakīrti's account as focusing on the practical aspect of mental events. It is the possibility of practical results brought about by a given cognition that primarily determines its status as valid. Dharmottara gives even more weight to pragmatic concerns when he further explains the preceding passage: "The meaning of this [preceding passage] is this: it is not apprehending the object that [makes a cognition] a right cognition but only obtaining a thing."[36] For Dharmottara, the nondeceptiveness of a mental episode is practical, not cognitive.[37] A cognition is nondeceptive inasmuch as it has the ability to bring about the appropriate possible practical results. For example, a perception of fire is valid inasmuch as it enables us to deal with the fire in the appropriate way (appropriateness being here a contextual notion). This nondeceptiveness is understood in a causal way: It is the result of the mental episode's causal connection with reality and in turn leads to the appropriate causal results. Thus, this account of nondeceptiveness does not seem to involve any explicit normative element.

This is not enough to explain the notion of validity. Important as they might be, practical considerations are not sufficient to determine knowledge. To illustrate this point, Dharmottara gives the following example: Imagine that we are seeking water on a hot day. We suddenly see water, or so we think. In fact, we are not seeing water but a mirage, but when we reach the spot, we are lucky and find water right there under a rock. Can we say that we had genuine knowledge of water? The answer seems to be negative, for we were just lucky. We did not obtain the object we were looking for. Thus, practical success is clearly not enough. We need a normative element as well. This is why, says Dharmottara, "[Dharmakīrti] speaks of [cognitions engaging] 'having determined their objects,' for [cognitions] apply [to their objects] in dependence upon previous realization."[38] In our example, our mental event concerning water is not valid because its success does not correspond to our previous determination of the seen object. We thought it was water when it was only a mirage. If practical concerns were enough for validity, cases similar to that described by Dharmottara would have to count as genuine knowledge!

The example used by Dharmottara is interesting in more than one respect. It is quite similar to the cases used by Gettier in his attacks against the classical Western definition of knowledge as justified true belief. Gettier has suggested examples that undermine this standard definition.[39] These examples are situations in which the criteria offered by the definition are satisfied but our intuitions tell us that there is no knowledge. Dharmottara's example is quite similar and hence can be appropriately described as Gettier-like in that it takes a putative definition of knowledge and brings a counterexample in which the criteria implied by the definition are met but we know that there is no knowledge.[40]

The conclusion that Dharmottara draws from this Gettier-like example is that we need both criteria (practical value and normative truth) to define validity (leaving aside for the time being the issue of novelty). Each criterion is necessary but not sufficient. Valid cognition is to be defined in practical terms with a normative addendum. Notice that, when we described the practical value on the basis of a causal connection, we always had to add a normative element. We talked, for example, about "appropriate causal results." But what does *appropriate* mean? In our example, the result we obtained was practically appropriate, but cognitively inappropriate since it did not agree with the cognitive determination of the situation. This shows that a causal account of knowledge can be made complete only by at least tacitly appealing to a normative element determined in intentional terms. This is what Dharmakīrti intends to capture in his account of valid cognition.

Before moving on, let us pause to notice the problems raised by Dharmottara's answer. The Gettier-like example does the job that Dharmottara intends it to, proving that practical value is not sufficient for validity. But it goes further than that and threatens Dharmottara's own account that a cognition is valid if the practical value of the object is determined truthfully. What is Dharmottara's account? Does he hold that validity = practical value + factuality? Presumably not, for that would include our example among valid cognitions, since the assumption that there is water is factual. Hence, it would satisfy both criteria (practical value and truth understood as factuality), and yet, it is clearly not valid. Thus, if Dharmottara wants his account to exclude Gettier-type cases, he must hold that here truth does not mean just factuality, but something stronger, what we could call *normative truth*; that is, truth in accordance with the proper standards of evaluation. The assumption that there is water is factually correct but relies on a faulty cognitive background. It infers from the vision of what looks like water the presence of water, neglecting the special conditions that could have allowed one to doubt the presence of water. Hence, such an assumption does not conform to the standards of evaluation and therefore does not satisfy the second criterion.

The Epistemological Role of Language

Having defined *valid cognition*, the epistemologist is faced with the even more important task of differentiating the types of valid cognition. Indian schools have conflicting views on this topic, revealing their deep metaphysical and religious differences. In accordance with their materialism, the Cārvāka school accepts only one type of valid means of cognition, perception (*pratyakṣa, mngon sum*). The Buddhist and the Vaiśeṣika accept two types of means of knowledge, perception and inference (*anumāna, rjes dpag*), the cognition of a fact through a related sign that correctly indicates this fact. The Sāṃkhya add a third means of knowledge to this list, verbal testimony (*śabda, sgra*). The Nyāya accept four means of knowledge, adding analogy (*upamāna, [dpe] nyer 'jal*).[41] This list of four means of valid cognition became the most authoritative, and even certain Buddhists[42] used it. The Prābhākaras accept five means, whereas the Bhāṭṭas and the Vedāntins accept six.

One of the main issues behind these differences concerns the epistemological status of verbal testimony or language (*śabda, sgra*). For orthodox Hindu thinkers, the means of valid cognition are not limited to perception and inference. Although the different Hindu schools disagree about the number of means to valid cognition, they almost all agree on verbal testimony as a separate means of valid cognition.[43] This assertion is an important point in their philosophies, for it is intimately connected with the validity of scriptures.

We have already encountered the Mīmāṃsā view that language in general is naturally meaningful and that Vedic revelation is an absolutely certain and self-certifying source of knowledge. It is the only means that humans have to understand *dharma.* The Nyāya agrees with the Buddhists that language is conventional, but nevertheless asserts with great strength the sui generis nature of verbal communication. Knowledge based on testimony is not a form of inference (despite Dignāga and Dharmakīrti) because it does not involve the knowledge of the relation of two facts as inference does. Since it cannot be reduced to any other means of valid cognition, verbal testimony must be accepted as an independent means of valid cognition. *Nyāya-sūtra* I.1.7 explains the epistemological status of testimony: "Verbal testimony (*śabda*) is the communication (*upadeśa*) from a trustworthy person (*āpta*)."[44] For the Nyāya, the authoritativeness of a statement is not intrinsic (as asserted by the Mīmāṃsā) but derives from the nondeceptiveness of its speaker. Knowledge based on verbal testimony imparted by trustworthy people (experts, *āpta*) can concern worldly as well as spiritual matters. In spiritual matters, the experts are the beings who have directly experienced the truth; that is, the Vedic *ṛṣis.* They reveal the hidden truth to ordinary beings. Hence, scriptures have their own independent validity that is not reducible to that of inference.

Buddhist epistemologists reject this view. They refuse to recognize language as a separate source of knowledge. Dharmakīrti argues that a meaningful expression is stated by a speaker with a definite intention, and the hearer can infer the speaker's intention from his words. If I say to you "this is my rocking chair," you can infer from my words the nature of my communicative intention. You cannot, however, infer that the object I am referring to is a rocking chair from my words only. To do this, you must first know the chair. Hence, knowledge based on communication is not a sui generis form of knowledge. The only sure information obtained from testimony concerns the speaker's intentions. The content must be confirmed independent of the testimony. Dharmakīrti states: "Since statements do not have any concomitance with real things, one [cannot] establish the [referred] object on their [basis]. They merely express the speaker's intention."[45] A statement does not have any necessary relation with its content. Assertions are not self-validating. At best, they can inform us of the speaker's subjective intentions. They can also be an indirect source of knowledge. Words are evidence that can serve as the basis for further inference. Valid cognition based on valid testimony understood as a direct understanding of the object expressed by a statement is to be rejected.

This answer leaves out two major difficulties in Dharmakīrti's system. First, it provides a counterintuitive account of the knowledge we can acquire through communication. We seem to be able to acquire information through communication with other people, but is this actual knowledge? For example, people learn a great deal about countries to which they have never been. Are these cognitions valid or not? The answer of the Buddhist epistemologist is not clear, as can be seen from the frequency and intensity with which the question is debated in the courtyards of Tibetan monasteries. The answer seems to be that these cognitions are not knowledge but mere opinions, as long as they are not based on a solid reasoning. The Nyāya idea that information can be known on the basis of the speaker's non-deceptiveness will not do for the Buddhists. For we can rely on the speaker only once we have established him or her to be trustworthy on a particular topic. To establish that person as generally trustworthy is of no help.

Second, this account seems to exclude religious scriptures as means of valid cognition. Dharmakīrti's view on this topic is complicated and may not even be fully consistent. Its analysis is well beyond the purpose of this book. Suffice it to say that Dharmakīrti attempts to solve the difficulty by differentiating between two types of situations. In most cases, we do not need scriptures. Experience or rational understanding is sufficient, at least theoretically. Still there are important cases, which Dharmakīrti describes as extremely hidden (*atyantaparokṣa, shin tu lkog gyur*), where ordinary reasoning is in principle powerless. Morality, for example, is not fully understandable rationally. According to most Indian thinkers, we cannot deduce moral rules and guidance but must find it in a scriptural tradition. For Dharmakīrti, however, not every moral tradition is equally valid. In particular, the established Hindu tradition is not reliable. Hence, we first need to establish by reason and experience the validity of a particular tradition by considering its general views and goals. Once we have decided on a particular tradition, we need to find a rational procedure to sort out the deceptive from the non-deceptive statements made by this tradition concerning extremely hidden matters. This is done by a special type of formal argument, in which we infer certain extremely hidden matters by establishing the validity of statements concerning these matters. For example, we infer that generosity is good since it leads to favorable results by relying on Nāgārjuna's statement in his *Precious Garland* that "through giving [one obtains] wealth and through ethical restraint happiness [i.e., happy rebirth]."[46]

The difficult question here is whether our understanding is valid in the technical sense of the term. Is our conclusion a form of inferential knowledge or just a correct and useful opinion? Most Tibetan thinkers seem to assume that this type of argument can support a genuine though unusual form of inference. There are reasons to believe that the opinions of Dharmakīrti and his followers may be different. Certain passages suggest that scriptures only approximate knowledge.[47] They cannot provide the certainty that valid cognitions require, for statements cannot attest to the validity of their content. Nevertheless, scriptures are cognitively important because they provide the only guidance that we can obtain in the vital domains of existence inaccessible to rational understanding.

Epistemological Typology

The importance of the typology of valid cognitions cannot be overstated. It is the foundation on which Dignāga's and Dharmakīrti's entire epistemological program rests.[48] By stating that there are only two types of valid cognition, they do not merely limit the number of acceptable types of knowledge, they also want to impose severe restrictions on the ways in which the two types of object posited by their ontology are understood. Whereas real things are apprehended only by perception, constructs are apprehended only by conceptions. In this way, Dharmakīrti prevents universals from becoming objects of perception, which would make them real. Perception can bear directly only on individuals, which constitute reality; unreal universals are only to be apprehended by inference. Thus, Buddhist epistemology is committed to a radical dichotomy between two types of valid cognition (*pramāṇa-vyavasthā*). This epistemological dichotomy is a consequence as well as a support of the ontological dichotomy between things and conceptual contents.[49] The former are real individuals and are apprehended accurately by perception. These real objects cannot be apprehended by thought, which conceives of things only through the intermediary of universals. Those are fictional, existing only inasmuch as they are constructed by conceptual activities. Hence, they cannot be apprehended by undistorted perception, otherwise they would be real.

Similarly, conception cannot apprehend real things, for it always proceeds by description. We do not conceive of things in their particularities, but only by providing general characteristics that we apply to particular things. For example, when I think about my chair, my thought apprehends an object by subsuming it under a characteristic provided by a description.[50] Even in the case where I seem to directly identify an object, as when I think "this is my chair," analysis shows that this referring act always presupposes some description in the background. *This* does not directly refer to its object but only identifies its object by subsuming the object under a general characteristic such as having a form, a color, and so on. Since such characteristics are not individuals, they are not real but merely constructs. Hence, thought can never be directly in touch with real individuals. It is limited to its own constructs. Thus, the dichotomy between the two types of knowledge is radical.

This typology of valid cognition is the keystone of Dharmakīrti's *pramāṇa* method; the whole system stands or falls on the cogency of its restriction of validity to perception and inference. Dharmakīrti does not intend to provide impressionistic explanations, but a complete account of the epistemic support of philosophical statements. Hence, he must show how all possible forms of knowledge can be included in perception and inference. But this is not enough. He must justify theoretically his demonstration by showing that this limitation of knowledge to perception and inference is not due to a momentary limitation of human capacities, but reflects the nature of reality. Because there are only two types of entity, there are only two forms of knowledge. In this way, Dharmakīrti's *pramāṇa* method is solidly established. The range of knowable objects is delineated, the nature of valid cognition is established, and the type of cognitions that are allowable are determined. In this way only well-grounded statements can be admitted. For a statement to be admissible it must be supported by a valid cognition, which must be either an observation or based on reasoning bearing a demonstrable connection with some observable fact, as when we infer the presence of fire from smoke. Any cognition that does not satisfy either requirement is eo ipso not valid.

Western epistemology usually defines *knowledge* as justified true belief, thus restricting the purview of knowledge to that which is true and justified. Buddhist epistemology goes essentially in the same direction. The requirement that a cognition be nondeceptive parallels the necessity for a belief to be true. Although there is no direct Buddhist equivalent of *justified*, the requirement that a cognition be either directly grounded in facts by observation or connected to observed facts is an equivalent for the necessity that a cognition be justified. In both systems, only a well-grounded belief or cognitive event can be accepted as knowledge. Although the Buddhist epistemology of valid cognition does not explicitly refer to the question of justification, there is a similar preoccupation with grounding epistemic practices. Cognitions are valid because they are grounded in reality. Perceptions are the foundations of knowledge because they reflect reality. They apprehend their objects evidently and are, as we will see, partly self-justified. Hence, they are in no need of further justification. Such is not the case with inference, which has no direct connection with reality. Hence, it is in need of being justified on the basis of its connection with perception. Because he holds that both forms of knowledge must be grounded in reality, it is quite appropriate to describe Dharmakīrti as a foundationalist.[51]

As we will see, this dichotomy raises many problems. This view was opposed by Hindus, for whom the different valid cognitions coalesce (*pramāṇa-samplava*). Hindu realists refused to accept the Buddhist idea that there are two different types of existent. Either things are real and they exist, or they are not real and there is nothing more to say. Accordingly, the different types of cognition do not relate to different kinds of objects. Instead, they relate in different ways to the same real things that make up the world.[52] Both Dignāga and Dharmakīrti rejected this commonsensical view and held to their point, despite its many problems. Hindu opponents responded by raising numerous objections. Dharmakīrti's followers attempted to respond to these criticisms. Later developments in Dharmakīrti's tradition such as the distinction between several types of object, which we will examine shortly, are related to these debates.[53]

We may wonder why Dignāga and Dharmakīrti make a move that is so problematic? First, such a radical dichotomy is in accordance with the epistemological atomism we already noticed in the Abhidharmic tradition. There sense perceptions are limited to their own particular objects.[54] A visual perception can see only a shape or a color and a bodily perception can apprehend only a touch. Such atomism is systematized by Dignāga. It is extended to include all forms of knowledge and connected with the twofold ontology of the tradition.[55] Second, this move is the logical consequence of their rejection of the reality of universals. Thought is unable to refer directly to reality and can do so only through concepts. For example, when we think about our favorite chair, we do not apprehend this object directly but only by identifying it through a general property, being a chair, which we apply to a particular situation. Since such a property does not really exist, such a thought is inherently distorting. It can conceive things, but in doing so it does not apprehend reality but only its own unreal constructs.

Before moving to the analysis of perception, which provides the foundation of Dharmakīrti's system, we need to further discuss Dharmakīrti's view in the light of the Tibetan understanding of valid cognition. In the process, we will explore further the two possible understandings of epistemic validity: practical and intentional. We will show that, although Dharmakīrti tends toward the former, he cannot do without the latter. In the process, we will make a few comparative remarks on Dharmakīrti's view of truth before showing the importance of the issue involved in this discussion.

17

Was Dharmakīrti a Pragmatist?

Valid Cognition and Its Object

In the preceding chapter, we determined that the Buddhist understanding of *pramāṇa* is nondeceptive cognition. We also paused to examine the typology of valid cognitions. Let us return to the concept of nondeceptiveness. In the process we will examine the conflicting interpretations of Tibetan thinkers, clarifying the relation between the two ways (the practical and the intentional) of understanding valid cognition, relating this question to the distinction between types of objects of valid cognition.

Distinguishing cognitions in terms of their objects is a standard move in epistemological thinking. The intentional nature of consciousness entails a relationship with an object. To say that we are conscious of an object does not, however, say anything about that object. A purely phenomenological approach might remain happily confined to the exploration of the nuanced ways in which objects appear to the mind. Epistemology, at least in its foundational mode, proceeds differently. It intends to provide a complete account of epistemic practices by relating them to their objects and to analyze the ontological status of these objects in order to decide whether cognitions are true or not.

The foundational mode of epistemology is at the center of Dharmakīrti's system. The validity of a cognition is determined by the ontological status of its object (*viśaya, yul*).[1] Perception, for instance, is valid because it apprehends veridically real things. The validity of inference is more problematic, since it only bears on pseudo-entities. How can factual thoughts be distinguished from mistaken ones when both bear on equally unreal constructs? Dharmakīrti's answer to this question, which we have already encountered, is that inference is a valid cognition when it apprehends constructs that apply to real entities. Mistaken constructs cannot be applied, and hence mistaken thoughts are not valid.

The difficulties involved in the notion of an object become apparent. Whereas, at first, the idea of a cognition taking something as its object seems unproblematic, further analysis shows that this is not the case. When Dharmakīrti says that thought does not take reality as its object, this concept of the object is not a straightforward phenomenological idea of something immediately present in the ken of the mind. Rather, a distinction must be made between the prima facie or direct object (*dngos yul*), which Dharmakīrti sometimes calls the *object of comprehension* (*meya, gzhal bya*), and the primary or main object (*yul gyi gtso bo*) of awareness to which cognition applies (*pravṛtti, 'jug pa*).

Later Indian and Tibetan scholars have systematized and greatly extended these distinctions, which in Dharmakīrti often remain implicit. Tibetan epistemologists call the latter the object of application (*'jug yul*) and the former the appearing object (*snang yul*). There is no unanimity concerning these objects; in this and the following chapter I delineate the conflicting explanations given by Tibetan thinkers regarding the objects of mental episodes. This chapter examines the conflicting interpretations of the concept of object of application presented by Tibetan thinkers. In the process we also further explore their understandings of the notion of nondeceptiveness. The notion of appearing object will be analyzed in the next chapter when we discuss the attempts made by Dharmakīrti's realist interpreters to explain the nondeceptiveness of inference.

Objects of application are said to be the objects to which our cognitions apply. But what does this mean? Tibetan thinkers have taken the word *apply* in two different ways. A cognition can be said to apply to an object when it either practically helps to appropriate this object or cognitively to reveal it. In accordance with their realism, Gyel-tsap, Kay-drup, and Ge-dün-drup emphasize the latter intentional aspect of valid cognition. According to their views, the object of application of a cognition is the object it identifies.[2] My favorite rocking chair, for example, can be apprehended by either perception or conception. In either case the chair is the object of application, since it is apprehended.[3]

Antirealists like Śākya Chok-den favor the causal and pragmatic approach to the object of application, which they understand not as the object apprehended, but as the object of practical concern. In the case of perception, both the realists and the antirealists agree that a real object is the object of application. For conception, however, the situation is quite different. For the antirealists, when I think about my rocking chair, I do not apprehend the chair itself, but only its unreal universal. Does this mean that the chair is not the object of application? No, for I am able to relate successfully to the chair through its concept. For antirealists, the rocking chair is not an object of application because it is apprehended, but because it is pragmatically appropriated. Here, cognition is a form of knowledge because it helps us deal successfully with our environment on the basis of a causal link with objects.

Ge-luk thinkers and the antirealists differ about how to explain the object of application. What is behind this opposition? Do Sa-gya antirealists reject the intentional understanding of mental episodes? Do Ge-luk realists reject an explanation of consciousness in causal terms? In the following pages, I will argue that the opposition is not absolute. The two sides differ in the emphasis placed on either the pragmatic or the intentional understanding of consciousness. This translates into exegetical differences about how to interpret Dharmakīrti's concept of nondeceptiveness. A more strictly philosophical issue is also at stake, which is the cognitive status of conceptual knowledge. In this regard, the pragmatic explanation is also an attempt to explain how thought can be valid in a world where its objective referents, the universals, do not exist. Thought in the form of inference is valid because it helps us to deal successfully with the world. The intentional interpretation insists that such a pragmatic interpretation does not suffice.

As already indicated, Dharmakīrti and most other Indian epistemologists (including Dharmottara) stress the practical dimension when explaining the nondeceptiveness of valid cognition; nevertheless, it is possible to find passages stressing another aspect. In *Commentary*, I:215, for example, Dharmakīrti describes nondeceptiveness in reference to scriptural statements as free of contradiction (*abhādhana, mi gnod pa*) from any other source of knowledge, perceptual or inferential. This explanation suggests that the nondeceptiveness of a statement, and of thought as well, is a function of its content, not just its pragmatic contribution.

This emphasis on the intentional component is difficult to explain in an antirealist framework. For how can we talk about thought knowing objects if it is strictly limited to pseudo-entities? There is a definite tension within Dharmakīrti's system between his sober ontology and the necessity to account for epistemic practices. This tension is the source of later realist interpretations. Because of his foundationalism, Dharmakīrti's system may not be able to fully repress its tendencies toward realism, despite its attempt to refute such a view. This chapter introduces this question by discussing the conflicting interpretations of the concept of object of application (*'jug yul*), which directly relates to that of nondeceptiveness. The discussion of realism is continued on into the next chapter, where it is the primary focus.

An Intentional Interpretation

Ge-luk thinkers emphasize the intentional aspects of epistemological concepts. Most[4] follow Gyel-tsap in defining valid cognition as "that cognition which is newly nondeceptive" (*gsar du mi bslu ba'i shes pa*).[5] This definition, also given by Ge-dün-drup,[6] is accepted as standard by the later authors of the textbooks in the important Ge-luk monasteries. It privileges the intentional explanation of consciousness by emphasizing the importance of the content of a cognition rather than its pragmatic contribution.

This intentional emphasis is particularly apparent in the interpretation that the Ge-luk tradition gives to the concept of nondeceptiveness. Whereas antirealist thinkers understand Dharmakīrti's concept of nondeceptiveness pragmatically, Ge-luk thinkers stress its cognitive importance. A cognition is nondeceptive if, and only if, it provides some new cognitive content. Although Gyel-tsap suggests that nondeceptiveness can also be interpreted in pragmatic terms,[7] he has been understood by his followers to characterize nondeceptiveness in intentional terms. This view, which is shared by Gyel-tsap, Ge-dün-drup, and most Ge-luk thinkers,[8] can be traced back to Cha-ba. His views are described by Śākya Chok-den: "The former party [Cha-ba] holds that the object of application is only that which is a true object. The meaning of truth is taken to be the absence of contradiction toward the object accordingly determined. Such [an object] can be either capable or incapable of performing a function. For [something] to be the object of application of a valid cognition, this [cognition] must eliminate the opposed superimposition."[9] For a cognition to be nondeceptive it must satisfy two criteria: It must identify its object correctly and be new. Let us examine these two conditions.

A valid cognition must newly realize things; that is, obtain the identified object (*bcad don thob pa*). Cha-ba takes this characterization to be intentional. A cognition epistemically secures its object not just by leading to the appropriate pragmatic result but by correctly identifying its object. For reasons we will examine later,[10] Cha-ba understands this in negative terms: In identifying its object, a valid cognition eliminates false superimpositions (*sgro 'dogs gcod pa*). A cognition is valid if, and only if, it apprehends its object in a way that is not contradicted by other cognitions. This intentional emphasis is not meant to deny to the object of application its practical importance. This practical connotation, however, is not conceived as constituting the full cognizance of the concept of object of application. Even Kay-drup, who tends to be skeptical of some of Cha-ba's epistemological explanations, agrees that a cognition must be understood intentionally. Or, to put in Tibetan terms, the nondeceptiveness of a cognition is its ability to eliminate false superimposition. To include practical concerns, which he understands to be central to Dharmakīrti's concerns, Kay-drup distinguishes two types of object of application: the purposeful object (*don du gnyer bya*) and the determined object (*yongs su gcod par bya ba*). The former is the object we try to appropriate. It can be different from the latter, which is the object as cognized. Thus, for Kay-drup, the meaning of nondeceptiveness is double: It is intentional with respect to the determined object and pragmatic with respect to the purposeful object.[11]

Kay-drup defines the object of application as "that object which exists in the way in which it is explicitly determined by a valid cognition."[12] This intentional understanding of the object of application (and of valid cognition, which is determined as a function of this object) is currently accepted by contemporary Geluk-ba thinkers. They hold that the object of application of a valid cognition is the phenomenon identified by that cognition.

This view, which emphasizes the normative and intentional aspect of the mental, goes together with the realism concerning universals asserted by these thinkers. Valid cognition identifies objects by way of their properties. For example, I see and identify a jar as a jar. For Cha-ba and his tradition, this is what being nondeceptive means. Even perception identifies its object in this way. It is nondeceptive inasmuch as it identifies the jar as a jar; that is, as instantiating the property of being a jar. Cognitions are determined to be nondeceptive when the identification of their objects as subsumed under a universal is correct. Hence, for these thinkers, intentionality entails the reality of some universals.

The Requirement of Novelty

Before examining the more pragmatically antirealist view of cognition, I would like to say a few words on the differences between Kay-drup and most other Ge-luk thinkers, who describe valid cognition as newly nondeceptive cognition. Thus, a memory, which is taken by almost all Indian epistemologists to be a typical example of a nonvalid conception, is excluded because it does not provide any new information. Ge-dün-drup claims that novelty is suggested by the Sanskrit etymology (*skad dod*) of *pramāṇa: pra* means first and *māṇa* means realization. Hence, valid cognition means new realization.[13] Kay-drup dissents, holding that novelty should not be an issue in defining valid cognition. He gives a different definition: "The defining property of valid cognition is the cognition that is nondeceptive with respect to the object that it [the cognition] realizes by its own power. Accordingly, [Dharmakīrti says] in the *Ascertainment of Valid Cognition:* '[Perception and inference are right cognitions] because they are nondeceptive with respect to the purpose [of the action] when [somebody] engages [in an object] having determined it.'"[14] According to Kay-drup, a valid cognition must be nondeceptive and ascertain its object by its own power; that is, independent of the cognitive content of another cognition. For example, imagine that I see smoke. My visual perception of the smoke will be valid if, and only if, three criteria are satisfied: (a) it correctly identifies the object, (b) the object has the ability to help me to achieve some possible practical result, and (c) the ascertainment is induced by the cognition's own power, not by another cognition (e.g., a memory of smoke).

For Kay-drup, a valid cognition does not require cognitive novelty but independent epistemic access to its object. A visual perception of my rocking chair, for example, accesses its object independent of my previous perception of that chair. A memory of that same chair does not have epistemic independence, for it mechanically repeats a previous cognition. Whether the information is new or not is irrelevant. If a perception sees a chair as it exists, that is, in its momentariness, then this perception is new in each of its moments. But since I am not necessarily aware of the momentary character of my chair, it is misleading to speak of cognitive novelty. If, for a cognition to be valid it must bring entirely new information, then my second moment of perceiving my chair is not valid. As we will see later, Gyel-tsap and most Ge-luk thinkers would support this second opinion.

How does this interpretation compare with its Indian sources?[15] Several passages in Dharmakīrti indicate that he holds that novelty is required for a cognition to be valid. In verse II:3.a. of his *Commentary,* he says: "Since it apprehends what is [already] held, relative [cognition] (*saṃvṛti-jñāna, kun rdzob shes pa*)[16] is not accepted [as a valid cognition]."[17] A relative cognition, that is, a conceptual cognition that does not rely on reasoning, is not valid because it can only repeat what has been already cognized. Thus, if we take this statement literally, a cognition has to apprehend an object not yet apprehended to be a valid cognition. For Dharmakīrti, however, novelty is not part of the definition of valid cognition.

It is simply a consequence of his view of perception. We find confirmation that Dharmakīrti requires novelty in *Drop of Reason*, where he also defines *valid cognition*: "With respect to this, valid cognition is only that which first sees an uncommon object."[18] Dharmakīrti further states that "Because [a recollection] apprehends an [already] completely seen aspect, it is not a valid cognition. [This is so for the following reason:] having seen the uncommon [real thing] one states '[this is] an uncommon thing' [but such a judgment] does not realize any previously unrealized object."[19] As we saw while examining Dharmakīrti's ontology, real things are individual objects that fulfill strict identity conditions explained in terms of spatio-temporal location and entity. These are the objects perception apprehends, a process that in turn induces perceptual judgments. These judgments realize already perceived objects and do not bring any new information to the cognitive process. Hence, they are not valid. Thus, there is clear evidence that for Dharmakīrti validity entails novelty, although novelty is not a definitional requirement for validity.[20]

This similarity with the mainstream of Ge-luk realism, however, should not blind us to the important differences in the epistemologies of antirealist and realist thinkers. The requirement of novelty as stated by Dignāga and Dharmakīrti was not meant to exclude the second moment of perception from being valid but the conceptual judgments that follow perceptions. The Nyāya take such judgments to be perceptual. Hence, their exclusion from validity is important for Dignāga and Dharmakīrti in maintaining the integrity of their system.[21] The definition of *valid cognition* as newly nondeceptive cognition and the discussion of whether the second moment of perception should be excluded from being valid are new developments not directly related to the refutation of the Nyāya view. They signal a paradigmatic shift in Buddhist epistemology.

Tibetan antirealists have noticed this shift and accordingly criticized the intentional view sketched previously, pointing out its discrepancies with the Indian sources it is meant to interpret. The realist intentional emphasis is particularly inappropriate in the case of perception, which cannot be explained in cognitive terms since it has no cognitive content. Therefore, if we look at the differences between Kay-drup's account, which is also defended by Gyel-tsap in his *Essence,* and the other Ge-luk accounts such as Ge-dün-drup's and Gyel-tsap's in *Revealing,* we find this paradoxical situation: The requirement of novelty defended by Gedün-drup is shared by Dharmakīrti but this does not make his view identical to Dharmakīrti's. Whereas the former excludes the second moment of perception from being valid, the latter does not even consider this as a possible issue! Thus, Kay-drup's account is in some way closer to Dharmakīrti, inasmuch as he holds that all perceptions are valid. This closeness, however, is only relative, for both Ge-luk accounts mark the rise of what I will describe as a new Buddhist epistemology, which is meant to solve the intractable difficulties in Dharmakīrti's system. This will become fully apparent when we consider the theory of perception. For the time being, let us examine the Sa-gya antirealist explanations of nondeceptiveness and the issues involved.

A Pragmatist Explanation of Nondeceptiveness

There is little apparent difference between realists and antirealists on this issue. Śākya Chok-den gives the same definition of the object of application as Ge-dün-drup.[22] The similarity is superficial, however, for Śākya Chok-den conceives this type of object not in intentional, but in practical terms. For him the object of application is the object that we can appropriate by relying on a cognition.

Śākya Chok-den differentiates the primary object of a valid cognition, its object of application, from its prima facie object. This object, sometimes called the *object of comprehension* or *appearing object*, is specific to the type of cognition: Real things are objects of comprehension of perception, and universals are objects of comprehension of inference. It is impossible for a conception to comprehend a real thing and equally impossible for a perception to cognize a conceptual construct.[23] This dichotomy makes it difficult, however, for the consistent antirealist to account for inference. If inferences do not comprehend real objects, how can they lead to successful action in the real world? And if they do not, how can they be valid, since pragmatic nondeceptiveness defines *validity*?

To solve this problem, Śākya Chok-den uses the distinction between primary objects of application and prima facie or direct objects. The exclusion of things from being objects of conception is said to concern the prima facie object of valid cognition. It does not apply to the primary object of application. For example, the conception of a chair has a chair as its primary object, but a construct, the universal chairness, as its prima facie object. Dharmakīrti excludes the conception from taking a real chair as its prima facie object. This does not exclude that the real chair is its primary object; that is, its object of application. Thus, all valid cognitions have real things as their objects of application. Dharmakīrti says: "Both [types of] valid cognition [perception and inference] have [real] things as their objects."[24] For a cognition to be valid it must enable us to deal with the real world. A cognition is nondeceptive if it delivers an object in a way that is practically adequate. Thus, a cognition's nondeceptiveness is less the expression of its cognitive apprehension of reality than a function of its causal relation to a real situation. Hence, both perception and inference can be valid, since they both relate to real things and contribute to successful practical action.

In this way, Śākya Chok-den contrasts his pragmatic understanding of nondeceptiveness and application from Cha-ba's intentional interpretation. Whereas the former emphasizes the intentional aspect of consciousness, claiming that a cognition applies to reality only inasmuch as it correctly apprehends it, Śākya Chok-den emphasizes a pragmatic understanding of nondeceptiveness. He agrees with Cha-ba, whose ideas are quite similar to those of Kay-drup or Ge-dün-drup, that a cognition is determined in relation to its object of application. However, he disagrees with Cha-ba's intentional rendering of this object. For Śākya Chok-den, "Such an object of application must be a specifically characterized phenomenon. Moreover, the meaning of being a valid cognition with respect to an object is not the elimination of a superimposition or the realization [of that object]. Rather, it is taken to be the nondeceptiveness with respect to this [object of application]. The meaning of this [nondeceptiveness] is the capacity to obtain this [object]."[25] A cognition is nondeceptive because it stands in appropriate pragmatic relation with reality. For example, the inference that the Vedic language is impermanent does not realize that the language is impermanent. It only understands the concept of impermanence in relation to the Vedic language. Nevertheless, this inference is nondeceptive and, hence, valid. How can it be nondeceptive toward a reality that it does not apprehend?

An inference is based on evidence perceived by the person who makes the inference. In our example, we study the Vedic language and realize that it has been produced. In this way, we are able to infer the impermanence of the Vedic language. This inference is nondeceptive because it is brought about by a perception that relates to reality and leads to further perceptions. Since this inference helps me to relate to these words in the appropriate way, it is nondeceptive. The inference's nondeceptiveness rests on a causal relation with reality through perception and consists of the inference's causal ability to bring about the right outcome. Śākya Chok-den triumphantly summarizes his point: "There is no scriptural [basis] for the explanation of nondeceptiveness [in terms of] realization of an object [for the following reason:] when arguments establishing that this [cognition] is nondeceptive with respect to that [object] are explained in the texts of the Knower of Reasoning (Dharmakīrti), [equivalents such as] obtaining that *(de thob pa),* indirectly relating to that (*de la rgyud nas 'brel ba*), relying upon that (*de la brten pa*), etc., are mentioned. Explanations such as '[this is nondeceptive with respect to that] because this realizes that' are not observed."[26] Cha-ba's interpretation, which is also supported by the Ge-luk tradition, that a cognition's nondeceptiveness consists of its ability to correctly apprehend the object does not correspond to the meaning of Dharmakīrti's texts. He and Dignāga explained nondeceptiveness in pragmatic terms, not in intentional terms. Moreover, argues Śākya Chok-den, Cha-ba's interpretation is unable to explain other difficulties in Dharmakīrti's system. For example, Cha-ba cannot explain how conceptions do not apprehend real objects and yet are valid. A solution is possible only if we think about applicability and nondeceptiveness in pragmatic terms. This, in turn, allows the inclusion of inferences, which do not apprehend reality, among valid cognitions.

A Pragmatic Theory of Truth?

Śākya Chok-den's pragmatic explanation of nondeceptiveness faces an obvious difficulty, for it seems to include among valid cognitions Gettier-like situations that are not valid and yet lead to adequate pragmatic results. In Dharmottara's example, the vision of a mirage that leads to the fortuitous discovery of water must be nondeceptive. And if so, how can we avoid including it among valid cognitions? Are not valid cognitions defined by being nondeceptive?

To this, Śākya Chok-den responds that Dharmottara's vision of the mirage is nondeceptive since it is pragmatically adequate. It is not valid, however, for the favorable pragmatic outcome does not correspond to the person's intentional determination. In our example, the person determined that he saw water, and he was wrong. He just turned out to be lucky. Although, his cognition was nondeceptive, it was not valid. Thus, for Śākya Chok-den, practical success is necessary but not sufficient for determining the validity of a cognition. A normative element is required. A mental state may not be valid just because it produces an adequate pragmatic result. We must evaluate its truth normatively, comparing its intentional determination with the real situation.

For Śākya Chok-den, pragmatic nondeceptiveness is a necessary but not sufficient condition of valid cognition. Based on Dharmakīrti's words in the *Ascertainment,* Śākya Chok-den defines *valid cognition* as "that cognition which is both nondeceptive and newly determines [its object]."[27] A cognition needs to meet three criteria to be valid: (a) nondeceptiveness understood in a practical way, (b) a normative idea of truth relying on the idea of intentionality, and (c) novelty. The first criterion is the most important and represents Dharmakīrti's understanding of nondeceptiveness as explained in *Commentary*, II:1. The second is necessary to avoid Gettier-like cases being included among valid cognitions. The third prevents memory from being included, for memory satisfies the first two criteria.

How does Śākya Chok-den's account compare with other views? I believe that his explanation is quite persuasive. It corresponds quite well to several important elements in Dharmakīrti's own explanation, especially as stated in the later *Ascertainment.* There Dharmakīrti gives an account that clearly parallels criteria (a) and (b) given by Śākya Chok-den. We can also assume that, in *Ascertainment,* Dharmakīrti intends the reader to add the criterion of novelty, which he discusses in other passages. Thus, Śākya Chok-den's account is close to Dharmakīrti's more thoughtful explanations.

Does this account also correspond to what Dharmakīrti had in mind in his earlier *Commentary*? I would argue that it corresponds to Dharmakīrti's pragmatic explanations of nondeceptiveness as stated in *Commentary*, II:1. I would also argue that, given this pragmatic account of nondeceptiveness, Devendrabuddhi's suggestion that we should take Dharmakīrti's two statements in *Commentary* as providing two alternative definitions is philosophically unsound, despite its literal plausibility. For, as we saw, the Gettier-like examples show that practical nondeceptiveness is neither sufficient nor equivalent to intentional normativity. Did Dharmakīrti misspeak when in *Commentary*, II:5 he used the word *or*, thereby suggesting that he is offering an alternative account of valid cognition? Or did he realize only later the problems involved in his earlier statements?

As is often the cases in determining authorial intentions, there is room for ample disagreement among commentators. Whatever the commentarial details, the most important conclusion seems to be the following. A coherent explanation of the validity of cognition must involve both pragmatic and normative dimensions.

Either criterion is a necessary but not a sufficient condition of validity. This is the unanimous opinion of Sa-paṇ and his followers.[28] They all agree that a coherent Dharmakīrtian account cannot avoid the normative, a point sometimes missed by those who described Dharmakīrti as a pragmatist. This is important, for it prevents a possible misunderstanding. Śākya Chok-den's pragmatic description of nondeceptiveness might mislead some into taking his view as implying a pragmatic theory of truth. This is not the case, however, for Śākya Chok-den defends a pragmatic interpretation of *nondeceptiveness*, not a pragmatic theory of *truth*.

In general, modern Buddhist scholars show a tendency to use fashionable philosophical descriptions to interpret the difficult ideas they encounter. I myself am not entirely innocent of such a misdeed. The description of Buddhist views as a form of pragmatism is, however, more than a fashion. It is a long-lasting confusion that needs to be clarified. Even classical scholars such as La Vallée Poussin and Rhys Davids have asserted that Buddhism is pragmatic in its theory of truth. In recent years, Kalupahana has emphasized the empirical and pragmatic aspects of Buddhism and undervalued the importance of tradition as a source of truth.[29] This description is also often applied to Buddhist epistemologists. Potter is ready to apply this description to most Indian philosophers when he asserts that they understand validity (*pramānya*) in terms of workability.[30] Mohanty responds that this is true only of Dignāga, Dharmakīrti, and their followers.[31] I believe that a little care in the use of philosophical vocabulary would clarify the confusion.

It is certainly true that a great emphasis is put on practical concerns in the Buddhist tradition. If the label *pragmatism* is meant to capture this emphasis, this is correct but not very significant. If this label is used with a greater precision, as referring to the positions defended by thinkers such as James, Pierce, or Dewey, I think it does not fit completely Dharmakīrti and his tradition.

One may object that my use of the label *pragmatism* is too restrictive. For example, in recent years Rorty has proposed a form of pragmatism based less on a theory of truth than a rejection of the relevance of such a theory. Rorty holds that the very idea of providing an account of truth and knowledge is an expression of the "Cartesian neurotic quest for certainty."[32] Truth and knowledge have no essence and hence, rather than attempt to define them, we should pay attention to the cultural and political consequences of the accounts we commit ourselves to. As Rorty puts it, "no wholesale constraints derived from the nature of the objects, or of the mind, or of language, but only those retail constraints provided by the remarks of our fellow-inquirers."[33]

Rorty's emphasis on the conventional nature of truth and knowledge raises serious philosophical questions. Can we reject an account of truth as easily as Rorty assumes? Are we not committed by the nature of our conceptual practices to certain accounts of truth? Rorty's view also raises interesting comparative questions. We could wonder, for example, whether such an account is compatible with Candrakīrti's Madhyamaka? One cannot but notice a certain family resemblance between these two thinkers. It is clear, however, that Rorty's new pragmatism is not applicable to Dharmakīrti, for our author takes ontology and the commitments it implies much more seriously than Rorty. Like Quine, Dharmakīrti believes that holding a certain view commits oneself to asserting the existence of certain types of entities. Hence, for Dharmakīrti, Rorty's pragmatic trivialization of the issue of truth and knowledge is not acceptable.

I believe that we, as modern Buddhist scholars, must be careful in our use of labels such as *pragmatist*, *empiricist*, or *deconstructivist*. These descriptions are of limited use for the comparativist, for they do not delineate eternal sides in the philosophical conversations of humankind. More modestly, they describe thinkers who have a substantial shared tradition of common references, concerns, and the like and who are historically connected. For example, it makes sense to describe Pierce, James, Dewey, and Rorty as pragmatists because of their common background and concerns. A term such as *pragmatist* is most useful not as a doxographical description, but as a description of a historically embedded tradition of inquiry. The task of the comparativist is precisely to bridge thinkers who do not share such a continuity.

Such a term is not impossible to use doxographically, but it requires a precise definition. For example, in this work I have used the term *realist* to refer to certain views about universals. Such a use requires great precision and clarity. Similarly, pragmatism can be used meaningfully to refer to a certain view of truth. This view is opposed to a correspondence theory of truth, which asserts that truth is the adequacy of knowledge (or proposition) to reality, and to a coherence theory, which asserts that truth consists in the internal coherence of knowledge. A pragmatist rejects these views to assert that knowledge is true only inasmuch as it leads to adequate pragmatic results. A locus classicus of such a theory is James's assertion that "the true is only the expedient in our way of thinking, just as the right is only the convenient in our way of behaving."[34]

If *pragmatism* is defined as a particular philosophical position rather than as an historically embedded tradition of inquiry, it appears that Dharmakīrti in his most mature account is not a pragmatist or at least that he should not be if he wants to remain consistent. He does not hold that "the rational purport of a word or other expression, lies exclusively in its conceivable bearing upon the conduct of life,"[35] the definition that Pierce gives of *pragmatism*. Although Dharmakīrti insists on the practical bearings of knowledge and language, he does not insist that their meanings come exclusively from practical concerns. Knowledge functions in relation to practical concerns, but its criteria are not exclusively pragmatic. Nondeceptiveness may be purely pragmatically understood, but in this case it cannot by itself constitute validity. Dharmakīrti's point is quite straightforward: Statements or cognitions that are true are useful and, therefore, nondeceptive. They are not, however, valid simply because they are useful. Jayatilleke makes a similar distinction in the context of early Buddhism: "We may conclude from this that the truths of Buddhism were also considered to be useful (atthasaṃhitaṃ) for each person until one attains salvation. . . . We may sum this up by saying that the truths of Buddhism were considered to be pragmatic in the Buddhist sense of the term, but it does not mean that Early Buddhism believes in a pragmatic theory of truth."[36] To put

Jayatilleke's point in a slightly different way, the depiction of Buddhism as pragmatic comes from a confusion between practical and pragmatic. Buddhism certainly insists on the practical consequences of knowledge, but a similar insistence is found in the Nyāya and other Indian traditions. This practical emphasis is different from a pragmatic theory of truth, according to which the expression "this is true" is interpreted as meaning "this leads to the appropriate results." In such a theory, the obtention of appropriate pragmatic results is not only a necessary but a sufficient condition of truth. I would argue that this pragmatic view differs from Dharmakīrti's, at least in his more lucid moments. I believe that Sa-gya commentators are quite right to emphasize that a cogent account of truth in Dharmakīrti's tradition requires both pragmatic and normative elements. Does this mean that they are committed to a so-called correspondence theory of truth?

To answer such a question would require that we clarify the meaning of such a theory. Considerable disagreement surrounds the meaning of such a theory or even whether there is such a theory. This is obviously not the place to enter into this discussion. If one understands such a theory to posit truth as a metaphysical correspondence between concepts and a reality determinable in abstraction from any conceptual scheme, then Dharmakīrti is not committed to such a theory. This is so because it makes no sense in Dharmakīrti's system to discuss reality in abstraction of any conceptual framework. Although such a reality exists, our concepts cannot capture it. Perception has access to such a reality, but it provides no cognitive content, as we will discover when we investigate Dharmakīrti's theory of perception. Hence, Dharmakīrtians are not committed to a correspondence theory of truth, at least as understood in the metaphysical sense, despite their acceptance of a normative theory of truth.

Reductionism and Intentionality

This explanation of valid cognition presents a plausible and coherent account of valid cognition. It does raise a question, however. If Dharmakīrti wants to introduce a normative element, why does he insist on the practical element when explaining nondeceptiveness? Why does he not just present a normative account? This is the view of most Ge-luk authors. For example, Ge-dün-drup describes nondeceptiveness in purely cognitive terms with no reference to a pragmatic dimension. Why can Dharmakīrti not accept such a simple and elegant account?

The answer has to do with the central issue of this book, the problem of universals and the difficulties raised by Dharmakīrti's antirealism. To illustrate this point, a Western parallel may be useful. In recent years, Quine has proposed an account of knowledge called *naturalized epistemology*.[37] Instead of speaking of knowledge in normative terms, Quine proposes that knowledge consists of appropriate stimuli responses. An object gives rise to a representation to which I assent in the appropriate way. A belief is not true because it is rationally warranted or justified but because it has the appropriate causal relation with its object. For a belief to be true has nothing to do with any intentional notion such the right mental content but is entirely a function of the causal chain in which this belief stands.

For Quine, this program has several goals. On the one side, Quine is a materialist who wants to eliminate our confused mental terminology (sometimes called *folk psychology*) and substitute for it well-established scientific notions. In this, Quine has little in common with Dharmakīrti, who is certainly no materialist. Quine is also, however, quite close to nominalism in his suspicion of any intentional account, which introduces a normative dimension that is difficult to account for in an antirealist philosophy.[38] Let us go back to our earlier example: We see a cow and think "this is a cow." Inasmuch as this belief refers to an individual, it can can be thought to stand in a causal relation to that individual. But the belief is not reducible to this causal relation. I see the same individual and think "this is a horse." The causal connection, which existed in the first case, is still there. Why is this second belief not true then? Because, answers Quine, it does not stand in the appropriate causal relation with its object.

This is where Quine's program of naturalized epistemology gets in trouble, as Putnam has convincingly shown. For, the introduction of a factor of "appropriateness" smuggles back the intentional element that Quine's program was meant to eliminate in the first place. What does it mean for a belief to stand in the appropriate causal relation with its object? In our example, the first belief stands in an appropriate relation with its object because there is an intentional "fit" between reality and what we think. There are many ways to spell out this "fitness" between mind and reality. I can say that my mental content corresponds to the real situation or that my mental state captured a property. I can also speak of a warranted belief or having the right concept, and so on. These descriptions are not equivalent, but they come to the same point: It is not possible to explain the difference between beliefs (a) and (b) without introducing a normative element.[39]

The normative element is described in many ways by philosophers. Plato speaks of ideas; Aristotle, of forms; Uddyotakara, of kinds; Dharmakīrti, of unreal universals; Kay-drup, of real universals; Wittgenstein, of rules and procedures; Sellars, of dispositions; and so forth. These descriptions are certainly not identical, but they are all attempts to capture the same normative element we examined when we introduced the problem of universals. In fact, a large part of the history of philosophy in the so-called East and West consists of never completely successful and yet always repeated attempts to capture this normative dimension. The reason for the elusiveness is that normativity is not reducible to temporal individual realities. In our examples, belief (a) is right because it fits with a norm, which goes beyond the present situation. Without such a time-neutral element, however one wants to describe it, we would be reduced to what Putnam calls the *solipsism of the present moment*.[40] Without a normative dimension, our statements would be reduced to being mere noises and our cognitive states would be no more than acceptance or rejection of such noises in the present moment.

Dharmakīrti understands the necessity of positing such a normative dimension. As a thinker steeped in the study of the meaningfulness of language, he realizes that we cannot give an account of language in terms of individuals. Without universals, language becomes a succession of meaningless noises. And yet, universals are troubling fellows. They do not follow Dharmakīrti's identity conditions. They are not determined in a spatio-temporal location. Neither are they determined in their entity. For example, cowness is neither brown, nor white, and so on. In short, it is not an individual. But what is it then? To be consistent with this antirealist ontology, Dharmakīrti ought to give an account of thought and language based on causal relations with individuals. And yet, he knows that this will not work. He sees that this is a self-refuting enterprise, if there ever was one. In short, he cannot do without universals. Hence, he reintroduces them as valid fictions, thus introducing an element of normativity.

This normative element is, however, limited to the conceptual domain. For, normativity derives from unreal universals. Hence, normativity is the domain of thought only and has no direct relation to real things. Real things are apprehended by the other type of valid cognition, perception. This latter type of cognition cannot, however, be appraised in normative terms in isolation from conception. As we will see later, perception has no cognitive content but just puts us in contact with bare reality. This, as we will also see, is a necessary consequence of Dharmakīrti's antirealism combined with his view that perception is undistorted. Since it accurately reflects reality and since reality is reducible to bare particulars, perception cannot provide any cognitive articulation and boils down to a passive encounter with things in their momentariness.

Dharmakīrti's theory of valid cognition is meant to account for the validity of both types of cognition. It must account for perception, which is the foundation of knowledge. Perception's validity is hard to account for, however, in cognitive terms, since this cognition is contentless. Hence, it is better appraised in pragmatic terms. Perception is valid in that it leads to appropriate results. This is not, however, sufficient, since this would include Gettier-like cases. To exclude them, Dharmakīrti needs to add a normative criterion. This criterion cannot be met, however, by perception itself, but only by conceptual judgments induced by perception. Perception passively holds an object that is categorized by conceptions. Only this latter type of cognition can provide the normative element we discussed. This is why Dharmakīrti says: "[Perception and inference are valid cognitions] because they are nondeceptive with respect to the purpose [of the action] in the application [toward an object] after having determined it."[41] I take this to be Dharmakīrti's final statement about the nature of valid cognition, as explained by Śākya Chok-den. A cognition is valid if, and only if, it has the ability to bring about some possible practical results in accordance with the intentional determination of the appropriated object. This determination is normative in that it refers to standards that allow us to decide whether this cognition is correct or not. This normative element, however, is not part of the fabric of reality. It comes from our conceptual frameworks, which arise as the result of our experiences. Hence, the normative element is not arbitrary or purely a priori. Nevertheless, it is not dictated by reality itself.

Dharmakīrti's system is based on the strict dichotomy between the perceptual and the conceptual viewpoints. This duality is fundamental, for it reflects the ontological difference between the real and the conceptual domains and the ways in which these two domains can be appropriated. As in any other epistemological system, a central element of this system is the explanation of the nature of knowledge. For Dharmakīrti, such an account must include both perception and conception. In doing so, Dharmakīrti cannot avoid taking either of the two standpoints existing in his system. In his first account (*Commentary*, II:1), Dharmakīrti takes the standpoint of perception, showing that it is valid inasmuch as it is pragmatically nondeceptive. This account also includes inference but only from the perceptual standpoint. That is, according to this first account, inference is valid inasmuch as it leads to appropriate results. Dharmakīrti's second account (*Commentary*, II:5) views validity from a conceptual standpoint. In doing so, Dharmakīrti provides a cognitive and normative account of knowledge. A cognition is valid inasmuch as it reveals a hitherto unknown object. This account includes perception. A perception is valid inasmuch as it reveals an object. Since perception does not have any cognitive content, its revealing is limited to inducing the right kind of conceptualization. This is the second way of accounting for the validity of cognitions. In his later *Ascertainment,* Dharmakīrti seems to bring together these two standpoints. In doing so, however, he has to take either of the two standpoints. In accordance with his antirealism and the foundational role of perception in his system, he chooses the real-perceptual perspective, but adds a normative dimension.

This explanation of Dharmakīrti's accounts of valid cognition may strike the reader as rather different from the one given by other scholars. In the preceding chapter, we saw Katsura's explanation of Dharmakīrti's two accounts. For him the first reflects a conceptual standpoint and the second reflects a perceptual one. Thus, his account and mine seem to be contradictory. Whereas Katsura holds the first account to be conceptual and the second to be perceptual, I hold the opposite view. The reason for his view is the following. According to Dharmakīrti's first account, nondeceptiveness is established in relation to objects of practical concerns, the objects of application understood practically. These objects are real and their links with valid cognitions are causal. This causal link between real objects and cognitions ensures that the appropriation of real objects remains in touch with reality. But, can we really say that a cognition appropriates a real object? The problem with this account is that it contradicts a fundamental point of Buddhist ontology, as pointed out by Lo Ken-chen.[42] The practical appropriation of an object presupposes that this object has some duration. We cannot appropriate an infinitesimal moment. Thus, appropriation concerns only objects of commonsense and excludes real objects, which are a succession of infinitesimal moments. As such, real objects cannot be appropriated. It is only under their conceptual descriptions that they can become objects of practical concern. Descriptions, however, are conceptual and do not capture reality. Thus, it looks as if the pragmatic nondeceptiveness, which Dharmakīrti places at the center of his ontology and epistemology, cannot encompass the real.

Śākya Chok-den deals with the problem by describing the object of nondeceptiveness as a "specifically characterized phenomenon together with its continuum."[43] Things are the objects of application of cognitions only inasmuch as they endure. That is, real things are not objects of application in and of themselves, but they are so under certain conceptual descriptions. Thus, Dharmakīrti's description of cognitions as appropriating objects is a conceptual description of the cognitive process, which, for Śākya Chok-den, is to be understood in causal terms. Realizing this point, Katsura takes Dharmakīrti's pragmatic account of validity to reflect a conceptual standpoint. Following Śākya Chok-den, I take Dharmakīrti's pragmatic account to be a convenient description of the cognitive process made from the point of view of perception. To say that a cognition is pragmatically nondeceptive with respect to a jar, for instance, is a convenient description of a causal process involving the interaction of infinitesimal moments of matter and awareness. Since Dharmakīrti's pragmatic account does not explicitly involve a universal, it reflects reality; and his cognitive account reflects a conceptual standpoint. Who is right?

I believe that we are both right in a certain way, for our differences come less from a misunderstanding of Dharmakīrti than from an attempt to struggle with the problems raised by the radical dichotomy between real and conceptual domains. This is the basis of Dharmakīrti's system as well as its fundamental problem. To give an account of knowledge, Dharmakīrti must be able to bring together the two halves of the dichotomy. But, far from succeeding, Dharmakīrti seems only to reduplicate the basic dichotomy. Dharmakīrti tries to solve his problem by the concept of *arthakriyā*, a term that, as we saw earlier, is ambiguous, for it designates both the causal abilities of things and their practical functions.[44] These two connotations, however, do not go together. Whether *arthakriyā* in its former sense refers to real things, its latter meaning is limited to the conceptual way of understanding things. Thus, the basic dichotomy between the real and the conceptual is reduplicated by Dharmakīrti when he describes the real. Only the ambiguity of the concept of *arthakriyā* masks Dharmakīrti's inability to escape from the problems created by his overly dichotomous system.

Hence, neither Katsura, who describes Dharmakīrti's pragmatic nondeceptiveness in conceptual terms, nor I, who describe nondeceptiveness in causal terms, is wrong. Both descriptions capture one half of the concept of *arthakriyā* and its epistemological use. Katsura's description of the cognitive nature of cognitions as reflecting a real standpoint is not wrong, for inasmuch as a cognitive content is correct it must reflect reality. Since only perception reflects reality, it is quite logical to think about the cognitive content as deriving from perception, as Katsura does. This solution, however, is problematic, for perception provides nothing more than a passive encounter with reality. Cognitive content comes from conception. Hence, my description of the intentional nature of cognitions as being conceptual is quite justified, for it captures the requirement that any cognitive content must refer to some norm and as such can be only conceptual.

In the following chapters, I further explore the inconsistencies of Dharmakīrti's dichotomous system. In particular, I focus on Dharmakīrti's attempts to join the two halves of his system. This endeavor is essential for the success of his system. As we just saw, an account of the validity of cognitions requires a normative element, which perception cannot provide. It also requires a relation with reality so that normative concepts can be connected with the real. Conception alone cannot provide such a link. Hence, Dharmakīrti's only solution is to coordinate the real-perceptual and conceptual halves of his system, which are powerless in isolation to account for *pramāṇa,* the central topic of Dharmakīrti's work.

The next chapter will deal with this problem from the conceptual angle. I will analyze how Dharmakīrti brings normativity, which is conceptual, back in touch with reality. This is not a small problem, for conceptual validity is not easy to explain. Since universals are all equally unreal, how can one concept be more appropriate to the situation than another? Let us examine Dharmakīrti's famous answer through an example that has challenged the imaginative verve of his commentators. In the process, we will see the problems of this answer. This will provide a justification for the revisions proposed by Buddhist realists, who want to establish a connection between thought and reality stronger than antirealism would allow.

18

Can Inference Be Valid?

Dharmakīrti on the Validity of Thought

The problem of the validity of thought is one of the central difficulties of Dharmakīrti's system. Thought provides the normative and cognitive element in Dharmakīrti's epistemology. Thought is also, however, mistaken and cut off from reality, since it apprehends only conceptual constructs, which do not really exist. How can concepts provide a normative dimension, since they do not seem to have any bearing on reality? Dharmakīrti's answer is mostly practical and conventional. Concepts are valid inasmuch as they are pragmatically useful mistakes. Dharmakīrti replies to an objection that, if conceptuality is distorted, it cannot help us appropriate real things: "All [conventions] about things depend on mutually nonidentical [things]. Therefore, they are eliminative subjects and are related to things. [These conventions] are the basis [on which one can] obtain things just as the aforementioned[1] inference. Although other, that is, [nonfactual conceptions] are similar inasmuch as they are distorted, they [differ inasmuch as they] do not [deliver things], just like [trying to find] jewels from [the clue provided by] the light of a lamp."[2] For Dharmakīrti, the practical validity of concepts derives not from a pre-established harmony, but because we form concepts by being exposed to experience. By using conventions derived from our experiences, we can achieve our practical ends. Conceptual cognitions are pragmatically nondeceptive since they lead to practical success.

Nondeceptiveness does not come about because conceptions reflect reality accurately, for inferences are mistaken (*bhrānta, 'khrul pa*), but because of their causal connection with reality via perception. We must distinguish between nondeceptiveness (*avisaṃvādi, mi slu ba*), which is a function of the appropriate causal relation that a cognition has with reality, and nonmistakenness (*abhrānta, ma 'khrul ba*), which is a function of the cognition's accurate apprehension of things as they are.[3] An erroneous conception, such as the apprehension of smoke as permanent, and an inference[4] do not differ in their inability to provide an adequate representation of reality. In this respect, both fail. Where they differ is in their connection with reality. The conception of smoke as permanent is the result of inner mistaken tendencies, rather than that of experience. Hence, we cannot achieve our goals by relying on the idea that smoke is permanent. By contrast, the inference of the existence of fire on seeing smoke has an adequate connection with reality. It is formed on the basis of successful experiences and leads to further success. Hence, it is nondeceptive. The practical validity of inference is a function of its relation to perception, which in turn is connected to reality.[5]

Dharmakīrti illustrates his point by a double example: the apprehension of the light of a lamp as being taken as a jewel and the apprehension of the light of a jewel as being taken as a jewel.[6] The first example illustrates how a conception can be wrong: If we mistake the light of a lamp for an actual jewel, no useful result can be expected. Misled by a partial similarity, we project inappropriate concepts.[7] Dharmakīrti says: "When [one sees] the glitter of a jewel, one rushes [impelled] by the belief that [this is] a jewel. Although both [cognitions][8] are equally wrong, there is a difference in [their ability] to perform a function."[9] This unusual example has excited the imagination and exegetical skill of commentators. Let us examine Go-ram-ba's summary of the different positions in turn.[10] He distinguishes three interpretations: one can take Dharmakīrti's example to be about (1) an inference, (2) a perception, or (3) a wrong cognition.

1. According to Go-ram-ba, Dharmakīrti's direct disciple Devendrabuddhi and his student Śākyabuddhi hold that Dharmakīrti's example as well as its meaning concerns the validity of inference. The example is an inference from effect to cause: We infer the presence of a jewel from the light of that jewel. The light is the evidence that indicates the presence of the cause, the jewel. This example illustrates, according to this interpretation, the more general point that inference is nondeceptive despite being mistaken (since it does not apprehend real individual objects but only unreal constructs).[11]

2. According to Go-ram-ba, the later commentator Prajñākaragupta holds the example to be a perception of the light of a jewel as an actual jewel. The example illustrates the validity of inference by comparing inference to a perception that is partially mistaken, but practically nondeceptive. Kay-drup disagrees with this rendering of this second interpretation, for he thinks that it is unlikely that an accomplished thinker such as Prajñākaragupta would take as perception a mental episode apprehending a glitter as an actual jewel. According to Kay-drup, Prajñākaragupta's position is that the example refers to the perception holding the glitter and inducing the inference of the presence of the jewel. Kay-drup holds that, in fact, Devendrabuddhi, Śākyabuddhi, and Prajñākaragupta explain Dharmakīrti's example in the same way.[12]

3. According to Go-ram-ba, Dharmottara takes the example to involve a comparison between the pragmatic value of an erroneous cognition (*log shes*) and that of an inference. When we see the glowing light of a jewel, we think "this is a jewel." This is a mistake, however, for the light of a jewel is not a real jewel. Nevertheless, if we act on our mistake, we can obtain the real jewel. Similarly, inference is pragmatically valid. Although both inference and wrong conception are mistaken, since they apprehend constructed properties that are not part of the fabric of reality, they can be the support of successful practical actions.[13]

Go-ram-ba criticizes (1) for not fitting the example closely enough. The inference of the light of a jewel does not match the example, which requires holding the glitter to be an actual jewel. An inference does not hold the glitter to be an actual jewel, for then it would be a false conception. Moreover, he says, the example of an inference does not answer the opponent's objections to which Dharmakīrti is responding in the text. The adversary is arguing that since all inferences are mistaken they cannot be valid. It would not be convincing to argue that inference in general is valid because some particular inferences are valid, for this is precisely what the adversary denies![14]

Against (2) Go-ram-ba argues that a perception also does not fit the example because a perception does not hold the glitter to be a jewel. The perception of a jewel's glitter is no more the perception of a jewel than the vision of a coiled rope is the perception of a snake. If the example is about the judgment induced by the perception, then it is not about a perception but about a wrong conception.[15] This is indeed, according to Go-ram-ba, what the example is about.

Following Dharmottara, Go-ram-ba explains that if we were to see the glitter through the chink of a door, we might react in different ways. The careful person understands that this is not a real jewel but may indicate the presence of a jewel. Others might get excited and think that there really is a jewel. Such a conception can lead to successful action despite being erroneous. For Go-ram-ba, the apprehension of a jewel with respect to a jewel's glitter is no less erroneous than a similar apprehension with respect to a lamp's light. They are equally mistaken. They are also equally unable by themselves to cause us to obtain a real jewel. What then is the difference between valid and nonvalid conceptions? Go-ram-ba answers: "Although the inference realizing the impermanence of sound and the wrong apprehension of sound as permanent are equally mistaken, there is a difference in their being valid cognitions or not. For example, the mind that apprehends a jewel's glitter as a jewel and the mind that apprehends a lamp's light as a jewel are equally wrong cognitions. Nevertheless, there is a difference in their being [able] or not to support further valid cognitions [enabling one] to appropriate their objects of application. Such is the unequaled thought of [Dharmakīrti's] root text. Let the ones who rely on the meaning investigate."[16] Despite the puzzling details of Dharmakīrti's example, the gist of his answer is clear: The only factor that differentiates the conceptions we hold to be factual from others is their practical success. This success consists of its capacity to bring forth a more valid mode of cognition; namely, perception. Valid conceptions, that is, inferences, allow us to gain experience of things as they are through perception.

We are now able to explain in relation to inference what Dharmakīrti means when he describes valid cognitions as being "nondeceptive with respect to the purpose [of the action] in the application [toward an object] after having determined it."[17] Let us take the example of the inference of the presence fire from the presence of smoke. This determination is valid, not because it truly mirrors reality, but because it relates adequately to the perceptions of smoke and fire. It is caused by the perception of smoke and leads to the perception of fire. These relations to perception make the conceptual determination of an object adequate.

A Major Difficulty in Dharmakīrti's System

This explanation, however, creates serious difficulties within Dharmakīrti's system that we already alluded to. Being produced by perception and in turn producing further perceptions cannot ensure that our concepts are in touch with reality. Perception can give rise to right as well as wrong conceptions. For example, we may see a mountain several times and notice minute changes. From this experience we may infer (a) the mountain is impermanent since it changes and (b) the mountain is permanent since it has not changed for the most part. Both cognitions (the second is not called *inference* in Indian epistemology since it is faulty) are caused equally by valid experience. Both may lead to further valid perceptions. How can we distinguish the first valid inference from the latter conception, which from a Buddhist point of view has no validity whatsoever?

Although Dharmakīrti's introduction of a causal link with reality is meant to account for the objectivity of our conceptual activities, it does not explain how conceptions operate nonrandomly. We need something more that allows us to distinguish (a) from (b). We could look at the kind of relation involved in both cases. We could say that in case (a) the relation is adequate, whereas in (b) it is not. But what do we mean by *adequate*? This is where the normative must be introduced, for there is no way to specify the type of relation needed independent of intentionally determined norms. Those norms, however, do not exist in reality but derive from our conceptual framework. How can they help us to cope with reality?

Dharmakīrti's solution is to coordinate perception and conception. The former provides the contact with reality. The latter provides the norm. Together, they allow us to distinguish truth from falsity. In (a), the relation is adequate because there is a fit between the way things exist and our conceptual determination. In (b) such a fit is missing. This solution is, however, far from obvious, since they do not apprehend the same object. Dharmakīrti explains: "All the cognitions generated from the sense bases have as their object individuations (*viśeṣa, khyad par*). It is impossible for words to relate to these individuations."[18] Language, and hence thought, can directly bear only on unreal conceptual contents. It does not apply directly to the reality given to sense perception. On the other hand, perception does not apprehend unreal universals. Hence, the epistemological gap between perception and conception is radical. How can they be coordinated?

A possible answer could be to posit that an appropriate connection between the two takes place when they relate to an object of application common to both. Perception apprehends this real object and conception applies to it, although it does not apprehend it. In this way, perception and conception can be matched, since they relate to the same real object. This solution, however, just postpones the problem, for the supposedly common object is apprehended differently by perception and conception. Whereas the former apprehends the real object, the latter is limited to an unreal universal. What then guarantees that conceptions apply to real objects that they never grasp? We are caught in a vicious circle.

A similar conclusion is reached upon investigating the normativity required for knowledge and truth. A normative dimension is not found in perception, which is without cognitive content, but in the concepts constructed by thought. Thought, however, is mistaken, since it apprehends unreal constructs. How can its norms be true? Dharmakīrti answers through the example of the jewel. Though mistaken, thought is valid inasmuch as it leads to perception, which is unmistaken. But perception does not provide much in terms of knowledge and truth. It is the foundation of knowledge but it is not cognitive in and of itself. It induces only conceptual categorization, which provides the cognitive dimension. Hence, we are back to the conceptual domain. This is what I perceive to be the greatest difficulty in Dharmakīrti's system. To answer the charge that the denial of real universals makes conceptuality arbitrary he needs to link concepts to reality. To do this he needs to stitch back together the two halves of his system, the real-perceptual and the conceptual. He needs to coordinate perception and conception, providing a synthesis between the two types of knowledge. His system, however, seems to exclude such a possibility, since these two types of cognition are limited to radically different types of object. This is the problem described by Sa-paṇ through a pithy expression: how to coordinate blind conception and dumb perception.

There is here an obvious parallel with Kant's statement that intuitions without concepts are blind and concepts without content (i.e., intuition) are empty.[19] For Kant, sensible intuition (Dharmakīrti's perception) does not provide any cognitive content. Hence, it is blind. Similarly, concepts divorced from the contact with reality provided by sensation are without cognitive content. Knowledge comes only through the synthesis of sensation and understanding (Dharmakīrti's inference). The parallel between Sa-paṇ's formulation of Dharmakīrti and Kant's formula must, however, be properly understood. The similarity between the two thinkers concerns the problem they face, not their solutions. They both understand that bare sensation does not provide any cognitive content, which comes from concepts. Their common problem is how to coordinate sensation and thought, which are powerless in isolation from each other. Kant solves the difficulty by providing a model of knowledge in which the two types of knowledge, sensation and understanding, are coordinated to synthesize increasingly abstract objects of knowledge. Senses provide the material that is integrated in ever more abstract cognitive schemes by the understanding. In the process, we come to grasp an already categorically articulated phenomenal reality.

In contrast, Dharmakīrti does not find it possible to synthesize perception and conception. By virtue of his typology of valid cognition, Dharmakīrti refuses to conflate the two types of valid cognition and their objects. He is committed to limiting conception to unreal universals and perception to real individuals. Hence, conceptions cannot organize the sensory material delivered by the senses. They are limited to conceptual constructs that are induced by perception but remain separate from it. This is well captured by Sa-paṇ's description of dumb perception and blind conception. But here I am running ahead of myself, for to tackle this problem we will need to examine Dharmakīrti's theory of perception. For the time being, let me sketch out another response to this problem, that of the Buddhist realist. To account for the necessity to link thought and reality and justify a normative dimension, Buddhist realists offer their often tortuous reinterpretations of Dharmakīrti. This realism finds its epistemological expression in two important moves that transform the basic terms of the system:

1. One way to justify conceptuality and its relation to perception is to break the isolation of thought and assert that conceptions relate to reality, albeit differently from perception.
2. The second way is to transform the meaning of perception, so that it can provide an articulation of reality grasped and elaborated by conceptions.

These two moves constitute what I describe as a *new epistemology*, which I see beginning in India with thinkers such as Dharmottara and Mokṣākaragupta and continuing in Tibet with the tradition of Ngok and Cha-ba. Although these two moves go in the same direction, they do not entail each other logically. Thus, Dharmottara seems to adopt the second without the first. Moreover, despite these two views being consequences of a realism regarding universals, they do not necessarily entail such an ontology. Mokṣākaragupta argues for the latter move when he asserts that universals are indirectly perceived by perception, without drawing the realist consequences of his assertion.[20] Nevertheless, both historically and philosophically, these two epistemological moves often have been associated with a realist ontology. In Tibet, Cha-ba and his followers assert the reality of universals as a basis for their new epistemology. Within the Ge-luk tradition, both points have been defended in relation to a realist ontology.

When Dzong-ka-ba discusses this crucial point in Dharmakīrti's thought, he raises two sets of questions, which he polemically designates the qualms raised by "those with searching minds" (*rtog ldan*) and those raised by "unsubtle minds" (*blo mi zhi ba*).[21] The first group notices the major problem created by Dharmakīrti's description of conceptuality, without interpreting Dharmakīrti as an antirealist. The second group raises similar questions, but rushes to adopt the antirealist interpretation that Dzong-ka-ba finds objectionable.

The problems raised by Dzong-ka-ba have occupied us throughout this work: Dharmakīrti's thought seems to deny the reality of universals, making it impossible to establish a viable epistemology. In particular, if one holds that universals, which are the contents of thought, are unreal, then it becomes difficult to explain how reality can be understood by thought. If, on the other hand, one holds that the objects of thought are real, then how can one avoid falling into the reification of abstract entities?[22] The Ge-luk tradition attempts to solve this quandary by elaborating one of the distinctions used to support its realist interpretation.

A Realist Answer

The first key epistemological move made by the realists is to break the isolation of thought by reinterpreting the concept of the object of thought. This reinterpretation concerns two types of object, the appearing object (*snang yul*) or its equivalent, the held object (*gzung yul*), and the object of application (*'jug yul*). These concepts, which can be traced back to Dharmottara, have been stressed by Tibetan epistemologists as part of an elaborate typology of object, which we will examine later, first proposed by Cha-ba. They are meant to account for and underline the cognitive aspect of cognition, the fact that consciousness reveals objects.

For Cha-ba and his followers, this explanation plays a particularly important role in their epistemology, for it provides a way to strengthen the connection between thought and reality. Thus, the intentional interpretation of the object of application examined earlier and the explanations of the concept of appearing object that follow are intended as realist explanations of how thought apprehends reality. According to this account, the conception of my rocking chair, for example, is not strictly enclosed in the realm of concepts, as antirealists maintain. Although this conception primarily apprehends the object universal of chair, it also applies to a real chair. Antirealists agree with this last statement but understand it in pragmatic terms. My thought of a chair applies practically to a real chair. By contrast, Cha-ba understands application in intentional terms. That is, the thought of a chair applies to the real chair in that it apprehends it. In this way, Cha-ba and his disciples offer a realist explanation of the relation between thought and reality. Instead of being limited to unreal constructs, thought is said to apprehend reality itself through the mediation of constructs.

This description of thinking, which is in accordance with commonsense, raises difficult interpretive questions within Dharmakīrti's tradition, which strongly emphasizes the distorted nature of conceptuality. If it is true that thought is mistaken in its apprehension of its objects, how can we still maintain that it apprehends reality? Moreover, how can we make this explanation compatible with Dharmakīrti's assertion that thought's apprehension does not mirror reality?

Following Cha-ba, Tibetan realists have attempted to resolve this difficulty by a complicated scholastic analysis of the concept of appearance that rests on the distinction between appearance (*snang ba*) and the appearing object (*snang yul*). According to this analysis, both perception and conception have their appearing objects: Whereas real things (both individuals and properties) are the appearing objects of perception, conceptual entities (object universals) are those of conception. In the latter case, a distinction must be made between appearance and the appearing object. Kay-drup describes this appearing object as the direct object of thought: "The held object of conceptual thought is that object that appears to a conceptual thought as if it existed in front of us. Moreover, it is the object that appears continuously as an object universal. Therefore, from the point of view of conception, the appearing and held objects are only objects [indicated by] words (*sgra don, śabdārtha*)."[23] The appearance of an object to a conceptual mental episode is a conceptual construct. It appears as the real object, but in reality is just the object universal (also characterized as an object [indicated] by words) previously described.[24] This is identified technically as the appearing object (*snang yul*) and recognized by Tibetan realists as unreal. This recognition does not entail that whatever appears to a conceptual mental episode must be unreal. The notion of something appearing to a conceptual state of mind is a complex notion in which two elements have to be distinguished: the appearance itself, that is, the object universal, which is the appearing object, and the object that appears.

The appearing object of a conception (*rtog pa'i snang yul*), understood in a technical sense, is necessarily unreal. It must be distinguished from the real object that appears to that conception (*yul de rtog pa la snang ba*). Accordingly, a jar, for example, appears to a conceptual cognition but is not its appearing object, which is the object universal of the jar. This artificial distinction is made to conciliate the Ge-luk view of thought and language as partially reflecting reality with Dharmakīrti's assertion that thought does not take real things as its objects of comprehension (*meya, gzhal bya*).[25] According to this interpretation, Dharmakīrti did not intend to exclude that real things appear to thought but only that they are their appearing objects in the technical sense of the word. Only object universals are the appearing objects of conceptual thought. Real entities are not appearing objects of thought even though they appear to it.

A conceptual consciousness cannot make such a distinction, because a conceptual thought is inherently mistaken with respect to its appearing object (*snang yul*). Thought cannot ascertain its own appearance, which is the object universal of the object that it conceives, because it is mistaken with respect to it. How are we aware of this conceptual appearance? Gyel-tsap answers that this is not a result of the thought itself but of its self-cognition, for the conceptual appearance is implicitly determined by self-cognition. Referring to Dharmakīrti's description of ascertaining consciousness (*Commentary*, I:57), Gyel-tsap says: "Those who hold that this passage teaches that in our system the held object of an ascertaining consciousness must be [its] object of ascertainment have not understood anything of this topic, because the Logician [Dharmakīrti] has repeatedly asserted that the held object of a conceptual cognition is the object of comprehension of a self-cognition, which is a perception."[26] The held object of thought is not ascertained by thought, which apprehends the external object via this object, but by its self-cognition, which implicitly identifies it while explicitly experiencing the thought.

Since it is mistaken, thought cannot correctly identify this appearance. This does not mean that a conceptual consciousness is completely mistaken. Although it is mistaken inasmuch as it does not distinguish the two aforementioned appearances, it is not mistaken with respect to the object it conceives (*zhen yul*), here, a jar. Although a conceptual appearance appears to such a consciousness as being a jar, this consciousness does not apprehend such an appearance as being a jar. Otherwise, such a consciousness would be completely mistaken to the extent of being an example of wrong cognition.[27] The distortion imposed by conceptual thought is in the appearance of the object, not in the object conceived by thought.

Kay-drup says: "A conceptual consciousness relates to [literally, engages in] an external jar by conceiving [its object] in reference to the appearance [of something] as a jar. [Such a consciousness] does not relate [to its object] through conceiving the appearance [of something] as jar as [being] a jar."[28] We do not think of the appearance as being a jar, but rather, we think of a jar on the basis of a confusion between the appearance, that is, the object universal, and the real thing. This confusion is described as the "mixing of appearance and denomination as [being] one" (*snang btags gcig tu 'dres*).[29] The word *appearance* refers to the real object such as a jar as it appears to perception. *Denomination* refers to the object [indicated by] words, the object universal. Conception apprehends the object delivered by perception through concepts. In this way, the manifold is organized in conceptual patterns. In doing so, thought does not take the conceptual content for the real thing, but, rather apprehends the real thing by using the conceptual construct.

This explanation partially differs from what Dharmakīrti seems to have in mind. For him, the distortion of thought does not lie just in the appearance of its object but in the way in which it conceives its object. A conception of a jar, for instance, is not mistaken just because the appearance of a jar appears as a real jar, but because it conceives of a particular object as instantiating a general property. For Ge-luk thinkers, this is not a mistake, since such a particular does instantiate such a property. Accordingly, thought relates to real phenomena, which appear to it. For example, the conception of a jar is not just dealing with a self-constructed concept, but with the real fact of being a jar (*bum pa dngos gnas pa*). This insistence that thought is in contact, albeit in a distorted way, with reality is a natural consequence of the realism of the Ge-luk tradition. Since some universals are real and since thought determines them, thought is not completely cut off from reality, as asserted by antirealists. Ge-luk thinkers are unanimous in agreeing with Gyel-tsap that real things appear to thought as well as to perception, albeit in a different way. Answering the objection that if specifically characterized phenomena appear to conceptual cognitions, those would be perceptual since they would be perceived evidently, Gyel-tsap says: "Although perception and conceptual cognition are similar in that specifically characterized phenomena appear [to both], the ways in which those appear differ. [This is so] for the following reason: whereas [a real thing] appears to conceptual cognition as undetermined [literally, mixed], a thing such as blue appears to perception as [having] the uncommon essence of a [real] thing, that is, as being determined [unmixed] in time and space with respect to other [things]."[30] Real things appear to both perceptual and conceptual cognitions, but whereas they appear to perception as they are, they appear indirectly and in a distorted fashion to conception. The denial that thought reflects reality amounts, for Ge-luk thinkers, to a rejection of the validity of thought, which is at the basis of Dharmakīrti's assertion of the validity of inference.[31]

The assertion that thought relates to real entities is difficult to sustain within a system that emphasizes the mistaken character of thought and its radical difference from perception. The difficulties of the Ge-luk interpretative move are clear in the rather contorted nature of the distinction between the appearing object of conception and the object that appears to conception. Such a distinction, which is typical of the subtle but sometimes overly complex style of Tibetan scholasticism, is hard to make sense of.

We should not, however, jump to the conclusion that this interpretation is purely ad hoc. The constraints under which Dharmakīrti's realist interpreters work lead them to make complicated distinctions, but we should resist the temptation to reject their ideas as being purely artificial. The value of a thought is not, after all, a function of the ease of comprehending it. Good thinking takes time. The necessity to interpret Dharmakīrti's system against the grain is also a source of strength, for it obliges these thinkers to make the best possible use of the conceptual resources of Dharmakīrti's system.

In our case, the distinction between the appearing object and the object that appears helps to underline an important point in Dharmakīrti's system, namely, the different ways in which perception and conception apprehend their objects. Perception is said to operate through the power of appearance (*snang stobs kyis 'jug pa*). That is, we perceive an object by the power of that object impinging on our consciousness. Since perception operates by the power of appearance, everything appearing to it must have equal status as far as appearance is concerned. Thus, it is not possible to say that something appears to perception through something else. Hence, all phenomena appearing to a nonconceptual consciousness are its appearing objects. In the case of a conceptual cognition, the external object appears only through the mediation of the object universal. Conception is said to operate by the power of grasping an object (*zhen stobs kyis 'jug*). Accordingly, the status of the external object as far as appearance is concerned is secondary to that of the object universal.

Despite this relation to Dharmakīrti's system, the distinction between the appearing object of conception and the object that appears to conception remains odd. If the direct object of conception is not the real object but the object universal, why should we say that the real object appears to thought? This objection, often raised in the courtyards of Ge-luk monasteries, is usually answered in one of two ways: either in reference to technical notions such as the distinction between explicit and implicit levels of realization (*dngos dang shugs la rtogs pa*), or by stating that the denial that objects appear to thought is tantamount to denying the validity of thought. Both arguments, however, will not do, for they both beg the question.

The latter argument is hardly convincing, in that it presupposes that the validity of thought cannot be explained without assuming that thought is somehow able to apprehend real objects. But this is precisely the major point of contention between realists and antirealists. Hence, this argument is circular and the whole exercise is nothing but an internal technical interpretation in which the most important point is assumed rather than argued for.

The former argument is equally problematic, although less obviously so. It rests on a distinction between two cognitive levels: Whereas some objects are known because they appear to consciousness, others are known although they do not appear. The argument can then be stated thus: Real objects must appear to thought because, otherwise, they would be the implicit objects of conceptions. Such implicit realization, however, presupposes that an object is explicitly realized by the conception. Such an object could be only the object universal. Since conception, however, is mistaken with respect to this object, it cannot be said to correctly identify it. Therefore, one must admit that real objects are the objects explicitly realized by thought.

This argument runs into the problem that the distinction between explicit and implicit levels of realization must first be established. Second and more important, the argument is circular, for it rests on the assumption that conceptions realize real objects. Since such a realization is not implicit, it must be explicit. Antirealists, however, deny precisely the assumption that thought apprehends reality, even indirectly. For them, thought can at best lead us to practical success despite its strict cognitive limitations.

Conclusion

Our discussion has come back to its starting point: The difficulty that an antirealist philosophy has in accounting for epistemic practices. Dharmakīrti's restrictive ontology makes an elaboration of a credible account of knowledge difficult. This is, however, Dharmakīrti's main concern, as it had been Dignāga's. Both authors came at a time when Indian philosophy had turned toward epistemology as a way of defending older doctrines. The question of knowledge, phrased in terms of what is *pramāṇa,* is seen as central to the philosophical quest. To achieve this, Dharmakīrti must demonstrate that his system can account for the richness and objectivity of human knowledge. The first part of Dharmakīrti's answer is his explanation of the negative nature of conceptual knowledge and his attempt to preserve some practical validity to this form of knowledge, despite its inherent distortion.

Such practical validity is, however, hardly satisfactory as an epistemological answer. Moreover, it fails to satisfy our intuition that thoughts are more than useful devices to cope with the world. We feel that ideas are not just useful mistakes but actually constitute knowledge. Impressed by these arguments, Buddhist realists attempt to elaborate a system in which these intuitions will receive their due place. This requires that thought be described as bearing on reality itself. Within Dharmakīrti's system, however, this is highly problematic. Once thought has been explained through its relation to unreal constructs (the object universals), it is difficult to explain its relation to reality. That is, once we separate the real and the conceptual and declare that thought is limited to the latter, it is hard to explain how thought can have any bearing on the former. Such an account would be feasible within a nonfoundational system that refuses to separate constructs from reality. In Dharmakīrti's system, however, such a distinction is fundamental. Consequently, the cognitive status of thought is always problematic at best.

As a problematic form of knowledge, thought (i.e., inference) must be grounded on an unproblematic form of knowledge, which in Dharmakīrti's system is perception, our only undistorted epistemic access to reality. Accordingly, the other part of Dharmakīrti's epistemology consists of his explanation of the foundation of knowledge through a theory of perception, to which we now turn our attention.

Part II

Perception

19

Philosophy of Perception

Representationalism and Its Problems

An important dimension of our situation as embodied beings is our interaction with a physical environment. Our privileged, though not unique, channel to gather information about this world is through our physical senses. Knowledge derived from the senses is described as perception (*pratyakṣa, mngon sum*).[1] Although sense perception is not the only type of perception in Buddhist epistemology, it is the paradigm of perceptual experience. Therefore, a study of the nature, scope, and object of perception focuses primarily on sense perception.

In our daily life, we commonly assume that we have unproblematic access to our environment through our senses. Our ontological investigation has shown, however, that the objects of commonsense are problematic within a systematic philosophy. Many Buddhist philosophers, for instance, deny that they even exist. Hence, philosophy cannot take for granted the commonsense view of perceptual knowledge. Ayer remarks that our perceptual knowledge goes well beyond the sensible experiences that give rise to it.[2] Although this claim is debatable,[3] we cannot assume that we know what perception is without examination.

Post-Cartesian philosophy distinguishes three positions on the nature of perceptual experience: direct realism, representationalism, and phenomenalism. Although these positions do not necessarily exclude each other, they represent three distinct strategies adopted by Indian and European thinkers to explain the relation of perception to its object. Let us examine the nature and rationale of these distinctions and how they relate to Dharmakīrti's theory of perception.

Direct realism, as articulated, for example, by Reid,[4] holds that perception does not require mediation; it is in direct contact with physical reality. Among Indian schools, the Nyāya offers a view typical of direct realism. We have direct access to commonsense objects, substances together with their qualities and properties. The Buddhist Vaibhāṣika school defends a related, but different view, which proposes a direct contact between perceptual consciousness and its object. Its view, however, is also phenomenalist, for it holds that the object of perception is not a commonsense thing, but a *sensibilia*. Among Tibetan traditions, the Ge-luk theory of perception also belongs to this category, but differs from the Vaibhāṣika view in that it holds that perception directly apprehends commonsense objects. It also differs from the Nyāya position in its insistence on a strict causal theory to account for the relation between perception and its object.

Whereas the realist asserts that perception puts us in direct contact with physical objects, representationalism and phenomenalism deny this, arguing that perception has only a mediated access to its object. Representationalism and phenomenalism assert that we have direct acquaintance only with perceptual objects, called *ideas*, *sensations*, *sense data*, or *percepts*. A few observations will be enough to indicate the nature of representationalist's and phenomenalist's preoccupations.

Let us, following Moore's careful study,[5] examine our perceptions of an envelope. When we both examine our experiences, we discover that they are not identical. Whereas I saw the envelope from a certain angle, with a certain shape and color, you saw it differently. If what we each saw is the envelope, how could we see it differently? Representationalists and phenomenalists explain this discrepancy as a distinction between the direct objects of our varied experiences and the unique objects (the envelope itself) that we assume we see directly, but that in fact we see only indirectly. Moore calls these direct objects *sense data*: "But now, what happened to each of us, when we saw that envelope? I will begin by describing part of what happened to me. I saw a patch of a particular whitish color, having a certain size, and a certain shape, a shape with rather large angles or corners and bounded by fairly straight lines. These things: this patch of a whitish color, and its size and shape I did actually see. And I propose to call these things, the color and size and shape, *sense-data,* things given or presented by the sense—given in this case by my sense of sight."[6] Sense data are the perceptual entities that we apprehend when we have a visual experience, regardless of whether the object that we believe we are seeing exists or not. For example, when a torch is turned rapidly, we see a circle of fire, although there is no circle. Representationalists and phenomenalists explain this experience by positing the existence of a circle-of-fire-looking datum, which we apprehend directly.

Now, what is the relation between these perceptual entities and the physical objects we commonly accept? The representationalist explains this relation in terms of representations caused by external objects. In our example, the turning of a torch causes the representation of a circle of fire through which we apprehend the object. In this case, the apprehension is mistaken, since the representation does not correspond to the cause of the perception. Classic representationalism is Locke's view that to perceive an object is to have a sensible idea in the mind caused by and resembling that object. Locke says: "It is evident that the mind knows not things immediately, but only by the intervention of the ideas it has of them. . . . The mind . . . perceives nothing but its own ideas."[7] There are various problems in Locke's account, some of which directly relate to our inquiry. First is the problem of the time gap between object and perception and the related argument of the veil of perception. Based on scientific considerations relating to the time that our nervous system requires to process perceptual information, Russell and Lovejoy have argued that this time gap proves the imperceptibility of external objects. Since the objects we perceive no longer exist when they are perceived, they are only inferred or postulated.[8] The cogency of this argument is, however, open to discussion, for it rests on the premise that perception must be simultaneous with its object, which limits perception to internal representations. Among Buddhist philosophers, the time-gap problem comes out of a different background, but is no less urgent: Since objects and perceptions are momentary, they can never be simultaneous. How can we apprehend things if they have ceased to exist when we perceive them? Dharmakīrti and his followers propose conflicting solutions that illustrate the difficulties representationalism and causal theory face.

Any account that posits a strict causal relation between objects and perceptions faces the same difficulty, which is not just the result of philosophical distortions but reflects the tension between several of our intuitions. On the one hand, we hold the commonsense view of perception as an awareness directed to an immediately present object. On the other hand, we also assume that perception is the result of a contact with external reality. We saw this tension in Dharmakīrti's account of the nondeceptiveness of valid cognitions. There, intentional and causal accounts are in tension. Whereas the former emphasizes the presence of the object to cognition, the latter undermines this immediacy by stressing the time gap between the object and the subject implied by a causal relation. Direct realist interpreters, particularly Cha-ba and his direct followers, have emphasized the former account, whereas Dharmakīrti and his Sa-gya interpreters have stressed the latter. Both, however, have had to combine these two elements, for they recognize that a viable account of mental life must include both.

Nevertheless, it remains true that the time-gap problem has a greater urgency for representationalism than for other views. Objects cause representation but remain unperceivable. This is the famous argument of the veil of perception, which can be summarized as follows: Since objects are not apprehended directly but only through the intermediary of sensory objects, it logically follows that external objects remain hidden behind the veil of perception. Many philosophers have held this objection to be decisive against representationalism and causal theories.

This argument, however, is far from decisive. In recent years, Grice has shown that a causal theory is not logically committed to hold that real objects are unperceivable.[9] Following him, modern analytical philosophers have recognized that the imperceptibility of external objects is not a logical consequence of representationalism. Dicker explains: "It should be noted, however, that representationalism does not entail the unperceivability of physical things. There would be no *inconsistency*[10] in holding that 1) only ideas are immediately perceived, 2) physical things are perceived by the senses (though not immediately perceived), 3) ideas resemble physical things. The most that can be said is that representationalism *suggests*[11] that the objects represented are not themselves perceived."[12] As we will see, Go-ram-ba makes a similar argument in his defense of the Sa-gya theory of perception against Ge-luk objections. For Go-ram-ba, the veil of perception argument is inconclusive. It does not follow that objects are not perceivable because they are not directly apprehended. Rather, they may be perceived in a way that is different from what we take for granted.

The second, and perhaps the more difficult and important, question facing representationalism concerns the nature of representation. For Locke, a representation is a sensible idea (to be differentiated from a complex idea, which stands for a universal). A simple idea represents an external object by virtue of looking like it. This resemblance is not obvious, however, for how can physical objects resemble perceptual objects, which have no size, shape, or position. Is it feasible to argue that an idea can stand for an object merely by virtue of being similar? For example, an image of a person represents that person through physical similarities. This type of representation is based on similarities but is different from the representation of objects in the mind. Cognitive representations do not involve merely chains of images and reflections but require intentionality, which in turn provides a normative dimension. Cognitive activity is not a passive mirroring of the object but an active categorization of the object. Locke's idea of representation qua similarities does not account for the intentional nature of knowledge.

Post-Kantian representationalists hold out a more sophisticated form of representationalism, in which sensible objects and representations are distinguished. Sellars, for instance, differentiates impression or sensation from perception. A sensation involves merely appearances and is not by itself intentional. To say that a person has a sensation of blue does not entail that this person sees blue or knows blue. The sensation of blue presupposes a kind of mental fact that is known directly, what other theorists call a *datum*. This sensible object is directly sensed but does not yield any knowledge over and above the knowledge that we have a blue impression. In particular, such a datum does not represent an external blue object. To see a blue object requires the acquisition of complex concepts (the concept of spatio-temporally located object, the concept of the different colors, the understanding of standard and nonstandard conditions of observation, etc.). Only when the datum is integrated in this complex cognitive context can it be taken to represent an external object.

Phenomenalism attempts to bypass the difficulty of explaining the relation between representations and external objects by retaining the concept of sense data, but eliminating the idea of representation. Sense data no longer stand in for physical objects but are their constituents or, better, their replacements. The phenomenalist holds that all that is available to us are actual or potential data that we may notice among our perceptual experiences. There is no chair, for example, beyond that collection of data. Rather, the idea of chair is a convenient way to regulate the variegated field of sense data. The direct acquaintance of these data provides direct knowledge. When I sense a blue datum I know that someone is having the experience of a blue object. Such experience may be mistaken with respect to an external object (assuming that there such an object) but it is indubitable with respect to the blue datum which is given to consciousness.

Most modern sense-data theories such as Moore's are phenomenalist in the sense described here[13] and quite compatible with a causal account. For example, it is quite feasible to argue that commonsense objects are nothing but an arrangement of data and that those data are caused by external objects. Moreover, contemporary thinkers, such as A. J. Ayer have defended a linguistic version of phenomenalism, where the issue between conflicting theories of perception is seen to concern more statements about external objects than about the objects themselves. In Ayer's view, objects are described in terms of data without entailing any commitment to a position on the nature or lack thereof of external objects.[14] Thus, phenomenalism is far from being committed to idealism. It remains true, nevertheless, that in its classical forms,[15] phenomenalism shares a common ground with idealism. Both doctrines dissolve the objects of commonsense into perceptual entities.

Representationalism and Realism in Indian Philosophy

Related distinctions can be made in the field of Indian epistemology, although the similarities are only partial. The fundamental divide is between those who argue that cognition has an aspect (*ākāra, rnam pa*) and those who deny it.[16] The former hold that cognition does not apprehend its object nakedly, but through an aspect. For its proponents, "knowledge is made possible by virtue of the objective reality leaving an impress of its likeness on the mirror of consciousness."[17] This view, called *sākāravāda*, includes the Sāṃkhya, Vedānta, and Sautrāntika-Yogācāra schools.[18] In most of its forms, sākāravāda is similar to the rejection of direct realism by Western representationalists or phenomenalists. It asserts the mediated character of cognition, the recognition that perception apprehends its object through the mediation of a mark left by the object on consciousness. Not all accounts holding to such a view are committed, however, to a rejection of direct realism. Some doctrines hold that an explanation of perception requires the idea that cognition apprehends its object by bearing the mark of its object. This idea is felt to be compatible with the assertion that a cognition directly apprehends its object. Such a view, defended by the Ge-luk tradition (and by Aquinas as well), is a form of sākāravāda as well as a form of direct realism. In most of its expressions, however, sākāravāda is incompatible with direct realism.

On the other side, the Nirākāravādins, among them Nyāya-Vaiśeṣika, Vaibhāṣika, Mīmāṃsaka, and Jain, hold that there is no intermediary. Consciousness is amorphous and does not change with its object. It is like a light that reveals the object and its properties without undergoing any change in its form. Perception is direct, without any intermediary aspect.[19] According to the Nirākāravādins, if there were such an intermediary, we would not be seeing external objects but merely their representations. For the Nyāya, consciousness of a given object has no other form than that of the object itself. This, in turn, implies that consciousness is not intrinsically reflexive. These two theses, that cognition is formless and not self-manifesting, together constitute the heart of Nyāya epistemological realism, which is a consequence of the ontological realism basic to the Nyāya tradition.

Among the Buddhists, the Vaibhāṣika school holds that consciousness does not need the mediation of aspects, for it has a direct apprehension of external reality. This view is an example of direct realism, since it asserts the immediate contact between consciousness and the external world. Let us notice that this qualification should be nuanced, for the Vaibhāṣika position differs from classical realism, which is essentially a vindication of our commonsense intuition. We do not feel at all uncomfortable in holding that we perceive objects such as apples and chairs. The realist defends this intuition by asserting that perception directly contacts these objects. The Vaibhāṣika position differs. It does not hold that we perceive objects of common sense but their sensible qualities, such as color and touch. For instance, I do not see an apple but the color of that apple. This view is realist in that it asserts my apprehension of the color as direct. It is, however, phenomenalist in that it denies perception of the objects of commonsense.

The view held by Proponents of Aspects (sākāravāda) is quite different. For Dharmakīrti, as for Dignāga before him, consciousness does not apprehend external objects directly but only through the mediation of aspects. An aspect is the reflection or mark of the object in consciousness. Our sense consciousness does not directly perceive a blue color but captures the form of the object, which leaves its imprint on consciousness. The aspect is the form of the object stamped on cognition that allows us to differentiate among our experiences. Bandyopadhyay explains the nature of the aspect: "It is the cognitive object-form that determines knowledge as capturing the object. This object-form assures me that I know the object. As long as the form of the object remains confined to the external thing it cannot be looked upon as given to knowledge. But when the external object confers its form upon cognition, it (the form) becomes the *cognitive object-form* which alone finally helps in manifesting the object as known to the knower."[20] To be aware of an object means to have a mental state that has the form of this object and is cognizant of this form. The aspect is the form or epistemic factor that allows us to distinguish mental episodes. Without aspects, we could not distinguish, for instance, a perception of blue from a perception of yellow. Thus, the role of the aspect is crucial in Dharmakīrti's system, for it explains the nature of consciousness. Consciousness is not the bare seeing that the realist and commonsense imagine but the apprehension of an aspect, which stands for an external object in the field of consciousness; hence, my description of Dharmakīrti as a representationalist.

A major problem for Dharmakīrti's view is to explain the relation between the aspects and the external objects that caused them. Take the example of the perception of a multicolored object. Is there a one-to-one correspondence between the parts of the multicolored object and its aspect? If so, there must be as many aspects as there are visible parts in the object. But in this case, our impression of dealing with a unitary object becomes hard to account for. Is the aspect globally produced by the multicolored object as a whole? This answer is not easy to maintain in the context of Buddhist ontology, where there is a strong tendency to reduce entities to their components. From this perspective, the notion of a multicolored object acting as a cause becomes little more than a convenient description for the causal action of its parts.

An even more difficult problem is the nature of the representational relation between the direct object of consciousness and the external object. Like in other forms of representationalism, Dharmakīrti's perception has access to external objects only via the mediation of directly apprehended objects, the aspects. These aspects are perceptual objects with which we have direct acquaintance, not unlike Locke's ideas. But whereas Locke holds these ideas to stand for external objects and their apprehension to be by themselves cognitive, Dharmakīrti posits a more complex relation between direct and external objects. For him, the apprehension of these directly given objects is not by itself cognitive, because perception is contentless. Perception passively holds its object without determining it and merely induces appropriate conceptualizations. For example, we sense a blue object that we categorize as blue. The perceptual aspect (the blue aspect) is not yet a representation, since its apprehension, the perception of blue, is not yet cognitive. Only when it is interpreted by a conception does the aspect become a full fledged intentional object standing for an external object. Hence, it looks as if Dharmakīrti is bound to maintain that perceptual aspects are transformed retrospectively into representations by conceptions, a highly uncomfortable position given the foundational status of perception.

When pressed by these problems, Dharmakīrti shifts to a Yogācāra framework, following Dignāga's example and his strategy of ascending scales of analysis. This perspective denies that there are any external objects over and above the direct objects of perception. This view is phenomenalist in that it reduces external objects to conceptually interpreted data. Data are not taken to stand for external objects since nothing exists independent of consciousness. In its denial that perceptions are produced by external causes, this view is idealist. This theory is, however, counterintuitive. Hence, Dharmakīrti refers to it only occasionally and prefers to argue on the assumption that external objects exist. Thus, his theory of perception has a peculiar two-tiered structure in which he presupposes the existence of external objects, which ultimately he rejects to propound a form of idealism.

Of these two layers, the more important is the first one, the so-called Sautrāntika theory, which is best described as a form of representationalism. Consciousness has no direct access to external objects but grasps objects via the intermediary of an aspect, being caused by and representing an external object. The Sautrāntika view is sometimes replaced by a Yogācāra view, which holds that representations are not produced by external objects, but by internal tendencies. This shift allows Dharmakīrti to bypass the difficulties involved in explaining the relation between internal perceptions and external objects. Since there is no external object, the problem of the relation between representations and external objects does not arise. At this level, his philosophy of perception can be described as phenomenalist, since it holds that there is no external object outside of data (aspects).

Dharmakīrti does not often refer to this phenomenalist view, preferring to examine perception more conventionally. This reliance on an approach that is rejected in the final analysis is due to the nature of his project, to develop a Buddhist epistemology integrated within the mainstream of Indian philosophy. Such an account must refer primarily to ordinary epistemic practices, and since these practices assume that external objects exist, it is easier to explain knowledge using a framework that assumes their existence.

Dharmakīrti seems to understand his philosophy as a defense of Buddhist principles in relation to a very specialized philosophical milieu sharing a common language. His participation in a conversation in which Buddhist principles cannot be taken for granted obliges him to formulate his thought within the well-accepted framework of Indian epistemology, as defined in the Nyāya system, where external objects are assumed. Therefore, he assumes external objects to exist in most explanations of perception. It is this view of perception that I examine. Its central element is the notion of aspect, a concept that requires further elaboration.

Aspects and Reflexivity

Aspects are relevant to both conceptual and nonconceptual cognitions. In the former case, an aspect is taken to stand for the property assumed to be instantiated by the represented object. Since such a property does not exist in reality, the representation has no direct relation to the actual object; hence, the description of thought as being mistaken. Similarly, perception is an awareness of the aspect of the object, for its access to reality is not direct. There is, however, a major difference between conception and perception. Whereas the former can arise completely independent of the presence of the objects it conceives, the latter requires the presence of these objects. Thus, contrary to conceptual representations, perceptual aspects have a direct correspondence with the objects they represent. On the basis of such a one-to-one correspondence, perception can be said to hold the object itself, even though it is aware of only the aspect, which is not the object; hence, its description as being unmistaken (*abhrānta, ma 'khrul ba*). Conception is mistaken because it conceives of its object without a direct correspondence between its aspect and the represented object.

The epistemological importance of aspect is clear: It stands as intermediary between experience and object. Consciousness has cognitive capacities, due to its direct contact with aspects. Furthermore, it is differentiated by the form it assumes and apprehends. This aspect, however, is not external to consciousness. It is the form under which an external object presents itself to consciousness. But it is also the form that consciousness assumes when it perceives its object. Thus, an aspect is a representation of objects in consciousness, as well as the consciousness that sees this representation.

This double nature of aspects is a consequence of being an intermediary between the external world and consciousness. To perform this role, it must partake of both domains. That is, it must both look like external objects and be of the nature of consciousness. This double nature is marked in the word *ākāra (rnam pa)*, meaning form and quality; that is, the form through which the object is seen. The word also means aspect, that is, the aspect under which consciousness sees the object. *Ākāra* is the aspect of the object in the consciousness as well as the aspected consciousness itself. The implication of this analysis is that perception is inherently reflexive. As Mohanty says: "Knowledge, being essentially self-manifesting, can only manifest that with which it identifies itself by assuming its form."[21] Awareness takes on the form of an object and reveals that form by assuming it. Thus, in the process of revealing external things, cognition reveals itself. Dharmakīrti expresses this idea by saying that cognition is self-luminous (*svayam prakāśa, rang gsal ba*); that is, self-presencing and, hence, inherently reflexive. He says: "The result is said [by Dignāga] to be self-cognition, for when one considers the nature of [self-cognition] it is identical with cognition of an object."[22] From one side, consciousness has an externally oriented feature called the *objective aspect* (*grāhyākāra, bzung rnam*). This is the form that a mental state assumes in order to bring about knowledge of an external object. The second side is the internal knowledge of our own mental states. It is called the *subjective aspect* (*grāhakākāra, 'dzin rnam*), the feature that ensures that we are aware of the objective aspect, the representation of the object. However, these two parts do not exist separately. Rather, each mental state consists of both and, hence, is necessarily reflexive.

The idea that cognition is necessarily reflexive must be integrated further within Dharmakīrti's epistemology. Since the self-cognizing feature of a mental state brings knowledge of this mental state, it is valid. Since it is not inferential, it looks like it is a third type of valid cognition. To ward off this unwanted consequence, the reflexive feature of awareness is described as a particular type of perception called *self-cognition* (*svasaṃvedana* or *svasaṃvitti, rang rig*). The category of perception is thus extended to include four types of perception: sensory, mental, yogic, and self-cognizing perceptions.[23]

Self-cognition can be compared to what Western philosophers call *apperception*; namely, the knowledge that we have of our own mental states.[24] It is important to keep in mind, however, that here apperception does not necessarily imply a separate cognition. For Dharmakīrti, apperception is not introspective or reflective, for it does not take inner mental states as its objects. The self-cognizing or self-presencing factor of every mental episode brings us a nonthematic awareness of our mental states. For Dharmakīrti, reflexivity does not require a special type of cognition but is the necessary consequence of his analysis of perception in which a subjective aspect beholds an objective aspect, which represents the external object within the field of consciousness. Self-cognition is nothing over and above this beholding. By including apperception in perception, Dharmakīrti can claim that self-cognition is valid (as we will see later, the most important valid cognition) without jeopardizing the twofold typology of valid cognition. Moreover, he draws our attention to the fact the validity of the self-cognizing factor of a mental episode is not reducible to that of the episode itself. For example, when I wrongly conceive of the moon as being made of green cheese, my thought is not valid. But I am aware that I have this thought. Hence, my apperception is valid, though it is not a separate awareness. This is what Dharmakīrti means when he says: "The [mind] understands by itself its own nature."[25] Self-cognition is nothing but the self-revealing aspect of a mental episode. It is the intuitive presence that we feel we have toward our own mental episodes. We may not be fully aware of all the aspects and implications of our experiences, but we do seem to keep track of them. Tibetan scholars express this idea by saying that there is no person whose mental states are completely hidden to himself or herself. This limited self-presence is not due to a metaphysical self but to apperception. Since apperception does not rely on reasoning and is valid, it is taken to be a form of perception. It does not constitute, however, a separate cognition. Otherwise, the charge that the notion of apperception opens an infinite regress would be hard to avoid.

Dharmakīrti's ideas are not unlike those Western philosophers who have argued that consciousness implies self-consciousness.[26] According to Locke, a person is conscious of his or her own mental state. He defines consciousness as "the perception of what passes in a man's mind."[27] Leibniz criticizes Locke, pointing out that this view leads to an infinite regress, for if every cognitive act implies self-awareness, self-knowledge must also be accompanied by another awareness and so ad infinitum.[28] This infinite regress, however, is harmful only if knowledge of one's mental states is assumed to be distinct from knowledge of external objects. This is precisely what Dharmakīrti denies. A consciousness is aware of itself in a nondual way that does not involve the presence of a separate awareness of consciousness. The cognizing person simply knows that her or she cognizes without the intervention of a separate perception of the cognition. This is the function of apperception, which thus provides an element of certainty with respect to our mental states. It does not necessarily, however, validate these states. For example, we seem to be seeing water without knowing whether our seeing is factual or not. In this case, we know that we have an experience, but we do not know that we know. The validity of a cognition is not internal or intrinsic to that cognition but is to be established by practical investigation. By tasting the water (or discussing it with other people) we know our perception was correct. Hence, Dharmakīrti said: "But validity is established through conventional [practices] (*vyavahāra, tha snyad*)."[29] Thus, the question of whether we know directly that we know or not involves two separate questions: (a) Do we know that we have experiences? (b) Do we know that these experiences are true?[30] Whereas the first question concerns the problem of the self-presencing of cognition, the second concerns the question of whether validity is internal or external to cognition.[31] The acceptance of apperception entails a positive answer to (a), but does not require a positive answer to (b). Dharmakīrti rejects the Mīmāṃsā idea of intrinsic or internal validity. Similarly, the acceptance of the idea of internal validity does not require that of self-presencing. For example, Kumārila claims that cognitions are internally valid. They are presumed valid in normal circumstances. Only under special conditions, such as a contradiction to something we know, do we need further validation. Hence, validity is not due to external conditions. Truth is normal; error is the exception. Some other philosophers, such as the Advaitins, accept both self-presencing and self-validity, whereas others (Naiyāyika) answer negatively on both questions.

The Foundational Significance of Aspects

Now that we have philosophically situated Dharmakīrti's theory of perception, let us deepen our reflection on the importance of aspects as immediate objects of consciousness so that the link between this aspect of our inquiry and our central preoccupation, the problem of universals, becomes clear. Like the sense data posited by some Western philosophers, aspects are meant to explain how consciousness can perceive external objects with which it is not in direct contact. How can perception, which is internal, relate to external objects? The answer given by Indian or Western representationalists is that perception relies on mediation by an intermediate element such as aspects or sense data.

The larger question is not just about the relation between external and internal aspects of reality, but about the very possibility of epistemological thinking. Systematic epistemology requires that different forms of knowledge be grounded in reality. Within Dharmakīrti's epistemology, knowledge is constituted by perception, through which we experience reality, and inference, which relates to reality on the basis of the evidence provided by the former. Since inference is distorted, it cannot act as the foundation of knowledge. As we saw earlier,[32] its validity can be appraised only in relation to that of perception. Thus, perception provides the only unproblematic access to reality required by a systematic description of epistemic practices. The whole weight of Dharmakīrti's epistemological program rests on a satisfactory account of the unmistaken nature of perception. Once the epistemological status of perception is secured, inference can be grounded in reference to perception.

The foundational status of perception corresponds to the intuitions we commonly have about the immediacy of our perceptions. We have the "gut feeling" that we are in touch with some directly given reality. We also have an intuitive grasp of a fundamental difference between concrete entities and abstract objects (such as properties), and we feel that our grasp of reality owes nothing to these abstract objects. We also feel that the reality we perceive is composed of commonsense objects such as mountains, trees, animals, and chairs. Finally, we feel that these three intuitions—namely, being directly in touch with reality, having a conceptually unmediated contact with it, and dealing with commonsense reality—are perfectly consistent.

Epistemological analysis reveals that this assurance is mistaken. Perception of commonsense objects implies that we perceive entities that belong to a categorical scheme. Objects are not given as mountains, trees, animals, and chairs but are interpreted as such. This interpretation requires the involvement of abstract entities, which we feel should be excluded from the purview of perception. Hence, it is clear that the beliefs we hold onto concerning the immediacy of our perception are largely mythical. At least one among these three intuitions must be given up.

Systematic epistemologists try to find a more secure foundation for our feeling of immediacy by sifting through these beliefs, separating the ones we can keep from the one we have to abandon to provide a coherent account. Realists (regarding universals) usually discard the second intuition, accepting that our perception is not just an apprehension of concrete objects but also involves abstract entities. This commitment to abstract entities sometimes translates into a direct realist view of perception, which allows them to hold onto commonsense as much as possible.[33] Perception puts us in direct contact with external objects characterized by abstract entities. Perception is articulated and propositional and apprehends universals as well as particulars.

Antirealist epistemologists, who are uncomfortable with abstract entities, tend to keep the second intuition. They also are not ready to let go of the feeling immediacy altogether. Hence, they tend to discard the third one and adopt a representationalist or phenomenalist view of perception.[34] The experience of commonsense objects is not immediate but rests on some objects of immediate experience, which we conceive as being commonsense objects. We usually do not differentiate the objects of immediate experience from the conceptual interpretations, which we superimpose on the perceptual core of the experience. Differentiating objects of direct experience from conceptual overlays allows representationalists and phenomenalists to avoid the contradictions mentioned previously and save our intuition of immediacy (although not in its original form).[35] Perception can be securely grounded on these objects of immediate experience.

Thus, the discovery of objects of immediate experience is a crucial part of the representationalist's and the phenomenalist's systematic quest for immediacy. It allows them to claim that, although we do not perceive directly commonsense objects, our intuition of immediacy is not completely mistaken, since we immediately perceive some entities that form the basis for further conceptual interpretations. It also ensures a secure foundation for our perceptions. Although we might misperceive things, we can at least be sure about the immediate objects of our consciousness. This preoccupation with the epistemological status of the immediate object of perception is related to Sellars' Myth of the Given. Knowledge can be accounted for by reducing cognitions to contacts between the mind and the type of entities whose nature is to be immediately present to consciousness. Other forms of knowledge can then be explained in relation to a perception that is securely grounded in reality through the intermediary of these entities immediately given to consciousness. Rorty explains: "Knowledge is either of the sort of entity naturally suited to be immediately present, or of entities whose existence and properties are entailed by entities of the first sort (and which are thus 'reducible' to those of the first sort)."[36] We can know things in two ways: either by acquaintance or by inference. In the first case, we know objects by direct observation of a special type of object, such as sense data, whose very presence provides indubitable knowledge. Other forms of knowledge are inferences resting on this self-authenticating form of knowledge. This is, as Sellars puts it, "the heart of the Myth of the Given."[37] Notice that, for Sellars, the myth is not that there are perceptual objects distinct from commonsense objects but that sensing those is a form of knowledge. Appearances and impressions are not intentional entities; to sense them does not entail that we know them.

In a Western context, sense data theories have been associated with a preoccupation about certainty, a question at the center of the epistemological discussion during the seventeenth century.[38] How can we be sure that we know anything at all? Descartes' famous *cogito* answers by finding indubitable justificatory grounds (the certainty that I am thinking) from which the whole edifice of human knowledge can be reconstructed. British empiricists did not accept Cartesian rationalism (or at least what they perceived to be his rationalism) and attempted to appease this Cartesian anxiety in another way. For them, the foundation of knowledge is the immediate certainty of sensory impressions available through introspection. Reid sums up the spirit of this view: "All systems that have been invented . . . suppose that we perceive not external objects immediately, and that the immediate objects of perception are only certain shadows of external objects. These shadows or images, which we immediately perceive . . . since the time of Descartes have commonly been called ideas, and by Hume, *impressions*."[39] Human beings are locked in the cave or prison of their senses. Their problem is to bridge this gap between the inside and the outside. The solution is to posit entities that are the indubitable objects of perception. Locke calls them *ideas*; Hume, *impressions*; and Moore, *sense data*.

Similarly, Dharmakīrti understands aspects to be the immediate objects of awareness. His account differs, however, from that of empiricists in several respects. There is an obvious difference in context. Dharmakīrti set forth his idea of aspect not to respond to skeptics but to offer a systematic account of epistemic practices that vindicates Buddhist principles and shows them to be compatible with a complete explanation of knowledge.[40] The basic problem is to answer the question, How can knowledge be possible in a world of individuals? The nature of perception is explained in terms of the immediate objects, the aspects, which do not themselves provide knowledge. Perception, that is, a sensing of bare particulars, is valid only inasmuch as it is able to induce appropriate forms of conceptualization that provide cognitive content to our experiences. Thus, the direct objects of perception are not foundational in the sense usually accepted by data theorists, but they do provide an indubitable starting point, the direct acquaintance we have with our own mental states. In this, Dharmakīrti shares in the foundationalist tradition of thinkers who have attempted to ground knowledge. Let us examine in greater detail Dharmakīrti's description of perception before exploring the problems that his account raises.

The next chapter considers Dharmakīrti's definition of perception as being nonconceptual and unmistaken, where I analyze some interpretive issues surrounding his view. Chapter 21 deepens our reflection of Dharmakīrti's view by examining Dharmottara's attempts to account for the validity of perception. I return to one of the central problems of Dharmakīrti's epistemology, the coordination between perception and conception. I show that, given Dharmakīrti's view of perception as nonpropositional, it is very hard to explain how perception can be a form of knowledge at all. I examine Dharmottara's answer, which opens a new revisionist trend in Buddhist epistemology. Chapter 22 follows this new epistemology in Tibet, where I analyze some of Cha-ba's most important contributions to this movement: his sevenfold typology, his distinction between perception simpliciter and valid perception, and his view of perception as an active propositional form of knowledge. Chapter 23 analyzes the ways in which the Ge-luk tradition has appropriated Cha-ba's ideas. It also introduces Sa-gya critiques, particularly those of Śākya Chok-den, who presents a useful although not always disinterested historical presentation of the early stages of Tibetan epistemology. Chapter 24 examines Sa-paṇ's critique of Cha-ba's views, where I will show how Sa-paṇ greatly insists on the nonpropositional nature of perception, thus offering a more conservative interpretation of Dharmakīrti. The next three chapters further investigate the difference between the new and old epistemologies. Chapter 25 focuses on the subject of apperception, showing how the conflicting Sa-gya and Ge-luk analyses reflect a different theory of perception. In the process, the question of whether Ge-luk views are realist or not is raised. Chapter 26 continues this analysis, focusing on the problem of whether external objects are perceivable. This is a difficult question for representationalism and, consequently, Ge-luk realism has used it to support its views. Finally, Chapter 27 concludes by relating the concept of representation to Dharmakīrti's Yogācāra views. This leads to a few remarks concerning the soteriological content or lack thereof of Dharmakīrti's epistemology.

20

Dharmakirti's Account of Perception

The Nyāya Theory of Perception

Understanding Dharmakīrti's theory of perception requires placing his ideas in their context, which is the Nyāya theory of perception. A full discussion of this theory, which evolved considerably under the impact of critiques from Buddhists and others, is beyond the scope of this work. Here I offer only a simplified presentation of the Nyāya theory, a version that might not have been accepted by most of Dharmakīrti's Naiyāyika contemporaries but that nevertheless captures the essential element in the Nyāya theory. This theory of perception was first propounded by Vaiśeṣikas and subsequently came to be acknowledged as the most complete account of perception in Indian philosophy.[1]

The Nyāya discussion of perception relates to Gautama's *Nyāya-sūtra* (I:4) in which four criteria differentiating perception from other types of cognitions are given: A cognition is perceptual if, and only if, it is (a) produced from contact between the senses and the object, (b) nonverbal (*avyapadeśya*), (c) nonerroneous (literally, nonwandering, *avyabhicāra*), and (d) definite (or determinate, *vyavasāyātmaka*), that is, not doubtful. These criteria of perception, which have given rise to many discussions among Naiyāyikas, constitute the background for most other discussions as well, including Dharmakīrti's.

The first requirement for perception is not especially problematic in the Indian context, where contact between sense and object seems to have been the dominant metaphor both for perception and knowledge in general. We come to know things by sensing them. This empirical form of knowledge may not be the whole extent of our epistemic activity, but it is the most basic form of knowledge for most Indian philosophers (with the exception of the Grammarians, who hold communicative knowledge to be more basic). The modality of this contact, however, may be problematic, especially in the case of sight or hearing. For the Nyāya, the senses are said to go out, reach for, and contact their objects. The visual sense, for example, extends to its object to illuminate it. This idea of a contact between senses and objects seem to have originated in the Vedas, where senses are compared to lesser deities (*devata*) who would be sent out by the major gods, particularly Indra. Hence, senses are called *forces at the disposal of Indra* (*indriya*). Philosophically speaking, senses are forces in that they serve the knowing self by going out and contacting the object. Buddhists reject this mythological background and the idea of going out (particularly in relation to vision and hearing) but have kept the term.[2]

The second criterion is meant to exclude verbal judgment from being perceptual. Since it relies on linguistic conventions, it cannot be perceptual. The third criterion excludes the cases of perceptual illusions, as when I mistake a fish for a piece of silver. Since such a cognition is mistaken it cannot be a perception, which is a type of valid cognition. Finally, the fourth criterion excludes from perception cases in which we cannot decide the nature of what we see, as for example, when we are in a state of extreme confusion. These descriptions are not, however, accepted by all Nyāya commentators. The last three criteria have been the focus of protracted debates.[3] Whereas earlier Nyāya commentators such as Uddyotakara tend to take the definition to be conjunctive (all perceptions must satisfy all four criteria), later ones such as the polymath Vācaspati-Miśra (tenth century) argue that it is disjunctive, referring to two types of perception (determinate and indeterminate, more on this later). Rather than analyze these differences and trace the evolution of the Nyāya views, let us summarize what is most distinctive about the Nyāya theory of perception. This will provide a context within which to assess Dharmakīrti's theory and its later developments.

A primary implication of Gautama's four criteria is that sense perception is central to a Nyāya theory of perception. Although perception may not be limited to sense cognition, such cognition provides the paradigm for discussing other types of perception. This is also true for Dharmakīrti. Although he accepts three other forms of perception (mental, self-cognition, and yogic), he holds sense perception to be central. Mental perception is understood through its similarities with sense perception. Self-cognition is described as the reflexive factor of sense cognition. Even yogic perception (*yogipratyakṣa, rnal 'byor mngon sum*) is not thought to offer a fundamentally different paradigm.[4] Dharmakīrti rarely discusses yogic perception, and does not use it to exemplify the salient features of perception. Rather, he assumes that yogic perception shares the characteristics of perception which are exemplified best by sense perception.

The greatest difference between the Nyāya and Dharmakīrti is that, whereas the former accepts the existence of perceptual propositional knowledge, the latter rejects it. Let me explain. When we first see a jar, for example, we merely sense the object. At this stage, we do not understand its nature. We do not remain at this unarticulated stage, however, but begin to form a perceptual judgment[5] and see the object as a jar. No longer is our experience a mere sensing, for it articulates two elements: an individual (this), and a general property or universal (being a jar). This form of knowledge is propositional, for it predicates a property of an individual. Later Nyāya accounts of perception (as with most orthodox schools) call this perception *determinate* (*savikalpaka, rtog pa can*), as distinguished from the mere sensing of the object, which is called *indeterminate* (*nirvikalpaka, rtog med can*) perception. Only nonverbal judgment is included in perception.[6] For the Nyāya, verbalization is not a source of knowledge in the case of perception, for it is just an externalization of what has been conceived already by perceptual judgment, which does not depend on language to apprehend its objects. This last point is obviously controversial and bound to be refused by the antirealist. It is nevertheless necessary to the success of the Nyāya extreme realist program.

Jayanta gives a particularly lucid exposition of the subject, which serves as our reference point throughout this discussion as representing a typical Nyāya view.[7] The first stage of perception is nonconceptual and nonpropositional. In it, the particular object (a splay-bottomed, bulbous object able to hold water), together with its kind (being a jar) and the relation of inherence that binds the two together, is given but not articulated. In the second stage, judgment arises, which articulates the content of the previous experience. We then see the bulbous object *as* a jar. On the basis of this perceptual judgment we are able to verbalize "this is a jar," at which point the judgment is not perceptual any more but verbal. However, this verbal judgment is connected to reality by the immediately previous judgment linking the particular object to its category.

The key element of the Nyāya view is this mediation between perception and verbalization. This linkage is in harmony with the realism of this school, which holds that since we experience universals, they really exist. Moreover, since they exist, these universals must be perceived in the way in which they are conceived. Therefore, perception contains two elements: an apprehension of the particular, which we perceive directly during the first moment of perception when the content of perception has yet to be articulated, and an understanding of its categorical nature, which comes at the second moment when we articulate the elements given to our experience. To put it briefly, perceptual knowledge concerns universals as well as individuals.

This credible account of experience is not acceptable to Buddhist antirealists such as Dharmakīrti, for it entails a realist acceptance of abstract universals. This leads to a crowded ontology as well as a view of perception as apprehending both concrete and abstract entities. Dharmakīrti holds that this mediatedness is conceptual and, hence, irrelevant to perceptual experience, which is a sensing of bare reality. To succeed in elaborating an epistemology based on Buddhist principles, Dharmakīrti's epistemological program (inherited from Dignāga) must elaborate a credible alternative to this generally accepted Nyāya theory. This task is more difficult than it might seem, because Dharmakīrti agrees with the Naiyāyikas that indeterminate perception (the only type of perception in Dharmakīrti's system) is merely a sensing. Hence, perception provides no articulation of reality. Thus, Dharmakīrti cannot accept the empiricist view that all knowledge derives from the senses. He must grant thought some role. To meet the epistemological challenge of the Nyāya, Dharmakīrti must use the resources that his restrictive (and reductionist) system acknowledges: dumb perception and blind conception. He must hope that the combination of these two elements, which are powerless in isolation, can fully account for knowledge.

In presenting his case, Dharmakīrti shows that the rival account is flawed. He develops a detailed critique of the Nyāya determinate perception, showing it to rest on the assumption that universals are real, whereas in reality they are nothing but conceptual constructs not directly relevant to our experiences. The centrality of the assertion that perception cannot be determinate is underlined by the definition of perception given by Dharmakīrti. This famous definition will serve as the starting point of our discussion of perception.[8]

Dharmakīrti's Definition of Perception

In defining perception as a cognition that is unmistaken (*abhrānta, mi 'khrul pa,* or undistorted, *avyabhicāri*) and free from conceptions (*kalpanāpoḍha, rtog pa dang bral ba*),[9] Dharmakīrti asserts his opposition to the Nyāya view of determinate perception. He also defends Dignāga's definition, which was heavily criticized by defenders of Hindu orthodoxy. Dignāga said: "Perception is free from conception, which consists in joining name and kind [to the object]."[10] For the Buddhist epistemologist, perception is differentiated from other cognitions primarily by its nonconceptual character. Conception does not apply to the individual reality of phenomena but addresses their general characteristics. Since these are only constructs, they cannot be true reflections of reality. For perception to be undistorted, therefore, it must be totally free from conceptual elaborations. This implies a radical separation between perception, which holds the object as it is in the perceptual ken, and interpretation of this object, which introduces conceptual constructs into the cognitive process. This requirement that perception be nonconceptual is the cornerstone of Buddhist theory of perception. It is made explicit by Dignāga's definition of perception as a nonconceptual cognition.[11]

An obvious and immediate problem this definition faces is how cases of distorted cognition (which are not perception), such as seeing a double moon, are to be excluded from perception. Hindu thinkers focused on this difficulty to discredit Dignāga's account of knowledge.[12] In response Dharmakīrti adds the qualification "unmistaken" to his definition, by which he claims to capture Dignāga's true intention. In this way, a mental state must be nonconceptual and unmistaken as well to be a perception.

Modern scholars give conflicting appraisal of Dharmakīrti's reinterpretation of Dignāga's definition. Some argue that it represents a substantial departure from Dignāga's thesis that mistakes are always conceptual. Others dispute this interpretation, arguing for a greater degree of continuity between the two thinkers. I will leave these discussions, which I have examined elsewhere.[13] Suffice to say that the later tradition reads Dignāga through Dharmakīrti's eyes, thus adding the word *unmistaken* to the definition of perception. In this way, a central point of Dharmakīrti's theory is made clear: Perception must be undistorted.[14]

Another issue that has occupied traditional commentators is the interpretation of Dharmakīrti's "unmistaken." Dignāga's commentator Jinendrabuddhi holds that perceptions do not need to be always unmistaken. For example, when we see a white conch as yellow under the influence of jaundice, our perception is mistaken. Nevertheless, we are able to correctly identify the conch. Therefore, this mental episode is valid and cannot be but a perception (since it is nonconceptual).[15] Similarly, Vinītadeva holds that the unmistakeness here means nondeceptiveness and thus does not imply complete absence of distortions.[16]

Dharmottara criticizes Vinītadeva on the following grounds. Since perception is a subspecies of valid cognition, we already know that it must be nondeceptive. If unmistakeness were to mean nondeceptive as argued by Vinītadeva, the definition would become redundant. Dharmottara also criticizes Jinendrabuddhi for not understanding that the vision of a yellow conch cannot perceive a conch, because such an object must be white and nothing white is perceived. Therefore, in this case, nothing seen qualifies as a conch. Moreover, perception operates on the totality of the object without making differences, which are necessarily conceptual. Therefore, either we see a conch with its full set of qualities (among them, white) or we do not see the conch at all.[17]

The main issue that occupies Jinendrabuddhi and Vinītadeva concerns the relation between Dharmakīrti's definition and his two-tier system. Is his definition of perception compatible with both Sautrāntika and Yogācāra systems? If by *unmistaken*, he means complete absence of any mistake, his definition is incompatible with a Yogācāra understanding of perception. This is so because, according to the latter school, ordinary perception is mistaken inasmuch as it apprehends objects as existing externally. Hence, Dharmakīrti's definition would exclude the second tier of his system.

Dharmottara accepts this latter consequence. For him, Dharmakīrti's definition strictly reflects the Sautrāntika point of view and is not compatible with the Yogācāra view that sense perceptions are mistaken. The exclusion of the Yogācāra view is clear from Dharmakīrti's statement that "Correct [cognition] is produced from the power of the [external] object."[18] Since Dharmakīrti explicitly rejects external objects, there is no reason to insist that Dharmakīrti's definition must include the Yogācāra standpoint.[19] For Dharmottara, Dharmakīrti's unmistakeness must be understood in relation to the way things appear to consciousness. A perception is unmistaken inasmuch as its object appears as it is.

Kay-drup, who does not always agree with Dharmottara, has a similar view. He also points out that Dharmakīrti gives different explanations in his *Commentary* and in his *Ascertainment.* Whereas in the former, Dharmakīrti describes perception as unmistaken simpliciter, in the latter, perception is understood in relation to the different causes of mistake (*'khrul rgyu*): "Here, perception is unmistaken and free from conceptions. [This means that] a perception is a cognition that is nonconceptual and not produced as mistaken [under the influence of causes of mistakes such as] ophthalmia, quick turning [of a fire brand], being disturbed by being in a [moving] boat, etc."[20] Causes of mistakes are said to be of four types: (a) The cause of mistake might be in the basis (*rten la yod pa*), that is, in the senses affected by some disease such as ophthalmia; (b) the cause of mistake might be in the object (*yul la yod pa*), as in the case of a quickly turning fire brand creating the illusion of a circle; (c) the cause of mistake might be in the location (*gnas la yod pa*), as in the case of seeing trees moving from a moving ship; and (d) finally, the cause of mistake might reside in the preceding condition of the cognition (*de ma thag rkyen la yod pa*), as in the case in which we see things red under the influence of an intense anger.[21]

According to Kay-drup, the *Commentary*'s explanation differs from the *Ascertainment*'s. The former is given in relation to the way things appear to a perceptual mental episode and is not meant to include the Yogācāra view. The latter, which possibly reflects a greater maturity on Dharmakīrti's part, is given as a function of the causes of mistakes and thus includes the two tiers of Dharmakīrti's theory of perception. The mistake that affects perception in Yogācāra philosophy is not one of the four causes of mistakes that are superficial (*phral*) or adventitious (*glo bur*). A profound (*phug*) and innate (*lhan skyes*) mistake makes us see objects as existing externally. This is an inherent mistake (*ngo bo nyid kyis 'khrul pa*) due to the latencies deposited in our stream of consciousness. A mental state needs not be free from this type of mistake to be a perception.

Dharmakīrti's Arguments

Whatever is the exact interpretation of Dharmakīrti's unmistakeness, the fundamental point of disagreement between Dharmakīrti and his Nyāya opponents hinges on the other element of the definition of perception, the requirement that perception be nonconceptual. Dharmakīrti devotes a great deal of effort to demonstrate the nonconceptual character of perception. Here, I will not present his arguments in their textual order but will attempt to logically reconstruct them.

On the basis of phenomenological considerations, Dharmakīrti shows that nonconceptual states exist and that they are empirically different from conceptual ones. He first argues that the nonconceptual character of perception is proven by experience: "The fact that perception is devoid of conceptuality is proven by perception itself. All [beings'] conceptualizations rely on names [and] are established by themselves individually. Having withdrawn one's mind from everything one abides calmly in oneself. Yet, form is seen by the mind, [and this] cognition is born from the senses. [When] thoughts slowly return, one [is able] to identify one's own conceptuality [and recognize that] the previously mentioned [conceptual] state does not come from the senses."[22] Dharmakīrti is describing here what some modern philosophers have called *perceptual reduction*.[23] We empty our mind without closing it completely to the external world. In this state of liminal awareness, things appear to us but we do not identify them. We merely let them go. When we come out of this stage, the usual conceptual flow returns and with it the conceptualization that allows us to identify things as being this or that. This experience shows,[24] Dharmakīrti argues, that identification is not perceptual but is due to internal conceptualization. In a state of perceptual reduction, perception takes place but not conceptualization. Hence, perception is a nonconceptual sensing onto which interpretations are added by our stream of conceptions. Due to the speed of the mental process, the untrained person usually cannot differentiate conceptual from nonconceptual cognitions.[25] Only on special occasions, such as in some form of meditation, can a clear differentiation be made. There, the flow of thought gradually subsides, and we reach a state in which there is a bare sensing of things. In this state, shapes and colors are seen barely; that is, as they are delivered to us through our senses without the adjunctions of conceptual interpretations. When one gradually emerges from such a nonconceptual state, the flow of thoughts gradually reappears, and we are able to make judgments about what we saw during our meditation. One is then also able to make a clear differentiation between the products of thoughts and the bare delivery of the senses.

Dharmakīrti then proceeds to establish, still on the basis of phenomenological considerations, an empirical difference between conceptual and nonconceptual states of mind. When we think of an object, we have only a blurred cognition of that object, whereas when we perceive the object we have a vivid apprehension of it. This difference is given in our experience and verifiable by introspection. It is due to the presence or absence of the cognition's object. Perceptions are vivid because they are produced by the presence of their objects. Conceptions are unclear (*aniyata, mi gsal ba*) because they do not rely on the presence of the object they conceive.[26] Before continuing, let us notice that Dharmakīrti's argument does not exclude the existence of degrees of clarity between conceptions, some of which might be clearer than others. Nevertheless, they are all unclear in comparison to perception. They become completely vivid only when they become nonconceptual. Dharmakīrti says: "To that which is connected to a conception, the object cannot appear clearly. Given a mind that is distorted, there is no clear [appearance of its] object for any consciousness that is mixed with words."[27] As long as a cognition remains connected with language, its object cannot appear completely vividly, for the concept used by this cognition to apprehend the object obstructs the vision of the mind. Hence, the complete adequation of the mind to the object that is characteristic of perception is impossible for any consciousness that relies on concepts or language.

In these first stages, Dharmakīrti's phenomenological arguments have established the following. Nonconceptual states are possible. They differ empirically from conceptual ones, a difference due to the reliance or lack thereof on the presence of the object. Dharmakīrti proceeds to show that, contrary to what most Hindu thinkers assume, nonconceptual states arise independent from and untainted by concepts. "[Thoughts] connect [to their objects] by remembering a linguistic sign independent of the external object. Similarly, an eye-consciousness arises directly from the [object] independent of the linguistic sign."[28] Perception is solely dependent on real objects. It does not rely on the recollection of a linguistic sign (*samaya, brda*) but apprehends things as they are. Here, Dharmakīrti's main target is the view that perceptual knowledge depends for its production on the object as well as on the recollection of a linguistic sign. This view is held by the Grammarians, for whom knowledge is necessarily linguistic.

To refute this view, Dharmakīrti proposes a complicated argument based on causal considerations. This argument is convincing only if one presupposes the acceptance of the Buddhist theories of causality and impermanence. Throughout his demonstration Dharmakīrti assumes the principle of momentariness, according to which both objects and perceptions exist unchanged for only a single moment, as well as the principle of necessary concomitance between causes and objects. That is to say, he assumes that once the causal set is completed, the effect has to come to existence in the next moment. Finally, Dharmakīrti also presupposes the Buddhist understanding of the set of causes necessary to generate a perception. Sense perception requires an object that acts as its object condition (*ālambana-pratyaya, dmigs rkyen*), an empowering condition (*adhipati-pratyaya, bdag rkyen*), which is the sense basis, and an immediately preceding condition (*samanantara-pratyaya, de ma thag rkyen*), which is the preceding moment of mental cognition.[29]

If a perception relied on the recollection of a sign, we would be faced with the following dilemma (by virtue of the momentariness of cognitions): Either recollection would arise simultaneously with the sense perception and then would have no influence whatever on the perception (by virtue of the principle that causes must precede their effects) or it would arise before the sense perception. In the latter case, it would have to arise before the moment of contact between object and sense, for once this contact takes place, sense perception always arises immediately after. This is so because in this case its set of three conditions is fulfilled (by virtue of the invariable concomitance between causes and effects). Hence, nothing can prevent the sense perception from arising. However, the previous presence of recollection would be irrelevant since its object would be different from that of perception; recollection could have no significant influence on sense perception. Therefore, perception arises independent of and untainted by concepts, which at best remain peripheral to the perceptual process.[30] By contrast, conceptions rely on quasi-entities, which are made present to the mind by the very fact that they are considered. Since real objects do not behave in this way, the objects of conceptual cognitions must be different; that is, fictional. They are, in fact, the universals imagined by the Naiyāyikas to be real. Dharmakīrti summarizes: "Its [i.e., perception's] object is only the specifically characterized. The specifically characterized is the [kind of object] whose nearness or remoteness creates a difference in the cognition. That alone ultimately exists because it has causal efficiency, the defining property of things. Other [phenomena] are generally characterized, they are objects of inference."[31] Dharmakīrti's conclusion emphasizes the link between epistemology and ontology. The assertion of the nonconceptual character of perception is the epistemological counterpart of the ontological rejection of universals. By demonstrating the nonconceptual character of perception, Dharmakīrti supports his rejection of realism. Dharmakīrti does not, however, present a very detailed account of knowledge. It is relatively easy to imagine how Dharmakīrti's nonconceptual perception cognizes the objects of sense spheres described in his ontology. It is more difficult to imagine how common experience comes out of this encounter with bare particulars. It is important to keep in mind that Dharmakīrti does not claim that bare contact with reality, which happens in perception, can explain human knowledge on its own.

Dharmakīrti shares basically the same view as the Nyāya concerning indeterminate perception. Bare perception does not provide us with a picture of the reality in which we live. As a Buddhist, Dharmakīrti sees philosophy as a therapy for our illusions as well as being a way to assert the value of Buddhist insights. As a systematic philosopher, Dharmakīrti does not completely renounce the task of accounting for what we commonly understand as knowledge. His solution seems to be a combination of perception and conception. This solution is, however, not clearly stated. Preoccupied with refuting the Nyāya account of perception, Dharmakīrti maintains an essentially negative strategy. To elaborate a detailed epistemology of perception based on his mostly polemical remarks, let us examine a more candid explanation given by Dharmottara.

21

A New Epistemology Begins: Dharmottara on Perception

Dharmottara as a Commentator and an Innovator

The preceding chapter delineated some of the issues involved in Dharmakīrti's definition of perception. Let us explore the implications of this definition by examining Dharmottara's explanation of the epistemological status of perception. In the process, a new trend in Buddhist epistemology associated with him will become visible. I do not intend to provide a complete history of the development of this new epistemology. Although Dharmottara is an important figure, he is certainly not the only one and might not even be the most important. The few historical flashbacks provided are meant to suggest, rather than describe, an evolution and to show that later developments in Tibet are not local aberrations or the product of some "indigenous spirit" asserting itself. Rather, these developments happen within the conceptual continuity of the Indian tradition and as a function of its problematic. Tibetans elaborate an epistemology that differs from Dharmakīrti's largely due to their historical position in the tradition. Conceptual changes such as the ones we have been examining throughout this work are due not just to the creativity of individuals or change of venue but occur within a historical and conceptual environment that sustains the efforts of their proponents.

Dharmottara's new ideas arise as a response to the objections raised by Dharmakīrti's orthodox opponents. In proposing these ideas, he clarifies Dharmakīrti's views but also goes beyond them, for a simple commentary to Dharmakīrti's text cannot resolve the difficulty. Dharmottara has to innovate, thereby expanding the conceptual resources of his tradition and contributing to a new trend in Dharmakīrti's epistemological tradition. Since he is a commentator, Dharmottara does this while explaining Dharmakīrti's intentions.[1] The double nature (exegetical and innovative) of Dharmottara's attempt is not unique, but it is a good example of the commentarial style of Indian philosophy, in which innovations are proposed as interpretations of an original system. Commentators are led, like other philosophers, to expand the conceptual resources of the system they rely on. Their particularity is that they do not see the original system as merely a source of inspiration but as actually containing these later developments.

The Validity of Perception

Dharmakīrti's epistemological project is based on the distinction between distorted conception and unmistaken perception. Since conception's epistemic access to reality entirely rests on perception, the epistemological status of the latter is a crucial question. The validity of perception consists in its being nondeceptive, that is, in its ability to lead us to successful practical actions. For example, our perception of a blue color is valid because it allows us to choose the right color for the suit we want to make. In the case of perception, however, practical validity is not as straightforward as one might think. Achieving practical purposes depends on correctly describing the objects we encounter. It is not enough to see an object that is blue; we must also see it *as* being blue. Hence, Dharmakīrti speaks of cognitions as being "nondeceptive with respect to the purpose [of the action] in the application [to an object] after having determined it."[2] To be nondeceptive, a cognition depends on the appropriate identification of the object as being this or that. Perceptions, however, do not identify their objects since they are not conceptual. Hence, they cannot categorize their objects but only hold them without determining them. Categorization requires conceptual thought under the form of a judgment (*adhyavasaya, nges shes*). Such judgment subsumes its object under an appropriate universal, thereby making it part of the practical world where we deal with long-lasting entities that we conceive as parts of a determined order of things.

Since our practical actions rely on the categorization of objects operated by conceptual judgment, it seems reasonable to assert that our experiences are valid only inasmuch as they are properly categorized. Categorization makes experiences pragmatically useful, and judgment brings about categorization. Hence, judgment should be included in the category of perception since it brings about perceptual knowledge. This is the view defended by the Nyāya, which holds such judgment to be determinate (*savikalpaka, rtog pa can*) perception. This form of perception, however, cannot be accepted by Dharmakīrti without undermining his epistemological edifice. For, it would lead to an impossible choice: Either this judgment is perception, but then it is undistorted and its objects, the universals, must be real. Or, this judgment is not perception but some other type of valid cognition. Since this judgment relies only on experience and not reason, it cannot be inferential. Therefore, if it were valid, it would constitute a third type of valid cognition and thus contradict the restriction of validity to inference and perception.

Another solution could be proposed: Perceptual judgment is not valid per se, for it does not have any independent epistemic access to external objects. Nevertheless, perception depends on it to apprehend its objects. Even this solution, however, is not acceptable to a strict Dharmakīrtian. For, since categorization is conceptual, it is false. Therefore, the validity of perception cannot depend on such a false cognition without threatening its foundational role in Dharmakīrti's system. The validity of conception can be established only in relation to an unproblematic form of knowledge. If the validity of perception required that of conception, what would then be the foundation of such conception? Since there is no third type of valid cognition, the validity of perception cannot be made dependent on that of conception. It must come from perception itself.

This is problematic, however, because perception by itself cannot convey any usable information. Remember Dharmakīrti's phenomenological reduction, in which the mind was reduced to its bare perceptual level. At that stage, meditators continue to have perceptual experiences, but only when thoughts return are they able to determine the objects that appeared. Perception is unable to determine its object by itself and its own identity as a perception of this object. Only when the object is categorized by judgment as, for example, being blue, does the perception receive its identity of being, for example, a perception of blue.[3] It is as if the validity of the perception is retroactively attributed to the perception by conception.

A similar point is made by Sellars in his refutation of the myth of the given. Contrary to the empiricists, who hold that knowledge is given to the senses, Sellars argues that knowing involves a conceptual process of categorization. We do not know things by sensing them, for perception does not deliver full objects but only impressions. Impressions are not forms of knowledge, but become so when they are integrated within our categorical scheme. For example, when we are hit on the head, we first have an impression that is not by itself cognitive. We just have a sensation of pain. This sensation becomes cognitive once it is integrated to a conceptual scheme in which it is explained as being an impact on a certain part of our body due to certain causes and so forth. Only then does the impression of being hit become fully cognitive. Prior to this, the impression, or to use Dharmakīrti's language, the aspect, does not represent anything yet. It becomes a representation only when conceptually interpreted.

In the description of perception we presented the aspect as being a representation of the object, but this is only partially accurate. An aspect represents an external object only inasmuch as it is conceptually interpreted. Just by itself, the aspect is not cognitive, as shown by the experience of perceptual reduction. Its function is to induce the appropriate perceptual judgment, which will interpret the aspect, thereby making it fully representative.

This situation creates a problem for Dharmakīrti's foundationalist epistemology. For Dharmakīrti, conceptions can be forms of knowledge only inasmuch as they rely on the undistorted grasp of reality of perception, which is their foundation. But how can Buddhist epistemologists hold that perception is foundational if its cognitive status is derived from its appropriation by conception? How can they even argue that perception is valid if experience becomes cognitive only by interpretation? Is not the validity of experience due to conception rather than perception? Dharmottara answers: "A conceiving [consciousness induced] by the power of a perception conceives that [we] see a thing, not that we conceptualize [it]. Moreover, seeing is what is done by perception; it is the function of perception. Accordingly, the nature of conceptual cognition [of] a hidden thing is to conceptualize, not to see. Experience establishes that the function of conceptual cognition is to conceptualize. Therefore, [in the case of a judgment, such a conceiving consciousness] leaves aside its own function and exhibits that of perception. From [that it follows] that only a perception is a valid cognition with respect to the thing to which the conceiving consciousness has become perceptual."[4] Dharmottara's solution is to recognize that perception is not cognitive by itself. It just holds its object and induces the appropriate conceptualization, thereby creating a fully cognitive situation. The validity of the experience is still due to perception, argues Dharmottara, because the conception induced by perception does not count as a conception. A conceptual cognition that is a perceptual judgment is not carrying on its proper function, which is to conceive or imagine a momentarily hidden object. Rather, it is carrying on the function of perception, which is to see an object. In perceptual judgment, we conceive that we see an object not that we imagine it. In such judgment, the function of seeing, which is perceptual, is taken over by conception, which is induced by perception, thereby making the object available to us. In being induced by perception, conception leaves aside its proper function, which is to imagine an object, and, so to say, assumes that of perception, which is to see an object. This shows, according to Dharmottara, that in this case only perception is valid even though its object is made available to us only through the intervention of a conception. This is so because in this case conception is assuming the function of perception and hence has no independent epistemic function. Hence, the validity of the whole experience is entirely due to perception. The conception that categorizes the object does not count, since it is not carrying out its proper function, which is to imagine the object rather than see it.

Dharmottara must reach this rather unconvincing conclusion to avoid accepting the Nyāya idea of a determinate perception, for that would be tantamount, for him, to the acceptance of a conceptual perception. The Nyāya view accepts the first moment of perception, Dharmakīrti's bare sensing, as valid, but also holds the judgment that follows to be valid in its own right. Dharmottara's solution is hardly satisfactory, however, for several reasons. First, it ignores that according to Buddhist epistemology conceptuality is not the passive internalization of perceived objects but an act of active construction that reflects the spontaneous and creative side of human understanding. Second, Dharmottara's solution assumes rather than establishes a distinction in the functions of perception and conception. It presupposes that conceptual cognitions function to conceptualize, that is, conceive, construct, imagine, and so on, following the Buddhist repudiation of realism. Since the objects conceived by thought are not part of reality, they must be constructed or imputed.

This view is quite different from the Nyāya view that objects conceived by thought are real, for the function of thought is not limited to imagining but is closely linked with reality. Thought is able to understand the general and abstract aspects of reality, which are not accessible to bare perception. Without this, human knowledge would be reduced to the sensing of bare particulars. Due to their commitment to a sparse ontology, Buddhist epistemologists cannot agree with the rather convincing Nyāya account of human knowledge. Their philosophy privileges the particular over the general: Reality is made up of a plurality of elements, and generality is, at best, the result of atomic aggregation (when it is not a figment of the imagination). This emphasis on the particular expresses itself on the epistemological level, where perception is valued over conception. This is where we can see the difficult articulation of the ontological and epistemological levels of a philosophical system. Although the two are not separable, they pull in different directions. Whereas ontology favors an economy of sparsity that devalues the general, epistemology tends to privilege it.

This situation can give rise to two attitudes: We might choose, as do the Naiyāyikas, not to sacrifice the integrity of the epistemological level and to pay the price of a crowded ontology. Or, like the Buddhists, we might refuse to pay this price and try to patch things up when it comes to epistemology. There, thought is given limited validity as inference but is denied any other cognitive role. Thought infers the real but does not apprehend it, because it is deprived of any direct access to it. Therefore, Dharmottara must deny that in the perceptual process thought has any validity of its own.

Third, Dharmottara's explanation, even more than Dharmakīrti's, assumes that conceptions and perceptions work together. For a conception to assume the function of prior perception, conceptions and perceptions must operate in relation to exactly the same object. For example, I see an object that I categorize as a blue thing. For this categorization to have any relevance to the perceptual experience, it must relate to the seen object. This is, however, impossible since, for Dharmakīrti, conceptions cannot apprehend the objects of perception.

The only link that can be posited between the two is causal. Such an explanation, however, cannot account for the coordination between perceptions and conceptions. A causal link cannot guarantee that our concepts are in touch with reality. The simple fact that I think "this is a fire" after seeing an object does not ensure that I saw a fire. I can have such an idea after seeing a red patch. Nor does my seeing a fire ensures that my idea applies to the fire I saw. What is required is that my perception and conception of fire cognitively bear on the same real object. In this way, the application of the appropriate concept can be differentiated from the inappropriate one. Such an epistemic coordination between perception and conception, however, is in principle outside Dharmakīrti's system, predicated as it is on a strict dichotomy between these two types of valid cognition on the basis of their having different objects.

We came across this problem while examining the objective basis of conceptual activities.[5] We noticed that the real problem of Dharmakīrti's philosophy is not that it does not offer an explanation of the objectivity of conceptions but that, rather, his explanation contradicts one of the most basic assumptions of his system, the absolute dichotomy between the only two forms of knowledge, perception and inference. Not only is there nothing in common between these two types of cognition, but even their objects are totally different. How can they be coordinated given these assumptions?

This difficulty does not concern only the explanation of the epistemic status of conception but also that of perception. Perception can be cognitive only in relation to conceptual interpretations. This presupposes that the two types of cognition can be cognitively coordinated or that a bridge between the two can be built. Without such an explanation, Dharmottara's theory of perception cannot stand. I believe that he sees the problem quite well and attempts to deal with it in other parts of his work. In the following pages, I look at two attempts to establish a bridge between perception and conception. The first passage attempts to deal with the problem by establishing an object common to both types of cognition, thereby bringing some degree of cognitive coordination. The second passage attempts to build a bridge between the two types of cognition by giving to perception a more active role. Instead of being purely passive, perception becomes cognitively active. This transformation marks a new trend in Buddhist epistemology, whose significance will become clearer when we examine Tibetan theories of perception.

Bridging the Gap Between Perception and Conception

Jñānagarbha and others have attempted to establish a link between perception and conception through the intermediary of mental perception (*mānasa pratyakṣa, yid kyi mngon sum*), which is one of the four types of perception accepted by Buddhist epistemologists. In this scenario, a sense perception gives rise to a mental perception, which transforms into a conceptual thought. Since sense perception is a different type of experience than conception (which is mental), it cannot give rise to a conception without the intermediary, mental perception.

Dharmottara does not accept the necessity of an intermediary. The validity of sense perception consists of its capacity to induce judgment. If an intermediary were necessary, sense perception could not produce judgment and would not be valid. Mookerjee explains Dharmottara's opinion: "The very validity of sense perception depends on this generative efficiency of itself and it can be regarded as an efficient cause of knowledge only if it exercises a function, . . . the generation of conceptual knowledge itself. If you suppose a *tertium quid* between the two cognitions, you will only make the indeterminate sense perception an inefficient, abortive fact, which is absurd."[6] For Dharmottara, there is no need to postulate an intermediary between sense perception and thought. In any case, the existence of a transitional mechanism does not answer the question raised by Dharmakīrti's epistemology: How can thought and perception refer to the same reality when their objects are different?

Dharmottara's solution is to finesse the restrictions imposed by Dharmakīrti on the objects of perception and conception by distinguishing between different types of object:

> There are two types of object of cognition: the held and the conceived. Conceptual cognitions apprehend a superimposed nature and ascertain the specifically characterized phenomenon that resembles this [imputed entity].

> Sense perceptions apprehend moments, and the ascertainment generated by its (perception) power ascertains [this object], thinking that it sees a continuum [of] momentary parts. Here, the held object is different but not the object of application, for both [perceptions and conceptions] engage only in specifically characterized phenomena by conceiving [of] them. Therefore, that object which is held by perception is not obtained, for it is not possible to obtain a [single] moment. Nevertheless, the ascertainment generated by the power of perception takes as its object the continuum of moments held [by perception]. Since this [continuum] is the object ascertained, there is no difference in the object of application conceived by both perception and inference.[7]

This important passage is quite puzzling, for it seems to attribute ascertainment to perception itself. But let us deal with Dharmottara's points in their order. Dharmottara first differentiates two types of object: held and conceived objects. The first is the direct object understood in terms of appearance, which we described as a prima facie or direct object.[8] Both perception and inference have held objects; namely, the individual moments and the unreal imputed nature, respectively.[9] Those are the objects directly held by consciousness.

The objects to which we relate on the practical level are different. They are objects conceived by cognition; that is, objects about which we gain certainty and to which we apply our efforts. They also constitute objects of [practical] application (*'jug yul*), which we also described as primary objects.[10] The restriction imposed by Dharmakīrti on the object of valid cognitions does not apply to this second type of object. Here both perception and conception conceive of the same real object, which has the capacity to perform a practical function. Thus, a certain unity of the cognitive process is established and perception is made more cognitive. In this way, Dharmakīrti's radical dichotomy is saved and reinterpreted as applying to the direct objects of cognitions, and the cognitive status of perception can be established on the basis of its indirect bearing on the conceived object apprehended by conception.

The singularity of Dharmottara's presentation is his attribution of a conceived object to perception, an idea that even his Tibetan followers will not adopt. What does he mean by that? Is Dharmottara saying that perception itself determines its object? Or is he saying that it induces judgment that determines its object? The former would be very surprising, for it contradicts a basic tenet of Dharmakīrti that perception does not determine its own object. The latter would leave open the problem of the coordination between the two types of cognitions.

But the problems faced by Dharmottara do not stop there. For, as he acknowledges, the object conceived directly by conception and indirectly by perception cannot be the real object. A real object exists moment by moment and, hence, cannot be integrated in our practical world, which assumes duration. The things we use in daily life are not the discrete moments that constitute reality, but the continua. These, however, are not real, as our analysis of Dharmakīrti's ontology has shown.[11] Therefore, how can they serve as the real objects in relation to which perception and conception can be coordinated? Or did Dharmakīrti hold that the coordination necessary to the establishment of the epistemic status of perception pertains to the unreal conceptual domain?

We apprehend commonsense objects as performing certain functions. These are not, however, the actual functions performed by real objects but the conceptual interpretations of these functions. That is, we project on a momentary reality concepts that help us to deal with it. Some of these concepts help us categorize these momentary objects whereas others bring some stability without which practical action would be impossible. Through these stabilizing concepts we see things as continua and impute on them a common function that brings unity to their discrete components.[12] Dharmottara says: "That which is obtained by perception is just the continuum. [For] one cannot obtain moments."[13] Valid cognitions, which apply practically to reality, take these synthetic constructs as their objects. In doing so, they do not relate to momentary reality but only to its conceptual interpretations, for discrete moments cannot be practically appropriated.

Thus, Dharmottara's difficulty in establishing the foundational status of perception remains. Such status cannot be established in relation to practical objects, for they are unreal. Perception's hold on reality must be explained in relation to the other type of object, the moments that are held by consciousness individually. These held objects do not, however, provide guidance in the practical world. Such guidance is found only at the level of the conceived object (the object of application). Such a level, however, is conceptual and thus irrelevant, according to the conceptualist, to reality. The problem of coordinating perception and conception remains.

Dharmottara's solution could be that coordination is achieved because perception, which directly perceives real moments, also indirectly cognizes practical objects. This, however, would be problematic, for it would entail that perception determines its object and thus contradict Dharmakīrti's explicit denial that perception determines reality.[14] If, on the other hand, perception merely induces judgment that conceives of the moments held by perception as practical objects, our problem is still unsolved. For all that has been achieved is a coordination of perception and conception in relation to conceptually constructed practical objects. The relation of this coordinated perception and conception to reality is still problematic.

Does Perception Determine Its Object?

Another passage from Dharmottara seems to indicate another attempt to secure the epistemic status of perception by attributing to it a more active role in the cognitive process. The epistemic status of perception is a function of its ability to lead to practical success. We identify through experience that certain actions, such as touching a fire with our hands, lead to suffering. How can experience inform us about the real world if it is devoid of any interpretation and, hence, of any cognitive content? Is not perception the mere presence of objects without determination, devoid of understanding and practically ineffective? Dharmottara answers:

> Ideas such as "this," [i.e.,] "this leads to happiness, that leads to suffering," are ascertained as perception. [For] when something is determinate, the person who establishes a practical convention determines the proximate object as leading to happiness. That which is said to lead to happiness or suffering is the object of application. . . . Such an application must have ascertainment. The opponent thinks that because perception does not [ascertain anything], it [cannot] engage [in practical activities]. The master [Dharmakīrti responds that] this is true for the things that are subsuming or subsumed. In order to show that both determinate and indeterminate perceptions are causes of application [in practical activities], the master said "this fault is not present." There are two types [of cases in which] there is no object of application: Sometimes, a perception does not take [anything] as its object of application due to its not [being able] to ascertain the nature [of the object. At other times], indeterminate perception does not take [anything] as object of application due to the lack of proximity of a precedingly seen activity [i.e., due to the lack of habituation]. . . . Accordingly, determinate perception separately ascertains the location, time, and aspect [of the object]. Moreover, the cognition that is produced by the power of indeterminate [perception] ascertains that which is held by perception.[15]

This passage is even more puzzling than the preceding one, for it seems to reintroduce the idea of determinate (or conceptual) perception, which Dharmakīrti so abundantly refuted. It is, therefore, difficult to interpret such a passage. One must wonder how serious Dharmottara can be in proposing a type of perception that so clearly contradicts Dharmakīrti's theory of perception. A possible interpretation would be that Dharmottara is referring to the fact that certain perceptions induce judgment that takes over their perceptual functions, while others require further investigation.

Although his formulation is surprising and problematic, Dharmottara's intention is here again to explain the epistemic status of perception by proposing a more active model of perception. To support this idea of a cognitive active perception, Dharmottara differentiates two types of perception: determinate and indeterminate. Although he is not very explicit about how the distinction is drawn, we can assume that he means something like this: Determinate perceptions identify their objects as this or that (or at least contribute to their identification directly), whereas indeterminate perceptions can only sense their objects without producing an immediate judgment. For example, the perception present in the experience of perceptual reduction induces no certainty in us at the time of the experience. Only afterward are we able to recollect the object (i.e., its touch as it was experienced at that time). Hence, it is indeterminate. Similarly, where we lack habituation, we may not able to categorize the situation we encounter. At such times our perceptions are indeterminate.

By contrast, determinate perceptions are able to induce direct determination of the nature and function of the objects they perceive. For example, I see a round object that I identify as a pot. This ascertainment requires previous acquaintance with the nature and the function of the object. Nevertheless, this identification of the object is due not to the conception following the perceptual experience but to the perception itself, which is able to ascertain (or lead to direct ascertainment of) the location, time and aspect of the object it perceives. Perception does not just passively hold its object but actively brings about some cognitive content, either directly (determinate perception) or indirectly (indeterminate perception).

Dharmottara does not dwell in detail on this idea, and we can only speculate on the implications of attributing a more active role to perception. We must wonder about the ontological implications of this serious revision of Buddhist epistemology. We remember a passage in which Dharmottara seems to introduce real universals by distinguishing between the imaginary universals posited by extreme realism (as independent from their instances) and those accepted by moderate realism (as dependent on their instances). Does Dharmottara have this in mind when he distinguishes entities that are subsumed or subsume other entities, from entities that are objects of both types of perception? Or does he want to exclude all universals that are posited by reasoning as objects of perception? Although this passage seems to suggest the second alternative, it is unclear.

In either case, Dharmottara's ideas represent a change from Dharmakīrti's idea of perception as the sensing of individual qualities. Perception is less a contact with bare reality, which is then clothed by concepts, than an active application toward objects of practical concern already determined at the perceptual level. This is what I have described as the second[16] move of a new epistemology (*tshad ma gsar ma*), which starts in India and continues in Tibet with Ngok, Cha-ba, and their tradition.

Before going on to examine further developments of this new trend in Tibet, let us pause to speculate briefly on the possible influences that prompted Dharmottara to use unorthodox epistemological concepts. For, although I claim that Dharmottara is an important figure of this new epistemology, I do not hold that it originated with him. I will here mention a single name, Śubhagupta (650–750 C.E.).

Śubhagupta is a critic of Dharmakīrti. He is usually classified as a Vaibhāṣika, although his theory is rather different from the usual epistemology of this school. Śubhagupta distinguishes two stages in the cognition of external objects. The first stage is nonconceptual, in which we contact aggregated atoms without imposing any form. In the second, conceptual stage, a mental cognition imposes a coarse (*sthūla, rags pa*) form on the aggregation of atoms. This form is the product of a synthesis and, therefore, illusory. Depending on this synthesis (in which sense and mental cognitions are involved), we apprehend things as extended in space and time. Śubhagupta's theory differs from the usual Vaibhāṣika view, which denies that cognition has any aspect at all. Śubhagupta does not deny that determinate perception has an aspect but asserts that this aspect is false or illusory (*alikākāra, rdzun pa'i rnam pa*) because it does not correspond to reality. Objects exist atomically despite their being perceived as extended. The extended aspect cannot be true and must be the result of distortions.

Dharmottara, who is also a False Aspectarian,[17] seems to defend a similar position. Like Śubhagupta, he asserts two types of perception. However, Dharmottara might not have accepted Śubhagupta's description of the formation of the false aspect through a synthesis between sense and mental consciousness. Dharmottara might have avoided this idea, which drew a lot of criticism from Dharmakīrti's followers (Prajñākaragupta in particular). However, the resemblance is real, and it is not impossible that Dharmottara developed his ideas under Śubhagupta's influence. At any rate, it provides some context for Dharmottara's development of a new epistemology. It also shows that the new epistemology developed by Tibetans was not due to their inability to understand Indian philosophy but to their pursuit of a long revisionist tradition already started in India. Confronted by the tensions of Dharmakīrti's system, Indian authors had to develop new interpretations. Tibetans continued their efforts, as we will see in the next chapter.

22

Tibetan New Epistemology

Cha-ba's Epistemology of Perception

The new trend, seen earlier in Dharmottara, developed in Tibet as a new epistemology (*tshad ma gsar ma*) through the works of Ngok and Cha-ba. The problem with the study of their ideas is that their works are not available, so we must rely on secondhand sources, usually Śākya Chok-den's rich presentation. Śākya Chok-den, however, is not always fair. He clearly has an axe to grind against some of his contemporaries and predecessors. Using the works of Cha-ba and others, he argues that the views of his contemporaries are actually distorted renderings of the original Dharmakīrtian views due to their reliance on misinterpretations of that tradition. For example, he denounces the Ge-luk identification of held and appearing objects, claiming that it is not Dharmakīrti's view but Cha-ba's invention. In this case, he also argues that his contemporaries did not even get Cha-ba right! Thus, while Śākya Chok-den brings us worthwhile information, it would not be wise to accept it uncritically. Another problem with Śākya Chok-den is that he tends to overemphasize for polemical purposes the differences between Tibetan thinkers and their Indian predecessors. He also assumes, as commentators often do, that his sources present a uniform view. But, in the (we hope) provisional absence of original material, Śākya Chok-den is our best resource, and I will assume generally that "he got Cha-ba right."

One of the particularities of Ngok's and Cha-ba's new epistemology is that it makes an important but controversial distinction between perception (*mngon sum*) and valid perception (*mngon sum gyi tshad ma*). In Dharmakīrti's works, perception is one type of valid cognition, and he never suggests that some perceptions are not valid. By contrast, Ngok and Cha-ba holds that perception is not necessarily valid although it is always undistorted.[1] Although elements in Dharmottara suggest such a move, their distinction is quite new in Buddhist epistemology.

In general, most Buddhist epistemologists agree that cognitions require both nondeceptiveness and novelty to be valid.[2] But whereas Dharmakīrti and his classical commentators understand nondeceptiveness in pragmatic terms, Ngok and Cha-ba understand it in an intentional sense. Assuming that validity is to be understood in those terms, they define a valid cognition as a mental episode that newly realizes (*gsar du rtogs pa'i blo*), that is, identifies, its object. Two criteria are implied by this definition: (a) A cognition must identify its object (criterion of cognitive success) and (b) this identification must be novel (criterion of novelty).

This definition is problematic in relation to perception, for not all perceptions fulfill these two criteria, according to these thinkers. For example, suppose that I am staring at a painting. The first moment is valid according to these thinkers, since it provides new information. But what about the second and the following ones? They are veridical but they do not meet the two previously delineated criteria, since they contribute nothing new to the epistemic process. Hence, they are not valid in the technical sense of the term, since they are not knowledge generating. Therefore, they are not forms of perceptual knowledge. Take another problematic example: I distractedly listen to music while writing this chapter. When this task is over, I have no recollection of what I listened to. I just have a vague memory of listening to some music. Was my musical perception valid? It certainly does not seem to determine anything and, hence, it is not valid by virtue of failing the first criterion.

To account for these problems, Ngok and Cha-ba distinguish valid perceptions from nonvalid and yet unmistaken perceptions. That is, certain perceptions contribute knowledge while others do not, although they are veridical. To develop Ngok's idea, Cha-ba proposes two new types of perception. The second moment of my seeing a painting in the first example is described as a subsequent perception (*bcad shes*). It is not valid because it brings no new information. My hearing music in the second example is described as an inattentive cognition (*snang la ma nges pa*).[3] It does not induce certainty with respect to its object and, therefore, is not valid (in the technical sense of the word).[4] Nevertheless, both types of cognitions are perception because their objects appear without any distortion.

Among the two criteria implied by Cha-ba's definition of *valid cognition*, the criterion of novelty is accepted by most Indian epistemologists. The criterion of cognitive success, however, is more problematic. Let me elaborate this important point that will provide a view of the nature of Cha-ba's new epistemology. According to Cha-ba, a cognition must correctly identify its object to be valid. Technically, this process of correct identification is described as the elimination of false superimpositions (*sgro 'dogs gcod pa*) and understood as being equivalent to the obtainment of the identified object (*bcad don thob pa*). Cognitions are valid if, and only if, they eliminate the appropriate false superimpositions and thus epistemically secure the object being identified.[5] False superimpositions can be eliminated in two ways: by relying on reasoning or by experience. Whereas the first is characteristic of inference, the second is how valid perception identifies its object. That an inference, which is a conceptual valid cognition, eliminates superimpositions is unproblematic within Buddhist epistemology. Elimination by experience, however, is rejected by Sa-paṇ and his followers, for whom it is a contradiction in terms, because elimination is a conceptual task performed by judgment (or by inference) but that cannot be performed by perception itself.

Let me explain what is meant by *elimination of superimposition* with a concrete example, using the vocabulary of Cha-ba and his tradition. I return home and see my favorite rocking chair. My visual consciousness immediately identifies this object as my favorite rocking chair. This mental state realizes (*rtogs*), that is, correctly identifies or determines (*bcad*) this object and induces certainty (*nges pa*, more on this latter). Determination consists of the elimination of the idea that this object is not my favorite rocking chair.[6] A cognition that determines its object is said to be nondeceptive. If, on top of this, it is novel, then it is valid; that is, it is knowledge generating. Hence, Cha-ba defines *valid perception* as "that cognition which eliminates superimpositions with respect to a previously unrealized thing by the power of experience."[7]

Thus Cha-ba explains how both perception and conception can be cognitively successful. If we believe Śākya Chok-den, Cha-ba seems to think that eliminating a false idea requires actual contact (*phrad pa*) between the false idea and the perception. At the second moment the false view is made powerless, and at the third moment it is eliminated.[8] Not every follower of the new epistemology, however, holds this rather mechanistic view. In particular, Ge-luk thinkers, who agree that understanding an object involves eliminating a superimposition, assert that the superimposition does not have to be directly present to be eliminated.[9] Therefore, elimination of superimposition does not necessarily mean that I must first have a false idea, which is later chased out of my mind. Rather, it means that I implicitly understand that the object apprehended (*'dzin stangs kyi yul*) by this false view (the pseudo-fact that this object is not my favorite rocking chair) does not exist. Exposing the falseness of the superimposition is its elimination. Put positively, my visual consciousness correctly identifies the object.

Why is this rather simple idea of correct identification put in such negative jargon? This question will be answered extensively in a later chapter while explaining Sa-paṇ's refutation of the Tibetan new epistemology.[10] Suffice to say that this negative description is meant as an interpretation of Dharmakīrti's views. These are, however, quite different. For Dharmakīrti, perception is passive. It is the holding of an object within its ken or the sensing of an object given in its bare particularity. The active integration of the object within a categorical framework does not happen at the perceptual level but is the product of conceptuality. Dharmottara tries to find ways to impart a more active role to perception, which is not for him limited to passive holding but includes an element of ascertainment.

A similar idea is at work in Cha-ba's elimination of superimposition. Cha-ba sees perceptual knowledge as actively presenting us with commonsense objects already integrated into a categorical scheme and not just with bare particulars. I am not just seeing a color and a shape that I interpret conceptually as a chair, I am seeing my favorite rocking chair. Thus, the activity of perception is not limited to inducing judgment (as Sa-paṇ holds) but actively determines its objects. We could imagine Cha-ba agreeing with Schopenhauer's argument that "the sensation does not separate itself clearly from the idea which is constructed out of it, as the raw material, by the understanding."[11] Antirealists are mistaken in assuming that perception (Schopenhauer's sensation) is limited to bare particulars. Experience shows that "we see things themselves quite directly, and indeed as lying outside us."[12]

The description of a more active cognition is not limited to perception but concerns both types of valid cognition. It does not, however, change the cognitive role of conception, which is conceived by both realists and antirealists as active. When applied to perception, the idea of an active cognition modifies the very idea of perception in its most meaningful expression, for it extends the capacities of perception beyond the mere holding of an object. Hence, Cha-ba's idea of perception is rather different from Dharmakīrti's and indeed represents a new development. This new epistemology is, however, not without sources in the Indian Buddhist tradition. We saw a related idea in Dharmottara, who, however, did not go as far. Dharmottara seems to have differentiated two levels of perception, in which the first (indeterminate) resembles Dharmakīrti's idea of perception. The second, however, introduces a more active view of it. Even so, Dharmottara maintains that apprehending an object within the perceptual ken is the function of perception per se (especially in its first moment). A similar move is found in Mokṣākaragupta, who asserts that perception can indirectly cognize universals. Perception passively holds the individual object but in the process determines its properties. This determination is not direct but is the by-product of the perceptual process.[13]

Can we further trace sources for Cha-ba's new view of perception? Sa-paṇ's *Auto-Commentary* mentions the view of followers of Śaṃkarānanda as holding that a valid cognition "merely eliminates an opposed superimposition with respect to a characteristic of the entity [of the object]."[14] This view also holds that a valid cognition does not take part in "establishment and refutation" (*dgag sgrub byed*), which is a purely conceptual matter. What does this mean? It is by no means easy to understand this position. Nevertheless, the following interpretation seems quite plausible: Perception does not apprehend a bare object, but delivers an object with distinguishing characteristics. We then put a label on the object, which is, however, already marked. Labeling is not the function of perception, but is done on the basis of a differentiation already present in perception.

We might wonder, who are these followers of the Brahmin Śaṃkarānanda (*bram ze rjes 'brang*) mentioned by Sa-paṇ? Śākya Chok-den suggests that they are only Cha-ba and other Tibetans.[15] We should, however, be suspicious of Śākya Chok-den's tendency to deny the Indian credentials of his opponents' ideas. I suspect Sa-paṇ is referring to an Indian source, possibly Śaṃkarānanda himself, but this is difficult to decide, since the relevant part of the latter's commentary is not extant in Tibetan. In any case, it seems quite plausible that Śaṃkarānanda held such a view, which is in harmony with his realist comments we saw while investigating the problem of universals. Therefore, Śaṃkarānanda is possibly a source (behind Dharmottara) for the theory that perception involves cognitive activity.

In harmony with his view of perceptual knowledge as apprehending an already articulated reality, Cha-ba's view on universals is that of a moderate realist. Perception apprehends a chair as being a chair. Consequently, chairness, or rather, being a chair, is a universal that is real and is substantially identical with its particulars.[16] Cha-ba does not accept, however, the Nyāya or the Sāṃkhya extreme realist view that universals exist independent of their particulars. Similarly, Cha-ba rejects the Nyāya idea of a determinate perception, for he holds perception to be nonconceptual. His understanding of nonconceptuality, however, is different from Dharmakīrti's. Contrary to Dharmakīrti's epistemological view that any propositional content is conceptual, Cha-ba understands nonconceptuality in a psychological sense. For him, a cognition is nonconceptual if, and only if, it does not involve the noticeable presence of a conceptual cognition. Hence, he can claim to reject the Nyāya view while at the same time maintaining the existence of a propositional perception. Nevertheless, his model of perception is close to the Nyāya view of a determinate perception.

Ge-luk Views of Perception

Cha-ba's views greatly influenced the Ge-luk tradition. His moderate realism is the source of the Ge-luk view we examined earlier.[17] His new epistemology has been taken over by this latter tradition. Although the Ge-luk thinkers do not follow completely Cha-ba's epistemology, the view of a more cognitively active perception seems to be universally agreed on among scholars belonging to this tradition. Both Gyel-tsap and Kay-drup repeatedly describe the elimination of superimposition as the function of a valid cognition. For example, to explain that a visual consciousness is not able to understand the impermanence of form, despite understanding form, Gyel-tsap says: "Despite the fact that there is no difference in the relation between the eye sense basis and all [the qualities of form such as] the impermanence of form, [a perception of form] is a newly non-deceptive consciousness with respect to form through the appearance of the aspect of the object [form]. Only this is fit to establish the valid cognition realizing form as a valid cognition. [This is so] because the fact that a sense consciousness apprehending form understands form but not sound is due to the appearance [of an object to] the mental episode which has or does not have the [relevant] aspect which is able to eliminate superimposition."[18] A perception holds form with all its intrinsic qualities, such as impermanence,[19] which act equally as causes of the perception (via the sense basis). Why does consciousness understand form, but not its impermanence? The aspect appearing to the mental episode can remove falsities of form but not of impermanence, which is too subtle. Deluded by the rapid succession of similar moments, which are in reality different from each other but appear similar,[20] ordinary beings view things as being stable. They understand the fundamental instability of things only when this succession of similar moments is broken (such as when an object breaks). Therefore, their perceptions cannot apprehend the impermanence of things, even though things appear to their perceptions as impermanent. Only noble beings can ascertain things as they appear to them. Dharmakīrti says: "The great mind ascertains all the aspects [of a thing] by merely seeing [it]."[21] Only noble beings can directly understand the subtle impermanence of things, because they are able to eliminate the superimposition of permanence.[22]

Their vision is not impeded, and they see things as they are.

Kay-drup disagrees with Gyel-tsap on the meaning of Dharmakīrti's "great mind," which he does not restrict to noble beings. A great mind is "the wise person who is able to eliminate by the power of reasoning a superimposition on the nature of things."[23] His understanding of epistemic validity is, however, similar to that of Gyel-tsap's. Explaining one of the two types of object of application by valid cognition, Kay-drup speaks of "the object [determined by] the elimination of superimposition by valid cognition."[24] For both thinkers, as well as for other Ge-luk scholars, the explanation of valid cognition as the elimination of a superimposition is an obvious truth. This has important consequences for their understanding of perception. As such, it constitutes a new conception of perception that is much closer to the common understanding than Dharmakīrti's idea of bare perception.

Implicit and Explicit

Another feature of the new epistemology is the distinction between explicit (*dngos su rtogs pa*) and implicit realization (*shugs la rtogs pa*). This distinction is an important interpretive device that was probably elaborated by Cha-ba or his followers. Conceptually, the distinction between explicit and implicit levels of understanding is necessitated by the problems raised by the new view of perception as cognitively more active which threatens to contradict Dharmakīrti's basic theorem that validity is limited either to perception or inference. Since perception's role is not limited to a bare sensing but involves the full identification of objects, the purview of this type of cognition expands dramatically. Not only are universals included, but even certain characteristics usually described as conceptual. For example, when I identify a pot, I am also aware that this pot is not a nonpot. This negation, however, is not part of the fabric of reality but merely conceptually added. How can perception understand this artificial construct?

The solution lies in the distinction between implicit and explicit realization, which we already encountered in our investigation of the meaning of negation. We saw that Ge-luk thinkers speak of nonimplicative negation (*med dgag, pratiṣedha*) being understood implicitly, and we noticed the difference in Śāntarakṣita's idea that nonimplicative negations are understood by implication (*arthāpati, don gyis rtogs pa*). Let us examine this concept in relation to perception.

The translation of the concept of *dngos su rtogs pa* is a major problem because not every thinker uses the term in the same sense. Bo-dong presents an interesting analysis of the word *dngos* for which he finds five meanings: (a) *dngos* = actual in opposition to *btags pa ba* (metaphorical); (b) *dngos* = principal in opposition to *zhar* (secondary); (c) *dngos* = explicit, that is, clearly indicated by words and so forth (*sgras zin sogs kyis gsal bar mtshon pa*) in opposition to *shugs* (implicit); (d) *dngos* = direct, that is, without intermediary in opposition to *rgyud* (indirect); and (e) *dngos* = self in opposition to *gzhan* (other).[25]

For Cha-ba and later thinkers of the Ge-luk tradition, the description of a cognition as *rang yul dngos su rtogs pa* concerns Bo-dong's third meaning of *dngos*. This is, however, not accepted by thinkers (such as Sa-paṇ) who refuse to make the distinction between implicit and explicit understanding. They hold that the term *dngos* is not to be taken in the (c) sense but in the (d) sense. In keeping with this complicated situation, I will translate *dngos su rtogs* as "direct realization" when dealing with the views of thinkers who reject the idea of an implicit realization (to be explained shortly) and as "explicit realization" when dealing with thinkers who accept this idea.

In his critique of early Tibetan epistemologists, Sa-paṇ takes this idea of implicit realization as a central point of the differences between him and his contemporaries. For Sa-paṇ, perception does not eliminate superimposition, for its function is strictly limited to the passive appearance of things. Accordingly, the distinctions we make on the basis of our perceptual experiences are the products of our conceptualization. The view of Cha-ba and his followers is quite different. For them, the role of perception is not limited to a passive reflection of objects but includes the determination of these objects. Our assertions and denials about things are made not just on the basis of a causal connection with perceptions. Rather, positive or negative judgment recaptures the cognitive content already contained in perceptual understanding. This cognitive content can be determined in two ways: explicitly or implicitly. An object is said to be explicitly realized (*dngos su rtogs pa*), that is, understood, if it appears to the cognition (perception or inference) that determines it. If it is determined without appearing to this cognition, it is said to be realized implicitly (*shugs la rtogs pa*).

These two realizations occur simultaneously. For example, my seeing a pot involves both aspects: explicitly I am aware of the pot as a pot, and implicitly I also understand the difference between pot and nonpot. Hence, I am said to realize that the pot is not a nonpot. This understanding is implicit because this nonimplicative negation (pot not being nonpot) does not appear to our eye consciousness. Another example is the understanding of the absence of a pot by a visual consciousness apprehending a spot on which there is no pot. Implicit understanding is posited to explain these facts without contradicting the basic tenet of Buddhist epistemology that valid cognitions can be perceptual or inferential. Since the absence of a pot is not seen by perception, it cannot be apprehended by perception. Nor is it understood by inference, for we need not reason to understand that there is no pot in front of us. The problem is solved by positing a second (implicit) level of perceptual knowledge. A phenomenon (such as the absence of pot) can be understood implicitly by perception without being perceived. Similarly, inference can identify an object without inferring it.[26]

This idea of an implicit understanding is taken over by Ge-luk-ba epistemologists. Kay-drup explains: "The meaning of explicit realization of a given object is this: a valid [perception] is directed toward that object and induces certainty by the power [of that object's] aspect appearing [to the perception] without having to rely on any later cognition. The meaning of implicit realization [of a given object] is this: a valid [perception] is not presently directed toward that object but eliminates superimpositions toward that object in accordance with the circumstances by the power of explicitly comprehending its object. Thus, it will be [able] to induce certainty [toward the implicitly realized object] without having to rely on another valid cognition by merely directing its mind [to that object]."[27] The two levels of understanding are differentiated according to whether the object understood (i.e., toward which mistaken superimpositions are eliminated) appears to the perception or not. For example, when I look at my desk I do not see any elephant. According to the proponents of the new epistemology, my visual perception explicitly realizes (*dngos su rtogs*) the desk that is without elephant in front of me. This sense perception is not explicitly aware of the mere absence of elephant. Nevertheless, after seeing the desk, I have no doubt as to whether there was or was not any elephant on it. This is the sign, according to Ge-luk thinkers, that the visual perception implicitly understands the absence of elephant while explicitly seeing the desk, even though this mere absence did not appear to perception. This mere absence is implicitly identified by the perception. Otherwise, the identification of the absence of elephant that takes place (since we do not have doubt any more) would have to be an inference, since it is valid and is not a perception.

The acceptance of two types of cognized object has the consequence that perceptions can be valid with respect to objects they do not perceive. Gyel-tsap says:

> In general, every valid perception is a perception and every valid inference is a conceptual cognition. Nevertheless, when related to a particular object, [a perception] is a valid perception but is not a perception with respect to its implicit object. [Similarly, an inference] is a valid inference but is not a conceptual cognition with respect to [this implicit object]. This is indicated by passages such as: "It is a perception with respect to a specifically characterized phenomenon" and "That cognition which apprehends the object [indicated by] words is accepted as a conceptual cognition with respect to this [object]."[28] [This is so] because it is explained that [a cognition] is a perception with respect to [a given object] only if the specific characteristics of this [object] appear [to this cognition]. [Similarly, a cognition] is conceptual with respect to [a given object] only if [this cognition] apprehends its object [designated by] words.[29]

It is a basic principle of Buddhist epistemology that a valid cognition is either a perception or an inference. This principle does not apply, however, to the objects understood implicitly. An object such as a jar is identified by a perception, which is thus valid. That is, this cognition contributes to our knowledge of the jar. This knowledge is at two levels. Explicitly, we see the jar. Implicitly, we identify this jar as not being a nonjar. Hence, this cognition is valid (in the technical sense of the word) with respect to this implicitly identified (conceptual) fact, for it is knowledge generating. Such a fact is not, however, seen and hence cannot be said to be perceived. This leads to Gyel-tsap's seemingly bizarre statement that a cognition is a valid perception with respect the object implicitly realized, although it is not a perception with respect to that object. The statement makes perfect sense, however, if we understand validity to be evaluated in terms of an epistemic contribution. The cognition of a jar does make a contribution by making us understand that a jar is not a nonjar. Such a cognition does not, however, perceive such a fact.

In this way, the followers of Cha-ba's new epistemology conciliate their more active view of perception with the restrictions of Dharmakīrti's system, according to which real things concern perception and unreal entities concern inference. According to the new model, perception identifies explicitly real things and implicitly unreal constructs. By positing a distinction between explicit and implicit, Dharmakīrti's restriction is shown to concern only the explicit level, leaving the epistemologist free to elaborate a model in which perception is no more a mere sensing but is a full-fledged propositional knowledge.

Epistemological Typologies

Another important characteristic of Cha-ba's approach is his elaboration of new epistemological typologies called *typology of mental states* (*blo rigs*).[30] Among those, the most important is his sevenfold typology. Cha-ba understands this division of mental states to be definitive in number (*grangs nges*); that is, that every cognition is included in one of these seven categories. His seven categories are as follows: doubt (*the tshom*), false cognition (*log shes*), inattentive cognition (*snang la ma nges pa*), subsequent cognition (*bcad shes*), perception (*mngon sum*), inference (*rjes dpag, anumāna*), and correct assumption (*yid dpyod*).

He argues for the comprehensiveness of his typology in the following way. When we cognize, we are either hesitating or not. Undecided cognitions are forms of doubt. All other types of cognition are unhesitating. Unhesitating cognitions are either false or factual. Factual cognitions either do or do not contradict a superimposition, and in this latter case are inattentive cognitions. Cognitively, active cognitions identify an object that is already realized (subsequent cognition) or a new object. In this latter case, the new object can be perceived in either of two ways: by seeing the object (perception) or by not seeing the object. In this case, the cognition either relies on a reason and is inferential or does not rely on a reason and just correctly assumes the nature of its object.[31]

Cha-ba's distinction between perception and valid perception can now be better understood. Cha-ba asserts that perception can be of three types: valid cognition (*tshad ma*), subsequent cognition (*bcad shes*), and inattentive cognition (*snang la ma nges pa*). As explained previously, the distinction between the first two types of perception and inattentive cognition lies in the active cognitive ability or lack thereof of them. The distinction between the valid perception and subsequent cognition derives from the second criterion set by Cha-ba for being a valid cognition; namely, that of novelty. For example, the first moment of my seeing my rocking chair is valid. The following moments are not, for they merely realize the same object as the first moment.

This presentation of mental states is accepted by many Tibetan thinkers. Bo-dong, for example, differentiates perception from valid perception: Whereas the former merely holds its object, the latter identifies it. Although valid perception does not ascertain (*nges*) its object (for then it would be conceptual), it determines its object by eliminating superimpositions. If, as Sa-paṇ claims, perception could not eliminate wrong views, then, absurdly, yogic perception could not root out delusions, for this presupposes a capacity to eliminate false superimpositions.[32]

While there seems to be general agreement on the idea that perception is cognitively more active than Dharmakīrti would have it, the Ge-luk tradition is divided regarding Cha-ba's sevenfold typology and the distinctions that it entails. Although these differences are rather technical, they alert us to the fact that the Ge-luk tradition is not monolithic. Although united on many topics, Ge-luk thinkers have substantial disagreements. In the domain of logic and epistemology, two currents can be distinguished. The first tradition is usually associated with Gyel-tsap, defended by the authors of the monastic textbooks (*yig cha*) and accepted by the majority of scholars. It is closely associated with the tradition of the Collected Topics, which derives from Cha-ba's Summaries. Hence, it follows the latter's views on most points, with some minor modifications.[33]

The second alternative tradition is usually associated with Kay-drup, although we saw that this exclusive attribution is probably mistaken (since Gyel-tsap defends similar views in commentary on Sa-paṇ's *Treasure*). The views of this alternative tradition have not been integrated into most monastic textbooks, which rely on Cha-ba's typology and the new concepts it introduces. This alternative current is closer to Sa-paṇ's more literal interpretation. Its similarity with the latter's epistemology is, however, limited to the eschewal of posited entities such as subsequent and inattentive cognitions, on the ground that these are Tibetan inventions without basis in Dharmakīrti's works. It does not extend to the conception of perception as a passive holding of the object, as explained by Dharmakīrti and Sa-paṇ. Both trends in Ge-luk epistemology accept Cha-ba's characterization of perception as cognitively active. Similarly, they both agree on the other two fundamental points of Ge-luk epistemological thinking; namely, that there are real universals and that conceptions are not limited to constructs but cognize reality, albeit indirectly. Thus, although the differences between these two currents are real, they should not be overemphasized, for their philosophical significance is limited. Therefore, I will only briefly explore the differences between these two currents concerning the concept of subsequent cognition and its Indian source. In addition to underlining a certain diversity within the Ge-luk tradition, this topic will also reveal the extent to which the theory of perception of this tradition has moved away from Dharmakīrti's original model.

The views defended by the two subtraditions result from their respective views on valid cognition. The Collected Topics tradition holds that a cognition requires novelty to be valid. This requirement, which is defended by Gyel-tsap in *Revealing,* is rejected by Kay-drup who holds that novelty is not a part of the definition of valid cognition.[34] Accordingly, the cognition of subsequent moments of perception is seen differently by both sides. Suppose that I gaze at my rocking chair for several moments. The first moment of perception is a valid cognition according to both sides. That is, it is knowledge generating. But, according to the Collected Topics tradition, the second moment is not valid because it does not introduce a new element to the cognitive process. This failure to generate new knowledge does not cast any aspersion on its veridicality. Hence, it is a subsequent cognition.[35]

The author of Dre-bung Lo-sel-ling's textbook, Paṇ-chen Sö-nam-drak-ba, defines *subsequent cognition* as "that nonvalid cognition which realizes something already realized by the valid cognition that induces it."[36] A subsequent cognition is a mental episode that identifies its object because it determines the object previously determined by a valid cognition. The only difference between a valid cognition and a subsequent cognition is that, whereas the former contributes to the epistemic process, the latter is not knowledge generating. Hence, it is not valid.

The Collected Topics tradition holds that this view of subsequent perception is based on Dharmottara, particularly his assertion that valid cognitions identify objects that have been previously unknown to the knower. Dharmottara says: "Although mere realization [of an object] is application (*pravṛtti, 'jug pa*) [to this object], there is no valid cognition with respect to [an already] realized object, for a person is made to engage [in an object] by the very first showing of this object of application independently of anything else. . . . Therefore, all valid cognitions take as their objects only [previously] unrealized things. Consequently, since the very moment of first perception or inference ascertains the continuum of things that are able to perform a function, they can take [these things] as [their] objects of application. Therefore, the later continuation of those [moments of cognition] that do not make any separate [epistemic] contribution are to be excluded [from being] valid cognitions."[37] Dharmottara argues that only the first moment of a given perception can be a valid cognition. The cognitions of the same type that arise following the first moment are not valid since they do not contribute anything to the epistemic process. Most Ge-luk thinkers take Dharmottara's statement as supporting their view that the second moment of a perception is a subsequent cognition.

Kay-drup, while not denying that this could be Dharmottara's view, points out that if this really were his opinion, Dharmottara would be contradicting himself. This is so because he asserts that a mental perception is valid although it perceives only the latest instant of a continuum already ascertained by sense perception. If the second moment of perception were not valid due to its apprehension of an already ascertained object, how could a mental perception, which Dharmottara holds to be valid, in fact be valid?[38] The most charitable interpretation of Dharmottara's remarks about the next moments of perception being invalid is to take them to refer to judgments induced by perception. We should, nevertheless, note that the less charitable interpretation is not without support in Dharmottara's writings. It corresponds to Dharmottara's insistence on a more cognitively active perception.

Kay-drup adamantly rejects the existence of nonvalid perceptions, which is, nevertheless, accepted by most later Ge-luk thinkers.[39] According to him, the second moment of perception is valid because it perceives its object through its own power. That is, the second moment makes the same contribution as the first. It does not rely on a previous cognition to apprehend its object, as does recollection, for example. For Kay-drup, the concept of subsequent cognition should be limited strictly to the repetitions of previously acquired item of knowledge, as in the case of memory. It is appropriate for a recollection, which Dharmakīrti calls *relative cognition* (*saṃvṛtijñāna, kun rdzob shes pa*),[40] not to be valid, for it reasserts the conclusion of a previous valid cognition. Such is not the case of the second moment of perception, which apprehends reality independent of any other cognition.[41]

This difference is significant from more than one perspective. From a philosophical point of view, the issue is whether a cognition does or does not generate knowledge. Gyel-tsap's view is that only the first moment of seeing an object provides new information. Subsequent moments apprehend the continuous existence of the object and hence add nothing new to the epistemic process. These moments merely renew the acquaintance that we already have with the object. Hence, they are not valid, despite being veridical.

Psychologically, novelty is also an important factor. It differentiates the first moment of perception from the second. When we see a new object our attention is drawn to the object and our mind is alert. Such keenness is difficult to sustain when we experience something we are already acquainted with. Collingwood describes the feeling of novelty of the first discovery: "The first discovery of a truth, for example, differs from any subsequent contemplation of it, not in that the truth contemplated is a different truth, nor in that the act of contemplating it is a different act; but in that the immediacy of the first occasion can never again be experienced: the shock of its novelty, the liberation from perplexing problems, the triumph of achieving a desired result, perhaps the sense of having vanquished opponents and achieved fame, and so forth."[42] After the first encounter with a new object, we tend to lose the freshness. The object becomes something usual and attention may fade, thereby impairing our ability to fully understand the nature of the object. The reason for this is that subsequent perceptions make no cognitive contribution. Hence, our attention tends to slack, and we fall in a pattern of repetition. This is why subsequent perceptions are not, for Gyel-tsap, knowledge generating. Hence, they are not valid in the technical sense of the word.

Kay-drup disagrees, arguing that the main issue is not whether the information is new or not but whether the cognition has the same cognitive access to its object or not. Subsequent perceptions apprehend their objects exactly in the same way as the first moment. They make the same contribution as the first moment. Their not being new does not entail that they do not generate knowledge. Moreover, if novelty were the issue, we could have only one valid perception of a single object. Then every time we see this object, our mental state would not be knowledge generating. This is false, argues Kay-drup, since such cognitions bring new information. We notice subtle differences we have missed earlier or take stock of the continuous existence of the object. Hence, independent access to an object is the issue for determining the epistemic status of a cognition, not novelty.

The issue separating the two views is also interpretive. Dharmakīrti and other classical figures (Dignāga, Devendrabuddhi, Śākyabuddhi, Prajñākaragupta, etc.) describe perception and inference as subdivisions of valid cognition, thus suggesting that both are valid. They also seem to support the requirement of novelty. For them, there is no contradiction. Perception is constantly perceiving its object anew because it passively holds an object that is changing at every moment. Its epistemic status is not to be appraised in terms of cognitive contribution, but merely in terms of its ability to induce adequate forms of conceptualization. Therefore, for these classical thinkers, the question of knowing whether perception is always valid or not does not arise.

Dharmottara and some later Indian and Tibetan thinkers seem to have a different view of perception, one that accords to it not only the capacity to passively hold its object but also the ability to actively apprehend it. Consequently, these thinkers emphasize that perception is not a passive holding of its object, but an active identification of the cognitive patterns exhibited by the object. Since the objects perceived by the first and second moments of perception exhibit the same pattern, the objects of these two moments are found to be essentially the same (despite having undergone imperceptible changes due to their momentariness). This is why Gyel-tsap (and possibly Dharmottara), by accepting the criterion of novelty, deny that subsequent perceptions are knowledge generating and assert the existence of perceptions that are not valid. Kay-drup rejects the idea that subsequent moments of perception are not valid, yet he shares the same basic understanding of perception.

That neither Gyel-tsap nor Kay-drup tries to use the doctrine of momentariness to resolve their debate reveals the transformation the concept of perception has undergone. For Dharmakīrti, perception is a passive holding of an object that is constantly produced anew. Since its object is always new, perception, which passively reflects this momentary reality, is always valid. For the proponents of the new epistemology, perception actively apprehends its object by identifying its epistemically salient features. For instance, when we look at a jar for several moments, we identify the object as a jar. While doing so, the jar undergoes minute transformations that we fail, however, to register. Since these changes do not affect the object's epistemically salient features, subsequent perceptions register no new information. For Dharmakīrti, this failure does not affect the epistemic status of these perceptions since perception cannot in principle determine its object. For the new epistemologists, since perception can be cognitively active, failure to provide new information entails the exclusion from being valid.

We measure the difference between Dharmakīrti's description of perception as a passive holding and some of his later interpreters' view that perception identifies its object. The former view is a logical consequence of the antirealism central to Dharmakīrti's tradition. The latter view represents a paradigm shift within the epistemology of this tradition, which is a consequence of the realism developed by later thinkers. Objects are not bare particulars but elements of an articulated cognitive order that partly reflects reality. Such a shift is not without justification. It represents an attempt to solve the epistemological problems raised by Dharmakīrti's antirealism. The depiction of perception as cognitively active is meant to respond to objections that if perception is inarticulate it cannot be valid. Dharmakīrti's solution is to combine perception and conception, but as we saw, this will not do. To solve these problems, later revisionist thinkers transformed perception into a cognitively active agent. In doing so, these thinkers provided a picture of perceptual knowledge more attuned to commonsense, which is intuitively more satisfactory than Dharmakīrti's idea of bare sensing. In doing so, however, they transformed the original concept they intended to capture.

23

Cha-ba's Philosophy of Mind

Cha-ba's Typologies of Objects

The preceding chapter has shown the evolution of the concept of perception among Tibetan thinkers. It has examined the transformations brought about by the new epistemology started in India and expanded by Cha-ba. The central issue was the transformation of perception from a passive nonconceptual receptivity into an active cognitive process. Our next important task is to examine Sa-paṇ's critique. Before going into this, however, I will pause to examine Cha-ba's typology of objects (*yul, viṣaya*). I examine this topic less for its philosophical importance than for its enormous influence in the Tibetan tradition. Its adoption by other thinkers has had important consequences on the development of their own theories of perception. While they have not necessarily agreed with Cha-ba, they have shared his basic vocabulary. No study of Tibetan epistemology can pretend to any degree of completion without such an explanation. Some of my less Tibetologically inclined readers may want to skip this chapter and move directly to Sa-paṇ's critique.

Cha-ba's typology of objects comprises of four types of object: the held object (*gzung yul*), the appearing object (*snang yul*), the object of application (*'jug yul*), and the conceived object (*zhen yul*). To understand the epistemology implied by this typology, we have to remember the distinction between two traditions of commentators: the realists, who insist on the intentional aspect of mental states and tend to favor a phenomenological approach, and the antirealists, who tend to minimize this element and stress the pragmatic importance of knowledge.[1] Cha-ba stands squarely in the former camp.

His fourfold typology offers a partly phenomenological description of awareness that supports his realist vision of mind as being in contact with real objects. Cha-ba and his tradition examine all the four types of object from the point of view of how they appear to our prereflective experience. Their explanations stress the intentional nature of mental states, explicating it in two ways. Mental episodes are object directed in that objects appear to them, and they apprehend these objects. The definition of *consciousness* as "that which is clear and cognizing" is meant capture this double aspect of intentionality. It emphasizes that any mental state must have these two characteristics: It must reveal an object and apprehend it. The first two types of object (appearing and held objects) are defined in terms of the mind's ability to reveal an object, whereas the last two (object of application and conceived object) are defined in terms of the mind's ability to determine an object.

Unfortunately, this typology is not as systematic as one may wish. For, whereas the first three types of object concern all cognitions, the fourth one (conceived object) concerns only conceptions. Let me illustrate this through the example of the perception of my favorite rocking chair. This perception both reveals and apprehends the chair, which is an instance of the first three types of objects. It is the object of application of my perception since it is apprehended by it. The chair is also its appearing object and held object since it is the object whose appearance determines the mind as cognizing its object.[2] This chair is not, however, the conceived object of that perception, for such a mental episode does not conceive but rather perceives its object. The conceptual judgment that follows ("this is a great chair") takes the same chair as its object. Of this judgment, the chair is an instance of each of the last two types of object. It is neither of the first two, however, for only the object universal of the chair can be the appearing object for this mental episode. On the other hand, the object universal of the chair is not the object of application or the conceived object of this cognition, for the latter does not conceive of the object universal but of the chair.[3]

This rather involved description presents a realist view of mental life depicted in accordance with commonsense intuitions. This realism is in harmony with Cha-ba's Madhyamaka interpretation of Buddhist epistemology. Contrary to Dharmakīrti, Cha-ba insists that epistemology must respect commonsense. As a Mādhyamika, Cha-ba holds that neither perception nor conception are ultimately real. Hence, neither can be studied from an ultimate standpoint. They can be understood only conventionally.[4] To brush aside common conventions as being confused or the products of ignorance is neither desirable nor feasible, for it would prevent us from gaining the only tenable understanding.

Cha-ba's Madhyamaka orientation translates into his preference for a Vaibhāṣika theory of perception. The Vaibhāṣika view is a "naive" form of direct realism. It holds that perception not only directly sees the external object that it perceives but coexists with it, despite that the latter causes the former. For example, my perception of a blue patch is caused by the patch with which it nevertheless coexists. Otherwise, argue Vaibhāṣikas, perception could never see an external object. For it cannot see an object with which it is not causally related, and neither could it see an object with which it has a causal relation, since that object already would have disappeared when perception comes to be.

The Sautrāntika causal theory of perception is quite different. It rests on the view of causation according to which causes cease to exist when their effects come into existence. This view is the logical consequence of the Sautrāntika radical view of momentariness, according to which there is no real duration but only a succession of infinitesimal moments. The application of this view to perception makes it very difficult to explain how perception directly perceives external objects. Since objects have ceased when perceptions of them arise, how can they be perceived? The Sautrāntika response grants that external objects do not appear directly (*dngos su mi snang*) but are represented by aspects which are similar to them.

Cha-ba denies the validity of the Sautrāntika theory of perception as counterintuitive. His argument is similar to the one raised by Berkeley against Locke, although the conclusions reached by these two thinkers are radically different. Cha-ba asks how in the Sautrāntika system we can determine that objects and perceptions are similar if we do not have access to these objects independent of the perceptions? How can we determine them to be causes and effects if we do not have direct access to the external objects?[5] Moreover, if the external thing does not exist when the perception comes to be, it would be hidden and could not be taken as an object by that subject.[6]

Cha-ba did not invent these arguments. He borrowed them from the Yogācāra objections against the Sautrāntika view. But, whereas the Yogācārins and Berkeley use them to establish an idealist epistemology, Cha-ba argues for a Madhyamaka epistemology following common conventions. Accordingly, he emphasizes the importance of a phenomenological understanding of cognition as being concordant with commonsense. This is reflected in his insistence that the held object (*gzung yul*) and the appearing object (*snang yul*) are the same. Śākya Chok-den gives us the following paraphrase of Cha-ba's position: "The master Cha-ba asserts that what is called *held object* is the appearing object. [This object] only exists simultaneously with the consciousness that takes it as its object because a nonsimultaneous subject and object [relation] is not tenable. The thesis of the Sautrāntika that an object arising before the consciousness casts its aspect (*rnam pa gtod pa*) on the consciousness is not correct, for how would you refute the assertion that [a type of supersensory being called] a flesh eater casts its aspect on consciousness! [One may answer that] such a flesh eater is neither established by perception nor inference. But this also applies to the "hidden" object (*don lkog na mo*) posited to exist.[7] Therefore, it is asserted that there are three types of held objects: specifically characterized phenomena, object universals, and nonexistents clearly [appearing]."[8] The point of the example of the flesh eater is not that there is no such thing as a flesh eater (*sha za*), i.e., a ghost, but that we ordinarily cannot assert the presence of such an entity, for it is unobservable. The Sautrāntika assertion of the existence of external objects that are in principle unobservable is similar to asserting that there are flesh eaters in front of us inasmuch as both claims cannot be substantiated. According to the Sautrāntika causal theory, the external object is neither directly (*dngos su*) nor nakedly (*rjen par*) apprehended by the perception and remains, in a way, "hidden." Cha-ba argues that this amounts to the introduction of an unobserved entity. If this is allowable, why not say that perception is produced by a flesh eater? If one answers that a flesh eater is neither established nor inferred, then the invisible external object would also be excluded, for it is also neither observed nor inferred.

For Cha-ba, the held object of perception is the object that appears to that perception and with which it coexists. The only coherent way to account for perception, according to Cha-ba, is to remain as much as possible in touch with common sense while explaining the tenets of Buddhist epistemology. Still, some distinctions have to be made in the ways things appear to the mind. Things do not appear in the same way in perceptions, thoughts, or illusions (the vision of falling hair due to ophthalmia). Accordingly, Cha-ba distinguishes three different types of appearing objects: (a) real things that are the appearing objects of perceptions, (b) object universals that are the appearing objects of conceptions, and (c) nonexistents that are the appearing objects of deluded nonconceptual cognitions (*rtog med log shes*). And yet, all three types of cognitions have their own appearing (or held) objects.

The Ge-luk tradition has adopted many of Cha-ba's realist ideas such as his view of an active perception, his typology of objects, and the like. Ge-luk thinkers do not accept, however, Cha-ba's peculiar combination of Madhyamaka philosophy with a Vaibhāṣika theory of perception. Gyel-tsap and Kay-drup follow Sa-paṇ's description of Dharmakīrti's system as Sautrāntika-Yogācāra.[9] While discussing perception, they follow Sa-paṇ in adopting the Sautrāntika causal theory of perception. This shows that the views held by Gyel-tsap and Kay-drup are not identical with those of Cha-ba. Although it shares in the new paradigm developed by Cha-ba, Ge-luk epistemology does not completely follow the latter's views but, rather, often attempts a reconciliation between his more innovative approach and Sa-paṇ's more literal rendering of Dharmakīrti. This peculiar synthesis is not only the result of particular philosophical choices but also a reflection of the particular historical position of the tradition and the hermeneutical constraints under which Tibetan thinkers work.

And yet on the topic of the object, Ge-luk thinkers adopt Cha-ba's typology tout court. This creates a peculiar situation in which some of Cha-ba's concepts are used to make points opposed to his views. *Object* is defined in the Ge-luk tradition (as by most Tibetan thinkers) as "that which is cognized by mind."[10] Like Cha-ba, Ge-luk thinkers distinguish between appearing and held objects, which are the objects revealed by conception, and objects of application and conceived objects, which are the objects apprehended by cognitions. Kay-drup says: "Appearing and held objects are equivalent. With respect to this, the appearing and held objects of nonconceptual cognitions are the objects whose aspects clearly and explicitly appear to that nonconceptual cognition. Accordingly, from the point of view of nonconceptual cognitions, appearing and held objects are the external objects [in the case of sense perceptions] and the cognitions [in the case of self-cognitions]. The subjects [cognizing those] are most of the other cognitions[11] and the self-cognitions."[12] Like Cha-ba, the Ge-luk tradition understands the notion of object realistically, at least as far as perception is concerned. The appearing object of perception is the real object that appears to it. Since such an object is held by the perception as it is, it appears with all its characteristics (being produced, being impermanent, etc.), although those are not necessarily identified as such by the perceiving person. The object as it is identified by the perceiving person is the object of application (perceptions do not have conceived objects).

One of the distinctive features of this new epistemology is that its proponents maintain that perception itself identifies its object, or to speak more technically, it eliminates wrong superimpositions. We perceive objects as they appear and we identify them through our experiences. Hence, real objects are both the appearing and the held objects of perception. This commonsense view of an object must be modified, however, when dealing with conceptions to account for the distorted nature of thought. Although external objects appear to conceptions, they do not appear as they are. Hence, they are not the appearing and held objects of conceptions but the objects of application and conceived objects. Only object universals can be the appearing objects of conception. Hence, unlike perception, conception is not fully phenomenologically transparent.

There is universal agreement within the Ge-luk tradition on this identification of held and appearing objects. Some minor differences remain on whether all cognitions require an appearing object or not. Like Cha-ba, Paṇ-chen Sö-nam-drak-ba holds that all cognition (including nonconceptual wrong cognition) has an appearing object, although this object may be a nonexistent.[13] Kay-drup disagrees with this view, holding that some cognitions such as the vision of falling hair under the influence of ophthalmia have no appearing object, since they do not rely on the presence of an external object[14] and are produced only by malfunctions of the senses. Ge-dün-drup and Gyel-tsap hold that all mistaken nonconceptual cognitions are without appearing objects. They argue that, for example, the seeing of a double moon is without any appearing object. This is so because no existing object appears to it. The moon does not appear to such a cognition, otherwise the mental episode would be partly unmistaken.[15] It is clear, however, that these do not amount to serious differences, for these thinkers all agree on the main point; namely, the equivalence of held and appearing objects.

Śākya Chok-den's Polemical Use of History

Cha-ba's typology of objects, which had been (and still is) enormously influential in establishing the vocabulary of Tibetan epistemological enquiry, came under strong criticism from Sa-paṇ and his followers. Sa-paṇ criticizes Cha-ba's identification of held and appearing objects on the grounds that, for Dharmakīrti, a held object can be only the external object acting as the cause of the perception (and, therefore, nonexistent when the perception comes to be). Dharmakīrti says: "Besides the entity which is the cause [of the perception] what could be called *held* [*object*]? That which appears to the mind is said to be held."[16] Relying on Dharmakīrti's view that the held object is the object directly producing the perception, Sa-paṇ argues against Cha-ba that if object universals and nonexistents were held objects, they would have to produce their cognitions directly. Therefore those cognitions would be unmistaken, since they would be produced by the power of real things. Moreover, if a quasi-phenomenon such as a vision of falling hair due to ophthalmia were a held object, it would be a public object and would have to be observable by other people like, for example, a jar.[17] Therefore, Cha-ba's threefold classification is not defensible. In reality, only real things, which are the objects of our practical concerns, are objects.

Sa-paṇ's followers have developed his critical remarks and mobilized them against the adoption of Cha-ba's typology by later epistemologists (mostly Ge-luk thinkers). The most devastating critique is doubtlessly Śākya Chok-den's, which skillfully uses historical arguments to undermine the positions of his adversaries. Śākya Chok-den sharply criticizes the fourfold typology of objects elaborated by Cha-ba and taken over by Ge-luk thinkers on two grounds: (a) as being a Tibetan creation unsupported by Indian sources and (b) as being philosophically unsustainable. Śākya Chok-den does not reject the whole typology but only certain of its aspects. In this section, I will examine his critique of the appearing object that marks his rejection of the direct realism defended by his adversaries.

According to Śākya Chok-den, among the four types of object only two, the held object (*gzung yul*) and the object of application (*'jug yul*), are identifiable in Indian sources. The appearing and the conceived objects are Tibetan creations.[18] Śākya Chok-den claims that Indian texts speak of objects appearing to the mind, but nowhere does he find formalized the concept of an appearing object. Hence, Cha-ba's presentation cannot be accepted as a bona fide interpretation of Dharmakīrti since it is not found in Dharmakīrti's own works. It is even absent from the writings of authoritative commentators. How can it be taken seriously in a tradition where philosophical truth must proceed in the form of a commentary?

Śākya Chok-den presents a few philosophical arguments against Cha-ba's position, mostly restating the points already made by Sa-paṇ. He argues that the held object is the external object that causes a sense perception.[19] For Śākya Chok-den, as for other Sa-gya thinkers, the held object can be the direct cause (*dngos rgyu*)[20] of only a sense or mental perception. This is what Ge-luk-bas describe as the held thing (*gzung don*) and consider to be the object condition (*dmigs rkyen, ālambana-pratyaya*) of perceptions of external objects. Only sense perceptions have held objects, other types of cognition do not.[21]

Śākya Chok-den's real interest in the matter was not to refute Cha-ba's position. Rather, Śākya Chok-den wanted to show that views presented by his contemporaries as true renderings of Dharmakīrti's original thought were, in fact, reflections of previous Tibetan mistakes. Combining historical evidence and philosophical analysis to undermine the legitimacy of the views of one's contemporaries is by no means unique to Śākya Chok-den, although he was probably the most systematic practitioner of this approach in Tibet. Sa-paṇ and Dzong-ka-ba used a similar technique when they referred to their opponents as "previous Tibetan [thinkers]" (*bod snga rabs pa*), implying with them that a new period in the history of the tradition was beginning and that old interpretations were being superseded by more accurate ones. Śākya Chok-den, however, went further. He analyzed in detail the views of past masters to undermine his contemporary opponents' views, showing them to be the distorted by-products of historical developments rather the true interpretations they claim to be. In his criticism of the notion of appearing object, Śākya Chok-den showed that his opponents were not only repeating Cha-ba's past mistakes in identifying held and appearing objects, but that they even got him wrong. That is, Cha-ba's intentions had been misunderstood by those who adopted his vocabulary without realizing what they were buying into.

According to Śākya Chok-den, Cha-ba's presentation of the four objects was not meant as an explanation of a Sautrāntika theory of perception, but as its refutation. Cha-ba asserted the equivalence of these two objects to refute a causal theory, intending to propose an alternative, the Vaibhāṣika theory.[22] Later thinkers, however, have kept this equivalence to explain the very theory that Cha-ba refuted. Śākya Chok-den sarcastically comments: "Cha-ba's followers establish the presentation of held and appearing objects in accordance with Cha-ba's system while accepting the Sautrāntika system. This is piling one mistake on top of the other."[23] The equation of appearing and held objects is a way of stressing a theory of perception fully commensurate with commonsense. We seem to have the intuition that we directly perceive objects that exist as we perceive them. For Cha-ba, the held object is the object seen in the present moment. To stress that the object held by perception is not "hidden," but appears to awareness as it is, Cha-ba created the new concept of the appearing object.

This identification of held and appearing objects is sustainable, Śākya Chok-den argues, only if one denies the Sautrāntika causal theory of perception. For his Ge-luk opponents, who hold a causal theory, to accept the equivalence of appearing and held objects is nothing short of amazing, for it contradicts the very purpose of asserting such an equivalence. If the object held by perception is its cause and exists prior to it, then it cannot appear to it, for it ceases to exist when its effect, the perception, comes to be. Hence, it remains "hidden" to perception, which apprehends its representation. If the object held by a perception appears to it, then it cannot be the cause of that perception (as understood by Sautrāntikas). To maintain both is incoherent!

Critical Appraisal

What should we think of Śākya Chok-den's devastating impeachment of the legitimacy of the fourfold typology of objects? Is Śākya Chok-den right that the concepts of appearing and conceived objects are Tibetan creations with no support in Indian sources?[24]

Go-ram-ba does not agree with Śākya Chok-den and finds sources for the concepts of appearing and conceived objects.[25] This assertion is not, however, as convincing as one might hope. As Śākya Chok-den points out,[26] these sources refer to the concepts of appearing (*snang ba, pratibhāsa*) and conceiving (*mngon par zhen pa, abhiniveśa*), which clearly exist in Dharmakīrti's works,[27] but do not formally distinguish between appearing objects and other type of objects. Since Go-ram-ba does not provide an analysis to show that these passages necessitate these concepts, we cannot admit them as sources for the notions of appearing and conceived objects.

It might seem, therefore, that Śākya Chok-den has a justifiable claim that both these concepts are Tibetan. This, however, assumes that concepts not found in Dharmakīrti are eo ipso Tibetan creations, thus overemphasizing the unity of the Indian tradition, something Śākya Chok-den repeatedly does. We might agree that the notions of appearing and conceived objects are not found in Dharmakīrti. This does not necessarily make them into Tibetan deformations of Indian originals. We already saw evidence that Dharmottara clearly asserted a conceived object when he says: "Cognitions have two types of object, held and conceived . . ."[28] Clearly, Śākya Chok-den is wrong that the concept of conceived objects is a Tibetan creation, since Dharmottara unambiguously asserts and uses it.

Similarly, Śākya Chok-den goes too far when he asserts that the equivalence of the held and appearing objects is without support in Indian original sources. His attempt to trace this idea back to Cha-ba's refutation of the causal theory of perception is a definite contribution to the intellectual history of Tibetan Buddhism. His polemical motivation pushes him to overlook the complexity of the Indian tradition. In doing so, he also reflects the religious assumptions of traditional Buddhists, who hold that their tradition does not just provide useful guidelines but is true. In a Buddhist tradition, this assumption is not without problem, for many teachings tend to undermine any absolute claim to truth and teachings may contradict each other. Nevertheless, practically Tibetan traditions tend to limit these warnings against absolutism to the theoretical sphere and assume that Indian sources are entirely true and coherent.

We should not push this point too far, however, for traditional scholars are aware of the great diversity in the Indian Buddhist tradition. Hence, they know that it is not possible to hold that the whole of the Indian Buddhist tradition is coherent and right. Some interpretation is required to account for the diversity of the tradition. This is usually done through a doxographical ranking. For example, Ge-luk commentators recognize that Dharmakīrti is not a Mādhyamika. Hence, they are ready to recognize that his teachings are not entirely true, for, according to them, truth is understood according to Nāgārjuna's Madhyamaka teachings. Nevertheless, they will assume that, unless otherwise specified by some more important texts such Nāgārjuna's or Candrakīrti's, Dharmakīrti is completely right in his presentation of more specifically logico-epistemological points. This is why these scholars feel completely justified in arguing for a particular interpretation on the basis of its being true, despite the thinness of textual evidence, as we saw in the case of the Ge-luk interpretation of Dharmakīrti as a realist. Similarly, Tibetan commentators will also assume that Dharmakīrti is completely right in his interpretation of Dignāga and that his accredited commentators are right when they interpret him. Thus, there is a definite tendency toward an assumption of unity in the tradition that, from a modern perspective, seems ahistorical.

This is not to say that Tibetan commentators are unable to think historically or that they refuse to see diversity when they see it. Śākya Chok-den's critique shows that traditionally Tibetan scholars have understood their tradition historically. Moreover, when confronted with discrepancies between their official interpretations and details of Indian texts, many traditional scholars are quite ready to grant that the Indian tradition is more diverse than is commonly recognized. Thus, the difference between modern and traditional scholars is not a matter of kind but of degree. Both types of scholars are able to understand texts as making truth claims as well as being historical products. And yet, there is a tendency among traditional scholars to overemphasize the coherence of the Indian tradition.

Śākya Chok-den's inference from the claim that Cha-ba's ideas are without any support in Dharmakīrti's texts to the claim that Cha-ba's ideas are Tibetan inventions and thus not worthy of consideration within a tradition in which philosophical truth is commentarial is a very effective strategy. In such a tradition, the accusation of being fabricated (*rang bzo*) is tantamount to rejection. Śākya Chok-den's assumption that, since Cha-ba's ideas are not found in Dharmakīrti they cannot be found in other Indian authors is not warranted, for it assumes that, everything else being equal, the views of later commentators are similar to Dharmakīrti's. We have seen that the idea of a held object (*gzung yul*) is found in Dharmottara.[29] Śākya Chok-den claims that Dharmottara does not assert that held and appearing objects are equivalent, since a held object is an external object impinging on consciousness. However, Dharmottara does not restrict the concept of held object to the external objects of sense perception (as Śākya Chok-den wants us to believe). For Dharmottara, inferential cognitions also have a held object, which is the unreal conceptual appearance. Having explained the difference between the held and the conceived objects of perception, Dharmottara describes the held object of inference: "Similarly, inference operates by conceiving its appearance, which is not the [external] object, as the appearing thing. Therefore, [the object] it apprehends does not exist in reality. Moreover, [inference] apprehends a superimposed entity as a specifically characterized phenomenon. Therefore, the so-called object of application of an inference is a specifically characterized phenomenon and [its] held [object] does not exist in reality."[30] Dharmottara establishes a parallel between perception, which does not conceive the object (the individual moments) that it holds, and inference, which conceives an object that is different from its held object. Whereas perception conceives an unreal continuum on the basis of a real appearance, inference conceives of a real thing on the basis of an unreal appearance, the unreal held object. This passage, as well as others,[31] shows that, for Dharmottara, the held object is not necessarily an external object and can be understood in terms of appearance.[32] The held object of a perception is the appearing moments of the object and that of an inference is the conceptual appearance mistaken as the real thing.

Whatever Cha-ba's particular views of perception, the assertion that held and appearing objects are equivalent is intelligible not only within the direct realism of the Vaibhāṣika school. It also makes sense within Dharmottara's attempt to develop an epistemology in which perception and conception are more connected with each other. It is, therefore, quite logical for the Ge-luk tradition, which continues Dharmottara's program, to keep this equivalence.

Nonetheless, Śākya Chok-den's analysis captures a real tension in the epistemology of his Ge-luk adversaries who attempt to present a realist interpretation of an antirealist system. In particular, the realist assumption that we see things directly is difficult to reconcile with a causal account that assumes a time gap between perception and its object. Direct realism and the causal account pull in different directions. In the Vaibhāṣika view defended by Cha-ba, there is no such difficulty since the causal relation between the external object and its perception is understood differently. There, things are assumed to have real duration[33] and hence a causal relation between object and perception does not conflict with their coexistence. Thus, the description of a mental episode as bearing on an object that appears to it can proceed safely since the object is present to the mind that perceives it. Such an explanation is more problematic, however, in a Sautrāntika theory of perception, which denies that the object is present when the mental episode is produced. How can the former appear to the latter in a system where the time gap between perception and its object is radical? Śākya Chok-den's presentation of objects makes quite clear this tension to which we will have the occasion to return.[34] For the time being, let us continue our investigation of the Sa-gya critique of the new epistemology developed by Cha-ba and his followers.

24

Sa-paṇ's Critique of the New Epistemology

Sa-paṇ's Rejection of Cha-ba's Typology

The preceding chapters introduced some of the main ideas of the new epistemology elaborated by later Indian and Tibetan scholars. We also started to examine some of the criticisms offered by Sa-paṇ's disciples. We have yet to examine Sa-paṇ's own reaction to the new epistemology. According to the traditional account, as a consequence of studying with Śākya Śrībhadra, Sa-paṇ realized that the epistemology accepted by most Tibetan thinkers differs from Dharmakīrti's original model. He resolved to expose these differences by writing the *Treasure*, a work that follows the outline of Cha-ba's *Summary*, but rejects any idea not found in Dharmakīrti's writings.

In his *Treasure,* Sa-paṇ severely criticizes Cha-ba's sevenfold typology for departing from Dharmakīrti's presentation. In an attempt to retrieve the original thought of Indian texts on logic and epistemology, which he argues was compromised by these Tibetan elaborations, Sa-paṇ objects to such fabrications on the ground that they lack a solid basis in the original texts. Accordingly, Sa-paṇ sets out to refute the sevenfold typology of mental states elaborated by early Tibetan masters.

For Sa-paṇ, cognition is either valid or not. If it is not valid, it belongs to one of three categories traditionally known to Indian Buddhist scholars: false conception (*log rtog*), nonrealizing mental state (*ma rtogs pa'i blo*), or doubt (*the tshom*). Sa-paṇ focuses his criticism on three of the seven divisions: correct assumption (*yid dpyod*), inattentive cognition (*snang la ma nges pa*), and subsequent cognition (*bcad shes*). Let us briefly analyze his complete rejection of correct assumption as well as its astonishing misinterpretation by later scholars in their attempt to reconcile the views of the *Treasure* with those of the Summaries.

A correct assumption is a mental state that holds its object without sufficient evidence. For example, when I am told that my neighbor had an accident, I do not know it for a fact since I have have neither seen the accident nor am I able to infer it. Rather, I am just content to assume that this is the case. Such a mental state is described by early Tibetan epistemologists as a correct assumption (*yid dpyod*).[1] It is a correct cognition that lacks the grounding in reality that would make it a form of knowledge. It is the Tibetan equivalent of Plato's *doxa,* the mere opinion opposed to certain knowledge.

Sa-paṇ does not accept this concept of correct assumption. He claims that it is a pseudo-category that can be dissolved into one of the already existing categories (doubt or cognition relying on reasoning). He says: "Correct assumption does not rely on evidence. If it is a mere assertion, it is a [form of] doubt. However, if it relies on evidence, it must be either valid or [relying on] one of the three invalid [evidences]."[2] For Sa-paṇ, doubt is not limited to a psychological state in which we feel hesitant but includes all forms of indecisive awareness. He claims that, if the mental state assumed to be a correct assumption is a mere assertion that does not rely on any justificatory evidence, it must be a form of doubt.[3] If, on the other hand, it relies on evidence, it must rely on either correct or incorrect evidence. He further claims that, in the first case, it is an inference since it correctly understands its object in reliance on correct evidence. In the second case, it is a wrong cognition, depending on one of three types of incorrect evidence (*rtags ltar snang*). In either case, correct assumption does not constitute a separate epistemological category.[4]

What is interesting in Sa-paṇ's refutation is not its intrinsic philosophical merit, for it is not decisive. There is room to argue that a mental state assuming some facts is not a form of doubt. Why would an unfounded but correct opinion be a form of doubt? This seems to be a problematic extension of the concept of doubt. Hence, the concept of correct assumption is defensible on philosophical grounds. More significant is the way in which Sa-paṇ's passage has been misinterpreted by some later Ge-luk texts. There, it is cited in support of the existence of correct assumption. This is nothing short of amazing, since this passage is a clear refutation of the concept of correct assumption. Napper has given a translation of Sa-paṇ's passage that accords with the sense in which this text is (mis)understood by these scholars: "Correctly assuming consciousnesses are not more than three: not depending on a sign—being only an assertion it can turn into doubt—depending on a 'correct' sign, or [depending on] a facsimile of a sign."[5] Ge-shay Sam-pel's interpretation, which is reflected in Napper's translation, is unfortunately not exceptional in the contemporary Ge-luk tradition. His text is a compilation of the standard points in later Ge-luk monastic textbooks pertaining to the genre of literature called *Typology of Mental States (blo rigs*). It reflects the accepted views of Dre-bung Lo-sel-ling monastery, though it is not an official textbook. His interpretation is, nevertheless, quite spectacular in the deformations that it imposes on the text. This example is illustrative of the difficulties that many Tibetan scholars have accepting Sa-paṇ's *Treasure* literally, steeped as they are in the vocabulary of the new epistemology.[6] It also shows the tendency of Ge-luk scholars to coopt Sa-paṇ into their tradition, claiming that he has been misunderstood by later Sa-gya scholars such as Go-ram-ba or Śākya Chok-den.

Let us notice, however, that the more lucid members of the tradition do not give in so easily into such a temptation. Although they do try to coopt Sa-paṇ, they do not use recourse to such a blatant misinterpretation. Kay-drup does not seem to use the concept of correct assumption at all. Gyel-tsap mentions correct assumption once without, however, referring to Sa-paṇ.[7] Moreover, in his commentary on Sa-paṇ's *Treasure,* Gyel-tsap correctly interprets Sa-paṇ's comments as being a refutation of correct assumption, not an endorsement.[8]

Sa-paṇ also criticizes Cha-ba's conception of subsequent cognition (*bcad shes*), as we discussed earlier. Sa-paṇ grants that subsequent cognition exists, but does not accept it as a division of nonvalid cognition. For Sa-paṇ, subsequent cognitions are nonrealizing cognitions. He rejects the idea that subsequent cognitions have any cognitive role. They merely repeat a previous cognition without contributing to the identification of an object. Hence, it is not even a realization of a previously realized object, as Ge-luk thinkers would have it. Sa-paṇ compares the identification of an already cognized object to cutting a tree already cut.[9] Just as something that is already established and not forgotten does not need to be re-established, something previously understood cannot be understood unless one forgets it in the meanwhile.

Sa-paṇ is particularly critical of the idea of the second moment of a perception as a subsequent cognition. Since perception merely holds its object and since this object is in constant transformation, the subsequent moments of perception are as valid as the first moment.[10] Therefore, no perception can ever be a subsequent cognition. Only the conceptions that are recollections (*dran shes*) of something previously realized can be subsequent cognitions.[11]

The Case of Inattentive Cognition

Sa-paṇ rejected correct assumption as a fabrication that on investigation falls into one of the three aforementioned categories (false conception, nonrealizing mental state, and doubt). He also has refused to accept subsequent cognition as representing a distinct element in his typology of nonvalid cognition. When he rejects inattentive cognition it is on the grounds that though such exists, it is misdescribed as invalid by Tibetan epistemologists, who wrongly assign it to a separate category. Even more than the other two, this mistake clearly reveals the difference that separates Cha-ba's new epistemology from the more classical model that Sa-paṇ attempts to retrieve.

Cha-ba's idea of an inattentive cognition as a separate type of perception derives from his idea that valid perceptions determine their objects. Since some perceptions seem to be unable to do so, a separate category (inattentive cognition) must be created. For example, I distractedly listen to music while writing this chapter. When this task is over, I have no recollection of what I listened to. I just have a vague memory of listening to some music. Cha-ba argues that my hearing is not able to induce recollection because it fails to determine its object. Nevertheless, it is neither mistaken nor conceptual. Hence, it is a perception. Sa-paṇ agrees with this last point but refuses to accept that this perception represents a different type of perception. For him, perception never determines anything to begin with. Therefore, there is no need for a special category such as "inattentive cognition" to refer to perceptions that do not determine their object. My listening consciousness is just a normal perception. Sa-paṇ says: "If inattentive cognitions were not valid, all perceptions would be nonvalid because ascertainment is denied with respect to perception."[12] Perception does not ascertain its objects nor does it determine them. It just holds the objects, which are then determined by judgment induced by it. For example, a mass appears to my visual consciousness. At this stage I am uninformed about the object I see without determination. Sa-paṇ compares this stage to the seeing of a stupid person who does not understand anything.[13] This passive holding of the object is the function of perception and establishes it as valid: "Therefore, valid perception does not need to ascertain [an object] since it is nonconceptual. Perception is established as valid by its being unmistaken and free from conceptions."[14] For Sa-paṇ (as for Dharmakīrti and other classical epistemologists), perception ascertains nothing since it reflects the reality of the object without adding anything. Ascertainment (*nges pa, niścita*) is restricted to conception, which is absolutely different from perception. Therefore, it is impossible for a perception to determine an object.[15]

In creating the pseudo-category of inattentive perception, Cha-ba and others miss the simple fact that perception does not ascertain or determine anything. They see that certain perceptions induce immediate certainty, while others do not. Since the former perceptions seem to determine their objects and the latter do not, there must be something in them that accounts for this difference. The perceptions that are unable to induce certainty must be, argue these thinkers, a different type of perception.[16] Therefore, these thinkers invent a special category (inattentive cognition), not understanding that all perceptions are inattentive, since a real thing appears without being ascertained.[17]

According to Sa-paṇ, these thinkers are under the misapprehension that valid perceptions determine (*bcad*) their objects, and that, therefore, a special category is needed for perceptions that do not determine their object. Since perceptions do not determine anything, however, a perception unable to induce immediate certainty is no less valid than a perception able to do so. Hence, there is no need for a new category. Moreover, if one wants a category for perceptions that do not induce immediate certainty, one does not need to create such a category, for it already exists. The distinction between internally and externally valid cognitions (*rang las nges dang gzhan las nges kyi tshad ma*)[18] accounts for the differences in the cognitive capacities of different valid perceptions. A perception able to induce immediate ascertainment is an internally valid cognition (*rang las nges*). A perception unable to do so is an externally valid cognition (*gzhan las nges*). In either case, the validity of the perception is identical, for it consists of the holding of the object as it is. Whether we can reach a clear judgment or not does not depend on the content of perception, for perception is contentless. Rather, such a difference is function of our overall cognitive situation and ability to induce the appropriate conceptualization, which enables us to categorize the objects encountered in experience.

Ascertainment Is Conceptual

As we saw in our examination of the *apoha* theory, the nature of conceptual activity is negative. A judgment such as "this is a cow" is a conclusion reached by the elimination of an individual from the category to which it does not belong. To mark this negative nature, Buddhist epistemologists describe judgment as consisting of the elimination of false superimpositions (*sgro 'dogs gcod pa*). This negative language is used to signal that things are not determined as they are in reality. Characterizing a thing as this or that[19] is not the expression of the reality of the thing but is a result of a process of conceptualization. To support his point, Sa-paṇ quotes Dharmakīrti:

> *Question*: How is it that perception holds without ascertaining?
> *Answer*: No perception ever ascertains [anything, for] what is apprehended [by perception] is not ascertained.
> *Question*: But, what is [the function of perception]?
> *Answer*: The appearance [of the object] to it [the perception]. It is not the case that perception apprehends or does not apprehend [its object] by ascertaining or not ascertaining [the object]. Ascertaining [cognitions] are quite different. They ascertain some [aspects of the object] and do not ascertain other [aspects of the object]. Therefore, their applications are different [and this explains the fact] that they apprehend or do not apprehend [this or that aspect of the object].[20]

Dharmakīrti distinguishes perception and ascertainment through their different functions. The former's function is to let reality appear as it is without adding or subtracting anything. Hence, perception beholds its object in its totality. The function of conception is to determine the object appearing to the senses as being this or that. This ascertaining cognition relates to its object in a partial way by determining its object as possessing or lacking certain selected characteristics.

Ge-luk epistemologists (probably following Cha-ba) interpret Dharmakīrti's words as referring to two modes of cognitive operation. Perception operates by the power of appearance (*snang dbang gis 'jug*) and conception, by the power of ascertainment (*nges dbang gis 'jug*). These thinkers hold that this does not mean that perception does not determine its object, but only that determination is not its main function. Similarly, real things appear to conception but, since this is not conception's main function, conception does not operate by the power of the appearance of real things (*snang dbang gis mi 'jug*).

Sa-paṇ, by contrast, takes Dharmakīrti's words ("no perception ever ascertains . . .") literally. There is no question of differentiating primary and secondary functions: Holding the object is the sole function of perception, which contributes to our understanding of the world only indirectly, by inducing ascertainment. By itself, perception is totally powerless to determine anything. Since perception does not discriminate, it is valid with respect to the object as a whole. The perception of a pot is valid with respect to the color of the pot as well as to its impermanence.[21] Perception reveals the presence of a lumpy thing, which is then conceptualized as a pot because it is different from nonpots. Viewing the pot as a pot, as impermanent and so on, is accomplished by conception, which differentiates the object by elimination. That a perception is or is not able to bring about certainty is due to the conceptual state of the person and has nothing to do with the perception itself. When one's mental states are free from the causes of error, one is able to ascertain all the aspects of the object, as stated by Dharmakīrti when he refers to the great mind that ascertains all the aspects of its object.[22] Why is it then that we, ordinary beings, do not understand that the pot is impermanent?

The answer is that causes of error are present, preventing us from understanding the pot as impermanent. In this case, the cause is often described as the arising of different similar moments (*'dra ba gzhan byung*). That is, we are deluded in believing that the object we perceive endures because there is a rapid succession of similar moments. This external cause also presupposes an internal one, the inability to realize the changing nature of reality. We first overcome this obstacle through an inference, which ascertains the object to be impermanent, differentiating it from all nonimpermanent things. Meditative practice allows us to cultivate further this understanding and transforms it into a more direct insight of the changing nature of things.

This presentation, which seems to be faithful to Dharmakīrti's ideas, raises an obvious objection which Sa-paṇ does not address explicitly. Perception of sound is said to be valid with respect to the impermanence of sound. It is also said that, since impermanence is not ascertained, we need the support of a reasoning to infer it. How can an inference understand an object (sound's impermanence) already cognized by perception? Is inference not then a subsequent cognition? Śākya Chok-den answers: "No, because whereas the former valid cognition [perception] holds a specifically characterized phenomenon, the latter [inference] apprehends the elimination of impermanence. Both [cognitions] operate on the same object of application (*'jug yul*) because they operate on this very sound's impermanence which is a specifically characterized phenomenon."[23] As Dignāga and Dharmakīrti repeatedly emphasize, perception and inference comprehend different objects: Whereas perception relates to real things, inference apprehends only constructs on the basis of an inherent mistake (*ngo bo nyid kyis 'khrul ba*) albeit one necessary to practical activities. A thing conceived by thought is no more than a "conventional denomination [given] to the mere conceptual elimination of the contradictory of the object (the non-*x*)."[24] Accordingly, the object apprehended by the perception of sound and that of the inference of the sound as impermanent are different even though the objects to which these two cognitions apply are similar. Therefore, since the inferential understanding of sound as impermanent cognizes a different object, it is a valid cognition. The mistake committed by Cha-ba and others in their explanation of perception is to forget the radical difference between perception and inference. Like Hindu thinkers, they confuse the functions of these types of cognition and argue from a misrepresentation of perception as having a determinative capacity. Referring to these Tibetan realists, Sa-paṇ concludes, rather flippantly: "They confuse the functions of perception and conception. That's all!"[25]

Explicit and Implicit

Another distinction revealing of the new epistemology is that between explicit and implicit levels of realization. Sa-paṇ is equally critical of this view of realization as another of those Tibetan inventions that obscures Dharmakīrti's original system. Sa-paṇ's refutation of this distinction is a logical consequence of his opposition to the idea that perception determines reality. For him, reality is beyond any determination, explicit or implicit. Determination is conceptual and has no bearing on reality.

Hence, it does not make sense to speak of an implicit level of realization by perception. According to the new epistemology, we explicitly perceive an object such as a jar and simultaneously realize implicitly that this object is not a nonjar. Such a realization implies that perception has content, that it is able to determine its object as being this and not being that. This, however, is impossible for Sa-paṇ, who holds that perception is not propositional, for it is limited to the bare holding of the object.

Sa-paṇ further argues that this distinction does not apply even to inference, for if there were such a thing as implicit realization, all inferential understandings would be implicit. This is so because, to understand its object, inference eliminates superimposition through the appearance of another phenomenon (an object universal).[26] Hence, inference necessarily involves the identification of an object through the appearance of another. Since this is the meaning of implicit realization according to new epistemologists, it would follow that inference would always be implicit in its realization. This is, however, impossible within their system, for the notion of implicit realization necessitates that of explicit realization. According to new epistemologists, an inference can have an implicit object only if it has an explicit one. But their definition of implicit realization is so broad (*khyab ches ba*) that it includes all inferences without being able to differentiate the two levels of realization.[27]

For Sa-paṇ, the distinction between explicit and implicit is another of these Tibetan creations based on a misunderstanding of the original sources. Indian texts speak of realization by implication (*don gyis rtogs pa, arthāpati*), which Indian thinkers do not understand to be simultaneous with explicit realization as do Tibetan thinkers. Rather, understanding arises after the initial valid cognition as an aftereffect of the valid cognition. For Sa-paṇ, the Tibetan idea of a simultaneous implicit and explicit realization is one more idea without support in Dharmakīrti's texts and one that, therefore, should be eliminated. It is for the very purpose of refuting views such as these that Sa-paṇ wrote the *Treasure*.[28]

Dharmakīrti's Problem and Sa-paṇ's Solution

This investigation has been dominated by the question of how perception, which is foundational in Dharmakīrti's system, contributes to knowledge.

According to Dharmakīrti, perception is powerless to inform us about the world and requires the cooperation of conception. Such cooperation is, however, in principle impossible within Dharmakīrti's radical dualism. Not only are perception and conception completely different, even their objects are distinct. Thus, far from resolving the problem, Dharmakīrti's epistemology seems to render it more intractable. Is there any way out of this predicament?

We have examined the elaboration of a new epistemology as an attempt to solve this problem. Perception is transformed from a nonpropositional contact with reality into an already articulated apprehension of the world. This "solution" entails, however, a revision of the tradition, for such a move is not compatible with Dharmakīrti's antirealism. Sa-paṇ attempts to resolve the difficulty without transforming the basic insight and terms of the system. In doing so, however, Sa-paṇ goes beyond what Dharmakīrti explicitly said and proposes his own solution. It is another example of the internal reconstruction and exploration of concepts which is the forte of Tibetan thinkers.

According to Sa-paṇ, the problem with perceptual knowledge stems from our necessary reliance on conceptual thinking, which is a result of our inability to relate to things as they are. Ordinary beings, unlike noble beings,[29] cannot operate by the power of meditative concentration. Instead, they relate to reality through the concepts they construct on the basis of their experiences. This necessarily entails distortions. Sa-paṇ describes this situation: "The valid cognitions of ordinary beings engage in [desirable activities] and withdraw [from undesirable ones] from just ascertainment. Noble beings [absorbed in] nonconceptual states are said to act by [the power of] concentration."[30] Buddhist philosophers do not see our reliance on distorted concepts as an insurmountable limitation to the human condition, but as the result of our minds' domination by ignorance (*avidyā, ma rig pa*). Noble beings, who have eliminated this ignorance or are in the process of doing so, can enter nonconceptual states in which their actions become spontaneously attuned to reality. This type of activity, which prefigures the unfathomable way in which a Buddha relates to reality, is a direct and undistorted relation to reality.

In the absence of an unmediated link to reality, ordinary beings act by relying on conceptual constructs. Inasmuch as these creations relate successfully to reality (and are not totally imaginary), they proceed through judgment of the type "this blue pot is beautiful" and so forth. The nature of such judgment is the subject of contention between the different epistemologies. The Nyāya school takes them to be a determinate perception. Tibetan realists take such judgment to conceptualize the cognitive content already present in the perceptual act. Sa-paṇ understands such judgment, which is induced by perception, to introduce an epistemic content by ascertaining (i.e., conceptually categorizing) its objects.

For Sa-paṇ, ordinary knowledge is achieved by applying the proper concept to the reality given to us by perception. It is not achieved by mere perception but requires active categorization on our part. Accordingly, perception does not determine the situation as it is cognitively understood, but brings about certain forms of conceptual activity in which we apply or withdraw certain concepts we have previously learned. These concepts are not given to perception but constructed in relation to language and previous experience. Thus, they are forms of memory rather than mere interiorizations of reality. For example, the judgment "this blue pot is beautiful" does not come about just by mere acquaintance with the object but is the result of a conceptual elaboration in which previously learned concepts are applied by excluding contrary assumptions such as "this is not blue," "this is not a pot" and "this is not beautiful." This conceptual activity is not arbitrary but it does not reflect reality directly. It consists of the induction by perception of the categorization of the objects of experience on the basis of previous learning. Recognizing reality is also an act of re-cognition.

This epistemology, however, leads to a major difficulty. Perception gives the object as it is but is not able to determine what it is. Conception determines and understands the object by subsuming it under a universal but does not see it. Knowledge of the external world cannot be boiled down to a bare encounter with reality but necessitates both seeing and conceiving and, therefore, requires the cooperation of these two cognitive elements, which are powerless in isolation. This cooperation is, however, problematic in Dharmakīrti's system, in which perception and conception relate to entirely different objects. How can the two work cognitively together? Sa-paṇ answers through a pithy metaphor: "Sense consciousness is like the fool who sees. Conception is like a blind skillful speaker. Self-cognition is like [a person] with complete senses, who introduces one to the other."[31] Perception is like the fool. It sees the objects but is unable to characterize them. This is the job of conception, the blind and clever person skilled in describing what he or she does not see. The cooperation between the two requires an intermediary because perception and conception do not apprehend the same things. Sa-paṇ finds this intermediary in the reflexivity of apperception, or to put it in Dharmakīrtian terms, self-cognition (*rang rig, svasaṃvitti*).

This reflexive factor is the pivot and warrant that ensures that conceptions operate on the objects given to perceptions, thereby indirectly keeping in touch with reality. Since it inheres in perception as well as in conception, apperception can act as an intermediary without breaking the restriction imposed on the number of allowable types of knowledge. It realizes the aspects of the two cognitions and keeps track of the epistemic continuity between them. We know that a conception of blue applies to the blue patch that we see because apperception ensures that the concept is induced by the appropriate perception.

Thus, according to Sa-paṇ, the final word in Dharmakīrti's system is *apperception*, which links perception and cognition. Apperception ensures the union of the two components of knowledge, dumb perception and blind conception, by keeping track of the continuity of our psychic life.[32] Under the guidance of apperception, conception can help perception by remembering previously learned concepts in appropriate ways. Moreover, apperception is the warrant of our knowledge about the world; it is indubitable. Although we can be mistaken about the nature of the objects of our perceptions, we cannot be mistaken in our immediate awareness of our experiences.

For Sa-paṇ, the final answer to the question about the feasibility of knowledge in the absence of real universals is apperception. Here again, there is a striking structural similarity with Kant's argument. Like Sa-paṇ, Kant is preoccupied with explaining knowledge, an enterprise that presupposes unity in the face of a sensory manifold. We do not know things as they are given to our senses. Rather, we passively receive a stream of impressions, which we synthesize through active conceptual appropriation, thus linking the unconnected sensory elements. The question is then, If this process of unification is due to the understanding, what structure allows the unification of the manifold? How does the sense of unity that we experience about mental life come about, if all we have is a series of sensory inputs and concepts? A causal connection or association of ideas, as argued by Hume, is not enough to explain unity.[33] Imagine two people, A and B, who exhibit a curious relationship: When A sees fire, B feels heat; when A sees bacon, B smells it; and so on. Such an unlikely situation would raise questions about the causal connection between A and B. We might even posit some psychic influence. But the one thing we would not be led to suppose is that A and B are one mind, for when B smells bacon A does not smell it and vice versa.[34] Hence, a causal connection or association of ideas is not enough to explain the way in which percepts and concepts are unified.

Kant's view is quite complex but one element, namely, his appeal to apperception, is particularly relevant here. If a manifold of sensory experiences is to acquire unity, Kant argues in response to Hume, these experiences cannot just be causally connected but must be thinkable by the same subject to which the unified knowledge is given. The synthetic unity of a manifold entails the unity of the knowing subject, which Kant calls the *transcendental unity of apperception* or self-consciousness. This apperception, which is to be distinguished from the empirical reflective sense of self that we gain from introspection, does not require that we be constantly aware of our mental states. All that is required for the unity of knowledge is that this self-consciousness be possible. As Kant puts it, the sense of "I think" must be able to accompany all my presentations, otherwise something would be presented to me that would mean nothing to me.[35]

Much in this answer is alien to the Dharmakīrtian spirit that animates Sa-paṇ's work. The idea of a transcendental apperception, which rests on a transcendental self, directly contradicts the doctrine of no-self, which argues in a Humean spirit that unity is largely illusory. Similarly, the idea of a synthesis of the sensory manifold is anathema to Dharmakīrti, who insists on the radical dichotomy between perception (sensation) and inference (the understanding). There is, however, a similarity in the preoccupation of the two authors; namely, how to construct the unity that knowledge requires and that is not given at the sensory level. There is also partial similarity in the structure of the arguments. In both authors apperception allows the unification of the sensory manifold. Their answers to these common preoccupations are, however, worlds apart. Whereas for Kant apperception is the transcendental possibility of the "I think" and presupposes a transcendental self, for Sa-paṇ apperception is the nonthematic, but nevertheless empirical, reflexive awareness of mental states existing within a selfless field of consciousness.

For Sa-paṇ, this self-presencing of conceptual mental events guarantees their objectivity. Although there is no correspondence between concepts and reality, thought is not arbitrary but causally grounded in reality through perception. A mere causal link or association of ideas, however, is not sufficient to ensure objectivity. Something stronger is needed to warrant the link between perception and conception. If Sa-paṇ is right, Dharmakīrtians find this link in apperception, which ensures the unity of our psychic life. Let us further explore this notion of reflexivity and its implications by examining Dharmakīrti's arguments supporting self-cognition and how Tibetan commentators explain them.

25

Perception and Apperception

Dharmakīrti on the Self-Presencing of Mental States

Dharmakīrti's representationalism centers on the concept of the aspect through which objects are perceived. Objects are apprehended through the imprints that their contact with the senses leave on consciousness. Thus, when perceiving external objects, consciousness is actually cognizing itself. Reflexivity is the condition for any cognitive activity. This is a basic tenet of Dharmakīrti's system first propounded by Dignāga. Both thinkers take great pains to prove this point, on which their theories of perception and their idealist metaphysics rest.[1]

This view that cognition is self-revelatory (*svaprakāśa, rang gsal ba*) or self-presenting is shared by the Prābhākara Mīmāṃsakas and the Advaita Vedāntins. According to their view, knowers know that they are aware of a cognized object because a cognition reveals itself to the knowing self. The reflexive nature of cognition is not accepted by the Naiyāyikas and the Baṭṭha Mīmāṃsakas, who maintain that cognition of an object does not necessitate awareness of that cognition. The Nyāya holds that perception is usually followed by an awareness of that perception. Thus, knowers usually are informed of their own mental processes by apperceptions that apprehend perceptions. However, this inner recognition may not arise due to a change in the knower's interest and expectation.[2]

Several arguments are presented by Dharmakīrti to establish the reflexive nature of consciousness.[3] One of his main arguments concerns the nature of suffering and happiness as it reveals the deeper nature of mental states. For Dharmakīrti, suffering and happiness are not external to consciousness, but integral to our awareness of external objects. For example, we do not get burned and afterward feel pain. Rather, our perceptions are colored from the very start by our sensations. Our perceptions arise with a certain tone feeling, be it pleasant, unpleasant, or neutral.[4] Thus, suffering and happiness are feelings experienced through the same mental states that apprehend external objects. They are not experienced separately from the objects we see, although they are different from them. How is a single mental state able to apprehend an external object and experience a sensation?

Dharmakīrti answers that this points to the dual nature of mental states. A mental episode apprehends an object, for example, food, which we find pleasant.

In doing so, the mental state is associated with a pleasant feeling.[5] In perceiving the external object, the food, we immediately know "how it feels" to taste this object. In this single mental state, two aspects can be distinguished. The first is the external object or, rather, its representation, revealing itself. This aspect is described as the objective aspect (*grāhyākāra, gzung rnam*). The second aspect is the apprehension of this appearance. This is the subjective aspect (literally, "holding aspect"; *grāhakākāra, 'dzin rnam*), which Dharmakīrti describes as self-cognition. Dharmakīrti says: "Therefore, happiness, etc., is commonly understood as [an experience of objects] because it has the appearance of objects being transferred onto itself and is experienced. [Happiness] does not, however, directly cognize the external object [but] cognizes itself through being merely produced from an [external] object."[6] Objects are not cognized directly but by an indirect process in which they produce their perceptions. These directly apprehend the representations of the objects. The term *apprehension of external objects* refers to this causal process in which an external object induces a mental state to experience itself under a certain aspect. Hence, when we are aware of something, we are at the same time cognizant of this awareness. This self-awareness is not objectified, so we are not aware of ourselves in quite the same way as we are aware of external objects. Nevertheless, our own experiences are integrated into the continuity of our mental life without any necessary mediation. We do not have to think that we experience, for we are unthematically and immediately aware of this fact.

For Dharmakīrti, a mental state thus has two functions. It apprehends an external object (*ālambana, dmigs pa*). This process is not, however, direct, but results from the causal influence of the object, which induces cognition to experience (*anubhava, myong*) its representation. The mind does not experience an external object but beholds an internal representation that stands for an external object. Hence, Dharmakīrti says: "Therefore, for all cognition, observation and experience are different."[7] Cognition cannot be reduced to a process of direct observation but involves holding an inner representation. This beholding is not, however, an apprehension in the usual sense of the word, for the two aspects of a single mental episode are not separate. It is an "intimate" contact, a direct acquaintance of the mental state by itself through which we experience our mental states at the same time as we perceive things.

Among Western philosophers, Sartre provides a somewhat similar account of consciousness. Like Dharmakīrti, and unlike Kant or Husserl, Sartre offers a nonegological (i.e., selfless) model of consciousness that explains reflexivity without presupposing the existence of a unitary self. He argues that reflexivity does not require the existence of a transcendental ego,[8] which would organize the variety of perceptions and thoughts as if it existed behind each mental episode. The unity of mental life can be explained by the reflexivity of an impersonal or prepersonal field of consciousness. The various thoughts and perceptions we have are organized as ours on the basis of the reflexive awareness we have of them. Recollection is made possible because our mind is also cognizant of its own seeing. Sartre explains: "Indeed, the existence of consciousness is an absolute because consciousness is conscious of itself. That is, the type of existence of consciousness is to be conscious of itself. And consciousness is aware of itself *inasmuch as it is conscious of a transcendent object.*[9] Hence, everything is clear and lucid in consciousness. The object with its characteristic opacity is before consciousness. Consciousness is purely and simply conscious to be conscious of that object; such is the law of its existence. We must add that this consciousness–except in cases of reflective consciousness which we will insist on later–is not *positional,* that is, that consciousness is not its own object."[10] For Sartre, the unity of mental life is the result of consciousness's awareness of itself. The mind is aware of other objects and, in the process, reveals its presence. This self-presencing is not, however, thematic. That is, we are not aware, except in cases in which we reflect on ourselves, of our awareness. Nevertheless, we are cognizant of our mental states. This is what Sartre describes as nonpositional self-consciousness; that is, the reflexivity of a mental state that does not set itself up as an object but rather becomes aware of itself through being aware of an object.

A similar view is embraced by Dignāga and Dharmakīrti with their doctrine of self-cognition or apperception, whose importance must be clear by now.[11] A number of questions, however, are left unanswered in their view: Is apperception a cognition, and if so, does it have an object? What is the nature of the relation between the two aspects of consciousness? And last, if consciousness's awareness of objects is a cognition of itself, how can we speak of the perception of external objects? These questions are not explicitly addressed by Dharmakīrti. To explore them, let us involve Tibetan commentators, starting with a discussion of whether self-cognition is a subject or not.

Does Self-Cognition Have an Object?

Self-cognition or apperception makes us aware of our mental states without thematizing them. As such it is certainly not a subject in the usual sense of the term. Can we then say that apperception is really an apprehending subject, that is, that it has an object? And if apperception is not a subject, how can we say that it is a cognition?

On this difficult point, Tibetan epistemologists have given contradictory answers, which reflect intra- as well as intersectarian differences. Most of Sa-paṇ's followers argue that apperception has no object. It does not observe anything but rather is the experience of an inner representation. It is an awareness not because it observes an object but because it is the self-presencing of a mental state. To put it in Dharmakīrtian terms, self-cognition is the luminosity of consciousness itself. Yak-dön, the fourteenth century reviver of Sa-paṇ's antirealism, seems to have been the first to clearly state this view in Tibet. He explains: "As for self-cognition, it is not the type of self-cognition in which cognizer and cognized [could be] distinguished, but it is the very [nature of consciousness] being merely produced as cognition that is different from matter. Therefore, self-cognition has no object."[12] Mental states apprehend their objects only through the intermediary of aspects, which are internal representations of the object apprehended indirectly by the cognition. For Yak-dön, apperception is the reflexive or subjective aspect of mental episode that is aware of the representations produced within consciousness by external objects. The ability of mental states to cognize their objects is what separates them from material objects. Mental states are intentional, they are directed toward objects, which they apprehend. For Yak-dön, this intentionality is not a direct contact between cognition and the external world but results from the ability of mental states to become aware of the representations produced within themselves by external objects. This ability to behold representations is due to apperception, the reflexive apprehension of representations internal to the cognition. Since apperception is not a separate mental state, it does not have an object distinct from itself; it is just the reflexive aspect of a mental state.

This view is quite similar to Sa-paṇ's brief comments in his *Auto-Commentary*. There, he rejects "that which cognizes an object" as the definition of *mental state* (*blo, buddhi*) on the grounds that it is both circular and does not include self-cognition, which is mental without having an object. For Sa-paṇ, self-cognition does not take itself as its object:

> *Question*: Is not self-cognition the object?
> *Answer*: It is contradictory for something to be [both] subject and object. Therefore, explanations of self-cognition as having an object [as in the example of the self-revealing of the lamp] are metaphorical.[13]

A subject-object relation requires that object and cognition be distinct. If self-cognition were its own object, it would have to be distinct from itself. However, we become cognizant of our mental states without the conscious realization that we are aware, as is illustrated by the example of the lamp that self-reveals while revealing other objects. The lamp does not light itself like it does external objects. It merely reveals its presence in the act of making objects clear. Similarly, consciousness does not take itself as an object, but merely self-cognizes while being aware of other objects.[14]

This view is not shared, however, by all followers of Sa-paṇ. Despite his representationalism, Go-ram-ba disagrees with this view on the following grounds. Take the example of the recollection of an experience. Since this recollection is a subsequent cognition, its object (the experience) must have been realized by a previous cognition, which cannot be but apperception itself. Therefore, apperception must have an object. Moreover, argues Go-ram-ba, as self-cognition is a valid cognition it must be intentional. It must be directed toward something and, hence, must have an object. To cover his differences with Sa-paṇ's clear assertion that self-cognition has no object, Go-ram-ba engages in an exegetical exercise typical of scholastic commentarial traditions. He interprets Sa-paṇ's comments not as denying that apperception has an object, but as rejecting the idea that a thought qua thought (and not qua cognition) can be the object of its own apperception. The object of the apperception of a conceptual cognition is not the latter's identity as a conception, but its identity as a mental state; that is, its clarity.

Kay-drup defends a similar point, although his view of perception and apperception radically differ from Go-ram-ba's. Kay-drup argues that if apperception had no object it could not be nondeceptive (*mi slu ba, avisaṃvādi*) with respect to a real thing. Moreover, the rejection of apperception's object contradicts the example given by Dharmakīrti. For if a lamp does not reveal itself, how is it that we see it? And if does reveal itself, does it not light itself? Similarly, apperception reveals itself in the process of revealing other objects. In the process, it must cognize itself and, hence, must take itself as its own object.

The view that apperception has an object is not surprising in Kay-drup, who, as we will see shortly, is a direct realist and argues for a reflective view of apperception. It is more surprising in an author such as Go-ram-ba, who argues for representationalism and a nonreflective view of apperception. How can apperception have an object in such a view since it does not apprehend anything, not even itself? Is not apperception an experiencing of an inner mental state, a process to which the subject-object distinction simply does not apply? Although the assertion that apperception has an object is difficult to sustain in Go-ram-ba's perspective, it corresponds to his particular approach, which is to show that representationalism is compatible with a phenomenological respect for the commonsense view of mental processes.

This difference among Sa-paṇ's orthodox commentators should also remind us not to overemphasize the inter-sectarian differences among Tibetan epistemologists. My description of the conflict between Sa-paṇ's followers and their realist contemporaries should not mask that there are important intrasectarian differences as well. Although, in Book I, I insisted on the former type of difference (since there seems to be relative unanimity among thinkers of each group about the issue of universals), here I have tried to correct that impression by bringing to our attention the intrasectarian differences as well.

The similarities between Kay-drup and Go-ram-ba are quite real. They should not hide, however, the deeper differences over the analysis of perception and apperception. This is no surprise, given their different theories of perception. Whereas Go-ram-ba holds the representationalist view sketched previously, Kay-drup holds a direct realist view. This difference is brought out next in our discussion, on the nature of and relation between the two aspects, objective and subjective. I ask the reader to bear with me through this exceedingly technical discussion, for it reveals often unnoticed but important differences between the Sa-gya and Ge-luk theories of perception.

Go-ram-ba's Representationalism

Go-ram-ba defines *self-cognition* as "that subjective aspect which apprehends the nature of [the cognition] itself."[15] This characterization is accepted by most of his contemporaries.[16] This unanimity, however, hides deep differences concerning the nature of aspects and apperception that often remain buried under the common definition and the exegetical details. These differences surface on the rather obscure question of whether every cognition is a self-cognition with respect to its own nature (*shes pa yin na rang gi ngo bo la rang rig yin pas khyab*). To explain this rather involved issue, which reveals important differences between Sa-paṇ's followers (*sa lugs*) and Cha-ba's followers (*cha lugs*), including the Ge-luk tradition, let us first examine Go-ram-ba's remarkably clear explanation before examining the Ge-luk objections.

As explained earlier, Go-ram-ba's theory of perception is representationalist. Perception only indirectly apprehends an external object through the direct apprehension of its aspect. The directly seen "object" is not the external object, contrary to what the direct realists assert, but the objective aspect of the perception. We perceive real things only inasmuch as we perceive their representations, which are similar to them. Go-ram-ba says: "That which appears to the sense consciousness as [existing] simultaneously [with the consciousness and as being] external, as if separate [from it], is labeled an external object by ordinary people. This is in reality the objective aspect, which is accepted by Sautrāntikas as being cast [on consciousness] by the external object. Proponents of Mind-Only hold that, in the absence of an external object, consciousness itself appears as the held [thing] under the power of latencies that cast [an aspect on consciousness]."[17] Instead of analyzing perception as a direct contact with an external object, Go-ram-ba describes perception as an immediate contact with an internal representation through which the external object is indirectly perceived.

This view, I would argue, is not unlike Dharmakīrti's own view. It provides an analysis based on the idea of internal objects that does not presume the status of external objects. Such analysis can be understood in representational terms and is then compatible with the Sautrāntika acceptance of an external world, or it can be interpreted as phenomenalist in accordance with the Mind-Only rejection of such a world. Both philosophies hold that consciousness cognizes itself as having a certain aspect, which is part of itself, but disagree on the causal process that gives rise to the cognitive process. Whereas Sautrāntikas assert that the objective aspect is a copy as well as an effect of an external object, proponents of Mind-Only reject this object, which is not observable independent of the aspect, as an unobservable metaphysical pseudo-entity (to use a fashionable language) and assert that perception is the product of internal tendencies.[18]

The consequence of Go-ram-ba's analysis is that perception is nothing but the apprehension of this objective aspect. It is perception apprehending itself. Go-ram-ba explains: "The subjective aspect is the appearance [of the cognition] as apprehending the object's aspect and the internal experience [of this appearance] as pleasant or unpleasant. This [aspect] is reified by common folks as the self that uses [external objects]. It is not reified as the used held [thing]."[19] Apprehension of real objects is an apprehension of their representations by the internal aspect of the cognition. In the final analysis, perception of objects boils down to apperception, the subjective aspect apprehending the representation (objective aspect). Consequently, every cognition is an apperception with respect to the representation of its object. Hence, it is an apperception with respect to its own form since the representation is nothing else than the form taken by the perception itself. Even a conceptual cognition is an apperception with respect to its own form. The distortion that affects a conception does not affect its cognizing nature (*svarūpa* or *svabhāva, rang gi ngo bo* or *rang bzhin*), but only its mode of apprehension. Its fundamental purity, which is manifested in its presence to itself, is not affected by the distortions that it imposes on external objects. As such it is a mode of perceiving, not conceiving.

Finally, before concluding Go-ram-ba's presentation, a last technical point must be made. Although Go-ram-ba appears to be saying that all cognitions are self-cognitions, in reality he is not. For him, that all cognitions are self-cognizing with respect to their representations does not entail that all cognitions are self-cognition. This rather technical distinction is made to ward off the following unwanted consequence: If an inference were a self-cognition it would be a form of perception and hence nonconceptual. Since it is conceptual, it cannot be a self-cognition, although it plays an apperceptive role toward its own cognizing nature.

The explanation of cognition as a self-cognition with respect to its own cognizing nature is only alluded to by Sa-paṇ, who defines *self-cognition* as "the nonmistakeness of consciousness with respect to its [cognizing] nature."[20] This view is more clearly articulated by Go-ram-ba and Śākya Chok-den, who see it as a major issue that opposes them to the Ge-luk revisionist interpretations. Both Go-ram-ba and Śākya Chok-den refute Gyel-tsap extensively on this issue, designating him "the [author of] the *Extensive Explanation*," a rather unusual occurrence in Tibetan scholarship, where usually positions rather than people are criticized.[21] Why did they find this issue so important?

As with the problem of universals, this issue became a focus for polemical activities. By delineating the differences that separate them from Dzong-ka-ba's followers on this question, Go-ram-ba and Śākya Chok-den stressed the particularity of their own tradition, which they probably perceived as threatened by syncretic tendencies found in the dubious interpretations of Sa-paṇ's thought. They considerably reinforced the distinction between the epistemological views of the Sa-gya tradition, as interpreted by Yak-dön and Rong-dön, and the Ga-den-ba interpretations of Dzong-ka-ba, Gyel-tsap, and Kay-drup. In doing so, they also contributed to the institutional separation of the two traditions. Henceforth, the demarcation was clear, and the two schools were set on the separate courses they have followed until the present day.

This conflict over apperception has, however, a more properly philosophical significance. Ge-luk and Sa-gya thinkers are separated in their understandings of the notion of aspect and their theories of perception. Sa-gya thinkers are representationalists, whereas Ge-luk-bas hold a form of direct realism, as they do not think that the direct object of perception, the objective aspect, is an internal representation. To explore this difference, let us first examine Gyel-tsap's sharp and influential attack against the position taken by Sa-paṇ's followers. Then we will analyze Kay-drup's comments, which reveal the implications of the differences between his (and Gyel-tsap's) position and that of Go-ram-ba.

A Ge-luk Understanding of Dharmakīrti's Aspects

Throughout their works, both Gyel-tsap and Kay-drup denounce the view according to which every mental episode is a self-cognition toward its own cognizing nature. Gyel-tsap rejects this view in the form of an extremely technical discussion, which is a classic of the Tibetan scholastic literature. His objection can be summarized as follows.

Let us take the example of an inference. If this inference were a self-cognition of its [cognizing] nature, it would be a perception of either its subjective aspect, the self-cognition of that inference, or its objective aspect, which is the inference itself. In both cases, the inference would be a perception and, therefore, free from conception. This is so for the following reason: If an inference were a self-cognition toward its own objective aspect, it would have to be a self-cognition simpliciter, because it would have to perceive internally a cognition (itself, that is, the cognition qua objective aspect). This, according to Gyel-tsap and Kay-drup, is the very definition of *self-cognition*. Gyel-tsap further pursues the argument, stating that if the adversary answers that an inference is an inference of its objective aspect and a self-cognition of its subjective aspect, the same fault (that an inference becomes nonconceptual) follows, for objective and subjective aspects are indiscernibly substantially identical.[22] Hence, when one appears to a perception, the other must also appear to that perception, for this is the meaning of being indiscernibly substantially identical.[23] Therefore, the unwanted consequence that an inference is nonconceptual still follows.

As we notice, this argument is highly technical and the issue is far from clear. We may wonder what the disagreement is about. Are Gyel-tsap and his opponents locked in a semantic debate over different ways of describing the same thing or are they involved in a substantive debate? The strong reactions that Gyel-tsap's criticisms provoked point to the second alternative. It is not easy, however, to see exactly what the real difference between Gyel-tsap and his opponents is. Let us unpack his statement by explicating his presuppositions. Here again, Kay-drup will prove an invaluable resource, for, as often, his remarks clarify what Gyel-tsap assumes.

The key difference between the Sa-gya and Ge-luk views of perception concerns the way they understand the objective aspect; that is, the appearance of the object to the perception. We ordinarily identify this appearance with the external object itself, that which is "in front of our eyes." This identification is, however, problematic in view of the time-gap problem. Since the object is the cause of the perception and since cause and effect cannot coexist, the external object cannot exist when the perception is produced. How can it then be said to be be perceived?

For Go-ram-ba, the solution to the time-gap problem is that perception does not directly cognize the external object but only its representation. The direct object of perception is the appearance of the object. This appearance is the objective aspect, which is usually confused with the real external object. This identification is, however, mistaken, for the appearance is just a representation of the external object. It is internal to the awareness, being nothing but the form that the awareness takes under the influence of the external object.[24] The part of the awareness that witnesses this taking such a form, that is, the cognition qua apprehender of the objective aspect, is the subjective aspect. According to Go-ram-ba's representationalism, awareness of an object must be analyzed as the interaction of three elements: the subjective aspect, the objective aspect and the external object. Perceiving an external object is for a mental episode to be aware of its arising under the form of a representation, the objective aspect, which stands for the external object by which it is produced. The act of awareness consists of the grasping of the objective aspect by the subjective aspect. In this process, the external object is not directly perceived. Its contribution to the epistemic process is only causal, the production of an internal representation that stands for the external object.

Gyel-tsap disagrees with this analysis of perception, which separates the appearance of the object from the object itself. For Gyel-tsap, the appearance of an object to a perception is not a representation. The appearance is the transparent revealing of the external object itself. The act of being aware of an object is not a three-term relation but a two-term relation. It involves a cognition and an external object. There is no intermediary, no appearance or internal object whose direct presence allows us to cognize indirectly an external object.

This realist analysis seems, however, to raise the following question: If consciousness perceives the external object itself, what is the role of the objective aspect? Kay-drup answers: "As [I] have already established through reasoning, the objective aspect of this or that cognition is only this or that cognition."[25] According to his view, the objective aspect is not a representation but is just the cognition qua awareness of an external object. The subjective aspect is the cognition qua awareness of itself as perceiving subject.

According to the Ge-luk analysis, each cognition has two parts, an external factor (*kha phyir lta'i cha*), the objective aspect, which perceives the external object, and an internal factor (*kha nang lta'i cha*), the subjective aspect, which perceives the objective aspect. In the case of a sense perception, the perception itself is the objective aspect since the outward looking part of the mental state cognizes an external object. The objective aspect is in turn apprehended by the second part of the perception, the subjective aspect. This subjective aspect is apperceptive and keeps track of the experiences of the cognizing person. But notice that here the meaning of *apperception* has shifted. Whereas for Sa-gya representationalism apperception is reflexive, it is now reflective or at least thematic. It is an inner awareness of a mental state and as such implies a double intentionality: external apprehension of an external object and internal apprehension of the mental state.

A classical objection against such a view is that it opens the door to an infinite regress. If the objective aspect needs a subjective one, this latter one will in turn require another aspect apprehending it. To avoid this objection, Ge-luk thinkers go back to Dharmakīrti's explanation, emphasizing that apperception is not a separate cognition. In doing so, however, they do not seem to realize that they are using Dharmakīrti's terms in a rather different way. Instead of presenting apperception as a necessary consequence of a representationalist analysis of cognition, they are forced into a more artificial position, arguing that the two aspects, the cognition qua external perception and the cognition qua internal apperception, are two aspects of the same mental state, which can be distinguished only on the basis of their functions. Since these functions are exclusive of each other, external and internal cognitions are distinct, although they do not exist separately. It is clear, however, that this explanation is not completely persuasive. It seems to hide the problem rather than solve it. Ge-luk thinkers themselves do not find it convincing and, hence, have no qualm leaving out the idea of apperception when they move to Candrakīrti's Madhyamaka philosophy.

Before proceeding, let us briefly reflect on the original debate: Is cognition a self-cognition with respect to its own cognizing nature? For Go-ram-ba, the answer is bound to be positive, because every cognition is in final analysis the subjective aspect. External objects cannot appear directly to consciousness without the intermediary of a representation, the objective aspect. The act of awareness consists in the apperception of this representation by the subjective aspect.

For Gyel-tsap and Kay-drup, this answer will not do. In accordance with their direct realism, Gyel-tsap and Kay-drup hold that perception is not the sensing of an internal representation, but the apprehension of an external object. Hence, in final analysis, perception boils down to the objective aspect. Since it apprehends an external object, perception is foremost the externally oriented factor of a perceptual episode. It is called *objective aspect* because it is the aspect of a perceptual state that apprehends the object. And, although it does not exist apart from its own apperception, it is not identical with it either. Each cognition has two functions, an external orientation and an internal apprehension of itself. Only the latter is apperceptive.[26] Moreover, among these two functions, the external one is primary.

This explanation faces several problems. If consciousness is aware of the external object itself, why should we bother to introduce the notion of aspect into the analysis? Why should we discuss the likeness of the mind and the object if this likeness is not an intermediary between the mind and the external world? Moreover, why do Ge-luk thinkers insist on keeping the doctrine of self-cognition, which does not seem necessary to explain the nature of perception? Why introduce self-cognition in an analysis of the direct relation between perception and the world?

In considering Ge-luk views, we must keep in mind the double nature of their project, which is philosophical as well as commentarial. These views are not independent philosophical elaborations, but interpretations of Dharmakīrti's thought. Hence, one obvious answer to our questions is that the notions of aspect and self-cognition are introduced by Ge-luk thinkers to explain Dharmakīrti's ideas. As such, however, the Ge-luk analyses do not fare very well. It is quite clear from the passages we examined that Dharmakīrti's view is better captured by the Sa-gya analysis than by Gyel-tsap's and Kay-drup's philosophically astute, but textually unlikely, interpretations.

However, these interpretations are not purely exegetical but are philosophical as well. In a tradition in which truth is found through commentaries, interpretation plays a larger role. Interpreting Dharmakīrti's text is the means through which truth, in our case, epistemological truth, is appropriated. Hence, a commentary on Dharmakīrti's theory of perception must satisfy two demands: It must reflect Dharmakīrti's ideas, but more important, it must be true, at least within the limits of Dharmakīrti's doxographical commitments. Let us examine Kay-drup's insightful comments in the light of these two conflicting demands.

Representationalism, Realism, and Causal Theories

Kay-drup objects to the Sa-gya interpretation of Dharmakīrti's theory of perception not on exegetical but on philosophical grounds. For him, the Sa-gya analysis is not receivable because it leads to the complete separation between cognition and object. According to this analysis, the aspect is a representation through which an external object is mediatedly perceived and stands between the world and awareness, like a curtain (to use Kay-drup's word) or (to use a classical expression in Western philosophy) a veil.[27] Kay-drup says: "Accordingly, the cognition held by a self-cognition is called an objective aspect, which is, after all, nothing but the cognition itself. It has already been well established that the appearance of an aspect does not refer to an aspect that would, like a curtain, [stand] between the cognition and the object, but to the very [cognition] produced as having the aspect. This is the view of both Sautrāntikas and Cittamātrins."[28] If the appearance of an object in a perception were a representation that stood for an external object, the cognition would not apprehend this object. It would be walled off from the external world by the curtain of representations which would stand between perception and reality. Hence, the Sa-gya interpretation of perception as being the apprehension of an internal representation cannot be true. It is philosophically unsound and cannot correspond to Dharmakīrti's own view, which is normative for Buddhist epistemology.

For Kay-drup, the aspect, which Sa-gya thinkers take to be an opaque representation, must be at least partly transparent. In the case of a conception, this transparency is limited, but in the case of a perception, it is complete. The object appears as it is to perception, which apprehends this object directly without any intermediary. This is direct realism, the view that mind is directly in contact with the real world. It differs, however, from the usual forms of direct realism in that it involves the notion of aspect, which in turn implies a notion of similarity. The aspect is similar to the external object, which is apprehended by the cognition. In that, Ge-luk thinkers differ from the views of the Vaibhāṣika. This school holds that there is no likeness between mental states and objects. Cognition apprehends its object nakedly (*jen par*), without the presence of any aspect. Awareness holds the object in a direct contact with reality without bearing in itself the mark of its apprehension of the object.

Direct realism is often posited to avoid the problem of the time gap raised by causal theories. If objects cause perception, how can the latter apprehend the former when the former have already disappeared? Direct realism's usual answer is that awareness and object coexist. In the Buddhist context, the Vaibhāṣika defends this view. Though this school does not deny that objects cause perception, they understand this causal relation in a rather loose way. Accordingly, object and subject coexist despite being cause and effect.

Ge-luk realism is different from these usual forms of direct realism, which it judges to be naive. Ge-luk thinkers take the time-gap problem seriously and dismiss the Vaibhāṣika view as reflecting an incoherent view of causality. They take Dharmakīrti's view of causality very seriously, holding that causes and effects never coexist,[29] and attempt to present a theory of perception in which the apprehension of the external world is made compatible with the time gap necessarily implied by a strictly causal account of the relation that exists between the object, the cause, and the perception, its result. To accomplish this, Ge-luk thinkers use Dharmakīrti's notion of aspect. Here the commentarial ingenuity and philosophical creativity of the Ge-luk tradition come together. Although no bona fide commentary of Dharmakīrti can ignore this notion, the Ge-luk adopt it because they find it useful to respond to the time-gap problem. Hence, even when explaining their theory of perception in the context of the study of Madhyamaka, that is, outside of Dharmakīrti's system, Ge-luk thinkers still use the notion of aspect, despite the very limited use of this term by their sources, Nāgārjuna and Candrakīrti.

To explain how perception can apprehend an external object that does not exist any more at the time when perception comes to be, Ge-luk thinkers use the notion of aspect. A perception is caused by an external object that is not apprehended nakedly. In the process, the perception comes to bear the marks of the object that it perceives. In this way, the perception is allowed to cognize its objects, which have already disappeared. To perceive an object is to be affected causally by this object. Cognition bears a form similar to that of external objects, but the likeness of the appearance is not representational. Rather, it is the likeness of the cognition to the external world. A cognition is like an external object in that it bears the impression of the external object.[30]

The causal connection between the external object and its perception does not entail a form of representationalism, which in the views of these theorists entails the acceptance of the existence of a veil between consciousness and the external world. As Kay-drup argues, the veil theory is not a necessary consequence of a causal theory of perception, although, in his view, it is entailed by representationalism. The likeness of the mind to the external world is not some kind of veil standing between mind and the world. Rather, it is the perceptual experience itself produced in us by our confrontation with the external world. It is the form that the mind takes in its encounter with external reality.

But notice that apperception plays little role in this analysis. It is posited on the basis of further commentarial considerations but is not implied by the analysis of perception. Whereas for Dharmakīrti and Go-ram-ba, apperception is implied by the representational analysis of perception, for Ge-luk thinkers apperception does not seem to be required by their realist analysis of perception. It is merely added as a supplementary factor to an analysis of mind that does not seem to require it. Ge-luk thinkers realize that this apperception cannot be a separate cognition. Hence, they argue that it is the second, subjective, part of a mental episode. But this second aspect is not entailed by their analysis of perception. Rather it seems to be required for commentarial purposes only and seems to lead to the unwanted consequence of a double intentionality.

Hence, contrary to the notion of aspect, which plays an important role in the Ge-luk tradition where it is kept even while investigating perception, in Madhyamaka, the notion of apperception is much more artificial. It is posited on a mostly commentarial basis, to account for Dharmakīrti's theory of the four types of perception. Ge-luk thinkers make only limited use of the notion of apperception. For example, Gyel-tsap describes apperception as the basis of denomination of the person as subject. Our mental life is more than a causal succession of mental events. It seems to have a coherence, which allows us to act as subjects in a world of objects. This ability is not based on the existence of a substantial self, but on the ability of the mind to cognize itself. Apperception enables us to apprehend things, thinking "I cognize this and that."[31] Nevertheless, these arguments, which are important for Dharmakīrti, are not taken very seriously by Ge-luk thinkers, who quickly forget them when the topic moves to Madhyamaka philosophy. Ge-luk thinkers are not really committed to the idea of apperception, which they consider to be a reflection of Dharmakīrti's lingering foundationalism and hence a limitation to his usually impeccable authority, which is to be overcome by the study of Candrakīrti's Madhyamaka.[32]

Sa-paṇ's followers hold quite different views. They hold that apperception is not reflective, but reflexive. It is not a supplementary factor but is entailed by the analysis of perception itself. Since perception apprehends an internal representation, it apprehends itself. Unsurprisingly, Sa-gya thinkers hold to the idea of apperception when explaining a Madhyamaka view of perception. Like their Ge-luk adversaries, they use Dharmakīrti's analysis, although their understanding is quite different. Hence, for them, apperception is not the expression of a lingering foundationalism, but the irrefutable consequence of a representationalist analysis of perception.

The Soteriological Implications of Apperception

For some Sa-gya epistemologists, apperception has an important soteriological role in explaining the nature of yogic perception (*yogipratyakṣa, rnal 'byor mngon sum*). This is a difficult topic within Dharmakīrti's tradition. Given the receptive and nonpropositional nature of perception, the notion of a yogic perception seems to be a contradiction in terms. For if perceptions are passive and entirely lack cognitive content, how can there be yogic perceptions, which eliminate all obscurations? If perception cannot eliminate wrong views, how can yogic perception root out delusions, since this constitutes an elimination of superimpositions?[33] How can yogic perception merely hold its object, while at the same time realizing the topics central to Buddhist soteriology such as suffering, impermanence, and no-self?

Dharmakīrti provides only partial and brief answers,[34] and they seem to be in tension with his general theory of perception. He takes yogic perception to be an extension of the inferential understanding we can gain through reasoning on topics such as suffering, impermanence, and no-self. When conceptual understanding of these topics is deepened and intensified through the practice of tranquility (*śamatha, zhi gnas*) and insight (*vipaśyanā, lhag mthong*), it gradually becomes clearer until it is completely vivid. At this stage, the insight thus gained is so clear as to be nonconceptual. Since such an insight is correct as well as non-conceptual, it must be perceptual. Dharmakīrti does not discuss the obvious problems that arises from this explanation, which seem to contradict his description of concepts as mistaken. How can conceptual cognitions, which are mistaken, become directly grounded in reality and hence undistorted, merely by becoming vivid?

Tibetan commentators have dealt with this issue, and their discussions lay out possible solutions. According to Śākya Chok-den, their views fall into two groups.[35] Cha-ba, and their followers have emphasized the cognitive nature of yogic perception. For them, yogic perception actively identifies an object such as impermanence, suffering, or no-self. Dharmakīrti's descriptions of yogic perception as an extension and enhancement of inference support their view that perception is not merely passively holding its object. Like other valid perceptions, yogic perception identifies its object by eliminating false superimpositions (*sgro 'dogs gcod pa*). Hence, for these realists, there is no difficulty in positing a transformation of conceptions, which already cognize reality albeit in a distorted way, into yogic perceptions through the practice of tranquility and insight.

Antirealists present a different view. In accordance with their view that perception is passive, they tend to emphasize the receptive character of yogic perception. Yogic perception is less an active cognizing than a heightened state of receptivity reached through the elimination of obscurations. This state of receptivity, which is explained as being objectless, is sometimes related to apperception. This idea seems to have originated with the first patriarch of the Dri-gung-ba (*'bri gung pa*) branch of the Ga-gyü school, Dri-gung Jik-den-gong-bo (*'bri gung 'jig rten mgong po,* 1143–1217). For him, the pure nondual awareness that constitutes the path, the wisdom of the Great Seal (*phyag chen, mahāmudrā*), is apperceptive.[36] It is a state in which the mind of the yogi does not apprehend any object but merely abides in its luminosity. From this comes the idea of relating such abiding in clarity to the concept of apperception. Yogic perception, then, is a state of pure apperception in which all conceptualization has been eliminated and in which the nonconceptual state of the mind is clearly revealed. Similarly, Śākya Chok-den explains yogic perception as apperceptive. For Śākya Chok-den, this is the Sa-gya view, the only way to make sense of the notion of yogic perception. Although yogic perception is sometimes described as having an object, this is a metaphorical description of the purely apperceptive state that is reached by the elimination of self-grasping.[37]

Śākya Chok-den is rather brief in his explanation of how apperception fits into the framework of Buddhist practice. His words suggest, however, the following picture. Through the practice of tranquility the mind is calmed. The conceptual network that usually agitates the mind ceases and the clear nature of the mind, that is, its apperceptive character, is more in evidence. Such a state of clarity, however, is only provisional. To have long lasting soteriological effects it must be conjoined with insight, so that wrong conceptions can be eliminated. In the process the yogi attains a state of extreme clarity and sharpness in which the mind becomes fully transparent to itself.[38] Such a state is not a mere blankness of mind or a momentary withdrawal from conceptualization obtained through concentration, but a heightened state of clarity and sharpness that has cognitive implications. Such a state is cognitively meaningful in that it is reached by the understanding of no-self and brings about the uprooting of illusions concerning the nature of the self. It is not, however, in and of itself cognitive. Hence, it is best described as a purely apperceptive state in which the clear nature of the mind is fully revealed.

This explanation, which gives a plausible account of yogic perception, does not seem to originate with Dharmakīrti. He explains yogic perception in relation to inference, without establishing a connection between apperception and yogic perception. Moreover, Dharmakīrti speaks of the clear nature of the mind in a soteriological context but does not seem to connect this clarity with apperception. Hence, the notion that yogic perception is apperceptive probably originates in sources other than Dharmakīrti's writings. A connection between wisdom and self-cognition appears in several Indian texts, which speak of self-cognizing wisdom (*rang rig pa'i ye shes*). This does not seem, however, to be a direct reference to the type of self-cognition posited by Dharmakīrti. All this suggests that the connection between yogic perception and apperception was made later. Nevertheless, this conncection does not fall outside of Dharmakīrtian ideas, as we will see in Chapter 27, where we examine the soteriological implications of Dharmakīrti's system.

Before entering into this discussion, however, we need to deepen our understanding of the differences between Ge-luk direct realism and Sa-gya representationalism by examining the question of whether or not external objects are perceptible. If objects are not directly observable but just represented, should we then say that objects are not really perceived? Tibetan thinkers have argued at length about this problem. They have also debated on the related but distinct issue of whether or not external objects are hidden. Working through their analyses on these questions will allow us to dispell the confusion that often surrounds this difficult issue in Dharmakīrti's thought.

26

Are External Objects Perceptible?

Are Objects Hidden or "Hidden"?

Commonsense views perception as an immediate contact with an object directly present to our awareness. We have seen, however, that this simple view is problematic in more than one respect. The preceding chapter has investigated some of the difficulties in accounting for immediacy. Direct realism and representationalism attempt to preserve our intuition of immediacy but account for it in different ways. Whereas the former holds that external objects are directly perceived, the latter introduces an intermediary element, the internal aspect, which is the direct object of awareness. Awareness is in direct contact with a representation that stands for an external object, which remains outside of its direct grasp.

Immediacy is also difficult to account for when we reflect on the causal relation between an external object and perception. There we seem to be faced with another quandary. On the one hand, we seem to think about perception as being an awareness of the presence of external objects. On the other hand, we also assume that perception is caused by external reality. Now, if objects cause perception, the former cannot be directly present to the latter, since this would require that causes (objects) and effects (perception) exist at the same time. This is impossible in Dharmakīrti's system, where reality is momentary. Hence, there is a tension in Dharmakīrti's account, which we already noticed while investigation the non-deceptiveness of valid cognitions.[1] There, intentional and causal accounts pull apart. Whereas the former emphasizes the object directedness of cognition, the latter undermines this immediacy by stressing the time gap between the object and the subject. Among Dharmakīrti's Tibetan realist interpreters, Cha-ba and his direct disciples have tended to minimize the importance of the causal element and preserve as much immediacy as possible. Ge-luk thinkers have not followed this trend and have tried to combine an intentional view of perception with a more coherent causal account. In their view, in perception we are immediately aware of the external world through a causal process influenced by the external object.

In harmony with their rejection of commonsense as a framework for epistemological inquiry, Sa-paṇ and his tradition stress causal accounts, even suggesting a radical reinterpretation of our usual epistemic vocabulary. Their position illustrates the paradox of theoretical systematization, which aims at explaining our common intuitions but ends up destroying them. This paradox is quite clear in the case of the theory of perception that attempts to account for our feeling of perceiving external objects but often ends by denying that we can be in direct contact with these external entities. Therefore, one wonders how far should one push the philosophical analysis (done here in terms of causality) of the perceptibility of external objects at the expense of commonsense?[2]

Sa-paṇ does not answer this question. We must turn to his commentators and their debate with Ge-luk opponents to see what they propose. Both sides agree that perception involves the presence of aspects but they disagree about the nature of these aspects. Their disagreement focuses around two issues: (a) Are external objects perceptible or are they just inferred? (b) Are external objects hidden from perception? This second issue seems at first to be identical with the first, but the situation is complicated by the use of a special term, "*hidden*" (*lkog na mo*), by Sa-paṇ and others[3] to describe the objects of of perception. Sa-paṇ says: "Sautrāntikas [establish] a "hidden" thing as object of comprehension and a cognition that is generated as having an aspect similar to [that] object."[4] This term has been the focus of conflicting interpretations among Tibetan epistemologists, who have debated at length whether external objects are completely perceptible, hidden, or only "hidden"! I first briefly document this discussion, which underlines the close relation between the ontological and epistemological issues. Realism concerning universals and duration are not just ontological issues but have epistemological consequences. This leads me to examine the related question of the perceptibility of the external world. The conflicting views adopted by Tibetan thinkers allow me to throw some light on this question, which is a classical philosophical quandary as well as a difficult issue in the interpretation of Dharmakīrti's thought. It also allows me to break away from the binary opposition between realism and antirealism to document some of the numerous intrasectarian debates among Tibetan thinkers.

The Tibetan word used by Sa-paṇ to describe external objects is not the usual word for hidden (*lkog gyur, parokṣa*), but a derivative (*lkog na mo*). It has probably been coined by Tibetan thinkers to signal a different meaning for hidden in this context from what it usually means in Buddhist epistemology, the objects of inference which are hidden to ordinary perception. What is the meaning of "hidden" as given here? Since in this case recourse to the dictionary proves disappointing, let us first investigate the objections raised by thinkers belonging to the current of the new epistemology (Cha-ba, Gyel-tsap, etc.) toward the use of "hidden" to describe external objects and the conflicting responses given by Sa-paṇ's followers.

As we observed in the preceding chapters, a consistent tendency within the new epistemological paradigm defined by Cha-ba is to interpret Dharmakīrti's views in harmony with commonsense. This is well in evidence in the description of perception as determining its object rather than merely holding it in the ken of perception. In Cha-ba's writings, this view is translated into a Vaibhāṣika view that maintains that external objects and their perceptions are simultaneous. In holding this view, Cha-ba is following commonsense in asserting that we see objects that face us. He bitingly argues that if perception of external objects is produced by "hidden" objects, then why not posit that they are produced by some mysterious entities such as flesh-eating ghosts?[5] Since both external objects and ghosts are equally hidden, what is the difference between them?

Although he does not accept Cha-ba's view that external objects and perceptions are simultaneous, Gyel-tsap agrees that external objects are fully perceptible. Consequently, he explicitly rejects the use of the word "*hidden*," which he interprets as meaning hidden simpliciter: "Some early commentators on [Dharmakīrti's] *Ascertainment* speak of the acceptance by Sautrāntikas of a "hidden" object. This does not [correspond] to this system [in which] perception is accepted as a present subject. External [objects], which directly cast their aspects [that are] similar [to the objects], are accepted as evident and not as hidden. When presenting the Mind-Only teaching the master [Dharmakīrti] posits his system according to the False Aspectarian [school], whereas he follows the Sautrāntika system when positing external objects."[6] Gyel-tsap believes that the mind perceives external objects by being marked by them. This explains how perception can occur in the absence of direct contact with an external object. The time gap is bridged by the impression left on cognition by the external object. This imprint is not an immediate object but the result of the cognitive process. Hence, Gyel-tsap rejects the idea that external objects are somehow less than fully perceptible. For Gyel-tsap, the idea that external objects are "hidden" is a Tibetan invention with no basis in any authoritative Indian source.

An Unstable Compromise: Go-ram-ba's Representationalism

Go-ram-ba's view is quite different, despite some superficial similarities. Go-ram-ba agrees that external objects are perceptible through the intermediary of their aspects, which are similar to the objects. But, whereas Gyel-tsap holds that perception directly cognizes its object, Go-ram-ba understands perception to directly bear on the representation of its object, but not on the object itself. Accordingly, Go-ram-ba holds that external objects are "hidden." This expression does not mean that objects are wrapped away (or, to use Kay-drup's words, exist behind the curtain of the aspect), but simply refers to the existence of objects before they are perceived. "*Hidden*" does not mean hidden in the normal sense, as some (like Śākya Chok-den) think, for only universals are hidden in the usual sense of the word.[7] Since objects cast an aspect similar to themselves on consciousness, they are not hidden from the consciousness, to which they are revealed via their aspect.[8] "*Hidden*" refers to the way in which these objects are perceived through their representations. Go-ram-ba says: "[It may seem that] a sense perception apprehending blue cognizes the appearance [of something that exists] simultaneously and as if separate. It is not that awareness itself appears that way as [is asserted by] the True Aspectarians. Rather, an aspect established in opposition [to awareness] by a 'hidden' external object appears."[9] For Go-ram-ba, "*hidden*" refers to the fact that the external object is delivered to consciousness through its representation. Although it might appear that perception results from the encounter of subject and object, in reality consciousness does not directly cognize (*dngos su mi rig*) the object. Perception is produced only as having a resemblance to the object, which remains inaccessible to consciousness except through its representational aspect. For Go-ram-ba, the similarity between object and consciousness is the crucial element in the Sautrāntika theory of perception, for it ensures that perception is not locked up in its own appearance, as conceptions are. As we will see, Śākya Chok-den's analysis differs in that it rejects similarity even within the Sautrāntika framework. How can an aspect, which is the imprinted consciousness, be similar to an aggregation of atoms, he asks?

As a consistent representationalist, Go-ram-ba explains perception as the direct apprehension by consciousness of an internal object. Perception does not perceive the external object directly, only its representation.[10] Go-ram-ba's opinion is similar to Shah's description of Dharmakīrti's view: "Dharmakīrti observes that cognition directly experiences the form of the external object reflected in itself and not the external object itself; or, only metaphorically is it said that cognition grasps the external object which in fact simply causes this reflection. Really speaking, cognition does not grasp the external object, it grasps merely its own form."[11] Consciousness is not in direct contact with the external world but only with an internal representation caused by the external object. Hence, the external object is "hidden" although not completely hidden.

Go-ram-ba's peculiar use of "*hidden*" marks his position within the field of Tibetan epistemology. His view attempts to preserve some of the phenomenological integrity of consciousness. But whereas Gyel-tsap and others do this by transforming Dharmakīrti's representationalism into a direct realism, Go-ram-ba wants to integrate the phenomenological dimension within representationalism. Go-ram-ba wants to maintain some validity to our ordinary epistemic vocabulary, which reflects our intuition of consciousness as being directed toward external objects. Therefore, he is unwilling to let go of common expressions such as *consciousness perceives a color*. He understands that such an expression cannot be explained in terms of a direct cognitive contact between perception and the external color. Yet he is unwilling to let go of such an expression as just being a convenient way to describe a causal process. Accordingly, he describes the color as being "hidden."

The Difficulties of Representationalism

Despite its idiosyncratic use of the word "*hidden*," this representationalist view is familiar to students of Western philosophy. Unsurprisingly, it faces some of the same objections encountered by its Western proponents. First, if it is true that consciousness apprehends only the internal representation of external objects, can we still maintain that those objects are perceptible? Do we not perceive only aspects that we infer or interpret as external objects? Go-ram-ba argues that the view that external objects are only inferred, which is defended by Śākya Chok-den, is not compatible with the Sautrāntika assertion of the reality of external objects. For if external objects were only inferred, they would not be objects of perception and hence could not be real (by virtue of the equivalence in Dharmakīrti's system of being real and being an object of perception).

According to Go-ram-ba's Sautrāntika theory of perception, external objects are perceived through the similar representational aspects they cast on consciousness.[12] Objects are perceived as they are (i.e., as external objects), although not directly,[13] for that would entail a surrender to direct realism. One might argue that, if only the aspect is directly apprehended, the object cannot be perceived. This objection is met by Go-ram-ba by an analysis of the expression *to perceive an object* (*yul mngon sum du rtogs pa*). Go-ram-ba points out that this expression does not mean to "realize an object directly," but to realize an object without relying on an argument. Hence, nothing in the term itself implies a direct contact between perception and the external world. It remains true, nevertheless, that Go-ram-ba's view contradicts our common intuition of having an immediate and unproblematic access to the external world. But it may be, after all, that our intuition is just false!

A second difficulty besetting causal theories of perception relates to the classical time gap argument. Since objects and perceptions are related causally, they cannot coexist. This argument is particularly compelling in a tradition like Dharmakīrti's for which the momentariness of all things is a basic premise. In this view, both an external object and perception cannot last for more than an instant. Moreover, since the former causes (and hence must pre-exist) the latter, they cannot coexist even for a moment. Hence, it is impossible to find a time at which consciousness perceives the object. When the object exists, consciousness has yet to come to be, and when the latter perceives its object, the former has already disappeared.

Go-ram-ba responds by pointing out that this objection rests on an investigation performed in terms of action and agent. It is, however, well known that, for Buddhists, agent, action, and object of action do not really exist but are merely conventions. Therefore, it is no surprise that external objects fail to be perceived when analyzed from this point of view. Go-ram-ba says: "It is not correct that when investigated, things are not apprehended for the following reason: The presentation of subject and object [in the case of, for example,] the realization of an object by a sense consciousness, and so forth, is posited in dependence on an agent and object of an action and those do not really exist."[14] The performance of an action presupposes duration: The agent acts on an object that is thereby changed. Since real things are momentary, there is no time for a real action to take place. Ideas about agent and action are just convenient but misleading ways to talk about a reality that consists of the succession of moments. Since the identity of a phenomenon as subject or object relies on its identity as agent or object of action, it must be unreal. Therefore, when analyzed in this way, external objects are not perceived. This is not, however, the meaning of "*hidden*," but rather a consequence of the doctrine of momentariness, which entails a general rejection of the reality of actions. Although not perceived when analyzed in terms of agent and object of action, external objects are perceived in reality.[15]

This response is certainly consistent with the Buddhist rejection of the reality of the distinction between agent and action. We may, however, wonder whether Go-ram-ba's response is credible. If distinctions of action and object of action have only conventional reality, how can we say objects are perceived in reality? This expression becomes just a convenient way of describing a momentary process in which perceptions are produced by objects. What does this causal process have to do with our commonly accepted ideas of seeing an object? Here again, our phenomenological intuitions are hardly satisfied!

Let us note that the Ge-luk theory of perception is faced with the same problem raised by the time-gap argument. Its realism concerning duration is, however, better equipped to deal with the difficulty. Like Go-ram-ba, Ge-luk thinkers hold that the time gap between object and subject is radical. They reject Cha-ba's idea of the coexistence of subject and object. If the former is the cause of the latter, it is incoherent to speak of them as existing at the same time. Contrary to Go-ram-ba, however, they do not deny the reality of duration. Real objects endure under the form of continua. Hence, they can be perceived as continua, even though their individual moments cease to exist before being apprehended. Kay-drup explains: "The held thing has [already] disappeared when the cognition [comes to be]. Nevertheless, there is no fault of not holding [the already gone object] for the following reason: the presentation of sense consciousnesses and their held things [as being] subjects and objects is established from the point of view of the period that has as its parts the times [in which] the consciousnesses and their held things [exist]."[16] From the point of view of the causal relation of individual moments, object and cognition do not coexist and our notion of subject and object cannot be maintained. Nevertheless, when the object is considered in its duration (as a continuum), we can speak of its being perceived by consciousness understood as a continuum. In this way, the phenomenological integrity of consciousness is maintained within a strict causal account.

Kay-drup's response also underlines the opposition between Ge-luk realism and Sa-gya reductive antirealism. Whereas for Go-ram-ba and other Sa-gya thinkers, the perceptual process is reducible to its atomic components and their causal connections because there is nothing real outside of them, for Ge-luk thinkers the real is not entirely reducible to its atomic components. Although nothing exists independent of these components, extension in time and space is real (and so are universals). Reality is not made up just of atomic elements that we order according to our predispositions, interests, and the like, but also contains categorically determined entities. This realism allows for an epistemology more attuned to our common intuitions. Perception does not apprehend groups of atomic elements that we misinterpret as commonsense objects but delivers objects that are parts of an at least partially given order of things.

Are External Objects Inferred?

This view leads Gyel-tsap to take a clear and unsurprising position on the second issue of this chapter, the question of whether external objects are perceptible or not. Although intimately related to the issue of whether external objects are hidden or not, this second issue involves a few twists of its own. For Gyel-tsap, external objects are perceptible and therefore do not need to be inferred. In his realist perspective, this view is quite logical.[17] We would expect Ge-luk thinkers to be unanimous in holding that objects are directly perceptible since they are direct realists. Such, however, is not the case.

Kay-drup surprisingly holds the opposite position denying that external objects are perceptible. Such a view is less surprising in a representationalist such as Śākya Chok-den, whose position we will investigate later. It is, however, much more striking in a thinker such as Kay-drup, who refuses the curtain view of perception and insists that external objects directly appear to consciousness. He holds, however, that although objects directly appear, they are not realized as such by ordinary beings. What Kay-drup seems to mean is that ordinary beings do not perceive objects in their externality. Otherwise, argues Kay-drup, the idealist philosophers of the Mind-Only school could not reject the existence of an external world.[18] The externality of the world is to be proven in the Sautrāntika system, it is not given to sense consciousness. Hence, Dharmakīrti provides several arguments establishing the existence of the real world in the Sautrāntika system.[19]

Almost equally surprising is Go-ram-ba's view that external objects are perceptible. Given his consistent representationalism, one may have expected him to side with Śākya Chok-den and Kay-drup to assert that external objects are not perceptible. As Go-ram-ba realizes, however, this view, which is tempting, cannot be sustained in Dharmakīrti's system. Go-ram-ba explains:

> *Objection*: If sense perception establishes external objects, what is the reason for the reason [stated by Dharmakīrti]: "[External objects] are established through [the fact that] consciousness ceases [in the absence of an object]."[20] *Answer*: [Relying on passages in Dharmakīrti such as] "The appearance [of an object] as blue is seen. There is no external object apart [from this appearance]."[21] [Proponents of] Mind-Only show that the simultaneous appearance to sense consciousness [of something] as being an external object is the held aspect of the sense consciousness. There is no other blue [object]. In [this context], Sautrāntikas establish [their view] in this way: Although the simultaneous appearance [of an object to a consciousness] is the held aspect [of that consciousness,] there is a blue [object] that produces this [consciousness. This is so] because, otherwise, there would be a unmistaken visual consciousness apprehending blue even in places where blue is unobserved. It is not the case that in the Sautrāntika system external objects are not established by perception and must be proven.[22]

As mentioned previously, Dharmakīrti's works contain arguments that purport to establish that the external world exists in the Sautrāntika system. As Go-ram-ba points out, however, this reasoning has to be understood within its own context; that is, the Mind-Only argument against the production of appearances by external objects. According to this argument, the only element to which we have empirical access is the appearance of the objects. But the Mind-Only proponents can easily point out that this appearance is nothing but the aspect of the cognition. It is no more than a representation, which is part of the cognition. Hence, the Sautrāntikas must agree that we do not see directly the external objects that are supposed to exist before we perceive them. For the Mind-Only school, assuming such objects is a useless metaphysical presupposition.

Against this idealist argument, which disqualifies the appearance as irrelevant to the existence of external objects, the Sautrāntikas state their counterargument: Perception must rely on external objects, for it does not arise in a place where those are not observed. This argument is not given to explain how we infer an unobservable external world, but because the adversary has discounted the appearance as irrelevant to the issue by pointing out that appearance is part of consciousness. This is a move crucial in the idealist strategy because it discounts the intuitions that support the acceptance of the external world. Once appearances are brushed aside, external objects can be proven to exist only by an argument. For Sautrāntikas, this does not mean that, in general, these objects are not observable but, rather, that they are to be demonstrated by reasoning once they have been discarded by the idealist. Thus, for the Sautrāntika, the external world is not beyond the veil of appearance; on the contrary, it is so obvious that idealist philosophers miss it.

Go-ram-ba's excellent explanation is helpful for understanding a delicate point of Dharmakīrti's system. Some interpreters, both traditional and modern, think that the external world is not directly accessible to us and furthermore that the external world is only a logical presupposition in the Sautrāntika part of Dharmakīrti's system. Some even see it as either a transcendental principle or an unreal superimposition. These scholars are mistaken in both regards, for they forget that external objects are said by Dharmakīrti to cause their perceptions.[23] Since they are effective they must be real and, therefore, objects of perception.

How Hidden Can "Hidden" Be?

An example of the problems created in Dharmakīrti's system by the assertion that external objects are not perceptible is provided by Śākya Chok-den's analysis. There he proposes a radical view, which attempts to push the representationalist analysis of perception to its limits by eliminating ordinary notions of appearance. Let us examine his views and see how the attempt to go beyond appearance leads to idealism. In doing so, we will keep in mind that Śākya Chok-den's move beyond appearance is not an unintended consequence of his analysis, but a deliberate attempt to emphasize the soteriological content of Dharmakīrti's tradition. This will lead to our last chapter, where the depth of Dharmakīrti's soteriological intentions will be probed.

Following the familiar strategy of ascending scales of analysis, Śākya Chok-den analyzes the causal theory of perception and its implications by distinguishing three levels of inquiry:

> 1. At a commonsense level, objects such as jars and the like are said to exist. At this preanalytical level, external objects appear to perception and, hence, are not hidden. At this level, constructs can be said to appear to conceptual cognition. Even at this level, however, self-cognition is said to be without an object, and real things are excluded from appearing to conceptions, for those can apprehend only constructs.[24]
>
> 2. At a deeper level, however, these naive ideas cannot stand. When further examined, objects of commonsense disappear and the color of the fire is distinguished from the fire. Epistemologically, the different uses of the word *appear* have to be distinguished as well. Śākya Chok-den distinguishes three possible meanings of the word *appear*: to appear directly (*dngos su snang ba*), to appear in a hidden way (*lkog tu snang*), and to appear without appearance (*snang ba med pa'i tshul gyis snang*). The first concerns the appearance of external objects such as colors to perception and is the only actual appearance. In its second sense, the term *appearance* metaphorically designates that thought conceives object universals by excluding the contradictory of the object conceived. Finally, the third use of the word *appear* refers metaphorically to the cessation of conceptualization in yogic experience.[25] The analysis, however, cannot stop there. Ontologically, as we already noticed,[26] even sensibilia such as color are not real.
>
> 3. At a deeper level, therefore, only infinitesimal components are real. Epistemologically, at this level, the concept of an object appearing becomes impossible to apply even to external sensibilia. This is so because perception does not directly apprehend (*dngos su mi rig*) real things but only their representations. At this level, cognitive activity boils down to the causal interaction of momentary particles with momentary mental states. Since subject and object do not coexist, no object directly appears (*dngos su mi snang*) to the cognition or is directly cognized (*dngos su mi rig*). Therefore, objects remain hidden (*lkog gyur, parokṣa*) to their perceptions. Their presence must be inferred by an analysis of the causes necessary to the production of perceptions.[27]

As we saw with his ontology,[28] Śākya Chok-den does not think that these three levels of analysis are exclusive. Rather they function at different levels of analysis. When discussing epistemology, the first two levels are preferably used, for they are closer to the way we commonly conceive of things. These two levels are not, however, sustainable, for when the analysis is pushed, even entities such as color and taste, which we usually think we perceive, are shown to be fictional. Hence, the description of perception as apprehending such an object cannot withstand critical examination and must be replaced by a more ontologically grounded description. How can we then describe how cognition takes place?

Perception can be described in relation to its object from two standpoints. Cognitively, it has an object of application (*'jug yul*), which is the object we are striving for. Although this object is described as real, in fact it is not. An object of application is the concept that we apply to a momentary reality to bring the stability necessary to our practical endeavor. Remember that Śākya Chok-den explains nondeceptiveness in relation to objects of practical concern. Also notice that this description is not unproblematic, for such objects, which are supposed to be real, are in fact conceptual constructs since they have duration.[29] Thus, although Śākya Chok-den maintains that cognitions relate to real objects of application, he recognizes that this description fails to capture the epistemic process in its reality. Because a description is conceptual, it necessarily reflects our ways to conceive things rather than reality itself. What is then the real object of perception?

Ontologically, perception relates to a held object (*gzung yul*), which is its object condition (*dmigs rkyen, ālambana-pratyaya*). This object is nothing but the atoms that cause a perception to arise under a certain aspect. Hence, an expression such as *consciousness apprehends a color* must be understood as a convenient description of a causal process in which momentary atoms cause moments of consciousness to arise. Descriptions in terms of subject and object (or agents and objects of action) are just convenient ways to characterize a causal process in which momentary phenomena influence the production of other phenomena. A consistent explanation of consciousness requires that one goes beyond the limited and contradictory vocabulary of ordinary commonsense.[30]

Other thinkers have refused this overly reductionistic approach since it undermines the phenomenological integrity of mental states.[31] Against Śākya Chok-den, Lo Ken-chen points out that such a view, which is meant to explain Dharmakīrti's Sautrāntika view, leads to idealism. For, if we deny that external objects appear, then we have no ground for asserting that they exist.[32] This leaves us with no alternative other than to completely deny that external objects exist. By problematizing intentional notions such as appearance and apprehension, this reductionist view undermines our epistemic vocabulary, which rests on the intuition that we perceive objects external to our consciousness. These differences within the Sa-gya tradition remind us that the differences between Tibetan epistemologists are not only intersectarian. My description of the conflict between Sa-paṇ's followers and their realist contemporaries should not mask the fact that there are important intrasectarian differences as well.

A question, however, remains for Śākya Chok-den's radical approach. If common notions of the mind are to be rejected, what distinguishes mental phenomena from other phenomena? That is, does the rejection of folk psychology entail the rejection of the intentional character of consciousness? The answer is unambiguously negative. Contrary to modern opponents of folk psychology, Śākya Chok-den does not attempt to reduce the mind to material phenomena. His opposition to common sense is not inspired by materialism, like many contemporary accounts, but by his attempt to make Dharmakīrti's system as consistent as possible. If any ideological agenda lay behind his interpretations, it is not materialism but idealism, which he considers to be central to Dharmakīrti' soteriology. How can he then explain intentionality?

Here again, the answer rests on apperception in relation to which intentionality is reinterpreted. Intentionality cannot be explained in relation to external objects but only as a process of apperception. Perception of a shape, for instance, is not an apprehension of an external object (*don rig*), as we ordinarily conceive it to be, but is awareness cognizing itself under the causal influence of external atoms. Śākya Chok-den says: "First, the real object of comprehension is the external "hidden" object that exists before the consciousness to which an external object appears. The conceived [object of comprehension] is that [object] imagined to exist simultaneously with the consciousness. Second, the real result is only the self-cognition that perceives the aspect of the object. The conceived [result] is that [self-cognition] conceived to be a cognition of an external object."[33] In first approximation (levels 1 and 2), perception is said to relate to external objects through representational aspects. External objects remain "hidden," for they cease to exist when they are perceived. They are conceived to be the real objects of practical concern that coexist with consciousness. This explanation, which adopts the conceptual standpoint of practical application, however, is not complete, for it fails to capture the ontological support of the cognitive process. For, how can consciousness perceive something that has stopped existing? More accurately, perception is not a subject perceiving an external object but a succession of moments of awareness cognizing themselves as having this or that aspect. Only from a conceptual point of view can this self-cognizing process be described as the cognition of an external object.

Although radical, this analysis is philosophically valuable, for it shows the problems and tensions inherent in Dharmakīrti's theory of perception. The problem of the perceptibility of the external world illustrates the difficulties in giving an epistemological account of consciousness in an antirealist system. Śākya Chok-den attempts a solution by pushing Dharmakīrti's philosophy to its limits, showing that the description of consciousness as an intentional entity can be understood to refer only to apperception, for any analysis of consciousness in relation to an external object leads to unsolvable difficulties. Since the external world cannot appear to perception, it is hidden in the true sense of the word. It is inferred on the basis of the evidence that perception of external objects (to retain a word emptied of its content) arise only on certain occasions. Since even when other conditions, such as preceding moments of consciousness and a sense basis, are present, sense consciousness does not arise, we must infer that there is a supplementary condition, the external object.

The paradoxical conclusion of this analysis is that the real character of the external object is not cognized by the sense consciousness, which cognizes only itself, but through the inference that establishes that perception requires the support of an external object. This object, however, remains hidden and can be perceived only indirectly.[34] Śākya Chok-den says: "Accordingly, the system of the Proponents of Perceptual Non-Duality[35] posits inference as the true realization of [external] objects and perception as a metaphorical realization of [external] objects . . ."[36] Śākya Chok-den takes great delight in this paradoxical conclusion, but we must wonder whether he is going too far. By rejecting ordinary phenomenological notions, Śākya Chok-den denies us access to the real world and encloses us in an unbreakable solipsistic isolation. According to Śākya Chok-den's epistemology, inference, which is conceptual, does not actually (*song tshod la*) apprehend real phenomena. Since it takes an object universal as its object, an inference is strictly bound to the unreal, and we only imagine (*rlom tshod la*) that we realize real things.[37] Thus, according to Śākya Chok-den's analysis, we never realize external objects, for we are cognizant only of our mind and of its conceptual creations.[38]

This quasi-solipsism is not unwelcome by Śākya Chok-den, who thinks that Dharmakīrti's system is strongly tilted toward idealism. For Śākya Chok-den, Dharmakīrti's so-called Sautrāntika theories, which often are the primary focus in his work, seem to be a way to build a bridge with the Yogācāra idealism. For example, the acceptance of the Sautrāntika theory of perception seems to be a way to bring about the awareness that, although we commonly assume that there is an external world, we actually have little evidence supporting this view. This realization opens the door to the Mind-Only idea that the objects of perception are not external but of the nature of the mind.

We must, however, wonder about the importance of this point for Dharmakīrti. If Dharmakīrti really holds this philosophy, why does he not say so and why does he focus instead on a contradictory view? Why does he insist on providing us with incompatible ontologies? These questions suggest that the defense of idealism might not have been Dharmakīrti's foremost concern. To get better insight into Dharmakīrti's metaphysics and understand its soteriological implications, let us once more investigate the views of Dharmakīrti's tradition in doxographical terms.

27

Epistemology, Metaphysics, and Religion

Yogācāra in Dharmakīrti's Thought

Throughout this investigation of Dharmakīrti's thought we have relied on doxographical categories, which play an important role in Tibetan interpretations of Dharmakīrti. As we observed earlier, using categories that were coined a long time after Dharmakīrti to describe his thought is not unproblematic. Nevertheless, these descriptions can help us understand the general thrust of some of his difficult ideas as well as underline the diversity that Dharmakīrti introduces in accordance with what I have described as a strategy of ascending scales of analysis. In the next few pages, I focus on distinguishing the conflicting doxographical descriptions of Dharmakīrti's thought among Tibetan thinkers. I show how these interpretations reflect in general the larger philosophical outlook of the authors and in particular the type of Madhyamaka philosophy to which they subscribe. Instead of the opposition between realists and their adversaries, I distinguish three groups: (a) the followers of Sa-paṇ and the Ge-luk tradition, who under the influence of Candrakīrti view the Yogācāra as an inferior view of reality to which Dharmakīrti subscribes; (b) the early Tibetan epistemologists, who favor a Madhyamaka interpretation of Dharmakīrti not yet influenced by the growing ascendency of Candrakīrti in Tibet; and (c) the proponents of some form of a Yogācāra-Madhyamaka synthesis, who see Dharmakīrti as offering an important source of insight into the nature of reality.

Of the first group, most Tibetan commentators have used doxographical categories extensively to understand Dharmakīrti's puzzling attitude toward external objects. Because Dharmakīrti ultimately seems to reject the existence of external objects, which he accepts at another level, Sa-paṇ, Go-ram-ba, Gyel-tsap, and Kay-drup have described Dharmakīrti as a Yogācārin who defends a Sautrāntika position for essentially strategic reasons throughout most of his work. This description allows these thinkers to use Dharmakīrti's logic and epistemology without having to accept his view of reality. In doing so, they represent a current of thought in Tibet that enthusiastically adopts Dharmakīrti's logico-epistemological concepts but rejects his idealist philosophy. All these thinkers, who are committed to

Candrakīrti's philosophy, accordingly insist on a doxographical interpretation of Dharmakīrti that allows them to adopt his epistemology while discarding his ontology, a move not without problems. Since Dharmakīrti is a Yogācārin and since their ultimate view is held to be Prāsaṅgika-Madhyamaka, his idealism can be attributed to an inferior system superseded by a higher truth and therefore left aside.

The second group consists of earlier Tibetan epistemologists, such as Ngok and Cha-ba, who are critical of Sautrāntika and Yogācāra views and interpret Buddhist epistemology in a nonidealist Madhyamaka way. Cha-ba emphasizes the agreement between Madhyamaka thought and commonsense and holds that epistemology should follow this standpoint. Accordingly, Cha-ba argues for a Madhyamaka epistemology that follows a Vaibhāṣika view on the conventional level.

Against this interpretation Sa-paṇ insists on the first view, presenting Dharmakīrti as a Yogācārin who uses Sautrāntika ideas as a bridge to his system. This description of Dharmakīrti is accepted by most later Sa-gya interpreters as well as the Ge-luk tradition. This work largely reflects the opinions of this group, which by now have become dominant among Tibetan scholars of epistemology. The meeting of minds between Ge-luk thinkers and Sa-paṇ is not fortuitous. Throughout this work, I have emphasized the opposition between the Sa-gya and Ge-luk interpretations despite the Ge-luk efforts to claim Sa-paṇ's authority. Due to the nature of my topic, the problem of universals and its epistemological consequences, I have depicted this Ge-luk claim as unconvincing. By now, the reader probably sees the Ge-luk attempt to include Sa-paṇ as a cover-up typical of a tradition of commentarial philosophy in which there is a strong propensity to hide a novelty by appealing to some authoritative figure.

This in fact has occurred regarding the doctrine of universals and the theory of perception. The Ge-luk claim to have captured Sa-paṇ's "true thought" is no more valid in these cases than the claim to have the "true interpretation" of Dharmakīrti's philosophy. This Ge-luk failure to truly understand Sa-paṇ's thought, however, is limited to the domains of logic and epistemology. From another angle, Ge-luk thinkers are quite right to claim Sa-paṇ, for they share with him important commonalities. They have a common commitment to Candrakīrti as providing the interpretive key to Nāgārjuna's philosophy. They also emphasize rational thinking, insisting on the soteriological value of reasoning. Although other Tibetan traditions are certainly not irrationalist, Sa-paṇ and Dzong-ka-ba are in a class of their own in their insistence on reasoning as a guide to religious experience. They are also similar in their insistence that sūtra and tantra be separated. For both of them, the latter does not imply a different view of reality but merely a different way of implementing the Madhyamaka view understood à la Candrakīrti. In several respects, Dzong-ka-ba is closer to Sa-paṇ than some of the thinkers I have described as Sa-paṇ's orthodox interpreters. This applies particularly to Śākya Chok-den, whose propensities toward the emptiness-of-other view are at odds with Sa-paṇ. The proximity between Sa-paṇ and the Ge-luk tradition is apparent also in the sympathy with which the latter has accorded Sa-paṇ's criticism of some views associated with the Great Seal (*mahāmudrā, phyag chen*) and Great Perfection (*rdzogs chen*) traditions.[1]

Thus, the Ge-luk acceptance of Sa-paṇ's doxographical interpretation reflects important commonalities between the Sa-gya and Ge-luk traditions. This has often been misunderstood for political reasons. Ge-luk thinkers have tended to assume complete identity between their views and Sa-paṇ's. They often have cast themselves as Sa-paṇ's true heirs. Sa-gya thinkers, on the contrary, have tended to minimize similarities in their opposition to the Ge-luk claim to politico-religious supremacy in Tibet. The philosophical truth seems to lie somewhere in the middle. The Ge-luk claim to incarnate Sa-paṇ's spirit is justified as far as the general spirit of the tradition, though certainly not regarding several epistemological points.

Finally, with regard to the third group, not all Tibetan thinkers have accepted Sa-paṇ's doxographical interpretation of Dharmakīrti based on the supremacy of Candrakīrti's view. Many Tibetan thinkers have tended to be less enthusiastic toward Candrakīrti, who historically was not the central figure depicted by many Tibetan scholars, and more favorable towards Śāntarakṣita's use of Yogācāra in Madhyamaka.[2] Such thinkers take the Yogācāra philosophy as either valid in its own right or as an indispensable propaedeutic leading up to the Madhyamaka goal of establishing the insubstantiality of all phenomena including mind. This group tends to see Dharmakīrti as a Mādhyamika or at least as importantly contributing to the philosophy of this school.

This current of thought is not a unified tradition but contains a diversity of views ranging from the most radical emptiness-of-other to more moderate accounts. For example, the modern Nying-ma scholar Mi-pam Gya-tso (*mi pham rgya mtsho,* 1846–1912) falls in the last category. Following Śāntarakṣita, he builds a Madhyamaka system in which Dharmakīrti's Yogācāra philosophy is accepted as an accurate description of conventional reality but not of ultimate truth understood as the lack of essence of all phenomena. Still, Mi-pam holds that external objects do not exist even at the conventional level. This is quite different from the Ge-luk view, which holds that external objects exist conventionally, thus tending to rely more on the Sautrāntika element in Dharmakīrti's thought. Mi-pam also downplays the separation between Śāntarakṣita's Madhyamaka view and Candrakīrti's Prāsaṅgika by asserting that the different Madhyamakas share the same view of emptiness and differ only on the method of communicating the teaching of emptiness.[3]

This current also contains a much more radical interpretation of Mahāyāna thought than Mi-pam's which describes itself as the Great Madhyamaka. This loaded description has been claimed by a variety of groups. Rong-dön and Go-ram-ba claimed that their interpretation is the true Great Madhyamaka. Here, I am referring to a different view, which asserts that the true Madhyamaka is the emptiness-of-other view. This is presented as Nāgārjuna's true view, not to be confused with Candrakīrti's interpretation, which represents at best a partial (small!) Madhyamaka. The view of this radical group is that essencelessness, which others take to be emptiness, is limited, for it does not apply to the ultimate. Only conventional phenomena are essenceless. Ultimate truth is the true Absolute, which is of the nature of Buddha's gnosis (*ye shes, jñāna*). This is, according to this view, the message of the third Turning of the Wheel found in texts such as the *Tathāgatagarbha-sūtra,* the *Saṃdhinirmocana-sūtra*, or the *Mahāparinirvāna-sūtra,* which, contrary to what Dzong-ka-ba and others have asserted, do not reflect a provisional Mind-Only standpoint but bring the truly ultimate perspective, superseding the view of the second Turning of the Wheel found in the *Prajñāpāramitā* literature.[4]

This view was systematically developed by Dol-bo-ba (1292–1361). It became closely associated with the Jo-nang-ba school and has been the focus of intense controversies in Tibet. Many Ga-gyü teachers, including the Seventh Karma-ba Chö-drak-gya-tso, have been sympathetic to this view, which is easily combined with the Great Seal approach favored by their tradition. In the later part of his life Śākya Chok-den also displayed a keen interest in this view, though we already noticed that his view is not to be assimilated to Dol-bo-ba's. After the middle of the seventeenth century this view fell into disfavor for political reasons (the close association of Tāranātha, the foremost teacher of the Jo-nang-ba, with the forces of Tsang). This trend was reversed by Si-tu Chö-gi-jung-ne (*si tu chos kyi 'byung gnas,* 1700–1774) under the influence of the Nying-ma abbot Ka-tog Tse-wang-nor-bu (*ka' thog tshe dbang nor bu,* 1698–1755).[5] Under their influence, the view of the emptiness-of-other spread through the Ga-gyü and the Nying-ma schools. It strongly influenced the nineteenth Nonsectarian (*ris med*) movement of Jam-gön Kong-trul and Jam-yang Kyen-tse-wang-po. We must keep in mind, however, that this label covers a variety of views, which do not necessarily share the absolutization of gnosis apparently advocated by Dol-bo-ba.

The Sa-gya and Ge-luk schools have tended to look less favorably on this view. Thinkers such as Tu-gen have vigorously opposed it describing it as a non-Buddhist absolutization of emptiness. They hold that no authoritative Indian thinkers ever held such a view, which they find reminiscent of Vedāntic monism.[6] As we saw earlier,[7] this hostility has at least as much to do with the political situation of the seventeenth century as with philosophical concerns. Although Dzong-ka-ba repeatedly expressed his opposition to the Jo-nan-ba interpretation of Yogācāra sūtras and commentaries in his *Essence of Good Sayings,* he did not pronounce the kind of excommunication that became customary after the seventeenth century. The Sa-gya thinkers adopt a more moderate view, although they equally reject the claim of the supporters of the emptiness-of-other to represent the true Madhyamaka. They fall between Ge-luk excommunication and Ga-gyü and Nying-ma acceptance or sympathy, viewing emptiness of other neither as Madhyamaka, as claimed by its proponents, nor as the crypto-Hindu monism described by Ge-luk thinkers. Rather, emptiness-of-other is described as the kind of Yogācāra False Aspectarian view that we will examine shortly.[8]

In general, the thinkers who have tended to favor a Yogācāra-influenced Madhyamaka approach have tended to emphasize the metaphysical value of Dharmakīrti's system. This is particularly true of the proponents of emptiness-of-other, who have always been keen to find as many Indian antecedents as possible to support their besieged view. It is also true of Śākya Chok-den, who presents Dharmakīrti as a Mādhyamika philosopher offering a complete metaphysico-soteriological system. Although in his *Defeater*, Śākya Chok-den does not defend the emptiness-of-other view, which he espoused in his later years, he comes quite close to it. For him, Dharmakīrti's philosophy is not just a Yogācāra view that is superseded by the Prāsaṅgika view enthusiastically adopted by most Tibetan thinkers (his rival Go-ram-ba included). Śākya Chok-den considers Dharmakīrti to be offering a meaningful Madhyamaka view.

Other than Śākya Chok-den, this view is best represented in Tibet by Chö-drak-gya-tso, who influenced the former. Chö-drak-gya-tso describes Dharmakīrti's philosophy as the expression of the highest truth, whose clearest expression is found in the tradition of the *tathāgatagarbha*. He understands Dharmakīrti to be expressing the same view found in the five works attributed to Maitreya as well as in the collection of praises (*bstod tshogs*) attributed to Nāgārjuna. According to this view, the ultimate truth is not emptiness in its negative aspect, but the pure and ineffable nature of awareness, which is clear and luminously present to itself. Such a pure and luminous nature is nothing but the self-cognition propounded by Dignāga and Dharmakīrti. It is the gnosis that is ultimately the ground of ineffable reality.[9] This tradition finds a source for this interpretation in Dharmakīrti's comment: "Mental states have a clear luminous nature. [Their] stains are adventitious."[10] This passage is part of an argument establishing the possibility of liberation. Dharmakīrti is responding to the objection that, although it might be possible to eliminate temporarily obstructions such as desire and ignorance, they will come back. Dharmakīrti answers by pointing to the luminous nature of the mind. The stains that obstruct this purity are adventitious. They do not participate in the purity of the awareness, but only cover it. Since they do not affect the luminous nature of mental states, the obstructions have nowhere to remain in the mind once it is purified. Hence, they cannot come back.

Chö-drak-gya-tso and Śākya Chok-den take this passage to indicate Dharmakīrti's acceptance of the same kind of view found in the tradition of the *tathāgatagarbha*. This tradition emphasizes the importance of the pure nature of mental states, stressing the adventitious character of obstructions, which merely hide the purity of awareness without affecting it. Chö-drak-gya-tso and Śākya Chok-den identify this purity of the mind with Dharmakīrti's self-cognition, the self-presencing of the mind through which they explain yogic perception. Is this is Dharmakīrti's view? It is difficult to answer based on such a short passage. Given Dharmakīrti's refusal to connect his soteriological references to his Yogācāra view and his views on yogic perception,[11] it is difficult to attribute to him such a view. Nevertheless, the convergence is quite real, contrary to what one may first suspect. Although Dharmakīrti is no proponent of the emptiness-of-other, elements in his system, particularly his view on apperception, go in the same direction.

To better understand the important questions raised by this interpretation, let us deepen our doxographical analysis by introducing new distinctions and subdivisions between the views we have described as Sautrāntika and Yogācāra. These distinctions directly relate to our central concern, the nature of perception and its relation to the concept of aspect.[12]

True or False Aspect?

Concerning the notion of aspect, Dharmakīrti's Indian and Tibetan followers can be divided into two categories: those who hold that aspects are real entities, the True Aspectarians (*satyākāravādin, rnam bden pa*), and those who deny it, the False Aspectarians (*alīkārāvādin, rnam par rdzun par smra ba*).[13] The former view is compatible with a so-called Sautrāntika view that perception provides undistorted access to the external world. Since external objects exist, the cognition that validates them, perception, must be undistorted. And so must the aspects that provide the basis for the conceptual interpretation of reality brought about by perception. Consequently, the adoption of a Sautrāntika view commits one to a True Aspectarian view of perception.

The converse, however, is not true. The adoption of a True Aspectarian view does not commit one to the Sautrāntika acceptance of the reality of external objects. Thinkers who deny the reality of the external world hold that perception is mistaken, since objects appear to us as existing independent of their perception. These thinkers differ, however, on the degree of distortion. Among these thinkers the True Aspectarians, who take a Mind-Only view, hold that perception is mistaken with respect to the externality of its objects. According to their view, this distortion does not affect the nature of perception itself. The objective aspect held by a mental state is substantially identical with consciousness and hence real. The False Aspectarians reject this distinction and hold that the representation of objects in consciousness is itself a deluded construct. For them, aspects do not really exist, but are superimposed on the luminous nature of consciousness. Such a nature is ineffable, utterly beyond the duality of subject and object. Thus this view is described by Śākya Chok-den as Yogācāra but not as Mind-Only.[14]

In the next pages, I further analyze these notions and their use in the Tibetan tradition to describe Dharmakīrti's view. Following Tibetan commentators, I ask whether Dharmakīrti is a True or False Aspectarian while keeping in mind the anachronistic character of the question. Let us notice, however, that this investigation is a bit more complex than it may seem, for Tibetan commentators disagree on the way to characterize these differences. Most Tibetan thinkers differentiate True from False Aspectarians on the basis of the acceptance or refusal of the reality of aspects, which seems a well-established criterion in both later Indian and Tibetan sources. Even Kay-drup and Dzong-ka-ba assumes this criterion that I will follow.[15]

Gyel-tsap and most later Ge-luk thinkers, however, disagree with this well-established way to draw the distinction. Making the unusual claim that he has the support of Dzong-ka-ba's authority for his analysis,[16] Gyel-tsap asserts that, since

False Aspectarians are Yogācārin, they must admit the reality of consciousness even in its deluded states. Therefore, False Aspectarians cannot refuse the reality of aspects. Therefore, the subject of dispute between True and False Aspectarians cannot be whether aspects are real or not. Gyel-tsap proposes that the dispute is about the truthfulness of perception regarding the status of commonsense objects.[17] True Aspectarians claim that the appearance of objects as commonsense objects, covering their parts and so on, is not distorted by ignorance (*ma rig pa'i bslad pa ma zhugs*). False Aspectarians do not deny, according to Gyel-tsap, that commonsense objects exist. They do deny, however, that their appearance as such is uncontaminated.

This way of distinguishing True from False Aspectarians is hard to understand. It excludes from the debate any ontological issue. But what then is the debate about? In the usual way of drawing the difference between these two groups, which has wider acceptance and is closer to Indian texts,[18] the debate is easier to pin down than for Gyel-tsap. The debate is about the ontological status of the aspect, and there is obvious disagreement between the two sides. Whereas True Aspectarians understand this object as consciousness "impersonating" external objects, False Aspectarians maintain this appearance does not rest on anything real.

On the question of where Dharmakīrti fits in, there is some confusion. Kay-drup asserts that Dharmakīrti is a True Aspectarian. Kay-drup grants that there is contradictory evidence and that different Indian commentators have come to conflicting conclusions. For instance, he notes that Dharmottara and Prajñākaragupta interpreted Dharmakīrti as a False Aspectarian.[19] Kay-drup prefers to follow here, as he often does, Devendrabuddhi and his disciple Śākyabuddhi, who take Dharmakīrti to be a True Aspectarian.

Contrary to Kay-drup, who asserts that Dharmakīrti is a True Aspectarian, Gyel-tsap follows Dharmottara and claims that Dharmakīrti is a False Aspectarian, pointing to several passages[20] more in accordance with the logic of this system. For instance, if all the sense perceptions of ordinary beings are indeed mistaken, how can one differentiate a part that is polluted by ignorance from one that is not? Sa-paṇ and Go-ram-ba share a similar view, although they disagree with Gyel-tsap on the way to make the distinction between the two groups. They conclude that Dharmakīrti's ultimate view is False Aspectarian. Sa-paṇ, for example, holds that Dharmakīrti is a Sautrāntika when he accepts the existence of external objects and a False Aspectarian when he denies it.[21] For him, although it is true that Dharmakīrti's texts contain both True and False Aspectarian views, Dharmakīrti must follow the latter view, which is superior.

Chö-drak-gya-tso also describes Dharmakīrti as a Yogācārin; that is, False Aspectarian. His interpretation of Yogācāra philosophy, however, is quite different from that of Sa-paṇ and Go-ram-ba. For him, Yogācāra is a Madhyamaka philosophy belonging to the *tathāgatagarbha* tradition. Chö-drak-gya-tso bases his remarks on the final passages of Dharmakīrti's *Commentary*. There, Dharmakīrti laments about the fate that awaits his peerless treatise, which "like water in the ocean, will merge in my body and disappear."[22] Such a comment is taken by Chö-drak-gya-tso to refer to Devendrabuddhi, who mistakenly interpreted Dharmakīrti's *Commentary* according to the Mind-Only (i.e., True Aspectarian) view.[23] For Śākya Chok-den, the right way to understand Dharmakīrti is as a False Aspectarian. His detailed analysis of this question is worth examining.

Śākya Chok-den on Yogācāra

Śākya Chok-den discusses the status and nature of aspects by drawing further doxographical distinctions, which support his view of Dharmakīrti's method as an analysis by ascending scales. Rather than going into the details of this discussion, let me just summarize its main issues. The main point at stake here is the following: Is the aspect through which objects are represented in consciousness real or not. The True Aspectarians answer that they are, but this raises another question: What is the correspondence between the aspect and reality?

According to one view, there is a one-to-one correspondence between the diversity of external objects (such as the colors, for example, in a multicolored patch) and the internal diversity of the cognitive aspects. Therefore, an external object appears by casting its form on consciousness, whose structure mirrors the structure of the external object. Another view, which Śākya Chok-den favors, rejects this correspondence between consciousness and its object. The aspect is a unity, and the diversity of external objects is cognitively irrelevant despite its causal importance.[24]

Making this distinction between these two views strengthens Śākya Chok-den's point that Dharmakīrti's system has an overall coherence with a soteriological thrust. According to his model of an ascending scale, Śākya Chok-den considers these two views, which both assume the reality of external objects as well as aspects, as steps toward understanding the final view, that of Yogācāra False Aspectarian. The first view establishes the existence of an aspect, which is understood to be similar to a real thing. The second moves up to argue that aspect and external reality are not similar. Whereas aspect is reflexive, external reality consists of infinitesimal particles of inert matter, the only link between external reality and our inner world being causal. This view is very close to the Mind-Only doctrine. We could say that it is a Sautrāntika view on its way to idealism and corresponds to the idea of the Sautrāntika view as a bridge to Mind-Only and Yogācāra.[25] It reduces the external object to a pure metaphysical presupposition, with no relation to commonsense. Why not say that the cause producing the aspect is not an invisible external object but an internal propensity and that reality consists of self-cognizing awarenesses mistaken for external perceptions, as asserted by the Mind-Only view?

This last view (True Aspectarian) is still, however, an attempt to think about consciousness as relating to an object. Although the external object is left behind, this view still holds to an internal object, the objective aspect, which it asserts is real. We must let go of this last attachment and realize that the aspect is not consciousness but a construction. Any duality, even internal, is fictitious. Ultimately, only awareness freed from every illusion of duality of object and subject is real. This is the final False Aspectarian view, which Śākya Chok-den describes as Madhyamaka and attributes to Prajñākaragupta.[26] This view is obviously quite different from the more sedate doxographical descriptions of Dharmakīrti by Sa-paṇ or Gyel-tsap.

We can see the great diversity among Indian and Tibetan commentators about the exact nature of Dharmakīrti's Yogācāra philosophy and we may wonder about the reasons for such extensive disagreement. Why is there so little agreement about whether Dharmakīrti is a True or False Aspectarian? An initial approach might question the utility of interpreting Dharmakīrti in terms of schools that did not exist until well after his demise. As we have seen earlier, doxographical considerations have limited value and should not act as the sole guide for our interpretations. We should not, however, go so far as to deny any validity to such considerations. Even if we reject the schema of interpretation in terms of tenet systems, we still will be saddled with passages in Dharmakīrti presenting conflicting assessments of the status of aspects. Rather than entirely reject this schema, let us approach this problem by considering one of the basic characteristics of Indian philosophy: its commentarial style.

The Importance of Yogācāra in Dharmakīrti's Thought

Dharmakīrti understands his work to further Dignāga's tradition of Buddhist logic and epistemology. Positing aspects is meant to advance the epistemology of perception. It explains how internal consciousness and external objects can interact in the perceptual process. By introducing aspects, Dharmakīrti (like Dignāga before him) can support his theory of perception, thus establishing the epistemological basis for a Buddhist philosophy expressed in terms that connect with standard Indian philosophical concepts.

Explaining the interaction of consciousness and object using aspects as the intermediary raises a new question, one that besieges any representationalism: What is the relation between external reality and the aspect that plays the role of intermediary? Dharmakīrti seems to offer several contradictory answers: He first answers from a False Aspectarian perspective (*Commentary,* III:209–219), arguing that the aspect is unreal, but then moves to give the opposed True Aspectarian answer (*Commentary,* III:220–222). We naturally wonder which one Dharmakīrti chooses.[27]

His two conflicting answers to the same question could be a contradiction overseen by the author. This is unlikely since these two answers are given in the same passage. That Dharmakīrti gives two answers seems to indicate something else. It could be that Dharmakīrti does not believe in either explanation. In this case, he would share a Madhyamaka view similar to Śāntarakṣita, who offers a sustained critique of both views as a preparation to the Madhyamaka.[28] Or, it could be that Dharmakīrti does not consider this point very important.

I will argue that this last explanation is closer to Dharmakīrti's ideas. To put it bluntly, Dharmakīrti does not care very much whether aspects are real or not as long as the answer supports his main concern, which is to respond to the Nyāya contention that the absence of substantial wholes contradicts our experience of unitary objects. By using the notion of aspect, Dharmakīrti shows that the absence of substantial wholes is not incompatible with common experiences. As long as Dharmakīrti can answer the Nyāya qualm, he has accomplished his task, the defense and development of Dignāga's system. Because Dharmakīrti's philosophy is foremost a commentary, it displays a great deal of opportunism. It adopts conflicting views as alternative interpretations provided they prove useful to the more important task of furthering the aims of the tradition.

This does not imply that Dharmakīrti and his disciples are irrational or blind to logical contradiction, only that their rationality operates under different constraints. Dharmakīrti and his followers value logical coherence as much as modern philosophers. They are, however, less prone to be guided in their reasoning by strictly logical considerations, giving more weight to commentarial considerations. This affects their style of reasoning, pushing them to accommodate various interpretations when this furthered their aims. I believe that this is the case in the question of True versus False Aspectarians. The acceptance of either view is fine as long as it is conducive to the fulfillment of the aims of Dharmakīrti's tradition.

The relevant question at this point seems to be this: What are these aims? Let us examine several possibilities with the understanding that they do not exclude one another. An obvious answer points to the soteriological background of Dharmakīrti's enterprise, a concern generally shared by many Indian thinkers. In this view, the scheme of ascending scales becomes soteriologically oriented. They lead the thinker from a lower view of reality to a higher realization of nonduality. This seems to be Śākya Chok-den's understanding of Dharmakīrti.

My own view is different. I accept Śākya Chok-den's model of ascending scales but hold this model to be more epistemological than soteriological in its intent. Soteriological considerations are relevant, but they should not be overemphasized, for they might prevent us from seeing that the primary goal of Dharmakīrti and his traditions is not soteriological. It is more general, for it is an attempt to formulate a Buddhist epistemology in terms that are relatively tradition neutral and thus have broad acceptance. It is important to note that Dharmakīrti does not introduce Yogācāra elements in his overall schema on the basis of their soteriological applications. It might be tempting to speculate with Gyel-tsap, Śākya Chok-den, and other commentators that this is actually what Dharmakīrti has in mind.[29] Nevertheless Dharmakīrti does not explicitly relate his Yogācāra views to soteriological considerations. Nor does he relate his soteriological considerations, which are expressed in *Commentary* II,[30] to his Yogācāra ideas. When discussing his soteriology, Dharmakīrti refers to selflessness of persons, but not to emptiness understood as the absence of duality (*advaya, gnyis med*) between subject and object. Hence, it is doubtful that the scheme of ascending scale is primarily soteriological. Rather, it seems to be intended to perform several functions.

The notion of aspects is relevant to Dharmakīrti's Yogācāra system because it may help to avoid some of the more extreme consequences of idealism expounded by earlier Yogācāra teachers. By denying external objects, classical Yogācāra tends to offer a fairly extreme view, which is open to the following objection: If there is no external object, how can there be a consciousness that perceives it? The notion of aspect is meant to answer this qualm. Although consciousness does not perceive external objects, it perceives their aspects under the influence of internal propensities. Although there is no external object, there is an objective correspondent to the experience of those objects, and thus the unwanted consequence of the unreality of consciousness is avoided.

It should remain clear, however, that discussing Yogācāra metaphysics is not Dharmakīrti's prime concern. It is an important but nevertheless secondary element, which relates to and supports the main issue on his agenda,[31] the development of an epistemology that philosophically articulates basic Buddhist principles. Aspects are introduced mostly for epistemological reasons: to explain the interaction of internal consciousness and external objects. In the process certain difficulties arise that can be solved by the use of Yogācāra ideas. The emphasis, however, remains on the side of epistemology. It thus appears that Dharmakīrti's system is mainly logical and philosophical. How does his thought relate to the soteriological dimension that usually characterizes Buddhist thought?

Philosophy and Soteriology in Dharmakīrti

Throughout this work, I have tried to elucidate the philosophical content of Dharmakīrti's ideas. My main focus has been to underline the genuine philosophical character of thinkers belonging to Indian logico-epistemological traditions. Some interpreters who are similarly impressed by Dignāga's or Dharmakīrti's philosophical acumen may feel that religious considerations should not enter into such discussions, for such considerations might distract us from understanding what is genuinely philosophical in these authors.

I would like to make clear that I do not agree with this view. We should resist the temptation to reduce Dharmakīrti to the models offered by contemporary academic philosophy. To discard the soteriological particularities of these thinkers in the name of philosophy would assume that a system can be philosophical only if it conforms to what is acceptable to contemporary minds. The loss of the soteriological dimension would seriously reduce the interest offered by a system such as Dharmakīrti's. It would also seriously reduce the purview of philosophy itself. The implicit assumption seems to be that only a purely philosophical system can be of interest to a philosopher, but I do not see anything supporting this rather positivist view of philosophy (nobody has proposed excluding Plato, Aquinas, or

Berkeley from the canon of philosophy). I also fear that the ignorance of the context in which an author writes is bound to distort our understanding of that author.

Moreover, the attempt to understand Dharmakīrti in isolation from his religious context seems to rely on the assumption that religion and philosophy were always clearly separable, a presupposition that is historically mistaken. We should not forget that the creation of academic philosophy came rather late during the Enlightenment. Even Descartes and Hobbes did not think of themselves as philosophers but as contributors to the development of mathematics and mechanics, as well as instigators in liberating intellectual life from the shackle of ecclesiastical institutions. As Rorty says: "The idea of 'philosophy' itself, in the sense in which it has been understood since the subject became standardized as an academical subject in the nineteenth century, was not yet at hand. . . . It was not until Kant that our modern philosophy-science distinction took hold."[32] Academic philosophy is the result of the gradual separation of philosophy from religion and science. The first separation was the work of the Enlightenment, whereas the second, the separation of philosophy from science, arose as a consequence of Kant's work. Therefore, we speak of academic philosophy only in a context in which religious and philosophical concerns are separated. Such a distinction does not make sense if religion and philosophy are not differentiated, as in ancient India.

Admitting the philosophical legitimacy of soteriological intentions, however, does not close the question. Although it is clear they pay more than lip service to the spiritual concerns of their tradition, how crucial to Dignāga and Dharmakīrti are these concerns? Both modern and traditional scholars are divided on this issue. Several modern scholars have gone to great pains to deny any soteriological relevance to Dharmakīrti's tradition. Conze is probably the most extreme advocate of the secular view when he says that logic was studied "in order to vanquish one's adversaries in controversy, and thereby to increase the monetary resources of the Order."[33] Conze's opinion that only a small minority among Buddhists took Dignāga or Dharmakīrti's works seriously seems inaccurate to say the least. A cursory glance at the language of later Buddhist authors is enough to show their enormous influence, extending well beyond the limits of the Dignāga-Dharmakīrti school.[34] Most Indian and Tibetan Buddhist thinkers did not perceive Dignāga and Dharmakīrti to stand outside the Indian Buddhist tradition. Other Western scholars such as Steinkellner and Tillemans have taken a view more sympathetic to the spiritual implications of Buddhist epistemologists' discussions. Nevertheless, uncertainty remains about how to appreciate the importance of the spiritual concerns underlying these epistemological discussions.

The Tibetan tradition is similarly divided on this issue. Atiśa's disregard for logic and epistemology influences a number of Tibetan Buddhist thinkers, who downplay the spiritual implications of Buddhist epistemology. For Atiśa epistemology is not useful for developing the realization of the true nature of reality, the means of actualizing the supreme good of religious life.[35] Rather, such realization is to be found in Madhyamaka philosophy, which is the final truth of Buddhism. Since the works of epistemologists are not conducive to such a realization, they have no direct soteriological value. They were relevant to the Indian context, where Buddhists had to defend their positions against Hindu attacks, but they lost relevance in Tibet where Buddhism dominated the intellectual landscape.

Although many later Tibetan thinkers do not completely follow Atīśa's unequivocal repudiation, they are reserved about the soteriological relevance of the logico-epistemological tradition. Many tend to see logic and epistemology as one of the five branches of knowledge (*rig pa'i gnas, vidyāsthāna*) without intrinsic religious value, on a par with grammar and poetry. Several Dak-po Ga-gyü (*dwags po bka' brgyud*) masters tended toward this attitude, such as Gam-po-pa, the founder of the tradition, and his followers Tsul-trim-nying-bo (*tshul khrims snying po,* 1116–1169) and the latter's disciple Shang Tsal-ba (*zhang tshal pa,* 1123–1193).[36]

Bu-dön also seems not to have included Dharmakīrti's logico-epistemological tradition among Buddhist teachings, placing it among other branches of knowledge.[37] Although this would seem to indicate that, for Bu-dön, Dharmakīrti's tradition is basically secular, one should be careful about such assessments. As D. Jackson rightly argues, by itself the inclusion of logic and epistemology into a branch of knowledge separate from the inner knowledge, which is Buddhism, does not prove that the author holds that logic and epistemology are non-Buddhist topics.[38]

Such an assumption is certainly not warranted in the case of Sa-paṇ, contrary to Stcherbatsky's assertion.[39] Although he does not emphasize the soteriological value of Dharmakīrti's works, Sa-paṇ considers Dharmakīrti's ideas to belong to the Yogācāra tradition. Moreover, when he examines in *Commentary* II, the proof of the existence of past and future lives and of the Buddha's authority on the basis of his spiritual attainments,[40] he describes Dharmakīrti's explanation of the ways in which attachment binds beings to cyclic existence and critical acumen leads them to liberation. Like later Ge-luk thinkers, Sa-paṇ understands Dharmakīrti's reasoning to refer not only to liberation from passion but to full omniscience.[41] He does not, however, insist on the overall religious significance of Dharmakīrti's works as much as Dzong-ka-ba does. Although Sa-paṇ's view of logic and epistemology is not secular (a proof of omniscience is hardly a secular topic), the religious element is not prominent.

The only major scholar among Sa-paṇ's followers who seems to have held to a secular view of Dharmakīrti's thought is Dak-tsang, who advanced an interpretation calling into question Dzong-ka-ba's insistence on the soteriological relevance of Dharmakīrti's thought. Dak-tsang argues that, if one were to accept the soteriological relevance of Dignāga's thought on the basis of his having a stanza of homage at the beginning of his work, one might as easily demonstrate that the science of grammar also possessed a divine origin.[42] For Dak-tsang, the religious intentions of Dignāga or Dharmakīrti are not in question but limited to homages (for the former) or special works (for the latter). Their main works are not directly concerned with Buddhist doctrines. Thus, their content cannot be taken as directly relevant to Buddhist doctrines.

Many Tibetan thinkers, however, take a diametrically opposed view. They emphasize the soteriological relevance of Dharmakīrti's tradition, stressing the importance of its religious goals. The most vocal supporters of the religious significance of Dharmakīrti's works are found in the Ge-luk tradition.[43] Starting with Dzong-ka-ba and his two disciples, Gyel-tsap and Kay-drup, Ge-luk thinkers insist that Dharmakīrti's tradition is essentially soteriological. For them, it constitutes part of the Mahāyāna tradition, and as such it is not understandable outside of the structure of the path as explained in the literature of the gradual path (*lam rim)* started by Atīśa and emphasized by the Ga-dam-ba (*bka' gdams pa*) tradition.

There is some uncertainty about how this more spiritually oriented interpretation of Dharmakīrti originated. Van der Kuijp argues that the first Tibetan thinker to emphasize the soteriological aspect of Dharmakīrti's tradition was Drigung Jik-den-gong-bo. Jik-den-gong-bo, best known for his works on the tradition of the Great Seal and his devotional hymns to Tāra, sees in Dharmakīrti's system a path to full Enlightenment. Although most elements of Dharmakīrti's epistemology have no direct soteriological relevance, self-cognition and yogic perception reveal the true liberational perspective of his tradition. These two types of perception include the traditional Buddhist meditative practices of tranquility (*zhi gnas, śamatha*) and special insight (*lhag mthong, vipaśyanā*) and provide the means for breaking through to the Bodhisattva path of seeing.[44]

Although Ge-luk thinkers have not followed Jik-den-gong-po in his description of Dharmakīrti as a Mādhyamika, they share his emphasis on the religious aspect of Buddhist epistemology. Gyel-tsap explicitly connects the Buddhist path as described by Dharmakīrti to the three types of individual described in the graduated path literature.[45] This strong emphasis on the religious aspect of Dharmakīrti is shared by other Ge-luk thinkers who insist on the central role of Dharmakīrti's soteriological intentions.[46]

Conclusion

The existence of a dispute in the Tibetan tradition over the role of Dignāga's and Dharmakīrti's spiritual intentions should alert us to the necessity of exercising great care in dealing with this issue. I believe that a solution to this question will find elements of truth in both views, thus striking a balance between two extreme positions. One extreme would present Dignāga and Dharmakīrti as purely secular thinkers, considering only the parts of their works without soteriological relevance. Such an interpretation, whether inspired by a Madhyamaka (as opposed to a logical and epistemological) preoccupation with the realization of emptiness or by a modern secular humanism, ignores important elements in these thinkers. Dharmakīrti devoted a whole chapter of his master work, the *Commentary on Valid Cognition,* to demonstrating the validity of his religious tradition. Although Dignāga was far less explicit, his homage praising Buddha as a source of valid cognition indicates the soteriological implications of his logical and epistemological work.[47] Valid cognition can be the final realization of truth achieved by an enlightened being, but it can also be the practical knowledge that rests on purely empirical grounds and, therefore, does not appeal to any authority.

Direct reference to a religious context, however, is not the only level at which the works of Buddhist epistemologists have soteriological implications. Throughout this work, I have argued that we should understand Dignāga and Dharmakīrti as exploring the epistemological consequences of the basic principles of Buddhist philosophy. We have seen how their ontology embodies the basic Buddhist tenets of impermanence and dependent arising. In elaborating a Buddhist epistemology that can compete with the dominant Nyāya school and other Hindu systems, these thinkers formulate Buddhist views in generally accepted philosophical terms. Inasmuch as it continues the overall project of a tradition whose primary goal is liberation, their project is soteriological. It has religious implications in that it elaborates the basic traditional Buddhist doctrines of impermanence and dependent arising.

It is clear, however, that many of the problems they deal with have no direct soteriological relevance. Therefore, the soteriological character of their works should not be overestimated. We should avoid the other extreme in our appreciation; that is, understanding Dignāga and Dharmakīrti as being exclusively preoccupied by religious questions. Their works formulate principles that are philosophical in the most restrictive sense of the word as well as embodying broader spiritual concerns. Their place in the overall history of human thought is neither that of precursors to modern secular philosophy nor that of Buddhist theologians. Rather, for these thinkers, soteriological concerns are part of their overall logico-epistemological project, which has intrinsic philosophical value.

CONCLUSION: PHILOSOPHY AS AN EDUCATION OF THE MIND

Realism and Antirealism as Interpretations

Before parting company with my patient reader, I would like to reflect on the significance of this inquiry into the Indian and Tibetan traditions of epistemology. We began by delineating the general structure of Dharmakīrti's system: It is based on a distinction between real things, which are individuated by their identity conditions, and the objects of concepts, which have no such criteria of identity. This ontological dichotomy is paralleled by an epistemological distinction between perception, which relates to real individual things as they are, and inference, which deals with conceptual constructs. According to this system, only perception can relate directly to reality; the cognitive range of conception is limited to the unreal objects of concepts. Central to this system, which I have described as conceptualist for its reliance on conceptually created pseudo-entities, are two related tenets: (a) the antirealist distinction between individuals, which are real, and universals, which are conceptual and linguistic constructs; and (b) the limitation of perception to the former and conception to the latter.

Dharmakīrti's system is based on the correlation of ontological with epistemological realms. It attempts to provide a viable system of logic and epistemology within an antirealist framework that embodies the basic Buddhist principles of impermanence and selflessness. The antireificationist concern contained in these basic Buddhist ideas, however, does not easily harmonize with Dharmakīrti's purpose. Denying the reality of universals leaves Buddhist logic with little in the way of ontological support. If reasoning relies on general statements that refer to unreal universals, how is possible to reach conclusions regarding the real based on such reasoning? By segregating the conceptual from the real, Dharmakīrti encloses thought in a self-regulated arena removed from reality.

A parallel problem affecting Dharmakīrti's conceptualism is the reliance of its epistemology on the primacy of perception as providing undistorted access to reality. Conception is a secondary form of knowledge, valid only inasmuch as it relates to the real entities accessed by perception. The problem with this schema is that, according to Dharmakīrti, perception provides no useful information since it has no propositional content. Accordingly, perception requires the cognitive cooperation of conception to provide guidance in the practical world. This is highly problematic, however, for the two forms of knowledge do not bear on the same objects. Hence, it is hard to conceive how they could cooperate.

Dharmakīrti's followers were left with the task of confronting these dilemmas. They attempted to solve the problems by modifying certain concepts without abandoning the Buddhist framework. In doing so, they adopted a variety of strategies that fall into two broad categories. Some attempted to solve the problems while remaining as close as possible to Dharmakīrti's original ideas. In India, Devendrabuddhi and Śākyabuddhi represented this conservative tendency. They responded to objections from Hindu opponents through glossing Dharmakīrti's texts. In doing so, they did not venture very far from Dharmakīrti's own formulations. In Tibet, Sa-paṇ's tradition represented a similar attempt to answer critiques without major transformations to Dharmakīrti's framework. These thinkers proposed new ideas but were careful to keep them in close relation with Dharmakīrti's own concepts. For example, when Sa-paṇ proposed self-cognition as the pivotal element explaining the cooperation between perception and conception, he offered views that do not change fundamentally the terms of Dharmakīrti's system, regardless of whether or not Dharmakīrti intended this idea.

Quite different is the revisionist strategy noticeable in thinkers such as Dharmottara and Śaṃkarānanda. Under pressure from the Nyāya critique, these thinkers introduced new ideas that gradually transformed the basic terms of the system. For example, Dharmottara brought into the Buddhist framework realist ideas based on the distinction between two types of universals: the properties posited by extreme realism, that is, existing independent of the individuals that instantiate them, and the properties posited by moderate realism, that is, existing in dependence of these individuals. Dharmakīrti's rejection of the reality of universals was then taken to refer to the first type of universal and did not preclude the reality of properties such as impermanence, which are of the second type of universal. Similar changes were introduced in the theory of perception. Instead of Dharmakīrti's accurate but passive encounter with bare reality, perception became more actively cognitive.

Early Tibetan thinkers such as Cha-ba continued and radicalized this realist reinterpretation of Dharmakīrti, which later gained wide acceptance in Tibet. In India, realism seems to have remained a marginal element. It was suggested by certain authors, but does not seem to have led to a systematic reinterpretation of Dharmakīrti's system as in Tibet. There, it became widely accepted and at times dominated the tradition. Starting with Cha-ba, a long tradition of realist interpretation of Dharmakīrti developed in Tibet. The Ge-luk tradition represents this revisionist current in the contemporary Tibetan tradition.

The realist reinterpretation of Dharmakīrti's system takes place at both the ontological and epistemological levels. To establish a foundation for a more integrated epistemology, universals are introduced and characterized as properties, depending on their instances. This ontological move is paralleled on the epistemological level by the relaxation of the requirement that perception relate only to real individuals. Instead, perception is now said to relate to universals as well as to individuals. Moreover, using the phenomenological distinction between explicit and implicit ways of understanding allows these Tibetan epistemologists to strengthen the connection between conception and perception. Instead of being two modes of cognition operating in separate domains, perception and conception relate to the same range of entities. Thus, the problems raised by the dichotomy between conception and perception are overcome.

This interpretation, however, significantly modifies the meaning of *perception*. No more is perception an inarticulate contact with reality whose bareness guarantees its being correct. Perception is now a propositional form of knowledge whose main difference from the other form of knowledge is that it is psychologically nonconceptual. Whereas for Dharmakīrti perception is epistemologically and psychologically free from concepts, for Tibetan realists perception takes conceptual creations as its object; hence it is not epistemologically beyond concepts, although it remains psychologically nonconceptual.

The realist reinterpretation of Dharmakīrti's (and Dignāga's) theory of perception results in a transformation of the very meaning of the basic terms of the epistemological system. This shift is paralleled by a similar change in the meaning of the basic ontological concepts. Specifically characterized phenomena are no longer things whose reality is a function of their individuality. Instead of being strictly limited to individual objects, reality includes universals as well. This again represents a transformation of the original meaning of the concept.

Throughout this work I have insisted that these changes are not arbitrary. That is, they are not due to the mistakes of individuals but to the internal evolution of the tradition. Nevertheless, it remains that the moderate realism adopted by many Tibetan thinkers is quite different from Dharmakīrti's conceptualism and, therefore, from a historical perspective is heterodox. Although it claims to be the authoritative interpretation, the realist understanding of Dharmakīrti cannot claim to reflect accurately the philosophy of this thinker. It certainly captures elements of his thinking, but fails to convey its overall antirealist thrust. This does not mean that this tradition is not a valuable resource for modern interpreters of Dharmakīrti. Gyel-tsap, Kay-drup, and Ge-dün-drup present rich and well-informed theoretical and exegetical discussions. Their works offer well informed explanations of Dharmakīrti's system and close glosses of his texts, which often can be read against the realist biases of their authors, a sure sign of great scholarly quality.

Different is the contribution made by Sa-paṇ's tradition. Although its claims to represent completely and accurately Dharmakīrti's thought fly in the face of the historical and, hence, contingent nature of tradition, its main views remain close to those of Dharmakīrti in many respects. Despite the great historical distance between Dharmakīrti and Sa-paṇ, the latter exemplifies a tradition of inquiry that has preserved most of the basic terms of the system and attempts to struggle with difficulties while remaining within this framework. As such, Sa-paṇ's description of the mediating function of self-cognition and Śākya Chok-den's insistence on the diversity in Dharmakīrti's ontological views are important contributions for modern interpreters. This does not mean, however, that the Sa-gya views are identical to Dharmakīrti's. For instance, our study of the *apoha* theory showed that, in attempting to explain Dharmakīrti's view, the Sa-gya tradition had reached a formulation closer to Dignāga's view of language than to Dharmakīrti's view.

Therefore, the lesson that I draw from this interpretive encounter is not the simplistic conclusion that one tradition got Dharmakīrti right and the other got him wrong, but rather that both make valuable contributions. In fact, I would argue that the greatest insight into the Indian originals gleaned from Tibetan sources does not come from considering individual commentators or schools in isolation. Rather it comes from a broader appraisal of the overall Tibetan development of logic and epistemology. For example, it is quite difficult to correctly evaluate the contributions of Ge-luk thinkers without contrasting their views with those of their Sa-gya opponents. Once this contextualization has been done, the Tibetan commentarial tradition becomes indeed a source of great insight.

Philosophy as an Education

Such an interpretive assessment leaves unresolved another important question; namely, the philosophical value of realist and antirealist views. It is quite true that historically, moderate realism has remained largely outside the main stream of Buddhist logic and epistemology. Although this reflects on its claims to be the authoritative interpretation of Dharmakīrti, it does not prejudice the cogency of the position.

The strength of antirealism lies in the economical nature of the ontology it presupposes. When explaining how individuals share common traits, antirealism does not give in to the temptation to posit some type of special entity (universal) that accounts for this commonality. It attempts to explain the existence of commonality without presupposing the existence of anything other than the individual objects with which we are acquainted. This economical explanation appears quite satisfactory on the ontological level, for it does not require the intervention of entities that are not parts of common experience. When explaining, for example, how Mary and Paul are human beings, antirealism does not presuppose the existence of some humanity equally shared by both. Rather, it accounts for the fact that both individuals are human by pointing to their similarities. Such an explanation accounts for the existence of commonalities without going beyond the ways in which we have learned to use concepts in actual life.

However satisfactory such a view may seem at first, it faces a number of difficulties, particularly at the epistemological level. Can the antirealist account for knowledge that pertains to the universal as well as to the individual? Can the antirealist account for the normativity implicated in knowledge? Within Indian and Tibetan traditions, the normativity of knowledge is discussed in relation to the problem of universals. Buddhist antirealists recognize that even perception, which is the primary form of knowledge, indirectly relies on the presence of universals.

Although these thinkers may declare that universals are not involved in the perceptual process, they must recognize that those universals are necessary to the propositional articulation of perceptual experiences. Hence, they are involved in any form of knowledge.

Dharmakīrtian antirealism finds it difficult to account for the nature and role of universals. If universals are relevant to perception, how could they be unreal? The antirealist answer is that universals are constructed by human minds in their encounter with the world. This raises further problems, however. If universals are just mental creations, how can they provide the norms without which there is no possibility of differentiating truth from falsity? The Dharmakīrtian response we have examined here is practical. Norms are created when we mistakenly apply concepts to reality. But the question remains: If norms are useful mistakes, how do we differentiate useful mistakes from useless truths?

Moderate realist interpretations of Dharmakīrti are largely attempts to resolve such difficulties. By reintroducing universals into the fabric of reality, realism explains knowledge in accordance with common experience. For example, we know that this is a text when we are able to subsume this particular object under the property of being a text. On the ontological level, such an operation relies on the existence of real individuals and some type of properties; and epistemologically, on the cooperation between perception and conception. In such a perspective, knowledge becomes less problematic, and thought and language can be assumed to describe reality accurately.

As for the price, such a move sacrifices the elegant ontology of the system. Reintroducing general entities into the fabric of reality weakens and blurs the precision of the criteria for reality adopted by Dharmakīrti. Instead of being able to clearly distinguish real individuals from unreal universals, one is left without distinct criteria to determine what is real and differentiate it from what is merely conceptually added. Extreme realists do not face this problem, for they assert the reality of properties independent of any empirical considerations. Unwilling to reify properties to this extent, moderate realists hold that universals exist in dependence on individual objects. They then face the difficult problem of clearly articulating the relation between individuals and universals, a situation I have described as the moderate realist's predicament. As far as I can see, this problem has not been solved with satisfaction by Tibetan scholars. Hence, in the final analysis, realist reinterpretations do not seem to be able to present a completely successful system either. The reintroduction of universals provides significant answers to certain epistemological problems, but it also introduces new difficulties.

The impossibility of reaching a final solution to this kind of problem may be felt as a disappointment. We may think that a problem such as that of universals should be solvable, like any other problem confronting human ingenuity. At various times and in various places, philosophers have announced the discovery of solutions to major problems, only to look on as their later colleagues disregard their views and raise the issues again. In the case of the Indian and Tibetan traditions, we observe a similar scenario. The problem of universals has been raised again and again and alternative solutions proposed. None of them, however, has been considered completely satisfactory, although each can be defended. The debate continues with all sides arguing that they have found the right solution.

The repetition of such a scenario across cultures suggests that problems such as these are of a peculiar nature. The problem of universals is not empirical. Appealing to some hitherto unknown facts or new theory is of little help. Defensible solutions are proposed but philosophers keep arguing, for the conflict is not just about finding a solution but also about what would a solution look like if we were to find it. The problem of universals is like a riddle in which we feel that we are confronted by something quite deep and yet we cannot even imagine what it would be like to have a resolution.

Some readers well acquainted with the problems of Western philosophy but less familiar with the study of non-Western philosophies may feel disappointed by the outcome of our inquiry here. Being familiar with the Western tradition, such readers expect Western philosophical inquiries to be inconclusive. They hope, however, to find in non-Western traditions the solutions unavailable in their own. As a scholar of the philosophical aspect of Tibetan traditions, I am often asked whether Tibetan thinkers have found some new philosophies not yet known to the West. The question seems to me to betray a false and dangerous expectation concerning non-Western traditions. The temptation is strong for Western readers to look to other traditions with the hope of finding some solution to the problems that their tradition has not been able to resolve. Such an expectation is dangerous because it is mistaken and hence bound to be disappointed and may even end in a dismissal of non-Western traditions. What is important to realize is that the disappointment that invariably follows such expectations is not due to the failings of these traditions. Rather, it is due to a lack of understanding of what a philosophical problem is.

The usefulness of an inquiry such as this one is to illustrate once more that philosophical problems are not deep questions awaiting final solutions. Rather, they are riddles that arise from the ways in which humans think. Wittgenstein captures the peculiar nature of philosophical problems when he says: "The problems are solved, not by giving new information, but by arranging what we have always known. Philosophy is a battle against the bewitchment of our intelligence by means of language."[1] The problem of universals, for example, does not await some new discovery or way of thinking. Rather, this problem is generated out of the way humans think. In particular, it arises from some deep compunctions that lie at the basis of our ways of thinking. Hence, a "solution" can come only from the examination and deflation of such compunctions, not from any new solution.

This point has been made quite clearly by some of Wittgenstein's best interpreters such as Stanley Cavell and Cora Diamond.[2] We do not need to repeat here their analyses but we do need to appreciate the importance of their insights for the study of non-Western philosophical traditions. Their analyses show that the expectation of uncovering solutions to philosophical problems in non-Western traditions is profoundly misplaced, not because these traditions lack the sophistication to arrive at a solution. Rather, the fundamental mistake is to assume that such a solution exists in the first place. The further assumption that this solution is in the possession of non-Western traditions can only disappoint, for it is based on a fundamental misunderstanding of what philosophy is about. Thus, to appreciate non-Western philosophical traditions we need to understand what can be learned from philosophical inquiry. Otherwise we will be disappointed. But then the question is, Why study these traditions if they do not offer anything new?

This question is certainly legitimate. Finding an answer, though, depends on answering a more general question: Why bother with philosophy at all? Facing the disappointment of the philosophical inquiry, the temptation is strong to proclaim the end of philosophy. Rorty and others have done so, claiming that Wittgenstein has shown the futility of engaging philosophical questions. They claim that philosophical problems are either intellectual confusions or questions that are relevant only as long as science is not sufficiently developed to provide richer avenues of inquiry. Historically, there was a role for philosophy. It raised questions that were taken over in a clearer way by the sciences. This role is over, however; hence there is no longer any role for philosophy. The greatest mistake, according to these thinkers, would be to believe that there are long lasting philosophical problems. Wittgenstein has shown, they claim, that this idea is a delusion, a nostalgia for the period in which philosophers played a role.[3] In this perspective, non-Western thinkers such as Dharmakīrti or Kay-drup are to be left aside like Plato or Aristotle, as interesting but irrelevant monuments of a past that "we" have left behind long ago.

There is no need to say that I do not share this view, which I take to be diametrically opposed to Wittgenstein's insight. More relevant, I understand this book to tell a different story. It shows that, far from being irrelevant, thinkers such as Dharmakīrti or Kay-drup illustrate the importance of the study of philosophy in general, and non-Western philosophy in particular. Confronting their difficult ideas is certainly not about to reveal some philosophical "silver bullet," but brings about a greater maturity to our thinking. By confronting ourselves with philosophical problems, we learn how to raise new questions, how to problematize what we usually take for granted. To philosophize is to question common notions, to recognize the difficulty where we usually just quickly pass over. The value of philosophy lies not in the answers we can come up with but in the questions themselves, for they open new ways of looking at reality.

The art of thinking is not limited to finding right or wrong answers. Rather it consists in the ways in which we deal with problems, and this in turn depends on our ability to raise questions. Thus, to think is not to answer but to question. This is what Plato and others have called *dialectics*, the art of thinking through conducting a dialogue of questions and answers. Gadamer emphasizes the central role of questioning: "We cannot have experiences without asking questions. Recognizing that an object is different, and not as we first thought obviously presupposes the question whether it was this or that. From a logical point of view, the openness essential to experience is precisely the openness of being either this or that. It has the structure of a question."[4] Becoming experienced in life does not depend on finding some previously overlooked fact but on raising questions we had not considered previously concerning the most common objects of our experience. This is what we can learn from philosophy in general. This is also what we can learn from studying Dharmakīrti's tradition.

The value of studying Dharmakīrti's tradition is that it raises questions about the ways in which we think about our most common activities. This is why Dharmakīrti and his followers use trivial examples, which we usually take for granted, and raise searching questions concerning how we think about them. The benefit in studying authors such as Dharmakīrti or Kay-drup is not to reach final answers, although this is what some of these authors themselves attempt to do. The benefit of spending the time and effort to go through their complicated analyses is the education that we receive in the process. To follow their views is a way to train our minds to make fine analytical distinctions and do rigorous investigation. In doing so, we develop our critical abilities and come to question our most cherished assumptions. The questions these philosophers raise are good to think about, not because they bring final clarity but because they oblige us to grow. To paraphrase Cavell, in the face of these authors we are children; we do not know how to go with these questions, what ground we may occupy. In this light, "philosophy is the education of grownups."[5]

This conclusion is not just my own post-Wittgensteinian view, but has also been reached by several, although by no means all, of the authors we have studied. Dharmakīrti and his direct Indian followers took their own attempts very seriously. They thought they could really solve epistemological problems and in the process silence once and for all their Hindu critics. Most Tibetan authors do not share this view. Due to their lack of contact with India, they may have the historically mistaken view that Dharmakīrti managed to crush the Hindu opposition. Even this, however, does not count in their minds as solving philosophical problems. Tibetan interpreters insist on understanding Dharmakīrti in relation to his own philosophical system, but they consider his project impossible. In the end, Dharmakīrti's analyses do not succeed in solving philosophical problems. This work has illustrated two attempts, the realist and the anti-realist, to make sense of his system. Both come up against unsurmountable difficulties.

Most Tibetan commentators take this failure as an indication that Dharmakīrti's enterprise cannot succeed. This failure is no reason for abandoning his system, though, for its value derives not from the final answers it brings but from its educational value. In Tibetan educational practices, understanding Dharmakīrti's system and its difficulties leads the student of Buddhist philosophy toward an understanding of what most Tibetan scholars consider a deeper philosophy of the Mahāyāna tradition, the Madhyamaka insight into the essencelessness of all phenomena. By way of conclusion, let me say a few words concerning the ways Tibetan thinkers understand the relation between the study of Dharmakīrti and the understanding of Madhyamaka philosophy. This will allow us to flesh out the ways in which Dharmakīrti's philosophy is an "education for grownups" in the Tibetan tradition.

Epistemology and the Madhyamaka Critique

Most Tibetan thinkers consider Madhyamaka as the most profound Buddhist philosophy. By this they do not mean that it is a better system in the usual sense. Rather it is a critique of systematic thought. It is a skepticism toward the possibility of doing philosophy on the basis of assuming that philosophical inquiry must proceed by securing the foundations on which it is possible to elaborate a complete architectonics. This suspicion of the idea of a foundation has obvious consequences for systematic epistemology. It is directly opposed to Dharmakīrti's foundationalism, which rests on the idea that certain phenomena have an essence that individuates them. Dharmakīrti bases his study of *pramāṇa* (knowledge) on an ontology at the center of which lies the opposition between real things, determined by their individual causal capacities, and conceptual constructs, which are essenceless.

Dharmakīrti's system, as depicted in this work, is foundationalist. It attempts to give a complete and systematic account of the types of knowledge in relation to their objects. Cognitions must be grounded in and limited to definite types of objects, entailing stringent conditions for validity. To be valid, a cognition must be either a direct reflection of reality or bear on an object that has a demonstrable relation with reality. These epistemic requirements disqualify most of what we normally consider valid as insufficiently grounded in reality and thereby exclude it from being knowledge. Tillemans explains: "it is difficult to resist the impression that the Buddhist, especially as explained by Dharmakīrti, sets his standards almost impossibly high. It should be apparent that no one, Buddhist or non-Buddhist, can in practice inferentially or empirically test for himself all rationally analyzable propositions on which he must make a decision."[6] Such a problem is typical of the epistemological approach, which aims at a systematic analysis of common epistemic practices by grounding them on certain types of object but ends up eliminating most of what is commonly held as knowledge on the grounds that it does not satisfy preconditions inspired by the desire to ground these practices.

This is precisely how Candrakīrti reproaches Dignāga.[7] Candrakīrti's critique of Buddhist epistemology (the philosophical interest of which extends well beyond its limited historical role)[8] is based less on phenomenological considerations than on ontological (or, rather, antiontological) considerations. Although Dignāga's epistemology is not meant as a full-fledged metaphysics, it cannot avoid ontological commitments due to its stress on strict criteria of validity and its insistence on grounding knowledge in reality. It is this project Candrakīrti finds objectionable.

Candrakīrti impeaches the systematic character of Dignāga's thought for the reason that it contradicts conventions and common linguistic usage. For him, epistemology should not aim at systematicity but should simply follow common human usage. It is not possible to logically regiment epistemic practices, as Dignāga attempts to do. For Dignāga a cognition is admitted as valid if, and only if, it hits a real object in the world. This truth-hitting characteristic can be obtained in two ways: It can be the result of a direct contact between a real object and a perception, or it can be the result of an indirect relation between reality and consciousness through the mediation of some reasoning. By declaring that only truth-hitting cognitions are valid and that this truth hitting can be achieved in only two ways, Buddhist systematic epistemology attempts to secure the foundation of knowledge. Candrakīrti disagrees with the premise of this project.

For Candrakīrti, the desire for completeness and the longing for secure foundations lead Dignāga to elaborate an epistemology that does violence to common practices. According to Dignāga's theory, for example, an object of commonsense such as a pot is conceptually constructed by welding together different elements such as color, taste, and touch into a synthetic unity. Therefore, such an object is not real and cannot be perceived.[9] This is obviously counterintuitive, argues Candrakīrti, for we do feel that we perceive objects such as pots and chairs. Nevertheless, fascinated by rigorous philosophical reasonings, the logicians are ready to deny such obvious commonsense facts. Siderits gives this excellent rendering of Candrakīrti's stance:

> If the Buddhist epistemologist is seeking to regiment our epistemic practices from within, he is engaged in a hopeless task, for the goal of complete consistency based on secure foundations (Dignāga's thesis of the two prameyas [objects of comprehension] and their pramāṇas [valid cognitions]) is unattainable. Candrakīrti's critique is meant to bring out this fact, and his description of his strategy is apt. He is a world-elder (lokavṛddha), one who upholds our common-sense conventions as adequate to their assigned tasks. He does so by refuting those arguments which purport to contradict some portion of the saṃvṛti. His procedure has its rationale in the fact that we cannot engage in criticism of accepted epistemic practices unless we are in possession of reliable procedures for testing the truth of our assertions, and such procedures may be developed only by scrutinizing the popular conventions with respect to pramāṇa and prameya.[10]

The mistake of so many epistemologists originates out of their theoretical compulsion, which cannot but lead them into a hopeless position.

Since Buddhist epistemology aims to explain knowledge, it must account for common epistemic practices. In such an endeavor, respecting common usage is not just one among several considerations. It is the primary guideline of the inquiry, without which the whole enterprise is called into question. For if we go beyond common usage, we are left with no objects to which our philosophical inquiry could apply. Contradicting common usage deprives us of any means to test an account, for if we cannot trust common sense, on what basis can we assess competing theoretical claims? As Siderits puts it, "in the absence of conventional linguistic behavior there are no objects available for philosophical scrutiny."[11]

For Candrakīrti, epistemology should aim not at completeness and systematicity but at providing a rich account of common practices (one is reminded here of Geertz's idea of thick description).[12] Accordingly, Candrakīrti rejects several elements of Dignāga's project. He makes two especially important points, which I mention in turn with brief elaborations. First, he rejects the definition of *perception* as being free from conception (*kalpanāpodha, rtog pa dang bral ba*) because it leads to the absurd situation in which what is commonly held to be a perception (seeing a pot) is denied perceptual status.[13] For example, when I see a round, bulky object that has the capacity to hold water, I think "this is a pot." According to Dignāga (and Dharmakīrti), this judgment is not a perception since it is conceptual. This, however, drives the epistemologist into the difficulties we have examined earlier. As Candrakīrti rightly argues, this is one of the several unfortunate consequences of unduly restricting the category of perception to fit philosophical considerations. Although Buddhist epistemology aims to provide an account of human epistemic practices, its fascination with theoretical elaborations ends in singling out as the best representatives of perception cognitions that only philosophers would recognize as perceptual.

Second, Candrakīrti also objects to the strict epistemological dichotomy defended by Dignāga and his followers. He does not believe that perception and inference relate to categorically different entities. Following common usage, Candrakīrti does not see any reason to deny the capacity of conceptions to apprehend real objects, which are considered by Dignāga's tradition to be the preserve of perception. Rather than follow the Buddhist epistemologists in their attempt to regiment human practices, Candrakīrti is ready to side with the Nyāya philosophy, which is more respectful of common conventions. Like the Nyāya, Candrakīrti allows for the conflation of valid cognitions (*pramāṇa-saṃplava*). Perception and inference can relate to the same objects without any restrictions. He also seems to accept their typology of four types of valid cognition, in which comparison (*upamāna, dpe nyer 'jal*) and verbal testimony (*śabda, sgra*) are added to perception and inference to give a better account of ordinary practices. In addition Candrakīrti shares the Nyāya view of perception and accepts nonconceptual as well as conceptual states as being perceptual.[14] Rather than follow what he considers the misguided effort of Dignāga's tradition to reform Nyāya by producing a better, more secure epistemology, Candrakīrti is ready to side with the Nyāya and use the ideas that are more attuned to common usage.

His endorsement of Nyāya philosophy is limited, however. Candrakīrti accepts neither the metaphysical commitments of this philosophy nor its tendency to reify and multiply entities. For him, the starting point of the Nyāya, respecting common usages and practices, is correct. Nyāya philosophy goes wrong, though, when it attempts to give a metaphysical account of common usages by reifying their objects. Candrakīrti shares the respect for common practices but he does not believe that they need ontological justification. In this respect, the Nyāya reification of entities is no less misguided than the more economical conceptualism of the Buddhist epistemologists. They both proceed from a foundationalist belief in the necessity to ground epistemic practices by relating them to some well-defined realm of existence. Whereas Naiyāyikas attempt to accomplish this through a categorical articulation of reality, Buddhist epistemologists distinguish real individuals from conceptual constructs. Both attempts are equally misguided in going beyond appearance to reach for some hypothetical ultimate standpoint.

Prāsaṅgika and Epistemology: Dzong-ka-ba's Realism

Candrakīrti's Madhyamaka critique is directed not merely against the ontology of Dignāga's tradition, it can be applied to the entire epistemological tradition inspired by Dignāga. Although Candrakīrti does not necessarily reject the study of epistemic practices, he is certainly skeptical about systematic epistemology. Most of the Tibetan scholars we have examined here share the gist of his view about reality (with the exception of Śākya Chok-den in the later part of his life and Chö-drak-gya-tso). They take him to have begun a new tradition of Madhyamaka, the so-called Prāsaṅgika subschool, although they are aware that the term itself is a Tibetan creation.[15] Although Tibetan thinkers markedly differ on the way in which Prāsaṅgika is differentiated from its rival Svātantrika, they mostly agree that Candrakīrti's tradition provides the most authoritative interpretation of Nāgārjuna's thought.

Why do then so many Tibetan thinkers place such emphasis on the study of Dignāga and Dharmakīrti's system, which Candrakīrti criticized so openly? Why do they use a system with which they only partially agree and which seems in tension with the deconstructive implications of their philosophy? Why have Tibetan philosophers not followed Candrakīrti's rejection of Buddhist epistemology in favor of the Nyāya, as advocated by their favorite interpreter of Madhyamaka philosophy? To fully answer this question we would need to delve into a historical description of the roles of Candrakīrti and Dharmakīrti in late Indian and early Tibetan scholarship.[16] Since this is well beyond our purview here, let me briefly examine the ways in which Ge-luk and then Sa-gya traditions understand the relation between Dharmakīrti's thought and their overall Madhyamaka philosophy.

Although Ge-luk scholars do not accept Dharmakīrti's overall philosophical outlook, they find in him two essential elements to support their project. These are the conceptual resources supporting an investigation into of reality, which is to be carried on following Candrakīrti's lead, based on an analysis of our ways of knowing, and an educational discipline that prepares the students to move to the Madhyamaka analysis.

The first point is probably the more important, but to examine it in detail would require extensive discussion of Madhyamaka concepts and their relation to the logico-epistemological tradition. Suffice it to say that Dzong-ka-ba made extensive use of ideas such as contradiction (*'gal ba, virodha*) and relation (*'brel ba, saṃbandha*), which are borrowed from the epistemological tradition. As well, Dzong-ka-ba uses the concept of valid cognition (*tshad ma, pramāṇa*) to support the idea that phenomena derive conventional validity from being observed by valid cognitions. These concepts play an essential role in Dzong-ka-ba's

Madhyamaka, even though they have been elaborated primarily by non-Mādhyamika thinkers.

These concepts are not exclusive to the logico-epistemological tradition, for Mādhyamikas also discuss the nature of valid cognition. However, Ge-luk discussions of this concept are often based rather closely on Dharmakīrti's ideas. When Ge-luk thinkers deal extensively with questions relating to epistemology, logic, or the philosophy of language, they use Dharmakīrti's texts as their source and tend to downplay his differences with Candrakīrti. For example, Ge-luk thinkers hold that Candrakīrti's acceptance of four types of valid cognition should not be taken literally. For them, the fourfold typology is compatible with the twofold one that is central to the Buddhist epistemological program. The two typologies, which seem to conflict, are made compatible by including two supplementary types of valid cognition (comparison and testimony) within inference. This move illustrates quite well the tendency of Ge-luk thinkers to use Dharmakīrti's categories when analyzing epistemic practices. They also tend to emphasize the importance of logical notions such as consistency and contradiction, which is in harmony with their commitment to realism and its emphasis on the importance of thought.

This usage of Dharmakīrti's concepts and ideas is not unproblematic for Ge-luk thinkers since they accept Candrakīrti's type of Madhyamaka philosophy, which is quite opposed to the account of Buddhist epistemologists. This tension is usually overlooked in the Ge-luk tradition, where Candrakīrti's remarks on epistemology often end up paradoxically as little more than footnotes to a revised Dharmakīrtian epistemology. This catholic inclusivism and the concomitant insistence on the lack of contradiction between the different aspects of Buddhist tradition is fundamental to Dzong-ka-ba's approach. Indeed his is an impressive attempt to harmonize the often conflicting teachings of Indian Buddhism. This emphasis on the compatibility of the conflicting Buddhist philosophies has resulted in the attempt to conciliate doctrines that are not really compatible, as in the case of Candrakīrti's and Dignāga's analyses.

This tendency to underestimate the significance of differences between the views of the Dignāga-Dharmakīrti tradition and Candrakīrti has been often reproached to this tradition. Dak-tsang, for example, levels this criticism against Dzong-ka-ba when describing the numerous (up to eighteen) contradictions that he finds in him: "The cause for such a burden of contradictions [in Dzong-ka-ba's writings] is that, despite [Candrakīrti's and others'] statements again and again [that phenomena exist] only for the world without analysis, [Dzong-ka-ba] applied reasoning and proved [their valid conventional existence] due to the force of his habituation to logic."[17] The Sa-gya scholar reproaches Dzong-ka-ba for using the idea of valid cognition in Prāsaṅgika philosophy. For Dzong-ka-ba, phenomena have conventional existence because they are conventionally established by valid cognitions. This is unacceptable to Dak-tsang, who argues that such a reference to a concept borrowed from the logico-epistemological tradition is inappropriate in the context of Prāsaṅgika philosophy. Concepts borrowed from the logico-epistemological tradition cannot be automatically applied to the analysis of epistemic practices within Prāsaṅgika for they are incompatible with it.[18]

It should be recognized that Dak-tsang's statement is polemical. Although the Ge-luk tradition certainly emphasizes the value of Buddhist logic and epistemology, it would be erroneous to believe that this is particular to the tradition. The acceptance of Dharmakīrti as providing the main resource in the study of logic and epistemology is shared by other Tibetan traditions, although possibly not to the same degree. In fact, it could be argued that the use of epistemological categories is widespread among post-Dharmakīrtian Mādhyamikas, both in India and in Tibet. Like the Ge-luk traditions, other Tibetan schools also tend to emphasize the coherence and unity of the Buddhist tradition. They similarly tend to assume that reliable Indian sources share a single authoritative view, a presupposition that often impedes their commentarial work.

Go-ram-ba, for example, demonstrates a similar impulse to use Dharmakīrtian categories when dealing with epistemic processes. He criticizes Dzong-ka-ba for not differentiating between the Prāsaṅgika idea of valid cognition and Dharmakīrti's idea; however, when analyzing the way in which inference relates to emptiness, Go-ram-ba uses the concept of object universal, even though its acceptance in Madhyamaka is highly problematic. Go-ram-ba's point is that inference does not apprehend emptiness itself, as Dzong-ka-ba believes. Emptiness lies beyond the grasp of thought and language, which has access only to the object universal of emptiness.

This point, which is by now familiar within Dharmakīrti's philosophy, has no obvious place in Madhyamaka, especially when understood from Candrakīrti's perspective. Based on the distinction between the "real" and the "conceptual," the notion of object universal seems tied down to the foundationalist standpoint of the epistemologists. Nevertheless, Go-ram-ba is quite happy to use this notion to strengthen his analysis of emptiness as being beyond thought and language.[19] My teacher Ge-shay Nyi-ma Gyel-tsen used to puzzle his students by asking them whether Candrakīrti's philosophy could accommodate the *apoha* theory. His students (myself included) would rush to answer positively, reasoning that conceptions relate to their objects negatively. It was unthinkable to imagine that a Mādhyamika would side with the Nyāya against Buddhist epistemology and assert that conception is able to relate directly to its object. It is clear to me now that my teacher was on to something not recognized by many Tibetan thinkers, irrespective of their sectarian affiliation.[20]

The second way the Ge-luk tradition has used Dharmakīrti's basic categories is educational. This propaedeutical use of Dharmakīrti has several dimensions. The main value of Dharmakīrti's system from the Ge-luk perspective is to introduce a certain number of important ideas. For example, it provides the student with a view of reality in which external existence is asserted. This is an important point for Ge-luk thinkers, because they differentiate theirs from other Tibetan interpretations of Madhyamaka philosophy by their uncompromising rejection of any view resembling the Mind-Only doctrine. For Ge-luk-bas, things such as pots and trees exist externally because they are the object conditions of the perceptions that apprehend them. The system proposed by the Collected Topics, through which Ge-luk students are introduced to Buddhist philosophy, allows the presentation of Buddhist ontology and epistemology in terms of such externally existing things. This view is stressed in the Ge-luk tradition.

The most important way in which Dharmakīrti's system is used by scholars of the Ge-luk tradition, though, is in relation to their view of emptiness. The Ge-luk tradition uses Dharmakīrti's Sautrāntika philosophy as a stepping stone toward the understanding of their own version of Candrakīrti's Prāsaṅgika view. Contrary to other Tibetan schools, the Ge-luk tradition does not hesitate to claim that, according to Madhyamaka philosophy, things exist. This view appears at first a shocking contradiction of the most fundamental Madhyamaka tenet, that things neither exist nor do not exist. The Ge-luk-bas' point is that Nāgārjuna's attack against the view that things exist is in fact directed at what Ge-luk thinkers refer to as the object of negation *(dgag bya)*, ultimate existence *(don dam par yod pa)*, real existence *(bden par grub pa)*, or intrinsic existence *(rang bzhin gis grub pa)*. According to this interpretation, Nāgārjuna is negating the putative real existence of things, not their conventional existence. Things do not truly exist, but they do exist nevertheless because they have a conventional validity that can be ascertained.[21] Since they are observed by valid cognitions, things exist.

For the Ge-luk approach, understanding a mode of existence that does not imply real existence is the most crucial step in the process of understanding emptiness. Positing this mode of existence allows them to interpret Nāgārjuna in a way that preserves the conventional validity of things. This is done by setting the object of negation, real existence, as the target of Madhyamaka reasoning. What does it mean for things to exist really? According to Dzong-ka-ba, phenomena would really exist if they had an identity by virtue of their own essence, independent of any conceptual framework. Things do not exist in such a way, for they can be identified only in dependence on conceptual activities. To use a simple expression, they exist only nominally. That is to say, the identity of things can be specified, because these things can be talked and thought about within the framework of agreed upon practices. The object of negation is to be understood by contrasting this nominal mode of existence with the way we grasp things.[22] The difference between the two is what students of Madhyamaka recognize as the object of negation, the putative object grasped by their own minds.[23] To recognize the all-important object of negation, the students must first gain a rough understanding of nominal existence. Then they are able to contrast the way in which they usually grasp onto reality from the way in which things exist. In this way, the implications of the putative object of negation, real existence, are understood.[24]

In this perspective the understanding of nominal existence is of great importance. According to Dzong-ka-ba, failure to identify such a mode of existence leads to the assumption that existence can be only real existence, which is one of the biggest obstacles to understanding the Madhyamaka view. Therefore, positing nominal existence as being different from real existence and as fulfilling the meaning of existence is a crucial move in Ge-luk philosophy. It allows this tradition to reconcile the antisubstantialist character of Buddhist philosophy with commonsense. This important move occurs in the intellectual life of students first while studying Dharmakīrti's system understood in a realist way. By differentiating nominal from real existence in the Sautrāntika system, the student prepares for a similar (but more subtle) distinction within Madhyamaka philosophy. In the Prāsaṅgika system all things are said to exist nominally, for they all lack real existence. In the Sautrāntika system by contrast, only entities such as object universals have nominal existence. Nominal existence in Sautrāntika is restricted to certain phenomena and posited on the basis of the real existence of some things, so it is easier for students to familiarize themselves with the concept of nominal existence in this system. Once nominal existence is understood in this context, the understanding can be deepened and applied to the more subtle Madhyamaka notion of conventional existence.

By allowing conventional validity but refusing ultimate validity to things, Dzong-ka-ba proposes an interpretation of Madhyamaka thought that is realist but still maintains its liberational value. In an essenceless reality, the only possible ontology applies to conventions delineated through agreed upon practices. Practitioners must rely on these conventionalities in two ways. They must take them as the framework for practices other than the realization of emptiness. They must also consider conventionalities in understanding emptiness. In particular, this involves attending to the mind as it reaches beyond the objects agreed upon in our practice to cling to things as being more than convenient designations. By noticing what the mind grasps onto, practitioners identify the object of negation and become well positioned to understand its nonexistence. In this way it is possible to separate conventional from ultimate validity. Things do not have an intrinsic essence, but they do have a validity that is not the mere product of ignorance. This sifting through of appearances to eliminate reification yet preserve what is valid in common experience constitutes the essence of Dzong-ka-ba's philosophy. His approach is realist in that it attempts to preserve the reality implied by common sense. It is moderate in that it refuses to hypostatize commonsense intuitions: it takes them to be valid only within the critique of substance that runs throughout the Buddhist tradition. Now we can understand some of the more far-reaching implications of the moderate realism we have analyzed throughout this work.

Go-ram-ba's Suspicion of Language

Quite different is the Sa-gya approach, which accentuates the antirealist character of Madhyamaka. This is hardly a surprise, for this emphasis is in harmony with this tradition's interpretation of Dharmakīrti's philosophy. Whereas the Ge-luk approach rests on a respect for common sense, the Sa-gya tradition sets forth a view that radically undermines common understanding, which is seen to consist of a network of reifications due to ignorance. Accordingly, the Sa-gya tradition insists that concepts apply only to conventional reality. Ultimate truth in Madhyamaka is completely beyond the reach of concepts. It is utterly ineffable, in the strong sense of the word.[25] Hence for the Sa-gya tradition in general and Go-ram-ba in particular, the key concept in Madhyamaka philosophy is not the absence of real existence but freedom from elaborations (*prapañca, spros pa*). Ultimate truth is utterly beyond the reach of elaboration.

As its name indicates, Madhyamaka philosophy takes as its central and self-descriptive motive the idea of a middle ground avoiding extremes. There is nevertheless room for considerable disagreement among various interpreters on the exact way in which extremes are to be identified and rejected. Unsurprisingly, Ge-luk and Sa-gya traditions disagree on this topic. Both understand the Middle Way to be the emptiness of all phenomena; that is, that all phenomena lack essence. This essencelessness is understood differently by the two traditions, however.

For Dzong-ka-ba, all phenomena are essenceless in that they do not really exist, even though they exist conventionally. The meaning of the doctrine of the Middle Way reflects this understanding. Phenomena are said to abide in the middle, for they transcend the extremes of eternalism and nihilism. Phenomena transcend the extreme of eternalism inasmuch as they are devoid of real existence. They also transcend the extreme of nihilism inasmuch as they exist conventionally. Thus, for Dzong-ka-ba, the Middle Way is reached by negating real existence in a way that preserves the limited validity of conventional practices.

Like Dzong-ka-ba, Go-ram-ba also relies on Candrakīrti, but he emphasizes another aspect of his thought. Instead of stressing the validity of conventionalities like Dzong-ka-ba, Go-ram-ba emphasizes the distorted nature of conventionalities. He criticizes Dzong-ka-ba's approach as only a partial overcoming of extremes. For Go-ram-ba, rejecting real existence is not sufficient to reach the Middle Way, for denying real existence is itself an extreme. The extreme of nonexistence also must be overcome. When we negate real existence, we come to hold to its nonexistence. This in itself is a kind of negative essence and hence it must be transcended to reach the Middle Way. Since holding to phenomena as not really existing involves a conceptual determination, it is a form of grasping. Reaching the Middle Way necessitates transcending all forms of grasping. Hence, it necessitates transcending all conceptual elaborations.[26]

By *elaboration*, Go-ram-ba means more than holding to things as really existing or understanding emptiness to imply a commitment to a positive entity. He means all signs, positive or negative, through which objects can be conceptualized.[27] Thus, to hold that phenomena do not really exist is an elaboration, for it is a conceptualization. Although it is soteriologically useful, it is not a realization of emptiness. As long as we remain restricted to a conceptual description of reality, either positive or negative, we cannot be said to have realized emptiness. Such realization is achieved when the mind completely transcends any description and goes beyond any kind of mental movement (*sems kyi rgyu ba*). Everything short of this complete overcoming of conceptuality, achieved only by the realization of emptiness through yogic perception, is not the Middle Way. Prior to such an experience, we are limited to conceptualizing emptiness. Such an understanding is not the view of emptiness but just assumed (*rlom*) to be the view of it, much like in Dharmakīrti's system where thought does not really conceive of reality but is just assumed to conceive of it.

In accordance with this radical rejection of conceptuality, Go-ram-ba offers a critique of ontology that further diverges from Dharmakīrti's views than does Dzong-ka-ba. On the topic of causality, for example, Go-ram-ba rejects Dharmakīrti's view that causes and effects are radically different. For Go-ram-ba this view, which is accepted by Ge-luk thinkers within their analysis of Madhyamaka, rests on the assumption that real things have an essence that can be pinned down. This is certainly Dharmakīrti's view, as we have seen. Within the Madhyamaka framework, however, such a view makes no sense since phenomena cannot be pinned down in terms of sufficient and necessary conditions. Hence, causes and effects are neither identical nor different. They are beyond the reach of any description that presupposes essential identity or difference.[28] Similarly, when explaining the Prāsaṅgika view of valid cognition, Go-ram-ba sides with Candrakīrti against Dharmakīrti and the Svatāntrika Mādhyamikas who follow him. For Go-ram-ba, there are four valid cognitions, not just two, as with Dharmakīrti, Bhavya, and Dzong-ka-ba.[29] Those cognitions are not valid in their own right, however, but only from the limited and fundamentally distorted viewpoint of conventional truth.

It would be wrong to infer that Go-ram-ba completely rejects Dharmakīrti's heritage. Like most later Indian and Tibetan Buddhist philosophers, Go-ram-ba's vocabulary is profoundly influenced by Dharmakīrti. For instance, he often uses Dharmakīrti's descriptions in differentiating perceptual from conceptual understanding. Whereas the former is an actual realization of emptiness, the latter is just a determination of the concept of emptiness, not of emptiness itself. Hence, far from rejecting Dharmakīrti, Go-ram-ba emphasizes the aspect of Dharmakīrti's thought that supports his emphasis on the utter failure of concepts to capture the ultimate and the consequent ineffability of reality. Here again, we realize some of the soteriological implications of the Sa-gya antirealism. Although the Dharmakīrtian opposition between the real and the conceptual cannot be maintained in a Madhyamaka framework, antirealism remains important in allowing us to understand the way in which thought and language function in the quest for the Middle Way. In particular, antirealism calls our attention to the limits of thought and language. Recognizing their limits does not entail rejecting thought and language but leads us to understand that we can get in touch with reality by using thought and language only in a self-canceling or self-consuming way.

Buddhist Epistemology as an Education

Although both the Ge-luk and Sa-gya traditions disagree on a number of relevant issues, they agree on what they see as the great educational value of studying

Dharmakīrti's epistemology. They perceive Dharmakīrti's system as offering the most systematic philosophical presentation of foundationalism in Buddhist philosophy. Hence it is also the ideal training ground to lead students from an unquestioning assent to the essentialization of reality to a skeptical questioning of it. Having understood Dharmakīrti's system, which is based on the difference between a reality definable in terms of essence and a projected essenceless conceptual realm, the student is shown how this distinction leads to unsolvable difficulties. Those difficulties do not come from incidental limitations of the system but from its assumption that real things are defined by their essences. Demonstration of this insight occurs in numerous debates analyzing Dharmakīrti's system on its own terms. In this way the crucial problems we have examined in this work, such as the relation between perception and thought and the difficulty of accounting for our experiences in terms of a reductionist typology of valid cognitions are exposed. This leads the student to the suspicion that what is wrong with Dharmakīrti's system does not come from the intellectual limitations of its author but from his essentialist assumptions.

Because Tibetan thinkers profoundly admire Dharmakīrti, they value the difficulties students encounter in dealing with the inextricable problems created by his system, which are symptomatic of the entrapment of foundational thinking. Precisely because of its philosophical rigor, Dharmakīrti's system exemplifies the type of problems encountered by any systematic and foundationalist thought. Since Dharmakīrti is consistent with his ontology and limits the number of valid cognitions, it is easy to uncover the difficulties his consistent philosophy creates. Thus, by using Dharmakīrti's system as the testing ground of essentialism, Tibetan traditions bring their members to realize the difficulties that such a mode of thinking entails. This leads students to the central insight of Madhyamaka teaching, the essencelessness of all things. This is, perhaps, a Tibetan Madhyamaka version of Cavell's education for adults.

Tibetans also use Dharmakīrti's thought in another way, to provide a useful analysis of thought and language. This is the issue about which realists and their opponents disagree, even within a consideration of Madhyamaka philosophy. Whereas the Ge-luk tend to insist on the intelligibility of reality to thought, the Sa-gya usually emphasize the gap between reality and thought. But what difference do these opposing views make once we have reached Madhyamaka?

As we have seen, realism and antirealism imply different ontologies. Whereas the former includes properties within the fabric of reality, the latter reduces reality to individuals. Within the Madhyamaka philosophy this ontological difference is less important. This tradition's emphasis on essencelessness reduces the importance of ontological choices. Deciding between realism and its opposite represents not a choice between two sets of well-defined entities but between two different descriptions of the same essenceless reality. Since neither tradition accepts Dharmakīrti's view as ultimate, their ontological differences often remain largely exegetical.

The ways in which these traditions understand language, however, is another matter. Realism and antirealism have important implications for how these traditions articulate their understanding of Nāgārjuna's teachings of essencelessness. This is not to say that one tradition understands essencelessness and the other does not. I believe that both traditions offer different but valuable insights into Madhyamaka. They differ, however, on what we could describe as the "cognitive management" of these Madhyamaka insights.

Realism insists on the ways in which reality is intelligible to thought and language. This does not mean that reality is transparent to thought and language, but that these can be taken as leading toward a goal that they may not fully grasp but that they can give us descriptions on which we can partly rely. Thought and language provide a global philosophical analysis that can be used to avoid mistakes and develop an understanding of reality. By contrast, antirealism does not trust thought and language to the same degree. It stresses the distorting nature of concepts. Thought and language should not be seen as leading to a deeper truth. These are powerless to describe reality, and we should not even try to have them do so. Concepts cannot give us an accurate vision of reality. All we can do is to use them pragmatically in our agreed upon practices. In the realm of understanding the empty nature of reality, concepts can be used only in a self-canceling way.

Hence, I believe that, inasmuch as there is some truth in this picture, we should see these two traditions not as opposed enemies, as we often have here for the sake of exposition. Rather, they suggest alternative understandings of how we manage to communicate and understand similar insights in ways that are neither fully adequate nor totally inappropriate.

NOTES

Introduction I. A Few Methodological Considerations

1. D. S. Ruegg, "On the Reception and Early History of the dbu ma (Madhyamaka) in Tibet," in M. Aris and A. Suu Kyi, eds., *Tibetan Studies in Honor of Hugh Richardson* (New Delhi: Vikas, 1980), pp. 277–79, 278. Ruegg distinguishes four periods in the development of Buddhism in Tibet: (a) preliminary assimilation (eighth–ninth centuries), the early propagation *(snga dar)*; (b) full assimilation (tenth–fourteenth centuries), systematization of the doctrines; (c) classical period (fourteenth–sixteenth centuries); and (d) scholastic period (sixteenth–twentieth centuries), systematization of textbooks, (often epigonal) efforts to reach definitive exegesis of interpretations previously elaborated.

2. Following Paul Ricoeur, I am using the word *interpretation* to refer to any act of comprehension of a historically or culturally alien text that involves a combination of understanding and explaining. Any fullfledged exegesis of a text, especially a difficult and, therefore, alien text, is an interpretation. Therefore, interpretation does not denote a loose or associative approach to the text but refers to any act of understanding a text. See *Interpretation Theory* (Forth Worth: Texas Christian University Press, 1976).

3. J. N. Mohanty, "Understanding Some Ontological Differences in Indian Philosophy," *Journal of Indian Philosophy* 8, no. 3 (1980): 205–17, 205. Reprinted by permission of Kluwer Academic Publications.

4. In a way, every thinker relies on a tradition, whether he or she adopts it or rejects it. The Indian situation differs from the pre-Hellenistic tradition in that this reliance is defined within the institution of the teacher-disciple relationship through which the tradition evolves. The idea in such a tradition is less to find the truth than to defend the truth that already has been found. This is not unlike some of the Hellenistic traditions, the Epicureans in particular.

5. M. Fishbane, "Inner Biblical Exegesis" in G. Hartman and S. Budick, eds., *Midrash and Literature* (New Haven, Conn.: Yale University Press, 1986), pp. 19–37, 19.

6. G. Scholem, *Messianic Ideas in Judaism* (New York: Shocken Books, 1971), p. 287.

7. The increasing role of textbooks with their endless fine-tuning of definitions in later Tibetan tradition is certainly an illustration of the excesses of scholasticism. Nevertheless, the tradition has managed to avoid becoming overwhelmed by such derivative activities, thus keeping alive the spirit of inquiry among its students. This is especially the case in the study of logic and epistemology where the role of textbooks is extremely limited.

8. Hans-Georg Gadamer, *Truth and Method* (New York: Crossroad, 1975), p. 264.

9. Alasdair MacIntyre, *Whose Justice, Which Rationality* (Notre Dame, Ind.: University of Notre Dame, 1988), p. 367.

10. J. Z. Smith, *Map Is Not Territory* (Leiden: Brill, 1978), pp. 240–64, 240.

11. See F. Boas, "The Limitations of the Comparative Method of Anthropology," 1896, reprinted in F. Boas, *Race, Language, and Culture* (New York: Macmillan, 1940), quoted in Smith, ibid., p. 262.

12. J. Z. Smith, *Imagining Religion* (Chicago: University of Chicago Press, 1982), p. 35.

13. Wilhelm Dilthey, *Gesammelte Schriften* (Stuttgart, 1926, 1958), VII.225. quoted in Smith, ibid., p. 242.

14. Smith, ibid., p. 35.

15. What Gadamer describes as *Vorurteile*, prejudgments and prejudices (*Truth and Method*, pp. 245–53).

16. I do not think that comparison needs to be symmetrical across cultures, for it is manifold, working at several levels. Nevertheless, at the most advanced stage, comparison becomes symmetrical and involves the recognition of similarities and differences in both directions.

Introduction II. Dharmakīrti's Tradition in India and Tibet

1. As usual in ancient India, Dignāga's exact dates are not possible to establish. Vidyabushana gives 450–520 C.E. but Hattori puts Dignāga later (480–540). S. Vidyabhusana, *A History of Indian Logic* (Delhi: Motilal Banarsidas, 1978), p. 270; M. Hattori, *Dignāga, on Perception* (Cambridge, Mass.: Harvard University Press, 1968), p. 4.

2. Here again the dates are fairly uncertain. The traditional account is that Dharmakīrti was the disciple of Dignāga's disciple Iśvarasena and tends to emphasize the proximity of the two authors. Several modern scholars tend, on the contrary to emphasize their distance. Frauwallner gives the usually accepted dates of 600–660 C.E. for Dharmakīrti. E. Frauwallner, "Landmarks in the History of Indian Logic," *Wiener Zeitschrift für die Kunde Süd und Ostasiens* 5 (1961): 137–41. Based on a cross reference in Bhavya, Lindtner, however, puts Dharmakīrti, disciple of Dharmapala (530–561) and Iśvarasena (480–540), significantly earlier (530–600), thus lending some support to the traditional account. C. Lindtner, "Apropos Dharmakīrti, Two Works and New Dates," *Acta Orientalia* (1980): 27–37.

3. R. Rorty, *Philosophy and the Mirror of Nature* (Princeton, N.J.: Princeton University Press, 1979).

4. J. Lukasiewicz, *Aristotle's Syllogistic from the Standpoint of Modern Formal Logic* (Oxford: Clarendon Press, 1959), p. 14. Also see I. M. Bochensky, *History of Formal Logic* (New York: Chelsea, 1961), p. 3.

5. R. Carnap, *The Logical Syntax of Language* (New York: Harcourt, 1959), p. 258.

6. Even in the discussions of logical topics, Indian thinkers remain more concerned with practical understanding than with formal validity. This concern is noticeable in their presentation of formal arguments. In fact, Indian formal arguments are not axiomatic reasonings. They are more accurately compared to systematic rhetorical arguments. This comparison better accounts for the vital part played by the example in Indian formal argument. Examples are not intended to provide axiomatic proof but to support a rhetorical argument. See T. Tillemans, "Sur le Pararthanumana en Logique Bouddhique," *Asiatiche Studien* 38, no. 2 (1984): 73–99, in which the author shows the fundamental difference between Buddhist formal arguments and Aristotelian syllogisms, emphasizing that the first is primarily not a deductive structure whereas the second indubitably is. Throughout this work I have avoided using the word *syllogism* in reference to the type of systematized rhetorical arguments used by Indian and Tibetan thinkers to avoid the confusion with Aristotelian syllogistic.

7. I am following the helpful schema suggested by R. Jackson, *Is Enlightenment Possible?* (Ithaca, N. Y.: Snow Lion, 1993).

8. See K. Battacharya, *The Dialectical Method of Nāgārjuna* (Delhi: Motilal, 1978, 1986).

9. This work will not examine in detail the nature and implications of the Yogācāra view, sometimes called *Cittamātra (sems tsam)* or *Mind-Only*. Modern scholars have tried to come to terms with this difficult topic. One interpretation is that this system is idealist. Another view is that this is a misinterpretation of a philosophy that emphasizes the mind dependency of perceptual elements but remains neutral as far as the status of external objects is concerned. I have not seen anything in the Tibetan tradition supporting the latter interpretation. As we will see in Book II, Sa-gya thinkers differentiate Cittamātra, which accepts the reality of ordinary mind, and Yogācāra, which accepts as real only the mind in its purity (the perfected nature, *pariniṣpanna, yongs grub*). Ge-luk thinkers reject this difference and assimilate these two views. Both groups, however, agree that both Yogācāra and Cittamātra philosophies are idealist. Therefore, throughout this work I have assumed that both Yogācāra and Mind-Only (whether they are the same or not) are idealist. In most sections, I use *Yogācāra* and *Mind-Only* without distinguishing them. For an analysis of the Ge-luk view of Mind-Only, see R. Thurman, *Tsong Khapa's Speech of Gold in the Essence of True Eloquence* (Princeton, N.J.: Princeton University Press, 1984). For a Sa-gya view, see van der Kuijp, *Contributions to the Development of Tibetan Epistemology* (Weisbaden: Franz Steiner, 1983). For the view of those who argue against the idealist interpretation, see A. Wayman, "Yogācāra and the Buddhist Logicians," *Journal of the International Association of Buddhist Studies* 2 (1979): 65–78; J. Willis, *On Knowing Reality* (New York: Columbia University Press, 1979); Y. Ueda, "Two Main Streams of Thought in Yogācāra Philosophy," *Philosophy East and West* 17 (1967): 155–65; B. C. Hall, "The Meaning of *Vijāpti* in Vasubandhu's Concept of Mind," *Journal of the International Association of Buddhist Studies* 9, no. 1 (1986): 7–23. An important middle view based on historical observations is provided by L. Schmithausen, "On the Problem of the Relation of Spiritual Practice and Philosophical Theory in Buddhism," in *German Scholars on India* (Bombay: Nachiketa, 1976).

10. The term is a part of the doxographical distinction between four schools, which is a later attempt by Indian and Tibetan commentators to bring order into the jungle of conflicting ideas in the commentarial literature. As such, this scheme is simplificatory and reductive. Hence, its applicability is limited. In particular, its retrospective application to an earlier thinker such as Dharmakīrti is problematic. Doxographical distinctions should be taken less as historical facts than as providing an interpretive framework in which the views of individual thinkers can be assessed. This schemata has narrow limitations but also some of the possibilities that have been well used by Tibetan thinkers. My usage of this schema is meant to capture the distinctions made by these thinkers and not as a critical analysis of the values of the tenet approach. Because I deal with the secondary literature, which assumes these distinctions, I will ignore the problems raised by doxographical considerations and assume their validity and applicability. For an analysis of the Tibetan doxographical literature, see Katsumi Mimaki, *Le Chapitre du Blo gsal grub mtha' sur les Sautrāntika (Présentation et édition)* (Kyoto: Zinbun Kagaku Kenkyusyo, 1979); *Le Chapitre du Blo gsal grub mtha' sur les Sautrāntika (Un essai de traduction)* (Kyoto: Zinbun Kagaku Kenkyusyo, 1980); and *Blo gsal grub mtha'* (Kyoto: Zinbun Kagaku Kenkyusyo, 1982). For a Ge-luk view of the topic, see Paul Jeffrey Hopkins and Geshe Lhundup Sopa, *Cutting Through Appearances: Theory and Practice of Tibetan Buddhism* (Ithaca, N.Y: Snow Lion, 1989).

11. M. D. Eckel, *Jñānagarbha's Commentary on the Distinction Between the Two Truths* (Albany: SUNY Press, 1987), p. 52.

12. With important transformations by Cha-ba (*phwya pa chos kyi seng ge*, 1182–1251). See later.

13. A translation of this chapter is found in M. Nagatomi, "A Study of Dharmakīrti's *Pramāṇavārttka*" (Ph.D., Harvard University, 1957) as well as in T. Vetter, "Der Buddha und Seine Lehre in Dharmakīrtis Pramāṇavārttika," in *Wiener Studien zur Tibetologie und Buddhismuskunde* 12 (1984), which examines verses 146.c–287.

14. Originally, the word may have designated a group of Buddhist thinkers who rejected the Vaibhāṣika reliance on Abhidharma. There is considerable disagreement, however, between scholars on the identification of this group. A. Bareau asserts that this school is a small and relatively unknown Hinayāna school that defends the positions articulated by Vasubandhu in his *Auto-Commentary on the Treasury of Manifest Knowledge* (*abhidharmakośabhāṣya, chos mgon pa'i mdzod kyi bshad pa*, P:5591, D: 4090). See *Les Sectes Bouddhiques du Petit Véhicule* (Paris: Ecole Française d'Extrême-Orient, 1955). S. Mookerjee, on the contrary, argues that the Sautrāntikas form an independent school that represents a transition between Hinayāna and Mahāyāna in *The Buddhist Philosophy of Universal Flux* (Delhi: Motilal Banarsidas, 1935, 1980). Similarly, Hattori sees this system defended by Śrīlāta in his *Vibhāṣā* as a bridge between the Sarvāstivāda and the Yogācāra schools. M. Hattori, "Realism and the Philosophy of Consciousness-Only," *The Eastern Buddhist* 21, no. 1 (1988): 41. The Ge-luk position represents in a way a compromise between these two views in an attempt to reconcile the conflicting evidence concerning the Sautrāntika school.

15. Ge-luk thinkers distinguish two subschools within Sautrāntika: those following scriptures *(lung gi rjes 'brang gi mdo sde pa)* and those following reasoning. See A. Klein, *Knowledge and Liberation* (Ithaca, N.Y.: Snow Lion, 1986), pp. 24–25.

16. One should also include in this tradition Karṇakagomin, whose work is extant in Sanskrit but has not been translated into Tibetan. This work, however, seems merely to restate Śākyabuddhi's explanations. See E. Steinkellner, "Miszellen zur erketnntnistheorisch-logischen Schule des Buddhismus I. zur Datierung Karnakagomin's," *Wiener Zeitschrift für die Kunde Südasiens* 23 (1979): 141–50; and "Philological Remarks on Śākyamati's Pramāṇavārttika," in *Studien zum Jaismus and Buddhismus, Gedenkschrift für Ludwig Alsdorf* (Wiesbaden: Steiner, 1981), pp. 283–95.

17. Stcherbatsky, *Buddhist Logic* (Leningrad, 1930; New York: Dover, 1962), vol. 1, pp. 39–47.

18. Jina (tenth–eleventh centuries C.E.) is Devendrabuddhi's most outspoken critic, accusing him of having inverted the order of the chapters of Dharmakīrti's *Commentary on Valid Cognition*. Stcherbastky, ibid., p. 44. For Jina, the "[Chapter on] Establishment [of Buddha] as Valid" (*pramāṇasiddhi, tshad mar grub pa*, traditionally the second) should be first and the "[Chapter on] Inference for Oneself" (*svārthanumāna, rang don rjes dpag*, traditionally the first) should be third, after the "[Chapter on Perception" (*pratyakṣa, mngon sum*, traditionally the third). In this work, I will follow the traditional order of the chapters, which has also been accepted by Frauwallner and Steinkellner. Although I for the most part use Miyaska's edition, I do not follow his order of chapters, which mirrors Jina's. See E. Frauwallner, "Die Reihenfolge und Entstehung der Werke Dharmakīrti's," in Kleine Schriften (Wiesbaden: Steiner, 1982), pp. 677–89; and E. Steinkellner, *Verse-Index of Dharmakīrti's Works* (Vienna: Arbeitkreis für Tibetsische and Buddhistische Studien, 1977).

19. Chief among them is Jītari (but also Mokṣākaragupta). See K. Shirasaki, "The Sugatamatavibhaṅgabhāsya of Jītari," *Bulletin of Kobe Women's University* 17, no. 1 (1984): 77–107. Jītari's case rests on an analysis of stanzas 4, 208–210, and 359 of the "Chapter on Perception" of Dharmakīrti's *Commentary*. Jītari's interpretation of the first passage parallels that of Ravigupta, who seems the only commentator to interpret this passage in a Madhyamaka way. Stanzas 208–210 are taken in a similar way by Prajñākaragupta and his commentators, whereas 359 is based on Śāntarakṣita, who, nevertheless, does not claim Dharmakīrti to be a Mādhyamika. See E. Steinkellner, "Is Dharmakīrti a Mādhyamika?" in D. S. Ruegg and L. Schmitthausen, *Earliest Buddhism and Madhyamaka* (Leiden: Brill, 1990), pp. 72–90.

20. chos grags chos mchog la sogs pas/ gzhung mang byas pa ji lta bu/ mu stegs rgol ba bzlog pa'i phyir/ mkhas pa rnams kyis byas pa yin// de bas don dam bsgom pa la/ tshad mas dgos pa med do zhes/ bdag gis gzhan du bkod pa na/ re zhig 'dir ni brjod mi dgos// Atiśa, *The Lamp of the Path to Enlightenment and Its Explanation (byang chub lam gyi sgron me dan de'i bka' 'grel*, Dharamsala: Council of Religious Affairs, 1969), 193.7–12.

21. We will examine later the debates among Tibetan thinkers about the religious significance or lack thereof of Dharmakīrti's system.

22. Earlier in the century, translations had been done by Sha-wa Lo-dza-wa Seng-ge-gyel-tsen *(zhwa ba lo tsā ba seng ge rgyal mtshan)* in collaboration with Vasudhararakṣita and by Ma Lo-dza-wa Ge-way Lo-drö *(rmā lo tsā ba dge ba'i blo gros)* in collaboration with Subhūtiśrīśānti. E. G. Smith, Introduction to *Tshad ma rigs gter gyi 'grel ba'i rnam bshad rigs lam gsal ba'i nyi ma* (Gangtok: Sonam Kazi, 1970), pp. 1–12, 5.

23. The monastery of Sang-pu was the main center of scholarly activities for several centuries from Ngok onward. It later degenerated and was replaced by Ge-luk monastic universities such as Dra-shi-hlun-bo in the Tsang province of western Tibet and the three Seats [of Learning] *(gdan sa gsum)* of Ga-den, Dre-bung, and Se-ra in central Tibet. In more recent times, the study of Dharmakīrti's tradition was not undertaken in these monasteries but in Jang near Lhasa. There the monks from the three Seats met during winter and debated Dharmakīrti's works at length. This session acquired increasing prestige and completely superseded Sang-pu. A proverb indicates this quite well: "At Jang, one becomes learned, at Sang-pu, one begs food" *(jang la mkhas pa sbyang gsang phu la do blang)* in H. Stoddard, *Le Mendiant de L'Amdo* (Paris: Société d'Ethnographie, 1985), p. 151.

24. Kuijp, *Contributions*, pp. 31–34 and D. Jackson, "Biography of rNgog Lo-tsā-ba," in *Tibetan Studies* (Oslo: Institute for Comparative Studies, 1994), vol. 1, pp. 372–87.

25. Kuijp describes Cha-ba as a nonsectarian thinker associated mostly with the Ga-dam-ba. "Phya-pa Chos-kyi-seng-ge's Impact on Tibetan Epistemological Theory," *Journal of Indian Philosophy* 5 (1978): 355–69, 357.

26. Kuijp reports the existence of three summaries, among which the middling is the *Clearing*, which van der Kuijp describes as "the first indigeneous Tibetan text on logic and epistemology" (ibid., p. 357).

27. Since the Collected Topics fulfill an introductory purpose, they are probably more restricted in scope than the summaries, which were not only introductions but the main textbooks used in logico-epistemological studies in Tibet. Sa-paṇ's *Treasure* partially follows the expository order of the Summaries.

28. Whereas a formal argument attempts to prove a thesis, Cha-ba's statement of consequence merely draws the consequences from previous statements. It is used in debates with the aim of refuting an opponent by inducing a self-contradiction. Hence, it often takes the form of reductio ad absurdum, but does not necessarily do so. Consequently, the valid-

ity of a consequence is to be appraised differently from that of a formal argument. Whereas the latter is to be judged in terms of truth conditions, the former is to be appraised partly in terms of deductive correctness and partly in terms of whether it successfully undermines the opponent's position. A correct consequence according to Cha-ba's tradition does not prove anything but merely induces one's opponents into contradicting a previous statement. Formally, the consequence is distinguished by the use of the formula "it follows because" *(thal phyir)* as opposed to the "syllogistic" formula "it is because" *(te phyir).* See M. Goldberg, "Entity and Antinomy in Tibetan Bsdus grwa Logic I and II," *Journal of Indian Philosophy* 13 (1985): 153–99 and 273–304; T. Tillemans, "Formal and Semantic Aspects on Tibetan Buddhist Debate Logic," *Journal of Indian Philosophy* 17 (1989): 265–97.

29. For a history of the Sa-gya school, see Chogay Trichen, *The History of the Sakya Tradition* (Bristol: Ganesha Press, 1983).

30. *Differentiation of the Three Vows (ldom gsum rab byed),* in The Complete Works of the Great Sa-skya Masters (Tokyo: Toyo Bunko, 1968–69), vol. 5, pp. 297.1.1–323.2.6.

31. Jackson, *Entrance,* I.134. Dharmakīrti. *Commentary on Valid Cognition (pramāṇavārttika-kārikā, tshad ma rnam 'grel),* ed. Y. Miyasaka (Sanskrit-Tibetan), *Acta Indologica* 2 (1971–72). Dharmakīrti, *Ascertainment of Valid Cognition (pramāṇa-viniścaya, tshad ma rnam par nges pa),* D: 4211.

32. In *The Complete Works of the Great Masters of the Sa sKya Sect* (Tokyo: Toyo Bunko, 1968), vol. 5, pp. 155.1.1–167.1.6.

33. Such an attitude is frequent among modern Tibetans, who would not dare show disrespect for an important figure in their society but who might "interpret" his or her words rather liberally.

34. Jackson, *Entrance,* vol. 1, p. 137.

35. Ibid., pp. 138, 158.

36. shes ldan rnams 'di dag gi don phyin ci ma log par rtogs nas smra ba nyid ni deng sang kha ba can 'di na kho bo tsam stel/ Yak-dön-sang-gyay-bel, *Radiating a Thousand Lights, [a Commentary] Revealing the Suchness of [Sa-paṇ's] Treasure on the Science of Valid Cognition, a Commentary on the Thought of the Seven Treatises [of Logic] (sde bdun gyi dgongs 'grel tshad ma rigs pa'i gter gyi de kho na nyid gsal bar byed pa rigs pa'i 'od stong 'phro ba,* n.d.*),* p. 68.5–.6.

37. Sa-gya Paṇḍita *(sa skya paṇḍita), Auto-Commentary to the Treasure on the Science of Valid Cognition (tshad ma rigs gter rang 'grel),* in *The Complete Works of the Great Masters of the Sa sKya Sect* (Tokyo: Toyo Bunko, 1968), vol. 5, pp. 167.3.1–264.2.6.

38. Śākya Chok-den, *The Presentation of the Turning of the Wheel* (*chos kyi 'khor lo bskor ba'i rnam bzhag,* in *Collected Works*) (Thimphu, Bhutan: Kunzang Topgey, 1971), vol. 16, pp. 457–82, 469.6. Quoted in Jackson, *Entrance,* pp. 134, 157.

39. We will see this later when analyzing Sa-paṇ's critique of Tibetan epistemology.

40. Kay-drup, *Ornament of the Seven Treatises Clearing Mental Obscurity (tshad ma sde bdun gyi rgyan yid kyi mun sel),* Collected Works vol. 10 (Lhasa: Zhöl blocks, 1897; New Delhi: Guru Deva, 1982).

41. For the outline of the *Treasure,* see Jackson, *Entrance,* vol. 1, pp. 131–32.

42. Gyel-tsap, *Essence of Good Sayings, an Explanation of* [*Sa-paṇ's*] *Treasure on the Science of Valid Cognition* (*tshad ma rigs pa'i gter gyi rnam bshad legs par bshad pa'i snying po, bkra shis 'khyil,* n.d.). This text is not included in Gyel-tsap's collected works and one may wonder whether its attribution to Gyel-tsap is authentic. As I have argued elsewhere, however, I think this is not a sufficient reason to doubt this attribution. See the Introduction to *rGyal tshap's Rigs gter rnam bshad* (Kyoto: Biblia Tibetica,

1993). As I argue later, the philosophical content of this work is in accordance with the Ge-luk views on the topic. Moreover, this work was quoted by Gung-tang Jam-bel-yang (*gung thang 'jam dpal dbyangs*, 1762–1823), *A Ford for the Wise: An Explanation of the Difficult Topics of "Mind and Basis-of-All" (yid dang kun gzhi'i dka' gnas rnam par bshad pa mkhas pa'i 'jug ngog*, Collected Works (New Delhi: Ngawang Gelek, 1972), vol. 2, p. 38.b.2 in J. Wilson, "The Meaning of Mind in the Mahāyāna Buddhist Philosophy of Mind-Only (cittamatra): A Study of of a Presentation by the Tibetan Scholar Gung-tang Jam-bay-yang" (Ph.D. dissertation, University of Virginia, 1991), p. 670. Finally, this work was mentioned by A-gu Shay-rap-gya-tso (*a ku shes rab rgya mtsho*, 1803–1875) as having been quoted by Jam-yang-shay-ba (*'jam dbyangs bzhad pa*, 1648–1722): "rgyal tshab rje'i rigs gter dar ḍika legs bshad snying po grub mtha' chen mor lung drang." A-gu Shay-rap-gya-tso, *A List of Some Rare Books (dpe rgyun dkon pa'i 'ga' zhig gi tho yig)* in L. Chandra, ed., *Materials for a History of Tibetan Literature* (Kyoto: Rinsen, 1981), pp. 637–735, 675. Hence, I think that it is reasonable to tentatively assume that the attribution of this work is accurate. This commentary has probably not been included in the Collected Works because it focuses on a text, which is outside of Dzong-ka-ba's tradition.

43. Gyel-tsap, ibid., 2.b.2.

44. In the colophon, Gyel-tsap acknowledges his debt to Ren-da-wa, whose many teachings on Sa-paṇ's *Treasure* have enabled him to write his book (*Essence*, p. 151.a.1–.2). Interestingly enough, Gyel-tsap does not mention Dzong-ka-ba's name in this work written at the end of his life, a difference from his *Explanation*, where Dzong-ka-ba's authority is invoked several times.

45. Jackson, *Entrance*, vol. 1, p. 163.

46. Śākya Chok-den, *Commentary on the Entrance Gate for the Wise (mkhas pa'i 'jug pa'i rnam bshad)*, Collected Works (Thimphu, Bhutan: Kunzang Topgey, 1971), vol. 24, pp. 67–102.7, quoted in Jackson, ibid., vol. 1, p. 146.

47. Dor-jay Gyel-bo *(rdo rje rgyal po)*, ed., *Treasure on the Science of Valid Cognition (tshad ma rigs gter)* (Beijing: People's Printing Press, 1988) lists all the discrepancies between the root text and the *Auto-commentary*. They are mostly minor differences that do not affect the overall meaning of the text, at least regarding the topics covered in this book. For an example, see chapter 24.

48. 'grel ba 'di la bdag gi bla ma mkhas pa kha cig/ cha 'di rang 'grel min zhes bzhag par dka' gsungs yang/ mi shes pa kha cig gis rtsa ba dang 'gal ba skabs 'gar cung zad bcug pa yod par mngon pas/ nor ba mi 'dor du mi rung ba rnams dor la 'grel ba dang mthun par byas so/ (Gyel-tsap, *Essence*, 150.a.2–.3).

49. Gyel-tsap's clearest attempts to establish a realist interpretation of Sa-paṇ's *Treasure* are found in *Essence*, 23.a.6, 25.a.1–26.a.1 (see chapters 8 and 9) and 6.a.3 (see chapter 5).

50. For example, I will not refer extensively to the Seventh Kar-ma-ba Chö-drak-gya-tso (*chos grags rgya mtsho*, 1454–1506). I occasionally refer to his work of considerable breadth to supplement my discussion but do not systematically explain his views, which are very close to Sa-paṇ's.

51. I introduce other Sa-gya thinkers in reference to Go-ram-ba or Śākya Chok-den, either as further explaining their ideas (as, for example, Ngak-chö [*ngag dbang chos grags*, 1572–1641] and Lo Ken-chen [*blo mkhan chen bsod nams lhun grub*, 1456–1532]) or as being their sources (like Yak-dön [*g.yag ston sangs rgyas dpal*, 1348–1414] and Rong-dön [*rong ston śākya rgyal mtshan*, 1367–1449]).

52. D. Jackson, *The Early Abbots of 'Phan po Na-lendra* (Vienna: Arbeitkreis für

Tibetische und Buddhistische Studien, 1989), p. 21. For a biography, see Kuijp, *Contributions*, pp. 116–24.

53. See Collected Works, vols. 6, 7, and 13 (Thimphu, Bhutan: Kunzang Tobgey (1975). See also Kuijp, *Contributions*, p. 15.

54. Kuijp, ibid., pp. 13–14, 22, n. 56.

55. Śākya Chok-den, *Defeater of Bad Systems Through the Wheel of Reasoning, an Ornament to the Thought of [Sa-paṇ's] Treasure on the Science of Valid Cognition (tshad ma rigs gter gyi dgongs rgyan rigs pa'i 'khor los lugs ngan pham byed)*, in Collected Works, vols. 9 and 10, (Thimphu, Bhutan: Kunzang Tobgey, 1975).

56. For example, Śākya Chok-den, *The Explanation of the Essential Definitive Points, an Explanation of [Candrakīrti's] Introduction to the Middle Way (dbu ma la 'jug pa'i rnam bshad nges don gnad kyi ṭīkā)*, Collected Works, vol. 5 (Thimphu, Bhutan: Kunzang Tobgey, 1975) composed at the age of forty or forty-one. For the dating of Śākya Chok-den's works, see Kuijp, *Contributions*, p. 17, and T. Tillemans and T. Tomabechi, "Le *dBu ma'i byung tshul* de Śākya mchog-ldan," *Asiatische Studien* 49, no. 4 (1995): 891–918.

57. Śākya Chok-den, *The Dharma Treasury, an Ocean of Scriptures and Reasonings Ascertaining the Middle Way (dbu ma rnam par nges pa'i chos kyi bang mdzod lung dang rigs pa'i rgya mtsho)*, Collected Works, vols. 14 and 15 (Thimphu, Bhutan: Kunzang Tobgey, 1975) written at the age of forty-nine.

58. See chapter 27, where I discuss the role of emptiness-of-other in Buddhist epistemology.

59. The relevant passages are found in *Dharma Treasury*, vol. 2, pp. 221, 448, 452–57, 467, 494–97, 519–20.

60. Śākya Chok-den, *The Ocean of Music [of] the Speech of the Seven Treatises, an Explanation of the Science of Valid Cognition (tshad ma rigs pa'i rnam bshad sde bdun ngag gi rol mtsho)*, Collected Works, vol. 19, (Thimphu, Bhutan: Kunzang Tobgey, 1975).

61. Śākya Chok-den, *The Wish Fulfilling Mountain, a Discussion of the History of Madhyamaka (dbu ma'i byung tshul rnam par bshad pa'i gtam yid bzhin lun po)*, Collected Works, vol. 4 (Thimphu, Bhutan: Kunzang Tobgey, 1975) and *The Extensive Commentary on the Treatise Establishing the Definitive Meaning as One Through Explaining the Distinction Between the Two Traditions of the Great Charioteers (shing rta chen po'i srol gnyis kyi rnam par dbye ba bshad nas nges don gcig tu bsgrub pa'i bstan bcos kyi rgyas 'grel)*, Collected Works, vol. 2, (Thimphu, Bhutan: Kunzang Tobgey, 1975).

62. Śākya Chok-den, *The Luminosity That Clarifies as the Day, the History of the Systems of the Sūtra on Valid Cognition and How Its Treatises Arose (tshad ma'i bstan bcos kyi shin rta'i srol rnams ji ltar 'byung ba'i tshul gtam du bya ba nyin byed snang ba)*, Collected Works, vol. 19, (Thimphu, Bhutan: Kunzang Tobgey, 1975).

63. Tāranātha, *Twenty-One Profound Topics (zab don nyer gcig pa)*. For a short and easy overview of the significance of the emptiness-of-other view see Tsultrim Gyamtso, *Progressive Stages of Meditation on Emptiness* (Oxford: Longchen, 1986, 1988). For a more complete view, see D. S. Ruegg, *Le Traité du Tathāgatagarbha de Bu ston rin chen grub* (Paris: Ecole Française d'Extrême-Orient, 1973); D. S. Ruegg, "The Jo naṅ pas: A School of Buddhist Ontologists According to the *Grub mtha' śel gyi me long*," *Journal of the American Oriental Society* 83 (1963): 73–91; S. Hookham, *The Buddha Within* (Albany: SUNY Press, 1991).

64. It is revealing that several monasteries do not have complete textbooks on epistemology. Paṇ-chen Sö-nam-drak-ba (*paṇ chen bsod nams grags pa*, 1478–1554) is the only textbook author who has provided a complete explanation of Dharmakīrti's *Commentary*.

65. The reliance on textbooks varies according to the domain of study. In the study of Maitreya's *Ornament* many students put a great deal of reliance on textbooks. This seems to be due to at least two factors: the enormous complication of the topic and that this text comes rather early in the studies. In the study of Mādhyamika philosophy, students put less emphasis on textbooks and attempt to concentrate on Dzong-ka-ba's treatises. Textbooks, however, remain an important though limited source of understanding. The study of logic and epistemology is usually conducted outside of the monastery. Up to 1959, special sessions were held in Jang near Lhasa, during which the monks of the different monasteries debated on Dharmakīrti's texts and ideas. In such a gathering, the textbooks could be used only as secondary sources. The main source was usually Gyel-tsap's *Faultlessly Revealing the Path to Liberation, [a Complete Commentary on Dharmakīrti's] Commentary on Valid Cognition (rnam 'grel thar lam gsal byed)* (Banaras: Pleasure of Elegant Sayings Press, 1974–75). This text has been accepted by all as the most authoritative source. Although monks are often supposed to adopt the views defended in their textbooks, they do this on the basis of Gyel-tsap's, Kay-drup's, or Ge-dün-drup's texts. Accordingly, these texts are recognized as the primary authorities and are studied with great care. Some students even memorize entire sections of these texts. Finally, in the domain of Vinaya and Abhidharma, the reliance on textbooks is a minor factor. This is so because it is recognized that the dialectical style of these manuals is inappropriate to these topics in which textual investigation is more important than logical acumen. These texts require patient effort of exegesis rather than sharp dialectical investigation.

66. Here, a brief mention of one of my teachers, the late Nyi-ma Gyel-tsen *(nyi ma rgyal tshan)*, is appropriate. He was considered a great authority in the field of Madhyamaka and epistemology in the Ge-luk tradition. He had very little interest in textbooks and showed annoyance when a student would put a question based on the textbook of his monastery (Dre-bung Lo-se-ling). On the contrary, he would be delighted by questions relating to Indian texts or the works of Dzong-ka-ba and his disciples. His preference, however, was for questions (even the most stupid ones) based on personal reflections.

67. Ge-dün-drup, most often follows Gyel-tsap's explanations. His work, however, is useful because it explains rather clearly what Gyel-tsap means in his more terse commentaries.

68. The reason for this is that most of these writings are lecture notes taken by his disciples. The tradition considers that these notes cannot be taken always to reflect the author's views because they were written by somebody else (usually Gyel-tsap). The title of one of these works illustrates this: Dzong-ka-ba, *Extensive Memorandum on Valid Cognition [as] Heard by the Lord of the Dharma Gyel-tsap from the Lord [Dzong-ka-ba] (rgyal tshab chos rjes rje'i drung du gsan pa'i tshad ma'i brjed byang chen mo)*, in *Collected Works*, vol. 14 (Delhi: Ngawang Gelek, 1975–79).

69. Jang-gya also associates Gyel-tsap with Dharmottara and Kay-drup with Devendrabuddhi (*Presentation*, 213.13–.16).

70. Because his commentary on Sa-paṇ's *Treasure* refers to his two major works on Dharmakīrti's *Commentary* and *Ascertainment* (*Essence*, 9.a.3 and 20.b.6), this work must have been completed at the end of Gyel-tsap 's life. It is not impossible that it represents an upgraded version of an earlier work.

71. R. Thurman, *Life and Teaching of Tsong Khapa* (Dharamsala: Library of Tibetan Works and Archives, 1982), p. 8.

72. Tshul khrims skal bzang reports the special reliance that Ren-da-wa put on the study of Prajñākaragupta's *Ornament* in his "A History of Logical Studies in Tibet" *(tshad*

ma'i lo rgyus dar ṭika mdzes rgyan), Saṃbhāsā 7 (1986): 55–96, 81. We will see in Chapter 10 the role of Sa-paṇ's direct disciple U-yuk-ba-rik-bay-seng-gay (*u yug pa rigs pa'i seng ge*, ?–1253), who, contrary to his master, defended a realist interpretation of Dharmakīrti.

73. Tshul khrims skal bzang, ibid., pp. 80–81.

74. Gyel-tsap, *Revealing*, II.9.1.

75. Paṇ-chen Sö-nam-drak-ba disagrees with this description, for he holds that the overall intention of the text is Yogācāra with Sautrāntika passages. See *A Word Commentary Completely Revealing the Thought of the Extensive Treatise the Commentary on Prime Cognition (rgyas pa'i bstan bcos tshad ma rnam 'grel gyi bka' 'grel dgongs pa rab gsal)*, in *Collected Works*, vols. 1 and 2 (Mundgod: Loling Printing Press, 1989), vol. 2, 9.a.5. Among the Ge-luk textbooks, I have tended to use Paṇ-chen Sö-nam-drak-ba's text, which covers all four chapters of Dharmakīrti's *Commentary* and thus is the most extensive Ge-luk textbook in the field of logic and epistemology. I have rarely referred to Se-ra Jay-dzün-ba's (*se rwa rje btsun pa*, 1469–1544) text, which does not differ substantially from Paṇ-chen Sö-nam-drak-ba's on most topics. I have also rarely included the views reflected by the textbooks from Go-mang monastery, for they have been well studied by Klein. In general, however, I do not rely very much on textbooks but focus on the works of Gyel-tsap, Kaydrup, and Ge-dün-drup, the seminal thinkers of the Ge-luk tradition of logic and epistemology.

76. Steinkellner adopts an essentially similar point of view; see "Is Dharmakīrti a Mādhyamika?" p. 76.

77. As we will notice, historically the Sa-gya tradition has presented a much greater diversity of opinions than the Ge-luk tradition. This still may be true, although much less so due the increasing rigidity that divides the schools of Tibetan Buddhism (see later).

78. Gö Lo-dza-wa Shö-nu-bel (*gos lo tsā ba gzhon nu dpal*, 1392–1481) criticiced Bu-dön for not including the Nying-ma tantras in the canon. See H. G. Smith, Preface to *The Autobiographical Reminiscences of Ngag-dBang-dPal-bZang* (Gangtok: Sonam Kazi, n.d.), p. 5. For an account of Bu-dön's view, see G. Roerich, trans., *The Blue Annals* (Delhi: Motilal, 1949, 1979), p. 417.

79. Thurman, *Life*, p. 26.

80. According to Kenpo Gyatso, abbot of the Sa-gya monastery of Phurwala.

81. The grave difficulties experienced by Na-len-dra seem to have been another example illustrating the fate of monasteries in these times of crisis. Jackson, *The Early Abbots*, pp. 18–28.

82. T. Shakaba, *Tibet, a Political History* (New York: Potala, 1984), p. 88.

83. Ibid., p. 110.

84. E. G. Smith, "Introduction," *Kongtrul's Encyclopedia of Indo-Tibetan Culture* (New Delhi: International Academy of Indian Culture, 1970), p. 17.

85. Jackson, *The Early Abbots*, p. 29.

86. The Nying-ma school seems to have avoided such a fate. It thrived during this period, gaining the favor of the Fifth Dalai Lama, perhaps partly because he had connections with this school through his family.

87. A-gu Shay-rap-gya-tso, *A List of Some Rare Books*, in L. Chandra, ed., *Materials*, p. 674.

88. Several Jo-nang-ba texts, which had been sealed in the library of the Pun-tsok-ling *(phun tshogs gling)* monastery, were reprinted after 1874 with the permission of the Lhasa authorities. E. G. Smith, "Introduction," *The Autobiography and Diaries of Si-tu Paṇ-Chen* (New Delhi: International Academy of Indian Culture, 1968), pp. 1–17, 8. Go-ram-

ba's works were reassembled with great difficulty at the beginning of this century, although there is still some doubt as to whether all his works have been included. Śākya Chok-den's works were only recently found in Bhutan.

89. Jang-gya, *Clear Explanation of the Presentation of Tenets, a Beautiful Ornament of the Mount Meru of the Doctrine of the Muni (grub mtha' rnam par bzhag pa gsal bar bshad pa thub bstan lhun po'i mrzes rgyan).* Benares: Pleasure of Elegant Sayings Press, 1970), 104.14–.18, in A. Klein, *Knowing, Naming, and Negation* (Ithaca, N.Y.: Snow Lion, 1991), p. 140.

90. Some might be surprised by the inclusion of Tu-gen among the less sectarian Ge-luk scholars. His doxographical presentation of the tenets of the other Tibetan schools is certainly heavily tilted toward the Ge-luk viewpoint. His defense of the validity of the *Treasures (gter ma)* against his own teacher Sum-ba Ken-po Ye-shay-bel-jor (*sum pa mkhan po ye shes dpal 'byor*, 1702–1788), however, reflects a more open aspect of his personality. See M. Kapstein, "The Purificatory Gem and Its Cleansing," *History of Religions* 28, no. 3 (1989): 217–44.

91. See S. Ozment, *The Age of Reform* (New Haven, Conn.: Yale University Press, 1980), pp. 54, 60–63; and D. Knowles, *The Evolution of Medieval Thought* (New York: Vintage, 1962), p. 111.

92. The great debate that took place at Sam-ye *(bsam yas)* in the second half of the eighth century between the Indian party around Kamalaśīla and the Chinese party of Ho-shang Mo-ho-yen is one later example of such a public debate with important political consequences. See D. S. Ruegg, *Buddha-Nature, Mind and the Problem of Gradualism in a Comparative Perspective* (London: School of Oriental and African Studies, 1989), P. Demieville, *Le Concile de Lhasa* (Paris: College de France, 1952, 1987), and G. Tucci, *The Religions of Tibet* (London: Routledge and Kegan, 1980).

Chapter 1. Ontology and Categories

1. Throughout this work I use the word "valid" to mean "correct" or "right" in accordance with *Webster's Ninth New Collegiate Dictionary*: "Valid implies being supported by objective truth . . ." This colloquial use should not be confused with the more technical distinction made by modern logicians who distinguish validity from soundness. Similarly, I use "cognition" less to refer to a process through which knowledge is acquired than to imply a momentary mental state that apprehends an object. In doing so, I am following the current scholarly usage in Buddhist studies. I reserve "correct cognition" to translate *samyagjñāna (yang dag pa'i shes pa).*

2. See Chapter 16.

3. B. K. Matilal, *Perception* (Oxford: Clarendon, 1986), p. 35.

4. Hence, it will come as no surprise that many of the Western philosophers I involve in a comparison with Indian thinkers belong either to the Anglo-Saxon current of analytical philosophy or at least favor such an approach.

5. I have not used *direct perception* to translate *pratyakṣa, mngon sum* because this translation suggests a direct realist view of perception according to which consciousness directly apprehends external objects. Since I describe most Buddhist epistemologists (a shorthand for the members of Dignāga's and Dharmakīrti's tradition) as representationalists or phenomenalists (see chapter 19), I have used the more neutral *perception*, reserving the examination of whether perception is direct or not for the chapters on perception.

6. This division between ontology and philosophy of language is heuristic and artificial, for it is not possible to separate completely the two domains. Accordingly, my discussion in Part II, which will focus on the linguistic relevance of universals, will have to come back again and again to the ontological implications.

7. W. V. Quine, *From a Logical Point of View* (Cambridge, Mass.: Harvard University Press, 1953), p. 14.

8. R. Carnap, "Empiricism, Semantics, and Ontology" in P. Benacerraf and H. Putnam, eds., *Philosophy of Mathematics* (Englewood, N.J. : Prentice-Hall, 1964), pp. 223–48.

9. Quine, *From a Logical Point of View*, p. 13.

10. The reader should keep in mind that our discussions of Indian philosophy are just meant to contextualize Dharmakīrti. Hence, we will not attend to the full range of developments but just those relevant to the ideas of his tradition.

11. E. Frauwallner, "Die Erketnislehre des klassischen Sāṁkhyasystems," in *Kleine Schriften*, pp. 223–78. Larson and Bhattacharya put Vārṣagaṇa between 100 and 300 C.E. J. Larson and R. S. Bhattacharya, *Encyclopedia of Indian Philosophies* (Delhi: Motilal, 1987), vol. 4, p. 15.

12. Nga-wang-bel-den *(ngag dbang dpal ldan), Presentation of Conventional and Ultimate Truths in the Four Systems of Tenets (grub mtha' bzhi'i lugs kyi kun rdzob dang don dam pa'i don rnam par bshad pa)* (Benaras: Pleasure of Elegant Sayings Press, 1964), 56.1–56.2.

13. This school will not receive the treatment that its importance would warrant, as it is only in the process of being understood by modern scholars. Moreover, its links, or lack thereof, with Dignāga and Dharmakīrti still await full analysis. Hence, I have kept mentions of this school to a minimum.

14. S. S. Barlingay, *A Modern Introduction to Indian Logic* (Delhi: National, 1975), p. 5.

15. I often abuse this general term to refer to the many thinkers who follow or are influenced by Dharmakīrti's thought. To talk of Dignāga's or Dharmakīrti's school would be too restrictive, since many Mādhyamikas (in India as well as in Tibet) use Dharmakīrti's ideas when dealing with issues in epistemology, logic, or ontology despite not being members of the school. Since these thinkers are often included in my discussion, I use the suitably vague term of *Buddhist*, which the reader should understand in this context.

16. Jacob Klein thus describes the influence of Aristotelian categories in the West: "It is perhaps an unfortunate, if perhaps not surprising, historical accident that Aristotle's vocabulary acquired immeasurable weight and fetish-like character in its Latin rendering perpetuated in almost all modern tongues. It is perhaps no exaggeration to state that something like three-quarters of all scientific and philosophical terminology is either determined by Aristotle's latinized vocabulary or can be traced back to it" (J. Klein, "Aristotle, an Introduction," pp. 56–57).

17. For further reference, see Barlingay, *Indian Logic;* B. K. Matilal, *Logic, Language and Reality* (Delhi: Motilal, 1985); K. Potter, *Indian Metaphysics and Epistemology* (Princeton, N.J.: Princeton University Press, 1977); D. N. Shastri, *Philosophy of Nyāya-Vaiśeṣika and Its Conflict with the Buddhist Dignaga School* (Delhi: Bharatiya Vidhya Prakashan, 1976); Ganganath Jhā, *The Nyāya-Sūtras of Gauṭama* (Delhi: Motilal, 1912–19, 1984); H. Ui, *Vaiśeshika Philosophy* (Banaras: Chowkhamba, 1962); Wilhelm Halbfass, *On Being and What There Is* (Albany: SUNY Press, 1992).

18. A mode of inquiry that investigates objects on the basis of the way they appear to our prereflective experiences.

19. astitva jñeyatva abhidheyatva/ quoted in Potter, *Indian Metaphysics*, p. 48.

20. This is not even close to a comprehensive list of all possible ways of using the label *realism.* For example, H. Putnam recently offered another meaning of realism. In *Realism with a Human Face,* he opposes realism to Realism, that is, the metaphysical assumption that the entities and properties we perceive in the world exist independent of our perceptual and conceptual activities. Putnam's realism rejects this attempt, holding that reality as we conceive it and our thoughts are mutually coimplicative. *Realism with a Human Face* (Cambridge, Mass.: Harvard University Press, 1990). Similarly, M. Dummett argues against metaphysical realism in his famous "Truth," in *Truth and Other Enigmas* (Cambridge, Mass.: Harvard University Press, 1978), 1–24. Nevertheless, Dummett's understanding of *realism* seems to differ from Putnam's in that it entails a correspondence theory of truth. The reader will have to remember that, in this work, I am using *realism* in a simpler and more classical way to refer to the acceptance of real universals. This is the way in which medieval thinkers and many philosophers since then have understood the term.

21. Quine, *From a Logical Point of View*, p. 74.

22. D. Hume, *A Treatise of Human Nature*, in *The Philosophical Works of David Hume* (London: Longmans, 1886, 1964), p. 536.

23. The Nyāya goes as far as asserting that, since it is a new entity, a woven cloth is heavier than the sum of the weights of the threads. The difference is, however, too small to measure! Shastri, *Philosophy*, p. 128.

24. Ibid., p. 376.

25. Contrary to the most common usage in modern Western philosophy in which subject and predicate are thought to be linguistic entities, I distinguish the subject and predicate (which are the real objects) from the subject expression and predicate expression, which are linguistic items. For a similar usage of these terms, see P. E. Strawson, *Individuals* (London: Meuthen, 1969, 1971).

26. In the Nyāya system, a *dharma* is not always instantiable. For example, qualities *(guṇa)* are always particular characters. Hence, I avoid calling them "properties." For a discussion of the differences between Nyāya uninstantiable *guṇa* and the Western concept of instantiable quality, see Karl Potter, "Are the Vaiśeṣika 'Guṇas' Qualities?" *Philosophy East and West* 4, no. 3 (1954): 259–64; and "More on the Unrepeatability of Guṇas," *Philosophy East and West* 7, nos. 1 and 2 (1957): 57–60. See also Halbfass, *On Being*, pp. 113–38.

27. Shastri, *Philosophy*, p. 139. *Substance* is similarly defined in Western philosophy. Cottingham describes the cluster of properties usually associated with substance: "substance is the enduring subject of change, an essence or nature, the subject of predication, that which has independent existence" (J. Cottingham, *The Rationalists* [Oxford: Oxford University Press, 1988], p. 77).

28. This list of characteristics may surprise one in that one may argue that universals are not really a category since they are the preconditions of category. The Nyāya does not see universals in this way, for it insists on the primacy of concrete substances. Its realism is more empirically minded. It does not put as much emphasis on abstract entities as a Platonist would.

29. Similarly, Grammarians use the concept of substance in ways that partly differ from the Vaiśeṣika ontological approach. For the different meanings of substance, see Matilal, *Logic*, pp. 378–89.

30. Dharmakīrti, *Commentary*, II:84–86.

31. The Navya Nyāya will later concede the point to the Buddhist and hold that an

object possesses its different colors in a nonpervasive manner. This represents a sacrifice of the Old Nyāya view that the qualities of an object, like color and touch, entirely pervade their substance. For, if different qualities reside in different parts of the object, then the object is not one but is an aggregation of different elements as maintained by the Buddhists. Coming after the demise of Buddhism in India, the Navya Nyāya felt less compelled to assert the unity of wholes against Buddhist atomism. See Shastri, *Philosophy*, p. 258.

32. Wholes are posited by the Nyāya to resolve the question of how different parts can be articulated in a single object. It is meant to solve such a question as, Is the jar inhering in the first half the same as the one inhering in the second? The Nyāya answers by saying that when two halves of a jar are put together they create a new unity that cannot be distinguished in terms of parts. For, if the whole were not partless, the question of whether the jar inhering in the first half is the same as that inhering in the second would remain unanswered.

Chapter 2. Dharmakīrti's Ontology

1. See Plato, *Theatetus*, 156–157.c.

2. On the soteriological implications of selflessness, see S. Collins, *Selfless Persons* (Cambridge: Cambridge University Press, 1982), pp. 85–143.

3. Hume, *Treatise*, p. 534.

4. See Louis de la Vallée Poussin, *L'Abhidharmakośa de Vasubandu* (Brussels: Institut Belge Des Hautes Etudes Chinoises, 1971), II:222–38.

5. Ibid., IV:8.

6. This ontology is as close as Dharmakīrti comes to talking about the two truths. He does not refer explicitly to these specifically Buddhist concepts. One possible reason for this silence is that Dharmakīrti (and Dignāga before him) addresses non-Buddhist thinkers such as Naiyāyikas who are not ready to engage in a discussion within a two-tier framework. For them, all things have equal reality, and the Buddhist distinction does not make sense. Among Hindus, only later Vedāntins adopt a two-tier system, apparently under the influence of Buddhism.

7. In another work, *Drop of Logical Reason (hetubindu, gtan tshigs thigs pa)*, P: 5712, 337.a.8–357.a.3., Dharmakīrti proposes another reasoning based on the fact that a thing cannot have contradictory properties. Thus, the seed that is in the granary and is unable to produce a sprout must be accepted as different from the "same" seed later put in the soil and about to germinate. See N. Shah, *Akalaṅka's Criticism of Dharmakīrti's Philosophy* (Ahmedabad: L. D. Institute, 1967), pp. 45–59; and R. Gupta, "The Buddhist Doctrine of Momentariness and Its Presuppostions," *Journal of Indian Philosophy* 8, no. 1 (1980): 47–68.

8. phyis 'byung phyir na rgyu nyid min/ 'bras bu na yang ga la nges// (paścād bhāvān na hetutvaṃ phale 'py ekāntatā kutaḥ//). Dharmakīrti, *Commentary*, I: 33.cd. See also *Commentary*, I: 32.cd. My reading of Dharmakīrti is based on the Tibetan version, Tibetan commentaries (mostly Ge-dün-drup, *Good Sayings on [Dharmakīrti's] Commentary on Valid Cognition [tshad ma rnam 'grel legs par bshad pa]*, *Collected Works*, vol. 5 [Gangtok: Dodrup Lama, 1978–1981]), with reference to the Sanskrit version found in Miyasaka's edition and secondary sources such as S. Mookerjee and H. Nagasaki, *The Pramāṇavārttikam of Dharmakīrti* (Nalanda: Nava Nalanda, 1964), p. 81. I usually refer to whichever commentary or secondary source I use in a particular passage.

9. Dharmakīrti, *Commentary*, I:269.

10. rgyu med phyir na 'jig pa ni/ rang gi ngo bos rjes 'brel nyid/ (ahetutvād vināśasya svabhāvād anubandhitā/). Ibid., I:193.cd.

11. 'o na 'jig pa gang yin zhe na/ bshig pas zhig de dngos med mi 'dod kyi 'on kyang rang gyi rgyu las skad cig gcig skyes nas gnyis pa phan chad du mi sdod pa tsam la 'jig pa zer gyis 'jig pa zhes bya ba'i chos logs pa mi 'dod do/ de'ang rnam 'grel las/ dngos 'jig gzhan las ltos med phyir/ de shes don du sems gyis ni/ de yi tha dad sgro btags nas/ gnas skabs de rgyu med can bshad/ zhes gsungs pas so/ (Sa-paṇ, *Auto-Commentary*, 84.b.6–85.a.1). Quote is from ibid., I:276.

12. 'jig pa zhes bya ba'i sgra de 'jig rgyu bum pa'am shing lta bu dngos po la 'jug zhig nas med pa'ang la 'jug pa la chos kyi grags pas 'jig par bya ba rgyu dngos po'i skabs su rgyu med du gsungs pa ni 'jig pa nyid dngos po yin pas dngos po skyed pa la rgyu gzhan la mi ltos pa la dgongs la zhig nas med pa la 'jig pa 'dogs pa'i skabs su rgyu med ni rgyu gtan med pa la dgongs te 'jig pa de dngos med yin pa'i phyir ro/ (Sa-paṇ, *Auto-Commentary*, 81.b.5–.6).

13. Mimaki, *La Réfutation*, p. 32.

14. 'di ltar gang yod pa'am byas pa de thams cad mi rtag pa ste/ dper na bum pa la sogs pa lta bu'o/ sgra yang yod pa'am byas pa'o/ (Dharmakīrti, *Science of Debate [vadanyaya, rtsod pa'i rigs pa]*, P:5715, 365.a.5–.6; D: 4218, 327.a.1.

15. gang yod de 'jig bum pa bzhin/ sgra yang yod ces rang bzhin rtags/ (Sa-paṇ, *Treasure*, 10.b.6).

16. Buddhist logic differentiates three types of correct evidence: evidence from effect *(kāryahetu, 'bras rtags)*, evidence of identical essence *(svabhāvahetu, rang bzhin gyi rtags yang dag)*, and evidence of nonobservation *(anupalabdhihetu, ma dmigs pa'i rtags)*. See Go-ram-ba, *The Explanation of the Difficult Points of the "Treasure on the Science of Valid Cognition" That Completely Clarifies the Seven Texts (tshad ma'i rigs gter gyi dka' gnas rnam par bshad pa sde bdun rab gsal)*, in the *Complete Works of the Great Masters of the Sa sKya Sect* (Tokyo: Toyo Bunko, 1968), vol. 12:1.1.1–167.3.3 (*Ga*, 1.a–334.a), 49.b; and Gyel-tsap, *Revealing*, I.36.14–48.17 and I:16.18–28.8. See also Mimaki, *La Réfutation*, p. 229.

17. Sa-paṇ, *Auto-Commentary*, 80.b.3–.4. Some Tibetan thinkers have preferred, however, to avoid this formulation and use this fact of being produced as a reason. This choice is dictated by a different view about the meaning of the word *exist* (which we will investigate later) and does not affect the meaning of the reasoning.

18. E. Steinkellner, "Die Entwicklung des Kśanikatvānumāna bei Dharmakīrti," *WZKSO* 12–13 (1968–69): 361–77.

19. E. Steinkellner, *Dharmakīrti's Pramāṇaviniścayaḥ II* (Vienna: Verlag der Österreichishen Akademie der Wissenschaften, 1973), II.78.14–29; P:5710, 277.a.4–7; Mimaki, *La Réfutation*, pp. 270–71.

20. Dharmakīrti, *Science of Debate*, P: 5715, 365.a.7–.8. There Dharmakīrti says: "As for sound, whatsoever is existent or produced is impermanent as, for example, a jar."

21. Mimaki, ibid., pp. 31–35. According to Mimaki, Śāntarakṣita and Kamalaśīla represent an intermediary stage in which both types are equally used.

22. Mimaki, ibid., p. 33.

23. In some Tibetan traditions, Dharmakīrti's discussion of the reasoning from disintegration is integrated with the reasoning from existence as a reasoning establishing the forward pervasion *(rjes khyab sgrub byed)* of the reasoning from existence. Sa-paṇ explains that this reasoning is stated to refute the view that things disintegrate only when they meet

some special circumstances (such as when a jar is struck with a hammer). The reasoning from distintegration is then called *reasoning from nondependence (ltos med kyi gtan tshigs)*, for it infers that existing (or produced) things are impermanent because their disintegration does not depend on any adventitious cause but is inherent to the things themselves. Sa-paṇ, *Auto-Commentary*, 81.b.1–85.b.2.

24. According to Hattori, the concept of ability to perform a function as a criterion of reality does not appear in Dignāga's works. *Dignāga*, 14, 79.

25. M. Nagatomi, "Arthakriyā," *The Adyar Library Bulletin* [Madras], 31–32 (1967–68): 52–72.

26. don dam don byed nus pa gang/ de 'dir don dam yod pa yin/ (arthakriyāsamartham yat tad atra paramārthasat/) (Dharmakīrti, *Commentary*, III: 3.a).

27. yang dag pa'i shes pa ni/ skyes bu'i don thams cad grub pa'i sngon du 'gro ba can yin pas de bstan to/ (Dharmakīrti, *nyāya-bindu-nāma-prakaṇa, rigs pa'i thigs pa shes bya ba'i rab tu byed pa*, D: 4212, 231.b).

28. Nagatomi, "Arthakriyā," p. 56. Explained in this way, this criterion of reality is quite close to the common ideas about what counts as real.

29. We will discuss later the appropriateness of characterizing these quasi-entities as phenomena or existents.

30. In Vasubandhu, *svalakṣaṇa* and *sāmānyalakṣaṇa* are used in the context of the development of the application of mindfulness *(smṛtyupasthāna, dran pa nyer bzhag)*. The two types of characteristics refer to properties, such as being material, impure, or impermanent, that are singled out by meditative practice. Specific defining properties refer to characteristics such as being material that are restricted to the type of objects (body, feeling, consciousness, or mental factors) considered. General defining properties refer to characteristics such as being impermanent shared by several types of objects. Poussin, *L'Abhidharmakosá*, VI:158–59.

31. For Dignāga and Dharmakīrti, the word *lakṣaṇa* refers to that which is characterized. In general the *lyud* suffix *(ana)* in the word *lakṣaṇa* (defining property) has an instrumental sense. A defining property is that by which something is characterized. Here, however, the word *lakṣaṇa* is taken as having an accusative force. Go-ram-ba explains (*Explanation*, 17.b.7–18.a.1.) that the word *mtshan nyid (lakṣaṇa)* can apply to a characteristic or to the object characterized by this property. Dignāga and Dharmakīrti use the word in its second sense whereas Vasubandhu used it in its first sense.

32. This difference has been clarified by the Tibetan translators, who coined two different sets of words to make this distinction. In the context of the development of the application of mindfulness, they translate *svalakṣaṇa* as *rang gi mtshan nyid* and *sāmānyalakṣaṇa* as *spyi'i mtshan nyid*; that is, as "own defining characteristic" and "general defining characteristic." In most of Dignāga's and Dharmakīrti's texts, however, these two words are translated as *rang mtshan* and *spyi mtshan*. Accordingly, I use the translation "specifically characterized phenomenon" and "generally characterized phenomenon," which is not literal but broad enough to accomodate both realist and antirealist interpretations. I am quite aware of the misunderstandings that this translation may create. The words "specifically characterized phenomenon" may suggest that the *svalakṣaṇa* is a thing characterized by a property. Although this interpretation would be welcomed by Ge-luk thinkers, it does not fit Dharmakīrti's antirealism, which asserts that the predication of a property has no direct relevance to the reality of the thing it characterizes.

33. I am following the Sanskrit here. The Tibetan adds the qualification of ultimately and thus reads: "Those [phenomena] that are ultimately able to perform a function." Kay-drup

reports that, according to the translator Bang *(dpang)*, most Indian manuscripts omit the word *ultimately*. He adds that since Dharmakīrti's *Ascertainment* also omits the word, one should read "those [phenomena] that are able to perform a function." Kay-drup, *Ocean of Reasoning, An Extensive Explanation of [Dharmakīrti's] Extensive Commentary on "Valid Cognition" (rgyas pa'i btsan bcos tshad ma rnam 'grel gyi rgya cher bshad pa rigs pa'i rgya mtsho)*, Collected Works, vols. 8 and 10. Lha-sa: Zhöl blocks, 1897. New Delhi: Guru Deva, 1982, III:9.4–.5. Dak-tsang (*stag gtshang lo tsā ba*, 1405–?) relies on the word *ultimately* as an argument for differentiating ultimate *(don dam)* from conventional things *(kun rdzob pa'i dngos po)*. See *Treatise Called the Establishment of the Freedom from Extremes Due to Knowing All Tenets (grub mtha kun shes nas mtha' bral sgrub pa zhes bya ba'i bstan bcos)*. Also Śākya Chok-den, *Defeater*, II.29.3. See Chapter 4.

34. don dam don byed nus pa gang / de 'dir don dam yod pa yin / gzhan ni kun rdzob yod pa ste / de dag rang spyi'i mtshan nyid bshad/ (arthakriyāsamarthaṃ yat tad atra paramārthasat / anyat saṃvṛtisat proktaṃ te svasāmānyalakṣaṇe/) (Dharmakīrti, *Commentary*, III:3).

35. de ni gzhan las log pa yin/ de ni rgyu dang 'bras bur bshad/ de ni rang gi mtshan nyid 'dod/ de ni blang dor 'bras can pas/ skyes bu tham cad 'jug pa yin// (tasya vyāvṛttayo 'pare// tatkāryaṃ kāraṇaṃ coktaṃ tat svalkṣaṇam iṣyate/ tattyāgāptiphalāḥ sarvāḥ puruṣāṇāṃ pravṛttayaḥ//) (Dharmakīrti, *Commentary*, I:171.d–172). Frauwallner, "Beiträge zur Apohalehre I" in *Kleine Schriften*, pp. 406–49, 442. The Sanskrit is slightly different and reads: "These others are the exclusions of this. They are described as causes and effects. They are accepted as specifically characterized and generally characterized phenomena. All those that have as their fruits adoption [of desirable objects] and rejection [of undesirable ones] are [the objects] to which people apply [themselves practically]."

36. Dharmakīrti, *Commentary*, III:54.cd. See also Hattori, *Dignāga*, p. 80.

37. de'i yul ni rang gi mtshan nyid de/ don gang nye ba dang mi nye dag las shes pa la snang ba tha dad pa de ni rang gi mtshan nyid do/ de nyid don dam par yod pa ste dngos po'i mtshan nyid ni don byed nus pa kho na yin pa'i phyir ro/ (Dharmakīrti, *Drop of Reasoning*, P: 5711, 329.b.7–.8).

38. ci'i phyir mngon sum gyi yul kho na rang gi mtshan nyid yin/ 'di ltar rnam part rtog pa'i yul gyi me la yang mthong ba'i bdag nyid kho nar nges pa yin no zhe na/ de nyid don dam par zhes smos te/ don dam pa dang bcos ma ma yin pa ste sgro ma btags pa'i rang bzhin yin la/ des yod pas don dam par yod pa'o/ gang gi phyir don gang nye ba dang mi nye ba dag las snang bar gsal bar byed pa de nyid don dam par yod pa yin la/ mngon sum gyi yul de nyid yin pa de'i phyir de kho nar rang gi mtshan nyid yin no/ (Dharmottara, *Commentary*, D: 4231, 44.b.6–45.a.1).

39. In his master work *(Buddhist Logic)*, T. Stcherbatsky assimilates the specifically characterized to Kant's transcendant noumenon. He describes the specifically characterized as qualityless, without extension, unknowlable, a thing-in-itself (*Buddhist Logic*, vol. 1, pp. 85, 182, 185). I believe that this interpretation is mistaken, despite its superficial plausibility. It is contradicted by many references to at least partly empirically observable entities, such as Dharmottara's description of fire as an object of perception. A brief examination of Stcherbatsky's translation shows that the idea of transcendent thing-in-itself is superimposed on the different notion of at least partly empirically available reality. See, for example, how Stcherbatsky interprets this passage in Dharmottara: "the particular, (i.e., the unique moment, thing-in-itself) is the exclusive object of sense perception" (*Buddhist Logic*, vol. 2, p. 36). The notion of Kantian noumenon is here added to the text, which refers to entities that are available to the senses. I believe that Stcherbatsky's comparison of Dharmakīrti and

Kant is quite insightful but unfortunately focuses on the more problematic aspect of Kant's philosophy, his doctrine of a thing-in-itself, instead of discussing more fruitful avenues such as Kant's analysis of sensation and conception, and so forth. As will be shown in Chapter 15, the assimilation of the specifically characterized to a thing-in-itself is based on a misunderstanding of the claims that reality is ineffable.

40. gang phyir dngos kun rang bzhin gyis/ rang rang ngo bo la gnas phyir/ mthun dgnos gzhan gyi dngos dag las/ ldog pa la ni brten pa can// (sarve bhāvāḥ svabhāvena svasvabhāvavyavasthiteḥ/ svabhāvaparabhāvābhyāṃ yasmād vyāvṛttibhāginaḥ//) (Dharmakīrti, *Commentary*, I:40). Mookerjee and Nagasaki, *The Pramāṇavārtikam*, p. 91.

41. In *Clarification*, 21.b.3–6, Go-ram-ba indicates some of the sources for these three sets of criteria.

42. This terminology is found in Y. Kajiyama, *Introduction to Buddhist Philosophy* (Kyoto: Kyoto University, 1966), p. 56. Tibetan scholars often use the expression *unmixed in place (yul ma 'dres pa).* See Gyel-tsap, *Revealing*, I.78–79.

43. This first criterion does not apply to nonmaterial phenomena such as consciousness.

44. gzhan la gnas par 'gyur ba ni/ rang gi gnas las mi g.yo zhing/ de las gnas gzhan skye ba la/ gnas na shin tu rigs par ldan// (anyatra vartamānasya tato 'nyasthānajanmani/ svasmād acalataḥ sthānād vṛttir ity atiyuktimat/) (Dharmakīrti, *Commentary*, I:153).

45. Dharmakīrti's discussion contains a complicated example that is standard in Indian linguistics (ibid., III:486–95). A letter *(varṇa, yi ge)* is pronounced with a certain length. A long letter is composed of more parts than a short one. If these parts were not temporally determined, there could not be any difference in the apprehension of the length of the letters. For a detailed discussion, see Kay-drup, *Ocean*, III:193.b2–198.b.5. For some of the background of this discussion, M. Biardeau, *Theorie de la Connaissance et Philosophie de la Parole* (Paris: Mouton, 1964), pp. 177–91.

46. See E. Steinkellner, "Wirklichkeit und Begriff bei Dharmakīrti," *Wiener Zeitschrift für die Kunde Südasiens* 15 (1971): 179–210.

47. In this chapter, I assume that I can unproblematically hold commonsense objects such as cows to be real. In Chapter 4, we will see that such objects cannot be real according to most Buddhist epistemologists. The description about the reality of a cow becomes a convenient way of describing individual atoms arranged in a certain order or perceptibles such as colors or tastes.

48. dngos po la min dngos po kun/ rang rang ngo bo la gnas phyir// khra bo yi ni ngo bo gang/ de ni ser skya la yod min/ de 'bras yin min las bzlog pa/ gnyis ka la yang yod pa yin// (na bhāve sarvabhāvānāṃ svabhāvasya vyavasthiteḥ// yad rūpaṃ śābaleyasya bāhuleyasya nāsti tat/ atatkāryaparāvṛttir dvayor api ca vidyate//) (Dharmakīrti, *Commentary*, I:138.c–139. Ge-dün-drup, *Good Sayings*, 39.2–4. Frauwallner, "Beiträge," pp. 421–22.

49. See Chapter 7.

50. Dharmakīrti, *Commentary*, I:40.ab. See previously.

51. Quine, *From a Logical Point of View*, p. 71.

52. See Chapter 6.

Chapter 3. The Ambiguities of the Concept of Existence

1. Steinkellner describes two possible meanings of the concept of essence (*svabhāva)*: (1) capacity *(śaktiḥ, nus pa)*, that is, the capacity that things have to produce their effects; (2) causal complex *(hetusāmagri, rgyu tshogs pa)*, which Dharmakīrti prefers. The nature of a

thing is determined by the causal nexus that has the fitness *(yogyatā, rung ba)* to produce its effect. "Wirklichkeit," pp. 183–87.

2. don sgrub par byed pa'i dngos po gags (i.e., 'gags) kyang de mi gags (i.e., 'gags) pa'i phyir dang de las cung zad grub med pa'i phyir ro de nyid kyi phyir yod kyang spyi ni don ma yin no/ (Steinkellner, ed., *Dharmakīrti's Pramāṇaviniścayah II. Svarthanumana Teil I*) (Vienna: Verlag der Osterreichischen Academie der Wissenschaften, 1973), p. 26.

3. Hiromasa Tosaki relates this passage to *Commentary* III:53.d–54, where Dharmakīrti had argued that ultimately there is only one object of comprehension (Tosaki, *Bukkyo-Nishikiron no Kenkyū I and II*) (Tokyo: Daito-shuppan-sha, 1979, 1985), p. 135. For a discussion of this passage, see Chapter 18.

4. Tosaki translates: "because there is ascertainment of absence" (ibid., p. 136).

5. med pa gzhal bya ma yin phyir/ gcig nyid ce na kho bo'ang 'dod// med pa'ang nges phyir gzhal bya ni/ min la ma nges pa nyid dam/ (ekam evāprameyatvād asataś cen matañ ca naḥ// anekānto 'prameyatve hy abhāvasyāpi) (Miyasaka: 'sadbhāvasyāpi) niścayāt (or niścayaḥ)/) (Dharmakīrti, *Commentary*, III:64.c–65.b). Also Ge-dün-drup, *Good Sayings*, p. 179.1–3; and Tosaki, ed., *Pramāṇa.*

6. The same applies to the concept of entity *(rūpa, ngo bo)*, which sometimes refers to a real thing (*Commentary*, I:185). At other times, Dharmakīrti applies this word to nonthings as well, which are then described as having an unreal construct (ibid., I:133).

7. See Linsky, *Referring* (London: Routledge, 1971).

8. An important difference between Meinong and Dharmakīrti is that, whereas for Dharmakīrti universals are attributed a lesser status, for Meinong the distinction between existence and subsistence is a way to protest against our prejudice for the actual. This realist tendency finds its full expression in Meinong's thought when he attempts to distinguish a third kind of object in addition to existence and subsistence, which is beyond being and nonbeing. A square circle, for example, neither exists nor subsists. Nevertheless, since it is possible to predicate nonexistence of a square circle, such a quasi-entity must have some kind of "being," which Meinong describes as being beyond being and nonbeing. This reifying tendency for which Meinong is famous is absent in Dharmakīrti, who does not attribute any kind of quasi-being to nonexistents.

9. This word can be indifferently translated as conception, conceptual cognition, conceptual thought, thought, and conceptual consciousness.

10. This definition of existence goes back to Vātsyāyana's statement that anything properly cognized exists. N. Shah, *Akalaṅka*, p. 42.

11. Lo Ken-chen (*glo bo mkhan chen bsod nams lhun grub*, 1456–1532) was a disciple of Śākya Chok-den who later became quite critical of his master. His commentary, *The Sun, an Explanation Which Clarifies the Path of Reasoning, a Commentary to [Sa-paṇ's] Treasure on the Science of Valid Cognition [and] a Commentary on the Thought of [Dharmakīrti's] Seven Treatises and [Dignāga's] Sūtra (sde bdun mdo dang bcas pa'i dgongs 'grel tshad ma rigs gter gyi 'grel pa'i rnam bshad rigs lam gsal ba'i nyi ma)*, is often original and reflects his personal ideas.

12. rang mtshan 'dzin pa rtog med de/ spyi 'dzin pa rtog pa yin/ de la rang mtshan dngos po ste/ spyi ni dngos por grub pa med/ (Sa-paṇ, *Treasure*, 5.a.2).

13. A distinguished phenomenon is the real thing that is distinguished by a conceptual distinguisher *(ldog pa, vyāvṛtti)*. For example, a gray cow is differentiated from things of dissimilar (other animals) and similar (other cows) kinds. The conceptual difference between these things is a distinguisher.

14. In general, equivalence *(don gcig)* does not need to imply synonymity of terms. This

is especially true in the Ge-luk tradition, where mutual inclusiviness is the main criterion for equivalence. For example, being produced *(byas pa)* and being impermanent *(mi rtag pa)* are said to be equivalent even though they are not cognitively equivalent. See Dreyfus, *Some Considerations*, pp. 185–93. In the Sa-gya tradition, however, equivalence is stronger than mere coinclusivity and reserved for actual cases of synonymity *(don gcig ming gi rnam grangs)*. Sa-paṇ, for example, described being produced and being impermanent as one entity *(ngo bo gcig)* but not as equivalent, reserving equivalence for actual synonyms such as the morning star and the evening star (*Auto-Commentary*, 121.b.2).

15. rang gi mtshan nyid gsal ba dngos po rdzas log pa don dam pa zhes bya ba la sogs pa ni don byed nus pa rdzas phan tshun ma 'dres pa rgyu dang 'bras bur grub pa skye bu thams cad kyi blang dor bya ba'i 'jug yul yin pas dngos po don du don gcig pa yin te (Sa-paṇ, ibid., 44.a.2–.3).

16. gzhal bya rang mtshan gcig kho na (Sa-paṇ, *Treasure*, 3.a.1). We will re-examine this difficult question while discussing the definition of valid cognition.

17. dngos med ngo bo min pas yod min pas/ ngo bo med pas shes bya min/ des na dngos po bsal ba la/ dngos med ces ni btags par zad// (ibid., 6.b.6).

18. I assume for the time being that commonsense objects such as a table are real. We will have to revise this judgment in the next chapter, when we will see that a reference to the reality of a table cannot be taken at its face value. It is merely a convenient way to designate the reality of the elements composing the table.

19. spyir 'dod tshad mas gzhal mi nus (Sa-paṇ, *Treasure*, 7.a.2).

20. meyam tvekam svalakṣaṇaṃ/ (rang gi mtshan nyid gcig bzhal bya/) (Miyasaka, ed., *Pramāṇa*, III:53.d).

21. Bo-dong *(bo dong phyogs las rnam rgyal)*, *Explanation of the Presentation of Buddhist [Views on] Valid Cognition as Stated by [Dharmakīrti's] Drop of Reasoning (rigs thig las gsungs pa'i nang pa'i tshad ma'i rnam bzhag bshad pa)*, *Collected Works*, vol. 7, pp. I:576.2–78.5, 590.1–91.3, and 593.6.

22. Bo-dong's discussion is quite technical. One of his many arguments is that Sa-paṇ's view contradicts the fact that an object of comprehension is accepted as an indeterminate *(ma nges pa'i gtan tshigs)* reason with regard to sound being impermanent. An indeterminate reason is an indecisive reason in which the reason does not entail the predicate. For example, the object of comprehension is given by Dharmakīrti as a classical example of an indeterminate reason with respect to sound being impermanent because sound is an object of comprehension but that does not entail that it is impermanent. The acceptance of this example entails that object of comprehension is not equivalent to impermanent phenomena; that is, permanent phenomena must be objects of comprehension.

23. *blos rig par bya ba* is Sa-paṇ's own definition of an object in *Treasure*, 2.a.2. Since Sa-paṇ holds that inference *(rjes dpag, anumāna)* is a valid cognition despite being conceptual, he must accept that an inference has an object. Since, as we will see later, it is a basic tenet of Sa-paṇ's system that specifically characterized phenomena cannot be objects of conception (ibid., 5.a.2), the object of an inference can be only a generally characterized phenomenon (such as an object-universal) and, therefore, generally characterized phenomena are objects of comprehension. Thus, for Bo-dong, Sa-paṇ's exclusion of generally characterized phenomena from the realm of objects and existence directly contradicts his own system. Bo-dong, *Presentation*, I:591.4–93.3.

24. des na yul rang mtshan gcig kho nar 'dod pa ni/ rtag pa yang mi rtag par 'gyur na/ 'gal ba la mi 'khrul ba srid par 'gyur bas dngos po'i chos nyid thams cad dor bar 'gyur ba'i phyir te/ rgya cher 'chad par 'gyur ro// (Bo-dong, ibid., I:592.2–.3).

25. spyi mtshan gzhal byar ma yin par bsrgrub pa la sgrub byed gang bkod kyang nyes pa de nyid las ma 'das la/ 'di ni byang chub sems dpa' kāma la sī las/ dngos med la go bya go byed mi rung bar 'dod pa ni rang nyid 'joms par byed pa mtshon cha'i thabs bslab nyes pa dang 'dra bar gsungs pa de dang 'dra ba yin te/ (Gyel-tsap *[rgyal tshab]*, *Clarifying the Thought, a Major Explanation of [Dharmakīrti's] Treatise, the Ascertainment of Valid Cognition [bstan bcos tshad ma rnam nges kyi tika chen dgongs pa rab gsal]*, Part I, *Collected Works*, vol. 7 *[Ja]* [Delhi: Guru Deva 1982], 355.6–56.1). I ignore whether Gyel-tsap's quote is a real quote or just a paraphrase of Kamalaśīla.

26. Ngak-chö seems to have in mind Śākya Chok-den and Tuk-je-bel-zang *(thugs rje dpal bzang)*. This, however, is puzzling, for the former has explicitly denied that only specifically characterized phenomena are objects of comprehension! See *Defeater*, II.27.3–.4, and *Music*, p. 466.4–.3. The latter was a direct disciple of Go-ram-ba who wrote supplements *(kha skong)* to the latter's works. He composed a word commentary to Sa-paṇ's *Treasure*, which reflects very closely Go-ram-ba's views. See *Commentary on [Sa-paṇ's] Treasure on the Science of Valid Cognition Which Explains the Thought of [Dharmakīrti's] Seven Texts Together with [Dignāga's] Sūtra Called Clarifying the Path of Reasoning (sde bdun mdo dang bcas pa'i dgongs 'grel tshad ma rigs gter gyi 'grel pa rigs lam rab gsal)*, 12.3.

27. Ngak-chö (*ngag dbang chos grags*, 1572–1641), *Good Sayings Which Bestow the Splendour of Speech and Clarify the Meaning of the Thought of [Sa-paṇ's] Treasure on the Science of Valid Cognition (tshad ma'i rigs gter gyi dgongs don gsal bar byed pa'i legs bshad ngag gi dpal ster)*, *Collected Works*, vol. 3 (Delhi: Ngawang Topgya, 1983), 29.a.3–b.6.

28. gzhal bya gnyis yod nas gnyis su gsungs pa ma yin gyi/ 'jal tshul gyi sgo nas mngon gyur gyi rang mtshan rang gis 'jal ba dang/ lkog gyur gyi rang mtshan gzhan las 'jal ba la dgongs nas gnyis su gsungs pa yin te (Sa-paṇ, *Auto-Commentary*, 29.a.4–5). Sa-paṇ is here closely following Dharmakīrti's epistemological idea (which we will examine later) that the two types of valid cognition relate to two types of object, specifically and generally characterized phenomena. However, the latter do not exist as objects of comprehension in the same way as specifically characterized phenomena, which have their own intrinsic identity.

29. See Chapters 11–14.

30. Sa-paṇ, *Auto-Commentary*, 81.a.2–.3.

31. dngos med kyi yod pa de ci/ don byed nus na dngos por 'gyur la/ mi nus na med pas yod par ming btags kyang med pa nyid yin no/ (ibid., 81.a.3–.4).

32. yod pa'i don ma grub pa'i phyir yod pa'i btags pa ba (Lo, *Sun*, 217.1).

33. yod pa nyid kyi mtshan nyid ni don byed nus yin la/ (ibid., 216.2). Similarly, Sa-paṇ says, "Dharmakīrti says 'the defining property of existant is that which is able to perform a function' [and] this is indeed so" (*Auto-Commentary*, 81.a.5). Lo also quotes from several other sources: Dharmakīrti's *Drop of Reasoning*, the works of Dharmakīrti's commentators such as Śāntarakṣita, Prajñākaragupta, and so on, as well as from other classical Buddhist texts such as the Bhavya's *Blaze of Logic* (*Sun*, 216.2–18.2).

34. Dharmakīrti, *Commentary*, I:206.

35. 'o na tshad mas dmigs pa yod pa'i mtshan nyid khas mi len pa'am/ len na shes bya thams cad mi rtag par thal lo zhe na/ de de'i mtshan nyid du khas len mod/ ldog pa'i chos rnams tshad mas dmigs par bshad pa de yang/ sel ngor dmigs pa la bsam pa yin gyi/ spyir tshad mas dmigs pa go chod pa ma yin te kun mkhyen ye shes kyis ma bzung ba'i phyir ro/ 'o na ji skad du/ med pa ma yin sgra sbyor phyir/ zhes bshad ma yin nam she na/ de yang sel

ngor med pa ma yin pa la bsam pa yin te/ (Śākya Chok-den, *Music*, 540.4–.6).

36. A similar view is taken by the Seventh Karmapa Chö-drak-gya-tso, who describes universals as being objects of comprehension from a conceptual point of view *(sel ngor gzhal bya)*. Quoting Śākyabuddhi as saying that "universals are not independently objects of comprehension" *(spyi gzhal bya rang rgyud pa med)*, Chö-drak-gya-tso argued that universals are conventionally objects of comprehension. *The Ocean of Text on the Science of Valid Cognition That Gathers the Water of All the Good Sayings (tshad ma legs par bshad pa thams cad kyi chu bo yongs su 'du ba'i rigs pa'i gzhung lugs kyi rgya mtsho*, n.d.*)*, I.325.1–326.2.

37. 'dir kha cig sgra ji bzhin du/ yod na mi rtag pas khyab par khas len pa ni bod kyi tha snyad la cung zad mi bde ste sgra mi rtag par bsrub pa la rtags su bkod pa'i yod pa dang dngos po gnyis rgya gar na bh'a wa zhes skad dod gcig tu yod pas 'ga' zhig tu dngos po dang 'ga' zhig tu yod pa bsgyur ba yin gyi sel ngor yod pa la yang yod pa'i tha snyad sngon gyi lo ts'a ba rnams kyis mang du gsungs pa'i phyir te/ spyi yod par ni rab tu bsgrags/ (Go-ram-ba, *Clarification*, 68.6–69.2). The quote is from Dharmakīrti, *Commentary*, I:70.b.

38. We will see a similar case concerning the words *viśeṣa* and *bheda*.

39. A potentially more significant fact, namely, that the Tibetan *dngos po* also translates the Sanskrit *vastu* goes unnoticed by Go-ram-ba. Although *bhāva* and *vastu* often have the same meaning, one could argue that *bhāva* corresponds more to the things as existing and *vastu* to things as having the capacity to perform a function.

40. Dharmakīrti, *Commentary*, I:70, 136, 180, etc.

Chapter 4. The Purview of the "Real"

1. See Chapter 2.

2. Poussin, *L'Abhidharmakośa*, I:22.

3. Traditionally, Buddhists distinguish three realms of conditioned existence: the Desire realm, dominated by the desire for sense objects; the Form realm, where the pleasures of meditative absorbtion prime; and the Formless realm, which is immaterial. Moreover, the composition of matter differs in the first two realms. Whereas matter in the desire realm has eight components, there are no smells or tastes in the Form realm.

4. Poussin, *L'Abhidharmakośa*, II:144–46.

5. Following the Tibetan doxographical tradition, I use the word *Vaibhāṣika* to refer to the position that might be more accurately described as *Sarvastivāda.*

6. This is the famous definition of ultimate truth given by Vasubandhu in his *Kośa* (VI:4). See Poussin, *L'Abhidharmakośa*, VI:139–140.

7. Hattori, "Realism," pp. 23–60, 39. This difficulty in the Vaibhāṣika philosophy comes because this system seems to have grafted an atomic theory borrowed from the Vaiśeṣika to its original phenomenological analysis of matter. According to this earlier approach, material objects are understood from the way they appear to the different types of sense consciousness. The analysis of matter into atomic components represents a different approach that threatens to undermine the former phenomenological method.

8. Ibid., p. 40.

9. W. Sellars, *Science, Perception, and Reality* (Atlantic Highlands, N.J. : Humanities Press, 1963). The background of Sellars's view (philosophy's necessity to address Gallileo's scientific revolution) is, however, quite different from Vasubandhu's (Abhidharmic speculations).

10. The most famous and influential being Stcherbatsky in his *Buddhist Logic*, where he describes the specifically characterized in a Kantian way as an extensionless, durationless unique moment, the limit of all synthetic construction. It is the absolute particular, the thing-in-itself that underlies every efficient empirical reality. Although not accepting the Kantian overtone of Stcherbatsky's explanations, most modern interpreters of Dharmakīrti seem to have adopted the view that reality is limited to infinitesimal elements.

11. Chö-drak-gya-tso describes a coarse object as that object which is held to be one solid block by the conceptions arising after the experience. He distinguishes that object, which he also describes as an aggregate *(bsags pa, saṃcita)* from the special atoms (i.e., the atoms that stand in a collection). *Ocean*, I.284.5–285.2. There is, however, considerable confusion about the use of the word *coarse*, which sometimes refers to any object that has spatial extension.

12. This description is given from the point of view of those who deny that commonsense objects are real. For these thinkers, such objects are not given to perception but are constructed by conception. As we will see shortly, Ge-luk thinkers oppose this view and hold that such objects are real. For them, commonsense objects are not syntheses but collections of different elements. To avoid the confusion of commonsense objects, which are described by some as collections and by others as syntheses, with the collections of similar elements, I will use the word *collection* to refer to the latter. The former type of object will be called *commonsense objects* or *coarse objects*.

13. Dharmakīrti, *Commentary*, III:191.c–248.d.

14. Hattori identifies this reference as Vasubandhu, *Abhidharmakośabhāṣya*, I:10, Chinese version, T.1558, XXIX. *Dignāga*, p. 89.

15. bsags pa dag ni tshogs pa yin/ de spyi de la dbang po'i blo/ spyi blo don mi za bar yang/ rnam par rtog dang rjes su 'brel// (sañcitaḥ samudāyaḥ sa sāmānyaṃ tatra cākṣadhīḥ/ sāmānyabuddhiś cāvaśyaṃ vikalpenānubadhyate//) (Dharmakīrti, *Commentary*, III:194). Quoted in C. M. Keyt, "Dharmakīrti's Concept of the *Svalakṣaṇa*" (Ph.D. diss., University of Washington, 1980), p. 201.

16. The nature of determinate perception and its relation to universals will be investigated in Book II.

17. don gzhan dang ni mngon 'brel phyir/ rdul phran gzhan gang skye 'gyur ba/ de dag bsags bshad de dag ni/ shes pa skye ba'i rgyu mtshan yin// rdul phran gzhan dag med par ni/ rdul phran khyad par de yang med/ shes de gcig la nges min phyir/ spyi yi spyod yul can du bshad// (arthāntarābhisambhandhāj jāyante ye 'ṇavo 'pare/ uktās te sañcitās te hi nimittaṃ jñānajanmanaḥ// aṇūnāṃ sa viśeṣaś ca nāntareṇāparān aṇūn/ tad ekāniyamāj jñānam uktaṃ sāmānyagocaram//) (Dharmakīrti, *Commentary*, III:195–196). Keyt, "Dharmakīrti," p. 204. Let us observe that Dignāga had already given a similar answer to the same objection: "Since perception is produced through [the contact of sense] with several substances [namely, atoms], it is said that it takes a universal as its sphere of operation with respect to its sphere of activity. This does not [mean] that it constructs diverse [elements] into a unity." (Dignāga, *Compendium on Valid Cognition*, P:5790, 14.b.3–.4). Hattori, *Dignāga*, p. 26.

18. gal te skye mchad gcig yin yang/ cig car du ma 'dzin ma yin/ til sogs tha dad la ji ltar/ cig car 'dzin pa snang ba yin// (athaikāyatanatve 'pi nānekaṃ gṛhyate (Miyasaka reads dṛśyate) sakṛt / sakṛd grahāvabhāsaḥ kiṃ viyukteṣu tilādiṣu//) (Dharmakīrti, *Commentary*, III:197). Ge-dün-drup read the first verse as "skye mchad min yang" but Miyasaka's version makes more sense. See *Good Sayings*, 211.3.

19. This point is accepted by the Nyāya, which distinguishes a collection of threads from

a cloth through the absence or presence of a synthetic whole. See Shastri, *Philosophy*, p. 240.

20. In another passage (*Commentary*, III:200) Dharmakīrti uses the example of a butterfly, showing that a multiplicity of elements can produce a single impression. Dharmakīrti also argues (*Commentary*, I:104–105) that the relation between a collection and its parts is different from that between a universal and its individual instances. The parts of a multicolored object retain their own identity, even when they are parts of a collection. This is so because a collection is produced by addition of real elements, not by synthesis. On the contrary, universals are the products of synthesis. Hence, individuals do not retain their own identity in relation to them.

21. D. Malvania, ed., *Duveaka Miśra's Dharmottarapradīpa (Being a Sub-Commentary on Dharmottara's Nyāyabinduṭīkā, a Commentary on Dharmakīrti's Nyāyabīndu)*, Tibetan Sanskrit Works Series II (Patna: Kashi Prasad Institute, 1971), pp. 42–44 in Keyt, "Dharmakīrti," p. 274.

22. Dharmottara, *Commentary*, D: 4231, 45.a.5–.7. See Chapter 2.

23. There are twelve spheres, the six senses (five material and mental senses) and their six kinds of objects (the five objects of the senses and the objects of the mental consciousness). Here, *sphere* refers to the five objects of the senses such as form and sound. See Poussin, *L'Abhidharmakośa*, I:37, 43, 65.

24. Dharmakīrti, *Commentary*, I:34.

25. Chö-drak-gya-tso seems to use the collection view on the conventional level, that is, the level at which we can speak of objects appearing to consciousness. At a deeper level, however, such explanation must be understood to refer to the interaction of infinitesimal atoms and moments of consciousness. *Ocean*, 284.5–85.2 and 420.6–22.6.

26. don dam par don byed nus dang mi nus pa'i chos (Śākya Chok-den, *Defeater*, II.38.5).

27. See Chapter 1.

28. Śākya Chok-den's ideas on oneness and distinctiveness *(gcig dang tha dad)* are very different from the Ge-luk distinction between oneness (*gcig*, which is conceptual) and substantial oneness (*rdzas gcig*, which is real). For Śākya Chok-den, as for Sa-paṇ, oneness and substantial oneness are identical. Being impermanent and being produced are one thing in reality. Sa-paṇ, *Auto-Commentary*, 73.a.4–74.a.1. See Chapter 8.

29. yang lag gi rdzas mang po tshogs pa'i tshogs pa khyad par can dang skad cig rgyun thud pa'i rgyun can de rdzas gcig du khas len pa lta zhog/ spyir rdzas su grub par bshad pa sde bdun mdzad pa'i gzhung na med do/ 'o na rang lugs la cha bcas yin na rdzas gcig ma yin pas khyab pa khas len par nus sam zhe na/ so sor phye dgos te/ rdzas kyi cha du ma dang bcas pa la des khyab par khas len nus shing ldog cha du ma dang bcas pa la der khyab pa khas mi len pa'i phyir ro/ (Śākya Chok-den, *Defeater*, II.140.1–.3).

30. Ibid., II.412.7–13.1.

31. Dak-tsang, *Ocean of Good Explanation, a Treatise on the Establishment of Freedom from Extremes Through Knowing All Tenets*, 125.4–28.6.

32. Śākya Chok-den, *Defeater*, II.8.7–29.2. It is clear that from a practical point of view we cannot understand reality from an atomic view point. Nevertheless, it remains true, according to Śākya Chok-den, that such a description is what we are really referring to when we talk about the function performed by a jar.

33. ldan min 'du byed, viprayuktisaṃskāra (Śākya Chok-den, *Defeater*, II.418.6). Traditionally, the Abhidharma contains a list of fourteen elements such as obtention *(prāpti, thob pa)* that are neither material nor mental (hence their name, *nonassociated*, *vi-prayukta*)

but are composed *(saṃskāra, 'du byed).* Poussin, *L'Abhidharmakośa*, II:178–234. There is, however, no necessary limitation to their numbers. Śākya Chok-den, however, dramatically extends the purview of this catergory to include all extended objects. We will see that other Sa-gya thinkers do not agree with this.

34. Sa-paṇ seems to imply that such factors are not things in Dharmakīrti's system when he says: "Since things cannot be [anything] but either gross matter or cognition" *(dngos po bems rig gnyis las ma 'das pas)* (*Auto-Commentary*, 33.a.2). Lo Ken-chen states that Sautrāntika followers of Dharmakīrti assert that these factors are factor of superimpositions *(sgro btags)* (*Sun*, 51.a.3).

35. Sa-paṇ, *Auto-Commentary*, 44.a.2–.3 in Chapter 3.

36. tshog pa can ya gyal rnams 'dus pa las tshogs pa'i gong bu skye ba ni rdul phran las 'dus pa'i ri'am nas 'dus pa las phung po skye ba ltar phan btags nyid kyi rgyu 'bras yin te/ . . . rnam nges las/ tshogs pa rnam par 'jog pa yi/ rgyu tshogs pa can yin pas/ (Sa-paṇ, *Auto-Commentary*, 76.b.5–6). The quote is from *Ascertainment*, D: 4211, 214.a.3.

37. yul dang dbang po'i rdul phra rab/ tshogs pa'i skad cig ji snyad kyi/ myong ba'i rnam shes gang bskyed pa/ so so skye bo'i mngon sum yin/ (Sa-paṇ, *Treasure*, 4.b.3).

38. tsam tsam mang po ngas mi shes/ sngon po don la yod (reported in Sa-paṇ's biography written by Lho-ba-gun-kyen *[lho pa kun mkhyen]*, quoted in Go-ram-ba, *Clarifying*, 31.4). Many of Sa-paṇ's contemporaries held that mere blue is a negation, which is the negation of nonblue and is, therefore, different from blue. It is a universal despite being real. For a similar view, see Bo-dong, *Explanation of the Presentation of Buddhist [Views on] Valid Cognition as Stated by [Dharmakīrti's] Drop of Reasoning*, 673, 703, 788–91. We will come back to this disguised form of realism in Chapter 9.

39. Go-ram-ba explains: "[Śākya Śrībhadra] says that through this [statement] one can understand all the essential points of the *anyāpoha* [theory]" (gzhan sel gyi gnad thams cad des go gsung) (*Explanation*, 5.a.5).

40. Lo Ken-chen, *Sun*, 119.3–.4 and 120.4. Unfortunately, Lo Ken-chen equates coarse *(rags pa, sthūla)* with extended objects (or, as they would be called by Tibetan scholars, objects with spatial parts, *yul kyi cha dang bcas pa'i dngos po*). Although this choice seems to be merely semantic, it complicates the issue. Throughout this discussion, I restrict the word *coarse* to the commonsense objects. Therefore, I have used *extended* even when describing Lo Ken-chen's view that uses *coarse* instead.

41. Although he does not indicate any Indian source for his discussion, this distinction has been made in several authoritative texts. Vasubandhu, for one, asserts that the five sense consciousnesses have as their objects the specific characteristics of sense spheres but not those of substances (skye mched rang gi mtshan nyid kyi yul can yin gyi/ rdzas rang gi mtshan nyid kyi yul can ma yin no). As reported by Śākya Chok-den, *Defeater*, II.416.5. Dignāga also has a reference in *Compendium*, P: 5700, 14.b.1–.3. See also Hattori, *Dignāga*, pp. 1, 26. Dharmakīrti alludes to this distinction when he uses sesame seeds in a heap to illustrate that an apprehension of a collection of atoms is real. "Although they [belong] to the same sense sphere . . ." (*Commentary*, III:197.a). See earlier. This remark seems to imply that distinct elements can appear to the same perception only when they belong to the same sense sphere.

Lo Ken-chen explicitly finds support for his distinction in a remark by Sa-paṇ. It concerns the identity of being impermanent and being produced *(byas mi rtag).* Sa-paṇ describes this identity as "not being that [identity] known to the world [which talks about] one jar or [one] moon, but being the substantial identity of the sense spheres which is familiar [to] philosophical treatises" (de'ang 'jig rten la grags pa zla ba'am bum gcig lta bu ma yin gyi bstan bcos la grags pa'i skye mched kyi rdzas gcig yin no) (Sa-paṇ, *Auto-Commentary*, 51.a.1). Thus, commonsense objects are known to the world, while the substantial identity of sense spheres is known to philosophy.

42. Poussin, *L'Abhidharmakośa*, I:37, 40, 43, 65.

43. 'jug pa'i tshe rdzas dang dngos po la sogs pa'i tha snyad 'jug pa yod kyang/ bstan bcos su rang spyi so sor phye nas 'chad pa'i tshe dngos por ma grub ste/ bum sogs la yod pa'i skye mched kyi rdzas brgyad rang dbang du grub pas/ rtog med kyis mngon sum so sor bskyed pa ltar bum pa zhes bya ba gcig gis mngon sum bskyed pa med cing/ bzhi brgya pa'i 'grel bar phyogs glang sogs kyi bzhed pa ston pa na/ 'di la rtog ge pa rnams na re/ bum pa la mngon sum nyid yod pa ma yin kho na ste/ gzugs la sogs pa rnams kyi rang gi mtshan nyid ni bstan du med la/ mngon sum gyi tha snyad par bya ba'i mig la sogs pa'i rnam shes yul yin pa'i phyir mngon sum zhes bya bar 'dogs so/ bum pa ni yongs su btags pa tsam yin pa'i phyir rang gi mtshan nyid yod pa ma yin la/ gang la rang gi mtshan nyid yod pa ma yin pa la de ni dngos kyi gnas pa'i mngon sum mi srid la 'ba' zhig ma zad kyi/ de la btags pa'i mngon sum nyid kyang mi rung ngo zhes gsung (Lo, *Sun*, 120.5–121.3).

44. Poussin, *L'Abhidharmakośa*, I:(13.a), 23.

45. rgyun yang de ma yin te/ de la cha shes du ma yod pa'i cha shes re re nas rang 'bras su 'gyur pa'i shes pa rdzas so so bar bskyed par byed pa'i phyir dang cha shes thams cad 'dus nas rang 'bras shes pa rdzas gcig bsked par byed pa mi srid pa'i phyir/ (Go-ram-ba, *Explanation*, 22.b.4–.5).

46. Ibid., 47.b.3 and Śākya Chok-den, *Defeater*, II.140.1–2. Although Sa-paṇ did not apply these reasonings to the refutation of continuum, he used them against Tibetan realists (*Auto-Commentary*, 46.b.1–47.a.1). Go-ram-ba and Śākya Chok-den repeatedly assert that Sa-paṇ's critique of Tibetan realism also applies to Ge-luk realism, which differs from earlier versions in only minor points. Therefore, it seems quite reasonable to assume that their use of Dharmakīrti's reasoning against the reality of continua corresponds to Sa-paṇ's opinion.

47. The Sāṁkhya school asserts the primacy of Nature in relation to their philosophy of causality. The ultimate cause of everything makes possible the cooperation of separate conditions. See G. Larson, *Classical Sāmkhya* (Delhi: Motilal, 1979), pp. 160–67.

48. tha dad pa/ med na cig car skye 'jig 'gyur/ (abhede tu syātāṃ [Miyasaka reads sāyāṃ] nāśod bhavau sakṛt/) (Dharmakīrti, *Commentary*, I:167.cd). Ge-dün-drup, *Good Sayings*, 43.3.

49. rdzas gcig la skye 'jig tha dad pa'am rnam pa tha dad 'gal te/ rnam nges las/ de grub na ma grub pa'am rgyu tha dad pa ni de'i rang bzhin du rig (rigs pa?) ma yin no/ dngos po rnams kyi tha dad pa'am rgyu tha dad pa ni 'di kho na yin te chos 'gal bar gnas pa'am rgyu tha dad pa'o/ des kyang tha dad par mi grub na ni 'ga' gang las kyang tha dad pa med pas ril po rdzas gcig tu 'gyur ro/ (Sa-paṇ, *Auto-Commentary*, 46.b.6–47.a.1). This argument is applied by Sa-paṇ to universals but equally refutes real continuums.

50. The Ge-luk answer to this argument distinguishes substantial identity (literally, one substance, *rdzas gcig*) and simultaneous substantial identity (literally, one substance of establishment and abiding, *grub bde rdzas gcig*). Dharmakīrti's argument applies to the second identity (which can be forced on the Sāṃkhya since Nature is said to be partless and, therefore, must exist entirely in each individual) but not to mere substantial identity. Śākya Chok-den answers that the Ge-luk distinction is not found in Dharmakīrti's texts (*Defeater*, II.137).

51. Sa-paṇ, *Auto-Commentary*, 34.b.3–35.a.6. From this, Sa-paṇ deduces that the Mind-Only reasonings that refute the existence of atoms do not apply to partless moments, which are individually real but whose aggregation is thoroughly unreal.

52. Dignāga, *Ch'ü-yin-chia-she-lung*, stanza 6, in H. Kitagawa, "A Study of a Short Philosophical Treatise Ascribed to Dignāga," *Indo Koten Ronrigaku no Kenkyū: Jinna no taikei*, rev. ed. (Tokyo: Suzuki Gakujutsu Zaidan, 1973), pp. 430–39, 433.

53. The concept of merely being not one is found in Dharmottara, *Explanation of [Dharmakīrti's] Ascertainment of Valid Cognition*, D: 4229, 179.b.1. Gyel-tsap criticizes this distinction, arguing that there are only two ways of drawing a distinction: two things are either conceptually or really distinct. In the first case, they are distinct, whereas in the second they are distinct substances. There is no third way of drawing the distinction. For Gyel-tsap, Dharmottara's remarks about merely not being one refer to phenomena that are distinct within having the same entity *(ngo bo gcig la ldog pa tha dad).*

54. *bsil zer byed* is a poetic name of the moon.

55. It is also called *distinction* [from something] that is a [mere] negation of being one with [that something] *(gcig pa bkag pa'i tha dad).*

56. bum pa la sogs pa rang mtshan yin pas los rdzas su grub/ (Nga-wang-chö-drak, *Discourse Differentiating and [Making] Decisions in the Tenets of Ealier and Later Tibetan Learned Ones) (bod kyi mkhas pa snag phyi dag gi grub mtha' shan 'byed mtha' dpyod dang bcas pa'i 'bel ba'i gtam),* 88.2–3.

57. Go-ram-ba, *Explanation*, 21.a.6–b.1.

58. Ibid., 21.a.6. and 48.a.6. For a more detailed analysis of Go-ram-ba's and Ngak-chö's desperate efforts to reconcile them, see G. Dreyfus, "Ontology, Philosophy of Language and Epistemology in Buddhist Tradition" (Ph.D. diss., University of Virginia, 1991), pp. 155–58.

59. Śākya Chok-den, *Defeater*, II.30.5.

60. rdzas yod ces bya ba dang rang bzhin yod ces bya ba dang don dam par yod ces bya ba dag dang don gcig ste/ gang zag ces bya ba btags pa dang ming tsam dang tha snyad tsam du yod ces bya la/ rdzas dang rang bzhin du yod pa ma yin te/ (Lo Ken-chen, *Sun*, 122.5.6).

61. Śākya Chok-den, *Defeater*, II.36.5–39.7.

62. D. J. Kalupahana, "Aspects of the Buddhist Theory of the External World," *Ceylonese Journal of the Humanities* 1 no. 1 (1970): 103. Quoted in Keyt, "Dharmakīrti," 230.

63. Hattori, *Dignāga*, p. 89. Keyt, ibid., pp. 233–44.

64. Dignāga, *Investigation of the Object (ālambanaparīkṣā, dmigs pa brtags pa)*, P: 5703, 177.a–179.a.

65. In this context, this term seems to have, roughly speaking, the following meaning: An object is substantially existing if its perception continues to exist when its parts are removed. Here substantially existing is equivalent to ultimate existence *(paramārthasat, don dam du yod pa)* according to the Vaibhāṣika Abhidharma. In his *Auto-Commentary*, Dignāga says: "In the case of something substantially existing, its perception is not removed even when what is connected to it is removed, like in the case of color." That is, when a patch of color is divided in atoms, the individual parts remain colors, whereas the parts of, for example, a jar do not remain a jar (Dignāga, *Investigation of the Object*, P: 5703, 178.b.1–.2).

66. The first three levels are the acceptance of commonsense objects, sensibilia, and partless atoms.

67. de phyir don dang shes pa la/ rags snang yod min de bdag nyid/ gcig la bkag pa nyid phyir dang/ mang po la yang yod ma yin// (tasmān nārtheṣu na jñāne sthūlabhāsas tadātmanaḥ/ ekatra pratiṣiddhatvād bahuṣv api na sambhavaḥ/) (Dharmakīrti, *Commentary*, III:211). Material added from Ge-dün-drup, *Good Sayings*, 214.6–215.1.

68. tha dad med can shes pa yi/ tha dad snang ba bslad pa nyid/ (jñānasyābhedino

bhedapratibhāso hy upaplavaḥ/) (Dharmakīrti, *Commentary*, III:212.cd).

69. dngos rnams tha dad gnas pa 'di/ de tha dad la brten pa yin// de ni bslad pa nyid yin na/ de dag tha dad kyang bslad par 'gyur// (tadbhedāśrayiṇī ceyaṃ bhāvānāṃ bhedasaṃsthitiḥ/ tadupaplavabhāve ca teṣāṃ bhedo 'py upaplavaḥ//) (Dharmakīrti, *Commentary*, III:214). Material added from Ge-dün-drup, *Good Sayings*, 215.4–.5 and Go-ram-ba, *The Perfect Light Explaining the Meaning of the Words of the Extensive Commentary on [Dharmakīrti's] Valid Cognition (rgyas pa'i bstan bcos tshad ma rnam 'grel gyi ngag don rnam par bshad pa kun tu bzang po'i 'od zer)*, in *The Complete Works of the Great Masters of the Sa skya Sect*, vol. 11 (Tokyo: Toyo Bunko, 1968–69), 126.4.6–127.1.1.

70. In *Commentary*, III:211, Dharmakīrti denies that extension exists even subjectively. Further down (219–22), however, Dharmakīrti gives the opposite answer, providing us with two contradictory views: The true aspectarian *(satyākāra, rnam bden pa)* view that holds that the experience of extension is subjectively valid (i.e., it exists really from the side of consciousness), and the false aspectarian *(alīkākāra, rnam par rdzun pa)* view that denies this. We will come back to this point in Chapter 27.

71. des de nyid don btang snyoms can/ glang chen gzigs stangs nyid mdzad nas/ 'jig rten thugs ni 'ba' zhig gis/ phyi rol dpyod la 'jug par mdzad// (tad upekṣitatattvārthaiḥ kṛtvā gajanimīlanaṃ/ kevalaṃ lokabuddhyaiva bāhyacintā pratanyate//) (Dharmakīrti, *Commentary*, III:219). Ge-dün-drup, *Good Sayings*, 216.3–.4.

72. According to Ge-dün-drup, the passage (*Commentary*, III:209–19) reflects a view propounded by False Aspectarians *(rnal 'byor spyod pa ba rnam rdzun pa)* (*Good Sayings*, 214.2).

73. Dharmakīrti's example of the elephant's gaze illustrates that Buddha's common teachings, found in the "Hinayāna" canon, do not refer to emptiness (the absence of duality between subject and object) as the true nature of reality. According to the Mind-Only school, these teachings do not attempt to capture the full meaning of reality but are meant to satisfy the spiritual needs of people who cannot accept the ultimate truth.

Chapter 5. Ge-luk Thinkers on Specific Ontology

1. Kajiyama, *Introduction*, pp. 58–59. A similar distinction is found among later Jain thinkers arguing against the Nyāya idea that universals are omnipresent. See Dravid, *The Problem of Universals in Indian Philosophy* (Delhi: Motilal Banarsidas, 1972), p. 135; M. Hiriyanna, *Essentials of Indian Philosophy* (London: Allen and Unwin, 1949, 1985), p. 66; and N. Shah, *Akalaṅka's Criticism*, pp. 144–48.

2. Sa-paṇ, *Treasure*, p. 5.a.4. Lo Ken-chen explains a vertical universal as the conceptual unity of moments of a single thing. He also wonders about the source of these concepts, which are not found in Dharmakīrti's works, and quotes Lo-drö-tshung-may *(blo gros mtshungs med)* as asserting that they are found in Mokṣākaragupta (*Sun*, 135.2–.4) where indeed they are. See Kajiyama, *Introduction*, pp. 58–59.

3. khyab byed du 'gro ba'i spyi tsam/ (Śākya Chok-den, *Defeater*, II.30.4–.5).

4. Ibid., II.124.7–125.1. Sa-paṇ is usually quite strict about not introducing concepts in his discussion that are not directly traceable to Dharmakīrti. There are, however, some noticable exceptions, such as his treatment of defining property *(mtshan nyid, lakṣaṇa)*, which is based almost entirely on the ideas of early Tibetan thinkers.

5. *Kind-universal* will be explained while dealing with the problem of universals (Chapters 7–9), whereas *object-universal* will be examined while studying the negative way in which concepts are formed (Chapters 12–14).

6. This qualification has to do with a rather obscure point in Ge-luk philosophy that we will examine in Chapter 9. Ge-luk logic considers the generic pot as well as individual pots to be instances of pot. Thus, the generic pot (which is a universal) as well as individual pots (which are not universal) are collection-universals.

7. ya gyal du ma 'dus pa/ (Ge-dün-drup, *Ornament*, 378.1).

8. cha shas du ma 'dus pa'i gzugs rags pa/ (Pur-bu-jok, *The Presentation of the Collected Topics, the Magic Key Revealing the Meaning of the Texts on Prime Cognition, the Small Path of Reasoning*, 21.a.3).

9. rdul rdzas du ma 'dus pa la rags par snang ba'i sgro btags/ (Go-ram-ba, *Explanation*, 43.a.2).

10. Sa-paṇ, *Auto-Commentary*, 45.b.5–46.a.2.

11. Śākya Chok-den's position superficially resembles the Ge-luk view. Like this tradition, he holds that commonsense objects are not universals. The similarity ceases there, for whereas Gyel-tsap or Kay-drup hold commonsense objects to be real, Śākya Chok-den denies this. For him, they are parts of an intermediary realm between the real and the purely constructed. Ge-luk thinkers deny that such a category exists within the boundaries of Dharmakīrti's system. See Chapter 4.

12. They are included in the category of non-associated compositional factors (Śākya Chok-den, *Defeater*, II.30.4. and 412.4).

13. Lo Ken-chen, *Sun*, 65.b.3–.6.

14. Dharmakīrti, *Commentary*, III:196.cd. See Chapter 4.

15. rdul rdzas du ma cha shas su ldan pa'i gong bu/ (Kay-drup, *Ornament*, 30.b.4). Gyel-tsap makes a similar point (*Essence*, 6.b.3) and asserts that this is Sa-paṇ's view. Gyel-tsap draws on Sa-paṇ's argument against Tibetan views of the held object *(gzung yul)* of perception (see Chapter 22). There (*Auto-Commentary*, 26.b.6.), Sa-paṇ takes a jar as an example of an object that everybody can see. This clearly shows, Gyel-tsap argues, that for Sa-paṇ commonsense objects such as jars are real. The argument is not as decisive as it may first appear, for Sa-paṇ may be using here the word *jar* to refer to the form of the jar, which he probably holds to be real. See Chapter 4.

16. Literally, occasions that have several moments as their parts (skad cig du ma cha shas su ldan pa'i dus) (Kay-drup, ibid., 30.b.4).

17. Haribhadra, *Commnentary on the "Ornament of Higher Realization, Advice on the Perfection of Wisdom" (shes rab kyi pha rol tu phyin pa'i man ngag gi bstan bcos mngon par rtogs pa'i rgyan zhes bya ba'i 'grel pa)*, D: 3793, 78.b.1–104.a.7.

18. Kay-drup, *Ornament*, 29.a.3. This idea is expressed by Dharmakīrti in *Commentary*, I:161, and explained by Sa-paṇ, *Auto-Commentary*, 77.b.5–78.b.3.

19. Kay-drup adds that the fact that a whole does not appear as such to perception does not contradict that perception perceives things as they are, for this does not mean that perception has to see all the facts relevant to an object. Rather, it means that perception does not see anything in a distorted way as conception does (ibid., 30.a.2–.5).

20. spyi dang rags pa dang rgyun zhes bya ba ni sgro btags rdzas su ma grub pa'i spyi mtshan yin kyang spyi dang rags pa dang rgyun yin na rdzas su ma grub pa dang rang mtshan la sogs pa yin par mi 'gal zhing/ spyi mtshan yin pas ma khyab bo/ de'i phyir bum pa lta bu spyi yang yin rags pa yang yin rgyun yang yin rang mtshan yang yin la spyi mtshan ma yin no zhes shes par gyis shig/ (ibid., 34.a.1–.2).

21. We will come back, in Chapter 9, to the idea that substantial identity does not exclude distinctiveness. There, I will show the central role that this idea plays in the Ge-luk moderate realism.

22. Kay-drup, *Ornament*, 34.a.3–.5.

23. rang grub dus las dus gnyis par mi sdod pa (ibid., 35.a.1).

24. Contrast this with the classical idea that things endure only for a short moment. According to this more traditional way of viewing things, entities such as days and months are conceptual constructs.

25. rang grub pa'i dus las dus gnyis par mi sdod pa de tshes gcig dang tshogs na rang grub dus yud tsam sum bcu'i yun tshad du 'gyur la/ dus kyi thung ba'i mthar thug pa dang tshogs na khem pa gcig gi dus su 'gyur/ (Gyel-tsap, *Revealing*, I.116.17–.20).

26. Theoretically the difference between impermanent and permanent phenomena is well established. In practice, however, it is difficult to establish a clear difference beween phenomena that come and go due to their causes and phenomena that also come and go but not due to causes! This problem has been a classical topic of debate and is still often selected as the subject of debates. The Ge-luk tradition is perfectly aware of the difficulties of this view of permanence but uses these difficulties in the elaboration of its philosophy.

27. Pur-bu-jok, *Small Path*, p. 7.b.6.

28. Sa-gya and Ge-luk thinkers do not disagree on this but on what counts as a construct. For example, Sa-gya thinkers would argue that a continuum is a construct whereas Ge-luk thinkers would hold it to be real.

29. Dzong-ka-ba, *Door of Entrance to the Seven Treatises Clearing the Obscuration of [Those Who] Aspire (sde bdun la sjug pa'i sgo don gnyer yid kyi mun sel)*, (Banaras: Pleasure of Elegant Sayings Press, 1972), 2.4–.5.

30. mi rtag pa'i mtshan nyid du gsungs pa'i skad cig ma ni rang grub pa'i dus las dus gnyis par mi sdod pa yin gyi yud tsam zhig las mi sdod pa ni skad cig ma'i don min no/ de'i phyir lo rdzogs pa la zla ba cu gnyis rdzogs dgos shing de'i 'og tu de mi gnas pas rgyun thams cad kyang rang grub dus las dus gnyis par mi sdod pa'i skad cig ma yin no/ (Dzong-ka-ba, *The Ocean of Reasoning, a Complete Explanation of the Basic Treatise in Stanzas of the Middle Way, Called Wisdom (dbu ma rtsa ba'i tshig le'ur byas pa shes rab ces bya ba'i rnam bshad rigs pa'i rgya mtsho)* [Banaras: Pleasure of Elegant Sayings Press], 1973, 181.2–.6).

31. dper na sgras khyad par du byas pa'i mi rtag pa bum pa la rjes su mi 'gro yang mi rtag pa sgra bum gnyis ka la rjes su 'gro ba bzhin du/ dus snga ma na yod pa'i bum pa dus phyi ma na med kyang bum pa dus snga phyi gnyis su gnas pa yang mi 'gal lo/ (Dzong-ka-ba, *Ocean*, 181.6–.9).

32. This view of momentariness is not the same as the Vaibhāṣika idea that things endure unchanged before changing. The difference is clear in the respective views of these traditions on causality. Whereas the Vaibhāṣika school holds that causes and effects can coexist, the Ge-luk tradition accepts the Sautrāntika view that causes necessarily cease when their effects arise. This view creates difficulties in the Ge-luk system, for if things can exist for a long time as continua, some of their effects will be produced before they disappear. This tension is a favored topic of debate in the Ge-luk monastic universities. No amount of debate, however, can solve this problem, which comes from the attempt to combine two elements that pull apart; namely, commonsense and the doctrine of momentariness in its strict understanding.

33. kun tu tha snyad pa'i tshad ma. Go-ram-ba explains that this is the type of pragmatic valid cognition present in all ordinary beings, irrespective of whether they are influenced by a philosophical view, and that helps us in developing what is helpful and avoiding what is harmful. Other valid cognitions are those that are present only in people influenced by tenets as well as supramundane cognitions such as yogic perception (Go-ram-ba,

Explanation, p. 16.b.4–.6). Dharmakīrti refers to such valid cognition at the end of his first chapter of *Ascertainment*, when he says: "this [text] is an explanation of the nature of conventional valid cognition" *('di ni kun tu tha snyad pa'i tshad ma'i rang bzhin brjod pa yin no)*, (*Ascertainment of Valid Cognition*, D: 4211, 167.a.6.). Dharmakīrti adds that he has only partially explained ultimate valid cognition produced by thinking and meditating. C. Lindtner has argued that this refers to Dharmakīrti's choice not to put to the forefront his Yogācāra philosophy. "Marginalia to Dharmakīrti's Pramāṇa-viniścaya I–II," *Wiener Zeitschrift für die Kunde Südasiens* 28 (1984): 149–75. There is very little evidence supporting this view. Go-ram-ba's explanation that Dharmakīrti's epistemology explains how ordinary cognitions operate, leaving out yogic perceptions, which operate in a radically different way (through the power of meditation), seems more cogent.

34. Śākya Chok-den, *Music*, 471.6–.7.

35. kun rdzob 'jig rten grags pa la/ brten na tshad ma'i rnam bzhag 'gal/ (Sa-paṇ, *Treasure*, 3.b.2). See also *Auto-Commentary*, 32.b.5–33.a.2.

36. Ge-dün-drup, *Ornament*, p. 306.19–.20.

37. rtog pas btags pa min par rang ngos nas thun mong ma yin pa'i rang bzhin du gnas pa'i ngos po'o/ (Kay-drup, *Ornament*, I:21.b.2–.3).

38. Gyel-tsap says: "[Everything] that is specifically characterized abides determined [with respect to] entity, time, and location. This is the uncommon meaning-distinguisher (*don ldog*; i.e., definition) of the specifically characterized" (rang mtshan yin na yul dang dus dang ngo bo ma 'dres par gnas la/ de rang mtshan gyi thun mong ma yin pa'i don ldog kyang yin zhing/) (*Revealing*, I.78.7–9). Contrast this with the definition given by Gyel-tsap, *Revealing*, II.6.14–7.1. Taken at face value, this passage does indeed suggest that Gyel-tsap holds determinate existence to be the defining mark of reality. However, this passage does not represent his own position but that of an adversary (contrary to what several contemporary Ge-luk scholars assert; Klein seems to follow their opinion, in *Knowledge*, p. 46)! This is quite clear from what Gyel-tsap says in the passage right before this quote. Referring to his adversary, he says: "Hey, you people of small minds, have you not eaten any *datura* (an Indian hallucinogen)? You should wipe your eyes again and again and look. Now, I will examine *this* [position: Everything] that is specifically characterized abides determinate [with respect to] entity, time, and location. This is [supposed to be] the uncommon meaning-distinguisher (*don ldog*; i.e., definition) of the specifically characterized. [Existence] in a determinate location is [supposed to entail] that it is contradictory for something to exist in the west if it exists in the east . . ." (kye shes chung ba dag da du ra zos pa min nam mig yang dang yang phyis la ltos shig/ da ni 'di dpyad par bya ste/ rang mtshan yin na yul dang dus dang ngo bo ma 'dres par gnas la/ de rang mtshan gyi thun mong ma yin pa'i don ldog kyang yin zhing/ yul ma 'dres pa ni shar na gnas na nub na gnas par 'gal ba dang/) (*Revealing*, I.78.6–10). Gyel-tsap is here referring to his adversary's position according to which a thing exists in a determinate way only if it has a punctual existence. Only partless particles that last for a single moment exist in a determinate way. Macroscopic objects such as jars and trees are not specifically characterized because they exist in more than one place and endure through time. Accordingly, they are generally characterized phenomena. But Gyel-tsap holds a diametrically opposed position on the question of the reality of macroscopic objects, and he is describing the view of an opponent (*Revealing*, I.79.2–.18).

39. The meaning-distinguisher of a phenomenon is its defining property. The two meaning-distinguishers are the defining properties of specifically characterized and generally characterized phenomena.

40. don dam par don byed nus pa gang yin pa de chos can/ bstan bcos 'dir don dam par yod pa yin te/ rtog pas btags tsam min par yul rang gi sdod lugs kyi ngos nas grub pa'i phyir/ de las gzhan don byed nus stong chos can/ kun rdzob tu yod pa yin ste/ rtog pas btags tsam gyi tshul gyis grub pa'i phyir/ ji skad bshad pa'i don ldog gnyis po de dag rang mtshan gyi mtshan nyid dang/ spyi'i mtshan nyid du bshad pa'i rgyu mtshan yod de/ don ldog de gnyis kyi dbang gis mtshon bya gnyis thun mong ma yin par so sor 'jog nus pa'i rgyu mtshan gyis de ltar bshad pa'i phyir/ (Gyel-tsap, *Revealing*, II.6.14–7.1).

41. Kay-drup, *Ornament*, 32.b.3–33.a.6.

42. This is considered to be the defining property of phenomenon.

43. Dzong-ka-ba, *Door*, 8.

44. Dzong-ka-ba, *Ocean*, 181.6–.9. See previously.

45. Excluding the definition in terms of causal efficiency, which relates more to the concept of thing *(vastu, dngos po)* than to that of the specifically characterized.

46. Gyel-tsap, *Revealing*, I.80.3.

47. This is a point often raised in debates. Some scholars attempt a solution by reading into Gyel-tsap's text an acceptance of the sets of criteria as defining the real. It is clear, however, that this reading rests on a misidentification, as explained earlier.

48. Pur-bu-jok, *Small Path*, 8.b.2.

49. yul rang ngos nas grub pa'i gnas lugs kyi ngo bo ma yin par rtog pas btags tsam gyi chos su grub pa'o/ (Kay-drup, *Ornament*, 35.a.2).

50. Ibid., 21.a.4–.5.

51. There is a difficulty of translation here. Since Tibetan language has no articles, a word such as *bum pa* can mean *pot*, *the* pot, *a* pot, or even *being* a pot. I will return to this ambiguity in Chapter 9.

52. yul dang shes bya gzhal bya dang yod nges dang gzhi grub rnams don gcig/ (Ge-dün-drup, *Ornament*, 301.20–302.1. This list is found in the Collected Topics with one or two insignificant changes: Definite existence is usually replaced by existence, and phenomenon *(chos, dharma)* is added to the list.

53. In the Ge-luk tradition, two phenomena are equivalent *(don gcig)* if, and only if, they are coextensive. For example, thing *(dngos po)* and composed phenomenon *('dus byas)* are equivalent because everything that is one is also the other. For more detail on this way of describing the relation between two phenomena (or perhaps between the two classes defined by two phenomena), see Dreyfus, "Some Considerations on Definitions in Buddhist Tradition" (MA thesis, University of Virginia, Charlottesville, 1987).

54. yul gyi mtshan nyid/ blos rig par ba ba/ shes bya'i mtshan nyid/ blo'i yul du bya rung ba/ gzhal bya'i mtshan nyid/ tshad ma'i rtogs par bya/ yod nges kyi mtshan nyid/ tshad mas dmigs pa/ gzhi grub gyi mtshan nyid tshad mas grub pa/ (Ge-dün-drup, *Ornament*, 302.1–.4).

55. Klein, *Knowledge*, p. 181.

56. See Chapter 2.

57. Dharmakīrti, *Commentary*, I:186.d.

58. Ibid., IV:263.b.

59. 'jig la 'bras dang yod pa bzhin no/ zhes yod pa sgra mi rtag sgrub kyi rtags yang dag tu bshad pa ji ltar yin ce na/ yod pa dmigs pa las gzhan ma yin/ zhes pa ltar/ yod pa dang tshad mas dmigs pa don gcig tu byas pa'i yod pa ma yin gyi/ rang gi ngo bo rang dbang yod pa la yod pa'i sgra spyi sgra bye brag la sbyar nas/ de lta bu'i yod pa de sgra mi rtag par sgrub pa'i rtags yang dag tu bshad pa yin no/ de bas na yod pa la rnam pa gnyis te/ rang gi ngo bo sgrub par rang dbang ba'i rnam par yod pa dang/ dgag bya bcad pa tsam du yod

pa'o/ gnyis ka'ang tshad mas dmigs pa'i phyir yod pa mtshan nyid pa yin la/ 'on kyang sgra dog 'jug gi dbang du byas nas/ spyi sgra bye brag la sbyar te/ rang gi ngo bo sgrub par rang dbang gi sgo nas yod pa la yod pa zhes sgra sbyar nas/ yod pa sgra mi rtag sgrub kyi rtags yand dag tu bshad pa yin te/ (Kay-drup, *Ornament*, 12.a.2–.5).

60. In this work, I usually use the word *existence* to refer to mere existence, reserving the word *real* to designate the existence of effective things.

61. Kay-drup, *Ocean*, I:895.3–.6.

62. A similar difference exists between the two schools in the domain of Madhyamaka philosophy. Whereas Dzong-ka-ba asserts that the conventional existence of phenomena is not reducible to mere creation by ignorance, Go-ram-ba asserts that conventional phenomena are just creations of ignorance that are valid only for sentient beings under the power of illusion. See Dzong-ka-ba, *Extensive Stages of the Path to Enlightenment (byang chub lam rim chen mo)* (Dharamsala: Shes rig par khang, block); and Go-ram-ba, *Distinguishing the View, the Moonlight of the Essential Points of the Best Vehicle (lta ba'i shan byed theg mchog gnad gyi zla zer)* (Banaras: Sakya Press, 1988).

Chapter 6. Introducing Universals

1. Let me remind my reader that *realism* can be used in several ways. This work uses the term in relation to the problem of universals unless otherwise specified. See Chapter 1.

2. Sellars, "Empiricism and the Philosophy of Mind," in *Science*, p. 169.

3. N. Goodman, "A World of Individuals," in P. Benacerraf and H. Putnam, *Philosophy of Mathematics*, pp. 196–210.

4. Modern analytical philosophers argue about the semantic of proper names. Frege holds that proper names both denote and connote, like any any other meaningful items. Mill denies this and holds that proper names do not have any meaning. Their only function is to single out an object. Naiyāyikas and Buddhists do not make this distinction, but they would favor Frege's view, which is that names have a minimal sense. What is this sense? It is not a definite description, but the simple fact that a certain individual can be called in this way. For example, the sense of Moses is not that of being a person who guided the Hebrews out of Egypt but just the fact of bearing that name. I take that traditional authors would be sympathetic to this Quinean account.

5. J. L. Mackie, *Problems from Locke* (Oxford: Oxford University Press, 1976), pp. 130–39.

6. Quine is less a nominalist than Goodman. Although Quine is suspicious of abstract entities and is reluctant to use them to explain common experiences, he realizes that one cannot do without them in domains such as mathematics.

7. This does not meant that this is Wittgenstein's solution. A discussion of Wittgenstein's view on universals must take into account his general attitude toward philosophy, as we will see in our final conclusions.

8. Sellars, "Empiricism," p. 169.

9. Ibid., p. 168.

10. At this stage of our investigation, the word *concept* remains somewhat vague. In the chapters on the *apoha* theory, we will show that for Dharmakīrti concepts are mental representations that stand for an unreal property.

11. Quine, *From a Logical Point of View*, p. 15. Quine himself distinguishes realism, conceptualism and nominalism.

12. Monier-Williams, *Dictionary*, p. 309.2.

13. This is only an example, for an extreme realist is not commited to hold that redness exists but only that there is some real and independent property in relation to which redness can be assessed.

14. The Medieval quarrel over universals was not just philosophical but had important theological and political implications. Aquinas's realism allows a strong connection between human thought and reality. This becomes translated theologically into an affirmation of a link between God, human beings, and the world. Ockham's nominalism, on the contrary, denies that there is such a link, for, according to him, there is no natural link between human thought and reality. The relation between human beings and God is a contingent covenant. It is no surprise that the Church chose Aquinas's doctrine, which supports its authority, and condemned Ockham. See Ozment, *The Age*, pp. 54, 60–63, and D. Knowles, *Evolution of Medieval Philosophy*, p. 111.

15. He is an eighth century Jain philosopher who offers a moderate realist view as a middle path between Nyāya extreme realism and Buddhist antirealism. See Dravid, *The Problem*, pp. 130–54.

16. On Scotus, see G. Leff, *The Dissolution of the Medieval Outlook* (New York: New York University Press, 1976) and E. Bettoni, *Dun Scotus: The Basic Principles of his Philosophy* (Washington, D.C.: Catholic University Press, 1961).

17. See Chapter 9.

18. Sāṃkhya is monist in its assertion that all empirical reality is the emanation of Nature, but modifies this view by holding to the plurality of selves and their absolute separation from Nature.

19. I follow here the usage of the later Nyāya in identifying *sāmānya* and *jāti*. There is good evidence that Vātsyāyana held the two to be separate. Whereas *sāmānya* was an intensional notion, the principle according to which objects are divided into classes (cowness), *jāti* was extensional, the class of these objects so divided (the class of cows). See Barlingay, *Introduction*, pp. 87–88, 92; and Biardeau, *Theorie*, pp. 229–40.

20. A glimpse of the sociological context of this notion of type may be noteworthy. In opposition to the group of bald men, which is not a real type, that of brahmins is the example for a natural type. The Sanskrit *jāti* means primarily birth, indicating the group of people that share in a birth and a name.

21. Universal is also an ontologically significant category, especially in the old Vaiśeṣika school. Thinkers of this school were attempting to understand the ultimate components of material reality. For them, universals designate natural types (such as man or pine tree) and refer to individuals that are similar in some important and nonsubjective fashion. In the Nyāya school, the ontological role of universals is not as significant as their semantic role.

22. Real universals are opposed to imposed entities *(upādhi)*. For example, the group of prematurely bald men is an artificial construction that does not correspond to a natural type. A common property is recognized as a true type only if it is in accordance with the brevity of assumption *(kalpanā-lāghava)*. Thus, according to this later version of Nyāya realism, the predication of general terms requires the existence of some true universals but does not require that every general term correspond to such a universal. This view was developed as a response to the Buddhist criticism that the Nyāya view leads to an absurd multiplication of entities.

23. An entity must be noncomplex to be a generic property. Being a cook, for example, does not qualify as a generic property because it is made up by several properties. B. K. Matilal, *Epistemology, Logic, and Grammar in Indian Philosophy* (The Hague: Mouton, 1971), p. 72.

24. Later Naiyāyikas define *jāti* as having permanence, commoness, and inherence in many individuals. Dravid, *The Problem*, p. 16.

25. As is the case for substances, which continually disintegrate and re-emerge.

26. Dravid, *The Problem*, pp. 53–72.

27. There are conflicting theories of universals within the Jain tradition, as explained by Dravid, ibid., pp. 140–46; Shah, *Akalaṅka's Criticism*, pp. 144–48; and Hiriyanna, *Essentials*, p. 65.

28. Locke, *Essay Concerning Human Understanding*, "Of General Terms," p. 6, quoted in H. Staniland, *Universals* (New York: Anchor, 1972), p. 28.

29. This emergence of questions relating to language as the central focus of philosophical enquiry is a relatively new phenomenon in the West. It is described by Richard Rorty in *Philosophy and the Mirror of Nature* as a *linguistic turn*. Although language was obviously an important element of philosophical reflection for ancient Greek thinkers, questions relating to language were rarely given special philosophical significance. That place was usually reserved for mathematics, geometry, and science, which were considered paradigms of knowledge.

Chapter 7. Dharmakīrti on Universals

1. A considerable literature has developed around this topic recently. See E. Steinkellner, "On the Interpretation of the Svabhāvahetu," *Wiener Zeitschrift für die Kunde Südasiens* 18 (1974): 117–29. E. Steinkellner, "The Logic of the *svabhāvahetu* in Dharmakīrti's Vādanyāya," *Studies in the Buddhist Epistemological Tradition* (Vienna: Österreichische Akademie der Wissenschaften, 1991), pp. 311–24. R. Hayes, "On the Reinterpretation of Dharmakīrti's *Svabhāvahetu*," *Journal of Indian Philosophy* 15 (1987): 319–32; S. Matsumoto, "Svabhāvapratibandha," *Indogaku Bukkyogaku Kenkyū* 30 (1981): 498–4; S. Katsura, "*Svabhāvapratibandha* Revisited," *Indogaku Bukkyogaku Kenkyū* 30 (1981): 476–3. For more general background, see Steinkellner, "Wirklichkeit und Begriff" and Kajiyama, *Introduction*.

2. See Chapter 10.

3. See Chapter 8.

4. Dharmakīrti, *Commentary*, III:25–26. We can see here the polemical nature of Indian argumentations. Dharmakīrti does not argue from Nyāya premises but from his own. According to his system, if an entity is different from other entities it can be related to these entities only causally. This relation is what is called *tadutpatti*, *de byung 'brel*, or *relation of origination*.

5. Another argument pointing to the same lack of clear criteria for the identity of universals is offered by Dignāga (*Compendium*, V:17–18, P: 10.a.7–.8) and Dharmakīrti (*Commentary*, I:89–90). A universal is a single entity that is supposed by the realist to abide in a plurality of instances. Is it divisible or not? If it is, particulars would instantiate only part of the universal. For example, a cow would possess only a portion of cowness. If it is not, how can an entity abide in its entirety in different places and times? See R. Hayes, *Dignāga on the Interpretation of Signs* (Dordrecht: Kluwer, 1988), pp. 183, 282–87. Plato puts a similar argument in the mouth of the old philosopher Parmenides against his own theory of forms. *Parmenides*, 130.e–131.e.

6. gzhan nyid yin na de 'brel med/ de phyir rang bzhin med par grub/ med pa'i rigs su thal mi 'gyur/ de la ltos pa med pa'i phyir// de phyir ngo bo la brten nas/ ngo bo med pa'i

rigs brtags pa/ khyad par de la 'jug don can/ sgra rnams kyis ni rab tu bstan// (anyatve asambadhaṃ siddhā 'to niḥsvabhāvatā/ jātiprasaṅgo 'bhāvasya nāpekṣā 'bhāvatas tayoḥ// tasmād arūpā rūpānāṃ āśrayenopakalpitā/ tadviśeṣāvagāhārthair jātiḥ śabdaiḥ prakāśyate//) (Dharmakīrti, *Commentary*, III:27–28, Ge-dün-drup, *Good Sayings*, 170.6–71.4. This passage further proves that Dharmakīrti differentiates between conceptual contents, which are unreal but not completely nonexistent, and nonexistents.

7. de spyi khyad par zhes bya ba'i/ bye brag 'di ni blo don la/ de nyid la gzhang las ldog pas/ chos kyi bye brag rab tu brtag// (bhedas tato 'yam bauddhe 'rthe sāmānyaṃ bheda ity api/ tasyaiva cānyavyāvṛttyā dharmabhedaḥ prakalpyate//) (Dharmakīrti, *Commentary*, I:88). Ge-dün-drup, *Good Sayings*, 28.2. Frauwallner, "Beiträge," p. 389.

8. This notion is already found in the Sāṃkhya literature. See Patañjali, *Yogasūtra*, I.9 in J. Wood, trans., *The Yoga-System of Patañjali* (Delhi: Motilal, 1912, 1988), p. 26. It is also elaborately used by Bhatṛhari.

9. B. K. Matilal, *Logical and Ethical Issues of Religious Belief* (Calcutta: University of Calcutta, 1982), p. 95.

10. Hayes, *Dignāga*, p. 186.

11. Dravid, *Problem*, p. 345.

12. Ibid., p. 266.

13. Ibid., p. 289.

14. My discussion here largely borrows from Matilal, *Logical and Ethical Issues*, pp. 95–100.

15. Compare this to Quine's assertion that "Everything to which we concede existence is a posit from the standpoint of a description of the theory-building process, and simultaneously real from the standpoint of the theory that is being built," *Word and Object* (Cambridge, Mass.: MIT Press, 1960), p. 22.

16. The reader may wish to keep in mind that *real similarities* is my shorthand for "real things that share some degree of similarity in their functions."

17. Dharmakīrti, *Commentary*, I:108.c.

18. Gnoli, ed., *The Pramāṇa Vārttika of Dharmakīrti* (Rome: Ismeo, 1960), I:46.11.

19. gcig rtogs don shes la sogs pa/ don gcig sgrub la 'ga' zhig ni/ tha dad yin yang rang bzhin gyis/ nges te dbang po la sogs bzhin// dper sman kha cig tha dad kyang/ lhan cig pa'am so so yis/ rims la sogs pa zhi byed par/ mthong gi gzhan gyis ma yin bzhin// (ekapratyavamarśārthajñānādyekārthasādhane/ bhede 'pi niyatāḥ kecit svabhāvenendriyādivat// jvarādiśamane kāścit saha pratyekam eva vā/ dṛṣṭā yathā vauṣadhayo nānātve 'pi na cāparāḥ//) (Dharmakīrti, *Commentary*, I:73–74). Additions from Ge-dün-drup, *Good Sayings*, 25.4; Frauwallner, "Beiträge," p. 384.

20. This example is well known in Buddhist epistemology. It is given by several authors including Śāntarakṣita, who holds the same resemblance theory as Dharmakīrti. In view of the clear assertion by Dharmakīrti and Śāntarakṣita that essential resemblances exist, I find it difficult to understand Siderits's description of Śāntarakṣita's *apoha* philosophy as "an extreme form of nominalism which makes do without the relation of resemblance." See Mark Siderits, "More Things in Heaven and Earth," *Journal of Indian Philosophy* 10, no. 2 (1982): 186–208, 188.

21. Gnoli, ed., *Pramāṇa*, 40.22–41.4. Quoted in Keyt, "Dharmakīrti," p. 95.

22. D. Hume, *Treatise of Human Nature*, quoted in H. Staniland, *Universals*, p. 42.

23. Hindu thinkers hold that there is such a thing as a similarity *(sādṛśya)*. The Prabhākara school of Mīmāṃsā holds similarity to be a basic category of reality. The Bāṭṭha holds a middle ground between the Buddhist denial of objective similarity and the

Prabhākara emphasis of similarity as a fundamental building block of reality. See Nandita Bandyopadhyay, "The Concept of Similarity in Indian Philosophy," *Journal of Indian Philosophy* 10 (1982): 239–75.

24. Here, Dharmakīrti can be imagined answering Russell's qualm that "Having been forced to admit this universal (resemblance), we find it no longer worthwhile to invent difficult and implausible theories to avoid the admission of such universals as whiteness and triangularity" (B. Russell, "The World of Universals," quoted in M. Loux, "The Problem of Universals," in Loux, ed., *Universals and Particulars* [New York: Anchor, 1970], p. 14).

25. Mohanty has rightly emphasized the preponderant place of causal theories in Indian philosophy. He speaks of the dominance of a "peculiarly ontological causal attitude which prevails in most Indian schools, especially in the Nyāya-Vaiśeṣika. Even the epistemology is not free from causal considerations" (J. Mohanty, *Gaṅgeṣa's Theory of Truth* [Delhi: Motilal, 1966, 1989], p. 51).

26. Dharmakīrti, *Commentary*, I:72.

27. The philosophical background of the Nyāya objection is that production of a single effect cannot be explained without the presence of a common element pulling together the different causes, which are unable to produce the effect by themselves. This has in turn epistemological consequences, for knowledge itself is to be included in the domain of causality. Thus, the Nyāya objection that different causes require a common element to produce a common effect does not concern the production of merely external things but also that of knowledge. Perception, for example, is an effect produced by several causes (sense power, object, intention, etc.) and requires a single common element that pulls together the different causal factors.

28. E. Rosch, "Principles of Categorization," quoted in J. Haugeland, *Mind Design* (Cambridge, Mass.: MIT Press, 1981), p. 177.

Chapter 8. Sa-gya Antirealism and the Problems of Predication

1. Let me remind the reader that, in this work, the word *antirealist* is taken as referring to a rejection of real universals. My use of this term is unrelated to Dummett's argument against realism in his famous "Truth."

2. See Chapter 3.

3. They have neither spatio-temporal nor essential determination. Sa-paṇ, *Auto-Commentary*, 44.a.1–b.3. See also Chapter 2.

4. rigs mi mthun rnam par dpyad (bcad) tsam gyi ldog pa cig kyang/ (Śākya Chok-den, *Defeater*, II.118.4). Go-ram-ba gives a similar definition: the superimposition appearing as a single distinguisher that is different from phenomena of a discordant kind in relation to its individuals (rang gi gsal ba rnams la ltos nas rigs mi mthun las ldog pa'i ldog pa chig kyang du snang ba'i sgro btags), *Clarification*, 24.5.

5. I will discuss "unique" later in this chapter when I contrast universals and individuations.

6. Sa-paṇ, *Auto-Commentary*, 46.a.1.

7. Dharmakīrti's arguments against the Sāṃkhya are found scattered throughout his works. The most systematic critique is found in *Commentary*, I:163–79.

8. Its closest Indian equivalent is the position defended by the Jain philosopher Samantabhadra. Unfortunately, Tibetan authors have not given the Jain tradition the recognition that it deserves.

9. Sa-paṇ, *Auto-Commentary*, 46.b.3–47.a.1.

10. dngos dang dngos med gnyis ka la/ brten phyir spyi de'ang rnam pa gsum// (sāmānyaṃ trividhaṃ tac ca bhāvābhāvobhayāśrayāt//) (Dharmakīrti, *Commentary*, III:51.cd).

11. We will see that such shyness does not affect Kay-drup, who resolutely asserts the reality of some universals. Ge-dün-drup is less courageous. When the issue of real universals is raised, he answers that Dharmakīrti's refutation refers to universals as asserted by the Sāṃkhya and the Vaiśeṣika (*Ornament*, 359.19–360.11). He seems to shy away from the open admission that there are real universals.

12. bod dag gis shing spyi dngos po bar ma grub kyi shing dang dngos po'i gzhi mthun yod par khas len pa yin no zhes pa'i tshig gi sgrib gyogs ltar na shing gsal rnams kyi spyir 'gyur pa'i shing chos can du bzung nas dgag par bya'o/ (Go-ram-ba, *Explanation*, 55.a.1–.2).

13. Ibid., 49.a.4–53.a.3.

14. Dharmakīrti, *Commentary*, I:171.d. In this passage Dharmakīrti describes things as having discrete appearance, being real, differentiated phenomena, causes and effects, specifically characterized phenomena, and objects of practice and abandonment.

15. de ni gzhan las log pa yin/ zhes sogs kyi 'grel bshad du/ Śākya blos/ spyi zhes bya ba'i dngos po gyur ba ni cun zad kyang yod pa ma yin no/ gsung pa'i don dang 'gal mi 'gal soms shig/ (Go-ram-ba, *Explanation*, 55.a.4–.5).

16. I will leave aside the problem raised by a proposition such as "all sounds are impermanent."

17. Contrary to the most common usage in Western philosophy in which subject and predicate are considered linguistic entities, I distinguish the subject and predicate, which are real objects, from the subject expression and the predicate expression, which are linguistic items. I believe that this way of putting things is not completely unlike Strawson's. See *Individuals*.

18. Śākya Chok-den, *Defeater*, II.215.3–.4.

19. B. K. Matilal, *Logic, Language and Reality*, p. 274. Also pp. 269–84, 378–89.

20. In this chapter, I consider only the cases of predication that involve real phenomena such as sound, pot, or impermanence. The other cases can be easily explained once these more difficult ones have been understood.

21. Śākya Chok-den, *Defeater*, II.104.2–.3.

22. chos can gang la ltos nas spyi dang ldog pa la sogs par bzhag pa'i tshe/ chos can de la ltos pa'i blo chos kho na yin gyi/ don chos su 'gal ba'i phyir/ (ibid., II.104.3).

23. A thing is taken from a real perspective when it is taken from the point of view of how it appears to perception. I will explain the role of that distinction for Śākya Chok-den.

24. de ltar na sgra mi rtag ces dang/ sgra byas so zhes brjod pa'i tshe/ sel ngo'i byas pa dang mi rtag pa de snang ngo dang sel ngo gnyis ka'i chos can sgra la ltos pa'i spyi dang/ gzhan sel dang ldog pa sogs yin la/ de dang de brjod pa'i sgra de yang de la ltos pa'i rigs brjod kyi sgra dang/ chos brjod kyi sgra kho na'o/ (Śākya Chok-den, *Defeater*, II.104.7–105.1).

25. Ibid., *Defeater*, II.138.1. Go-ram-ba makes a similar point in *Clarification*, 32.2–5.

26. de la'ang gzhan las ldog pa dang/ gzhan las log pa zhes bya ba'i/ sgra dang nges pa nyid dag ni/ brda yi rjes su byed pa yin// (tatrāpi cānyavyāvṛttir anyavyāvṛtta ity api/ śabdāś ca niścayāś caiva saṃketam anurundhate//) (Dharmakīrti, *Commentary*, I:59). Also Frauwallner, "Beiträge," p. 387.

27. Sa-paṇ made a similar distinction between real *(don la gnas pa)* and conceptual (literally, eliminative, *sel ba*) substances (*Auto-Commentary*, 44.a.5).

28. Śākya Chok-den, *Defeater*, II.102.7–103.3.

29. Ibid., II.111.3.

30. Sa-paṇ says: "[Be] wise by differentiating when explaining and successful by mistaking [real things and concepts] as one when engaging in practical activities" ('chad tshe rnam par phye bas mkhas/ 'jug tshe gcig tu 'khrul bas thob/) (*Treasure*, 8.b.6).

31. Usually, the argument is stated as sound is impermanent because it is produced. There is an ambiguity in this formulation. Are we speaking about a particular sound, all sounds, linguistic sounds, or language? My formulation is meant to resolve the ambiguity and restores some of the contextual importance of the argument.

32. Śākya Chok-den, *Defeater*, II.113.6.

33. Ibid., II.149.4 and 288.5.

34. On this topic, see N. Bandyopadhyay, "The Concept of Contradiction in Indian Logic and Epistemology," *Journal of Indian Philosophy* 16 (1988): 225–46.

35. Śākya Chok-den, *Defeater*, I.532.3–.7.

36. See D. Perdue, *Debate in Tibetan Buddhism* (Ithaca, N.Y.: Snow Lion, 1992). Several Sa-gya scholars do not show much consideration for this kind of literature. Lo Ken-chen refers to the debates explained in these texts as childish games (*Sun*, p. 129.2). Modern scholars have started to explore this literature from a logical point of view, showing that it is far from being a childish game. It manifests an incipient but real interest into logic in the narrower sense of the word. See M. Goldberg, "Entity and Antinomy in Tibetan Logic (I, II)," *Journal of Indian Philosophy* 13 (1985): 153–99, 273–304 and T. Tillemans, "Formal and Semantic Aspects on Tibetan Buddhist Debate Logic," *Journal of Indian Philosophy* 17 (1989): 265–97.

37. Jam-hang-chok-hla-ö-zer, *The Key to Knowledge, Cause of the Roar of the Five-faced Lion that Destroys the Elephant of Faulty Adversaries, [and] Opens the Door to the Knowledge of the Collected Text of the Commentary on "Prime Cognition." (tshad ma rnam 'grel gyi bsdus gzhung zhes bya'i sgo 'byed rgol ngan glang po 'joms pa gdong nga'i gad rgyangs rgyu rig lde mig)*, 14.3–30.2.

38. The intension of a concept is the set of properties that make up this concept in opposition to its extension; that is, the things that fall under the concept. In the example of the concept of thing, thingness is the intension of the concept, whereas the individual things are its extension.

39. Ge-luk thinkers make this point by a rather technical distinction between two types of distinguishers: an own distinguisher *(rang ldog)* and a basis distinguisher *(gzhi ldog)*. The basis distinguisher of a phenomenon is its instance. For example, a blue pot is a basis distinguisher of pot. The own distinguisher (also called the general distinguisher, *spyi ldog*) is the conceptual identity of the thing and equivalent to the distinguisher of that thing. The tradition distinguishes another type of distinguisher, the meaning distinguisher *(don ldog)*, which is the definition of a phenomenon. For example, being able to perform a function is the meaning distinguisher of thing. In this way, the subject is unreal from the point of view of its own distinguisher, i.e., in its own identity, but is real from the point of view of its basis distinguisher (its instances).

40. sgra dang mi rtag pa dang byas pa zhes ldog pa tha dad blos phye ba yin gyi don la med do/ (Sa-paṇ, *Auto-Commentary*, 73.a.5).

41. Sa-paṇ polemically observes that this idea is similar to the Sāṃkhya view that Nature and the three qualities that compose it exist as one entity in things (ibid., 73.a.6, b.6).

42. The Ge-luk tradition differentiates one substance *(rdzas gcig)*, which applies only to real things, and one entity *(ngo bo gcig)*, which applies to conceptual entities as well. For

Sa-paṇ, this distinction does not hold since conceptual entities are only quasi-entities.

43. Sa-paṇ, *Auto-Commentary*, 73.b.2–.4.

44. See Chapter 2.

45. Śākya Chok-den, *Defeater*, II.122.1–7, 222.4.

46. The Ge-luk argument is that anything that exists *(x)* must be its own distinguisher because it is different from its contradictory (non-*x*). Sa-gya thinkers answer that this confuses being different with being a distinguisher.

47. gser bum bum pa yin no zhes brjod pa'i de'i tshe bum pa ldog pa sogs su khas len cing de ltar na yang rang gi ldog pa ma yin te/ gser bum gyi ldog pa la sogs par khas len pa'i phyir/ (Śākya Chok-den, *Defeater*, II.122.3–4, 222.4–.5).

48. log ldog dang spyi gsal mtshungs pa'i rtsod spang/ (Gyel-tsap, *Revealing*, I.94.9–.10).

49. rtog pas btags tsam gyi chos/ (Kay-drup, *Ornament*, 221.6).

50. rang gi rigs mi mthun pa las log cing rang dang rigs mthun pa nang las kyang ldog pa'i ldog pa gnyis tshogs/ (Śākya Chok-den, *Defeater*, II.118.4). Go-ram-ba gives the following definition: the superimposition that appears as the assemblage of two distinguishers [different] from [phenomena of] discordant as well as concordant kind (rigs mi mthun dang rang rigs mthun kyang las ldog pa gnyis tshogs su snang ba'i sgro btags) (*Clarification*, 25.2).

51. Śākya Chok-den, *Defeater*, II.119.5.

52. Gyel-tsap mentions this conception of universal and individuation as conceptual characteristics (i.e., distinguishers), which would seem to imply an antirealist view of universals, but this does not prevent him from adopting a realist view concerning universals (*Revealing*, I.95.10). Gyel-tsap argues that the fact of universals being distinguishers does not contradict the reality of universals without which reality would be reduced to absolute singularity (*Essence*, 29.b.2–6).

53. Śākya Chok-den, *Defeater*, II.118.4.

54. See Dreyfus, "Ontology," pp. 258–67.

55. Śākya Chok-den, *Defeater*, II.215.3. A similar view is expressed by Go-ram-ba, *Explanation*, 43.b.1–.2; and by Ngak-chö, *Bestower*, 99.6–.7.

56. mdor na bye brag zhes bya ba 'di ni rdzas so so ba rnams la zer ba ma yin gyi/ rdzas gcig po'i de'i steng tu brjod byed kyi sgra dang/ rtog pa don mthun gyi ldog pa mang por phye ba de'i tshe na/ ldog pa so so ba de rnams la/ bye brag ces bya la/ rdzas de'i steng tu de min rnam par bsal ba tsam gyi ldog pa gcig po de la spyi zhes bya ba yin no/ de las gzhan du rdzas kyi khyad par so so ba rnams bye brag yin no/ zhes bya ba 'di ni mu stegs bye brag pa'i lugs bla na med pa yin te/ (Śākya Chok-den, *Defeater*, II.126.6–127.1). The reference to the Vaiśeṣika view is puzzling, for this school differentiates individual objects, which are substances, from individuations, which are the real differentiating characteristics of a substance. Śākya Chok-den seems to be carried away by his rhetoric.

Chapter 9. Ge-luk Realism

1. I refer the reader to Chapter 6.

2. rang gi gsal ba du ma la rjes su 'gro ba'i chos/ (Pur-bu-jok, *Small Path*, 20.b.6). Compare this with the Nyāya restriction that a genuine universal must be realized in more than one individual. See Matilal, *Epistemology*, p. 73. Go-ram-ba criticizes this definition for using the word *manifold*, thereby implying that a universal must have at least three

instances (*Clarification*, 42.b.4). This criticism does not seem to be valid, for it confuses the word *many* as used by Sanskrit grammarians (singular-dual-plural) and the same word used in philosophical contexts (singular-plural).

3. rang gi rigs can du ma la rjes su 'gro ba'i chos/ (Pur-bu-jok, *Small Path*, 21.a.1). A similar definition is found in Dzong-ka-ba, *Door*, 34.8.

4. Here, an individuation is the individual that instantiates a given universal. The word I have translated as *individual* is *gsal ba (vyakti)* and literally means manifestation.

5. This akward way of putting things is a result of the translation from the Tibetan, which does not have any article. Whereas we talk about *a* jar, *the* jar, or *jars*, the Tibetan language talks about *jar (bum pa)*, without any distinction of article and often without distinction of number.

6. rang gi khyab byed du 'jug pa'i rang gi rigs yod pa can gi chos/ (Pur-bu-jok, *Small Path*, 21.a.5).

7. The translation of the concept of *tādātmya* presents some major problems. Let us first notice that the Tibetan translation is not literal, for literally *tādātmya* would be *de'i bdag nyid. Tādātmya* is sometimes translated as identity. See B. K. Matilal, "Review of C. Goekoop, The Logic of Invariable Concomitance in the Tattvacintāmani," *JAOS* 92 (1972): 171. Whatever translation one adopts, one must be aware that in any case we are not dealing with identity as it is understood usually, when identity is described as possessing reflexivity, transitivity, and symmetry. Therefore, if a is identical to c (a=c) and b=c, then a=b. This does not apply to objects related by *tādātmya*; although jar and impermanence, and flower and impermanence have such a relation, it is hardly suitable to deduce jar=flower! This does not mean that Tibetan philosophers have a different understanding of identity than we do but that *tādātmya* is not the exact equivalent of identity. Hence, my use of the term *essential identity*. For an explanation of the type of identity involved here, see T. Tillemans, "The 'Neither One nor Many' Argument for *Śūnyatā* and Its Tibetan Interpretations," in Steinkellner and Tauscher, *Contributions on Tibetan Buddhist Religion and Philosophy* (Vienna: Wiener Studien zur Tibetologie, 1983), pp. 305–17.

8. Pur-bu-jok, *Small Path*, 19.a.1–2.

9. The English word *impermanence* fails to express what the Tibetan *mi rtag pa* expresses. *Mi rtag pa* refers at the same time to impermanent things and to impermanence itself. Only a new word such as *impermanant* could bring across the full meaning of the Tibetan word!

10. The Naiyāyika is not committed to accept every general property as a real universal, but only to the thesis that some general properties, such as that of being a cow *(gotva, ba nyid)*, are real. Some general properties can be mere imposed properties *(upadhi)*.

11. One exception is Dzong-ka-ba in his first work on store consciousness *(kun gzhi rnam shes, ālayavijñāna)*. There, he quotes Sa-paṇ (*Treasure*, 18.b.5–19.a.1) as saying: "Thus, as long as one accepts a substantially established universal different from individuals, one cannot eliminate the faults that arise from being either the same or different" (des na ji srid gsal ba rnams ma gtogs pa'i spyi rdzas su grub par 'dod pa de srid du rdzas gcig dang tha dad brtags pa'i skyon spong mi nus so) (*Extensive Commentary on Mind and Store [Consciousness], [yid dang kun gzhi'i dka' ba'i gnas rgya cher 'grel pa]*. In Collected Works, vol. 18 [New Delhi: Ngawang Gelek, 1975–79], 19.b.1). This passage is not taken literally by later Ge-luk scholars, who interpret it not as a critique of realism, as it seems to be, but as a refutation of substantially existing relation *(rdzas su grub pa'i 'brel ba)*. For example, Gung-tang, following a favorite interpretive method, which I examine later, argues that Sa-paṇ in his *Treasure* is not denying that universals are real but that their rela-

tion with their particulars is real. See *A Ford for the Wise*, in Wilson, "The Meaning of Mind," p. 665. Dzong-ka-ba himself does not explicate this passage, which he uses in a discussion on a different topic, the relation between store consciousness and predispositions.

12. gsal ba rang mtshan rnams la rjes su 'gro ba'i spyi dngos por gyur pa dang dngos med gyur pa gnyis gnyis yod/ (Dzong-ka-ba, *Memorandum*, p. 201.3). Thus, it is clear that the realist passage found in Dzong-ka-ba's *Mind* does not reflect his mature point of view.

13. Gyel-tsap also presents a few brief textual arguments to establish his realist interpretation of Sa-paṇ's *Treasure*. (*Essence*, 23.a.6 and 25.a.1–26.a.1). See Chapter 8.

14. Ge-dün-drup, *Ornament*, p. 377.17–8.

15. spyi dang dngos po'i gzhi mthun yod par bstan/ (Jay-dzün Chö-gyi-gyel-tsen, *The Complete Revealer of Gyel-tsap, an Explanation of the Meaning of the Extensive Treatise, the Commentary on Prime Cognition; Elimination of Qualms with Respect to the Difficult Points of the First Chapter [rgyas pa'i bstan bcos tshad ma rnam 'grel gyi don 'grel rgyal tshab dgongs pa rab gsal zhes bya ba le'u dang po'i dka' ba'i gnas la dogs pa gcod pa]*, 103.b.5).

16. Only real things can have a relation of origination. The relation of essential identity is not limited to real phenomena but includes generally characterized phenomena as well. This limitation of relation to two types reminds of Quine's statement that "The intervening theory is composed of sentences associated with one another in multifarious ways not easily reconstructed even in conjecture. There are so-called logical connections, and there are so-called causal ones . . ." (*Words*, 11).

17. Pur-bu-jok, *The Presentation of the Collected Topics, the Magic Key Revealing the Meaning of the Texts on Prime Cognition, the Middle Path of Reasoning*, 5.b.2–.3.

18. See Chapter 2.

19. This is the same move described in the previous chapter of differentiating the phenomenon itself, which is permanent, from its instance, which is impermanent.

20. Aristotle draws the one-many distinction in four ways. He says: "Again, some things are one in number, others in species, others in genus, others by analogy." Things one in number are those that are identical individuals that we commonly consider identical. For example, we see a house and think "This is the same house I saw last year." Two human beings are one in species, for they have the same definition. Humans and animals are one in genus (they are both animals) but not one in species (*Metaphysics*, 1016.b.30–5). These four ways do not suffice to establish the type of distinction that moderate realism requires.

21. Jay-dzün Chö-gi-gyel-tsen distinguished six types of identity and difference: (1) substantial identity *(rdzas gcig)*, (2) essential identity *(rang bzhin gcig)*, (3) identity of being *(bdag nyid gcig)*, (4) identity in entity *(ngo bo gcig)*, (5) identity of equivalence *(don gcig)*, and (6) identity of distinguisher *(ldog pa gcig)* (*The General Meaning of the First Chapter [skabs dang po'i spyi don]* [Se-ra-jay Library, Block, n.d.], 102.b). Quoted in Tillemans, "The 'Neither'," p. 312. The list just given is not complete. A compilation of all the possible ways to differentiate one and many within the Ge-luk system would have at least ten items.

22. Conceptual entities have no substantial identity since they are not substances (i.e., causally efficient) but have essential identity *(rang bzhin gcig)* or its equivalent identity in entity *(ngo bo gcig)*. Most of what will be said about substantial identity, however, applies mutatis mutandis to the more general relation of essential identity.

23. The Collected Topics define one as a "phenomenon that is not distinct" *(so so ba ma yin pa'i chos)* and distinct as "phenomena that are distinct" *(so so ba'i chos)*. Here, *distinct*

refers to those phenomena that can be conceptually distinguished (Pur-bu-jok, *Small Path*, 8.a.6).

24. Substantial identity is not a necessary condition of identity either. Two constructs can be identical, even though they are not substantially so.

25. cha dang cha can chos can/ rdzas tha dad du thal/ blo ma 'khrul ba'i gzung ngor so sor snang ba'i phyir/ (Gyel-tsap, *Revealing*, I.101.15–.16).

26. kun la rdzas dang dngos brjod pa'i/ sgra yi khyad par de nyid do/ de phyir de dag brjod bya la/ khyad par gang yang yod ma yin// (bhedo 'yam eva sarvatra dravyabhāvābhidhāyinoḥ/ śabdayor na tayor vācye viśeṣas tena kaścana//) (Dharmakīrti, *Commentary*, I:62; in Tillemans, "The 'Neither'," pp. 313–14).

27. Kay-drup, *Ornament*, 24.b3–25.a.4.

28. Ibid., 34.a.5–32b.3. In fact, Śākya Chok-den's argument and Kay-drup's presentation of his opponent's position match each other point by point. This shows that Śākya Chok-den's arguments were not his own inventions but standard arguments already well established within his tradition.

29. gzhan yang rdzas gcig na gcig yin dgos par 'dod pa ni/ sgra dang sgra'i mi rtag pa sogs rdzas gcig pa rnams/ rang 'dzin mngon sum gyis gcig tu dmigs pa'i phyir dang/ blo ma 'khrul bas gcig tu dmigs na gcig yin dgos pa'i phyir snyam pa 'ba' zhig sgrub byed mthar thug par zad mod/ 'di ni blo ma 'khrul bas gcig tu dmigs pa dang/ tha dad du ma dmigs pa ma phyed pa yin te/ (Kay-drup, ibid., 25.a.4–.5).

30. Ibid., 25.b.1.

31. This is not to say that the Sa-gya school does not have its own arcane ways of drawing distinctions. See Chapter 4.

32. Buddhists present material phenomena as made of at least eight components: the four elements (earth, water, fire, wind), form, taste, smell, and touch (Poussin, *Abhidharmakośa*, II:[22],144).

33. Any material thing *(gzugs, rūpa)* belongs to one of the five spheres. Visible things belong to the form sphere.

34. The distinction in sphere is established in relation to the senses through which we gain access to these objects. Forms are objects made accessible by our eyes, etc.

35. Dharmakīrti, *Commentary*, I:139. See Chapter 2.

36. Go-ram-ba, *Perfect Light*, 42.a.1–.4.

37. Bo-dong, *Presentation*, I.703.2–.4. We will discuss Bo-dong's negative realism in Chapter 10.

38. Gyel-tsap, *Revealing*, I.13–.14; and *Essence*, 26.a.1. A similar argument is found in Kay-drup, *Ocean*, I:112.a.3–.4. Kay-drup introduces other textual arguments. See Dreyfus, "Ontology," 275–77.

39. This was made clear to me by recent discussion I had with several Ge-shays, who all argued for realism on the basis of logical arguments based on commonsense consideration. In fact, many members of the tradition implicitly recognize that their interpretation is based more on logical arguments than on textual analysis. They often state that reasoning is primary over exegesis in the study of Dharmakīrti's logico-epistemological system.

40. Gyel-tsap, *Revealing*, I.74.8–75.3.

41. As we will see when we examine Dharmakīrti's theory of perception, antirealism makes it difficult to account for perception as well.

42. Dzong-ka-ba, *Extensive Memorandum*, 183.1–186.6.

43. des na bum pa dang dngos po sogs rang gi gsal ba la rjes 'gro byed pa dang/ rang nyid yul dus rang bzhin ma 'dres pa yin pa la 'gal ba med pas/ dngos po yin na rang mtshan

yin pas khyab pa yin la/ rang mtshan yin kyang rang gi gsal ba la rjes 'gro byed pa'i spyi yin par mi 'gal zhing/ (Kay-drup, *Ornament*, 33.a.2–.3).

44. See Chapter 5.

45. Kay-drup, *Ornament*, 33.a.4–.5. Gung-tang uses a similar interpretive strategy when he argues that Sa-paṇ is not denying that particulars and universals can be real but that their relation can be. See previously and Wilson, "Meaning of Mind," p. 665.

46. There is a real similarity with Samantabhadra's view that universal and individuation are two relative aspects of reality.

47. spyi bden grub 'gog pa la yang tshul gnyis te/ phyi rol pas btags pa'i spyi gtso bo sogs ni/ bden pa dang tha snyad gnyis kar du 'gog pa yin la/ rang lugs kyi spyi ni bden grub 'gog pa yin gyi/ tha snyad du grub pa 'gog pa ma yin zhing/ (Kay-drup, *Ornament*, 40.a.1–.2).

48. In Sanskrit grammar, these two expressions are synonymous. The latter genitive form is taken to be the implicit structure of any predication. The actual examples used by Dharmakīrti and his commentators are "a cow not being a horse" and "a cow's non-horseness." Since these two statements involve negative properties, whose status we have yet to examine, I have preferred to use simpler examples.

49. gnyis kas gcig gcig brjod mod kyi/ brjod bya'i shan (Miyasaki reads "gzhan") gyi khyad par gyis/ rnam dbye tha dad 'byed pa yis/ tha dad don bzhin sgrub par byed// (dvayor ekābhidhāne 'pi vibhaktir vyatirekiṇī/ bhinnam artham ivānveti vācye leśaviśeṣataḥ//) (Dharmakīrti, *Commentary*, I:60). Frauwallner, "Beiträge," p. 378. *Good Sayings*, 22.6.

50. lha spyin dang ril ba lta bu brjod bya chos chos can rdzas tha dad pa dag la lha spyin gyi ril ba zhes sogs rnam dbye drug pa'i sgra lan mang du sbyor ba yang yang mthong goms pas shan rgyab pa'i shugs kyi khyad par yin no/ (Kay-drup, *Ocean*, I:81.b.2–3). Kay-drup, Ge-dün-drup, and Śākya Chok-den all interpret *shan* (*leśa*, usually small, weak) as influence, as in *shan rgyab pa* (to influence [in a negative way]).

51. Gyel-tsap makes a similar point (*Revealing*, I.97.2–.8).

52. khyad par gzhan ni spong ba dang/ mi spong ba dag de gnyis kyi/ brda yi bye brag rtogs pa po/ 'dod pa'i rjes su byed pa'i gzhi// (bhedāntarapratikṣepāpratikṣepau tayor dvayoḥ/ saṃketabhedasya padaṃ jñātṛvāñcānurodhinaḥ//) (Dharmakīrti, *Commentary*, I:61). Ge-dün-drup, *Good Sayings*, 22.6–.7. Frauwallner, "Beiträge," p. 378.

53. This explanation follows Śākya Chok-den, *Explanation*, 218.7–19.2 and Frauwallner, "Beiträge," p. 378.

54. Similarly, there is no intrinsic difference between particulars and universals.

55. Kay-drup, *Ornament*, 218.a.1.

56. sgra rnams ni smra ba po rang dbang med par byed pa ma yin gyi/ smra ba po'i brjod 'dod dang nyan pa po'i shes 'dod kyi rjes su mthun par ston par byed do/ de la yang khyad par gzhan spong zhes pa ni/ don de khyad chos gzhan gyi rten byed pa'i khyad gzhi lta bur blo yul du 'char ba spangs nas/ khyad chos lta bur ston pa yin la/ (Kay-drup, ibid., 218.a.6–b.1).

57. The psychologist Lev Vygotsky makes a similar distinction between the grammatical and the psychological subjects. Take the sentence *a clock falls*. The subject can be the clock or the action of falling, depending on the topic we are intersted in. See *The Collected Works* (New York: Plenum, 1987), pp. 251–52.

58. Śākya Chok-den, *Defeater*, I.223.5–27.6.

59. Ibid., I.225.1–.2.

60. See Chapter 8.

61. P. Geach attributes a similar view, which he calls a *two-name theory*; that is, the idea

that both subject and predicate expression name objects, to philosophers as diverse as Aristole, Ockham, and Mill (*Logic Matters* [Berkeley: University of California Press, 1972], pp. 48–52).

62. Similarly, Latin does not have articles. Geach asserts that this fact influenced the development of the theory of *presupostio* by medieval philosophers (P. Geach, *Reference and Generality* [Ithaca, N.Y.: Cornell University Press, 1962], 52–53).

Chapter 10. Realism in Buddhist Tradition

1. To characterize Ge-luk thinkers as outside Sa-paṇ's logico-epistemological lineage is true only inasmuch as they are not direct followers of Sa-paṇ. Nevertheless they see themselves as continuing his work. Consequently they avoid criticizing him as much as possible and are ready to interpret his words in order to make them consistent with their own views (see later).

2. bum pa thams cad bum pa ma yin pa las log par mtshungs pa la spyi zhes brjod de bum pa thams cad la khyab pa'i phyir/ (U-yuk-ba, *Treasure of Reasoning Explaining [Dharmakīrti's] Commentary on "Valid Cognition" [tshad ma rnam 'grel kyi 'grel pa rigs pa'i mdzod]* [Delhi: Sonam Gyaltsen, 1982], 31.b.4). Special thanks to Professor van der Kuijp from Harvard University for drawing my attention to this passage.

3. gnyis pa ni/ rnam rtog la bum pa tha dad kyi snang ba la gcig tu bzung ba de kho na yin te rigs mthun gcig tu bsres pa'i phir ro/ de nyid 'dir ston pa ni tha dad min pa lta bur snang zhes drang go/ (ibid., 31.b.5).

4. Go-ram-ba, *The Excellent Sun [on] the Meaning of the Words of [Dharmakīrti's] Extensive Treatise on Valid Cognition (rgyas pa'i bstan bcos tshad ma rnam 'grel gyi ngag don kun tu bzang po'i nyi ma)*, Complete Works of the Great Masters of the Sa sKya Sect (Tokyo: Toyo Bunko, 1968–69), vol. 11, 27.a.4–.7.

5. Bo-dong, *Presentation*, I.573.2–.5.

6. This attribution of a realist position to Bo-dong is confirmed by his distinction between "universals that are external real phenomena and concomitant with other real things and universals such as object-universals that are artificially related to individuals" (dngos po thun mong ba la spyir bzhag pa don gyi chos kyi rang bzhin dang rnam par rtog pas sbyar ba'i don spyi la sogs spyir bzhag pa/) (ibid., I.566.4).

7. Ibid., I.679.3.

8. I am not implying here that Bo-dong is directly addressing Gyel-tsap or Kay-drup, but that he has in mind a position similar to the one held by these thinkers, who hold a position in no way unique to them.

9. Ibid., I.692.1–.6. Let us notice that the Ge-luk distinction between the real identity of things and their conceptual identity as universals is meant to answer this objection. Pot and thing are one substance from the point of view of their identity as real things but not from their identity as individuation and universal.

10. Ibid., I.696.4.

11. Ibid., I.703.2–.4. Bo-dong supports his claim by a quote from Dharmakīrti's *Ascertainment* that refers to "mere thingness which is different from the nature of [its] contradictory" (de min rang bzhin las ldog pa'i dngos po tsam) (*Commentary* I:139), which we have discussed already, and is also a source that Bo-dong uses to support his interpretation.

12. In another passage (*Presentation*, I.791.4), Bo-dong describes a similar entity in rela-

tion to trees. Such a universal is not a nontree but is [also] not deprived of the ability to perform the function of tree (shing min las log pa'i zhing gyi don mi byed pa dang bral ba). As we will see when we examine the *apoha* theory, Bo-dong holds this entity to be the main elimination.

13. Ibid., I.673.3–.6. Bo-dong surprisingly describes these negative universals (which are usually called *differentiated, log pa*) as distinguishers in reference to several passages in which Dharmakīrti speaks of the differentiation from other real things. See *Commentary*, I:40, 139, III:165, etc.

14. Go-ram-ba, *Explanation*, 5.a.5.

15. Rik-bay-ray-dri, *The Flower Ornament of [Dharmakīrti's] Seven Treatises on Valid Cognition (tshad ma sde bdun rgyan gyi me tog)* (Beijing: Institute of Tibetan Studies, 1991), p. 64.

16. The next part of this work will show that the Ge-luk reliance on negative language to describe the process of naming does not stem from a similar attempt to escape difficulties by negatively disguising realism. Most Ge-luk thinkers (excluding Jam-yang-shay-ba and his followers, who hold that a non-nonthing is conceptual) hold that if non-nonthing (the equivalent of Bo-dong's mere thing) is a universal, so must be thing itself. All negative language can do is emphasize the conceptual nature of certain distinctions involved in the naming process. Also see Klein, *Knowledge*, pp. 167–68.

17. M. Hobbart, "Is God Evil?" in D. Parkin, *The Anthropology of Evil* (Oxford: Blackwell, 1985), pp. 165–93, 183.

18. It is clear, however, that, since the social and political aspects of the formation of the Ge-luk school have not been studied, my conclusions here remain tentative.

19. This was a critical time for the Ge-luk school, during which the political opposition with the other schools (particularly the followers of the Kar-ma-pa) became particularly acute. In 1486, Ge-dün-gya-tso (*dge 'dun rgya mtsho*, 1448–1542) created Ga-den Podrang *(dga' ldan pho brang)* in Dre-bung monastery. Shortly after, the Rin-pung forces supporting the Kar-ma-pa school occupied Lhasa and promoted an actively anti-Ge-luk policy. Although Go-ram-ba's and Śākya Chok-den's doctrinal efforts started before these momentous events, they were prepared for by a chain of events that started much earlier and culminated at the end of the century. See Shakaba, *Tibet*, pp. 87–92.

20. *tsang ngag pa* (?–1171).

21. phwya gtsang nas bzung ste deng sang gi bar du thams cad zhal 'cham par/ dngos po gzhir bcas kyi spyi dang bye brag rdzas gcig pa yin no/ (Śākya Chok-den, *Defeater*, II.134.7–135.1).

22. At this stage of our knowledge of the early Tibetan logico-epistemological tradition, it seems better to suspend judgment concerning Ngok's views and contributions to the development of realism in Tibet. Was he a realist himself? And if he was, to what extent? Similarly, his Madhyamaka view is hard to determine. Śākya Chok-den describes Ngok in his interpretation of Dharmakīrti as a Mādhyamika relying on Prajñākaragupta's *Ornament* without being a Prāsaṅgika or a Svātantrika. *History*, 29.3–30.4. In an earlier work, however, he describes Ngok as following Śāntarakṣita. *Music*, 745.2. This would make him a Svātantrika, according to the standard Tibetan doxographical scheme. In a third work, Ngok is depicted as a Mādhyamika following the conventions of the world (a depiction which applies better to Cha-ba than Ngok). See Jackson, *Entrance*, 166–67.

23. Śākya Chok-den, *History*, 33.1–.5 in Jackson, *Entrance*, 168. We will discuss this concept in Chapter 12 on the *apoha* theory.

24. Candrakīrti declares that universals are objects of perception and, therefore, con-

ventionally as real as particulars. Since ultimately both particulars and universals are unreal, Candrakīrti rejects the distinction between real individuations and unreal universals. Conventionally, the Nyāya account is satisfactory. The attempt by Buddhist logicians to find some things more real than others is fundamentally misguided. See L. de la Vallée Poussin, ed., *Mūlamadhyamakakārikās* (Osnabrück: Biblio Verlag, 1964), pp. 58.15–59.3, 75.2–5.

25. Kuijp, *Contributions*, p. 50.

26. Ibid., p. 69.

27. Jam-yang-chok-hla-ö-ser, *Collected Topics*, 53.7. This text, otherwise known as *The Collected Topics from the Ra-dö [Monastery] (rwa stod bsdus grwa)* presents a point of view similar to the other Ge-luk views here examined.

28. If there were any influence, it would be in the other direction. Some later interpretations of Madhyamaka had been influenced by Dharmakīrti's tradition in general and by realism in particular. This is particularly clear in the case of Dzong-ka-ba as we will see in our concluding remarks.

29. Go-ram-ba, *Clarification*, 4.b.4–.6.

30. *skal ldan rgyal po.*

31. Kuijp, *Contributions*, pp. 31, 33, 46.

32. See Chapters 3 and 5.

33. The reasoning, called *argument concerning having a companion (sadvittīya prayoga, gnyis bcas kyi sbyor ba)*, is a twisted attempt by the Cārvākas to prove their view that persons disintegrate at the time of death and do not reincarnate. See T. Tillemans, "Dharmakīrti on Some Sophisms," *Studies in the Buddhist Epistemological Tradition* (Vienna: Österreichische Akademie der Wissenschaften, 1991), pp. 403–18.

34. sgra dang bum pa'i khyad par gyis/ rtog na 'jig la'ang mtshungs she na/ ma yin 'jig pa sgrub pa yis/ sgra ni de ltar grub phyir ro// (tulyam nāśe 'pi cec chabdaghaṭabhedena kalpane/ na siddhena vināśena tadvataḥ sādhanād dhvaneḥ//) (Dharmakīrti, *Commentary*, IV:36). Translation, Tillemans, "Pramāṇa-vārttika IV (3)," *Etudes Asiatiques* 46, no. 1 (1993).

35. Similarly, in *Ascertainment*, Dharmakīrti refers to the establishment of impermanence (mi rtag pa nyid grub pas . . .) D: 4211, 192.b.6.

36. Dharmakīrti, *Commentary*, III:102–3.

37. Kajiyama, *Introduction*, 56–8.

38. Dharmakīrti, *Commentary*, I:40.a.

39. gang phyir dngos kun te/ gsal ba 'ba' zhig tu ma zad/ spyi yang yin no zhes bya ba don no/ (Śaṃkarānanda, *Explanantion of Commentary on 'Valid Cognition' [pramāṇa-vārttika-ṭīkā, tshad ma rnam 'grel gyi 'grel bshad]*, P: 5721, 181.b.5–6, D: 4223, 152.b.6). The Peking has *'ga' zhig tu* instead of *'ba' zhig*. Quoted in T. Tillemans, "On a Recent Work on Tibetan Buddhist Epistemology," *Asiatische Studien* 28, no. 1 (1984): 59–66, 64.

40. Eli Franco, "On the Interpretation of Pramāṇasamuccaya(vṛtti) I, 3d," *Journal of Indian Philosophy* 12 (1984): 389–400.

41. Dignāga, *Compendium*, P: 5700, 2.a.2–.3. Hattori, *Dignāga*, 25, 176–77.

42. Dignāga, ibid., 3.d. Sanskrit fragments in Hattori, *Dignāga*, 237.b.16–.18.

43. artha keyaṃ kalpanā nāma? nāmajātyādiyojanā// yadṛcchāsabdeṣu nāmnā viśito 'rtha ucyate ḍittha iti, jātiśabdeṣu jātyā gaur iti . . . (rtog pa zhes bya 'di ji lta bur zhig ce na/ ming dang rigs sogs bsres pa'o/ 'dod rgyal ba'i sgra rnams la ming gi khyad par du byas nas don brjod pa byed de lhas byin zhes bya ba dang/ rigs kyi sgra rnams la rigs kyi ste ba lang zhes bya ba dang . . .) (Dignāga, *Auto-Commentary*, P: 5702, 94.b.3–.4). Hattori, *Dignāga*, 25, 177.

44. G. Jha, trans., *The Tattvasaṃgraha of Śāntarakṣīta* (Delhi: Motilal, 1937, 1986), pp. 1218–21.

45. Since no name is mentioned by Kamalaśīla, I will assume that the position here described was shared by a group of thinkers.

46. Franco, "Interpretation," p. 390. Vetter, *Dharmakīrti's Pramāṇaviniścayaḥ 1. Kapitel: Pratyaksam*, 40.6–7. Dharmakīrti, *Ascertainment*, P: 5710, 252.b.4.

47. Kāmalaśīla, *Literary Commentary of [Śāntarakṣita's] Compendium on Reality*, P: 5765, 56.b.2, .4. S. D. Shastri, *Tattvasaṅgraha of Ācārya Śāntarakṣita with the Pañjikā* (Banaras: 1968), 451.9–.10.

48. Franco, "Interpretation," p. 391.

49. The three criteria, property of the position *(pakṣadharmatvam, phyogs chos)*, positive concomittance *(anvaya, rjes 'gro)*, and negative concomittance *(vyatireka, ldog pa)* are explained in Kajiyama, *Introduction*, pp. 63–70; Y. Kajiyama, "On the Theory of Intrinsic Determination of Universal Concomittance in Buddhist Logic," *Journal of the International Association of Buddhist Studies* 7, no. 1 (1958): 360–64; Mimaki, *La Réfutation*, pp. 46–51; R. Hayes, *Dignāga on the Interpretation of Signs*, pp. 142–54.

50. Mokṣākaragupta reinterprets the restriction of the purview of perception. Accordingly, one should not understand that only particulars are objects of perception *(svalakṣaṇam eva tasya viṣayaḥ, rang mtshan nyid de'i yul yin pa)* but that particulars are definitively objects of perception *(svalakṣaṇam tasya viṣaya eva, rang mtshan de'i yul yin pa nyid)*. Kajiyama, *Introduction*, pp. 56–58.

51. skad ma nyid dang gzhan gang zhig med na ji rang bzhin gi gtan tshigs kyis bsgrub par bya zhe na (Dharmottara, *Examination of Valid Cognition II [prāmānya-parīkṣā, tshad ma brtags pa]*, P: 5747, 248.b.5–b.6). Special thanks are due to Helmut Krasser from the University of Vienna for giving me this reference.

52. sgra'i skad cig ma nyid thams cad du ni med pa ma yin gyi/ 'on kyang skad cig ma nyid ma yin pa las ldog nas skad cig ma gcig du ma'i thun mong du brtags pa yin pa de 'dra ba med kyi sngon po la sogs pa'i khyad par so sor tha dad pa gang yin pa de ni yod pa kho na'o/ de ltar yin yang spyi gang yin pa de ni khyad par gyi bdag nyid kho na'o/ yod pa yin zin khyad par gyi mthar thug kho nar gzung bar bya ba yin no/ khyad par med dam ma gzung na spyi yang med dang ma gzung bar 'gyur ro/ de'i phyir khyad par yod na ni spyi yod la khyad par med na ni spyi yang med par 'gyur ro// (ibid., P: 5747, 248.b.6–249.a.6). I have not found any mention of this passage in Ge-luk texts.

53. Mokṣakaragupta mentions four characteristics of the universals according to Nyāya: universals are inherent in many individuals *(anekavyaktisamaveta)*, visible *(dṛśya)*, single (i.e., partless, *eka*), and permanent *(nitya)*. Such putative entities are completly nonexistent (Kajiyama, *Introduction*, p. 128). They are called *separate universals (spyi don gzhan)* in the Tibetan tradition to differentiate them from the things that are both real and universal.

54. A question which I have left unanswered is this: Why did realism, which was probably always a minority view in India, become so popular in Tibet? I am not sure that I can give a definite answer to this question. A relevant element is the ambiguity of the Tibetan language, which we examined in an earlier chapter. Another and more convincing answer is that the predominance of realism in Tibet is accidental. Cha-ba came across a realist interpretation, which he adopted. Later thinkers, who often did not have access to original Sanskrit texts, followed his opinions, which became well entrenched. If this explanation is right, the predominance of realism in Tibet is due less to philosophical necessity than to historical contingencies.

Chapter 11. Introduction to Apoha

1. M. Hattori, "Apoha and Pratibhā," in M. Nagatomi, B. K. Matilal, J. M. Masson, and E. Dimock, *Sanskrit and Indian Studies, Festschrift in Honor of Danie H. H. Ingalls* (Dordrecht: Reidel, 1980), pp. 61–73.

2. R. Hayes, *Dignāga on the Interpretation of Signs.*

3. S. Katsura, "Jñānaśrīmitra on *Apoha*," in Matilal and Devans, *Buddhist Logic*, pp. 171–81. Also "Dignāga and Dharmakīrti on Apoha," in E. Steinkellner, ed., *Studies in the Buddhist Epistemological Tradition* (Vienna: Österreichisch Akademie der Wissenschaften, 1991), pp. 129–46.

4. Ratnakīrti does not name any author as supporting these two extremes. Later, he criticizes Dharmottara for saying that words refer to external objects, thereby suggesting that Dharmottara is to be included in the positivists (D. Sharma, *The Differentiation Theory of Meaning in Indian Logic* [The Hague: Mouton, 1969], p. 93). Matilal attributes the negativist view to Prajñākaragupta, whom he presents as arguing that "names cannot have any positive fuction like 'locating' or 'referring to' the objects, i.e., the particular" (*Epistemology*, p. 46). See Prajñākaragupta, *Pramāṇavārtika with Prajñākaragupta's Commentary* (Patna: Kashi Prasad Institute, 1953), pp. 262–66 (being a commentary on stanzas III.163.cd–173), P: 5719, *Te*, 295.a.4–301.a.4.

5. A. Thakur, *Jñānaśrīmitranibandhāvalī* (Patna: Kashi Prasad Institut, 1959), pp. 201–32.

6. S. Katsura, "Jñānaśrīmitra," pp. 171–181.

7. Katsura traces back the idea expressed by Jñānaśrīmitra that negation and affirmation are simultaneous to Dharmakīrti's *Drop of Logical Reason* ("Jñānaśrīmitra," p. 174). Also see E. Steinkellner, *Dharmakīrti's Hetubinduḥ* (Vienna: Österreichische Akademie der Wissenschaften, 1967), pp. 21.20–28.3.

8. Quoted in Biardeau, *Theorie*, p. 43.

9. Originally, the discussion focused less about the concept of universal than about the notion of configuration *(ākṛti)*, which is a unique combination of parts exhibiting a certain typical pattern. Only gradually did the concept of configuration tend to drop out of the conversation, which became more focused on the question of universals. See Biardeau, ibid., and P. Scharf, "The Denotation of Generic Terms in ancient Indian Grammar, Nyāya, and Mīmāṃsā" (Ph.D. diss., University of Pennsylvania, 1990).

10. Matilal places Pāṇini and Kātyāyana between 500 and 100 B.C.E. Vyādi and Vājapyāyana must have existed after Pāṇini and before Kātyāyana (*Epistemology*, p. 97).

11. K. K. Raja, "*Apoha* Theory and Pre-Dignāga Views on Sentence-Meaning," in B. K. Matilal and R. Evans, *Buddhist Logic and Epistemology* (Dordrecht: Reidel, 1986), pp. 185–91, 187.

12. Matilal, *Epistemology*, p. 107.

13. Hattori, *Apoha*, p. 63. For more on Bhartṛhari, see Biardeau, *Theorie*, and K. A. S. Iyer, *Bhartṛhari* (Poona: Deccan College, 1969).

14. Here again, I am greatly simplifying by eliminating the concept of configuration that seems to have little relevance to the discussion with the Buddhist tradition. The Nyāya view of composite denotation explains signification in relation to three (not just two) elements: individuals, universals, and configurations. M. Gangopadhyaya, trans., *Nyāya* (Calcutta: Indian Studies, 1982), p. 162.

15. Dignāga, *Compendium*, V:2–9. Hayes, *Dignāga*, pp. 255–72.

16. Dharmakīrti argues against the Nyāya view: "To indicate individual [objects] is

difficult, beyond [our] capacities, and fruitless" (tha dad pa dag bstan pa ni/ dka' dang nus med 'bras med phyir/) (gauravāśaktivaiphalyād bhedākhyayāḥ/) (Dharmakīrti, *Commentary*, I:137.bc for Sanskrit and 138.ab for Tibetan). The Tibetan and the Sanskrit do not correspond in Miyasaka's edition. Addition from Ge-dün-drup, *Good Sayings*, p. 39.2–.3.

17. As we will see later, three views concern the primary meaningful linguistic unit: (1) Dignāga and the Grammarians assert that sentences are meaningful, word meaning being abstracted; (2) the Bhaṭṭa Mīmāṁsakas and the Naiyāyikas hold a "word plus syntax" theory and assert that the meaningful unit of language is the word, not the sentence; and (3) the Prabhākaras hold a middle position, well described as "related designation theory" by Siderits. Dharmakīrti is not very explicit on this question. Hattori thinks that Śāntarakṣita holds (2) but Siderits argues for (3). See Hattori, "Apoha," pp. 69–70 and Mark Siderits, "Sentence Meaning and Apoha," *Journal of Indian Philosophy* 13, no. 2 (1985): 133–51, 134.

18. Dharmakīrti, *Commentary*, I:92.ab. See also III:34, 39.

19. The intension of a concept are the properties that make up this concept in opposition to its extension; that is, the things that fall under the concept. In our example of the cow, the putative cowness is the intension of the concept cow whereas the individual cows are its extension.

20. A similar paradox affects some of their adversaries such as the Naiyāyikas, who hold a denotationist view within a realism about universals that would seem to favor a connotationist account (as held, for example, by Kumārila, who holds that language first and foremost signifies universals).

21. C. Geertz, *The Interpretation of Cultures* (New York: Basic Books, 1973), pp. 3–33.

22. Matilal, *Epistemology*, p. 45.

23. sgra las byung ba rjes dpag las/ tshad ma gzhan min de ltar de/ byas so bzhin du rang don la/ gzhan sel bas ni rjod par byed (Dignāga, *Compendium*, V.1, P: 5700, 9.b.5–.6). Hattori, *Pramāṇa*, p. 107.

24. Hayes, *Dignāga*, p. 252.

25. gang zhig tshig gi brjod pa 'di/ ngag las don du rnam par brtags/ ngag don so sor snang brjod gang/ de yis dang po nye bar bskyed (Dignāga, *Compendium*, V:45, P: 5700, 82.b.1–.2, in Hattori, trans., *Apoha*, p. 63).

26. Dignāga, *Commentary*, V:48.ab. P: 5700, 83.a.1. de yang ngag gi don gzhan las/ rnam par bcad pa'i don du 'dod.

27. I am following, here, Siderits's helpful discussion in "Sentence Meaning." My discussion focuses entirely on the Bhaṭṭa branch of the Mīmāṃsā, leaving out the other branch, the Prabhākara.

28. The basic text of this school, the *Mīmāṃsāsūtra* (I:15) states: "The relation between a word and its meaning, however, is innate" (autpattikas tu śabdasyarthena saṃbandhaḥ).

29. See J. Kristeva, *Le Language, cet Inconnnu* (Paris: Seuil, 1969), pp. 86–96.

30. *Śruti* (revelation) is distinguished from *smṛti*, the tradition.

31. The Buddhist answer differs from both the Mīmāṃsā and the modern secular skepticism. Buddhists attempt to find a way to maintain the role of scripture without granting it any privileged status. They do this by delineating a particular type of reasoning, which is reserved for cases such as the law of karma that are not accessible to ordinary reasoning. The question is whether this type of reasoning provides actual knowledge or merely useful guidance. See Chapter 16.

32. G. Bhatt, *Epistemology of the Bhāṭṭa School of Pūrva Mīmāṃsā* (Banaras: Chowkhamba, n.d.), pp. 282–83.

33. The Mīmāṃsā view holds to a nontheistic orthodoxy in which gods exist only in the function of the impersonal order of *dharma*. The Buddhists go further and radically deny them any privileged status.

34. Jhā, *Ślokavārttika*, Sūtra V.14.

35. Ibid., V.39. Kumārila's arguments are taken on one by one by Śāntarakṣita in his *Compendium on Reality*. Jhā, *Tattvasaṁgraha*, stanzas 915–81.

36. Jhā, *Ślokavārttika*, V.83–84; Jhā, *Tattvasaṁgraha*, *stanzas* 943–44.

37. Jhā, *Ślokavārttika*, p. 43; Jhā, *Tattvasaṁgraha*, stanza 923.

38. See Jhā, *Tattvasaṁgraha*, stanzas 982–1000 and *The Nyāya-Sūtras*, pp. 1036–1060 (*Nyāya-vārttika*, 2.2.63).

39. Steinkellner, "Wirklichkeit und Begriff bei Dharmakīrti," 179–210. Vetter, *Erketnisprobleme bei Dharmakīrti* (Vienna: Österreichischen Akademie der Wissenschaften, 1964). Also Hayes, *Dignāga*; Kajiyama, *Introduction*; Hattori, "Apoha"; Keyt, "Dharmakīrti," etc.

Chapter 12. Dharmakīrti on Concept Formation

1. Partial accounts of this chapter are found in Mookerjee and Nagasaki, *The Pramāṇavārttikam*; Zwilling, "Dharmakīrti on Apoha" (Ph.D., University of Wisconsin, 1976); and Keyt, "Dharmakīrti."

2. See Chapters 16 and 18.

3. See Chapters 19 through 21.

4. spyi brjod ngang tshul can sgra dang/ rtog pa'ang de dang don gcig na/ (sāmānyavācinaḥ śabdās tadekārthā ca kalpanā/) (Dharmakīrti, *Commentary*, III:183.ab). Additions from Ge-dün-drup, *Good Sayings*, p. 208.2.

5. E. Betti, "The Epistemological Problem of Understanding," in G. Shapiro and A. Sica, *Hermeneutics* (Amherst: University of Massachusetts Press, 1984), pp. 25–53, 31.

6. This is not a very popular view in contemporary Anglo-Saxon philosophy, where Wittegenstein's arguments have carried great weight. For example, see L. Wittgenstein, *Blue and Brown Books* (New York: Harper, 1958). A careful discussion of this view would go well beyond the scope of this work. For a spirited defense of this view, see E. D. Hirsch, *Validity in Interpretation* (New Haven, Conn.: Yale University, 1967).

7. Dharmakīrti, *Commentary*, I:92–94.

8. Dharmakīrti, *Commentary*, III:45.

9. This view obviously privileges the cases in which the speakers have an adequate knowledge of what they are talking about. These are the normal cases in which language is unproblematic. Most classical authors (Plato, Hume, Bhartṛhari, Dignāga, etc.) think that these cases are more important and meaningful than the many cases in which we do not necessarily have any idea what we are saying. In recent years, Wittgenstein, Ryle, Kripke, and others have offered accounts of language that do not privilege the normal cases. See Kripke, *Naming and Necessity* (Cambridge, Mass.: Harvard University Press, 1980) and Michael Devitt, *Designation* (New York: Columbia University Press, 1981). For the more classical view, cases where speakers do not really know what they are talking about do not show that clear ideas are irrelevant to linguistic understanding, for in these cases our utterance succeeds in signifying something only in reference to the normal cases.

10. See Chapter 6.

11. shes gang gang la sgra don 'dzin/ de ni de la rtog pa yin/ (śabdārthagrāhi yad yatra tajjñānaṃ tatra kalpanā/) (Dharmakīrti, *Commentary*, III:287).

12. rtog pa ni brjod pa dang 'dres rung ba snang ba'i shes pa ste/ Dharmakīrti, *Ascertainment*, P: 5710, 252.b.4. T. Vetter, *Dharmakīrti's Pramāṇaviniścayaḥ*, 40.6–7. Also in *Drop of Reasoning*, P: 5711, 329.b.4.

13. See Chapters 19 through 27.

14. Ge-dün-drup, *Ornament*, 37.2–6.

15. sgra don 'dres rung du 'dzin pa'i blo (ibid., 36.15–37.6). Pur-bu-jok gives a similar definition, adding the attribute conceiving *(zhen pa)*: "a conceiving consciousness apprehending a term-[universal] and an object-[universal] as suitable to be associated." See Napper, *Mind in Tibetan Buddhism* (Ithaca, N.Y.: Snow Lion, 1981), pp. 130–33; and Klein, *Knowledge*, pp. 117–23. Although this definition is inspired by Dharmakīrti's *Ascertainment*, it is by no means identical. Here, a number of issues will have to be unpacked gradually. One issue on which Dharmakīrti and his Ge-luk interpreters differ is the idea of appearance. Whereas Dharmakīrti is a representationalist, Ge-luk thinkers are direct realists (see Chapter 26). Another point of difference is their understanding of the concept of object universal (see Chapter 14.).

16. See Y. Kajiyama, *Introduction*, 40–43. This does not imply that these basic non-linguistic concepts remain once language has been acquired, for they become integrated within a linguistically determined conceptual apparatus. Thus, Dharmakīrti's idea of the role of language as fixing a concept seems to go very much against Locke's idea that there are certain basic concepts that are language independent and available to act as the bases of lingusitic activity.

17. Śāntarakṣita, *Compendium*, 1214–26.

18. Kay-drup, *Ornament*, 57.a.3.

19. Ibid., 59.a.3–b.1.

20. sra don 'dzin pa'i blo (ibid., p. 57.a.5). In view of Dharmakīrti's other mentions of the word in his *Commentary* (I:84, 205, III:169), Kay-drup's interpretation is to be preferred in the context of the *Commentary*.

21. Klein, *Knowledge*, p. 122.

22. Kay-drup particularly objects to another position that is currently accepted in the Ge-luk tradition; namely, the idea that some conceptions apprehend only term universals *(sgra spyi rkyang pa 'dzin pa)* and other conceptions apprehend exclusively object universals *(don spyi rkyang pa 'dzin pa)*. This position was, according to Go-ram-ba, elaborated by early Tibetan scholars (*Explanation*, 72.a.6).

23. Go-ram-ba, *Explanation*, 139.b.2.

24. As Steinkellner remarks, the concept of inherent fitness *(yogyatā)* is not a Mīmāṃsā term but appears in the grammatical literature. It is used by Dharmakīrti against this school, in particular against Bhartṛhari. See E. Steinkellner, *Dharmakīrti's Pramāṇaviniścayaḥ II*, n. 211, p. 220. Nevertheless, it corresponds to the Mīmāṃsā idea of innate capacity *(śakti)* that words have to signfy their meaning and hence is used by Dharmakīrti in reference to this latter tradition. Moreover, Dharmakīrti intends to refute more than one view by his use of *yogyatā*. Karṇakagomin mentions the Grammarians Maṇḍanamiśra and Bhartṛhari himself among the putative targets. See T. Tillemans, "Dharmakīrti on *prasiddha and yogyatā*," p. 3.

25. The example is given by Dharmakīrti's commentators. See Tillemans, ibid., p. 2.

26. This negative character of thought further separates Dharmakīrti from empiricists such as Locke.

27. de la ngo bor snang ba 'am/ don la de nyid du 'dzin pa/ gang de 'khrul pa thog med

pa'i/ dus can mthong goms kyis sprul yin// don rnams kyi ni spyi gang yin/ gzhan las log pa'i mtshan nyid can/ sgra 'di dag gis gang brjod pa/ de la ngo bo cun zad med// (tasyāṃ rūpāvabhāso yas tattvenārthasya vā grahaḥ/ bhrāntiḥ sānādikālīnadarśanābhyāsanirmitā// arthānāṃ yac ca sāmānyam anyavyāvṛttilakṣaṇaṃ/ yanniṣṭās ta ime śabdā na rūpaṃ tasya kiñcana//) (Dharmakīrti, *Commentary*, III:29–30). Additions from Ge-dün-drup, *Good Sayings*, 170.6–171.4.

28. Go-ram-ba, *Explanation*, 66.a.2.

29. There are several problems of interpretation concerning these few verses. I will examine them in the next chapter, while investigating the concept of objective elimination.

30. The word *pratibimbakam* can be taken either as an adjectival form meaning "that which pertains to the reflection" or can be just taken as referring to the reflection itself in an appropriate metrical form. The translation I have adopted here intends to preserve the ambiguity and vagueness of the original text itself and will be helpful in explaining why later Tibetan scholars disagreed on the status of this conceptual reflection.

31. phyi rol nus pa rnam gcod la/ reg pa med kyang sgra de ni// rnam par rtog pa'i gzugs brnyan ni/ de yi mthar thug rnams dang 'brel/ des na gzhan sel mthar thug phyir/ mnyan pa gzhan sel byed par brjod// ldog pa bzhin du sgra dag las/ shes la gzhan gyi gzugs brnyan snang/ gang de'ang don gyi bdag nyid min/ de 'khrul bag chags las byung phyir// (bāhyaśaktivyavacchedaniṣṭhātabhāve'pi tacchrutiḥ// vikalpapratibimbeṣu tanniṣṭheṣu nibadhyate/ tato 'nyāpohaniṣṭhatvād uktā 'nyāpohakṛc chrutiḥ// vyatirekīva yaj jñāne bhāty arthapratibimbakam/ śabdāt tad api nārthātmā bhrāntiḥ sā vāsanodbhavā//) (Dharmakīrti, *Commentary*, III:163.cd–165).

32. For comments on this confusion, see Sellars, "Empiricism," p. 161. There Sellars emphasizes how descriptions of language acquisition commits the fallacy of placing the learning person in an universe of already categorized objects. My fictional example does not describe language acquisition but the construction of a new concept. The question of how language is acquired is not addressed by Buddhist epistemologists.

33. This is what Dharmakīrti calls the *objective factor* in the object *(arthāṃśa, don gyi cha)*.

34. See Chapter 14.

35. C. E. Pierce, "Logic as Semiotic: The Theory of Signs," in R. Innis, ed., *Semiotics* (Bloomington: Indiana University Press, 1985), pp. 1–23.

36. Go-ram-ba, *Perfect Light*, p. 187.a.2.

37. de ni mnyan pas brjod pa na/ don gyi cha gang rtogs par 'gyur/ de ma rtogs na de don can/ brda byed pa ni don med 'gyur// sgras don cha ni ci brjod ces/ de la gzhan sel brjod par bya/ rnam pa de yang don la med/ de brjod ci ltar don brten yin// rjes 'gro can sgra rjes gro can/ don gyi 'bras yin don goms pas/ sprul de'ang rjes 'gro med pa can/ blo las tha dad med phyir ro// (tasyābhidhāne śrutibhir arthe ko'ṃśo 'vagamyate/ tasyāgatau ca saṃketakriyā vyarthā tadarthikā// śabdo'rthāṃśaṃ kam āheti tatrānyāpoha ucyate/ ākāraḥ sa ca nārthe'sti taṃ vadann arthabhāk katham// śabdasyānvayinaḥ kāryam arthenānvayinā sa ca/ ananvayī dhiyo 'bhedād darśanābhyāsanirmitaḥ//) (Dharmakīrti, *Commentary*, III:166–68. Ge-dün-drup, *Good Sayings*, 204.3–205.1. Go-ram-ba, *Light*, 187.a.2–b.1).

38. Dharmakīrti, *Commentary*, I:92.

39. Go-ram-ba, *Explanation*, 66.a.2.

40. Kay-drup, *Ocean*, III:69.a.4–70.a.2. Śākya Chok-den, *Explanation*, 474.5–.7.

41. Bhartṛhari proposes a related theory of superimposition *(adhyāropita)*, according to which we understand words by superimposing a word universal on the universal of its object (Dravid, *The Problem*, p. 227).

42. Dharmakīrti, *Commentary*, I:68–70. This is as close as Dharmakīrti seems to ever come to propounding a view of the two truths. Conceptual contents are the pseudo-entities held to be true by conceptual thought, which is *saṃvṛti* (*kun rdzob*; concealer); that is, concealing or relative cognition. Hence, they are truths for a concealer, *saṃvṛti-satya (kun rdzob bden pa)*, that is, relative truth, in opposition to what is given to perception.

43. This does not say whether some particular concepts are inborn or not. Śāntarakṣita seems to think so (See Ganganath Jhā, *Tattvasaṅgraha of Śāntarakṣita*, p. I.616). Whatever the answer given to this last question, it is clear that the Buddhist conception of mind is very different from that of empiricists. Mind is not a tabula rasa, but an active agent already conditioned and predisposed to do certain things at birth. The adoption of this view does not commit oneself to accepting that knowledge has a priori elements. Although dispositions are innate, they can receive their contents from empirical experience. Finally, let us observe that the use of the term *mind* is tricky. In the Buddhist context, this term refers to what should be more accurately described as mental episode or event. See Chapter 16.

44. Jhā, *Ślokavārttika*, 14.39.

45. de dngos sgro btags rtog pa yis/ gzhan las bzlog pa rtogs phyir yang/ sgra don gang yin de nyid ces/ brjod pa la ni 'gal ba med// shes pa sgra yis nges sprul pa/ de dag log par snang ba nyid/ don gyi cha la 'di rjes 'gro/ de ltar mnyan pa gzhan sel byed// (tadrūpāropagatyā'nyavyāvṛttādhigateḥ punaḥ/ śabdārtho'rthaḥ sa eveti vacane na virudhyate// mithyāvabhāsino vaite pratyayāḥ śabdanirmitāḥ/ anuyāntīmam arthāṃśam iti vāpohakṛc chrutiḥ//) (Dharmakīrti., *Commentary*, III:169–70). Additions from Ge-dün-drup, *Good Sayings*, 205.1–4; Go-ram-ba, *Light*, 187.b.1–4.

46. K. Jarter, *Presuppositions of Indian Philosophy* (Englewood Cliffs, N.J.: Prentice-Hall, 1963), p. 203. Quoted in Klein, *Knowledge*, pp. 179–80.

47. The Ge-luk tradition represents an exception in that it puts great value on the intellectual understanding of reality as a means for more direct experience. See Chapter 18.

Chapter 13. The Concept of Negation and the Evolution of the Apoha *Theory*

1. See Siderits, *"Apoha"*; "More Things in Heaven and Earth," *Journal of Indian Philosophy* 10, no. 2 (1982); and "Was Śāntarakṣita a Positivist?" in Matilal and Devans, *Buddhist Logic*, pp. 193–205. Also see J. L. Shaw, "Negation and the Buddhist Theory of Meaning," *Journal of Indian Philsophy* 6, no. 1 (1978): 59–77.

2. As Barlingay remarks, the word *abhāva* has several meaning: absence, non-existence, negation, contradiction (*Introduction*, p. 72).

3. D. Sharma, "Epistemological Negative Dialectices of Indian Logic—*Abhāva* versus *Anupalabdhi*," *Indo-Iranian Journal* 9, no. 4 (1966): 291–300. This article describes the differences within the Mīmāṃsā on the subject of absence as a separate means of cognition. For the Nyāya view, see Shastri, *Philosophy*, pp. 395–418 and Barlingay, *Introduction*, pp. 72–86. For a Ge-luk view, see Klein, *Knowledge*, pp. 141–82.

4. Śāntarakṣita, *Compendium*, 1004, P: 5764, 46.a.3. See later.

5. Verbally and nominally bound negation is the translation proposed by Matilal and is well adapted to the grammatical aspect of the discussion (B. K. Matilal, *The Navya-Nyāya Doctrine of Negation* [Cambridge, Mass.: Harvard University Press, 1968]), pp. 156–57.

6. For more on this topic, see Sharma, *Differentiation*, p. 34; J. F. Staal, "Negation and

the Law of Contradiction in Indian Thought," *Bulletin of the School of Oriental and African Studies* 25, no. 1 (1962): 55–66.

7. Y. Kajiyama, "Three Types of Affirmation and Two Types of Negation in Buddhist Philosophy," *Wiener Zeitschrift für die Kunde Südasiens* 17 (1973): 161–75, 167.

8. Śākya Chok-den indicates a few passages in Dignāga and Dharmakīrti (such as *Commentary*, IV:262) as sources of the distinction between these two types of negation (*Defeater*, I.477.3–8.2). However, Dharmakīrti does not seem to mention this distinction in reference to the *apoha* theory. We will see the significance of this difference in the next pages.

9. tathā hi dvividho'pohaḥ paryudāsa niśedataḥ/ dvividhaḥ paryudhāso'pi buddhyātmārthātmabhedataḥ// (D. Shastri ed., *Tattvasaṃgraha of Ācārya Śāntarakṣita with the Commentary "Pāñjika" of Shrī Kamalaśīla* [Banaras: Bauddha Bharati Series, 1968], vol. 1, p. 390.6–7) (I prefer Jhā's numeration of the stanzas. Accordingly, I will refer to only the page numbers in Shastri's edition). de ltar sel ba rnam gnyis te/ ma yin dgag dang med pa'o/ ma yin dgag pa'ang rnam gnyis te/ blo dang don gyi dbye bas so// (Śāntarakṣita, *Compendium on Reality [tattvasaṃgraha, de kho na nyid bsdus pa]*, p. 1004, D: 4266, P: 5764, 46.a.3).

10. A negation does not need to negate an existing object. A negation negates an object of negation *(dgag bya)*, which does not need to exist, as in the case of the absence of the son of a barren woman.

11. Śāntarakṣita, *Compendium*, 1009.

12. Gyel-tsap, *Revealing*, 130, 147, and *Essence*, 35.a.1. In the latter passage, Gyel-tsap argues that Sa-paṇ's assertion that eliminations are always conceptual is not meant to deny objective eliminations but to underline the conceptual nature of their identity as negations, which is different from their identity as real things. Gyel-tsap does not point to any textual support in Sa-paṇ's work for his distinction.

13. Ge-dün-drup, *Ornament*, 364–65.

14. This opinion is reflected in Klein's presentation of this view as accepted by all Geluk thinkers (Klein, *Knowledge*, p. 152–82). Strictly speaking, there is no single opinion on this topic shared by all major Ge-luk thinkers since, as we will see, Kay-drup denies that real things can be negations in his *Ornament*. However, Kay-drup changed his mind in his *Ocean*. His later vigorous defense of objective elimination indicates that the acceptance of the concept is important for Ge-luk epistemology.

15. ma yin dgag gyi gzhan sel gang zhig/ sgro ma btags par don rang gnos nas grub pa/ (Ge-dün-drup, *Ornament*, 364.10–.11). Jang-gya and Pur-bu-jok give equivalent definitions. See Klein, *Knowledge*, pp. 166, 147.

16. I have chosen to translate *pratiṣedha* as "negation" to mark that, for many thinkers, it is a concept and not a real thing. In the framework of Śāntarakṣita's and Ge-luk philosophy, however, "negative" would be more appropriate, for *pratiṣedha* also refers to real things being distinguished from other things. This may surprise an analytically trained philosopher, who is used to thinking of negation as a logical operator.

17. Not only are they substantially identical, they are so simultaneously from the point of view of place, time, and nature *(yul dus rang bzhin gang la ltos te grub bde rdzas gcig)*. That is to say, they are infallibly concomitant in place, time, and nature. See Klein, *Knowledge*, p. 124.

18. Go-ram-ba, *Explanation*, 58.a6–b1.

19. Kajiyama, trans., *Introduction*, p. 122. I am slightly puzzled as to why Mokṣākaragupta chose a jar as the example of a real thing. In doing so, he is probably referring to the real elements that make a jar.

20. In holding that a mental elimination is a real mental event, Śāntarakṣita differs from Ge-luk thinkers who take it to be an unreal object universal. See Chapter 14.

21. apoha ityeṣā saṃjñoktam (gzhan sel ces ming du bstan pa) (Śāntarakṣita, *Compendium*, 1009; P: 5764, 46.a.6; Shastri, *Tattvasaṃgraha*, p. 391).

22. etat mukhyat eva svalakṣaṇo 'anyapohavyapadeśa ityuktam bhavati (Shastri, *Tattva*, p. 392.9–.10). 'dis ni rang gi mtshan nyid gzhan sel bar bstan pa ni dngos yin no zhes bstan pa yin no/ (Kamalaśīla, *Commentary*, P: 5765, 422.a.2).

23. The question of what are the examples of such objective elimination for Śāntarakṣita is not exactly clear to me. It seems that some of Bo-dong's ideas might be partly relevant here. Referring to a passage from Dharmakīrti's *Ascertainment*, Bo-dong proposes "mere thing which is excluded from what has the nature of what it is not" (de min rang bzhin las ldog pa'i dngos po tsam) as an example of objective elimination (*Presentation*, I:703.4). For Bo-dong, however, such an entity is a universal, a view not accepted by Śāntarakṣita.

24. Dharmakīrti, *Commentary*, III:163.cd. See Chapter 12.

25. de la ci'i phyir gzhan sel zhes bya zhe na/ 'di la gzhan sel bar byed pa'i gzhi yin pas gzhan sel zhes bya ste/ Śākya blos/ re zhig gcig ni 'di la gzhan dang gzhan sel bar byed pa'i phyir rang gi mtshan nyid ldog pa kho na'o/ zhes so/ de yang sgra bshad pa'i dbang du byas pa yin gyi gzhan sel bar byed pa'i gzhi yin na gzhan sel yin pas khyab pa ni ma yin no/ (Ge-dün-drup, *Ornament*, 364.10–.14).

26. In the absence of a clearer indication, however, this conclusion cannot be more than tentative. Only further research will be able to decide the truth on this matter.

27. Here again, the reader should remember that the representations we are dealing with are conceptual.

28. tanupāśritya yajjñāne bhātyarthapratibimbakaṃ/ kalpako 'rthātmatā 'bhāve 'pyarthā ityeva niścitam// (Shastri, *Tattvasaṃgraha*, pp. 390.10–391.1). der rten shes pa'i snang ba gang/ don gyi gzugs brnyan rtog pa can/ don gyi bdag nyid min pa la/ don zhes bya bar nges pa yin// (Śāntarakṣita, *Compendium*, 1006, P: 5764, 46.a.4–.5).

29. de la brten nas zhes bya ba ni mi 'jigs pa la sogs pa dang mtshungs pa'i don de la brten nas te rgyur byas nas de nyams su myong ba'i stobs kyis skyes pa'i rnam par rtog pa'i shes pa gang yin pa de la de la don gyi rnam pa nyid kyi don gyi gzugs brnyan gang yin pa de'i bdag nyid du don gyi rnam pa snang ba de la gzhan sel ba zhes bya ba'i ming 'di btags so// (Kamalaśīla, *Commentary*, P: 5765, 421.a.6–.7).

30. pratibhāsāntarād bhedādanyavyāvṛttavastunaḥ/ prāptihetutayā. Shastri, *Tattvasaṃgraha*, 391.2–.3. snang ba gzhan las tha dad phyir/ gzhan las log pa'i dngos po ni/ thob pa'i rgyu las/ (Śāntarakṣita, *Compendium*, 1007abc, P: 5764, 46.a.5).

31. rgyu mtshan bzhis 'di sel ba zhes bshad pa yin te/ dngos su ni rnam par rtog pa gzhan gyis sgro btags pa'i snang ba gzhan las tha dad pas rang nyid snang ba'i phyir te/ (Kamalaśīla, *Commentary*, P: 5765, 421.b.1–.2).

32. Hattori, "Apoha," p. 68.

33. Dharmakīrti, *Commentary*, III:165. See Chapter 12.

34. In Go-ram-ba's interpretation, Dharmakīrti does not deny this connection but holds that this is not enough to explain the nature of conceptuality. One cannot reduce conceptuality to the functioning of representations. One must address the nature of concepts, which is different from that of representations.

35. Kamalaśīla, *Commentary*, P: 5765, 421.b.3.

36. tadrūpapratibimbasya dhiyaḥ śabdācca janmati/ vācyavācakabhāvo'yaṃ jāto hetuphalātmakaḥ// (Shastri, *Tattvasaṃgraha*, p. 392.5–.6). de yi ngo bo gzugs brnyan gyi/

sgro ni sgra las skye ba ste/ brjod bya brjod byed dngos 'di ni/ rgyu 'bras bdag nyid can grub pa'o/ (Śāntarakṣita, *Compendium*, 1012; P: 5764, 46.a.8–b.1).

37. blo de'i ngo bo'i gzugs brnyan de'i 'brel ba nyid sgra las skyes pa na ste byung ba na brjod par byed pa'i mtshan nyid kyis dngos po'i mtshan nyid de dbyad (i.e., dpyad) pa na rgyu dang 'bras bu'i dngos po'i bdag nyid kho nar grub ste 'di ltar sgra ni gzugs brnyan de bskyed par byed pa'i phyir brjod par byed pa brjod la/ gzugs brnyan de yang sgra las bskyed par bya ba yin pa'i phyir brjod bya'o// (Kamalaśīla, *Commentary*, P: 5765, 422.b.1–.2).

38. Śāntarakṣita, *Compendium*, 1019.

39. Śāntarakṣita, *Compendium*, 1063–65.

40. This assertion relies on Hayes's presentation of the *apoha* theory in the context of inference (*Dignāga*, pp. 111–216).

41. The connection between Śāntarakṣita and the Tibetan tradition does not seem to be due to Śāntarakṣita's stay in Tibet toward the end of the eighth century. Van der Kuijp remarks on the conspicuous and surprising absence of Śāntarakṣita's tradition in the later stages of the Tibetan logico-epistemological tradition, quoting Go-ram-ba to that effect (*Contributions*, p. 5). In the field of Madhyamaka, Śāntarakṣita's tradition was first well established but later (eleventh century) supplanted by Ba-tsap's Prāsaṇgika. See S. Karmay, *The Great Perfection* (Leiden: Brill, 1988), p. 3; and D. S. Ruegg, *Buddha-Nature, Mind and the Problem of Gradualism in a Comparative Perspective.*

42. Kamalaśīla, *Commentary*, P: 5765, 420.b.7–.8; Shastri ed., p. 320.

43. dgag bya dngos su bcad pa'i tshul gyis rtogs par bya ba/ (Ge-dün-drup, *Ornament*, 347.17).

44. dgag bya dngos su bcad pa'i tshul gyis rtogs par bya ba gang zhig/ dgag bya bkag shul du chos gzhan mi 'phen pa/ (ibid., 347.20–348.1). Klein has dealt at length with the Ge-luk presentation of these two types of negation. See *Knowledge*, pp. 175–82.

45. This view of emptiness as a nonimplicative negation is strongly criticized by Go-ram-ba as being only a partial view of emptiness. For Go-ram-ba, negation of true existence does not constitute emptiness, which is reached by negating all four extremes. The identification of emptiness as the negation of true existence does not go beyond the refutation of the first of the four extremes. Phenomena are not just empty of truly existing, but also of being not truly existing. See Go-ram-ba, *Distinguishing the View, a Moonlight of the Essential Points of the Supreme Vehicle (lta ba'i shan 'byed theg mchog gnad kyi zla zer)*, 41.6–52.3. On the four extremes, see D. Ruegg, "The Uses of the Four Positions of the *Catuṣkoti* and the Problem of the Description of Reality in Mahāyāna Buddhism," *Journal of Indian Philosophy* 5 (1977): 1–71. On Dzong-ka-ba's interpretation, see E. Napper, *Dependent Arising and Emptiness* (London: Wisdom, 1989) and Hopkins, *Meditation on Emptiness.*

46. Gyel-tsap, *Revealing*, I.147.12–.3. He also mentions the great Brahmin Śaṃkarānanda, who seems to have held that the absence of jar on nonjar is the nonimplicative negative of a jar. More on this later.

47. Ge-dün-drup, *Ornament*, 348.13–.4.

48. Ge-dün-drup, *Ornament*, 348.2–.13. Ge-dün-drup's position does not strike me as very convincing, for when asked what in this case is the basis on which one can estimate whether another positive phenomenon is or is not implied, he answers: the knowable *(shes bya)*. In this case, why not dispense altogether with a basis of estimation?

49. This goes the other way as well. Realism concerning negation does not entail an acceptance of real universals. Śāntarakṣita holds that there are real negations but rejects realism.

50. For Kay-drup as well as for all major Ge-luk thinkers, elimination and negation are equivalent.

51. 'dis ni rang mtshan sel 'dod pa'ang khegs shing/ 'dod pa de dag ni/ gzhan sel ba thams cad ni sgro btags su lan gcig ma yin par bshad pa'i slob dpon kyi gzhung lugs dag la mngon sum du bsnyon par byed pa yin no/ (Kay-drup, *Ornament*, 220.a.3–.4).

52. don gyi sel ba yin na sel ba btags pa ba yin pas khyab par 'dod pa slob dpon de dag gi dgongs par smra ba'ang slob dpon de dag gi gzhung lugs ma mthong bar gsal te/ (Kay-drup, *Ocean*, I:130.a.5–6).

53. Ge-dün-drup, *Ornament*, 364.11. *bum pa ma yin pa las log pa* can be translated as "that which is not a nonjar." If we consider the Sanskrit equivalent of *log pa*, *vyāvrtta*, the translation would be "that which is distinguished [from] the nonjar." I have used the second here to mark that such a thing is a real jar.

54. Klein, *Knowledge*, pp. 125 and 168.

55. Bo-dong, *Presentation*, I.798.1. Although they might disagree with Bo-dong's negative realism, most Ge-luk thinkers would agree with this last assertion. As we will see later, they hold that this type of elimination is the main support of the process of naming. Several also hold that the elimination of a real thing such as a jar must be an objective elimination.

56. See Chapters 8 and 12.

57. phyi rol nus pa rnam gcod la/ Dharmakīrti, *Commentary*, III:163.c.

58. Dharmakīrti, *Commentary*, III:164.

59. See Chapter 22.

60. Sö-nam-drak-ba, *Revealing the Thought*, I.89.a.3–91.b.3.

61. Go-ram-ba, *Explanation*, 136.a.6. Although this is clearly not Śāntarakṣita's idea, it remains to be seen whether this idea does not come from another later Indian source.

62. Śāntarakṣita, *Compendium*, 1010.

63. Ibid., 1019–21 and 1095–96. Shastri, *Tattva*, pp. 395, 416. This issue seems to separate Jñānaśrīmitra and Ratnakīrti from Śāntarakṣita. Whereas for Śāntarakṣita, the positive and the negative element are understood in succession, for Jñānaśrīmitra and Ratnakīrti, they are understood at the same time. See Sharma, *Differentiation*, p. 53. As Siderits rightly remarks, the situation betwen the pair Jñānaśrīmitra-Ratnakīrti and Śāntarakṣita is complicated because the two sides refer to different things by the word positive. Jñānaśrīmitra and Ratnakīrti refer to the real thing, which is cognized as qualified by a negation, whereas Śāntarakṣita refers to the reflection as the thing that is felt to be positive. Yet, the idea of a cognitive process in time distinguishes the two sides. The only way to reconcile them on this issue would be to assert that what Śāntarakṣita really meant is not a temporal succession, but an epistemological priority. However, this does not seem to be the case. Commenting on stanza 1021, Kamalaśīla says that there would be incongruity if both affirmation and negation were resultants of the same cognition.

64. The discussion of this question centers around *Commentary*, IV:230, where Dharmakīrti argues that, if real things were the direct support of affirmation and negation, any affirmation would eo ipso establish all the characteristics of the object. Most Sa-gya scholars take this to mean that affirmation and negation of something directly concern only concepts and not real entities. Refutation and affirmation do not relate to the way things are but to our conceptualization of them. Go-ram-ba, *Explanation*, 49.a.4–50b.2.

In his typical realist way, Kay-drup takes Dharmakīrti not to be denying that refutation and affirmation can be done on the basis of real things but to be denying the reality of the idea that real things can be refuted. Although real things are objects of both affirmation and negation, they are not so ultimately. If they were ultimately objects of affirmation, those things would have to be the object designated by words *(sgra don)*. Accordingly, the words designating them and the conceptual cognitions associated with them would be subjects engaging affirmatively *(sgrub 'jug)* and would have to bring knowledge of the real thing in all its aspects. Kay-drup, *Ornament*, 38.b.6–39.a.1.

65. tshad ma'i stobs kyis dgag sgrub byed pa'i dngos yul la sgrub pa dang dgag par 'jog pa'i tshe gnyis ka yang gzhan sel kho na yin te/ mgnon sum ni don rang mtshan snang ba tsam yin pas dgag sgrub byed mi nus kyi des drangs pa'i nges shes dang/ rjes dpag gis dgag sgrub byed pa'i phyir// (Go-ram-ba, *Explanation*, 134.a.6–b.1).

66. Śākya Chok-den, *Defeater*, I.484.5–.6. This label of mere negation is remarkable for implicative negation.

67. rnam bcad kho nar rtogs par bya gang zhig dgag bya bkag shul du chos gzhan 'phen pa/ (Śākya Chok-den, *Defeater*, I.488.2).

68. Such negation is defined as "that phenomenon which is to be realized by both elimination and inclusion" (rnam bcad yongs gcod gnyis sgo nas rtogs par bya ba'i chos/) (ibid., I.487.5).

69. Ibid., I.487.3–.5. In this perspective, all affirmations are implicative negations (ibid., I.488.5).

70. Also called *nonexistent elimination (med pa gzhan sel)*.

71. dgag pa'am sel ba gang zhig sgrub pa mi spong ba'am sgrub chos ma dor ba'o/ (ibid., I.488.5).

Chapter 14. Object Universal and Concept Formation

1. I am here following O. Pind, "Dignāga on *śabdasāmānya* and *śabdaviśeṣa*," in *Studies in the Buddhist Epistemological Tradition*, pp. 268–80.

2. See Chapter 12.

3. Let us notice that both views differ from Śāntarakṣita's ideas, although they borrow their terminology from him. Contrary to the Ge-luk-bas, Śāntarakṣita does not assimilate universals and appearances. And contrary to Sa-paṇ's followers, Śāntarakṣita does not limit elimination to conceptual constructs but holds that real entities can be actual eliminations.

4. This reasoning rests on the fundamental structure of Dharmakīrti's system, where unreal, permanent, and generally characterized are equivalent. See Chapter 2.

5. bum 'dzin rtog pa la bum pa ma yin pa las log par snang ba'i sgro btags kyi cha/ (Pur-bu-jok, *Small Path*, 21.a.2).

6. bum 'dzin rtog pa la gser bum bum par snang ba de yang sgra don yin la/ rang la snang ba de nyid bum pa ma yin pa las log par snang ba de yang sgra don yin no/ (Kay-drup, *Ornament*, 35.a.5–.6).

7. Hopkins, *Meditation*, pp. 347–49.

8. Kay-drup describes the reflection as "the appearance [of something] as not being a nonjar" (*Ocean*, III:68.b.6).

9. Ge-luk thinkers do not hold that all properties are real. For example, existing is not a real but a conceptual property. By contrast, being a thing is a real property. The Ge-luk point is that there are some properties that are real.

10. des na bum gsal rnams la rjes su 'gro' ba'i spyi dngos po ba dang dngos po ba ma yin pa gnyis yod de/ bum pa ni bum gsal rnams la rjes su 'gro ba'i spyi dngos por 'gyur pa yin la/ rtog pa la bum par snang ba de nyid bum gsal rnams la rjes su 'gro ba'i spyi dngos med du gyur pa yin no/ (Kay-drup, *Ornament*, 36.b.3–.4).

11. It is technically described as the appearing object *(snang yul)*. More on this in Chapters 17 and 25.

12. Dharmakīrti, *Commentary*, I:68–69.

13. Śākya Chok-den, *Defeater*, II.18.7.

14. gal te spyi yul du byed na rtog pa yin pas khyab kyang rigs spyi snang yul du byed na rtog pa yin pas ma khyab bo zhe na/ don spyir ma 'dus pa'i rigs spyi 'dod pa ni chur ma 'dus pa'i rgya mtsho 'dod pa dang mtshungs la/ slob dpon ngan pa'i dug chus myos pa'i blab chol yin te/ snang btags gcig tu 'khrul pa'i sgro btags las ma gtogs pa'i rigs spyi mi srid pa'i phyir/ (Go-ram-ba, *Explanation*, 47.a.6–b.1).

15. bum 'dzin rtog pa la bum pa ma yin pa las log par snang ba chos can/ bum pa'i gzhan sel min te/ bum 'dzin rtog pa'i shes rnam yin pa'i phyir/ (Śākya Chok-den, *Defeater*, II.180.6–181.1).

16. Śākya Chok-den, *Defeater*, II.18.6–19.4.

17. Appearance *(snang ba)* is real in opposition to elimination *(sel ba)*, which is superimposed.

18. 'o na bum 'dzin rtog pa'i bzung rnam de snang ba yin nam sel ba yin zhe na/ de la shes pa yin pa'i cha dang/ phyi rol bum par sgro btags pa'i cha gnyis las/ snga ma ni snang ba yin te/ bum 'dzin rtog pa rang gi ngo bo la rang rig mngon sum du song ba'i yul yin pa'i phyir/ phyi ma sel ba yin te/ sgro btags yin pa'i phyir/ (Go-ram-ba, *Explanation*, 65.a.2–.4).

19. Śākya Chok-den classifies an object universal as an implicative negation that implies a commitment to the existence of some positive entity. In this case, the positive entity whose existence is implied by the negation is the real object. For example, when we think about the words *this is my chair*, the mistaken identity superimposed on the appearance is a negation that implies a commitment to the existence of a positive entity; namely, the chair. The mere negation of nonchairness is a nonimplicative negation that is the object directly expressed by these words *(sgra'i dngos kyi brod bya)*. Such a distinction applies only in cases where words and thought assert something. In cases of pure negation *(dgag bya 'gog pa)*, the object universal is a nonimplicative negation (Śākya Chok-den, *Defeater*, II.190.1–.2).

20. Stanton, *Universals*, (New York: Anchor, 1972), p. 41.

21. rtog pa gang ji snyed pa thams cad rang gi yul la ngo bo nyid kyis skra shad dam rmi lam ltar gzhi med pa la 'khrul/ (Sa-paṇ, *Auto-Commentary*, 44.a.5).

Chapter 15. Philosophy of Language

1. Hayes, *Dignāga*, p. 257.

2. "On Sense and Reference," in Martinich, *The Philosophy of Language*.

3. See G. Evans, *The Varieties of Reference* (Oxford: Oxford University Press, 1982).

4. We will deal later with the conflicting opinions within the Ge-luk tradition on this topic.

5. mi 'thad de/ dngos su bstan na dngos su brjod pas ma khyab pa'i phyir te/ dngos su bstan pa'i don ni sgra de la brten nas dngos su go ba'i yul la 'jog cing/ dngos su brjod pa'i don ni/ sgra de thos pa'i nyan shes mngon sum gyi rjes su byung ba'i rtog pa la de dngos su snang ba la byed pa'i phyir ro/ des na bstan tshul la dngos bstan dang shugs bstan gnyis/ brjod tshul la dngos kyi brjod bya dang zhen pa'i brjod bya gnyis su phye ba ma 'dres par shes par gyis shig/ (Go-ram-ba, *Explanation*, 74.b.4–.6).

6. Let us observe that such a claim is not central to Buddhist tradition, contrary to a

common misperception. There is, in fact, very little mention of ineffability in the literature of Nikāya Buddhism. Paul Williams aptly describes the view of early schools: "Followers of the older schools seem to have been united in holding that all existents can be named. Buddhaghosa observed that there is nothing which escapes being named, for if we say that a thing is ineffable then that thing is thereby named 'ineffable'. Such a point was methodologically important, for liberation came from knowing the way of things and was thereby much facilitated by the completeness and adequacy of a *dharmic* list, which included all ultimate existents" ("Language," p. 2). The claim of the ineffability of reality is more important in the Mahāyāna tradition. For a very good view of the role of ineffability claims in Mādhyamika, see P. Williams, "Silence and Truth," *Tibet Journal* 1 (1981): 67–80.

7. khyad par rjes 'gro med pas na/ brda 'jug pa ni med phyir ro/ sgra rnams yul yang gang de nyid/ de rnams nyid ni sbyor bar byed// (ananvayād viśeṣāṇāṃ saṃketasyāpravṛttitaḥ/ viṣayo yaś ca hi śabdānāṃ saṃyojyeta sa eva taiḥ//) (Dharmakīrti, *Commentary*, III:128). Ge-dün-drup, *Good Sayings*, 194.3–6.

8. Part II of Book II will clarify the meaning of the notion of direct object.

9. Shastri, *Philosophy*, p. 346.

10. Rita Gupta, "Apoha and the Nominalist/Conceptualist Controversy," *Journal of Indian Philosophy* 13, no. 4 (1985): 384–98, 388.

11. Ibid., 390.

12. Stcherbatsky, *Buddhist Logic*, vol. 1, p. 63. Also see vol. 1, pp. 85, 150, 182, 185, and 190.

13. Dharmakīrti, *Commentary*, I:43–45. More on this in Chapters 20–24.

14. Napper, *Mind*, pp. 141–43.

15. A Buddha is sometimes described as a person of full engagement *(sgrub 'jug gyi gang zag)* in that he cognizes reality without relying on concepts.

16. Go-ram-ba, *Explanation*, 73.a.5.

17. Ge-dün-drup, *Ornament*, 367.1–.2.

18. Tibetan scholars agree on that much, but they disagree on the exact implications of the distinction between perception and conception. More on this in Chapters 18 and 21–24.

19. The following is taken from Siderits, "Sentence Meaning." For a good study of the general background of the discussion, see Raja, *Indian Theories of Meaning* (Madras: Adyar Library, 1963); Barlingay, *Introduction*, pp. 23–62; Biardeau, *Theorie*, pp. 175–203, 400–20.

20. Compare this view to Quine's statement that "even the sophisticated learning of a new word is commonly a matter of learning it in context. . . . It therefore remained appropriate . . . to treat sentences and not words as the wholes whose use is learned-though never denying that the learning of these wholes proceed largely by abstracting and assembling of parts" (*Word*, p. 13).

21. Hattori, "Apoha," p. 70; and Siderits, "Sentence Meaning," p. 142.

22. See Dharmakīrti, *Commentary*, III:485–503. For self-cognition, see Chapters 19, 24, and 25.

23. One may obviously speculate on the reason for this shift. Pind attributes it to an influence of Vasubandhu's Sautrāntika view of language ("Dignāga on *śabdasāmānya*," p. 279). For my part, I believe that Dharmakīrti's emphasis on causally linking language to reality and his interest in reference are also relevant to explaining this shift from Dignāga's holistic view of language as an internal phenomenon. Influences from other Indian thinkers such as Kumārila may also be relevant.

24. Dharmakīrti is quite aware that language is not possible without a concept of commonality. Words cannot be meaningful unless they signify some common fictional property. He does not seem, however, to use commonality to explain the formation of words, which for him are fictional sequences of sounds formed and understood by the activation of memory traces. In Tibetan terms, Dharmakīrti accepts object universals but seems to have little use for term universals, the fictional commonalities that unite and transcend individual articulations.

25. This constructive conception of language differentiates Dharmakīrti's philosophy of language from an empiricist view, according to which language is little more than an instrument to communicate what we conceive in the privacy of our minds.

26. sgra rnams kyis ni brdar btags ston/ de ni tha snyad ched du byas/ de tshe rang gi mtshan nyid med/ des na de la brdar ma yin// (śabdāḥ saṃketitaṃ prāhur vyavahārāya sa smṛtaḥ/ tadā svalakṣaṇaṃ nāsti saṃketas tena tatra na//) (Dharmakīrti, *Commentary*, I:92). Frauwallner, "Beiträge," p. 394.

27. tha dad kyang gang dngos chos kyis/ de 'dra'i rnam shes rgyu yi ni/ don de dag la shes pa des/ de ltar rtogs par gyur ba yin// tha dad tha dad min par ni/ rtog la shes pa'ang de bzhin no/ de phyir de 'bras med bral ba/ rjes 'gro dngos gcig yod ma yin// (vastudharmatayaivārthās tādṛgvijñānakāraṇaṃ/ bhede'pi yatra tajjñānāt tat [or tajjñānaṃ tān] tathā pratipadyate// jñānāny api tathā bhede 'bhedapratyavamarśane/ ity atat kāryaviṣleṣasyānvayo naikavastunaḥ//) (Dharmakīrti, *Commentary*, III:161–62), Ge-dün-drup, *Good Sayings*, 203.2–.5).

28. Gyel-tsap calls these factual thoughts "subjects that deliver specifically characterized objects" *(don gyi rang mtshan thob pa'i yul can)* and "factual conventions that are indirectly (via perception) related to specifically characterized phenomena" *(rang mtshan la rgyud nas 'brel ba'i tha snyad don mthun)* (*Revealing*, I.107.15–.16).

29. de byed min la de byed dang/ 'dra ba'i ngo bor snang ba can/ dngos po tha dad dngos tsam gyi/ sa bon can don med pa'i blo/ skyed par byed pa'ang de mi byed/ yongs spangs yan lag ngo bo'i phyir/ dngos po tha dad rten can phyir/ don la mi slu yod par 'dod// de phyir gzhan sel yul can te/ de byed brten pa'i ngo bo'i phyir/ (akāryakṛtitatkāritulyarūpāvabhāsinīṃ/ dhiyaṃ vastupṛthagbhāvamātrabījām anarthikām// janayanty apy atatkāriparihārāṅgabhāvataḥ/ vastubhedāśrayāc cārthe na visaṃvādikā matā// tato 'nyāpohaviṣayā tatkartrāśritabhāvataḥ/) (Dharmakīrti, *Commentary*, I:111–113.b). Ge-dün-drup, *Good Sayings*, 33.1–.3. Frauwallner, "Beiträge," p. 402. See also Dharmakīrti, *Commentary*, I:98. The expression *(vastupṛthagbhāvamātrabhījām)* expresses quite clearly the idea that an agreed-on convention is not the result of a common thing but of the individuality of the things themselves (the Tibetan *dngos po tsam gyi sa bon can* is more ambiguous).

30. This theory of reference should not be confused with modern theories of causal reference, which attempt to posit denotation on the basis of a direct connection between names and objects (Kripke's famous notion of rigid designation). Dharmakīrti does not believe in rigid or direct designation, for he holds that language necessarily requires conceptual mediation. Hence, he sides with Frege in holding that naming can never be direct. Nevertheless, because he is an antirealist, he needs to introduce a causal element in his theory to relate concepts, whose objects are fictional, to reality.

31. For example, see Shastri, *Philosophy*, pp. 363–68 and Stcherbatsky, *Logic*, vol. 2, pp. 299–308. It now becomes clear why Stcherbatsky's description of the specifically characterized as a Kantian thing-in-itself is inadequate. It ignores the limited but real referential ability of language. Although things are not capturable by thought or language, they provide the empirical basis for the elaboration of concepts. Hence, they are not completely unknowable.

32. Strictly speaking, we should talk about the color of a snowy mountain.

33. See Chapters 16 and 17.

34. F. de Saussure, *Course in General Linguistics* (New York: McGraw-Hill, 1959), p. 66.

35. sgra thos pa'i nyan shes kyi rjes su byung ba'i rtog pa la sgra 'dis don 'di brjod par 'dug go snyam pa'i brjod byed du snang ba la dngos kyi rjod byed dang/ brjod byar snang ba la dngos kyi bjod byar 'jog pa'i phyir ro/ (Go-ram-ba, *Explanation*, 76.b.2–.3).

36. Ibid., 76.a.6–b.1.

37. Śākya Chok-den, *Defeater*, II.212.3–.6.

38. As with other comparisons, the similarities between Buddhist antirealist epistemologists and Saussure are partial and limited. Contrary to Saussure's scientific idea of language as a system of signs, the Buddhists' idea of the negative character of language is not systematic. It comes from their commitment to the rejection of a metaphysics of substance.

39. Dharmakīrti's use of the notion of inner propensities *(vāsanā, bag chags)* as, for example, in *Commentary*, III:165 (see Chapter 12) does not seem to involve an idea of a priori, but rather, to be part of his mentalistic effort to causally link the internal domain of concepts to external reality.

40. For example, Śākya Chok-den, *Defeater*, II.149.4 and 288.5.

41. See Chapter 13.

42. Ge-dün-drup, *Ornament*, 360.13–.16.

43. As already previously noticed, Buddhist philosophers do not seem to mark any difference between proper and general names. The function of all names is identical; namely, to exclude individuals from being associated with certain classes.

44. de la brda sbyor ba'i dus su ba lang zhes pa'i brda dngos su ma sbyar yang de ba lang du mi go ba'i skyon med de/ dngos su ba lang ma yin pa las log pa la brda sbyar ba yin la/ tha snyad kyi dus su ba lang nag sgur sogs kyang ba lang ma yin pas las log pa yin pa'i phyir ro/ (Ge-dün-drup, *Ornament*, 361.11–.14). A similar point is made by Gyel-tsap, *Revealing*, I.116.5–.6.

45. brda sbyor ba'i yul ni/ ba lang zhes pa'i sgra brda sbyor ba na/ dkar zal lta bu rang mtshan gcig gzhir byas nas de'i steng du ba lang la brda sbyor ba yin la/ (Kay-drup, *Ornament*, 41.a.2–.3). The difference between the two thinkers comes from their opinions on objective elimination. Whereas for Gyel-tsap, objective elimination is an actual elimination, for Kay-drup in his *Ornament*, it is not, since a non-noncow is a negative way of characterizing a positive entity. Apart from this, the two thinkers share a similar realist view of language. We also remember that, in his *Ocean of Reasoning*, Kay-drup changes his mind and rallies to Gyel-tsap's opinion regarding objective eliminations as true eliminations.

46. My preceeding remarks about the difficulties of translating the Ge-luk position into English, which linguistically marks the difference between universals and particulars, apply to this section, too. See Chapter 9.

47. Kay-drup's mention of non-noncow as an objective elimination is remarkable in that he denies in the same text that any real thing can ever be an elimination. See Kay-drup, *Ornament*, 220.a.3–.4. A charitable interpretation of such blatant contradiction would be to accept, in the true spirit of the subtle distinctions favored by Tibetan scholasts, that there are objective exclusions but to deny that they are authentic exclusions.

48. des na ba lang zhes pa'i brda dkar zal gzhir byas nas sbyor ba'i tshe brda'i yul gyi gtso bo ni ba lang dang ba lang ma yin pa las log pa'i gzhan sel yin la/ dkar zal ba lang ma yin pa las log par snang ba'i sgra don kyang brda'i yul tsam du 'gyur ba yin no/ (ibid., 41.a.6).

49. Kay-drup defines a meaningful word as "that which makes its object understood through an agreed-on convention" (ibid., 205.b.2). A meaningful word reveals its object through the intermediary of the convention established when the term was introduced.

50. rang mtshan sgras rjod mi nus par 'dod pa la gnod pa mi bzad pa mang du yod kyang gong rnams su yang brjod zin la/ mtha' yas pa ni brjod par ni ga la nus/ 'on kyang rang mtshan ni sgra'i dngos kyi brjod bya ma yin te/ rtog pa'i snang yul du thal ba'i phyir ro/ (ibid., 216.a.1). This passage gives a small idea of Kay-drup's biting style, which does not generally appear in my rendering of his position.

51. A few Ge-luk thinkers such as Ge-dün-drup, Jang-gya, and the like go further and assert that real things can be the direct objects of thought. They make this claim because, as we already saw, they assert that real objects appear to conceptual thought. Accordingly, they assert that language directly signifies *(dngos su rjod)* things, although it does not describe them as they are (Ge-dün-drup, *Ornament*, 367.6–.7). Klein presents a good description of the different positions adopted by Ge-luk authors on this point. See Klein, *Knowledge*, pp. 184–96.

52. As when Dharmakīrti speaks of "an exclusion [found in] external [things]" in *Commentary* III:163.c. See Chapter 12.

Chapter 16. Dharmakirti's Epistemology of Valid Cognition

1. E. Gettier, "Is Knowledge Justified True Belief," in M. Roth and L. Galis, eds., *Knowing: Essays in the Analysis of Knowing* (New York: Random House, 1970).

2. Those are accepted as equivalent by the Buddhists. Other Indian schools have their own mental vocabularies. All agree, however, on the understanding of mental terms as designating fleeting cognizing entities rather than a mechanism.

3. The investigation of phenomena in accordance with the way in which they appear to the common precritical mind.

4. F. Brentano, "The Distinction Between Mental and Material Phenomena," in R. M. Chisholm ed., *Realism and the Background of Philosophy* (Atascadero, Calif.: Ridgeview, 1960), pp. 39–61, 50. The concept of intentional inexistence relates to a complex of ontological issues pertaining to the type of existence attributed to mental objects we have briefly examined in Part I and which need not detain us any further.

5. rnam shes yul 'dzin pa yi chos/ (viṣayagrahṇaṃ dharmo vijñānasya/) (Dharmakīrti, *Commentary*, II:206.c).

6. gsal shing rig pa/ (Jam-bel-sam-pel, *Summary*, 1.3).

7. Several Tibetan scholars interpret clarity as the observable nonmaterial nature of the mind that phenomenologically differentiates it from other observables.

8. Both appearance and apprehension can be correct or incorrect. There is no suggestion here of a given distorted by subjective apprehension as in some Naiyāyikas who hold that a sense cognition is always factual but can be distorted by thought. We will discuss a similar problem in relation to Dignāga's definition of *perception*.

9. The Sāṃkhya view is, however, monistic in its understanding of Nature, which is the universal substratum of all phenomena other than self. For a mental episode is seen as complex, involving two factors: the permanent and knowing Self, and the mental organ made of subtle matter and composed by elements such as *buddhi*, *manas*, etc. The mental event comes about through the conjunction of these two heterogeneous factors. To greatly simplify, we could say that, for the Sāṃkhya, the content of the mental event is provided by

the mental organs and the factor of awareness by the immobile Self. The Self illuminates the mental content, making it part of the field of consciousness.

10. The views of other schools differ. For example, the Nyāya does not accept the dualism of Nature and Self. Instead it holds that there is a plurality of entities, falling in the six or seven categories we examined earlier. According to this analyis, a mental event is the momentary property of the permanent Self and is enabled by the mental organ and other various conditions. Here again, we notice the reluctance of Hindu philosophers to boil down mental episodes to a single factor. This is partly due to their view that mental life involves a permanent Self. Since it also involves changes, it cannot be reduced to this single motionless factor.

11. Burrow argues that the root *mā* has the meaning to ascertain rather than to measure. Burrow, "Sanskrit Mā- to Ascertain," *Transactions of the Philological Society* [Oxford] (1980): 134–40.

12. Monier-Williams gives "before, forward, in front."

13. Hattori says: "The suffix *ana* of the word '*pramāṇā*' signifies *karaṇa*, the instrument or, according to Pāṇini, the predominant cause." See *Pāṇ* I, iv, 42 42: *sādhakatamaṁ karaṇam*; Hattori, *Dignāga*, p. 98.

14. P. Bilimoria, "*Jñāna* and *Pramā*," *Journal of Indian Philosophy* 13, no. 1 (1985): 73–102, 74.

15. See Matilal, *Perception*, pp. 101–7. Like other Indian epistemologists, Dharmakīrti does not take memory to be *pramāṇa*. See *Commentary*, III:185–88, 236, 503, as well as Śāntarakṣita, *Compendium*, 446–47.

16. In fact, a number of Sanskrit words *(adhyvasita, avabodha, gam, jñāna, etc.)* are translated by the Tibetan *rtogs*. I will often use *realize* or *understand* to translate these concepts. In this context, to realize an object means to correctly indentify this object as what it is. The identification does not need to be complete in order to be correct. For example, if I see the stone from afar I might be able to identify it as round but not as a stone. Yet, this perception is valid since it allows me to have an at least partially correct identification of the object.

17. Many philosophers feel that certainty is too restrictive; for example, students might know their lessons, yet become confused under examination. The students' loss of confidence does not mean that they have lost their knowledge, but only their certainty. To account for this type of confusing situation, these philosophers make the distinction between knowledge and knowledge claims. They argue that knowledge simpliciter does not require certainty, but knowledge claims do. In our example, students would still know their lessons, but would have lost the capacity to make a knowledge claim. A. D. Woozley, "Knowing and Not Knowing," *Proceeding of the Aristotelian Society* 3 (1952): 151–72; reprinted in G. Phillips, ed., *Knowledge and Belief* (Oxford: Oxford University Press, 1967). For the classical Indian philosophers, these students are in a state of confusion that excludes *pramā* or *pramāṇa* since they have lost their certainty.

18. I have left out the discussion of the requirement that a belief be justified. Although there is no direct equivalent in the Buddhist understanding of valid cognition, we will see later that the requirement that a cognition be either perceptual or inferential in order to be valid is roughly speaking equivalent to the requirement of justification.

19. yang dag pa'i shes pa ni/ skyes bu'i don thams cad 'grub pa'i sngon du 'gro ba can yin pas na de bstan to/ (Dharmakīrti, *Drop of Reasoning*, D: 4212, 231.b; P: 5711, 329.b.2–.3).

20. This is the etymology given by Vātsyāyana, who says: "the word *pramāṇa* signifies

the instrument because it is derived as 'this is rightly known'" (Gangopadhyaya, *Nyāya*, p. 12).

21. Ganganath Jha, *Pūrva Mīmāmsā* (Banaras: Benares Hindu University, 1942, 1964), p. 69.

22. Let us notice the ambiguity of the word *karaṇa*, which means both cause and reason or ground. The same ambiguity is also found in classical Greek, in which *cause (aitia)* can mean either a cause in the strict sense of the term or a justificatory ground.

23. I translate *pramāṇa* as "means of valid cognition" when used in the Nyāya sense of the word and as "valid cognition" when understood according to Buddhist ideas. When the word is used in the context of the *pramāṇa-phala*, I keep the original Sanskrit word. I also sometimes use the Sanskrit word when I refer to a common mention by Nyāya and Buddhist of the concept. Since this work mostly deals with epistemological matters, I have preferred this translation, which emphasizes the epistemic quality of *pramāṇa*, to others (such as authority), which might be more appropriate to the discussion of the Buddha being a *pramāṇa*. See Vittorio van Bijlert, *Epistemology and Spiritual Authority* (Vienna: Wiener Studien zur Tibetologie und Buddhismuskunde, 1989), pp. 115–20.

24. tshad ma bslu med can shes pa/ don byed nus par gnas pa ni/ (pramāṇam avisaṃvādi jñānam arthakriyāsthitiḥ/) (Dharmakīrti, *Commentary*, II:1.ab).

25. The Nyāya assert that knowledge is a quality of the self *(ātma)*. Only when I become conscious of something can I be said to know it. Therefore, knowledge is analyzed as a quality of a substance, self. Barlingay, *Introduction*, pp. 44–46.

26. Śākya Chok-den, *Music*, 604.4–.7.

27. ma shes don gyi gsal bye kyang/ (ajñātārthaprakāśo vā/) (Dharmakīrti, *Commentary*, II:5.c).

28. A *pramāṇa* is characterized by the Naiyāyikas as a factual *(yathārtha, don mthun)* presentational apprehension *(anubhava, myong ba)*. This presentation of the object can be either direct or indirect (by reasoning, language, or example). Hence, all four instruments of knowledge accepted in Nyāya (perception, inference, verbal testimony, comparison) are presentational and differ from memory, which is re-presentational and, therefore, not valid. Similarly, the Mīmāṃsā assert that memory is not valid. Kumārila states the orthodox Mīmāṃsā opinion when he defines *pramāṇa* as the apprehension of an object not yet known to the knowing self. (Although the Mīmāṃsā view seems similar to Dharmakīrti's position, there is a difference in that for the former *pramāṇa* has an instrumental connotation. See J. V. Bhattacharya, trans., *Jayanta Bhatta's Nyāya-Mañjarī* [Delhi: Motilal, 1978], pp. 33–39.)

29. Jain, Vedānta, and Prāsaṅgika seem to be the only schools to assert the validity of memory. At least in the case of the latter two, this difference seems to come from their view of validity. Instead of seeing validity as the determination of an object, these two schools understand it in terms of noncontradiction. Accordingly, memory is valid because it is not contradicted by any other items of knowledge. The Jain view is that memory is valid because it realizes something new; namely, the pastness of its object. Udayana convincingly shows, however, that this is a confusion since the pastness of the object is not remembered but experienced in the present. See Matilal, *Logic*, p. 208.

30. arthaprakāśo buddhiḥ. (C. Sharma, *A Critical Survey of Indian Philosophy* [Delhi: Motilal,1960, 1991], p. 192).

31. See Dreyfus,"Dharmakīrti's Definition of Knowledge and Its Interpreters," in *Studies in the Buddhist Epistemological Tradition* (Vienna: Österreichische Akademie der Wissenschaften, 1991), pp. 19–38, 26.

32. S. Katsura, "Dharmakīrti's Concept of Truth," *Journal of Indian Philsophy*, 12, no. 3 (1984): 213–35.

33. Śākya Chok-den, *Defeater*, II.294.7. See Chapter 17.

34. de dag gis don yongs su bcad nas 'jug pa na don bya ba la slu ba med pa'i phyir/ (Dharmakīrti, *Ascertainment*, P: 5710, 251.a.1–.2).

35. ji ltar 'jig rten na khas blangs pa'i don dang phrad par byed pa mi slu ba yin pa de bzhin du shes pa yang bstan pa'i don dang phrad par byed pas mi slu bar blta bar bya ba'o/ (Dharmottara, *Explanation*, D: 4229, 8.a.6).

36. de'i don 'di yin te/ dngos po 'dzin par byed pas ni yang dag pa'i shes pa nyid ma yin kyi 'on kyang dngos po thob par byed pa nyid yin no/ (Dharmottara, *Explanation*, D: 4229, 8.a.6–.7).

37. Here, Dharmottara seems to oppose Śāntarakṣita, who explains valid cognitions in terms of congruence with reality *(vastusaṃvādaḥ)* (Śāntarakṣita, *Compendium*, 2958).

38. don yongs su bcad nas zhes gsungs te/ 'dis sngar yongs su bcad pa la ltos nas 'jug pa'i phyir/ (Dharmottara, *Explanation*, D: 4229, 9.a.2–.3).

39. E. Gettier, "Is Knowledge."

40. Gettier's own example is strikingly similar to Dharmottara's. Imagine we see a clock that indicates two o'clock. It is in fact two, but unbeknown to us, the clock has been stuck at that time for one day. We do not have knowledge, and yet the criteria implied by the standard definition of knowledge in modern Western tradition (justified true belief) seem to be met.

41. Analogy makes us know facts hithertho unknown to us by examples. If we do not know what a *bos gavaeus (gavaya, ba min)* looks like, an expert can tell us that it looks like a cow. On the basis of the expert's words and of our perception of cows, we can come to know what a *bos gavaeus* is. Contrary to the Buddhist epistemolgists who reduce this form of knowledge to inference, the Nyāya (*Nyāya-Sūtra*, I.1.6) maintains that analogical cognition is not inferential because in analogy we do not know both terms of the comparison and are, therefore, unable to establish the relation between the two terms. See Gangopadhyaya, *Nyāya*, p. 18.

42. Some pre-Dignāga Buddhist epistemologists accepted the Nyāya list of four means of valid cognition. See H. Nagasaki, "Perception in Pre-Dignāga Buddhist Texts," in *Studies in the Buddhist Epistemological Tradition* (Vienna: Österreichische Akademie der Wissenschaften, 1991), pp. 221–26. Candrakīrti also seems to accept the same list of four, although not all Tibetan scholars agree on this.

43. Except for the Vaiśeṣika school, which shared the same view as the Buddhist. However, the Vaiśeṣika position on this topic, which does not accept the Buddhist radical epistemological dualism, did not receive much attention, and the Nyāya list of four means of valid cognition came to be regarded as the standard theory.

44. Gangopadhyaya, *Nyāya*, p. 19.

45. sgra dngos rnams dang lhan cig tu/ med na mi byung nyid med phyir/ de las don grub min de dag/ smra ba po'i bsam pa bston par byed// (nāntarīyakatā 'bhāvāc chabdānāṃ vastubhiḥ saha/ nārthasiddhis tatas te hi vaktrabhiprāyasūcakāḥ//) (Dharmakīrti, *Commentary*, I:213).

46. spyin pas longs spyod khrims kyis bde/ (dānād bhogaḥ sukhaṃ śīlāt) (Nāgārjuna, *Precious Garland [ratnāvalī, rin chen phreng ba]*). See M. Hahn, ed., *Nāgārjuna's Ratnāvalī*, Vol. 1, *The Basic Texts (Sanskrit, Tibetan, Chinese)*, Indica and Tibetica 1 (Bonn: 1982), V.38.

47. Śākya Chok-den, who holds this type of scriptural argument to be fully valid, quotes

Śākyabuddhi and Prajñākaragupta as saying that inference from scripture is just similar *(mthun pa)* to inference. It is not a based on an actual valid reason *(gtan tshigs dngos)* since there is no relation between the statement and the stated facts that could allow us to infer the validity of the statement. Prajñākaragupta's quoted words are "yid ches pa'i tshig ni 'bras bu dang mthun pa yin la/ grags pa ni rang bzhin dang mthun pa yin no/ ci 'i phyir ce she zhe na/ . . . der ni khas blangs pa'i 'brel ba yod pa yin gyi/ tshad mas grub pa ni min pas 'bras bu'i gtan tshigs dngos min no/" (*Defeater*, I.236.2–.3). Śākya Chok-den understands this statement more trivially to deny that inference from scripture is an inference proceeding from the power of the facts *(vastubalapravṛttānumāna, dngos po stobs shugs kyi rje dpag)*.

48. Although the Vaiśeṣikas accept only two types of cognitions, their position is far less radical than Dignāga's. Vaiśeṣikas do not advocate a radical dichotomy between two types of cognition that are entirely different. They also admit that perception can be either indeterminate and nonconceptual *(nirvikalpaka, rtog med)* or determinate and conceptual *(savikalpaka, rtog bcas)*. Thus, they admit a certain coalescence of the two types of valid cognition, for a determinate perception constitutes a bridge between the two types of knowledge, perception and inference.

49. This epistemological dualism in turn reinforces the basic ontological typology, which acts as the support of the traditional Buddhist doctrines of impermanence, dependent arising, and selflessness.

50. This description suggests that the identification is done through a definite description of the type "the chair, which is mine, which is there, etc." This is, however, only one possibility, for descriptions can be used in several ways as Donellan has shown. They can be used ascriptively (as in the preceding case) or referentially (as when we manage to refer to an object despite providing a mistaken description). In both cases, some description helps us to identify the object. See K. Donellan, "Reference and Definite Descriptions," *Philosophical Review* 75 (1966): 281–304.

51. See R. Jackson, "Matching Concepts," *Journal of the American Academy of Religion* 57, no. 3, (1989): 561–89.

52. Stcherbatsky, *Buddhist Logic*, vol. 2, pp. 301–8.

53. Dharmakīrti does not take this typology as a premise of his system but argues for it. In *Commentary* III:1–2, he argues in relation to the primary object of cognitions. In *Commentary* III:59–63, he argues in relation to the prima facie object of cognitions. See Dreyfus, "Ontology," pp. 680–88.

54. See Chapter 4.

55. See Dignāga, *Compendium*, P: 5700, 1.b.5–2.a.1 and Hattori, *Dignāga*, p. 24.

Chapter 17. Was Dharmakīrti a Pragmatist?

1. For the canonical background of the concept of objects, see A. K. Warder, "Objects," *Journal of Indian Philosophy* 3 (1975): 355–61.

2. This object is called *'dzin stangs kyi yul* (Napper, *Mind*, p. 100). Nonvalid cognitions can also have an object of application, although such an object does not need to exist. For example, the double moon is the object of application of the vision of a double moon.

3. When a cognition is conceptual, its object of application (understood in intentional terms) is called the *conceived object (zhen yul)*. For example, the absence of pot is the conceived object of the inference realizing this absence.

4. Kay-drup presents a slightly different account that I briefly analyze later. Also see Dreyfus, "Ontology," 637–79 and "Dharmakīrti's Definition," pp. 33–37.

5. Gyel-tsap, *Revealing*, I.229.15.

6. Ge-dün-drup, *Ornament*, 18.10. This definition is not too different from Cha-ba's own definition as reported by Śākya Chok-den. For Cha-ba, the defining property of valid cognition is: "that which contradicts and eliminates a false superimposition by an unmistaken mode of apprehension with respect to a previously unrealized true thing." (sngar ma rtogs pa'i don bden pa la mi 'khrul ba'i 'dzin stangs kyis bzlog pa'i sgro 'dogs dang 'gal ba'o) (Śākya Chok-den, *Defeater*, II.298.4–.5).

7. Gyel-tsap speaks of "nondeceptiveness with respect to an action" *(las la mi slu ba)*, *Revealing*, I.230.1.

8. This assumption is even stronger in some of the later Ge-luk textbooks, which take for granted that for a cognition to be nondeceptive it must realize its object. For a description of Cha-ba's view, see Śākya Chok-den, *Defeater*, II.297.7–299.1.

9. phogs snga mas/ 'jug yul ni don bden pa dang ldan pa kho na yin la/ bden pa'i don kyang/ ji ltar yongs su bcad pa'i don la gnod pa med la byed cing/ de la don byed nus pa dang mi nus pa gnyis ka yod cing/ tshad ma de'i 'jug yul du 'gro ba la des de la log phyogs kyi sgro 'dogs bsal ba zhig dgos par bzhed/ (Śākya Chok-den, *Music*, 462.5–.7).

10. See Chapter 22.

11. Kay-drup, *Ornament*, 65.a.3–b.5. See Dreyfus, "Ontology," pp. 670–79.

12. tshad mas dngos su bcad pa ji lta ba bzhin du gnas pa'i chos/ (Kay-drup, *Ornament*, 113.4). Kay-drup is here defining the object of application of valid cognition rather than the object of application in general.

13. Ge-dün-drup, *Ornament*, 18.12–.14. I have not found any Sanskrit source supporting this etymology. Although most Indian Buddhist thinkers hold that novelty is a requirement for epistemic validity, this requirement is not thought to be part of the etymology of valid cognition.

14. tshad ma'i mtshan nyid/ rang dbang du rang gis yongs bcad ba'i gzhal bya la slu ba med pa'i shes pa/ de ltar yang rnam nges las/ 'di dag gis yongs su bcad nas 'jug pa na don bya ba la slu ba med pa'i phyir ro/ zhes gsungs pa yin no (Kay-drup, *Ornament*, 64.b.4–.5). The passage from Dharmakīrti's *Ascertainment* is found in D: 4211, 152.a.4. See Chapter 16.

15. Although Dignāga is not explicit on this question, there are indications that he supports the requirement of novelty. When discussing that there are only two types of valid cognition, Dignāga argues that a limit must be set on what can count as an independent valid cognition, otherwise memory, which is well known to be nonvalid, would have to be valid. Dignāga says: "For example, memory, desire, aversion, etc., are not independent [literally different] valid cognitions with respect to a previously cognized thing" (dper na dran pa dang/ 'dod pa dang/ zhe sdang la sogs pa sngar rtog pa'i don la tshad ma gzhan ma yin pa bzhin no//) (Dignāga, *Auto-Commentary*, P: 14.a.2–.3). Hattori, *Dignāga*, pp. 25, 176. Quoted in Bijlert, *Epistemology*, p. 177. Implicit in this argument is that a cognition must provide a new content to qualify as valid cognition. The Nyāya criticism of the requirement of novelty also confirms that this requirement was considered a significant tenet of Dignāga's system. See Hattori, *Dignāga*, p. 82.

16. I believe that Dharmakīrti does not mean to include in "relative cognition" all types of conceptual cognition, for that would absurdly exclude inference from being valid. Hence, a relative cognition is conception that does not rely on a reason to conceive its object. The source for this term is found Dignāga's list of pseudo-perceptions *(pratyakṣābhāsa, mngon*

sum ltar snang), where he says "Mistaken cognition, relative cognition, . . ." (Dignāga, *Auto-Commentary*, 14.b.2–.3). Hattori, *Dignāga*, pp. 28, 180–81.

17. gzung ba 'dzin phyir kun rdzob ni/ mi 'dod blo ni tshad ma nyid/ (gṛhītagrahaṇān neṣṭaṃ sāṃvṛtaṃ dhīpramāṇatā/) (Dharmakīrti, *Commentary*, II:3.ab).

18. de la dang po yul thun mong ma yin pa mthong ba gang yin pa de kho na tshad ma yin no/ (tatra yad ādyam asādharaṇaviṣayaṃ darśanaṃ tad eva pramāṇam/) (E. Steinkellner ed., *Dharmakīrti's Hetubinduḥ*, pp. 4, 33.18–.19, 32.24–.25).

19. ji ltar yongs su mthong ba'i rnam pa 'dzin pa'i phyir tshad ma ma yin te/ sngar thun mong ma yin pa mthong nas/ thun mong ma yin pa'o zhes mngon par brjod pas ni sngon ma rtogs pa'i don rtogs pa med pa'i phyir/ (yathādṛṣṭākāragrahaṇān na pramāṇam, prāg asādhāraṇaṃ dṛstvāsādhāraṇa ity abhilapato 'pūrvārthādhigamābhāvād/) (Steinkellner, ed., *Dharmakīrti's Hetubinduḥ*, pp. 33.23–.25).

20. Similar conclusions can be drawn from other commentators. See Devendrabuddhi, *Commentary*, P: 5717, 4.a.2. See also later the passage 6.b.1–.2, as well as Śāntarakṣita, *Compendium*, 1298, and Kamalaśīla's commentary. Also, Prajñākaragupta, *Ornament* , P: 5719, 31.a.4–.5.

21. See Chapter 19.

22. Śākya Chok-den, *Defeater*, II.12.3–.4.

23. Śākya Chok-den, *A General Presentation of Valid Cognition [Called] "The Magical Diamond Key Opening the Treasury of [Dharmakīrti's] Seven Texts (tshad ma spyi'i rnam bzhag sde bdun gyi bang mdzod chen po'i sgo 'byed par byed pa'i rdo rje'i 'khrul 'khor gyi lde mig)*, Collected Works, vol. 19 (Thimphu, Bhutan: Kunzang Thobgey, 1975), 140.5.

24. tshad ma gnyis ka dngos po'i yul can (Dharmakīrti, *Ascertainment*, II:7.a). See Steinkellner, *Dharmakīrti's Pramāṇaviniścayaḥ*, II:26.

25. de'i 'jug yul la rang mtshan gyis khyab cing/ de la tshad mar song ba'i don kyang/ sgro 'dogs bcad dang rtogs pa la bya ba ma yin gyi/ de la mi slu ba la byed cing/ de'i don kyang de thob nus pa la bya/ (Śākya Chok-den, *Music*, 462.7–463.1).

26. mi slu ba'i don rtogs pa la 'chad pa la ni lung yod pa ma yin te/ rigs pa mkhyen pa'i gzhung du de de la mi slu ba'i sgrub byed 'chad pa na de thob pa dang/ de la rgyud nas 'brel ba dang/ de la brten pa dang/ de'i mthar thug pa zhes bya ba rnams bshad pa yod kyi/ de rtogs pa'i phyir zhes bshad pa ni ma dmigs pa'i phyir/ (Śākya Chok-den, *Defeater*, II.288.4–.6).

27. gsar du bcad pa dang mi slu ba gnyis tshogs kyi rig pa/ (Śākya Chok-den, *Defeater*, II.294.7). See also Dharmakīrti, *Ascertainment*, P: 5710, 251.a.1–.2 already discussed in Chapter 16.

28. There are disagreements, however, among Sa-gyas on how to explain nondeceptiveness. Should it be understood à la Śākya Chok-den in purely pragmatic terms or should it be understood as including both pragmatic and normative dimensions? Most other Sa-gya commentators have opted for the latter. Go-ram-ba criticizes his rival Śākya Chok-den for explaining nondeceptiveness in purely pragmatic terms (*Explanation*, 15.b.3). Go-ram-ba goes further and argues that the requirement of novelty is already contained in the concept of nondeceptiveness. Hence, he defines *valid cognition* as "nondeceptive cognition" *(dmi slu ba'i rig pa)* (*Explanation*, 116.a.3). Sa-paṇ seems to share Go-ram-ba's understanding of nondeceptiveness, which he explains as the appropriation of an object. *Appropriation* does not refer to the brute obtainment of an object but to the capacity to obtain the object on cognitively determining its nature (*Auto-Commentary*, 116.a.3–.4). For these thinkers, valid cognitions are always nondeceptive with respect to a real object of application, but this does not imply that every object with respect to which a cognition is

nondeceptive must be real. Therefore, the nondeceptiveness of a cognition and its objective referent, the object of application, cannot be understood in exclusively pragmatic terms. Nondeceptiveness requires an intentional connotation as well.

29. D. Kalupahana, *Nagarjuna: The Philosophy of the Middle Way* (Albany: SUNY Press, 1986).

30. See K. H. Potter, "Does Indian Epistemology Concern Justified True Belief?" *Journal of Indian Philosophy* 12 (1984).

31. Mohanty, *Theory*, p. 220.

32. R. Rorty, *Consequences of Pragmatism* (Minneapolis: University of Minnesota, 1982), p. 161.

33. Ibid., p. 165.

34. W. James, *The Meaning of Truth* (New York: Longmans, 1909), p. vii.

35. C. E. Pierce, "The Essentials of Pragmatism," in J. Buchler, ed., *Philosophical Writings of Pierce* (New York: Dover, 1955), p. 255.

36. K. N. Jayatilleke, *Early Buddhist Theory of Knowledge* (Delhi: Motilal Banarsidas, 1963, 1980), p. 358.

37. W. Quine, *Ontological Relativity and Other Essays* (New York: 1969), pp. 69–91.

38. Let me remind the reader that I am talking of Quine as an antirealist only in reference to the problem of universals. Quine has depicted himself as a solid realist inasmuch as he accepts the truths of science. He is, however, suspicious of abstract entities such as universals, mental content, and meaning.

39. H. Putnam, "Why Reason Can't Be Naturalized?" in *Realism and Reason* (Cambridge, Mass.: Harvard University Press, 1983), pp. 229–47.

40. Ibid., p. 246.

41. Dharmakīrti, *Ascertainment*, P: 5710, 251.a.1–.2. See Chapter 16.

42. Lo Ken-chen, *Sun*, 26.4. See also Katsura, "Dharmakīrti's Concept" and E. Mikogami, "Some Remarks on the Concept of Arthakriyā," *Journal of Indian Philosophy* 7, no. 1 (1979): 79–94.

43. rgyun dang bcas pa'i don rang mtshan rnams (Śākya Chok-den, *Defeater*, II.295.4).

44. See Chapter 2.

Chapter 18. Can Inference Be Valid?

1. This refers to a previous explanation (I.2–6) of the three kinds of reason (effect *['bras rtags]*, identical essence *[rang bzhin gyi rtags]*, and nonobservation reasons *[ma dmigs pa'i rtags]*).

2. dngos po rnams kyis de kun kyang/ phan tshun med la brten pa ste/ des na gzhan sel yul can dang/ gang la dngos dang 'brel yod pa// dngos po rnyed pa'i rten yin te/ rjes dpag ji skad bshad ji bzhin/ 'khrul par 'dra yang gzhan las min/ mar me'i 'od las nor bu bzhin// (sa ca sarvaḥ padārthānām anyonyābhāvasaṃśrayaḥ/ tenānyāpohaviṣayo vastulābhasya cāśrayaḥ// yatrāsti vastusambandho yathoktānumitau yathā/ nānyatra bhrāntisāmye 'pi dīpatejo maṇau yathā//) (Dharmakīrti, *Commentary*, I:80–81. Frauwallner, "Beiträge," p. 388).

3. See Chö-drak-gya-tso (*Ocean*, I.326.2 and 297.3–298.2).

4. In Dharmakīrti's system inferences are by definition correct. A mistaken inference is not called *inference*. Similarly, a mistaken perception is not a perception but a pseudo-perception.

5. The link between inference and reality is provided by the cognitions that apprehend the evidence, and are technically described as apprehensions of the evidence *(rtags 'dzin sems)*. See, for example, Chö-drak-gya-tso, *Ocean*, I.344.4–.6.

6. Dharmakīrti, *Commentary*, III:57. Commentators have had to develop a great deal of ingenuity to make sense of these examples. Prajñākaragupta explains the example as involving a situation in which the light is seen through a keyhole. The person sees a glow on the keyhole and thinks that this is a jewel (Keyt, "Dharmakīrti," pp. 127–28). See also Zwilling, p. 146.

7. Gnoli, ed., *The Pramāṇavārttika*, 43.5–.6; D: 4210, 285.a.3–.4.

8. The cognition of the jewel in reference to the jewel glitter and the conception of a jewel in reference to the light of a lamp.

9. nor bu sgron me'i od dag la/ nor bu'i blo yis mgnon gyur pa/ log pa'i shes par khyad par med kyang/ ji ltar don byed pa khyad yod// (maṇipradīpaprabhayor maṇibuddhyābhidhāvataḥ/ mithyājñānāviśeṣe'pi viśeṣo 'rthakriyāṃ prati//) (Dharmakīrti, *Commentary*, III:57). Go-ram-ba, *Perfect Light*, 162.a.3–164a.1.

10. Go-ram-ba, *Explanation*, 123.a.5–125.b3.

11. Go-ram-ba, *Explanation*, 123.b.1–.5.

12. Kay-drup, *Ornament*, 67.b2–68.a.2.

13. Go-ram-ba, *Explanation*, 124.a.3–.6.

14. Go-ram-ba, *Explanation*, 124.a.1–b.2.

15. Gyel-tsap comes to the same conclusion as Go-ram-ba and adopts Dharmottara's explanation of the example. His view differs, however, on the implications of Dharmakīrti's example, for he holds that inference is not completely mistaken, though it is distorted (*Revealing*, II.32.8–.19). Go-ram-ba also criticises U-yuk-ba for relating the example to valid cognition in which ascertainment is induced by others *(gzhan las nges kyi tshad ma)*. According to Go-ram-ba, this is irrelevant, for the conception of the glitter as a jewel is not a valid cognition (Go-ram-ba, *Explanation*, 124.b.2–125.a.1).

16. sgra mi rtag par rtogs pa'i rjes dpag dang/ sgra rtag 'dzin gyi sgro 'dogs 'khrul ma 'khrul pa yin min gyi khyad par med kyang tshad ma yin min gyi khyad par yod de/ dper na nor 'od la nor bur 'dzin pa'i blo dang sgron 'od la nor bur 'dzin pa'i blo gnyis log shes khyad par med kyang 'jug yul thob pa'i tshad ma gzhan gyi rten byed pa dang mi byed pa'i khyad par yod pa bzhin no zhes pa ni rtsa ba'i bla na med pa ste/ (Go-ram-ba, *Explanation*, 125.b.1–.3).

17. Dharmakīrti, *Ascertainment*, D: 4211, 251.a.1–.2. See Chapter 16. We will deal with the problem of the validity of perception in Chapter 21.

18. de phyir dbang po las skyes blo/ thams cad khyad par yul can yin/ khyad par rnams la sgra dag ni/ 'jug pa srid pa yod ma yin te// (tasmād viśeṣaviṣayā sarvaivendriyajā matiḥ/ na viśeṣeṣu śabdānāṃ pravṛttav asti sambhavaḥ//) (Dharmakīrti, *Commentary*, III:127).

19. E. Kant, *Critique of Pure Reason* (New York: St. Martin's Press, 1929, 1965), p. 93 (A51).

20. See Kajiyama, *Introduction*, pp. 56–58.

21. Dzong-ka-ba, *Extensive Memorandum*, 183.1.

22. Dzong-ka-ba, *Extensive Memorandum*, 183.2–184.5.

23. rtog pa'i gzung yul ni/ rtog pa rnams la rang rang gi mdun na 'dug pa lta bur snang ba'i yul gang yin pa ste/ de yang don spyi bar ma chod par snang ba'i yul gang yin pa'o/ des na rtog pa'i dbang du byas pa'i snang yul gzung yul ni sgra don kho na'o/ (Kay-drup, *Ornament*, 55.b.6–56.a.1).

24. See Chapter 14.

25. A similar point is made by Dzong-ka-ba (through Gyel-tsap). See *Extensive Memorandum*, 219.4–220.2.

26. gzhung 'dis rang lugs la nges shes kyi gzung yul la nges yul gyis khyab par 'dod pa ni rnam bzhag ma chags pas te/ rtog pa rnams kyi gzung yul rang rig mngon sum gyi gzhal bya rigs pa smra bas yang dang yang du gsungs pa'i phyir/ (Gyel-tsap, *Revealing*, I.93.13–.16). It is not exactly clear to me which of Dharmakīrti's repeated assertions Gyel-tsap is referring to.

27. Kay-drup, *Ornament*, 35.a.6–b.6.

28. rtog pa des rang la bum par snang ba la zhen nas phyi rol bum pa la 'jug pa yin gyi/ rang la bum par snang ba de phyi rol gyi bum par zhen nas 'jug pa ma yin no/ (Kay-drup, *Ornament*, 36.a.5).

29. Kay-drup, *Ornament*, 35.a.5

30. rtog pa dang mngon sum gnyis rang mtshan snang bar mtshungs kyang snang ba'i tshul mi mtshungs par thal rtog pa la 'dres par snang mngon sum la snang ba'i don sngon po lta bu de ni yul dus gzhan dang ma 'dres par thun mong ma yin pa'i dngos po'i rang bzhin te/ rang bzhin du mngon sum la snang ba'i phyir/ (Gyel-tsap, *Explanation*, 68.2–.3).

31. A similar opinion is expressed by Bo-dong, who asserts that real things are realized by inference. While discussing the concept of a conceived object *(zhen yul)*, he argues that, contrary to what Sa-paṇ and his followers hold, inference's realization of its object is not merely conceptual but relates to reality (*Presentation*, I.608.1–.3).

Chapter 19. Philosophy of Perception

1. Literally, the knowledge derived from the sense bases *(akṣa)*. See Matilal, *Perception*, p. 226. Jam-yang-shay-ba (*'jam dbyangs bzhad pa*, 1648–1721), in explaining the logicians' system, etymologized *prati* as dependent and *akṣa* as sense. See his *The Blaze of Hundred Lights on Valid Cognition Clarifying the Path to Liberation, a Decisive Analysis of [Dharmakīrti's] Commentary on Valid Cognition (tshad ma rnam 'grel gyi mtha' gcod thar lam rab gsal tshad ma'i 'od brgya 'bar ba)*, Collected Works 13 (Delhi: Ngawang Gelek, 1974), XIII.856.4.

2. A. J. Ayer, *The Central Questions of Philosophy* (London: 1973), pp. 81 and 89. A similar claim is made by Quine, "Epistemology Naturalized."

3. See P. F. Strawson, "Perception and Its Objects," in J. Dancy, *Perceptual Knowledge* (Oxford: Oxford University Press, 1988), pp. 92–112.

4. T. Reid, *Essays on the Intellectual Powers of Man* (Cambridge: Bartlett, 1850), vol. 1, part i, p. 12.

5. G. E. Moore, *Some Main Problems of Philosophy* (London: Allen and Unwin, 1953), pp. 28–51.

6. Ibid., p. 30.

7. John Locke, *Essay Concerning Human Understanding*, II.ix.4. Some modern scholars have denied that Locke really had a representative theory of knowledge, but he certainly has been taken as such by the empiricist tradition.

8. For helpful discussion, see R. M. Chisholm, *Perceiving: A Philosophical Study* (Ithaca, N.Y.: Cornell University Press, 1957), pp. 91–92; and J. W. Cornman, *Materialism and Sensations* (New Haven, Conn.: Yale University Press, 1971), pp. 218–27, 341–42.

9. H. P. Grice, "The Causal Theory of Perception," in Dancy, *Perceptual*, pp. 66–88.

10. Author's emphasis.

11. Author's emphasis.

12. Dicker, *Perceptual Knowledge* (Dodrecht: Reidel, 1980), p. 90.

13. This description of phenomenalism relies on Sellars, *Science*, pp. 60–105.

14. A. J. Ayer, *The Foundations of Empirical Knowledge* (London: Macmillan, 1940).

15. I am referring here to formulation of phenomenalism as found in G. Berkeley, "Principles of Human Knowledge," in *Principles, Dialogues and Philosophical Correspondence* (New York: Bobbs-Merrill, 1965), pp. 103–211; and J. S. Mill, *An Explanation of Sir William Hamilton's Philosophy* (Boston: Spencer, 1865), p. i.

16. J. Sinha, *Indian Psychology* (Delhi: Motilal Banarsidas, 1958, 1985) and Mohanty, *Reason*, pp. 34–41.

17. Mookerjee, *Universal Flux*, p. 77.

18. Candrakīrti's position on this question is not entirely clear. He seems to use the notion of aspect. See C. Scherrer-Schaub, *Yuktiṣaṣtikāvṛtti* (Bruxelles: Institut des Hautes Etudes Chinoises, 1991), pp. 152–56. His position would then be representationalist. This view, however, does not correspond to his overall commitment to a commonsense philosophy. Hence, it is not clear whether Candrakīrti uses it as an element in a refutation or whether he is really committed to it as an explanation of perception. Tillemans interprets the few passages referring to aspects as merely asserting that consciousness has a content without "taking the additional step of reifying that content into something which is naturally suited to be the immediately present *entity*" (*Materials*, p. 52).

19. See Y. Kajiyama, "Controversy Between the Sākāra- and the Nirākāra-vādins of the Yogācāra School," *Indo Bukkyo Gaku Kenkyu* 14. no. 1, (1965): 26–37.

20. Nandita Bandyopadhyay, "The Buddhist Theory of Relation Between Pramā and Pramāṇa," *Journal of Indian Philosophy* 7, no. 1 (1979): 51. Reprinted by permission of Kluwer Academic Publishers.

21. J. N. Mohanty, "Understanding Some Ontological Differences in Indian Philosophy," p. 209.

22. rang bzhin sems yin pa ni/ don rig de yi bdag nyid phyir/ rang rig pa 'bras bur bshad/ (svasaṃvedanaṃ phalam/ uktaṃ svabhāvacintāyāṃ tādātmyād arthasaṃvidaḥ//) (Dharmakīrti, *Ascertainment*, I:42b–d, in Vetter, *Dharmakīrti*, p. 90). P: 5710, 263.a.1–.2.

23. See later and Hattori, *Dignāga*, p. 94.

24. The term was coined by Leibniz to distinguish the reflective knowledge that we have of our mental states from perception, which is the representation of outer things. See S. Körner, *Kant* (New Haven, Conn.: Yale University Press, 1982), p. 61.

25. rang las rang gi ngo bo rtogs/ (svarūpasya svato gatiḥ/) (Dharmakīrti, *Commentary*, II.4.d).

26. From Aristotle, *De Anima*, III.2 to J. P. Sartre, *Being and Nothingness*, pp. lix–lxvii.

27. Locke, *An Essay*, II.ii, p. 19.

28. G. Leibniz, *New Essays Concerning Human Understanding* (New York: Macmillan, 1896), II.i, p. 19. For a modern criticism of self-awareness, G. Ryle, *The Concept of Mind* (London: Hutchinson, 1949), pp. 148–89.

29. tha snyad las ni tshad ma nyid/ (pramāṇyaṃ vyavahāreṇa/) (Dharmakīrti, *Commentary*, II: 5.a).

30. In Indian philosophy, truth is not limited to propositions, as it is often in the West, but is extended to perceptive experiences as well. See K. Potter, "The Background of Skepticism East and West," *Journal of Indian Philosophy* 3 (1975): 299–313.

31. This is a subject of intense debate in India. Roughly speaking, there are two kinds of answer. Some thinkers, such as those belonging to the Mīmāṃsā, maintain the internal or

self-validity *(svataḥ-prāmānya, tshad ma rang nyid kyis grub pa)* of knowledge and language, while others, such as the Naiyāyikas, have maintained that validity is external (or extrinsic, *parataḥ prāmāṇya, tshad ma gzhan gyis grub pa*) to language and cognition. Dharmakīrti does not extensively address this question aside from indicating that validity is conventional and, hence, extrinsic. His disciples were left the task of responding to the Mīmāṃsā (see *Ślokavārttika*, II.49–52) argument that if validity is extrinsic we would be caught in an infinite regress of validation. Śākyabuddhi's answer is to distinguish internally valid cognitions (literally, self-ascertained valid cognition, *svataḥ prāmāṇya, rang las tshad ma*) and externally valid cognitions (other-ascertained valid cognitions, *parataḥ prāmāṇya, gzhan las tshad ma*). In the process, he opens a new topic in Buddhist epistemology, which is further discussed by Śāntarakṣita and Dharmottara. See Śākyabuddhi, *Explanation*, D: 4220; P:5718, 91.a.6–b.2; Śāntarakṣita, *Compendium*, 2810–3122; and Dharmottara, *Explanation*, D: 4229,.10.a.5–11.b.4. Tibetans continue this trend by further expanding the topic. See E. Steinkellner, "Early Tibetan Ideas on the Ascertainment of Validity," in *Tibetan Studies* (Narita: Naritasan Shinshoji, 1992), pp. 257–74 as well as Dreyfus, "Ontology," pp. 721–45.

32. See Chapter 18.

33. The connection between realism concerning universals and direct realism is not necessary. A realist can hold a representational view of perception. Nevertheless, there is often a relation between these two types of realism. This is particularly true in the Indian and Tibetan contexts, where the two forms of realism go together, as in the Nyāya school and Cha-ba's tradition.

34. Here again, there is no necessary connection. I am referring here mostly to Dharmakīrti and his antirealist followers.

35. Or this is at least what the epistemologist wants us to believe. As will be clear later, the immediacy preserved by the epistemologist is quite different from the immediate reality we ordinarily perceive. Thus, the epistemological attempt to save common intuition seems to achieve the contrary result: Rather than preserve the commonsense intuitions it intends to validate, epistemology destroys them.

36. Rorty, *Philsophy and the Mirror of Nature*, pp. 104–5.

37. Sellars, *Science*, p. 169. See also Chapter 6.

38. The reason for this preoccupation is to be found in the cultural climate of the time. Epistemologists were attempting to resolve a cultural crisis that was the result of the disintegration of the old order due to factors such as the end of the domination of the Church, the great discoveries, religious fanaticism, etc.

39. Reid, *Essays*, II.vi. Author's emphasis.

40. This shows that a response to skepticism is not necessarily the essential motivation behind the theory of the given. Although this is often the case, sense data can also be posited as a result of a purely phenomenological reflection on what is given to perception, as shown by Moore's analysis.

Chapter 20. Dharmakīrti's Account of Perception

1. Chatterjee, *The Nyāya Theory of Knowledge*, p. 195.

2. Hattori, *Dignāga*, p. 37.

3. See C. D. Bijalwan, *Indian Theory of Knowledge* (New Delhi: Heritage, 1977), pp. 72–78.

4. Dharmakīrti, *Commentary*, III:282–287 and *Ascertainment*, D: 4211, 161.a.6–162.b.2.

5. In the Nyāya system, a perceptual judgment, which is nonverbal, must be distinguished from other types of judgment such as verbal (which articulates the already perceived) and inferential judgment (which infers a new fact).

6. To mark this distinction I will translate *savikalpa* as "indeterminate" when this word is used to designate a judgment accepted as perceptual in the Nyāya system. Taken in a strictly Buddhist context, this word would be translated as "conceptual." Since this translation would lose track of the important Nyāya distinction between perceptual and verbal judgment, I have preferred to use "determinate" when *savikalpa* is discussed according to the Nyāya sense of the word.

7. J.V. Bhattacharya, trans., *Jayanta Bhatta's Nyāya Mañjari*, pp. 136–209.

8. Another important point to which we will not be able to give the attention it deserves is the question of the etymology of the word *pratyakṣa*, which has given rise to numerous debates both inside and outside the Buddhist tradition. In *Compendium* I.1.4.ab, Dignāga explains that a perception relies on several factors such as sense and object. Among those, sense is responsible for differentiating perceptions. Hence, the name *pratyakṣa* is given after the sense *(akṣa, dbang po)*, which is its uncommon cause *(asādhārana hetu, thung mong ma yin pa'i rgyu)* in accordance with the Abhidharmic doctrine. Candrakīrti objects to such an etymology on the ground that common linguistic usage determines the perceptual nature of something from its object, not from its sense basis. For him, the term *pratyakṣa* primarily applies to objects that are fully evident to the senses. Thus, the quality of "perceptionness" (being a *pratyakṣa*) literally applies to perceptible objects and metaphorically to to perception. See Hattori, *Dignāga*, p. 77; and Siderits, "The Madhyamaka Critique of Epistemology I and II," *Journal of Indian Philosophy* 8 (1980): 307–35 and 9 (1981): 121–60.

9. Dharmakīrti, *Commentary*, III:300.cd and *Drop of Reasoning*, D: 4212, 231.b.2.

10. rtog pa dang bral mngon sum mo/ (Dignāga, *Compendium*, P: 5700, 2.a.2).

11. This requirement of nonconceptuality is criticized by Candrakīrti, who asserts that the perceptual character of a cognition does not come from some introspectable quality but from its object. In opposition to Dignāga's foundationalism, Candrakīrti holds that consciousness and object are mutually implicative. Therefore, perception cannot be defined by some internal characteristics but in relation to its external object. See Siderits, "The Madhyamaka Critique of Epistemology II," pp. 149–58.

12. See, for example, Uddyotakara's remarks in Jha, *Nyāya*, vol. 1, pp. 147–51.

13. Dreyfus, "Ontology," pp. 479–87.

14. Candrakīrti also attacks this view, which, according to him, agrees with neither common practices nor considerations pertaining to the ultimate. On the conventional level, Candrakīrti points out that perception is defined by its object, not by any internal or epistemological quality. Perception is the cognition that relates to perceptible objects. If we analyze perception in relation to the ultimate, the requirement of unmistakeness is even more impossible, since all ordinary cognitions are fundamentally mistaken with respect to the nature (or lack thereof) of their objects. Hence, the theory of perception of Buddhist epistemologists has no support on either the conventional level or ultimate level, and this is the reason why conventionally the Nyāya theory is preferable. See Siderits, "The Madhyamaka Critique of Epistemology II," pp. 149–58; and T. Tillemans, *Materials for the Study of Āryadeva, Dharmapāla and Candrakīrti* (Vienna: Arbeitkreis für die Tibetische und Buddhistische Studien, 1990), pp. 44–45, 176–79. I will make a few more remarks on Candrakīrti's theory of perception in Chapter 28.

15. Jinendrabuddhi gives other famous examples, such as the vision of moving trees

while being in a moving boat and the unclear apprehension of a blue color from afar. See Jam-yang-shay-ba, *The Blaze*, 680.1–681.2.

16. M. Gangopadhyaya, *Vinītadeva's Nyāyabindu-ṭīka* (Calcutta: Indian Studies, 1971), p. 83. See also Mookerjee, *Buddhist Philosophy*, pp. 277–78.

17. Jam-yang-shay-ba, *The Blaze*, 681.2–682.2. Jam-yang-shay-ba further explains that in general Jinendrabuddhi's explanations are not false, but that they are inappropriate to the occasion, which relates to the Sautrāntika view (*The Blaze*, 683.3–.6).

18. don gyi mthu yis ni/ yang dag skye ba yin pa'i phyir ro/ (Dharmakīrti, *Ascertainment of Valid Cognition*, D: 4211, 154.b.2).

19. Dharmottara, *Explanation*, D: 4229, 38.b.6–39.a.3.

20. de la mngon sum rtog pa dang bral ma 'khrul lo/ rab rib myur du bskor ba dang/ grur zhugs pa'i 'khrug pa la sogs pas 'khrul ba ma bskyed cing rtog pa med pa'i shes pa mngon sum yin no/ (Dharmakīrti, *Ascertainment*, D: 4211, 154.a.7–b.1).

21. Ge-dün-drup, *Ornament*, 38.3–.10.

22. mngon sum rtog pa dang bral bar ni/ mngon sum nyid kyis 'grub par 'gyur/ kun gyi rnam rtog ming rten can/ so sor rang gis rig bya yin// thams cad las ni sems bsdus nas/ nang gi bdag nyid g.yo med pas/ gnas na'ang mig gis gzugs dag ni/ mthong ba'i blo de dbang skyes yin// slar yang cung zad rnam rtog na/ kho bo rnam rtog 'di 'drar gyur/ ces rig sngar bshad gnas skabs kyi/ dbang po'i rtogs pa la med do// (pratyakṣaṃ kalpanāpoḍhaṃ pratyakṣeṇaiva sidhyati/ pratyātmavedyaḥ sarveṣāṃ vikalpo nāmasaṃśrayaḥ// saṃhṛtya sarvataś cintāṃ stimitenāntarātmanā/ sthito 'pi cakṣuṣā rūpam īkṣate sākṣajā matiḥ// punar vikalpayan kiñcid āsīn me kalpanedṛśī iti vetti (Miyasaka has icchā ceti) na pūrvoktāvasthāyām indriyād gatau//) (Dharmakīrti, *Commentary*, III:123–125. Ge-dün-drup, *Good Sayings*, 193.4–194.1.

23. R. Firth, "Sense-Data and Percept Theory," in R. Swartz, *Perceiving, Sensing and Knowing* (Berkeley: University of California Press, 1965), pp. 204–70.

24. Dharmakīrti assumes that this experience reveals what is usually going on in our minds but is left unnoticed. We could respond to Dharmakīrti that meditation creates a new experience. Dharmakīrti does not examine this objection, and we can only speculate how he would answer.

25. Dharmakīrti, *Commentary*, III:133. The argument about the speed of the mental process as a cause of mistakes is delicate in Dharmakīrti's works, for in some passages (*Commentary* III:135, 198–199) it is refuted and in others (*Commentary*, III:133, 140) it is used. Kay-drup suggests that Dharmakīrti accepts that the speed of the mental process can cause us to fail to differentiate states of mind that are in reality distinct. He does not, however, accept that speed can cause a perception to apprehend different things as one (Kay-drup, *Ocean*, III:313.1).

26. Paralleling Dharmakīrti's distinction between perception and conception by their difference in clarity, Hume differentiates impressions from ideas as a correction to Locke's confusion between those two. Sensations are those cognitions that perceive things vividly and with strength. Sensations are contrasted with ideas, which are the faint images that our mind makes from sensations. We receive impressions from the outside that we elaborate into more or less complex ideas. Contrary to Dharmakīrti, who stresses the distorted character of conception, Hume is impressed by the obvious resemblance between sensations and ideas. The latter seem to be copies of the former and derived from them (Hume, *A Treatise*, I.i.1).

27. gang gi phyir/ rnam rtog rjes su 'brel ba la/ don gsal snang ba yod ma yin/ rnam par bslad pa'i blo yang rung ste brjod pa dang 'dres pa'i shes pa thams cad la ni don gsal ba nyid ldog pa'i phyir ro/ (*Ascertainment*, P: 5710, 259.b.7).

28. phyi rol don la ltos med par/ brda dran pa las sbyor ba yin/ de bzhin brda la ltos med pa/ dngos nus nyid las mig blor 'gyur// (anapekṣitabāhyārthā yojanā [Miyasaka has: anapekṣitabāhyārthayojanā] samayasmṛteḥ/ tathā 'napekṣya samayaṃ vastuśaktyaiva netradhīḥ//) (Dharmakīrti, *Commentary*, III:185).

29. The doctrine of the reliance of perception on a set of three conditions is already found in the Pāli canon *(Majjhima Nikāya)*, I.190. See Jayatilleke, *Early Buddhist*, p. 745.

30. Throughout this argument Dharmakīrti does not differentiate psychological and epistemological immediacies. He implicitly assumes that the demonstration that perception is psychologically unmediated proves the complete absence of mediation. If recollection does not directly intervene, one can assume it is inoperative. This assumption is probably a consequence of the dominance of causal models in Indian epistemology. Most thinkers seem to understand cognition, or at least perception, as the result of a causal contact between sense and objects. It becomes difficult in such a model to explain influences that are not directly expressible in causal terms.

31. de'i yul ni rang gyi mtshan nyid de/ don gang nye ba dang mi nye ba dag las shes pa la snang ba tha dad pa de ni rang gi mtshan nyid do/ de nyid don dam par yod pa ste dngos po'i mtshan nyid don byed nus pa kho na yin pa'i phyir ro/ gzhan ni spyi'i mtshan nyid de/ de ni rjes su dpag pa'i yul yin no/ (Dharmakīrti, *Drop of Reasoning*, D: 4212, 231.b.4–.5).

Chapter 21. A New Epistemology Begins: Dharmottara on Perception

1. I do not mean here to convey the cynical idea that a commentator is necessarily or even often consciously disguising his or her innovations. On the contrary, the commentator genuinely believes that his or her explanations capture the essence of the system being explained. This is a characteristic of the commentarial style of philosophy.

2. Dharmakīrti, *Ascertainment*, P: 5710, 251.a.1–.2. See Chapter 16.

3. Dharmottara, *Commentary*, D: 4231, 46.a.4–b.2.

4. gang gi phyir mngon sum gyi stobs kyis byung ba'i zhen pas ni don mthong ba nyid du zhen par byed kyi/ rtog par byed pa nyid du ma yin no/ mthong ba yang don mngon sum du byed pa zhes bya ba mngon sum gyi byed pa yin no/ rnam par rtog pa yin te 'di ltar don lkog tu gyur pa rnam par rtog pa ni bdag nyid rtog par byed kyi/ mthong ba ma yin no zhes rtog pa'i bdag nyid yin par ni myong ba las nges pa yin no/ de bas na rang gi byed pa btang ste mngon sum gyi byed pa ston par byed pa las don gang la mngon sum du song ba'i zhen pa yod pa der mngon sum 'ba' zhig tshad ma yin no/ (Dharmottara, *Commentary*, D: 4231, 46.b.4–.6). The Tibetan differs somewhat from the Sanskrit but this does not seem to affect the meaning of this passage.

5. See Chapter 18.

6. Mookerjee, *Buddhist Philosophy*, pp. 314–15; and Stcherbatsky, *Buddhist Logic*, vol. 2, pp. 309–40. The concept of perceiving external objects mentally is a delicate point in Buddhist epistemology. What is the object of such a perception? Is it the object already perceived by sense perception or is it a new object? In the first case (Dignāga's view), mental perception would just repeat the experience of sense perception and would be redundant. In the second case (Dharmakīrti's view), it is hard to imagine the relation between mental perception and the external object. Dharmottara does not reject the idea of mental perception but holds that it plays no role. It is postulated due to being mentioned in a scripture. It has no autonomous philosophical role and is not logically warranted. See Tillemans, *Materials*,

pp. 286–87; and "Indian and Tibetan Mādhyamikas on *mānasapratyakṣa*," *Tibet Journal* 14, no. 1 (1989): 70–85. Among Tibetan thinkers, Gyel-tsap and most Ge-luk thinkers follow Dharmottara's views (*Explanation*, 159.4–165.6). Kay-drup, however, follows Sa-paṇ and prefers Prajñākaragupta's view (*Ocean*, III:404.2–412.5).

7. shes pa rnams kyi yul ni rnam pa gnyis te gzung ba dang zhen pa'o/ rnam par rtog pas ni sgro btags pa'i rang bzhin 'dzin cing de dang 'dra ba'i rang gi mtshan nyid nges par byed pa yin no/ dbang po'i shes pas skad cig ma 'dzin cing de'i stobs kyis bskyed pa'i nges pa ni skad cig ma de'i cha shes rgyun mthong ngo snyam du nges pa yin no/ de la gzung ba yul tha dad kyi 'jug pa'i yul ni ma yin te/ gnyi gas kyang der zhen pas rang gi mtshan nyid kho na la 'jug pa'i phyir ro/ de nyid kyi phyir mngon sum gyi gzung ba'i yul gang yin pa de ni thob par bya ba ma yin te/ skad cig ma de thob par mi nus pa'i phyir ro/ 'on kyang mngon sum gyi stobs las skyes pa'i yul nges pa'i gzung ba'i skad cig ma gang yin pa de rgyun yul du byed la/ de yang nges par byas pa'i don yin pa des na mngon sum dang rjes su dpag pa dag gis zhen par bya ba'i yul khyad par med pa yin no/ (Dharmottara, *Explanation*, D: 4229, 179.a.4–.6).

8. Dharmottara, *Explanation*, D: 4229, 38.b.4–.6 and 179.a.4–.7. See Chapters 17 and 20.

9. Dharmottara, *Commentary*, D: 4231, 44.b.2–.4.

10. See Chapter 17.

11. See Chapter 4.

12. As we saw in Chapter 4, this concept is found in Prajñākaragupta's discussion of Dharmakīrti, *Commentary*, II:100–1. See *Ornament*, 108.a.7–.8.

13. mngon sum gyis thob par bya ba yang rgyun nyid yin no/ skad cig ma ni thob par mi nus pa'i phyir ro/ (Dharmottara, *Commentary*, D: 4231, 44.b.2).

14. This seems to be Mokṣākaragupta's idea when he asserts that perceptions cognize universals indirectly. Accordingly, Dharmakīrti's rejection of a determinative function in relation to perception is interpreted as referring to the direct object of perception. See Kajiyama, *Introduction*, pp. 56–8.

15. 'di ni bde ba sgrub pa'o/ 'di ni sdug bsngal sgrub pa'o zhes 'di'o zhes mngon sum nyid du nges te/ yongs su bcad na tha snyad du byed pa'i skyes bu bde ba sgrub par byed pa nyid du nye ba'i don yongs su gcod pa yin no/ bde ba dang sdug bsngal sgrub par byed pa dag ces bya ba ni 'jug pa'i yul ston pa'o/ . . . 'jug par byed pa de la yang nges par byed pa nyid kyis khyab pa yin no/ mngon sum la ni yod pa ma yin pa'i phyir 'jug par byed pa ni ma yin no zhes bya ba ni pha rol po'i bsam pa'o/ slob dpon gyis kyang khyab par bya ba dang khyab par byed pa byed pa'i dngos po de bden yang/ rtog pa med pa dang rtog pa dang bcas pa'i mngon sum dag 'jug pa'i yan lag nyid du khyad par med par bstan pa'i phyir skyon 'di med de zhes bya ba gsungs so/ 'di la 'jug pa'i yul mi gnas pa ni rnam pa gnyis te/ de'i dus na nye ba'i rang bzhin ma nges pa'i phyir mngon sum gyis 'jug pa'i yul du byed pa ni mi nus pa'am/ gal te bya ba byed pa nyid sngar mthong ba nye ba ma yin pa'i phyir rnam par rtog pa med pa'i mngon sum gyis ma nges pas 'jug pa'i yul du mi byed/ . . . 'di ltar rnam par rtog pa dang bcas pa'i mngon sum gyis yul dang dus dang rnam pa so sor nges pa gtan la phebs pa yin la/ rnam par rtog pa med par yang de'i rjes su byed pa de'i stobs kyis skyes pa'i gtan la phebs pa'i shes pas mngon sum gyis gzung ba nges par byed pa yin no/ (Dharmottara, *Explanation*, D: 4229, 83.a.1–b.1). I am once more grateful to Helmut Krasser for kindly sharing with me this reference.

16. The first move is the realist description of thought as apprehending reality, thus effectively escaping enclosure in the conceptual realm, as asserted by antirealists.

17. As we will see later, False Aspectarians *(rnam par rdzun par smra ba)* deny that the aspect through which the object is seen is real.

Chapter 22. Tibetan New Epistemology

1. Cha-ba defines *perception* as "that cognition which is free from conceptions and unmistaken with respect to its held object" (rtog pa dang bral zhing rang gi bzung yul la ma 'khrul ba'i rig pa) (Śākya Chok-den, *Defeater*, II.376.5).

2. See Chapters 16 and 17.

3. Subsequent cognition and inattentive cognition are divisions in Cha-ba's sevenfold typology of mental states we examine later. The latter is to be distinguished from inattentive perception *(mngon sum yid ma gtad pa)*, which is an externally valid cognition *(gzhan las nges)*. The identification of this last item is, however, not without problem. See Dreyfus, "Ontology," pp. 720–45; and Steinkellner, "Early Tibetan Ideas," p. 20.

4. Śākya Chok-den, *Defeater*, II.382.3–.6.

5. See Chapter 17.

6. The elimination of a superimposition only concerns the relevant aspect of the perceived object. For instance, in our example, I see a chair as a chair and eliminate all false views or doubts concerning this. I might still, nevertheless, hold the chair to be permanent. This superimposition will be eliminated by the comprehension of the impermanence of the chair.

7. sngar ma rtogs pa'i don la myong stobs kyis sgro 'dogs gcod par byed pa'i rig pa (Śākya Chok-den, *Defeater*, II.388.2–.3). In 376.5, Śākya Chok-den omits the words *sngar ma rtogs pa'i don la*. I assume that this is an omission on his part and that the preceding formulation is correct.

8. Śākya Chok-den, *Defeater*, II.298.6–.7.

9. Commenting on Dharmakīrti's *Commentary* (I:50), Gyel-tsap interprets this passage to refute the idea that an eliminative subject *(sel ba'i yul can)* cannot exist without the direct presence of a superimposition *(sgro 'dogs dngos su med pa)* (Gyel-tsap, *Revealing*, I.88.10–.11).

10. See Chapter 24.

11. A. Schopenhauer, *World as Will and Idea* (London: Trübner, 1886), vol. 2, p. 188. The similarity between Cha-ba and Schopenhauer concerns their arguments against the opposition between a passive sensation and an active conceptualization, not their overall view.

12. Ibid., 188.

13. Kajiyama, *Introduction*, pp. 56–58.

14. rang gi ngo bo'i khyad par bzlog phyogs kyi sgro 'dogs sel ba tsam/ (Sa-paṇ, *Auto-Commentary*, 116.a.6).

15. Śākya Chok-den, *Defeater*, II.600.3.

16. Śākya Chok-den, *Defeater*, II.135.1.

17. See Chapter 9.

18. mig gi dbang po de gzugs kyi mi rtag pa kun dang 'brel bar khyad par med na'ang rang yul gyi rnam pa shar ba'i sgo nas gzugs la gsar du mi slu ba'i shes pa de kho na gzugs rtogs pa'i tshad ma de'i 'jog byed tshad mar rigs te/ gzugs 'dzin dbang shes kyi gzugs rtogs la/ sgra ma rtogs pa 'di ni sgro 'dogs gcod nus kyi rnam pa shar ma shar gyi blo'i snang ba'i dbang gis byas pa'i phyir/ (Gyel-tsap, *Explanation*, 259.5–260.1).

19. A problem often debated in monastic courtyards is the following one: Not all the qualities of an object are apprehended by a perception. For example, a visual consciousness does not apprehend the taste of a slice of bread. Dharmakīrti's statement (*Commentary*, I.45ab) that all qualities are apprehended must be qualified. Gyel-tsap describes those as

"qualities [that are] simultaneously identical substances" *(grub bde rdzas gcig pa'i yon tan)* (*Revealing*, I.86.1). Kay-drup criticizes this, arguing that if Gyel-tsap's qualification is right, a person feeling the touch of a pot in the dark would also perceive its form, since both are simultaneously identical substances (*Ocean*, I:760.1–.5). Kay-drup's criticism does not, however, seem to capture Gyel-tsap's real position, which is that, here, for two things to be simultaneously identical substances "requires them to be identical substances without over- or under-inclusion, provided that they have the capacity to cover [each other in relation to] time, entity and place/object" *(dus dang ngo bo dang yul go sa gnon pa'i nus pa yod na de yang khyab che chung med pa rdzas gcig pa dgos so)* (*Revealing*, I.84.15–.16). Later scholars understand this to refer to "simultaneously identical substances from the point of view of place/object, time and nature" *(yul dus rang bzhin gang la ltos ste grub bde rdzas gcig)*; that is, the qualities that are intrinsically indissociable from the object. They, however, disagree on how to interpret the word *yul* (hence my bizarre notation). Jay-dzün-ba thinks that this refers to a place, in the same way that the *yul* of *yul ma 'dres pa* does (*Stream of Sayings*, 108.a.6–.7). Paṇ-chen holds that, here, *yul* means object and refers to the held object (*gzung yul*, see later). For him, these are indissociable qualities that appear together to perception, are identical substance with each others' properties, and exist for the same duration. *Revealing the Thought*, I.74.b.1–.3).

20. Gyel-tsap is making the usual Buddhist point that the cause of this mistake is both internal (weakness of the mind) and external circumstances, leading to holding things to be permanent such as "the arising of similar other [moments] as cause of mistake" *('dra ba gzhan byung 'khrul rgyu)* (*Revealing*, II.49.17–8).

21. blo gros mthon nyid nas/ rnam pa thams cad nges par byed/ (vyavasyantīkṣanād eva sarvākārān mahādhiyaḥ//) (Dharmakīrti, *Commentary*, III:107.cd).

22. Gyel-tsap distinguishes gross and subtle impermanence. The first is what common people understand by impermanence (the death of somebody, the end of a period, etc.). The second relates to the changing nature of reality. Things do not abide unchanged for more than one moment. Their constant transformation constitutes the subtle level at which impermanence can be understood. Such understanding is accessible only by great minds, that is, noble beings, as stated by Śākyabuddhi (*Revealing*, II.50.15–.19).

23. rigs stobs kyis dngos po'i gnas lugs la sgro 'dogs gcod par nus pa'i mkhas pa dag/ (*Ocean*, III: 291.3).

24. tshad mas sgro 'dogs gcod pa'i yul/ (Kay-drup, *Ocean*, II: 57.6). A similar passage can be found in *Ornament*, 65.a.3–.6, which I will discuss in detail later.

25. Bo-dong, *Presentation*, I.611.5–613.2. A parallel in Western philosophy is the term *immediate*, which can be understood psychologically or epistemologically. An object is psychologically immediately perceived if it is apprehended without relying on the direct presence of conception. It is epistemologically immediately perceived if it is perceived by a direct contact that makes its perception indubitable. See Dicker, *Perceptual*, pp. 55–56. Although the ambiguities of *immediate* do not correspond to those of *dngos*, it is easy to see that they apply to our discussion. Ge-luk thinkers take perception to be immediate in the first sense, seeing perception as a psychologically nonconceptual state. Go-ram-ba and others tend to focus on the second meaning of the term and take perceptions' nonconceptuality in a more epistemological sense.

26. Śākya Chok-den, *Defeater*, II.369.2–370.2.

27. tshad ma de yul de la blo kha phyogs shing rnam par shar ba'i stobs kyis nges shes rjes kyi blo gzhan la stos med du 'dren pa ni/ yul de dngos su rtogs pa'i don yin la/ yul de la da lta glo (i.e., blo) kha phyogs kyang/ tshad ma des rang gi gzhal bya dngos su gzhal ba'i

stobs kyis yul de la skabs dang mthun par sgro 'dogs bcad tshar bas phyis blo kha phyogs pa tsam gyis tshad ma gzhan la ltos med du nges pa skye bar 'gyur ba ni/ shugs rtogs kyi don yin no/ (*Ornament*, 35.4–.6). See also ibid., 36.1–.3.

28. Dharmakīrti, *Commentary*, III:75.b. and 287.ab.

29. spyir mngon sum tshad ma yin na mngon sum yin pas khyab pa dang/ rjes dpag tshad ma yin na rtog pa yin pas khyab mod kyi/ rang gi mtshan nyid la mngon sum/ zhes pa de dang/ shes gang gang la sgra don 'dzin/ de ni de la rtog par 'dod/ ces pa'i gzhung 'di dag gis yul bye brag tu bkar nas rang gi shugs yul gang yin pa de la mngon sum tshad ma yin yang mngon sum min pa dang/ rjes dpag tshad ma yin yang rtog pa min par bstan te/ de la mngon sum yin na de'i rang gi mtshan nyid snang dgos pa dang/ de la rtog pa yin na de'i sgra don 'dzin par bshad pa'i phyir/ (Gyel-tsap, *Revealing*, II.38.13–.20). Kay-drup makes a similar point in *Ornament*, 36.3–37.5. See also Ge-dün-drup, *Ornament*, 321.9–322.18.

30. Go-ram-ba, *Explanation*, 35.b.1. This typology is presented by introductory textbooks, which are also sometimes called *Mental States and Awareness (blo rig)*. See L. van der Kuijp, "Miscellanea Apropos of the Philosophy of Mind in Tibet: Mind in Tibet Buddhism," *Tibet Journal* 10–11 (1985): 36–37; Napper, *Mind*, pp. 162–63. Since this type of text is the counterpart of an introduction to reasoning called *Typology of Reasons (rtags rigs)*, this spelling is probably deviant. These two types of text, which are parts of the textbooks of Ge-luk monasteries, introduce the student to the basic logical and epistemological concepts, which are later examined in greater detail while studying Dharmakīrti's texts. These introductory texts are important in that they provide the basic vocabulary for further studies. The student will feel free to use concepts such as inattentive cognition or correct assumption in reference to Dharmakīrti's texts, even though these concepts hardly appear in those texts. Sa-gya curriculum contains a study of *Typology of Reasons* (written by Lo Ken-chen) but there is no special study of the *Typology of Mental States*, which are examined in Sa-paṇ's *Treasure*.

31. Śākya Chok-den, *Defeater*, II.74.1–.3.

32. Bo-dong, *Presentation*, II.836.5–839.5.

33. Some thinkers, for example, hold that this typology is not a definite enumeration since some mental episodes (such as the compassion of a Bodhisattva) are left out. Jam-bel-sam-pel, *Summary of the Indispensable Points [in the] Presentation of Mental States and Awareness (blo rig gi rnam bzhag gnyer mkho kun 'dus)* (1975), 6.a.3–b.1. Most textbooks are not explicit on the question of whether the sevenfold typology is inclusive or not.

34. In *Essence* (80.a.6–b.6), Gyel-tsap does not speak of novelty.

35. The *bcas shes* (literally cognition of the [already] determined, also sometimes spelled *dpyad shes*, i.e., investigating cognition), is a transformation of the term *bcad pa'i yul can* (according to Śākya Chok-den, *Defeater*, II.89.3), which refers to the determining subject that follows a valid cognition and cognizes the same object as that valid cognition.

36. rang gi 'dren byed kyi tshad ma snga mas rtogs zin rtogs pa'i tshad min gyi rig pa/ (Paṇ-chen Sö-nam-drak-ba, *Revealing the Thought*, II:6.b.7). Jam-yang-shay-ba gives an equivalent definition: "that nonvalid cognition which is reliable and realizes that which has already been realized" (rtogs zin rtogs pa'i tshad min gyi mi slu ba'i shes pa) (*The Blaze*, 677.2).

37. yongs su gcod pa tsam 'jug par byed yin na yang/ gang gis dang po 'jug pa'i yul bstan pa de nyid kyis gzhan la ltos pa med par skyes bu gcug pa'i phyir rtogs pa'i don la tshad ma yod pa ma yin no/. . . . de'i phyir tshad ma thams cad ni ma rtogs pa'i don can kho na'o/ de nyid kyi phyir dang po'i mngon sum dang rjes su dpag pa'i skad cig ma nyid kyis don byed nus pa'i dngos po'i rgyun nges pas 'jug pa'i yul du byed nus pa'i phyir/ de'i

rgyun du gyur pa grub pa dang bde ba tha mi dad pa phyi ma rnams tshad ma yin pa spangs pa yin no (Dharmottara, *Explanation* D: 4229, 9.a.5–9.b.2).

38. Kay-drup, *Ornament*, 134.4. Dharmottara accepts, contrary to Gyel-tsap, that a mental perception is valid. He says: "Because he accepts [this mental perception] as valid, Dignāga explains the object of mental consciousness as being different [from those of sense perceptions]" *(tshad ma zhal gyis bzhes pa'i slob dpon phyogs kyi glang pos kyang yid kyi rnam par shes pa'i yul gzhan nyid yin par bshad/)* (*Explanation*, D: 4229, 108.a.5). Śākya Chok-den develops a long textual argument to the same effect in *Music*, 494.6–.7. He argues that Dharmottara in *Explanation*, D: 4229, 89.a.1–.2, cannot deny that subsequent moments of perception are valid because this passage refers to a passage in which Dharmakīrti says: "*Objection*: It follows that since former and latter [moments of] perception do not relate to different [thing], they are not valid cognitions. *Answer*: This is not so because [these moments make] *distinct* [epistemic] contributions with respect to what one seeks to establish" (mngon sum snga ma dang phyi ma rnams su 'ga' zhig la nye bar sbyor bar tha mi dad pa'i phyir/ tshad ma nyid ma yin par thal bar 'gyur ro/ zhe na/ ma yin te/ skad cig ma'i bye brag gis bsgrub par bya ba'i don du 'dod pa la grub pa bde ba tha dad pa'i phyir ro/) (*Drop of Logical Reason*, D: 4213, 239.b.4). However, Dharmottara reads this passage differently, as saying that "[these moments make] *nondistinct* [epistemic] contributions." Hence, the whole argument is difficult to evaluate. See Dreyfus, "Ontology," pp. 645–46.

39. See *Ornament*, 58.b.5–59.a.3. According to Kay-drup, if novelty were a requirement for validity, then people would have no valid cognition of sound once they had understood what sound is (presumably at a very young age). Moreover, the inference of the impermanence of the sound would also absurdly turn out to be a subsequent cognition, since it apprehends previously understood objects such as sound and impermanence. For more detail, see Kay-drup, ibid., 63.b–64.b. Another argument adduced by Kay-drup against the requirement of novelty is that if novelty were required for validity there could be no valid mental perception of sound *(sgra 'dzin mngon sum gyi tshad ma)* in ordinary beings. See ibid., 66.b.3–.4. Gyel-tsap expresses a similar opinion while extensively commenting on Sa-paṇ's refutation of subsequent perception (*Essence*, 20.a.4–21.b.4).

40. Literally, obscured cognition. See Chapter 17.

41. Here, Kay-drup is in agreement with Dharmakīrti's original system. A similar position is taken by Śākya Chok-den, who refutes the existence of a nonconceptual subsequent cognition (*Defeater*, II.85.5–96.1).

42. R. G. Collingwood, *The Idea of History* (New York: Oxford University Press, 1946, 1956), pp. 297–98.

Chapter 23. Cha-ba's Philosophy of Mind: Objects and Appearances

1. See Chapter 17.

2. Ge-dün-drup defines appearing object as "that phenomenon which is cognized through its mere appearing" (chos des snang tsam gyi sgo nas rig par bya ba) (*Ornament*, 312.10–.11).

3. Real objects cannot be the appearing objects of conceptions even though they appear to it. Similarly, object universals are not the conceived objects of conceptions. Otherwise, these conceptions would have to realize the object universals. This not possible, since they mistake those for real objects. See Chapter 18.

4. (Literally) Madhyamaka acting [in accordance with] the world *('jig rten grags sde dbu ma pa)* (Śākya Chok-den, *Ocean of Music*, 468.3). We should not rush to identify this as a Prāsaṅgika view, for, according to Śākya Chok-den, Cha-ba wrote extremely extensive refutations against the Prāsaṅgika view. See *History*, 33.4–5 and *Dharma Treasury*, I.518.5–523.3, where Cha-ba's arguments are carefully laid out.

5. Śākya Chok-den, *Ocean of Music*, 469.7–471.5.

6. Sa-paṇ, *Auto-Commentary*, 31.a.4. and Śākya Chok-den, *Ocean of Music*, 468.5–474.2.

7. Here, I differentiate hidden *(lkog gyur)* from "hidden" *(lkog na mo)*. External objects are said by certain philosophers to be "hidden." This claim should be distinguished from the assertion that external objects are hidden, i.e., unperceivable and must be inferred. See Chapter 26.

8. slob dpon phya pa na re/ gzung yul zhes bya ba ni snang yul la bya ba yin cing/ de yang yul can gyi shes pa dang dus mnyam kho na yin te/ dus mi mnyam pa yul yul can du mi rung ba'i phyir/ mdo sde pa shes pa'i snga logs su byung ba'i don gyis shes pa la rnam pa gtad par 'dod pa mi 'thad de/ 'o na sha zas don gyi rnam pa gtad par 'dod na ci 'gog/ sha za mngon sum dan rjes dpag gyis ma grub bo zhe na/ de ni snga logs na yod par 'dod pa'i don lkog na mo la yang mtshungs so/ de bas na gzung yul gsum ste/ don rang gi mtshan nyid dang/ don spyi dang med gsal ba'o/ zhes bzhad do/ (Śākya Chok-den, *Defeater*, II.3.5–4.3).

9. There is some minor disagreement within the Ge-luk tradition on how the two standpoints expressed in Dharmakīrti's text (Sautrāntika and Yogācāra) should be articulated. Whereas Gyel-tsap describes Dharmakīrti's text as expressing a view common to both schools (*mdo sems thung mong ba; Revealing*, II.9.1.), Paṇ-chen holds that these texts are really Yogācāra because no texts are common to both schools. There are, however, passages that reflect a Sautrāntika standpoint, but the global intention of the text is Yogācāra. *Revealing the Thought*, III.9.a.4–5). Paṇ-chen's point seems to be that, as a unified work, Dharmakīrti's *Commentary* is a treatise intended to introduce its audience to the Yogācāra view. Therefore, as a unified text it is a Yogācāra text, for the Sautrāntika passages are there only to support this final intention by asserting the conventional nature of conceptual objects. There is, however, unanimity in rejecting a Madhyamaka interpretation among Ge-luk interpreters.

10. blos rig par bya ba/ (Sa-paṇ, *Treasure*, 2.a.2; Kay-drup, *Ornament*, 26.4; Go-ram-ba, *Explanation*, 10.b.3).

11. *gzhan rig*; that is, all the cognitions that are not self-cognitions.

12. snang yul dang gzung yul don gcig la/ de la rtog med shes pa'i snang yul dang gzung yul ni/ rtog med shes gang la chos de'i rnam pa gsal bar dngos su shar ba'i sgo nas shes pa de'i yul du gyur ba rnams yin la/ de ltar na/ rtog med shes pa'i dbang du byas pa'i gzung yul dang snang yul ni/ phyi rol dang shes pa rnams yin cing/ yul can ni/ rtog med gzhan rig phal cher dang rang rig rnams yin no/ (Kay-drup, *Ornament*, 55.a.3–.5). A similar view is found in most Ge-luk presentations. See Ge-dün-drup, *Ornament*, 312.11–.12; Napper, *Mind*, pp. 28–29; Klein, *Knowledge*, pp. 38–39.

13. Paṇ-chen, *Revealing the Thought*, III:18.a.6–.7.

14. phyi rol gyi yul nye ba la mi ltos (Kay-drup, *Ornament*, 111.6).

15. Ge-dün-drup, *Ornament*, 311.17–.20.

16. rgyu yi dngos po ma gtogs pa/ gzung ba zhes bya ba ci yang med/ de la blo gang du snang/ de ni de yi gzung bar brjod/ (hetubhāvād ṛte nānyā grāhyatā nāma kācana/ tatra buddhir yad ābhāsā tasyās tadgrāhyam ucyate/) (Dharmakīrti, *Commentary*, III:224). Verses ab are quoted by Sa-paṇ in his refutation of Cha-ba, *Auto-Commentary*, 31.b.2.

17. Sa-paṇ, *Auto-Commentary*, 31.b.1–.6. These arguments will be made clear when we examine Sa-paṇ's view of perception in the next chapter.

18. Śākya Chok-den, *Defeater*, II.20.3–.5. We will see that Śākya Chok-den is only partially right here.

19. Śākya Chok-den, *Defeater*, II.8.6–.7. A similar view is found in Go-ram-ba and Bo-dong. See *Explanation*, 15.a.4–b.1 and *Presentation*, I.615.2–.6. This corresponds to Dharmakīrti's use of the terms. See *Commentary*, III:240.ab.

20. The direct cause produces its effect immediately after its disappearance, in opposition to the indirect causes *(brgyud rgyu)*, which are not immediately effective.

21. Yogic perception is able to perceive objects in the three times and, therefore, does not rely on an object casting its aspect on consciousness. Since self-cognition is simply the reflexive aspect of consciousness, it has no object at all. Mistaken nonconceptual cognitions are not the products of external objects but of internal or external causes of mistake. Finally, conceptions do not rely on the presence of a real thing and are, therefore, not the direct product of an external object.

22. In the absence of Cha-ba's texts, I find it difficult to decide whether he intended his view of perception as an interpretation of Dharmakīrti or as a refutation.

23. phya pa'i rjes 'brang dag gis/ mdo sde pa'i lugs khas blangs nas snang yul dang gzung yul gyi rnam par bzhag pa phya pa'i lugs bzhin du rang lugs su 'jog pa 'khrul pa'i steng du yang 'khrul gnyis pa brtsegs pa yin no/ (Śākya Chok-den, *Defeater*, II.7.6–.7).

24. Śākya Chok-den admits the legitimacy of the object of application and the held object.

25. Go-ram-ba traces the concept of appearing object back to Dharmakīrti, *Commentary*, I:68.ab. and I:125.ab. He finds mention of the same concept in reference to nonconceptual thought in *Ascertainment*, II.7.ab. The source for conceived objects is *Commentary*, III:55.ab (Go-ram-ba, *Explanation*, 13.a.2–b.1).

26. Śākya Chok-den, *Defeater*, II.20.4–.6.

27. For example, see Dharmakīrti, *Commentary*, III:55 and I:171.

28. shes pa rnams kyi yul ni rnam pa gnyis te/ gzung ba dang zhen pa/ (Dharmottara, *Explanation*, D: 4229, 179.a.4). Quoted by Go-ram-ba, *Explanation*, 11.a.5–.6. as a source for Cha-ba's views, which he rejects.

29. Dharmottara, *Explanation*, D: 4229, 179.a.4.

30. de bzhin du rjes su dpag pa yang rang gi snang ba don med pa la yang rang gi snang ba don du zhen pas 'jug pa'i phyir don med pa 'dzin pa yin no/ yang sgro btags pa'i don 'dzin pa na rang gi mtshan nyid du 'dzin te/ de bas na rjes su dpag pa 'di 'jug yul ni zhes bya ba rang gi mtshan nyid yin la/ gzung bar bya ba ni don med pa yin no/ (Dharmottara, *Commentary*, D: 4231, 44.b.2–.4).

31. Dharmottara, *Explanation*, D: 4229, 38.b.6–.7.

32. It seems that Dharmottara understands held object in two ways: in terms of appearance (as we just saw) and in terms of being an external object that causes the perception as, for example, when he says: "The very cause that has the capacity to produce a consciousness that has its aspect is said to be held . . ." (rang gi rnam pa can gyi shes pa skyed par byed pa'i rgyu nyid la gzung bar brjod par bya ba yin gyi/) (Dharmottara, *Explanation*, D: 4229, 108.a.1).

33. This is different from the Ge-luk view of the duration of objects under the form of continua. For the Vaibhāṣika, things endure in a stronger sense, for they do not change moment by moment. Hence, a cause can still exist after producing its object.

34. See Chapters 25 and 26.

Chapter 24. Sa-paṇ's Critique of the New Epistemology

1. Śākya Chok-den, *Defeater*, II.74.3–.7.

2. yid dpyod rtags la gtan mi ltos/ dam bca' tsam yang the tshom 'gyur/ rtags la ltos na yang dag gam/ ltar snang gsum las 'da' ba med// (Sa-paṇ, *Treasure*, 4.a.1–.2). Sa-paṇ's *Commentary* (35.b.5) has a different version: "yid dpyod rtags la ltos mi ltos/"; i.e., "Either a correct assumption relies on reason or not . . ." (quoted in Jam-bel-sam-pel, *Summary*, 6.a.1–.2). See also L. van der Kuijp, "Miscellanea," 37–38. My reading of the last line, which is different from van der Kuijp's, is based on Go-ram-ba, *Clarification*, 36.b.6, and on Sa-paṇ, *Auto-Commentary*, 172.4.1–.2. There, Sa-paṇ says: "If assumption relies on evidence, it does not [go] beyond four possibilities." He then enumerates these four possibilities as the three invalid evidences and one valid evidence. Therefore, I think that the word *three* refers to the three types of invalid evidence, not to three possibilities.

3. Sa-paṇ, *Auto-Commentary*, 36.b.2–39.a.6. For Sa-paṇ's sources in Dharmakīrti's writings, see Go-ram-ba, *Clarification*, 36.b.3–.5.

4. Go-ram-ba, *Clarification*, 36.b.1–37.b.5; and Śākya Chok-den, *Defeater*, II.76.3–80.5. According to Śākya Chok-den, *yid dpyod* is found in Dharmottara and in Śaṃkarānanda as conceptual investigation *(dpyod pa, vicāra)*. Accordingly, it can be either an inference or one of the three forms of nonvalid cognition *(tshad min gyi blo)*; namely, doubt, wrong conception, or nonrealization (Śākya Chok-den, *Defeater*, II.96.2–.3).

5. Napper, *Mind*, p. 98.

6. Jam-yang-shay-ba is noncommittal about the exact interpretation of Sa-paṇ's verses. He simply quotes the stanza while giving the opinion of a follower of [Sa-paṇ's] *Treasure*. Jam-yang-shay-ba's argument supporting the existence of correct assumption is that experience shows that there are two levels of understanding a fact hidden to perception. At first we understand it tentatively; only later, once we have been through a deeper process of reasoning, can certainty be reached (*The Blaze*, II.660.3–662.3). Jam-yang defines assumption as "that cognition which newly and single-mindedly ascertains a true object and which is not a certainty relying on either [perceptual] experience or evidence" (myong ba dang rtags la brten pa'i nges gang yang ma yin pa'i bden pa'i don la gsar du mtha' gcig tu nges pa'i rig pa de) (*The Blaze*, II.666.5).

7. Gyel-tsap, *Treasure of the Essence of Good Saying, a Commentary on [Dharmakīrti's Treatise] on Valid Cognition the Drop of Reasoning (tshad ma rigs thigs kyi 'grel pa legs bshad snying po'i gter)*, Collected Works, VIII.534.3.

8. Gyel-tsap, *Essence*, 17.b.1–19.a.4. Some contemporary members of the Ge-luk tradition realize that Sa-paṇ's quote has been completely misinterpreted by certain later authors, but they usually keep quiet about this for fear of hurting the pride that their fellow monks invest in the literature of their monastery. This shows the danger for modern scholars of relying too much on the literature of particular monasteries, leaving aside the most seminal authors such as Dzong-ka-ba, Gyel-tsap, and Kay-drup.

9. Sa-paṇ, *Auto-Commentary*, 40.a.6.

10. Sa-paṇ, *Auto-Commentary*, 40.a.2–42.a.5. We saw (Chapter 22) similar ideas in Kay-drup who shares Sa-paṇ's conception of subsequent cognition as exclusively conceptual. There is, however, a difference between the two thinkers: whereas for Sa-paṇ subsequent cognition is to be altogether excluded from the domain of realizing mental states, Kay-drup holds that subsequent cognitions realize their objects.

11. Sa-paṇ is not explicit about the meaning of *realize (rtogs pa)*. This word might be read as "determine" *(bcad)*. As we will see shortly, however, determination is limited to the

conceptual and hence inapplicable to perception. Śākya Chok-den, despite not always following Sa-paṇ, offers some helpful remarks when he differentiates determination and realization on the following grounds. The inference of sound as impermanent determines the sound's impermanence, but does not realize it, because it does not apprehend *('dzin pa)* it. Therefore, for Śākya Chok-den, realization consists of a correct apprehension of the object. Perception realizes the real object directly held. Inference realizes its direct object, the object universal, but determines its object of application (Śākya Chok-den, *Music*, 508.7).

12. gal te snang la ma nges pa/ tshad ma min na mngon sum kun/ tshad ma min pa 'gyur mngon sum la/ nges pa nyid ni bkag phyir ro/ (Sa-paṇ, *Treasure*, 4.a.6).

13. Sa-paṇ, *Treasure*, 7.a.5.

14. des na mgnon sum tshad ma yang/ rtog med phyir na nges mi dgos/ mngon sum rtog bral ma 'khrul ba/ nyid kyi tshad ma grub pa yin/ (Sa-paṇ, *Treasure*, 6.a.2). I am reading the genitive in the last verse as an agent: *nyid kyis grub*.

15. Sa-paṇ, *Auto-Commentary*, 51.b.4. Sa-paṇ rejects the distinction between conceptual and nonconceptual ascertainment proposed by an opponent.

16. Some Ge-luk thinkers define inattentive cognition differently. They recognize that perception does not ascertain its object, but they still hold that a valid perception determines its object. For example, Ge-shay Jam-bel-sam-pel, a follower of Paṇ-chen Sö-nam-drak-ba, defines *inattentive perception* as "a cognition to which a specifically characterized phenomenon, which is its object of application, appears, but that cannot induce certainty towards that [object]" (rang gi 'jug yul du gyur pa'i rang mtshan gsal bar snang ba yang yin de la nges pa 'dren mi nus pa'i rig pa) (Jam-bel-sam-pel, *Summary* 6.b.3). Jam-yang-shay-ba states a similar definition: "that cognition which has the clear appearance of a specifically characterized phenomenon but does not ascertain its object" (rang mtshan gsal snang can yang yin rang yul ma nges pa yang yin pa'i gzhi mthun par 'gyur pa'i rig pa) (*The Blaze*, 666.4–.5).

17. Sa-paṇ, *Auto-Commentary*, 66.b.6.

18. See Steinkellner, "Early Tibetan Ideas" and Dreyfus, "Ontology," pp. 721–45.

19. We would commonly talk about seeing a thing as this or that. According to Sa-paṇ, this is not an actual seeing but only a conceptual characterization of seeing.

20. da ni ji ltar ma nges pa mngon sum gyis kyang gzung yin zhe na/ mgnon sum gang gis kyang nges par byed pa ma yin te/ des gang zhig 'dzin pa de'ang nges pas ni ma yin no/ 'o na ci yin zhe na der snang bas so/ des nges pa dang ma nges pa'i dbang gis mngon sum gyis 'dzin pa dang mi 'dzin pa dag ma yin no/ nges pa rnams kyis de lta ma yin te/ 'ga' zhig nges kyang 'ga' zhig ma nges pas 'jug pa tha dad pas 'dzin pa dang mi 'dzin pa yin no/ (Dharmakīrti, *Auto-Commentary*, D: 4216, 278.a.5–.6; quoted by Sa-paṇ, *Auto-Commentary*, 39.b.3–.5).

21. Sa-paṇ, *Auto-Commentary*, 51.b.6.

22. Dharmakīrti, *Commentary*, III:107.cd. See Chapter 22.

23. ma yin te/ tshad ma snga mas mi rtag pa rang mtshan bzung la/ phyi mas mi rtag pa'i rang mtshan 'dzin pa'i phyir/ gnyis ka yang 'jug yul ni gcig la 'jug ste/ sgra mi rtag pa rang mtshan de nyid la 'jug pas so/ (Śākya Chok-den, *Ocean of Music*, 508.7).

24. rtog ngor de min rnam par bsal tsam la de'i tha snyad byed pa/ (Śākya Chok-den, *Defeater*, II.94.1).

25. de dag gis ni mngon sum dang/ rtog pa'i byed pa 'dres par zad/ (Sa-paṇ, *Treasure*, 16.a.4–.5).

26. don gzhan gyi rnam pa snang ba'i sgo nas sgro 'dogs gcod pa. This is what Sa-paṇ reports as the definition of *implicit realization* given by early Tibetan thinkers

(*Auto-Commentary*, 128.a.2). Ge-luk thinkers explain (but do not define) implicit realization as the realization of something whose aspect does not appear to that mental episode *(rnam pa ma shar ba'i sgo nas rtogs pa)*. There does not appear any significant difference between early Tibetan thinkers and Ge-luk-bas on this point.

27. Sa-paṇ, *Auto-Commentary*, 129.a.3.

28. Sa-paṇ does not address the question of whether the deformations he criticizes are the products of later Indian commentaries or Tibetan creations. He usually seems to work under the latter assumption, but this does not really matter for him. Since his task is the retrieval of Dharmakīrti's original system, he very rarely relies on other Indian commentators. He directly refers to Dharmakīrti's texts, most especially to his *Commentary*, a work cherished by Sa-paṇ.

29. *Ārya (phags pa)*; i.e., the persons who have obtained direct realization into the four noble truths.

30. so so skye bo'i tshad ma ni/ nges pa nyid las 'jug ldog byed/ 'phags pa rtog pa bral ba rnams/ ting nge 'dzin las byed par gsungs/ (Sa-paṇ, *Treasure*, 17.a.4–.5).

31. dbang shes lkugs pa mig can 'dra/ rtog pa long ba smra mkhas 'dra/ rang rig dbang po tshang ba yis/ gnyis po de'i brda sprod byed/ (Sa-paṇ, *Treasure*, 6.a.5).

32. Although Dharmakīrti does not explicitly express this view, he suggests it, particularly in *Commentary* III:489–503, when he discusses the role of self-cognition in bringing about the impression of length in phonemes by keeping track of the individual moments of hearing. See Chapter 15.

33. Hume says: "The mind is a kind of theatre, where several perceptions successively make their appearance; pass, re-pass, glide away, and mingle in an infinite variety of postures and situations. There is properly no simplicity in it at one time, no identity in different; whatever natural propension we may have to imagine that simplicity and identity . . . They are the successive perceptions only, that constitute the mind. . . . What then gives us so great a propension to ascribe an identity to these successive perceptions and to suppose ourselves possest of an invariable and uninterrupted existence thro' the whole course of our lives? . . . the true idea of human mind, is to consider it as a system of different perceptions or different existences, which are link'd together by the relation of cause and effect and mutually produce, destroy, influence, and modify each other. Our impressions give rise to their correspondent ideas; and these ideas in their turn produce other impressions. One thought chases another, and draws after it a third, by which it is expell'd in turn. In this respect, I cannot compare the soul more properly to any thing than to a republic or commonwealth . . ." (*Treatise*, pp. 534, 535, 541–42).

34. This example is taken from R. Wolff, *Kant's Theory of Mental Activity* (Cambridge, Mass.: Harvard University Press, 1963), p. 108.

35. Kant, *Critique*, p. 152 (B131).

Chapter 25. Perception and Apperception

1. Dignāga reasons to this conclusion from memory, which involves a past object as well as a past experience. The recollection of these two elements differs in their form. When I recollect my experience, I remember a subjective experience, which is something above the mere recollection of the object. This difference can be accounted for only if we posit that the original experience has two aspects, one (the objective aspect) oriented toward the external world and one (subjective aspect) directed inward (Hattori, *Dignāga*, pp. 28–31).

2. The argument against this position is that if a perception needs a distinct apperception to be known, then that apperception in turn will need another perception to be revealed. To this, the Nyāya answers: "It is necessary that a cognition cognizes an object, but it is only contingent that we have a cognition of cognition. Some cognitions [e.g., a cognition of a cognition] may simply arise and be not cognized, for the mind may be forced into another activity" (Matilal, *Perception*, p. 153).

3. Go-ram-ba mentions five reasonings developed by Dharmakīrti, in addition to the two already propounded by Dignāga (*Explanation*, 212.a.3–213.b.3). Among those five is the argument from the ascertainment of simultaneous observation *(lhan cig dmigs nges)* (*Explanation*, 213.b.3–218.b.3; Śākya Chok-den, *Defeater*, II.56.6–63.4; Gyel-tsap, *Complete Explanation*, 307.3– 319.3; Kay-drup, *Ornament*, 179.1–196.1).

4. Dharmakīrti, *Commentary*, III:249–267. This argument is directed against the Nyāya view. Arguments against the Sāṃkhya are found in *Commentary* III:269–288. For a summary, see Dreyfus, "Ontology," pp. 591–95.

5. I am greatly simplifying the description, leaving memory out of the picture. This does not change the analysis, for although memory is involved in determining our likes and dislikes, pleasantness and unpleasantness are actually experienced. For Dharmakīrti, a pleasant taste is not a conceptual projection on a neutral perception but is actually experienced as such.

6. de phyir bde sogs rang nyid la/ 'phos pa'i don ni snang ba dang/ de myong phyir na 'jig rten 'dogs/ phyi rol don ni dngos su min/ rang bdag rig byed 'di dag ni/ don las skyes pa tsam du zad/ (tasmāt sukhādayo 'rthānāṃ svasaṃkrāntāvabhāsinām/ vedakāḥ svātmanaś caiṣām arthebhyo janma kevalaṃ/) (Dharmakīrti, *Commentary*, III:266). In Ge-dün-drup, *Good Sayings*, 225.2–4, the Sanskrit is quite different. For one, it does not have verses 3 and 4, which are found are in Devendrabuddhi, *Commentary on Commentary on Valid Cognition*, D: 4229, 207.a.2. It also takes the term *appearance (avabhāsinām, snang ba)* to refer to objects and not to happiness, as does the Tibetan translation. Thus, the Sanskrit reads: "Therefore, happiness, etc., is that which cognizes itself, objects appearing as transferred onto itself. It is merely produced from an [external] object."

7. des na shes pa thams cad kyi/ dmigs myong tha dad yin/ (bhinne jñānasya sarvasya tenālambanavedane/) (Dharmakīrti, *Commentary*, III:460.ab).

8. Transcendental ego is the self that is the condition of the possibilities of persons. It is distinguished from the empirical self, which is identified with different elements of our personality (what Buddhists would describe as elements of the basis of designation of the person). The transcendental self is not given in experience but only as an a priori of our experiences as a person.

9. Author's emphasis. For Sartre, *transcendent*, not to be confused with transcendental, refers to intentionality, which he describes as "the essential principle of phenomenology" (*La Transcendance of the Ego* [Paris: Vrin, 1927, 1985], p. 28). A consciousness is produced as oriented toward a phenomenon that is different from it. Its object is transcendent because it is not reducible to consciousness and its content.

10. Ibid., p. 24.

11. See also Chapters 19 and 24.

12. rang rig pa'ang rig bya rig byed gnyis su phye ba'i rang rig pa ma yin gyi bem po las log nas rig par skyes tsam de nyid yin no/ des na rang rig la yul med do/ (Yak-dön, *Radiating*, 299.4–.5).

13. rang rig yul yin no zhe na/ rang la yul yul can 'gal lo/ des na rang rig la yul yod par shad pa ni btags pa ba yin no/ (Sa-paṇ, *Auto-Commentary*, 36.a.4).

14. Yak-dön, *Radiating*, 300.1–.6. The example is found in Dharmakīrti, *Commentary*, III:329. Similar views are expressed by Lo Ken-chen, *Sun*, 76.6, and Śākya Chok-den, *Music*, 479.4–.7. Śākya Chok-den argues that apperception cannot have an object in the cognitive sense of the word. Since it is a valid cognition, apperception must have, however, an object of application *('jug yul)* pragmatically understood.

15. rang gi ngo bo myong byed kyi 'dzin rnam/ (Go-ram-ba, *Explanation*, 162.b.2).

16. With the exceptions of Śākya Chok-den (*Defeater*, II.471.2–476.6) and Bo-dong (*Presentation*, I.940.1–.2).

17. dbang shes la rang dus su phyi rol rgyang chad ltar du snang ba/ 'jig rten pa rnams kyi phyi rol don gyi tha snyad byed pa'i snang ba 'di nyid gzung rnam yin la/ de nyid mdo sde pa rnams kyis phyi rol don gyis gtad par 'dod cing/ sems tsam pa rnams kyis gtod byed kyi phyi don med par bag chags kyi dbang gis shes pa nyid gzung bar snang bar 'dod do/ (Go-ram-ba, *Explanation*, 206.b.3–.4).

18. There is here an obvious similarity with Locke and Berkeley.

19. 'dzin rnam ni yul gyi rnam pa de 'dzin byed du snang zhing nang du sim gdung du myong ba 'di yin no/ de la 'jig rten pa rnams kyis longs spyod byed kyi bdag tu sgro 'dogs par byed kyi/ longs spyad bya'i gzung bar sgro 'dogs pa ni med do/ (Go-ram-ba, *Explanation*, 206.b.4–.5).

20. shes pa rang gi ngo bo la ma 'khrul ba/ (Sa-paṇ, *Auto-Commentary*, 135.b.3).

21. Go-ram-ba, *Explanation*, 163.a.4–165.b.4; and Śākya Chok-den, *Defeater*, II.476.7–486.7.

22. Literally, "the same simultaneous substance from the point of view of location, time, and nature" *(yul dang dus dang ngo bo gang la ltos kyang khyab mnyam grub bde rdzas gcig yin pa'i phyir)* (Gyel-tsap, *Explanation*, 173.3).

23. As Gyel-tsap points out, this is the implication of Dharmakīrti's assertion in *Commentary*, I:43–45, that a thing appears as it is (with all its intrinsic qualities) to a perception.

24. Go-ram-ba, *Explanation*, 206.b.2–.6.

25. shes pa de dang de'i gzung rnam ni shes pa de dang de nyid la brjod par/gong tu rigs pas legs par bsgrubs zin . . . / (Kay-drup, *Ornament*, 212.2). Here Kay-drup seems to be referring to ibid., 151.2.6.

26. Gyel-tsap, *Explanation*, 173.4–.6.

27. J. F. Bennett discusses what he calls the veil of perception doctrine in *Locke, Berkeley, Hume: Central Themes* (Oxford: Oxford University Press, 1971), pp. 68–70. For a response, see Mackie, *Problems*, pp. 51–55.

28. de ltar rang rig gzung bya shes pa'i gzung rnam zhes brjod pa gang yin pa de yang/ shes pa de nyid la brjod pa yin la/ rnam pa shar ba'i don rnam par skyes pa de nyid la brjod pa yin gyi/ yul dang shes pa'i bar na rnam pa grib ma lta bu yod pa min no zhes sngar legs par gtan la phab zin de nyid mdo sems gnyis ka'i grub pa'i mtha' yin la/ (Kay-drup, *Ornament*, 220.5–221.2).

29. The Ge-luk adoption of Dharmakīrti's analysis of causality goes further than this point. Even in the field of Madhyamaka, they continue to use his view, despite the deterministic and even essentialist overtone of Dharmakīrti's view of perception. As we will see in our conclusion, Go-ram-ba criticizes Dzong-ka-ba for using this view of causality in Madhyamaka, where the relation between causes and effects is not understood on the basis of necessary and sufficient conditions but in relation to linguistically embedded conventional practices.

30. To illustrate this view, the example of Aquinas may be useful. Like Kay-drup,

Aquinas holds a direct realist view of mind as being in direct contact with the external world. Like Kay-drup, he also holds the view that the mind bears the likeness of the object. This likeness is not, as one may think, representational, for it does not stand for the object. Rather, it is the mark of the attunement of the mind to the reality of the object. For Aquinas, an external object produces in the sense a likeness, which is in turn transmitted to an internal sense where it becomes available for further intellectual operations. As N. Kretzmann emphasizes, we should not be misled by Aquinas's mention of likeness. His view is not a mixture of realism and representationalism. Rather, it reflects an insistence on the fact that to apprehend an object is to be affected by this object. Thus, the likeness essential to sensory cognition does not compromise direct realism; the relation is causal but not representational. An important difference between Kay-drup and Aquinas derives from the latter's hylomorphic distinction between substance and form. For Aquinas, the likeness of the object in the mind is the form of the object. In this way, the mind can be said to be attuned directly to the very essence of the external object. Kay-drup does not make this distinction between form and substance. Hence, the form of the object taken by the cognition does not belong to the object but only to the cognition. It is the cognition being produced that exhibits the influence of the object (N. Kretzmann and E. Stump, *The Cambridge Companion to Aquinas* (Cambridge: Cambridge University Press, 1993), pp. 138–39). See also: N. Kretzmann, A. Kenny, J. Piborg, and E. Stump, *The Cambridge History of Later Medieval Philosophy* (Cambridge: Cambridge University Press, 1982), pp. 605–6; and G. Anscombe and P. Geach, *Three Philosophers* (Ithaca, N.Y.: Cornell University Press, 1961), pp. 94–105.

31. Gyel-tsap, *Explanation*, 172.1–.2.

32. For Dzong-ka-ba's view of the implications of self-cognition in Madhyamaka philosophy, see *Clarification of the Thought, an Extensive Treatise on [Candrakīrti's] Introduction to the Mādhyamika (dbu ma dgongs pa rab gsal)*, (Banaras: Pleasure of Elegant Sayings Press, 1973), pp. 281–307. Also P. Williams, "On Rang Rig," in Steinkellner and Tauscher, *Contributions on Tibetan Buddhist Religion and Philosophy* (Vienna: Wiener Studien zur Tibetologie, 1983), pp. 321–30.

33. Bo-dong, *Presentation*, II.836.5–839.5. A possible answer would be based on the distinction between elimination of a superimpostion by refutation of its object *(yul sun 'byung ba)*, which is a conceptual function, and elimination of the seed or root of the superimposition, which is a perceptual and not an eliminative function.

34. Dharmakīrti, *Commentary*, III:282–287, and *Ascertainment*, D: 4211, 161.a.6–162.b.2.

35. Śākya Chok-den, *Dharma Treasury*, II.548.7.

36. Kuijp, "Early Tibetan View," p. 63.

37. Śākya Chok-den, *Defeater*, II.17.7 and 20.1–.2 as well as *Dharma Treasury*, II.556.4. Sa-paṇ did not seem explicit on this topic.

38. S. U Pandita gives a brief description of such a state according to the Theravāda tradition. See *In This Very Life* (Boston: Wisdom, 1991), p. 204.

Chapter 26. Are External Objects Perceptible?

1. See Chapters 16 and 17.

2. There is here a parallel, familiar to students of Western philosophy, with Berkeley, who claims to base his views on a strict respect of commonsense and yet ends up with completely counterintuitive positions.

3. Ü-ba Lo-sel *(dbus pa blo gsal)* uses this expression while describing external objects (Mimaki, "Le Chapitre, Présentation," 192.24). Mimaki translates it as "invisible" ("Le Chapitre du Blo gsd grub mtha'," p. 147).

4. mdo sde pas don lkog na mo gzhal bya don dang 'dra bar skyes pa'i shes pa tshad ma/ (Sa-paṇ, *Auto-Commentary*, 151.b.2). Sa-paṇ's remarks are part of his brief presentation of valid cognition and its result, a topic we will briefly touch on in the next section.

5. See Śākya Chok-den, *Defeater*, II.4.1–.3 as explained in Chapter 23.

6. rnam nges kyi ṭi ka byed pa snga ma kha cig gis mdo sde pas don lkog na mo khas blangs par 'chad pa ni de'i lugs min te mngon sum da ltar ba'i yul can dang/ rang 'dra'i rnam pa dngos su gtod pa'i phyi rol mngon du gyur par 'dod kyi lkog tu gyur ba mi 'dod do/ slob dpon gyis sems tsam pa'i rnam bzhag mdzad pa'i tshe rnam rdzun pa'i lugs dang/ phyi rol kyi rnam bzhag mdzad pa'i tshe mdo sde pa'i lugs mdzad do/ (Gyel-tsap, *Explanation*, 67.5–68.1).

7. A similar argument is made by Lo Ken-chen, *Sun*, 44.3–45.4. Lo Ken-chen argues that this interpretation corresponds to Dharmakīrti's thought when he stated in his *Ascertainment*: "These cognitive phenomena do not not have (i.e., they have) cognitivity because they relate to [external] objects and because otherwise it would absurdly follow that [external] objects would be unperceived" (rig pa'i chos 'di ni don la reg pa dang mi ldan pa ma yin te/ de don tu sbyor ba'i phyir dang/ de las kyang don rnams ma rtogs par thal ba'i phyir ro) (cited in *Sun*, 45.6–46.1). Hence, for Lo Ken-chen, Dharmakīrti's view is that external objects are perceptible, albeit not directly. This is what *"hidden"* means.

8. Go-ram-ba, *Explanation*, 183.b.5.

9. sngo 'dzin dbang mngon la rang dus su rgyang chad ltar snang ba de shes pa yin la/ de yang rnam bden pa ltar shes pa nyid de ltar snang ba ma yin gyi/ phyi don lkog na mos tshur bzhag pa'i rnam pa snang ba'o/ (Go-ram-ba, *Explanation*, 182.a.5).

10. The difference between perception and conception is that in the case of perception the aspect and the object are similar, whereas in the case of conception they are not.

11. Shah, *Akalaṅka*, pp. 214–15.

12. rang ngos nas rang dang 'dra ba'i rnam pa gtod byed/ (Go-ram-ba, *Explanation*, 178.b.4).

13. dngos su ma rtogs/ (Go-ram-ba, *Explanation*, 183.a.5. and 199.b.2).

14. dpyad na dbang shes kyis don 'dzin pa mi 'thad de/ dbang shes kyis don rtogs pa sogs yul yul can gyi rnam bzhag 'di dag kyang bya byed la ltos nas 'jog la bya byed bden pa ma grub pa'i phyir/ (Go-ram-ba, *Explanation*, 195.a.3–.4).

15. For a searching critique of this distinction within the framework of the presentation of valid cognitions and its effects, see Kay-drup, *Ocean*, III:450.2–.6.

16. dbang shes rnams rang dus na rang gi gzung don 'gags la/ 'on kyang ma gzung ba'i skyon med de/ dbang shes rnams rang rang gi gzung don dang yul yul can du bzhag pa ni/ dbang shes rnams rang dus dang gzung don gyi dus gnyis ka cha shas dang ldan pa'i dus la ltos nas bzhag pa'i phyir/ (Kay-drup, *Ornament*, 151.5–.6).

17. Let us notice, however, that the issue is slightly more complex that one may expect. Gyel-tsap obviously agrees that objects are perceived evidently *(mngon sum du rtogs pa)*. He also holds that objects appear directly. He does not explicitly state this, however. This is so because he understands differently the expression *dngos su snang*, which I have translated as "appear directly" in reference to Go-ram-ba. For the former, this expression means "to appear explicitly," in accordance with his commitment to the distinction between explicit and implicit levels of realization made in Cha-ba's new epistemology. Nevertheless, Gyel-tsap rejects Go-ram-ba's view of mediation and hence we can infer that for him

objects are directly perceived. We should remember Bo-dong's analysis of the five meanings of the word *dngos*: (a) *dngos* = actual in opposition to *btags pa ba* (metaphorical); (b) *dngos* = principal in opposition to *zhar* (secondary); (c) *dngos* = explicit, i.e., clearly indicated by words, etc. *(sgras zin sogs kyis gsal bar mtshon pa)* in opposition to *shugs* (implicit); (d) *dngos* = direct, i.e., without intermediary in opposition to *rgyud* (indirect); and (e) *dngos* = self in opposition to *gzhan* (other).

18. Kay-drup, *Ornament*, 249.3–.4. This argument seems particularly weak.

19. Dharmakīrti, *Ascertainment*, D: 4211, 167.a.4. See later. Presumably, these arguments are only provisional for Dharmakīrti, who ultimately leans toward the Yogācāra view.

20. Dharmakīrti, *Ascertainment*, D: 4211, 167.a.4.

21. Dharmakīrti, *Commentary*, III:335.ab

22. 'o na dbang mngon gyis phyi don grub na/ rnam shes ldog pa las grub par 'gyur/ zhes rtags kyis grub pa'i rgyu mtshan ci yin zhe na/ sems tsam pas sngon por snang ba mthong ba yin/ phyi rol yan gar don yod min/ ces dbang shes la rang dus su phyi rol don du snang ba de dbang shes rang gi gzung rnam yin cing/ de las gzhan pa'i sngon po med par bstan pa na rang dus snang ba de gzung rnam yin kyang de bskyed par byed pa'i sngon po yod de/ gzhan du na sngon po tshad mas ma dmigs pa'i sa phyogs na yang sngo 'dzin mig shes ma 'khrul ba yod par thal zhes tshul gyis sgrub pa yin gyi/ mdo sde pa rang lugs la phyi don mngon sum gyis ma grub pas rtags kyis sgrub pa ni ma yin no/ (Go-ram-ba, *Explanation*, 179.a.4–.6).

23. Dharmakīrti, *Commentary*, III:224.

24. Śākya Chok-den, *Defeater*, II.16.7–17.1. For self-cognition, see Chapters 19 and 25.

25. Śākya Chok-den, *Defeater*, II.19.3.

26. See Chapter 4.

27. Śākya Chok-den, *Defeater*, II.36.5–39.7.

28. See Chapter 4.

29. See Chapter 17.

30. A similar point is made by the Seventh Kar-ma-pa Chö-drak-gya-tso, *Ocean*, I.422.2–.4, in referrence to Dharmakīrti, *Commentary*, III:308–309.

31. Go-ram-ba criticizes Śākya Chok-den's suspicion of phenomenological explanations for cognitive processes. He points out that his rival seems to collapse two meanings of appearance: (1) the ontological one, that is, appearance as opposed to elimination, and (2) the phenomenological one, that is, appearance opposed to apprehension (*Explanation*, 11.a.1–2). Go-ram-ba does not see any compelling reason to deny that universals appear to conceptual cognitions. Go-ram-ba distinguishes two ways in which an object can appear to a cognition: either by casting its aspect *(rnam pa gtod pa)* as external objects do, or by appearing nakedly in an aspectless fashion *(rnam med du dngos su snang ba)* as the objects of self-cognition and conception do (*Explanation*, 15.a.1–.4).

32. Lo Ken-chen ironically describes his adversary, presumably his master Śākya Chok-den, as "a modern Dignāga" *(phyog glang gsar ma)* (*Sun*, 26.4).

33. dang po song tshod kyi gzhal bya ni/ phyi rol gyi don lkog na mo don snang shes pa'i snga logs na yod pa de nyid yin la/ rlom tshod ni shes pa dang dus mnyam par rlom pa'o/ gnyis pa 'bras bu la song tshod ni/ don gyi rnam pa rig pa'i rang rig pa de nyid yin la/ rlom tshod ni phyi rol gyi don rig par rlom pa'o/ (Śākya Chok-den, *Defeater*, II.541.7–542.1).

34. Śākya Chok-den is adopting the view also defended by Kay-drup and Bo-dong, that we cannot know directly that the external world exists. His view, however, is much

more radical than Kay-drup's, for he not only denies that we can see objects as external (like Kay-drup) but that we can see any object at all.

35. *sna tshogs gnyis med su smra ba'i mdo sde pa* (literally, "Sautrāntika proponents of the absence of diversity") are opposed to *gzung 'dzin grangs mnyam par smra ba'i smdo sde pa* (literally, "Sautrāntika proponents of the equal number of held [objects] and holding [subjects]") (Śākya Chok-den, *Defeater*, II.541.1). We will discuss this distinction in the next chapter.

36. de ltar na rjes dpag don rtogs mtshan nyid pa dang/ mngon sum gyis don rtogs btags pa bar 'jog pa'i sna tshogs gnyis med . . . / (Śākya Chok-den, *Defeater*, II.554.2–.3).

37. Śākya Chok-den, *Defeater*, II.497.5–499.1. Śākya Chok-den defines inference as "that cognition which is nondeceptive with respect to its imagined hidden object of comprehension and which newly realizes its real hidden object of comprehension in dependence on its basis, an evidence that [satisfies] the three criteria" (rang gi rten tshul gsum pa can gyi rtags la brten nas song tshod kyi gzhal bya lkog gyur gsar du rtogs shing/ rlom tshod kyi gzhal bya lkog gyur la mi slu ba'i rig pa) (*Defeater*, II.497.5–.6).

38. Although Śākya Chok-den usually deals fearlessly with the most difficult questions, he does not address this reduction of his position to solipsism. Dharmakīrti denies that idealism necessarily involves solipsism. He argues that the inference of others' minds from their behavior is valid within an idealist framework as well as within a philosophy accepting the existence of external objects. Dharmakīrti, *Establishment of Others' Continua (saṃtānāntara siddhi nāma prakaraṇa, rgyud gzhan grub pa shes bya ba'i rab tu byed pa)*. P: 5716.

Chapter 27. Epistemology, Metaphysics, and Religion

1. See D. Jackson, "Sa-skya Paṇḍita the 'Polemicist': Ancient Debates and Modern Interpretations," *Journal of the International Association of Buddhist Studies* 13, no. 2 (1990): 17–116; and "Birds in the Egg and Newborn Lion Cubs," in *Tibetan Studies* (Narita: Naritasan Shinshoji, 1992), pp. 95–114. Also: M. Broido, "Sa-skya Paṇḍita and the Hva-shang Doctrine," *Journal of the International Association of Buddhist Studies* 10 (1987), 27–68; and R. Jackson, "Sa-skya Paṇḍita's Account of the bSam yas Debate: History as Polemic," *Journal of the International Association of Buddhist Studies* 5 (1982): 89–99.

2. Ruegg, "The Literature of the Madhyamaka School of Philosophy in India," in J. Gonda, *A History of Indian Literature* (Wiesbaden: Harassowitz, 1981), p. 90.

3. Mi-pam, *An Explanation of [Śāntarakṣita's] Ornament of Madhyamaka Called "Oral Transmission Rejoicing the Guru Manjuśri" (dbu ma rgyan gyi rnam bshad 'jam dbyangs bla ma bgyes pa'i zhal lung)* (New Delhi: Karmapa Chodhey, 1976).

4. On the three Turnings of the Wheel, see P. Williams, *Mahāyāna Buddhism* (London: Routledge, 1989), pp. 77–80, 96–109, as well as Ruegg, *Buddha-nature*. For a Ge-luk view of the question, see Thurman, *Tsong Khapa's Speech of Gold*. For an emptiness-of-other view, see Hookham, *The Buddha Within*.

5. See H. Richardson, "A Tibetan Antiquarian in the Eighteenth Century," *Bulletin of Tibetology* [Gangtok: Namgyal Institute of Tibetology] 4, no. 3, 5–8; and E. G. Smith, Introduction to *The Autobiography and Diaries of Si-tu Paṇ-Chen* (New Delhi: International Academy of Indian Culture, 1968), pp. 1–17, 8.

6. Ruegg, "The Jo naṅ pas."

7. See Introduction II.

8. Go-ram-ba explains that the proponents of the emptiness-of-other is the "best view of Mind-Only that has not quite reached the Madhyamaka [level]" *(sems tsam pa'i lta ba drag shos dbu mar cung zad ma slebs pa)* (*Distinguishing the View*, 34.4–.5). Nevertheless, Mi-pam, who at least at some level professes an emptiness-of-other view, is quite close to Go-ram-ba, who rejects the same view. Hence, the label *proponents of the emptiness-of-other* covers a vast variety of views, which range from attempts to integrate the third Turning of the Wheel into the Madhyamaka to much more radical rejections of emptiness of self.

9. This mind is empty of being limited and dependent but is not empty of self-identity (*rang bzhin, svabhāva*). Hence, it is called *emptiness-of-other* (Chö-drak-gya-tso, *Ocean*, I.667.1–678.2).

10. sems ni rang bzhin 'od gsal te/ 'dri ma rnams ni glo bur ba/ (prabhāsvaram idaṃ cittaṃ prakṛtyāgantavo malāḥ//) (Dharmakīrti, *Commentary* II:208.c; Ge-dün-drup, *Good Sayings*, 140.3).

11. Dharmakīrti presents yogic perception as an enhancement of inference and, hence, seems to be more a cognitively active mental state than a pure receptivity. See Chapter 25.

12. Here, *aspect* refers to the objective aspect *(gzung rnam)*, whose nature we have explored in the last two chapters.

13. The description of these two views is complicated because the latter is also sometimes called *rnam par med par smra ba*. Since the view of False Aspectarians differs from direct realism, the former should be clearly differentiated from the latter. For an analysis of the differences between these two views from an Indian perspective, see S. Moriyama, "The Yogācāra Refutation of the Position of the Satyākāra and Alīkākāravādins of the Yogācāra School I," *Bukkyo Daigaku Daigakuin Kenkyu Kiyo* 12 (1984), 1–58; Y. Kajiyama, "Controversy between the Sākāra- and the Nirākāra-vādins" and "Later Mādhyamikas on Epistemology and Meditation" in M. Kyota, ed., *Mahāyāna Buddhist Meditation: Theory and Practice* (Honolulu: University of Hawai Press, 1978), pp. 114–43; as well as K. Mimaki, *Blo gsal grub mtha'* , pp. 99–100; *La Réfutation*, pp. 71–72; Tillemans, *Materials*, pp. 41–42.

14. Śākya Chok-den, *Defeater*, II.569.2–.7 and 577.1–579.1. Go-ram-ba describes this view as the best of Mind-Only (*Distinguishing the View*, 34.4).

15. Kay-drup, *Ornament*, 100.1–.2. Kay-drup does not make the distinction between Yogācāra and Mind-Only.

16. Gyel-tsap, *Explanation*, 297.1–.2. Usually, Tibetan philosophers support their claims by providing well-established sources. Thus they avoid the use of oral communication, which is difficult to verify.

17. Gyel-tsap says: "The subject of the debate is the truthfulness or falsity of the appearance to sense consciousness of blue, yellow, red, etc., as extended, having the aspect of color, and covering its many parts which compose it" (dbang shes la sngo ser dmar sogs rags par snang ba dang/ kha dog gyi rnam par snang ba dang/ cha du ma 'dus pa'i go sa gnon pa'i tshul du snang ba 'di dag bden pa dang rdzun par rtsod gzhi yin te/) (Gyel-tsap, *Explanation*, 295.2).

18. Bo-dong, *Presentation*, II.81.3–82.3, 100.3–101.3. Ngak-wang-bel-den remarks that most texts, including those of Dzong-ka-ba, explain the difference as consisting of the acceptance or refusal of the reality (literally, "the thingness," *dngos po*) of the aspect (*Precious Jewel of Clear Thought, Annotations to [Jam-yang-shay-ba's] "Great Exposition of Tenets," Freeing the Knots of the Difficult Points [grub mtha' chen mo'i mchan 'grel dka' gnas mdud grol blo gsal gces nor]* [Banaras: Pleasure of Elegant Sayings Press, 1964], II.23.3–.4).

19. The former as False Aspectarian with Stains *(dri bcas)* and the latter as a False Aspectarian without Stains *(dri med)*. Kay-drup describes these two groups as asserting or denying that the Buddha has some false conventional appearance left in his continuum (*Ornament*, 100.2–.4).

20. Such as Dharmakīrti, *Commentary*, III:217, 330 (quoted by Gyel-tsap, *Explanation*, 294.4).

21. Sa-paṇ, *Auto-Commentary*, 151.b.5.

22. Dharmakīrti, *Commentary*, IV:286.d.

23. Chö-drak-gya-tso, *Ocean*, 674.2–.6.

24. Śākya Chok-den associates these two views with two subgroups of the True Aspectarians: the Proponents of Perceptual Duality (*gzung 'dzin grangs mnyam par smra ba'i smdo sde pa*; literally, "the proponents of the equal number of held [objects] and holding [subject]"), and the Proponents of Perceptual Nonduality (*sna tshogs gnyis med su smra ba'i mdo sde pa*; literally, "proponents of the absence of diversity") (*Defeater*, II.541.1). Śākya Chok-den does not mention the third subgroup often mentioned, the "Half-Eggist" *(sgo snga phyed tshal ba)*, who adopt a position of compromise between the two positions. Kay-drup draws this distinction between these groups. Proponents of Perceptual Nonduality assert that several aspects can appear to a single cognition. The Half-Eggists assert that only a single aspect can appear to a single consciousness. Finally, the Proponents of Perceptual Duality assert that several cognitions are needed to apprehend several aspects (*Ornament*, 99.5–.6). According to Ngak-wang-bel-den, Proponents of Perceptual Duality assert that many cognitions of a similar type *(rnam shes rigs mthun)* exist simultaneously as there are different aspects in the object. According to him, the particularity of Half-Eggists is that they refuse self-cognition and assert that objective and subjectal aspects are successive (*Annotations*, II.210.4–.6, 212.3–.6, and 216.3–.6).

25. Hattori, "Realism," p. 41.

26. Śākya Chok-den, *Defeater*, II.569.2–.7 and 577.1–579.1.

27. See Ge-dün-drup, *Good Sayings*, 214.2–217.2.

28. Ruegg, *The Literature*, p. 92.

29. For a study of the differences in the soteriology of Dharmakīrti and Gyel-tsap, see Jackson, *Is Enlightenment Possible?*, pp. 31–55.

30. For more on this, see van Bijlert, *Epistemology*, pp. 115–20. For a study of the Tibetan reception of this part of Dharmakīrti's work, see E. Steinkellner, "*Tshad ma'i skyes bu.* Meaning and Historical Significance of the Term," in Steinkellner and Tauscher, *Contributions on Tibetan Buddhist Religion and Philosophy* (Vienna: Wiener Studien zur Tibetologie, 1983), pp. 275–84.

31. It would be tempting to say that Dharmakīrti uses with equal opportunism Sautrāntika and Yogācāra views and is not preoccupied by the correctness of either. This easy explanation, however, is contradicted by *Commentary*, III:219, in which the Yogācāra view is presented as true, whereas the Sautrāntika view is only provisional. See Chapter 4.

32. Rorty, *Philosophy*, p. 131.

33. E. Conze, *Buddhist Thought in India* (London: Allen and Unwin, 1962), p. 265. Partial and one-sided as they might be, Conze's remarks are far from absurd. Logic and epistemology have had political implications in India as well as in Tibet. In both cultures, dialectics was developed in relation to public debates, which were important events in which the political authorities took part. In more recent times in Tibet, the Ge-luk school has used the power of dialectics to promote the interests of the tradition. Part of the prestige of this tradition has come from its very strong dialectical tradition, which has gone unmatched by the other traditions in recent times.

34. Let me remind the reader that such a label does not imply that Dignāga and Dharmakīrti were in total agreement on all significant issues, but that their positions are similar enough to allow us to speak of a single tradition of inquiry.

35. Atiśa, *Lamp*, 193.7–12. See Introduction II.

36. D. Jackson, "The Status of Pramāṇa Doctrine According to Sa skya Paṇḍita and Other Tibetan Masters: Theoretical Discipline or Doctrine of Liberation?" *The Buddhist Forum* 3 (1994): 85–129.

37. D. Ruegg, *The Life of Bu sTon Rin Po Che* (Rome: Ismeo, 1966), p. 37.

38. Jackson, "The Status of Pramāṇa Doctrine."

39. Stcherbtsky, *Buddhist Logic*, vol. 1, p. 46.

40. Sa-paṇ, *Auto-Commentary*, 136.a.2–150.b.2.

41. Sa-paṇ, *Auto-Commentary*, 147.b.3–150.a.2.

42. Jackson, "The Status of Pramāṇa Doctrine," p. 21.

43. The short-lived tradition of Bo-dong's followers also stressed the importance of the soterological aspect of Dharmakīrti's tradition.

44. Kuijp, "An Early Tibetan View of the Soteriology of Buddhist Epistemology," *Journal of Indian Philosophy* 15 (1987): 59. See Chapter 25.

45. Gyel-tsap, *Teaching on the Path of Valid Cognition (tshad ma'i lam khrid)*, Collected Works, vol. 5 (Delhi: Guru Deva).

46. Although the significance of this interpretation is quite clear, its origin is less obvious. Steinkellner speculates that the initiator of this religious interpretation might have been Dzong-ka-ba's teacher, Ren-da-wa (E. Steinkellner, *"Tshad ma'i skyes bu."*) Van der Kuijp rejects this idea as lacking evidence. He finds it extraordinary that Ren-da-wa would not be mentioned by Gyel-tsap or Kay-drup (Kuijp, "Studies in the Life and Thought of mKhas-Grub-rJe I," *Berliner Indische Studien* 1 [1985], 75–105).

47. On the implications of Dignāga's hommage, see Steinkellner, "The Spiritual Place of the Epistemological Tradition in Buddhism," *Nanto Bukkyo* 49 (1982): 1–18.

Conclusion: Philosophy as an Education of the Mind

1. L. Wittgenstein, *Philosophical Investigations* (Oxford: Basil Blackwell, 1952, 1984), p. 109.

2. S. Cavell, *The Claim of Reason* (Oxford: Oxford University Press, 1979) and C. Diamond, *The Realistic Spirit* (Boston: MIT, 1991).

3. R. Rorty, "Pragmatism and Philosophy," in K. Baynes, J. Bohman, and T. McCarthy, *After Philosophy* (Cambridge, Mass.: MIT, 1987), pp. 26–66.

4. Gadamer, *Truth and Method*, p. 362.

5. Cavell, *The Claim*, p. 125.

6. Tillemans, *Materials*, p. 34.

7. Candrakīrti's works seem to have been produced during the century that separates Dignāga and Dharmakīrti. Most of the information contained in this conclusion is derived from two excellent works: Siderits, "Madhyamaka Critique II" and Tillemans, *Materials*.

8. Candrakīrti's comments on epistemology do not seem to have received much attention in India at the time (sixth century). Even in Tibet, where, contrary to India, Candrakīrti's ideas are extremely important (from the twelfth century onward), his epistemological doctrines are not given much attention; they are considered to be footnotes on Buddhist epistemology understood à la Dharmakīrti. For example, Ge-luk thinkers mostly

use Dharmakīrti's system when they think about epistemological matters. They certainly know Candrakīrti's position, but tend to prefer the more elaborate doctrine of Buddhist epistemologists. As a result, they tend to minimize the differences between Candrakīrti and Buddhist epistemologists.

9. See P. Vaidya, ed., *Madhyamakaśastra of Nāgārjuna with the Commentary: Prasannapadā by Candrakīrti* (Dharbanga: Mithila Institute, 1960), 23, 28. The reader should also refer to my discussion of the lack reality of objects of commonsense in Chapter 4. There, I argue that Buddhist epistemologists might admit the reality of extended objects such as colors but not that of commonsense objects, which require a conceptual synthesis. To this effect I used Lo Ken-chen's account, which relies on Candrakīrti's critique as it is explained in his *Explanation of [Āryadeva's] Four Hundred on the Conduct of the Bodhisattva Practice.*

10. Siderits, "Madhyamaka Critique II," p. 147. Reprinted by permission of Kluwer Academic Publishers.

11. Ibid., p. 154. Candrakīrti's negative appreciation of the epistemological project strikes one as very similar to the view expressed by Wittgenstein in his *On Certainty* (New York: Harper Books, 1972). There, Wittgenstein undermines any attempt to understand knowledge as proceeding from secure foundations. The validity of human practices is due to their being part of actual contexts in which they have concrete applications. Conventional (to use Candrakīrti's language) practices do not need philosophical validation, which is the expression of a misguided craving for generality. For more on this antifoundationlist stance in contemporary philosophy, see R. Bernstein, *Beyond Objectivism and Relativism* (Philadelphia: University of Pennsylvania Press, 1983).

12. Geertz, *The Interpretation of Cultures.*

13. Candrakīrti briefly states his view on the topic in an argument directed against the teaching of the *Bhagavad Gītā*, in which the use of violence is commended in the performance of the duties of a king. He describes how the four means of valid cognition (perception, inference, analogy, and testimony) establish the existence of nonvirtuous deeds in kings and other beings whose positions in society entail an obligation to use violence (Vaidya, P., Madhyamaka-śāstra, 25.10–.12; quoted in Siderits, "Madhyamaka Critique II," p. 154).

14. This point, contrary to the former, is clearly recognized by Ge-luk thinkers such as Se-ra Jay-dzün-ba and Jam-yang-shay-ba in relation to the concept of mental perception. Candrakīrti seems to support a view of mental perception that is quite different from the epistemologists' idea. Since for Candrakīrti perception does not need to be nonconceptual, mental perception can be conceptual. For Candrakīrti, judgment associated with the senses (as when we think "this is blue" on seeing a blue object) seem to be perceptual. See Tillemans, *Materials*, pp. 286–88, and "Indian and Tibetan Mādhyamikas on *mānasapratyakṣa*." By accepting the existence of conceptual mental perception, Candrakīrti is able to make sense of the concept of mental perception, which is one of the most obscure notions in Buddhist epistemology.

15. Dzong-ka-ba, *Essence of Good Sayings, a Treatise Differentiating Between the Interpretable and the Definitive*, 139.

16. Another relevant point may be mentioned here; namely, that the type of deconstructive philosophy championed by Candrakīrti offers little support for constructive developments. Hence, thinkers interested in some form of (even weak) systematic thought will tend to move away from such an approach.

17. Hopkins, *Meditation*, pp. 539–40.

18. It is interesting to note that Dak-tsang's comments are meant to parallel Candrakīrti's comments in reference to the Buddhist logicians: "In conclusion, when this logician becomes intoxicated through imbibing the brew of dialectics, then, in his madness, he abandons the excellent path known as dependent origination and dependent designation, and completely fails to see through the collection of bad jokes propounding entities which is set forth in the Outsiders' treatises" (Tillemans, trans., *Materials*, p. 179).

19. Go-ram-ba, *Distinguishing*, 41.6–52.3.

20. A similar point can be made in relation to the Ge-luk and Sa-gya use of the notion of aspect, which is taken from Dharmakīrti's epistemology and used while explaining Candrakīrti without much reflection on whether this is compatible with his view. See Chapter 25.

21. Hopkins, *Meditation*, pp. 95–107.

22. Dzong-ka-ba, *Clarification*, 136.20–137.2.

23. Since real existence does not exist, it is not possible to talk about understanding it. It is, nevertheless, possible to identify the notion of real existence, understanding what real existence would "look like" if it existed. This understanding of this putative mode of existence, called *identification of the object of negation (dgag bya ngos 'dzin)*, is considered in to be the most crucial step in the process leading to an insight into emptiness.

24. Ge-luk-ba thinkers hold that according to Prāsaṅgika philosophy all phenomena have no ultimate reality and exist only conceptually. This does not contradict my description of their interpretations of Dharmakīrti as realist. This description refers to their views on the problem of universals in relation to Dharmakīrti's ideas. Ge-luk-ba thinkers hold a different view on universals in relation to Prāsaṅgika. In this philosophy nothing can be said to be real, including universals. They exist nominally in the same way any other phenomena exist. It would be a misunderstanding, however, to describe such a Prāsaṅgika view as conceptualist on the sole basis that universals are characterized as having conceptual existence. Conceptualism presupposes a distinction between real and conceptual entities, which are differentiated from the former as being less real. The Prāsaṅgika view denies this very distinction and therefore cannot be adequately characterized as conceptualism. If anything, a Prāsaṅgika view on universals is a form of realism, for it admits that conventionally universals have the same degree of reality as individual objects. Such a characterization, however, is not completely adequate for the Prāsaṅgika view, since this philosophy seems to want to avoid any ontological commitment to real entities.

25. This description applies only to the Sa-gya interpretation of Madhyamaka. In Chapter 15, we discussed how their understanding of Dharmakīrti's philosophy of language sets forth a weaker ineffability claim.

26. Go-ram-ba, *The General Teaching of the Profound Thought of All the Victors That Completely Clarifies the Definitive Meaning (rgyal ba thams cad kyi thugs kyi dgongs pa zab mo'i de kho na nyid spyi'i ngag gis ston pa nges don rab gsal)*, Complete Works of the Great Masters of the Sa sKya Sect (Tokyo: Toyo Bunko, 1968), vol. 14, 1.1.1–167.3.3 *Ca*, 1.a–209.a., 21.a.2.

27. Go-ram-ba, *Definitive Meaning*, 47.a.3.

28. Go-ram-ba, *Definitive Meaning*, 42.b. Go-ram-ba takes this distinction to be one of the sixteen differences he sees between Svatāntrika and Prāsaṅgika. None of these, however, amounts to a difference in the view of emptinesss. They stem from differences in the way in which the view of emptiness is produced or from differences in understanding the implications of the view of emptiness (Go-ram-ba, *Definitive Meaning*, 102.a.6–103.a.2).

29. Go-ram-ba, *Explanation*, 120.a.1.

GLOSSARY
TIBETAN - SANSKRIT - ENGLISH

Tibetan	*Sanskrit*	*English*
kun tu tha snyad pa'i tshad ma		conventional valid cognition
kun rdzob	saṁvṛti	relative (literally, "concealer")
kun rdzob tu yod pa	saṃvṛtisat	conventionally existent
kun rdzob bden pa	saṃvṛti-satya	relative truth (literally, "truth for a concealer")
rkyen	pratyaya	condition
lkog gyur	parokṣa	hidden; hidden objects
lkog tu snang		to appear in a hidden way
lkog na mo		"hidden"
skad cig ma	kṣaṇika	momentary; evanescent
skad dod		etymology
skur 'debs	apavāda; abhyākhyāna	nihilism; denial
skye mched	āyatana	sense sphere
kha nang lta'i cha		internal factor
kha phyir lta'i cha		external factor
khams	dhātu	elements
khyad par	bheda	distinction
khyad par gzhan spongs		eliminating other characteristics
khyad gzhi		basis of predication
khyad gzhi khyad chos sbyar ba		predication
khyab pa	vyāpti	pervasion; entailment
'khrul rgyu		causes of mistakes
gang zag	puruśa, pudgala	person
gang zag gyi bdag med	pudgalanairātmya	selflessness of persons
gong ma	ūrdhva	vertical
gong ma'i spyi	ūrdhvatālakṣaṇa	vertical universal
grangs can pa	sāṃkhya	Sāṃkhya (a Hindu school)
grangs nges		definitive in number
grub mtha'	siddhānta	tenets; tenet systems
grub dus		time of establishment

Tibetan	*Sanskrit*	*English*
grub bde rdzas gcig		simultaneous substantial identity
glo bur		adventitious
dgag sgrub gnyis tshogs		combination of both affirmation and negation
dgag sgrub byed		to refutate and establish
dgag pa	pratiṣedha	negation
dgag pa rkyang pa		mere negation
dgag bya		object of negation
dgag bya ngos 'dzin		identification of the object of negation
'gal ba	virodha	exclusive
'gal ba'i gtan tshigs	viruddhahetu	contradictory evidence
'gro tshul		criterion; standards
rgyang phan	cārvāka	materialist
rgyu tshogs	hetusāmagrī	causal complex, aggregate of causes
rgyu mtshan	hetu, nimitta	reason; sign
rgyud		indirect
rgyun	saṃtāna	continuum
sgra	śabda	verbal testimony, language, sound
sgra 'jug		explanation of sense
sgra don	śabdārtha	object-indicated by words
sgra spyi	śabdasāmānya	term universal
sgra bshad		explanation of the etymology
sgra'i gzhan sel		verbal exclusion
sgra'i yul ma yin	śabdasyāviśayaḥ	not directly denotable by language
sgras brjod rigs kyi sgo nas dbye ba		terminological division
sgrub ngag		statement of proof
sgrub 'jug	vidhipravṛtti	full (or affirmative) engagement
sgrub pa	viddhi	affirmation
sgrub bya'i chos	sādhyadharma	property of the probandum
sgro btags	samāropa	superimposition
sgro 'dogs	adhyāropa	superimposition
sgro 'dogs bcad pa		elimination of superimposition
brgyud rgyu		indirect cause
bsgrub bya	sādhya	probandum
bsgrub bya'i chos	sādhyadharma	property of the probandum
nges don	nītārtha	definitive meaning
nges pa	adhyavasaya; niścita	certainty

Tibetan	*Sanskrit*	*English*
nges pa 'dren pa		to induce certainty
nges shes	niścayajñāna	ascertaining consciousness
ngo bo	rūpa	entity
ngo bo nges pa	ākāraniyata	determinate with respect to its entity
ngo bo gcig	ekarūpatā	identical entity
ngo bo gcig la ldog pa tha dad		distinct distinguishers within having the same entity
ngo bo tha dad		different entity
dngos	mukhyat	direct; primary; true; principal; explicit
dngos kyi brjod bya		direct or actual signified
dngos dgal gcod pa		preclusion of one's contradictory
dngos rgyu		direct cause
dngos rtogs		explicit realization
dngos po	vastu; bhāva	thing
dngos po stobs shugs kyi rigs pa	vastubalapravṛttānumāna	inference proceeding from the power of facts
dngos po'i gnas lugs		nature of things
dngos med	avastu; abhāva	absence; nonthing
dngos yul		direct object
dngos su rjod		to directly signify
dngos su bstan pa		to explicitly indicate
dngos su snang ba		to directly appear
mngon gyur	abhimukī	evident
mngon sum	pratyakṣa	perception
mngon sum gyi tshad ma		valid perception
mngon sum rtog pa can	vikalpakapratyakṣa	determinate perception
mngon sum rtog med	nirvikalpakapratyakṣa	indeterminate perception
mngon sum ltar snang	pratyakṣābhāsa	pseudo-perception
gcig	abhinna; eka	one; oneness
gcig pa bkag pa'i tha dad		[being] distinct from sg. [in the sense of merely] not being one
bcad don thob pa		to obtain the identified object
bcad shes		subsequent cognition
cha	aṃṣa	part; factors
cha bcas		part owner; whole
chos	dharma	phenomenon; predicate
chos mngon pa	abhidharma	abhidharma
chos can	dharmin	subject; substratum
chos can brjod pa'i sgra		subject expression
chos brjod kyi sgra		predicate expression

Tibetan	Sanskrit	English
'chad pa		[critical/theoretical] explanation
'chad pa'i tshe		from a theoretical standpoint; critically speaking
'jig rgyu	vināśahetu	causes of destruction
'jig rten la grags pa	lokaprasiddha	reknown to the world
'jig pa	vināśa	disintegration
'jug pa		[practical] application
'jug pa'i tshe		from a practical point of view
'jug yul		object of application
rjen par		nakedly
rjes khyab	anvayavyāpti	forward pervasion
rjes 'gro	anvaya	positive concomitance
rjes dpag	anumāna	inference
rjod	vāc	to signify
rjod byed	vācaka	signifier
brjod bya	vācya	signified
gnyis snang nub pa'i tshul gyis rig		cognition of an object in a nondual way
gnyis su med pa'i stong pa nyid	advayaśūnyatā	emptiness of absence of duality [between subject and object]
gtan tshigs	hetu	reason
btags pa ba		metaphorical
btags yod	vijñapti-sat	nominally existent
rtag gcig rang dbang can gyi bdag		permanent, partless, and autonomous self
rtag pa	nitya	permanence
rtags	liṅga	evidence
rtags ltar snang		incorrect evidence
rtags yang dag	samyakliṅga	correct evidence
rten 'byung	pratītyasamutpāda	dependent arising
rtog pa	kalpanā	conceptual cognition
rtog pa can	savikalpaka	conceptual; determinate
rtog pa can gyi mngon sum	savikalpakapratyakṣa	determinate perception
rtog pa dang bral ba	kalpanāpoḍha	free from conception
rtog pas btags tsam		nominal; imputed by thought
rtog med can	nirvikalpakaka	nonconceptual; undeterminate
rtog med log shes		false nonconceptual cognition
rtogs	adhigam	to realize; identify; understand

Tibetan	*Sanskrit*	*English*
tha snyad	vyavahāra	convention
tha dad	bhinna	distinct
thad ka'i spyi	tiryaglakṣaṇa	horizontal universal
thal 'gyur	prāsaṅga	consequence
thug med	anavasthā	infinite regress
thun mong	sādhāraṇa	common
thun mong ma yin pa	asādhāraṇa	uncommon
the tshom		doubt
thogs pa med pa	apratigha	not limited by material obstacles
thob pa	prāpana	to obtain
mtho ris	svārga	[rebirth in] a fortunate condition
dam bca'	pratijñā	thesis
dus nges pa	kālaniyata	temporally determinate
dus ma 'dres pa	kālaniyata	temporally determinate
de byung 'brel	tadutpatti	relation of origination
de ma thag pa'i rkyen	samanantara-pratyaya	preceding condition
dong rang mtshan gyi gzhan gsel	arthātmaka-svalakṣaṇānyāpoha	objective elimination
don	artha	object
don lkog (gyur) na mo		"hidden" object
don gyi cha	arthāṃśa	objective factor in the object
don gyis rtogs pa	arthāpati	to realize by implication
don gcig	ekārtha	equivalent
don gcig la ming gi rnam grangs		equivalent and synonymous
don chos		real property
don mthun	yathārtha	factual
don dam bden pa	paramārtha-satya	ultimate truth
don du gnyer bya		purposeful object
don dam du yod pa	paramārthasat	ultimately existing
don ldog		meaning distinguisher; defining property
don spyi	artha-sāmānya	object universal
don byed nus pa	arthakriyāsamartham	able to perform a function
don smra ba		proponent of real external objects
don rig		cognitions of external objects
don la gcig		one in reality
don la mi gnas pa		not existing in reality
drang don	neyārtha	interpretable
dran par nyer bzhag	smṛtyupasthāna	application of mindfulness
dran shes		recollection
bdag	ātma	self

Tibetan	*Sanskrit*	*English*
bdag rkyen	adhipatipratyaya	empowering condition
bdag gcig 'brel	tādātmyasaḥbandha	relation of identical nature
bdag nyid gcig	ekātman	identity of being
bdag med	anātma	selfless
bdags gzhi		basis of designation
bden grub		real; really existent
'du ba	samavāya	inherence
'dus pa	saṃghāta	aggregate; collection
'dus byas	saṃskṛta	conditioned; compounded phenomenon
'dogs gcod		eliminate doubts
'dra ba	sādṛśya	similar
'dra ba gzhan byung 'khrul rgyu		the arising of similar other [moments] as a cause of mistake
'dres pa		indeterminate; mixed
rdul phran	paramāṇu	atom
rdul rdzas		atomic substance
ldan min 'du byed	viprayuktasaṃskāra	nonassociated compositional factor
ldog khyab	vyatirekavyāpti	negative pervasion
ldog pa	vyāvṛtti; vyatireka	distinguisher; negative concomittance
ldog pa ngos 'dzin		presentation of distinguishers
ldog pa gcig		identitical distinguisher
ldog pa tha dad		distinct distinguishers
ldog pa'i chos	vyatirekadharma	phenomena that exist as distinguisher
sdod lugs		mode of existence
brda	saṃketa	agreed upon convention; sign
bsdus grwa		Collected Topics
nam mkha'		space
nus pa	śaktiḥ	capacity; ability
gnod pa	bhāda	to refute
gnod byed	bādhaka	refuter
rnam mkhyen		omniscient consciousness
rnam 'gyur	parināma	manifestation
rnam gcod	vyavaccheda	preclusion
rnam pa	ākāra	aspect
rnam pa gtod pa		casting an aspect
rnam pa dang bcas par smra ba	sākāravāda	proponent of aspect
rnam par bden par smra ba	satyākāravādin	True Aspectarian
rnam par rdzun pa smra ba	alīkārāvādin	False Aspectarians

Tibetan	*Sanskrit*	*English*
rnam (pa) med (par) smra ba	nirākāravāda	proponent of no-aspect
rnam smin	vipāka	[karmic] effect
rnal 'byor mngon sum	yogi pratyakṣa	yogic perception
rnal 'byor spyod pa ba	yogācāra	Yogācāra
sna tshogs gnyis med su smra		proponent of perceptual nonduality
snang btags gcig tu 'dres		mixing of appearance and denomination
snang ba	pratibhā	appearance; intuitional meaning
snang yul		appearing object
snang la ma nges		inattentive cognition
dpe	dṛṣṭānta	example
dpe nyer 'jal	upamāna	analogy; comparison
spang blang		abandonment [of what is not desirable] and development [of what is desirable]
spyi	sāmānya	universal
spyi dngos po ba		real universal
spyi don gzhan		separate universals
spyi ldog		general-distinguisher
spyi gtso bo	prakṛti	primordial nature
spyi mtshan	sāmānyalakṣaṇa	generally characterized phenomenon
spyod pa ba	mīmāṃsā	Mīmāṃsā
phyin ci ma log pa	avaiparītya	unmistaken
phyogs	pakṣa	thesis
phyogs chos	pakṣadharmatā	property of the position
phrad pa	prāpaṇa	obtain
'phags pa	ārya	noble beings
bag chags	vāsanā	trace; propensity; latency
bems po		gross material object
bye brag	viśeṣa	individuation
bye brag pa	vaiśeṣika	Vaiśeṣika
blo	buddhi; dhī	mind; mental episode
blo chos		mental property
blo rigs		typology of mind
blo'i gzhan sel	buddhyātmakānyāpoha	mental elimination
dbang po	indriya	sense basis
dbang phyugs	īśvara	God; Creator
dbye chos		elements of a division
dbye gzhi		basis of division

Tibetan	*Sanskrit*	*English*
'byung 'gyur	bhautika	[phenomena] arising from elements
'byung ba	bhūta	element
'bras bu	kārya; phala	effect; result
'bras bu'i gtan tshigs	kāryahetu	reason of effect
'brel ba	saṃbhandha	relation
sbyor ba	prayoga	formal argument
ma 'khrul ba	abhrānta	unmistaken
ma grub pa'i gtan tshigs	asiddhahetu	unestablished reason
ma nges pa'i gtan tshigs	anaikāntikahetu	indeterminate reason
ma rtogs pa'i blo		nonrealizing mind
ma dmigs pa'i gtan tshigs	anupalabdhihetu	reason of non-observation
ma yin dgag	paryudāsa	implicative negation; nominally bound negation
ma rig pa	avidyā	ignorance
mi rtag pa	anitya	impermanent
mi 'dra ba	asadṛṣa	dissimilar; specific
mi srid pa	asambhava	impossibility
mi slu ba	avisaṃvādi	nondeceptive
ming	nāma	name; term
med dgag	prasajyapratiṣedha; niṣedha	nonimplicative negation; verbally bound negation
med pa gzhan sel		nonexistent elimination
myong ba	anubhava	experience; presentational apprehension
dmigs rkyen	ālambanapratyaya	object condition
dmigs pa	ālambana	observation
tshad 'bras	pramāṇa-phala	result of valid cognition
tshad ma	pramāṇa	valid cognition
tshad ma gzhan gyis grub pa	parataḥpramāṇa	external (or extrinsic) validity
tshad ma rang nyid kyis grub pa	svataḥpramāṇa	internal (or intrinsic) validity
tshad mar 'gyur pa	pramāṇabhūta	serving as valid cognition
tshad mas dmigs pa		observed by a valid cognition
tshad min gyi blo		nonvalid cognition
tshig don	padārtha	category
tshu rol mdzes pa	cārvāka	Hedonist
tshul gsum	trairūpya	threefold criteria
tshogs pa	samudāya	collection
tshogs spyi		collection universal
mtshan nyid	lakṣaṇa	defining characteristic
mtshan gzhi		illustration
mtshon bya	lakṣya	defined object
'dzin stangs kyi yul	muṣṭibandhaviṣaya	apprehended object

Tibetan	*Sanskrit*	*English*
'dzin rnam	grāhakākāra	subjective aspect
rdzas	dravya	substance
rdzas kyi skye mched		substance in relation to the sense spheres
rdzas gcig		substantantially identical
rdzas gcig la ldog pa tha dad		distinct within being the same substance
rdzas yod	dravyasat	substantially existent
brdzun pa	alīka	illusory
zhan	leśa	influence; weak
zhan rgyab pa		to influence [in a negative way]
zhar		secondary
zhi gnas	śamatha	tranquility
zhen pa'i brjod bya		conceived signified
zhen yul		conceived object
gzhan	para	other
gzhan stong		emptiness of other
gzhan las nges	parataḥprāmāṇya	externally valid cognition
gzhan sel	anyāpoha	elimination of other
gzhal bya	prameya; meya	object of comprehension; object of valid cognition
gzhi	ādhāra	substratum; basis
gzhi grub		established basis
gzhi mthun		common locus
gzhi ldog		basis distinguisher; illustration
gzugs	rūpa	matter
gzugs kyi skye mched	rūpāyatana	form-sphere
gzugs brnyan	pratibimba	reflection
gzung 'dzin grangs mnyam par smra ba		proponent of perceptual duality
gzung yul		held object
bzung rnam	grāhyākāra	objective aspect
bzo sbyor gyi rtags		twisted evidence
bzlog pa	parāvṛtti	exclusion
yang dag pa'i lta ba	samyag dṛṣṭi	correct view
yang dag shes pa	samyagjñāna	correct cognition
yan lag can	anavayin	whole
yig cha		textbook
yid	manas	mind
yid mngon	mānasapratyakṣa	mental perception
yid ches rjes dpag		inference from conviction
yid dpyod		correct assumption
yul	viṣaya	object
yul nges pa	deśaniyata	spatially determinate

Tibetan	*Sanskrit*	*English*
yul can		subject
yul dus rang bzhin gang la ltos·te grub bde rdzas gcig		identical simultaneous substance from the point of view of place, time and nature
yul ma 'dres pa		spatially determinate
ye shes	jñāna	gnosis
yongs grub	pariniṣpanna	perfected nature
yod pa	sat; bhāva	to exist; existence
yon tan	guṇa	quality
rags pa	sthūla	coarse [objects]
rang gi ngo bo la gnas pa	svarūpasthitayaḥ	abiding within their own entity
rang nyid gsal ba	svayamprakāśa	self-presenting; self-luminous
rang don rjes dpag	svārthānumāna	inference for oneself
rang ldog		own distinguisher
rang mtshan	svalakṣaṇa	specifically characterized phenomenon
rang bzhin	svabhāva, prakṛti	essence; own nature; Nature
rang bzhin gyi gtan tshigs	svabhāvahetu	reason of nature
rang las nges kyi tshad ma		internally valid cognition
rang rig	svasaṃvedana/svasaṃvitti	self-cognition; apperception
rigs	jāti	type
rigs mthun pa	svajāti	similar type
rigs pa	nyāya; yukti	reasoning
rigs pa can pa	nyāya	Nyāya
rigs pa'i rjes 'brang gi mdo sde pa		Sautrāntika following reasoning
rigs spyi	jāti-sāmānya	type universal
rung ba	yogyatā	fitness
reg bya'i skye mched		sense sphere of touch
rlom pa		to conceive; to imagine
rlom tshod kyi chos can		conceived subject
rlom tshod kyi rtags		conceived reason
rlom tshod la		from the conceptual standpoint
lam 'bras		path and result [tradition]
lam rim		gradual path
las	karma	action
lung	āgama	scripture
lung gi rjes 'brang gi mdo sde pa		Sautrāntika following scripture
log rtog		false conception
log pa		distinguished [phenomenon]
log shes		false cognition

Tibetan	*Sanskrit*	*English*
shin tu lkog gyur	atyantaparokṣa	thoroughly hidden
shugs rtogs		implicit realization
shes pa	jñāna	cognition, consciousness, awareness; mental episode
shes bya	jñeya	knowable
sa skya		Sa-gya
sa bon	bīja	seed
sa lugs		Sa-paṇ's system
sems tsam	cittamātra	Mind-Only
sel ngo		eliminative point of view
sel 'jug	apoha-pravṛtti	eliminative engagement
sel ba	apoha	elimination
sel ba'i yul can		elimanative subject
song tshod kyi chos can		actual subject
song tshod kyi rtags		actual reason
song tshod kyi gzhal bya		actual object of comprehension
song tshod la		in actuality
gsal ba	vyakti	individual
bsags pa	saṃcita	aggregate
lhag mthong	vipaśyanā	special insight
lhan skyes		innate

GLOSSARY
SANSKRIT - TIBETAN - ENGLISH

Sanskrit	*Tibetan*	*English*
atyantaparokṣa	shin tu lkog gyur	thoroughly hidden
advayaśūnyatā	gnyis su med pa'i stong pa nyid	emptiness of absence of duality [between subject and object]
adhigam	rtogs	to realize; identify; understand
adhipati-pratyaya	bdag rkyen	empowering condition
adhyavasaya	nges pa	certainty
adhyāropa	sgro 'dogs	superimposition
anavayin	yan lag can	whole
anātma	bdag med	selfless
anitya	mi rtag pa	impermanent
anubhava	myong ba	experience; presentational apprehension
anumāna	rjes dpag	inference
anyāpoha	gzhan sel	elimination of other
anvaya	rjes 'gro	positive concomitance
anvayavyāpti	rjes khyab	forward pervasion
apavāda	skur 'debs	nihilism; denial
apoha	sel ba	elimination
apoha-pravṛtti	sel 'jug	eliminative engagement
abhinna	gcig	one; oneness
abhimukī	mngon gyur	evident
abhyākhyāna	skur 'debs	nihilism; denial
abhrānta	ma 'khrul ba	non-mistaken
aṃṣa	cha	part; factors
artha	don	object
arthakriyāsamartham	don byed nus pa	able to perform a function
arthasāmānya	don spyi	object-universal
arthātmakasvalakṣaṇān yāpoha	dong rang mtshan gyi gzhan gsel	objective elimination
arthāpati	don gyis rtogs pa	to realize by implication
arthāṃśa	don gyi cha	objective factor in the object
alīkārāvādin	rnam par rdzun pa smra ba	False Aspectarian

Sanskrit	*Tibetan*	*English*
avidyā	ma rig pa	ignorance
avisaṃvādi	mi slu ba	nondeceptive
avaiparītya	phyin ci ma log pa	non-mistaken
asadṛṣa	mi 'dra ba	dissimilar; specific
asādhāraṇa	thun mong ma yin pa	uncommon
ākāra	rnam pa	aspect
ākāraniyata	ngo bo nges pa	determinate with respect to its entity
āgama	lung	scripture
ātma	bdag	self
āyatana	skye mched	sense sphere
ārya	'phags pa	noble beings
ālambana	dmigs pa	observation
ālambanapratyaya	dmigs rkyen	object-condition
upamāna	dpe nyer 'jal	analogy; comparison
ūrdhvatālakṣaṇa	gong ma'i spyi	horizontal universal
indriya	dbang po	sense-basis
eka	gcig	one; oneness
ekātman	bdag nyid gcig	identity of being
ekārtha	don gcig	equivalent
ekarūpatā	ngo bo gcig	identical entity
karma	las	action
kalpanā	rtog pa	conceptual cognition
kalpanāpoḍha	rtog pa dang bral ba	free from conception
kārya	'bras bu	effect; result
kālaniyata	dus nges pa; dus ma 'dres pa	temporally determinate
kṣaṇika	skad cig ma	momentary; evanescent
guṇa	yon tan	quality
grāhakākāra	'dzin rnam	subjective aspect
grāhyākāra	bzung rnam	objective aspect
cārvāka	rgyang phan	materialist
cittamātra	sems tsam	Mind-Only
jāti	rigs	type
jātisāmānya	rigs spyi	type-universal
jñāna	shes pa	cognition, consciousness, awareness; mental episode
jñeya	shes bya	knowable
tādātmya-saḥbandha	bdag gcig 'brel	relation of identical nature
tadutpatti	de byung 'brel	relation of origination
tiryaglakṣana	thad ka'i spyi	vertical universal
trairūpya	tshul gsum	three-fold criteria
deśaniyata	yul nges pa	spatially determinate
dravya	rdzas	substance
dravyasat	rdzas yod	substantially existent
dharma	chos	phenomenon; predicate

Sanskrit	*Tibetan*	*English*
dharmin	chos can	subject; substratum
dhātu	khams	elements
dhī	blo	mind; mental episode
nāma	ming	name; term
nitya	rtag pa	permanence
nimitta	rgyu mtshan gtan tshigs	reason; sign
nirākāravāda	rnam (pa) med (par) smra ba	proponent of no-aspect
nirvikalpakapratyaksa	mngon sum rtog med	non-determinate perception
niṣedha	med dgag	non-implicative negation; verbally bound negation
niścita	nges pa	certainty
niścayajñāna	nges shes	ascertaining consciousness
nītārtha	nges don	definitive
neyārtha	drang don	interpretable
nyāya	rigs pa	reasoning
pakṣa	phyogs	thesis
pakṣa-dharmatā	phyogs chos	property of the position
padārtha	tshig don	category
parataḥprāmāṇya	gzhan las nges	externally valid cognition
parataḥpramāṇa	tshad ma gzhan gyis grub pa	external (or extrinsic) validity
paramaṇu	rdul phran	atom
paramārthasat	don dam du yod pa	ultimately existing
paramārthasatya	don dam bden pa	ultimate truth
parāvṛtti	bzlog pa	exclusion
parināma	rnam 'gyur	manifestation
parokṣa	lkog gyur	hidden; hidden objects
paryudāsa	ma yin dgag	implicative negation; nominally bound negation
pudgala	gang zag	person
pudgalanairātmya	gang zag gyi bdag med	selflessness of persons
puruśa	gang zag	person; self
prakṛti	rang bzhin; spyi gtso bo	essence; own nature; Primordial Nature
pratijñā	dam bca'	thesis
pratibimba	gzugs brnyan	reflection
pratibhā	snang ba	appearance; intuitional meaning
pratiṣedha	dgag pa	negation
pratītyasamutpāda	rten 'byung	dependent arising
pratyakṣa	mngon sum	perception
pratyakṣābhāsa	mngon sum ltar snang	pseudo-perception
pratyaya	rkyen	condition
pramāṇa	tshad ma	valid cognition

Sanskrit	*Tibetan*	*English*
pramāṇaphala	tshad 'bras	result of valid cognition
pramāṇabhūta	tshad mar 'gyur pa	serving as valid cognition
prameya	gzhal bya	object of comprehension; object of valid cognition
prayoga	sbyor ba	formal argument
prasajyapratiṣedha	med dgag	non-implicative negation; verbally bound negation
prāpana	thob pa	to obtain
prāsaṅga	thal 'gyur	consequence
phala	'bras bu	effect; result
bādhaka	gnod byed	refuter
bīja	sa bon	seed
buddhi	blo	mind; mental episode
buddhyātmakānyāpoha	blo'i gzhan sel	mental elimination
bhāda	gnad po	to refute
bhāva	yod pa; dngos po	to exist; existence; thing
bhūta	'byung ba	element
bhautika	'byung 'gyur	[phenomena] arising from elements
bhinna	tha dad	distinct
bheda	khyad par	distinction
manas	yid	mind
mānasa-pratyakṣa	yid mngon	mental perception
yathārtha	don mthun	factual
yukti	rigs pa	reasoning
yogi pratyakṣa	rnal 'byor mngon sum	yogic perception
yogyatā	rung ba	fitness
rūpa	gzugs; ngo bo	matter; entity
rūpāyatana	gzugs kyi skye mched	form-sphere
liṅga	rtags	evidence
loka-prasiddha	'jig rten la grags pa	reknown to the world
vastu	dngos po	thing
vastubalapravṛttanumana	dngos po stobs skugs kyi rigs pa	operating by the power of facts
vāc	rjod	to signify
vācaka	rjod byed	signifier
vācya	brjod bya	signified
vāsanā	bag chags	trace; propensity; latency
vikalpakapratyakṣa	mngon sum rtog pa can	determinate perception
vijñaptisat	btags yod	nominally existent
viddhi	sgrub pa	affirmation
vidhipravṛtti	sgrub 'jug	full (or affirmative) engagement
vināśa	'jig pa	disintegration
vināśahetu	'jig rgyu	causes of destruction
vipāka	rnam smin	[karmic] effect

Sanskrit	*Tibetan*	*English*
vipaśyanā	lhag mthong	special insight
viprayuktasaṃskāra	ldan min 'du byed	non-associated compositional factor
viruddha-hetu	'gal ba'i gtan tshigs	contradictory evidence
virodha	'gal ba	exclusive
viṣaya	yul	object
viśeṣa	bye brag	individuation
vyakti	gsal ba	individual
vyatirekavyāpti	ldog khyab	negative pervasion
vyatireka	ldog pa	distinguisher; negative concomittance
vyatirekadharma	ldog pa'i chos	phenomena that exist as distinguisher
vyavaccheda	rnam gcod	preclusion
vyavahāra	tha snyad	convention
vyāpti	khyab pa	pervasion; entailment
vyāvṛtti	ldog pa	distinguisher; negative concomittance
śaktiḥ	nus pa	capacity; ability
śabda	sgra	verbal testimony, language, sound
śabdārtha	sgra don	object indicated by words
śabda-sāmānya	sgra spyi	term-universal
śabdasyāviśayaḥ	sgra'i yul ma yin	not directly denotable by language
śamatha	zhi gnas	tranquility
sat	yod pa	to exist; existence
satyākāravādin	rnam par bden par smra ba	True Aspectarian
samanantara-pratyaya	de ma thag pa'i rkyen	preceding condition
samavāya	'du ba	inherence
samāropa	sgro btags	superimposition
samudāya	tshogs pa	collection
saṃketa	brda	agreed upon convention; sign
saṃghāta	'dus pa	aggregate; collection
saṃcita	bsags pa	aggregate
saṃtāna	rgyun	continuum
saṃbhandha	'brel ba	relation
samyakliṅga	rtags yang dag	correct evidence
saṃvṛti	kun rdzob	relative (literally, "concealer")
saṃvṛtisat	kun rdzob tu yod pa	conventionally existent
saṃvṛti-satya	kun rdzob bden pa	relative truth (literally, "truth for a concealer")
saṃskṛta	'dus byas	conditioned; compounded phenomenon

Sanskrit	*Tibetan*	*English*
savikalpaka	rtog pa can	conceptual; determinate
savikalpakapratyakṣa	rtog pa can gyi mngon sum	determinate perception
sākāravāda	rnam pa dang bcas par smra ba	proponent of Aspect
sādhāraṇa	thun mong	common
sādhya	bsgrub bya	probandum
sādṛśya	'dra ba	similar
sādhyadharma	sgrub bya'i chos; bsgrub bya'i chos	property of the probandum
sāmānya	spyi	universal
sāmānyalakṣaṇa	spyi mtshan	generally characterized phenomenon
siddhānta	grub mtha'	tenets; tenet systems
sthūla	rags pa	coarse [objects]
svataḥpramāṇa	tshad ma rang nyid kyis grub pa	internal (or intrinsic) validity
svajāti	rigs mthun pa	similar type
svayamprakāśa	rang nyid gsal ba	self-presenting; self-luminous
svalakṣaṇa	rang mtshan	specifically characterized phenomenon
svasaṃvitti	rang rig	self-cognition; apperception
svabhāva	rang bzhin	essence; own nature; Nature
svārthānumāna	rang don rjes dpag	inference for oneself
svarūpasthitayaḥ	rang gi ngo bo la gnas pa	abiding within their own entity
hetu	gtan tshigs; rgyu mtshan	reason; sign
hetusāmagrī	rgyu tshogs	causal complex, aggregate of causes

BIBLIOGRAPHY

Indian and Tibetan Traditional Scholarship

A-gu Shay-rap-gya-tso *(a khu shes rab rgya mtsho). A List of Some Rare Books (dpe rgyun dkon pa 'ga' zhig gi tho yig).* In L. Chandra, ed., *Materials for a History of Tibetan Literature,* pp. 637–735. Kyoto: Rinsen, 1981.

Atīśa. *The Lamp of the Path to Enlightenment and Its Explanation (byang chub lam gyi sgron me dang de'i bka' 'grel),* D:3947, 3948, P: 5343, 5344. Dharamsala: Council of Religious Affairs, 1969.

Āryadeva. *Compendium of All the Essences of Wisdom (jñānasārasamuccaya, ye shes snying po kun las btus pa).* D: 3851, P:5251.

Bhavaviveka. *Commentary on the Essence of the Middle Way, a Blaze of Reasoning (madhyamaka-hṛdaya-vṛtti-tarkajvālā, dbu ma'i snying po'i 'grel pa rtog ge 'bar ba).* D: 3856, P: 5256.

Bo-dong *(bo dong phyogs las rnam rgyal). Explanation of the Presentation of Buddhist [Views on] Valid Cognition as stated by [Dharmakīrti's] Drop of Reasoning (rigs thig las gsungs pa'i nang pa'i tshad ma'i rnam bzhag bshad pa).* Collected Works, vols. 7 and 8. Delhi: Tibet House, 1973.

Candrakīrti. *Explanation of [Āryadeva's] Four Hundred on the Conduct of the Bodhisattva Practice (bodhisattva-yogācara-catuḥśataka-ṭīkā, byang chub sems dpa'i rnal 'byor spyod pa bzhi rgya pa'i rgya cher 'grel pa).* D: 3865, *Ya,* P: 5266.

Chim Jam-pel-yang *(mchims [*or *'chims] 'jam dpal dbyangs). Commentary on the Chapters of [Vasubandhu's] Treasury of Knowledge (chos mngon pa'i mdzod kyi tshig le'ur byas pa'i 'grel pa mngon pa'i rgyan).* Mundgod: Loling Printing Press, 1986.

Chö-drak-gya-tso *(chos grags rgya mtsho),* Seventh Kar-ma-pa. *The Ocean of Text on the Science of Valid Cognition That Gathers the Water of All the Good Sayings (tshad ma legs par bshad pa thams cad kyi chu bo yongs su 'du ba'i rigs pa'i gzhung lugs kyi rgya mtsho).* Thimbu, Bhutan: 1973.

Dak-tsang *(stag gtshang lo tsā ba). Ocean of Good Explanation, a Treatise on the Establishment of Freedom from Extremes Through Knowing All Tenets (grub mtha kun shes nas mtha' bral sgrub pa zhes bya ba'i bstan bcos rnam par bshad pa legs bshad kyi rgya mtsho).* Thimphu, Bhutan: Kunzang Tobgey, 1976.

Den-dar-hla-ram-ba *(bstan dar lha ram pa). The Account That Establishes That the Teacher Is a Person of Authority; the Jeweled Staircase Ascending to the Palace of Great Happiness (ston pa tshad ma'i skyes bur sgrub pa'i gtam bde chen khang bzang dzegs pa'i rin chen them skas).* Collected Works. Delhi: Guru Deva, 1971.

Devendrabuddhi. *Commentary on Commentary on Valid Cognition (pramāṇavārttika-pañjikā, tshad ma rnam 'grel gyi 'ka' 'grel).* D: 4217; P: 5717(b).

Dharmakīrti. *A Brief Work called "Drop of Reasoning" (nyaya-bindu-prakaraṇa, rigs pa thigs pa zhes bya ba'i rab tu byed pa).* D: 4212, P: 5711.

———. *Ascertainment of Valid Cognition (pramāṇa-viniścaya, tshad ma rnam par nges pa).* D: 4211; P: 5710.

———. *Commentary on Valid Cognition (pramāṇavārttika-kārikā, tshad ma rnam 'grel)* D: 4210, P: 5709, Y. Miyasaka, ed. *(Sanskrit-Tibetan). Acta Indologica* 2 (1971–72).

———. *Drop of Logical Reason (hetubindu, gtan tshigs thigs pa).* D: 4213; P: 5712.

———. *Establishment of Others' Continua (saṃtānāntara-siddhi-nāma-prakaraṇa, rgyud gzhan grub pa shes bya ba'i rab tu byed pa).* D: 4219, P: 5716.

———. *Science of Debate (vādanyāyaḥ, rtsod pa'i tshigs rigs pa),* D: 4218; P: 5715, 364.a.7–400.a.7

Dharmottara, *Examination of Valid Cognition II (prāmānya-parīkṣā, tshad ma brtags pa).* D: 4249, P: 5747.

———. *Explanation of [Dharmakīrti's] Ascertainment of Valid Cognition (pramāṇa-viniścaya-ṭīkā, tshad ma rnam par nges pa'i 'grel bshad),* D: 4229; P: 5727.

———. *Extensive Commentary on [Dharmakīrti's] Drop of Reasoning (nyāyabinduṭīkā, rigs pa thigs pa'i rgya cher 'grel ba).* D: 4231; P: 5730.

Dignāga. *Compendium on Valid Cognition (pramāṇa-samuccaya, tshad ma kun btus),* D: 4203; P: 5700.

———. *Auto-Commentary on the Compendium on Valid Cognition (pramāṇa-samuccaya-vṛtti, tshad ma kun las btus pa'i 'grel pa).* D: 4204; P: 5701.

———. *Investigation of the Object (ālambanaparīkṣā, dmigs pa brtags pa),* D: 4205; P: 5703.

Dzong-ka-ba *(tsong kha pa). Clarification of the Thought, an Extensive Treatise on [Candrakīrti's] Introduction to the Madhyamaka (dbu ma la 'jug pa'i rgya cher bshad pa dgongs pa rab gsal).* Banaras: Pleasure of Elegant Sayings Press, 1973.

———. *Door of Entrance to the Seven Treatises Clearing the Obscuration of [Those Who] Aspire (sde bdun la 'jug pa'i sgo don gnyer yid kyi mun sel).* Banaras: Pleasure of Elegant Sayings Press, 1972.

———. *Essence of Good Sayings, a Treatise Differentiating Between the Interpretable and the Definitive (drang ba dang nges pa'i don rnam par phye ba'i bstan bcos legs bshad snying po).* Banaras: Pleasure of Elegant Sayings Press, 1973.

———. *Extensive Explanation of the Treatise of the Ornament Together with Its Commentaries, a Golden Garland of Good Sayings (bstan bcos mngon rtogs rgyan 'grel pa dang bcas pa'i rgya cher bshad pa legs bshad gser gyi phreng ba).* Bylakuppe, India: Sera Monastery, block.

———. *Extensive Commentary on Mind and Store [Consciousness] (yid dang kun gzhi'i dka' ba'i gnas rgya cher 'grel pa).* In *Collected Works,* vol. 18. New Delhi: Ngawang Gelek, 1975–79.

———. *Extensive Memorandum on Valid Cognition as Heard by the Lord of the Dharma Gyel-tsap from the Lord [Dzong-ka-ba] (rgyal tshab chos rjes rje'i drung du gsan pa'i tshad ma'i brjed byang chen mo.* In *Collected Works,* vol. 14. Delhi: Ngawang Gelek, 1975–79.

———. *Extensive Stages of the Path to Enlightenment. (byang chub lam rim chen mo).* Dharamsala: Shes rig par khang, Block.

———. *The Ocean of Reasoning, a Complete Explanation of the Basic Treatise in Stanzas of the Middle Way, Called Wisdom (dbu ma rtsa ba'i tshig le'ur byas pa shes rab ces bya ba'i rnam bshad rigs pa'i rgya mtsho).* Banaras: Pleasure of Elegant Sayings Press, 1973.

Ge-dün-drup *(dge 'dun grub)*, First Dalai Lama. *Ornament of Reasoning, a Great Treatise on Valid Cognition (tshad ma'i bstan bcos chen po rigs pa'i rgyan).* Mundgod, India: Loling Press, 1985.

———. *Good Sayings on [Dharmakīrti's] Commentary on Valid Cognition (tshad ma rnam 'grel legs par bshad pa).* In Collected Works, vol. 5. Gangtok: Dodrup Lama, 1978–81.

Go-ram-ba *(go rams pa bsod nams sen ge). The General Teaching of the Profound Thought of All the Victors That Completely Clarifies the Definitive Meaning (rgyal ba thams cad kyi thugs kyi dgongs pa zab mo'i de kho na nyid spyi'i ngag gis ston pa nges don rab gsal)*, XIV. 1.1.1–167.3.3 *Ca*, 1.a–209.a. In the Complete Works of the Great Masters of the Sa sKya Sect. Tokyo: Toyo Bunko, 1968.

———. *Distinguishing the View, the Moonlight of the Essential Points of the Best Vehicle (lta ba'i shan byed theg mchog gnad gyi zla zer).* Banaras: Sakya Press, 1988.

———. *The Explanation of the Difficult Points of [Sa-paṇ's] Treasure on the Science of Valid Cognition That Completely Clarifies the Seven Texts (tshad ma'i rigs gter gyi dka' gnas rnam par bshad pa sde bdun rab gsal).* In *The Complete Works of the Great Masters of the Sa sKya Sect*, vol. 12, Tokyo: Toyo Bunko, 1968.

———. *Faultless Commentary on the Thought of the Seven Treatises and Their Sutra Revealing the Meaning of [Sa-paṇ's] Treasure of Reasoning (sde bdun mdo dang bcas pa'i dgongs pa phin ci ma log par 'grel ba tshad ma rigs pa'i gter gyi don gsal bar byed pa).* The Complete Works of the Great Masters of the Sa sKya Sect, vol. 11. Tokyo: Toyo Bunko, 1968–1969.

———. *The Excellent Sun [on] the Meaning of the Words of [Dharmakīrti's] Extensive Treatise on Valid Cognition (rgyas pa'i bstan bcos tshad ma rnam 'grel gyi ngag don kun tu bzang po'i nyi ma).* In *The Complete Works of the Great Masters of the Sa sKya Sect*, vol. 11. Tokyo: Toyo Bunko, 1968–69.

———. *The Perfect Light Explaining the Meaning of the Words of the Extensive Commentary on [Dharmakīrti's] Valid Cognition (rgyas pa'i bstan bcos tshad ma rnam 'grel gyi ngag don rnam par bshad pa kun tu bzang po'i 'od zer).* In *The Complete Works of the Great Masters of the Sa sKya Sect*, vol. 11. Tokyo: Toyo Bunko, 1968–69.

Gön-chok-jik-may-wang-bo *(dkon mchog 'jigs med dbang po). Precious Garland of Tenets (grub mtha'i rnam par bzhag pa rin po che'i phreng ba).* Mundgod, India: Loseling Printing Press, 1980.

Gong-drul-lo-drö-ta-yay *(kong sprul blo gros mtha' yas). The Encyclopedia, a Treatise Compiled from All Vehicles Excellently Teaching the Triple Training, the Treasury of the Scriptures (theg pa'i sgo kun las btus pa gsung rab rin po che'i mdzod bslab pa gsum legs par ston pa'i bstan bcos shes bya kun khyab).* New Delhi: International Academy of Indian Culture, 1970.

Gung-tang Jam-bel-yang *(gung thang 'jam dpal dbyangs). A Ford for the Wise: An Explanation of the Difficult Topics of "Mind and Basis-of-All" (yid dang kun gzhi'i dka' gnas rnam par bshad pa mkhas pa'i 'jug ngog)*, Collected Works, vol. 2. New Delhi: Ngawang Gelek, 1972.

Gyel-tsap *(rgyal tshab). Complete Explanation of the Sūtra on Valid Cognition (tshad ma mdo'i rnam bshad).* Collected Works, vol. 8. Delhi: Ngawang Gelek.

———. *Clarifying the Thought, a Major Explanation of [Dharmakīrti's] Treatise, the Ascertainment of Valid Cognition (bstan bcos tshad ma rnam nges kyi tika chen dgongs pa rab gsal)*, Part I. Collected Works, vol. 7. Delhi: Guru Deva, 1982.

———. *Essence of Good Sayings, an Explanation of [Sa-paṇ's] Treasure on the Science of Valid Cognition (tshad ma rigs pa'i gter gyi rnam bshad legs par bshad pa'i snying po)*. bkra shis 'khyil, n.d.; *rgyalntshab's Rigs gter unambshad*. Kyoto: Biblia Tibetica, 1993.

———. *Teaching on the Path of Valid Cognition (tshad ma'i lam khrid)*. Collected Works, vol. 5. Delhi: Guru Deva, 1982.

———. *Treasure of the Essence of Good Saying, a Commentary on [Dharmakīrti's Treatise] on Valid Cognition, the Drop of Reasoning (tshad ma rigs thigs kyi 'grel pa legs bshad snying po'i gter)*. Collected Works, vol. 8. Delhi: Guru Deva, 1982.

———. *Faultlessly Revealing the Path to Liberation, [a Complete Commentary on Dharmakīrti's] Commentary on Valid Cognition (tshad ma rnam 'grel gyi tshig le'ur byas pa'i rnam bshad thar lam phyin ci ma log par gsal bar byed pa)*. Banaras: Pleasure of Elegant Sayings Press, 1974–75.

Haribhadra. *Commentary on the "Ornament of Higher Realization, Advice on the Perfection of Wisdom" (abhisamayālaṃkāra-nāma-prajñā-pāramitopadeśa-śāstra-vṛtti, shes rab kyi pha rol tu phyin pa'i man ngag gi bstan bcos mngon par rtogs pa'i rgyan zhes bya ba'i 'grel pa)*, D: 3793, P: 5191.

Jam-bel-sam-pel *('jam dpal bsam 'phel). Summary of the Indispensable Points [in the] Presentation of Mind and Awareness (blo rig gi rnam bzhag gnyer mkho kun 'dus)*, n.p., n.d. block.

Jam-yang-chok-hla-ö-ser *('jam dbyangs phyogs lha 'od zer). The Key to Knowledge, Cause of the Roar of the Five-Faced Lion That Destroys the Elephant of Faulty Adversaries, [and] opens the Door to the Knowledge of the Collected Text of the Commentary on "Prime Cognition" (tshad ma rnam 'grel gyi bsdus gzhung zhes bya'i sgo 'byed rgol ngan glang po 'joms pa gdong nga'i gad rgyangs rgyu rig lde mig)*. Dharamsala, India: Library of Tibetan Works and Archives, 1980.

———. *The Blaze of Hundred Lights on Valid Cognition Clarifying the Path to Liberation, a Decisive Analysis of [Dharmakīrti's] Commentary on Valid Cognition (tshad ma rnam 'grel gyi mtha' gcod thar lam rab gsal tshad ma'i 'od brgya 'bar ba)*. Collected Works, vol. 13. Delhi: Ngawang Gelek, 1974.

Jang-gya Röl-bay-dor-jay *(lcang skya rol pa'i rdo rje). Clear Explanation of the Presentation of Tenets, a Beautifying Ornament of the Mount Meru of the Doctrine of the Muni (grub mtha'i rnam par bzhag pa gsal bar bshad pa thub bstan lhun po'i mrzes rgyan)*. Banaras: Pleasure of Elegant Sayings Press, 1970.

Jay-dzün-chö-gi-gyel-tsen *(rje btsun chos kyi rgyal mtshan). The General Meaning of the First Chapter (skabs dang po'i spyi don)*. Bylakuppe, India: Se-ra-jay Library, block, n.d.

———. *The Complete Revealer of Gyel-tsap, an Explanation of the Meaning of the Extensive Treatise, the Commentary on Prime Cognition; Elimination of Qualms with Respect to the Difficult Points of the First Chapter (rgyas pa'i bstan bcos tshad ma rnam 'grel gyi don 'grel rgyal tshab dgongs pa rab gsal zhes bya ba le'u dang po'i dka' ba'i gnas la dogs pa gcod pa)*. Bylakuppe, India: Se-ra Jay Monastery, n.d. block.

Jinendrabuddhi. *Explanation of [Dignāga's] Compendium on Valid Cognition (pramāṇa-samuccaya-ṭīkā, tshad ma kun las btsus pa'i 'grel bshad)*. D: 4268, P: 5766.

Kamalaśīla. *Literal Commentary of [Śāntarakṣita's] Compendium on Reality (tattvasaṃgraha-pāñjika, de kho na nyid bsdus pa'i dka' 'grel ba).* D: 4267, P: 5765.

Kay-drup *(mkhas grub). Ornament of the Seven Treatises Clearing Mental Obscurity (tshad ma sde bdun gyi rgyan yid kyi mun sel),* In *Collected Works,* vol. 10. Lha-sa: Zhöl blocks, 1897; New Delhi: Guru Deva, 1982.

———. *Extended Presentation of Valid Cognition and Its Result (tshad 'bras kyi rnam bzhag chen mo bzhugs pa'i dbu phyogs).* Collected Works, vol. 12. Lha-sa: Zhöl blocks, 1897. New-Delhi: Guru Deva, 1982.

———. *Ocean of Reasoning, An Extensive Explanantion of [Dharmakīrti's] Extensive Commentary on "Valid Cognition" (rgyas pa'i btsan bcos tshad ma rnam 'grel gyi rgya cher bshad pa rigs pa'i rgya mtsho.* Collected Works, vols. 8 and 10. Lha-sa: Zhöl blocks, 1897; New Delhi: Guru Deva, 1982.

Lo Ken-chen *(glo bo mkhan chen bsod nams lhun grub). Sun, an Explanation Which Clarifies the Path of Reasoning, a Commentary to [Sa-paṇ's] Treasure on the Science of Valid Cognition [and] a Commentary on the Thought of [Dharmakīrti's] Seven Treatises and [Dignāga's] Sūtra (sde bdun mdo dang bcas pa'i dgongs 'grel tshad ma rigs gter gyi 'grel ba'i rnam bshad rigs lam gsal ba'i nyi ma).* Reprint of Derge edition; Manduwalla, India: Ngorpa Center, 1985.

Mi-pam *(mi pham). An Explanation of [Śāntarakṣita's] Ornament of Madhyamaka Called "Oral Transmission Rejoicing the Guru Manjuśri" (dbu ma rgyan gyi rnam bshad 'jam dbyangs bla ma bgyes pa'i zhal lung).* New Delhi: Karmapa Chodhey, 1976.

Maitreya. *Treatise in Stanzas of Instructions on the Perfection of Wisdom Called "Ornament for Realization" (abhisamayālaṃkāra-nāma-prajñāpāramitopadeśa-śāstrā-karikā, shes rab pha rol tu phyin pa'i man ngag gi bstan bcos mgnon par rtogs pa'i rgyan zhes bya ba tshig le'ur byas pa).* D: 3786, P: 5184.

Nāgārjuna. *Basic Treatise in Stanzas of the Middle Way, Called Wisdom (prajñā-nāma-mūla-madhyamaka-kārikā, dbu ma rtsa ba'i tshig le'ur byas pa shes rab ces bya ba).* P: 5224, D: 3824.

Ngak-wang-chö-drak *(ngag dbang chos grags). Discourse Differentiating and [Making] Decision in the Tenets of Earlier and Later Tibetan Learned Ones (bod kyi mkhas pa snag phyi dag gi grub mtha' shan 'byed mtha' dpyod dang bcas pa'i 'bel ba'i gtam).* Thimphu, Bhutan: Kunzang Tobgyal, 1984.

———. *Good Sayings Which Bestow the Splendor of Speech and Clarify the Meaning of the Thought of [Sa-paṇ's] Treasure on the Science of Valid Cognition (tshad ma'i rigs gter gyi dgongs don gsal bar byed pa'i legs bshad ngag gi dpal ster).* Delhi: Ngawang Topgyal, 1983.

Ngak-wang-bel-den *(ngag dbang dpal ldan). Presentation of Conventional and Ultimate Truths in the Four systems of Tenets (grub mtha' bzhi'i lugs kyi kun rdzob dang don dam pa'i don rnam par bshad pa).* Banaras: Pleasure of Elegant Sayings Press, 1964.

———. *Precisous Jewel of Clear Thought, Annotations to [Jam-yang-shay-ba's] "Great Exposition of Tenets," Freeing the Knots of the Difficult Points (grub mtha' chen mo'i mchan 'grel dka' gnas mdud grol blo gsal gces nor).* Banaras: Pleasure of Elegant Sayings Press, 1964.

Paṇ-chen Sö-nam-drak-ba *(paṇ chen bsod nams grags pa). A Word Commentary Completely Revealing the Thought of the Extensive Treatise the Commentary on Prime Cognition (rgyas pa'i bstan bcos tshad ma rnam 'grel gyi bka' 'grel dgongs pa rab gsal).* Collected Works, vols. 1 and 2. Mundgod, India: Loling Printing Press, 1989.

Prajñākaragupta. *Ornament of [Dharmakīrti's] Commentary on Valid Cognition (pramāṇa-vārttikālaṁkāra, tshad ma rnam 'grel gyi rgyan)*, D: 4221, P: 5719.

Pur-bu-jok Jam-ba-gya-tso *(phur bu mchog 'byams pa rgya mtsho). The Presentation of the Collected Topics, the Magic Key Revealing the Meaning of the Texts on Valid Cognition, the Small Path of Reasoning (tshad ma'i gzhung don 'byed pa'i bsdus grwa rnam par bshad pa rigs lam 'phrul gyi lde mig las rigs lam chung ba rtags rigs kyi skor)*. Palampur, India: Library of Bkra Bshis Rjongs, block.

———. *The Presentation of the Collected Topics, the Magic Key Revealing the Meaning of the Texts on Valid Cognition, the Middle Path of Reasoning (tshad ma'i gzhung don 'byed pa'i bsdus grwa rnam bzhag 'phrul gyi lde mig rigs lam 'bring)*. Palampur, India: Library of Bkra Bshis Rjongs, block.

———. *The Complete Explanation of the Collected Topics, the Magic Key of the Path of Reasoning Revealing the Meaning of the Texts on Valid Cognition, the Great Path of Reasoning About Signs and Reasonings (tshad ma'i gzhung don 'byed pa'i bsdus grwa rnam par bshad pa rigs lam 'phrul gyi lde mig las rigs lam che ba rtags rigs kyi skor)*. Bylakuppe, India: Sera Jay's Library, block.

Rik-bay-ray-dri *(rig pa'i ral gri). The Flower Ornament of [Dharmakīrti's] Seven Treatises on Valid Cognition (tshad ma sde bdun rgyan gyi me tog)*. Beijing: Institute of Tibetan Studies, 1991.

Śākya Chok-den *(śākya mchog ldan). Commentary on the Entrance Gate for the Wise (mkhas pa'i 'jug pa'i rnam bshad)*. Collected Works, vol. 24. Thimphu, Bhutan: Kunzang Tobgey, 1975.

———. *Defeater of Bad Systems Through the Wheel of Reasoning, an Ornament to the Thought of [Sa-paṇ's] Treasure on the Science of Valid Cognition (tshad ma rigs gter gyi dgongs rgyan rigs pa'i 'khor los lugs ngan pham byed.* Collected Works, vols. 9 and 10. Thimphu, Bhutan: Kunzang Tobgey, 1975.

———. *The Dharma Treasury, an Ocean of Scriptures and Reasonings Ascertaining the Middle Way (dbu ma rnam par nges pa'i chos kyi bang mdzod lung dang rigs pa'i rgya mtsho)*. Collected Works, vols. 14 and 15. Thimphu, Bhutan: Kunzang Tobgey, 1975.

———. *The Explanation of the Essential Definitive Points, an Explanation of [Candrakīrti's] Introduction to the Middle Way (dbu ma la 'jug pa'i rnam bshad nges don gnad kyi ṭīkā)*. Collected Works, vol. 5. Thimphu, Bhutan: Kunzang Tobgey, 1975.

———. *The Extensive Commentary on the Treatise Establishing the Definitive Meaning as One Through Explaining the Distinction Between the Two Traditions of the Great Charioteers (shing rta chen po'i srol gnyis kyi rnam par dbye ba bshad nas nges don gcig tu bsgrub pa'i bstan bcos kyi rgyas 'grel)*. Collected Works, vol. 2 (Thimphu, Bhutan: Kunzang Tobgey, 1975.

———. *A General Presentation of Valid Cognition [Called] "The Magical Diamond Key Opening the Treasury of [Dharmakīrti's] Seven Texts (tshad ma spyi'i rnam bzhag sde bdun gyi bang mdzod chen po'i sgo 'byed par byed pa'i rdo rje'i 'khrul 'khor gyi lde mig)*. Collected Works, vol. 19. Thimphu, Bhutan: Kunzang Thobgey, 1975.

———. *The Luminosity That Clarifies as the Day, the History of the Systems of the Sūtra on Valid Cognition and How Its Treatises Arose (tshad ma'i bstan bcos kyi shin rta'i srol rnams ji ltar 'byung ba'i tshul gtam du bya ba nyin byed snang ba)*. Collected Works, vol. 19. Thimphu, Bhutan: Kunzang Tobgey, 1975.

———. *The Ocean of Music [of] the Speech of the Seven Treatises, an Explanation of the Science of Valid Cognition (tshad ma rigs pa'i rnam bshad sde bdun ngag gi rol mtsho).* Collected Works, vol. 19. Thimphu, Bhutan: Kunzang Tobgey, 1975.

———. *The Presentation of the Turning of the Wheel (chos kyi 'khor lo bskor ba'i rnam bzhag).* Collected Works, vol. 16. Thimphu, Bhutan: Kunzang Topgey, 1971.

———. *The Wish Fulfilling Mountain, a Discussion of the History of Madhyamaka (dbu ma'i byung tshul rnam par bshad pa'i gtam yid bzhin lun po).* Collected Works, vol. 4. Thimphu, Bhutan: Kunzang Tobgey, 1975.

Śākyabuddhi. *Explanation of [Dharmakīrti's] Commentary on Valid Cognition (pramāṇa-vārttika-ṭīkā, tshad me rnam 'grel gyi grel bsahd).* D: 4220, P:5718.

Sa-gya Paṇḍita *(sa skya paṇḍita). Differentiation of the Three Vows (ldom gsum rab byed). The Complete Works of the Great Masters of the Sa sKya Sect,* vol. 5. Tokyo: Toyo Bunko, 1968.

———. *Treasure on the Science of Valid Cognition (tshad ma rigs gter),* vol. 5, *The Complete Works of the Great Masters of the Sa sKya Sect.* Tokyo: Toyo Bunko, 1968.

———. *Treasure on the Science of Valid Cognition (tshad ma rigs gter),* ed. Dor-jay Gyel-bo *(rdo rje rgyal po).* Beijing: People's Printing Press, 1988.

———. *Auto-Commentary to the Treasure on the Science of Valid Cognition (tshad ma rigs gter rang 'grel). The Complete Works of the Great Masters of the Sa sKya Sect,* vol. 5. Tokyo: Toyo Bunko, 1968.

Śāntarakṣita. *Compendium on Reality (tattvasaṃgraha, de kho na nyid bsdus pa).* D: 4266, P: 5764.

Tsul-trim-kal-zang *(tshul khrims bskal bzang). The Beautifying Ornament Explaining the History of Prime Cognition (tshad ma'i lo rgyus dar ṭika mdzes rgyan).* Kyoto: Saṃbhāṣā 7, 1986.

Tuk-je bal-sang *(thugs rje dpal bzang). Commentary on [Sa-paṇ's] Treasure on the Science of Valid Cognition Which Explains the Thought of [Dharmakīrti's] Seven Texts Together with [Dignāga's] Sūtra Called Clarifying the Path of Reasoning (sde bdun mdo dang bcas pa'i dgongs 'grel tshad ma rigs gter gyi 'grel pa rigs lam rab gsal).* Rajpur, India: Sa-skya Center, 1985.

U-yuk-ba *('u yug ba rig pa'i seng ge). Treasure of Reasoning Explaining [Dharmakīrti's] Commentary on "Valid Cognition" (tshad ma rnam 'grel kyi 'grel pa rigs pa'i mdzod).* Delhi: Sonam Gyaltsen, 1982.

Yak-dön-sang-gyay-bel *(g.yag ston sangs rgyas dpal). Radiating a Thousand Lights, [a Commentary] Revealing the Suchness of [Sa-paṇ's] Treasure on the Science of Valid Cognition, a Commentary on the Thought of the Seven Treatises [of Logic] (sde bdun gyi dgongs 'grel tshad ma rigs pa'i gter gyi de kho na nyid gsal bar byed pa rigs pa'i 'od stong 'phro ba, n.d.).* Delhi: 1992.

Vasubandhu. *Stanzas of the Treasury of Superior Knowledge (chos mngon pa'i mdzos kyi tshig le'ur byas pa, abhidharmakośa-kārikā),* D: 4089, P: 5590. Banaras: Ge-luk-ba Press, 1972.

Modern Scholarship on Indian and Tibetan Traditions

Bandyopadhyay, N. "The Buddhist Theory of Relation between Pramā and Pramāṇa." *Journal of Indian Philosophy* 7, no. 1 (1959): 41–78.

———. "The Concept of Similarity in Indian Philosophy." *Journal of Indian Philosophy* 10 (1982): 239–75.

———. "The Concept of Contradiction in Indian Logic and Epistemology." *Journal of Indian Philosophy* 16 (1988): 225–46.

Bareau, A. *Les Sectes Bouddhiques du Petit Véhicule*. Paris: Ecole Française d'Extrême-Orient, 1955.

Barlingay, S. S. *A Modern Introduction to Indian Logic*. Delhi: National, 1975.

Bhatt, G. *Epistemology of the Bhāṭṭa School of Pūrva Mīmāṃsā*. Banaras: Chowkhamba, n.d.

Bhattacharya, J. V., trans. *Jayanta Bhatta's Nyāya Mañjari*. Delhi: Motilal, 1978.

Battacharya, K. *The Dialectical Method of Nāgārjuna*. Delhi: Motilal, 1978, 1986.

Biardeau, M. "La Définition dans la Pensée Indienne." *Journal Asiatique* 245 (1957): 371–84.

———. *Théorie de la Connaissance et Philosophie de la Parole*. Paris: Mouton, 1964.

Bijalwan, C. D. *Indian Theory of Knowledge*. New Delhi: Heritage, 1977.

Bijlert, V. van. *Epistemology and Spritual Authority*. Vienna: Wiener Studien zur Tibetologie und Buddhismuskunde, 1989.

Bilimoria, P. *"Jñāna* and *Pramā." Journal of Indian Philosophy* 13, no. 1 (1985): 73–102.

Bond, G. *The Words of the Buddha*. Colombo: Gunasena, 1982.

Broido, M. "Sa-skya Paṇḍita and the Hva-shang Doctrine." *Journal of the International Association of Buddhist Studies* 10 (1987): 27–68.

———. "Veridical and Delusive Cognition: Tsong-kha-pa on the Two *satyas*." *Journal of Indian Philosophy* 16 (1988): 29–63.

Burrow, "Sanskrit Mā- to Ascertain." *Transactions of the Philological Society*, (1980): 134–140.

Cabezon, J. *Buddhism and Language*. Albany: SUNY, 1994.

Chandra, L., ed. *Materials for a History of Tibetan Literature*. Kyoto: Rinsen, 1981.

Chatterjee, S. C. *The Nyāya Theory of Knowledge*. Calcutta: University of Calcutta, 1950.

Chogay Trichen. *The History of the Sakya Tradition*. Bristol: Ganesha Press, 1983.

Collins, S. *Selfless Persons*. Cambridge: Cambridge University Press, 1982.

Conze, E. *Buddhist Thought in India*. London: Allen and Unwin, 1962.

Dasgupta, S. *A History of Indian Philosophy*. Delhi: Motilal, 1922, 1975.

Demieville, P. *Le Concile de Lhasa*. Paris: College de France, 1952, 1987.

Dravid, L. S., and Dvivedin, V., eds. *Nyāyavārttikasya Bhūmikā*. Banaras: Kashi, 1916–1917.

Dravid, R. R. *The Problem of Universals in Indian Philosophy*. Delhi: Motilal Banarsidas, 1972.

Dreyfus, G. "Dharmakīrti's Definition of Knowledge and Its Interpreters." In *Studies in the Buddhist Epistemological Tradition*. Vienna: Österreichische Akademie der Wissenschaften, 1991, 19–38.

———. "Universals in Tibetan Tradition: A Conceptual Evolution." In *Tibetan Studies*. Narita: Naritasan Shinshoji, 1992, 29–46.

———. Introduction. rGyal tshap's *Rigs gter rnam bshad*. Kyoto: Biblia Tibetica, 1993.

———. "The Yogācāra Philosophy of Dignāga and Dharmakīrti," in collaboration with C. Lintdner. *Studies in Central and East Asian Religions* 2 (1989): 27–52.

———. "Ontology, Philosophy of Language and Epistemology in Buddhist Tradition." Ph.D. diss., University of Virginia, 1991.

———. "Some Considerations on Definition in Buddhism." MA., University of Virginia, 1987.

Eckel, M. D. *Jñānagarbha's Commentary on the Distinction Between the Two Truths*. Albany: SUNY Press, 1987.

Faddegon, B. *The Vaiśeṣika System*. Amsterdam: Mueller, 1918.

Franco, E. "On the Interpretation of Pramāṇasamuccaya(vṛtti) I, 3d." *Journal of Indian Philosophy* 12 (1984): 389–400.

———. "Was the Buddha a Buddha?" *Journal of Indian Philosophy* 17 (1989): 81–99.

Frauwallner, E. "Die Reihenfolge und Entstehung der Werke Dharmakīrti's." In *Asiatica, Festschrift F. Weller*. Leipzig: 1954, 142–154.

———. "Landmarks in the History of Indian Logic." *Wiener Zeitschrift für die Kunde Süd und Ostasiens* 5 (1961): 137–41.

———. "Die Erketnislehre des klassischen Sāṁkhyasystems." *Wiener Zeitschrift fur die Künde Sūdasiens und Archive für indische Philosophie*, 2 (1968): 83–139.

———. *History of Indian Philosophy*. Delhi: Motilal, 1973.

———. "Beiträge zur Apohalehre I." In *Kleine Schriften*. Wiesbaden: Steiner, 1982.

———. "Die Erketnislehre des Klassischen Sāṃkhyasystems." In *Kleine Schriften*. Wiesbaden: Steiner, 1982.

Gangopadhyaya, M. *Vinītadeva's Nyāyabindu-ṭīkā*. Calcutta: Indian Studies, 1971.

———. trans. *Nyāya*. Calcutta: Indian Studies, 1982.

Gnoli, R., ed. *The Pramāṇavārttika of Dharmakīrti*. Rome: Ismeo, 1960.

Goldberg, M. "Entity and Antinomy in Tibetan Bsdusgrwa Logic I and II." *Journal of Indian Philosophy* 13 (1985): 153–99, 273–304.

Griffiths, P. *On Being Mindess*. La Salle, Ill: Open Court, 1986.

Gupta, R. "The Buddhist Doctrine of Momentariness and Its Presuppostions." *Journal of Indian Philosophy* 8, no. 1 (1980): 47–68.

———. "Apoha and the Nominalist/Conceptualist Controversy." *Journal of Indian Philosophy* 13, no. 4 (1985): 384–98.

Gyamtso, T. *Progressive Stages of Meditation on Emptiness*. Oxford: Longchen, 1986, 1988.

Hahn, M., ed. *Nāgārjuna's Ratnāvalī*, Vol. 1, *The Basic Texts (Sankrit, Tibetan, Chinese)*. Indica and Tibetica 1. Bonn: 1982.

Halbfass, W. "More on the Unrepeatability of Guṇas." *Philosophy East and West* 7, nos. 1 and 2 (1957): 57–60

———. *On Being and What There Is*. Albany: SUNY Press, 1992.

Hall, B. C. "The Meaning of *Vijāpti* in Vasubandhu's Concept of Mind." *Journal of the International Association of Buddhist Studies* 9, no. 1 (1986): 7–23.

Harnotte, L. "Lakṣaṇalakṣaṇam in Annaṃbatta's Tarkasaṃgraha and Dīpikā." *South Asian Horizons* (1984): 118–27.

Hattori, M. "Apoha and Pratibha." In M. Nagatomi, B. K. Matilal, J. M. Masson, and E. Dimock, *Sanskrit and Indian Studies, Festschrift in Honor of Danie H. H. Ingalls*. Dordrecht: Reidel, 1980, 61–73.

———. *Dignāga, on Perception*. Cambridge, Mass.: Harvard University Press, 1968.

———. "Realism and the Philosophy of Consciousness-Only." *The Eastern Buddhist* 21, no. 1 (1988): 23–60.

Hayes, R. *Dignāga on the Interpretation of Signs*. Dordrecht: Kluwer, 1988.

———. "The Question of Doctrinalism in the Buddhist Epistemologists." *Journal of American Academy of Religion* 52, no. 4 (1984): 645–70.

———. "On the Reinterpretation of Dharmakīrti's *Svabhāvahetu*." *Journal of Indian Philosophy* 15 (1987): 319–32.

Herzberger, R. *Bartrhari and the Buddhists*. Dordrecht: Reidel, 1986.

Hiriyanna, M. *Essentials of Indian Philosophy*. London: Allen and Unwin, 1949 and 1985.

Hookham, S. *The Buddha Within*. Albany: SUNY Press, 1991.

Hopkins, J. *Emptiness Yoga*. Ithaca, NY: Snow Lion, 1987.

———. *Meditation on Emptiness*. London: Wisdom Publications, 1983.

——— and Lhundup, S. *Cutting Through Appearances: Practice and Theory of Tibetan Buddhism*. Ithaca: Snow Lion, 1989.

Inami, M., and Tillemans, T. "Another Look at the Framework of the *Pramāṇasiddhi* Chapter of the *Pramāṇavārttika*." *Wiener Zeitschrift für die Kunde Südasiens* 30 (1986): 123–42.

Iyer, K. A. S. *Bhartṛhari*. Poona: Deccan College, 1969.

Jackson, D. *The Entrance Gate for the Wise*. Vienna: Arbeitkreis für Tibetische und Buddhistische Studien, 1987.

———. *The Early Abbots of 'Phan po Na-lendra*. Vienna: Arbeitkreis für Tibetische und Buddhistische Studien, 1989.

———. "Sa-skya Paṇḍita the 'Polemicist': Ancient Debates and Modern Interpretations." *Journal of the International Association of Buddhist Studies* 13, no. 2 (1990): 17–116.

———. "Birds in the Egg and Newborn Lion Cubs." In *Tibetan Studies*. Narita: Naritasan Shinshoji, 1992, 95–114.

———. "The Status of Pramāṇa Doctrine According to Sa skya Paṇḍita and Other Tibetan Masters: Theoretical Discipline or Doctrine of Liberation?" *The Buddhist Forum* 3 (1991–1993): 85–129.

———. "Biography of rNgog Lo-tsā-ba." *Tibean Studies*, vol. 1, pp. 372–87. Oslo: Institute for Comparative Studies, 1994.

Jackson, R. "Dharmakīrti's Refutation of Theism." *Philosophy East and West* 36, no. 4 (1986): 315–48.

———. "Sa-skya Paṇḍita's Account of the bSam yas Debate: History as Polemic." *Journal of the International Association of Buddhist Studies* 5 (1982): 89–99.

———. "Matching Concepts." *Journal of the American Academy of Religion* 57, no. 3 (1989): 561–89.

———. *Is Enlightenment Possible?* Ithaca, N.Y.: Snow Lion, 1993.

Jarter, K., *Presuppositions of Indian Philosophy*. Englewood Cliffs, N.J.: Prentice-Hall, 1963.

Jayatilleke, K. N. *Early Buddhist Theory of Knowledge*. Delhi: Motilal Banarsidas, 1963, 1980.

Jhā, G. *Pūrva Mīmāṁsā*. Banaras: Benares Hindu University, 1942, 1964.

———, trans. *Ślokavārttika*. Calcutta: Asiatic Society, 1908, 1985.

———, *The Nyāya-Sūtras of Gauṭama*. Delhi: Motilal, 1912–19, 1984.

———, trans. *The Tattvasaṃgraha of Śāntarakṣīta*. Delhi: Motilal Banarsidas, 1986.

———, trans. *Śābara-Bhāṣya*. Baroda: Oriental Institute, 1973.

Kajiyama, Y. "On the Theory of Intrinsic Determination of Universal Concomittance in Buddhist Logic." *JIBS* 7, no. 1 (1958): 360–64.

———. "Controversy Between the Sākāra- and the Nirākāra-vādins of the Yogācāra School." *Indo Bukkyo Gaku Kenkyu* 14, no. 1 (1965): 26–37.

———. *Introduction to Buddhist Philosophy*. Kyoto: Kyoto University, 1966.

———. "Three Types of Affirmation and Two Types of Negation in Buddhist Philosophy." *Wiener Zeitschrift für die Kunde Südasiens*, 17 (1973): 161–75.

———. "Later Mādhyamikas on Epistemology and Meditation." In M. Kyota, ed., *Mahāyāna Buddhist Meditation: Theory and Practice*, pp. 114–43. Honolulu: University of Hawai Press, 1978.

Kalupahana, D. *Causality, the Central Philosophy of Buddhism*. Honolulu: University Press of Hawai'i, 1976.
———. *Nagarjuna: The Philosophy of the Middle Way*. Albany: SUNY Press, 1986.
Kalupahana, D. J. "Aspects of the Buddhist Theory of the External World." *Ceylonese Journal of the Humanities* 1, no. 1 (1970).
Kapstein, M. "The Purificatory Gem and Its Cleansing." *History of Religions* 28, no. 3 (1989): 217–44.
Karmay, S. *The Great Perfection*. Leiden: Brill, 1988.
Karunadasa, Y. *Buddhist Analysis of Matter*. Colombo: Dept. of Cultural Affairs, 1967.
Katsura, S. "Dharmakīrti's Concept of Truth." *Journal of Indian Philsophy* 12, no. 3 (1984): 213–35.
———. "Jñānaśrīmitra on *Apoha*." In B. K. Matilal and R. Devans, *Buddhist Logic and Epistemology*. Dordrecht: Reidel, 1969.
———. "Dignāga and Dharmakīrti on Apoha." In E. Steinkellner, ed., *Studies in the Buddhist Epistemological Tradition*, pp. 129–46. Vienna: Österreichische Akademie der Wissenschaften, 1991.
———. "*Svabhāvapratibandha* Revisited." *Indogaku Bukkyogaku Kenkyū* 30 (1981): 476–73.
Keyt, C. M. "Dharmakīrti's Concept of the 'Svalaksana'." Ph.D. diss., University of Washington, 1980.
Kielhorn, F., ed. *Mahābhaṣya*. Bombay: BSS, 1892–1909; Reprinted Poona: Bhardakar Oriental Research Institut, 1962.
Kitagawa, H. "A Study of a Short Philosophical Treatise Ascribed to Dignāga." In *Indo Koten Ronrigaku no Kenkyū: Jinna no taikei*, rev. ed. Tokyo: Suzuki Gakujutsu Zaidan, 1973, 430–39.
Klein, A. *Knowledge and Liberation*. Ithaca, N.Y.: Snow Lion, 1986.
———. *Knowing, Naming, and Negation*. Ithaca, N.Y.: Snow Lion, 1991.
Kuijp, L. van der. *Contributions to the Development of Tibetan Epistemology*. Wiesbaden: Franz Steiner, 1983.
———. "Phya-pa Chos-kyi-seng-ge's Impact on Tibetan Epistemology." *Journal of Indian Philosophy* 5 (1978): 355–69.
———. "Studies in the Life and Thought of mKhas-Grub-rJe I." *Berliner Indische Studien* 1 (1985): 75–105.
———. "Miscellanea Apropos of the Philosophy of Mind in Tibet: Mind in Tibetan Buddhism." *Tibet Journal* 10–11 (1985): 32–43.
———. "An Early Tibetan View of the Soteriology of Buddhist Epistemology." *Journal of Indian Philosophy* 15 (1987): 57–70.
Larson, G. J. *Classical Sāṃkhya*. Delhi: Motilal, 1969, 1979.
Larson, J., and Bhattacharya, R. S. *Encyclopedia of Indian Philosophies*, vol. 4. Delhi: Motilal, 1987.
Lindtner, C. "Atiśa's Introduction of the Two Truths, and Its Sources." *Journal of Indian Philosophy* 9 (1981): 161–214.
———. "Apropos Dharmakīrti, Two Works and New Dates." *Acta Orientalia* (1980): 27–37.
———. "Marginalia to Dharmakīrti's Pramāṇa-viniścaya I–II." *Wiener Zeitschrift für die Kunde Südasiens* 28 (1984): 149–75.
Lopez, D. *A Study of Svātantrika*. Ithaca, N.Y.: Snow Lion, 1987.
Malvania D., ed. *Duveaka Miśra's Dharmottarapradīpa (Being a Sub-Commentary on*

Dharmottara's Nyāyabinduṭīkā, a Commentary on Dharmakīrti's Nyāyabīndu. Tibetan Sanskrit Works Series II. Patna: Kashi Prasad Institute, 1971.

Matilal, B. K. "The Intensional Character of Lakṣaṇa and Saṃkara in Navya-Nyāya." *Indo-Iranian Journal* 8, no. 2 (1964): 85–95.

———. *Epistemology, Logic and Grammar in Indian Philosophical Analysis.* The Hague: Mouton, 1971.

———. *Logic, Language and Reality.* Delhi: Motilal Banarsidas, 1985.

———. *Logical and Ethical Issues of Religious Belief.* Calcutta: University of Calcutta, 1982.

———. *Perception.* Clarendon, 1986.

———. *The Navya-Nyāya Doctrine of Negation.* Cambridge, Mass.: Harvard University Press, 1968.

———. "Review of C. Goekoop, the Logic of Invariable Concomitance in the Tattvacintāmani." *JAOS* 92, no. 1 (1972): 169–73.

——— and Devans, R. *Buddhist Logic and Epistemology.* Dordrecht: Reidel, 1969.

Matsumoto, S. "Svabhāvapratibandha." *Indogaku Bukkyogaku Kenkyū* 30 (1981): 498-94.

Mikogami, E. "Some Remarks on the Concept of Arthakriyā." *Journal of Indian Philosophy* 7, no. 1 (1979).

———. "The Problem of Verbal Testimony in Yogācāra Buddhism." *Bukkyotaku kenkyu* 32 and 33 (1977).

Mimaki, K. *La Refutation Bouddhique de la Permanence des Choses et la Preuve de la Momentaneite des Choses.* Paris: Institut de Civilisation Indienne, 1976.

———. *Le Chapitre du Blo gsal grub mtha' sur les Sautrāntika (Présentation et édition).* Kyoto: Zinbun Kagaku Kenkyusyo, 1979.

———. *Le Chapitre du Blo gsal grub mtha' sur les Sautrāntika (Un essai de traduction).* Kyoto: Zinbun Kagaku Kenkyusyo, 1980.

———. *Blo gsal grub mtha'.* Kyoto: Zinbun Kagaku Kenkyusyo, 1982.

Miyasaka, Y., ed. *Pramāṇavārttika-kārikā (Sanskrit-Tibetan).* Tokyo: *Acta Indologica* 2, 1971–1972.

Mohanty, J. N. "Understanding Some Ontological Differences in Indian Philosophy." *Journal of Indian Philosophy* 8, no. 3 (1980): 205–17.

———. *Gaṅgeṣa's Theory of Truth.* Delhi: Motilal, 1966, 1989.

———. *Reason and Tradition in Indian Thought.* Oxford: Clarendon Press, 1992.

Mookerjee, S. *The Buddhist Philosophy of Universal Flux.* Delhi: Motilal Banarsidas, 1935, 1980.

——— and Nagasaki, H. *The Pramāṇavārttikam of Dharmakīrti.* Nalanda, India: Nava Nālandā Mahāvihāra, 1964.

Moriyama, S. "The Yogācāra Refutation of the Position of the Satyākāra and Alīkākāravādins of the Yogācāra School I." *Bukkyo Daigaku Daigakuin Kenkyu Kiyo* 12 (1984): 1–58.

Nagasaki, H. "Perception in Pre-Dignāga Buddhist Texts." In *Studies in the Buddhist Epistemological Tradition.* Vienna: Österreichische Akademie der Wissenschaften, 1991, 221–26.

Nagatomi, M. "A Study of Dharmakīrti's Pramāṇavārttka." Ph.D. diss., Harvard University, 1957.

———. "Arthakriyā." *The Adyar Library Bulletin* 31–32(1967–68): 52–72.

Nagatomi, M., Matilal, B. K., Masson, J. M., and Dimock, E. *Sanskrit and Indian Studies, Festschrift in Honor of Danie H. H. Ingalls.* Dordrecht: Reidel, 1980.

Napper, E. *Dependent Arising and Emptiness.* London: Wisdom Publications, 1989.
———. *Mind in Tibetan Buddhism.* Ithaca, N.Y.: Snow Lion, 1981.
Newland, G. "The Two Truths." Ph.D. diss., University of Virginia, 1988.
Nyanaponika Thera, *The Heart of Buddhist Meditation.* London: Rider, 1969.
Onoda, S. "The Chronology of the Abbatial Successions of the Gsang Phu Sne'u Thog Monastery." *Wiener Zeitschrif für die Kunde Südasiens* 33 (1989): 203–13.
Perdue, D. *Debate in Tibetan Buddhism.* Ithaca, N.Y.: Snow Lion, 1993.
Philips, S. "Dharmakīrti on Sensation and Causal Efficiency." *Journal of Indian Philosophy* 15, no. 3 (1987): 221–59.
Pind, O. "Dignāga on *śabdasāmānya* and *śabdaviśeṣa.*" *Studies in the Buddhist Epistemological Tradition.* Vienna: Österreichische Akademie der Wissenschaften, 1991, 268–80.
Potter, K. "Are the Vaiśeṣika 'Guṇas' Qualities?" *Philosophy East and West* 4, no. 3 (1954): 259–64.
———. "More on the Unrepeatability of Guṇas." *Philosophy East and West* 7, no. 1 and 2 (1957): 57–60.
———. *Presuppositions of Indian Philosophy.* Englewood Cliffs, N.J.: Prentice-Hall, 1963.
———. "The Background of Skepticism East and West." *Journal of Indian Philosophy* 3 (1975): 299–313.
———. *Indian Metaphysics and Epistemology.* Princeton, N.J.: Princeton University Press, 1977.
———. "Does Indian Epistemology Concern Justified True Belief?" *Journal of Indian Philosophy* 12 (1984).
Poussin, L. de la Vallée, ed. *Mūlamadhyamakākarikās de Nagarjuna.* Osnabruck: Biblio Verlag, 1970.
———. *L'Abhidharmakoça de Vasubandhu.* Brussels: Institut Belge des Hautes Etudes Chinoises, 1971.
———, ed. *Mūlamadhyamakakārikās.* Osnabrück: Biblio, 1964.
Pradhan, P., ed. *Abhidharmakośabhāṣyam of Vasubandhu.* Patna: Jayaswal Institute, 1975.
Radhakrishnan, S., and Moore, C. *A Sourcebook in Indian Philosophy.* Princeton, N.J.: Princeton University Press, 1957, 1973.
Rahula, W. *Le Compenium de la Super-Doctrine (Abhidharma-sammuccaya d' Asaṅga).* Paris: Ecole d' Extreme Orient, 1971
Raja, K. *Indian Theories of Meaning.* Madras: The Adyar Library, 1963.
Raja, K. K. "*Apoha* Theory and Pre-Dignāga Views on Sentence-Meaning." In B. K. Matilal and R. Devans, *Buddhist Logic and Epistemology*, pp. 185–91. Dordrecht: Reidel, 1969.
Renou, L. *Terminologie Grammaticale du Sanskrit.* Paris: Librairie Ancienne Honoré Champion, 1957.
Richardson, H. "A Tibetan Antiquarian in the Eighteenth Century." *Bulletin of Tibetology* [Gangtok: Namgyal Institute of Tibetology] 4, no. 3: 5–8.
Roerich, G., trans. *The Blue Annals.* Delhi: Motilal, 1949, 1979.
Rogers, K. "Tibetan Logic." M.A. diss., University of Virginia, 1980.
Ruegg, D. S. *La Théorie du Tathāgathagarbha et du Gotra.* Paris: École d'Extreme Orient, 1969.
———. "The Jo naṅ pas: A School of Buddhist Ontologists According to the *Grub mtha' śel gyi me long.*" *Journal of the American Oriental Society* 83 (1963): 73–91.

———. *The Life of Bu sTon Rin Po Che*. Rome: Ismeo, 1966.

———. *Le Traité du Tathāgatagarbha de Bu ston rin chen grub*. Paris: Ecole Française d'Extrême-Orient, 1973.

———. "The Uses of the Four Points of the *Catuṣkoti* and the Problem of the Description of Reality in Mahāyāna Buddhism." *Journal of Indian Philosophy* 5 (1977): 1–71.

———. "On the Reception and Early History of the dbu ma (Madhyamaka) in Tibet." In M. Aris and A. Suu Kyi, eds., *Tibetan Studies in Honor of Hugh Richardson*. New Delhi: Vikas, 1980, 277–79.

———. "The Literature of the Madhyamaka School of Philosophy in India." In J. Gonda, *A History of Indian Literature*. Wiesbaden: Harassowitz, 1981.

———. *Buddha-Nature, Mind and the Problem of Gradualism in a Comparative Perspective*. London: School of Oriental and African Studies, 1989.

Sāṅkrtyāyana, R., ed. "Pramāṇavārttikavṛtti of Manorathanandin." *Journal of the Bihar and Orissa Research Society* 24 (1938).

———, ed. *Pramāṇavārtika with Prajñākaragupta's Commentary*. Patna: Kashi Prasad Institute, 1953.

Śāstri, P., and Śukla, H., ed. *Nyāyabhāṣya*. Banaras: Kashi Sanskrit Series, 1983.

Scharf, P. "The Denotation of Generic Terms in ancient Indian Grammar, Nyāya, and Mīmāṃsā." Ph.D. diss., University of Pennsylvania, 1990.

Scherrer-Schaub, C. *Yuktiṣaṣtikāvṛtti*. Brusseles: Institut des Hautes Etudes Chinoises, 1991.

Schmithausen, L. "On the Problem of the Relation of Spiritual Practice and Philosophical Theory in Buddhism." In *German Scholars on India*. Bombay: Nachiketa, 1976.

Shah, N. *Akalaṅka's Criticism of Dharmakīrti's Philosophy*. Ahmedabad: Institute of Indology, 1967.

Shakaba, T. *Tibet, a Political History*. New York: Potala, 1984.

Sharma, C. *A Critical Survey of Indian Philosophy*. Delhi: Motilal, 1960, 1991.

Sharma, D. "Epistemological Negative Dialectics of Indian Logic—*Abhāva* versus *Anupalabdhi*." *Indo-Iranian Journal* 9, no. 4 (1966): 291–300.

———. *The Differentiation Theory of Meaning in Indian Logic*. The Hague: Mouton, 1969.

Shastri, D. *Pramāṇa-vārttika of Acharya Dharmakīrti with the Commentary "Vṛtti" of Acharya Manorathnandin*. Banaras: Bhauddha Bharati, 1968.

Shastri, D.N., *The Philosophy of Nyāya-Vaiśeṣika and Its Conflict with the Buddhist Dignaga School*. Delhi: Bharatyiya Vidya Prakashan, 1976.

Shastri, S. D. *Tattvasaṃgraha of Ācārya Śāntarakṣita with the Pañjikā*. Banaras: Bauddha Bharati Series, 1968.

Shaw, J. L. "Negation and the Buddhist Theory of Meaning." *Journal of Indian Philsophy* 6, no. 1 (1978): 59–77.

Shirasaki, K. "The Sugatamatavibhaṅgabhāsya of Jītari." *Bulletin of Kobe Women's University* 17, no. 1 (1984): 77–107.

Siderits, M. "Madhyamaka Critique of Epistemology I and II." *Journal of Indian Philosophy* 8 (1980): 307–35 and 9 (1981): 121–60.

———. "More Things in Heaven and Earth." *Journal of Indian Philosophy* 10, no. 2 (1982): 186–208.

———. "Was Śāntarakṣita a Positivist?" In B. K. Matilal and R. Devans, *Buddhist Logic and Epistemology*. Dordrecht: Reidel, 1969, 193–205.

———. "Sentence Meaning and Apoha." *Journal of Indian Philosophy* 13, no. 2 (1985): 133–51.

Sinha, J. *Indian Psychology.* Delhi: Motilal Banarsidas, 1958, 1985.

Smith, E. G. Introduction. *Kongtrul's Encyclopedia of Indo-Tibetan Culture.* New Delhi: International Academy of Indian Culture, 1970.

———. Introduction. *The Autobiography and Diaries of Si-tu Paṇ-Chen.* New Delhi: International Academy of Indian Culture, 1968, 1–17.

———. Introduction. *Tshad ma rigs gter gyi 'grel ba'i rnam bshad rigs lam gsal ba'i nyi ma.* Gangtok: Sonam Kazi, 1970, 1–12.

———. Preface. *The Autobiographical Reminiscences of Ngag-dBang-dPal-bZang.* Gangtok: Sonam Kazi, n.d.

Staal, J. F. "Negation and the Law of Contradiction in Indian Thought." *Bulletin of the School of Oriental and African Studies* 25, no. 1 (1962).

———. "The Theory of Definition in Indian Logic." *Journal of the American Oriental Society* 81 (1961): 121–26.

Stcherbatsky, T., and Obermiller, E., ed. *Abhisamayalamkara.* Osnabrück: Biblio Verlag, 1970.

Stcherbatsky, T. *Buddhist Logic.* Leningrad, 1930; New York: Dover, 1962.

———. *La Théorie de la Connaissance et la Logique chez les Bouddhistes Tardifs.* Paris: Geuthner, 1926.

Steinkellner, E. *Dharmakīrti's Hetubinduḥ.* Vienna: Österreichische Akademie der Wissenschaften, 1967.

———. "Die Entwicklung des Kśanikatvānumāna bei Dharmakīrti." *Wiener Zeitschrift für die Kunde Süd- und Ostasiens* 12–13 (1968–69): 361–77.

———. "Miszellen zur erketnntnistheorisch-logischen Schule des Buddhismus I. zur Datierung Karnakagomin's." *Wiener Zeitschrift für die Kunde Südasiens* 23 (1979): 141–50.

———. "Philological Remarks on Śākyamati's Pramāṇavārttika." In *Studien zum Jaismus and Buddhismus, Gedenkschrift für Ludwig Alsdorf.* Wiesbaden: Steiner, 1981, 283–95.

———. "Wirklichkeit und Begriff bei Dharmakīrti." *Wiener Zeitschriift für die Kunde Südasiens* 15 (1971): 179–210.

———. *Dharmakīrti's Pramāṇaviniścayaḥ II. Svārthānumana Teil I.* Vienna: Verlag der Österreichishen Akademie der Wissenschaften, 1973.

———. "On the Interpretation of the Svabhāvahetu." *Wiener Zeitschrift für die Kunde Südasiens* 18 (1974): 117–29.

———. *Verse-Index of Dharmakīrti's Works.* Vienna: Arbeitkreis für Tibetsische and Buddhistische Studien, 1977.

———. *Dharmakīrti's Pramāṇaviniścayaḥ II. Svārthānumana Teil I.* Vienna: Verlag der Österreichishen Akademie der Wissenschaften, 1979.

———. "The Spiritual Place of the Epistemological Tradition in Buddhism." *Nanto Bukkyo* 49 (1982): 1–18.

———. "*Tshad ma'i skyes bu.* Meaning and Historical Significance of the Term." In E. Steinkellner and H. Tauscher, *Contributions on Tibetan Buddhist Religion and Philosophy.* Vienna: Wiener Studien zur Tibetologie, 1983.

———. "Is Dharmakīrti a Mādhyamika?" In D. S. Ruegg and L. Schmitthausen, *Earliest Buddhism and Madhyamaka.* Leiden: Brill, 1990.

———. "The Logic of the *svabhāvahetu* in Dharmakīrti's Vādanyāya." In *Studies in the Buddhist Epistemological Tradition.* Vienna: Österreichische Akademie der Wissenschaften, 1991, 311–24.

———. "Early Tibetan Ideas on the Ascertainment of Validity." In *Tibetan Studies*. Narita: Naritasan Shinshoji, 1992, 245–56.

——— and Tauscher, H. *Contributions on Tibetan Buddhist Religion and Philosophy*. Vienna: Wiener Studien zur Tibetologie, 1983.

Stewart, B. "A Translation and Introduction to the 'Direct Perception' Chapter of Go-rams-pa's *Sde Bdun Mdo*." Ph.D. diss., Columbia University, 1983.

Stoddard, H. *Le Mendiant de L'Amdo*. Paris: Société d'Ethnographie, 1985.

Thakur, A. *Jñānaśrīmitranibandhāvali*. Patna: Kashi Prasad Institut, 1959.

Thurman, R. *Life and Teachings of Tsong Khapa*. Dharamsala: Library of Tibetan Works and Archives, 1982.

———. *Tsong Khapa's Speech of Gold in the Essence of True Eloquence*. Princeton, N.J.: Princeton University Press, 1984.

Tillemans, T. "The 'Neither One nor Many' Argument and Its Tibetan Interpretations." In E. Steinkellner and H. Tauscher, *Contributions on Tibetan Buddhist Religion and Philosophy*. Vienna: Wiener Studien zur Tibetologie, 1983, 305–17.

———. "On a Recent Work on Tibetan Buddhist Epistemology." *Asiatische Studien* 28, no. 1 (1984): 59–66.

———. "Sur le Pararthanumana en Logique Bouddhique." *Asiatische Studien* 38, no. 2 (1984): 73–99.

———. "On Scriptural Authority." In *Felicitation Volume for Professor A. Uno*. Tetsugaku, 1986, 31–47.

———. "Identity and Referential Opacity in Tibetan Apoha Theory." In B. K. Matilal and R. Devans, *Buddhist Logic and Epistemology*. Dordrecht: Reidel, 1989, 207–27.

———. "Indian and Tibetan Mādhyamikas on *mānasapratyakṣa*." *Tibet Journal* 14, no. 1 (1989): 70–85.

———. "Formal and Semantic Aspects on Tibetan Buddhist Debate Logic." *Journal of Indian Philosophy* 17 (1989): 265–97.

———. *Materials for the Study of Āryadeva, Dharmapāla and Candrakīrti*. Vienna: Arbeittais für die Tibetische und Buddhistische Studien, 1990.

———. "Dharmakīrti on Some Sophisms." In *Studies in the Buddhist Epistemological Tradition*. Vienna: Österreichische Akademie der Wissenschaften, 1991, 403–18.

———. "Pramāṇa-vārttika IV (3)." *Etudes Asiatiques* 46, no. 1 (1993): 437–67.

——— and Tomabechi, T. "Le *dBu ma'i byung tshul de Śākya mchog-ldan*," *Asiatische Studien* 49, no. 4 (1995): 891–918.

Tosaki, H. *Bukkyo-Nishikiron no Kenkyū I and II*. Tokyo: Daito-shuppan-sha, 1979, 1985.

Tshul khrims skal bzang. "A History of Logical Studies in Tibet" *(tshad ma'i lo rgyus dar ḍika mdzes rgyan)*. *Saṃbhāsā* 7 (1986): 55–96.

Tucci, G. *The Religions of Tibet*. London: Routledge and Kegan, 1980.

U Pandita, S. *In This Very Life*. Boston: Wisdom, 1991.

Ueda, Y. "Two Main Stream of Thought in Yogācāra Philosophy." *Philosophy East and West* 17 (1967): 155–65.

Ui, H. *Vaiśeshika Philosophy*. Banaras: Chowkhamba, 1962.

Vaidya, P., ed. *Madhyamakaśāstra of Nāgārjuna with the Commentary: Prasannapadā by Candrakīrti*. Dharbanga: Mithila Institute, 1960.

Vetter, T. *Erketnisprobleme bei Dharmakīrti*. Vienna: Österreichischen Akademie der Wissenschaften, 1964.

———. *Dharmakīrti's Pramāṇaviniścayaḥ 1. Kapitel: Pratyakśam*. Vienna: Österreichische Akademie der Wissenschaften, 1966.

———. "Der Buddha und Seine Lehre in Dharmakīrtis Pramāṇavārttika," *Wiener Studien zur Tibetologie und Buddhismuskunde*, 1984, 12.
Vidhyabhusana, S. C. *A History of Indian Logic*. Delhi: Motilal Banarsidas, 1970, 1978.
Warder, A. K. "Objects." *Journal of Indian Philosophy* 3 (1975): 355–61.
———. *Indian Buddhism*. Delhi: Motilal Banarsidas, 1970.
Wayman, A. "Yogācāra and the Buddhist Logicians." *Journal of the International Association of Buddhist Studies* 2 (1979): 65–78.
Williams, P. "Tsong Kha pa on *kun dzob bden pa*." In M. Aris and Aung San Suu Kyi, eds., *Tibetan Studies in Honour of Hugh Richardson*. Warminster, England: Aris and Phillips, 1979, 325–35.
———. "Some Aspects of Language and Construction in the Madhyamaka." *Journal of Indian Philosophy* 8 (1980): 1–45.
———. "On the Abhidharma Ontology." *Journal of Indian Philosophy* 9 (1981): 227–57.
———. "Silence and Truth." *Tibet Journal* 1 (1981): 67–80.
———. "On Rang Rig." In E. Steinkellner and H. Tauscher, *Contributions on Tibetan Buddhist Religion and Philosophy*. Vienna: Wiener Studien zur Tibetologie, 1983.
———. *Mahāyāna Buddhism*. London: Routledge, 1989.
Willis, J. *On Knowing Reality*. New York: Columbia University Press, 1979.
Wilson, J. "The Meaning of Mind in the Mahāyāna Buddhist Philosophy of Mind-Only (cittamatra): A Study of of a Presentation by the Tibetan Scholar Gung-tang Jam-bay-yang." Ph.D. diss., University of Virginia, 1991.
Wood, J., trans. *The Yoga-System of Patañjali*. Delhi: Motilal, 1912, 1988.
Zwilling, L. "Dharmakīrti on Apoha." Ph.D. diss., University of Wisconsin, 1976.

Western Thought

Anscombe, G., and Geach, P. *Three Philosophers*. Ithaca, N.Y.: Cornell University Press, 1961.
Ayer, A. J. *The Central Questions of Philosophy*. London: 1973.
———. *The Foundations of Empirical Knowledge*. London: Macmillan, 1940.
Baynes, K., Bohman, J., and McCarthy, T. *After Philosophy*. Cambridge, Mass.: MIT Press, 1987.
Bennett, J. F. *Locke, Berkeley, Hume: Central Themes*. Oxford: Oxford University Press, 1971.
Berkeley, G. "Principles of Human Knowledge." In *Principles, Dialogues and Philosophical Correspondence*. New York: Bobbs-Merrill, 1965.
Bernstein, R. *Beyond Objectivism and Relativism*. Philadelphia: University of Pennsylvania Press, 1983.
Betti, E. "The Epistemological Problem of Understanding." In G. Shapiro and A. Sica, *Hermeneutics*, pp. 25–53. Amherst: University of Massachusetts Press, 1984.
Bettoni, E. *Dun Scotus: The Basic Principles of his Philosophy*. Washington: Catholic University Press, 1961.
Boas, F. "The Limitations of the Comparative Method of Anthropology" [1896]. Reprinted in F. Boas, *Race, Language, and Culture*. New York: Macmillan, 1940.
Bochensky, I. M. *History of Formal Logic*. New York: Chelsea Publishing, 1961.
Brentano, F. "The Distinction Between Mental and Material Phenomena." In R. M. Chisholm, ed., *Realism and the Background of Philosophy*. Atascadero, Calif.: Ridgeview, 1960, 39–61.

Carnap, R. *The Logical Syntax of Language*. New York: Harcourt, 1937, 1959.
———. "Empiricism, Semantics, and Ontology." In P. Benacerraf and H. Putnam, eds., *Philosophy of Mathematics*. Englewood, N.J.: Prentice-Hall, 1964, 223–48.
Cavell, S. *The Claim of Reason*. Oxford: Oxford University Press, 1979.
Chisholm, R. M. *Realism and the Background of Phenomenology*. Atascaredo, Calif.: Ridgeview, 1960.
———. *Perceiving: A Philosophical Study*. Ithaca, N.Y.: Cornell University Press, 1957.
Collingwood, R. G. *The Idea of History*. New York: Oxford University Press, 1946, 1956.
Cottingham, J. *The Rationalists*. Oxford: Oxford University Press, 1988
Cornman, J. W. *Materialism and Sensations*. New Haven, Conn.: Yale University Press, 1971.
Dancy, J. *Perceptual Knowledge*. Oxford: Oxford University Press, 1988.
Diamond, C. *The Realistic Spirit*. Boston: MIT, 1991.
Demoss, D., and Devereux, D. "Essence, Existence, and Nominal Definition in Aristotle's Posterior Analytics." *Phronesis* 33 (1988): 133–54.
Devitt, M. *Designation*. New York: Columbia University Press, 1981.
——— and Sterelny, K. *Language and Reality*. Cambridge, Mass.: MIT Press, 1987.
Dicker, G. *Perceptual Knowledge*. Dodrecht: Reidel, 1980.
Davidson, D., and Harman, G., eds. *Semantic of Natural Languages*. New York: 1972.
Donellan, K. "Reference and Definite Descriptions." *Philosophical Review* 75 (1966): 281–304.
———. "Speaking of Nothing." *Phiosophical Review* 83 (1974).
Dretske, F. *Knowledge and the Flow of Information*. Cambridge, 1981.
Dummett, M. *Truth and Other Enigmas*. Cambridge, Mass.: Harvard University Press, 1978.
Eco, U. *Semiotics and the Philosophy of Language*. Blooomington: Indiana University Press, 1986.
Evans, G. *The Varieties of Reference*. Oxford: Oxford University Press, 1982.
Firth, R. "Sense-Data and Percept Theory." In R. Swartz, *Perceiving, Sensing and Knowing*. Berkeley: University of California Press, 1965.
Fishbane, M. "Inner Biblical Exegesis." In G. Hartman and S. Budick, eds., *Midrash and Literature*. New Haven, Conn.: Yale University Press, 1986.
Frege, G. "On Sense and Reference." In A. P. Martinich, *The Philosophy of Language*. New York: Oxford University Press, 1985.
Gadamer, H.-G. *Philosophical Hermeneutics*. New York: Crossroad, 1989.
———. *Truth and Method*. New York: Crossroad, 1985.
Geach, P. *Reference and Generality*. Ithaca, N.Y.: Cornell University Press, 1962.
———. *Logic Matters*. Berkeley: University of California Press, 1972.
Geertz, G. *The Interpretation of Cultures*. New York: Basic Books, 1973.
Gettier, E. "Is Knowledge Justified True Belief." In M. Roth and L. Galis, eds., *Knowing: Essays in the Analysis of Knowing*. New York: Random House, 1970.
Giddens, A. *The Consequences of Modernity*. Stanford, Calif.: Stanford University Press, 1990.
Gilson, E. *Histoire de la Philosophie Médiévale*. Paris: 1945.
Goodman, N. *The Problem of Universals*. Notre Dame, Ind.: Notre Dame University Press, 1956.
———. "A World of Individuals." In P. Benacerraf and H. Putnam, eds., *Philosophy of Mathematics*. Englewood, N.J.: Prentice-Hall, 1964, 196–210.

Grice, H. P. "Meaning." *Philosophical Review* 66 (1957): 377–88.
———. "The Causal Theory of Perception." In J. Dancy, *Perceptual Knowledge*. Oxford: Oxford University Press, 1988.
Gurwitsch, A. "On the Intentionality of Consciousness." In *Studies in Phenomenology and Psychology*. Evanston, Ill.: Northwestern University Press, 1966.
Guthrie, W. K. C. *History of Greek Philosophy*, vols. 4 and 5. Cambridge: Cambridge University Press, 1975, 1987.
Hamilton, E., and Cairns, H., eds. *The Collected Dialogues of Plato*. Princeton, N.J.: Princeton University Press, 1963, 1987.
Hartman, G., and Budick, S., eds. *Midrash and Literature*. New Haven, Conn.: Yale University Press, 1986.
Haugeland, J. *Mind Design*. Cambridge, Mass.: MIT Press, 1981.
Hirsch, E. D. *Validity in Interpretation*. New Haven, Conn.: Yale University, 1967.
Hobbart, M. "Is God Evil?" In D. Parkin, *The Anthropology of Evil*. Oxford: Blackwell, 1985, 165–93.
Hume, D. *An Essay Concerning Human Understanding*. New York: Colliers, 1962.
———. *A Treatise of Human Nature*. In *The Philosophical Works of David Hume*. London: Logmans, 1886, 1964.
James, W. *The Meaning of Truth*. New York: Longmans, 1909.
Kant, E. *Critique of Pure Reason*. New York: St. Martin Press, 1929, 1965.
Knowles, D. *The Evolution of Medieval Philosophy*. New York: Vintage, 1962.
Körner, S. *Kant*. New Haven, Conn.: Yale University Press, 1982.
Kretzmann, N., Kenny, A., Piborg, J., and Stump, E. *The Cambridge History of Later Medieval Philosophy*. Cambridge: Cambridge University Press, 1982.
Kretzmann, N., and Stump, E. *The Cambridge Companion to Aquinas*. Cambridge: Cambridge University Press, 1993.
Kripke, S. *Naming and Necessity*. Cambridge, Mass.: Harvard University Press, 1980.
Kristeva, J. *Le Language, cet Inconnnu*. Paris: Seuil, 1969.
Leff, G. *The Dissolution of the Medieval Outlook*. New York: New York University Press, 1976.
———. *William of Ockham: The Metamorphosis of Scholastic Discourse*. Manchester: Manchester University Press, 1975.
Leibniz, G. *New Essays Concerning Human Understanding*. New York: Macmillan, 1896.
Leonard, H. *Principles of Reasoning*. New York: Dover, 1967.
Linsky, L., ed. *Reference and Modality*. Oxford: Oxford University Press, 1971.
———, ed., *Semantics and the Philosophy of Language*. Urbana: University of Illinois, 1952.
———. *Referring* . London: Routledge, 1971.
Locke, J. *Essay Concerning Human Understanding*. Cleveland: Meridian, 1969.
Loux, M., ed. *Universals and Particulars*. New York: Anchor, 1970.
Lukasiewicz, J. *Aristotle's Syllogistic from the Standpoint of Modern Formal Logic*. Oxford: Clarendon, 1959.
MacIntyre, A. *Whose Justice, Which Rationality*. Notre Dame, Ind.: University of Notre Dame, 1988.
Mackie, J. L. *Problems from Locke*. Oxford: Oxford University Press, 1976.
Marras, A. *Intentionality, Mind, and Language*. Chicago: University of Chicago Press.
Martinich, A. P. *The Philosophy of Language*. New York: Oxford University Press, 1985.
McKeon, R. ed. *The Basic Works of Aristotle*. New York: Random House, 1941.

Metha, J. L. *Martin Heidegger: The Way and the Vision*. Honolulu: University Press of Hawaii, 1967, 1976.
Mill, J. S. *An Explanation of Sir William Hamilton's Philosophy*. Boston: Spencer, 1865.
Minsky, M. "A Framework for Representing Knowledge." In J. Haugeland, *Mind Design*. Cambridge, Mass.: MIT Press, 1981.
Moore, G. E. *Some Main Problems of Philosophy*. London: Allen and Unwin, 1953.
Olshewsky, T. *Problems in the Philosophy of Language*. New York: Rinehart and Winston, 1969.
Owens, J. *The Doctrine of Being in the Aristotelian Metaphysics*. Toronto: Pontifical Institute of Medieval Studies, 1951, 1957.
Ozment, S. *The Age of Reform*. New Haven, Conn.: Yale University Press, 1980.
Phillips, G., ed. *Knowledge and Belief*. Oxford: Oxford University Press, 1967.
Pierce, C. E. "Logic as Semiotic: The Theory of Signs." In R. Innis, ed., *Semiotics*. Bloomington: Indiana University Press, 1985, 1–23.
———. "The Essentials of Pragmatism." In J. Buchler, ed., *Philosophical Writings of Pierce*. New York: Dover, 1955.
Price, H. H. *Perception*. London: Meuthuen, 1950.
Putnam, H. *Realism and Reason* . Cambridge, Mass.: Harvard University Press, 1983.
———. *Realism with a Human Face*. Cambridge, Mass.: Harvard University Press, 1990.
———. *Words and Life*. Cambridge, Mass.: Harvard University Press, 1994.
———. "Why Reason Can't Be Naturalized?" In *Realism and Reason*. Cambridge, Mass.: Harvard University Press, 1983.
——— and Benacerraf, P., ed. *Philosophy of Mathematics*. Englewood, N.J.: Prentice-Hall, 1964, 223–48.
Quine, W. *From a Logical Point of View*, pp. 139–59. Cambridge, Mass.: Harvard University Press, 1953; New York: Harper, 1963.
———. *Ontological Relativity and Other Essays*. New York: 1969.
———. *Word and Object*. Cambridge, Mass.: MIT Press, 1960.
Realer, G. *The Systems of the Hellenistic Age*. Albany: SUNY Press, 1985.
Reid, T. *Essays on the Intellectual Powers of Man*. Cambridge: Bartlett, 1850.
Ricoeur, P. *Du Texte a l'Action*. Paris: Le Seuil, 1987.
———. *Interpretation Theory*. Fort Worth: Texas Christian University Press, 1976.
Robinson, R. *Definition*. Oxford: Clarendon Press, 1954.
Rorty, R. *Philosophy and the Mirror of Nature*. Princeton, N.J.: Princeton University Press, 1979.
———. *Consequences of Pragmatism*. Minneapolis: University of Minnesota Press, 1982.
———. "Review of G. J. Larson and E. Deutsch, eds., *Interpreting Across Boundaries*." *Philosophy East and West* 39 (1989).
Rosch, E. "Human Categorization." In E. Rosch and B. Lloyd, *Cognition and Categorization*. Hillsdale, N.J.: Lawrence Erlbaum, 1978.
Ross, D. *Aristotle*. New York: Barnes and Noble, 1923, 1964.
Roth, M., and Galis, L., eds. *Knowing: Essays in the Analysis of Knowing*. New York: Random, 1970.
Russell, B. *Mysticism and Logic*. London: Allen and Unwin, 1917.
———. *An Enquiry into Meaning and Truth*. London: Allen and Unwin, 1940.
———. *Introduction to Mathematical Philosophy*. London: Allen and Unwin, 1919, 1967.
———. *The Problems of Philosophy*. Oxford: Oxford University Press, 1912.
Ryle, G. *The Concept of Mind*. London: Hutchinson, 1949.

Sartre, J.-P. *La Transcendance of the Ego*. Paris: Vrin, 1927, 1985.

Saunders, J. *Greek and Roman Philosophy After Aristotle*. New York: Macmillan, 1966.

Saussure, F. *Course in General Linguistics*. New-York: McGraw, 1959.

Scholem, G. *The Messianic Idea in Judaism*. New York: Shocken Books, 1971.

Schopenhauer, A. *World as Will and Idea*. London: Trübner, 1886.

Sellars, W. *Science, Perception, and Reality*. Atlantic Highlands, N.J.: Humanities Press, 1963.

Shapiro, G., and Sica, A. *Hermeneutics*. Amherst: University of Massachusetts Press, 1984.

Smith, J. Z. *Map Is Not Territory*. Leiden: Brill, 1978.

———. *Imagining Religion* . Chicago: University of Chicago Press, 1982.

Staniland, H. *Universals*. New York: Anchor, 1972.

Stich, S. *From Folk Psychology to Cognitive Science*. Cambridge, Mass.: MIT, 1983.

Strawson, P. E. *Individuals*. London: Meuthen, 1969, 1971.

———. "Perception and Its Objects." In J. Dancy, *Perceptual Knowledge*. Oxford: Oxford University Press, 1988.

Swartz, R. *Perceiving, Sensing, and Knowing*. Berkeley: University of California Press, 1965, 1976.

Vygotsky, L. *The Collected Works*. New York: Plenum, 1987.

White, N. P. *Plato on Knowledge and Reality*. Indianapolis: Hackett, 1976, 1987.

Wittgenstein, L. *Blue and Brown Books*. New York: Harper Books, 1958.

———. *On Certainty*. New York: Harper Books, 1972.

———. *Philosophical Investigations*. Oxford: Basil Blackwell, 1952, 1984.

Wolff, R. *Kant's Theory of Mental Activity*. Cambridge, Mass.: Harvard University Press, 1963.

Woozley, A. D. "Knowing and Not Knowing." *Proceeding of the Aristotelian Society* 3 (1952): 151–72.

AUTHOR INDEX

Indian and Tibetan Traditional Authors

A-gu Shay-rap-gya-tso, 38, 469 n. 42
Atīśa, 21–23, 439–40, 467 n. 20

Ba-tsap Nyi-ma-drak, 19, 519 n. 41
Bhartṛhari, 137, 207–208, 211–12, 214, 218, 232, 266, 272, 498 n. 8, 513 n. 9, 514 n. 24, 515 n. 41
Bhavya, 19, 234, 460, 464 n. 2, 483 n. 33
Bhavyarāja, 196, 201
Bo-dong, 34, 507 n. 8, 508 n. 16
- on distinguishers, 508 n. 13
- on inference, 25, 482 n. 23, 535 n. 31
- on objective elimination, 246, 518 n. 23, 520 n. 55
- on ontology, 25–26, 78, 80, 155, 169, 179, 189–93, 482 nn. 22–23, 487 n. 38, 507 n. 6, 507 nn. 11–12
- on perception, 374
- on realization, 370–71, 554 n. 17, 555 n. 34
- and soteriology, 559 n. 43

Bu-dön-rin-chen-drup, 35, 472 n. 78
- on Dharmakīrti, 440

Candrakīrti, 19, 33, 51, 55, 195, 209–10, 428–29, 508 n. 24, 93, 560 n. 9
- on Dignāga, 451–55, 559 nn. 7–8, 560 n. 11
- on perception, 411, 453, 536 n. 18, 538 n. 8, 538 n. 11, 538 n. 14, 560 n. 14
- on valid cognition, 455, 529 n. 42, 560 n. 13

Cha-ba Chö-gyi-seng-gay, 22, 24–26, 32–33, 75, 115, 120, 136, 154, 165–66, 175, 189, 194–96, 246, 251, 253, 256, 276, 302–306, 322, 365–92, 413, 417–18, 429, 444, 466 n. 12, 467 n. 25, 467 n. 28, 510 n. 55, 531 n. 6
Chö-drak-gya-tso (Seventh Kar-ma-ba), 28–29, 37, 431–34, 454, 469 n. 50, 484 n. 36, 485 n. 11, 486 n. 25, 533 n. 3, 555 n. 30, 557 n. 9

Dak-tsang, 89, 91, 98, 108, 440, 455–56, 479 n. 33, 486 n. 31, 561 n. 18
Devendrabuddhi, 21, 31, 206, 291, 307, 317, 434–35, 444, 466 n. 18, 471 n. 69, 551 n. 6
Dharmakīrti: on affirmation and negation, 233–34, 520 n. 64
- and antirealism, 56, 71, 75, 82, 86, 478 n. 32
- ascending scales of analysis, 20, 49, 59, 83, 86, 90, 92, 98–99, 103–105, 337–38
- on aspects, 256, 341–43, 401
- on causality, 411, 460, 552 n. 29
- on commonsense objects, 89, 130
- on conception, 220–32, 286–91, 316, 514 n. 26
- as conceptualist, 131–33, 147, 218, 231, 272–80
- and connotationist view of language, 207–12, 272
- dates and life of, 1–5, 15–21, 464 n. 2
- on defining property, 478 nn. 31–32
- on distinguishers, 159, 167–68
- and emptiness-of-other, 29
- on elimination, 238, 246, 275–79
- exclusion (apoha), 145–47, 184, 187, 526 n. 52
- on existence, 82, 98–105, 196
- on extended objects and continua, 102, 360, 490 n. 70
- on external objects, 422
- as foundationalist, 210, 297, 412
- on generally characterized phenomena, 73–75, 157, 199
- on identity conditions, 69–72, 154
- on impermanence, 62–65, 73
- on individuals, 130, 176, 179
- on inference, 154, 196, 199, 291, 303, 312, 316–27, 352, 359–60, 531 n. 16
- Kant and, 320, 479 n. 39, 485 n. 10

Western Authors

SUBJECT INDEX